CONCISE

FOURTH

EDITION

# THE COMPOSITION OF EVERYDAY LIFE

## A GUIDE TO WRITING

**JOHN MAUK**

*Northwestern Michigan College*

**JOHN METZ**

*Kent State University at Geauga*

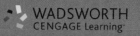
WADSWORTH
CENGAGE Learning·

Australia · Brazil · Japan · Korea · Mexico · Singapore · Spain · United Kingdom · United States

**WADSWORTH**
CENGAGE Learning™

**The Composition of Everyday Life:**
**A Guide to Writing**
**Concise Fourth Edition**
**John Mauk • John Metz**

Senior Publisher: Lyn Uhl

Publisher: Monica Eckman

Acquisitions Editor: Margaret Leslie

Senior Development Editor: Leslie Taggart

Development Editor: Stephanie Carpenter

Assistant Editor: Amy Haines

Editorial Assistant: Danielle Warchol

Media Editor: Janine Tangney

Senior Marketing Manager: Stacey Purviance

Marketing Coordinator: Brittany Blais

Senior Marketing Communications Manager: Linda Yip

Content Project Manager: Corinna Dibble

Senior Print Buyer: Betsy Donaghey

Rights Acquisition Specialist: Roberta Broyer

Design, Production, and Composition: Lachina Publishing Services

Cover Designer: Hahn Luu

Cover Image: © www.shutterstock.com

For product information and technology assistance, contact us at **Cengage Learning Customer & Sales Support, 1-800-354-9706**

For permission to use material from this text or product, submit all requests online at **www.cengage.com/permissions.** Further permissions questions can be e-mailed to **permissionrequest@cengage.com.**

Library of Congress Control Number: 2011937664

ISBN-13: 978-1-111-84051-8
ISBN-10: 1-111-84051-2

**Wadsworth**
20 Channel Center Street
Boston, MA 02210
USA

Cengage Learning is a leading provider of customized learning solutions with office locations around the globe, including Singapore, the United Kingdom, Australia, Mexico, Brazil and Japan. Locate your local office at **international.cengage.com/region**

Cengage Learning products are represented in Canada by Nelson Education, Ltd.

For your course and learning solutions, visit **www.cengage.com.** Purchase any of our products at your local college store or at our preferred online store **www.cengagebrain.com.**

**Instructors:** Please visit **login.cengage.com** and log in to access instructor-specific resources.

Printed in the United States of America
2 3 4 5 6 7 15 14 13 12

# Brief Contents

# Contents

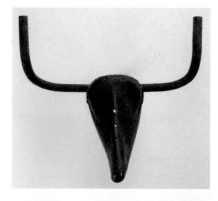

## Chapter 2  Remembering
                Who You Were        24

# Chapter 3  Explaining Relationships    60

# Chapter 4  Observing    92

## Chapter 7  Making Arguments        194

# Chapter 8  Responding to Arguments    244

# Chapter 9  Evaluating    280

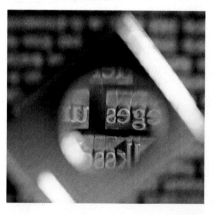

# Chapter 10  Searching for Causes   314

# Chapter 11  Proposing Solutions   350

## Chapter 12  Thinking Radically: Re-Seeing the World    382

## Chapter 15  Integrating and Documenting Sources    454

# Using *The Composition of Everyday Life* as a Thematic Reader

Here we suggest how readings from different chapters might be grouped together thematically. As you explore a particular subject (Education and Learning, for example), you might focus on a particular rhetorical aim (such as evaluating or proposing a solution). Or you might explore a subject area without a particular aim in mind, eventually discovering a specific topic and rhetorical aim.

## Education and Learning

Are students customers? What is the practical value of studying great works of literature? Is school too easy? The essays listed below explore the complexity of education and learning. Through reading, writing, and discussion, you might explore and come to think differently about education and its role in people's lives. You might discover an important point about education by exploring a memory, a relationship, an observation, a concept, and so on.

"Black Like I Thought I Was," *Erin Aubry Kaplan* (5)

"Have It Your Way," *Simon Benlow* (5)

"Floppy Disk Fallacies," *Elizabeth Bohnhorst* (7)

"What Orwell Didn't Know," *George Lakoff* (8)

"Entitlement Education," *Daniel Bruno* (8)

"Reality Check," *Alison Hester* (8)

"Is Google Making Us Stupid?" *Nicholas Carr* (10)

"Attending to the Word," *Deirdre Mahoney* (11)

## Justice and Equality

A quick survey of the readings about justice and equality suggests a range of areas: Native American rights, body type, legal drugs, the mentally and physically challenged, wildlife, and so on. These readings can help you identify and explain a relationship, analyze a concept (such as "justice" or "equality"), respond to an argument, identify a cause, propose a solution, and so on. What is justice, and how might exploring the concept of justice in today's world be of value? What revelatory idea about justice and equality might you discover and share with others?

"Cruelty, Civility, and Other Weighty Matters," *Ann Marie Paulin* (7)

"What Orwell Didn't Know," *George Lakoff* (8)

"*Star Trek:* Where No Man Has Gone Before," *Jaren Provo* (8)

"An Apology to Future Generations," *Simon Benlow* (12)

## Environment and Animals

These readings, which offer different ways of looking at the environment and animals, encourage you to explore ideas beyond your initial thoughts and beyond conventional beliefs. What is your relationship to the land? To the air? To the animals? How might you think differently about that relationship? And what might be the consequence of your new way of thinking?

"Americans and the Land," *John Steinbeck* (3)

"Heart of Sand," *Anne-Marie Oomen* (4)

"The Front Porch," *Chester McCovey* (4)

"World Gone Mad," *Derrick Jensen* (5)

"The Dog Delusion," *April Pedersen* (7)

"An Apology to Future Generations," *Simon Benlow* (12)

## Consumerism and Economy

Several readings in this book encourage you to think about yourself as a consumer. What and how do you consume? And what, if anything, do you produce by consuming? As with other subjects in CEL, you might spend an entire semester exploring this area, or you might explore it for just one assignment. It could be of great value to spend an entire semester exploring just one question: What does it mean to be a consumer?

"Selling Manure," *Bonnie Jo Campbell* (2)

"The Front Porch," *Chester McCovey* (4)

"Have It Your Way," *Simon Benlow* (5)

"The Real, the Bad, and the Ugly," *Cassie Heidecker* (5)

"Rise of the Image Culture: Re-Imagining the American Dream," *Elizabeth Thoman* (6)

"The Mighty Image," *Cameron Johnson* (6)

"Whales R Us," *Jayme Stayer* (7)

"What Orwell Didn't Know," *George Lakoff* (8)

"Entitlement Education," *Daniel Bruno* (8)

"Is Google Making Us Stupid?" *Nicholas Carr* (10)

"American Consumerism," *Jamie Bentley* (10)

"An Apology to Future Generations," *Simon Benlow* (12)

# America

These readings deal with America and being American. They allow you to explore the relationship between yourself and your country. (International students may find this subject to be especially interesting as they bring a unique perspective to the topic.) To what degree do the two—individual and country—influence each other? You can make observations, evaluate, identify causes, propose solutions, and so on. And, you can explore how America communicates with and influences you.

"Americans and the Land," *John Steinbeck* (3)

"Black Like I Thought I Was," *Erin Aubry Kaplan* (5)

"Rise of the Image Culture: Re-Imagining the American Dream," *Elizabeth Thoman* (6)

"The Mighty Image," *Cameron Johnson* (6)

"Whales R Us," *Jayme Stayer* (7)

"What Orwell Didn't Know," *George Lakoff* (8)

"Reality Check," *Alison Hester* (8)

"Talibanned," *Benjamin Busch* (9)

"American Consumerism," *Jamie Bentley* (10)

"Reverence for Food," *Rachel Schofield* (11)

"Cookies or Heroin?" *Marie Winn* (14)

# Self

Readings in this book encourage you to explore your own life in a way you have perhaps not done before. These readings about self go beyond mere expressive writing. They encourage you to connect with others, even though—or perhaps *especially when*—you are looking inward at yourself. You can explore how these readings, your own writing, and focused discussion with others helps you to see differently—to learn something about yourself and connect it to the world around you.

"Selling Manure," *Bonnie Jo Campbell (2)*

"Thrill of Victory . . . The Agony of Parents," *Jennifer Schwind-Pawlak* (2)

"How I Lost the Junior Miss Pageant," *Cindy Bosley* (2)

"Mugged," *Jim Crockett* (3)

"Delicate Friend," *Lauren Jackson* (3)

"Corpse Colloquy," *Justin Scott* (4)

"Cruelty, Civility, and Other Weighty Matters," *Ann Marie Paulin* (7)

"What Orwell Didn't Know," *George Lakoff* (8)

"*The Andy Griffith Show:* Return to Normal," *Ed Bell* (9)

# Others (Community)

Can we look at ourselves without looking at our community? Both subjects (self and others) explore relationships between the individual and his or her surroundings. What is community? How is community created? These readings will help you to explore what we commonly call *community,* to consider how it works, and to examine your place in it. An entire writing course might be an exploration of one very important question: What is the relationship between community and communication?

# Language and Culture

What is the relationship between language and culture? For example, how does the way that a group of people communicates affect their shared values, beliefs, customs, attitudes, and practices—and vice versa? (How, for example, does what a group values about education influence the way that group uses, and thinks about, language?) These readings and others will help you step back and explore the relationship between words, ideas, and actions. Through exploration of this subject, you might discover that your college writing class is something more than you had originally imagined it to be.

"Is Google Making Us Stupid?" *Nicholas Carr* (10)

"Attending to the Word," *Deirdre Mahoney* (11)

# Gender and Identity

What does it mean to be male or female? How does gender affect our identities? What influence can we have on issues of gender and identity? This group of readings can be used in combination with other reading groups—from America or pop culture, for example. Instead of exploring just gender and identity, you might narrow your focus to readings that relate to gender and identity *and* pop culture.

"Selling Manure," *Bonnie Jo Campbell* (2)

"How I Lost the Junior Miss Pageant," *Cindy Bosley* (2)

"The Thrill of Victory . . . The Agony of Parents," *Jennifer Schwind-Pawlak* (2)

"Delicate Friend," *Lauren Jackson (3)*

"Cruelty, Civility, and Other Weighty Matters," *Ann Marie Paulin* (7)

"Throwing Up Childhood," *Leonard Kress* (10)

"Celibate Passion," *Kathleen Norris* (12)

# Parents and Family

What role do our parents play in our lives? Such a question might be explored endlessly with interesting results for both writer and reader. You might spend an entire semester exploring issues about parents and family. Such a simple subject area can prove to be far more complicated   and interesting—than you first imagined. What might be the value of thinking analytically and finding public resonance regarding the subject of parents and family?

"Selling Manure," *Bonnie Jo Campbell* (2)

"How I Lost the Junior Miss Pageant," *Cindy Bosley* (2)

"The Thrill of Victory . . . The Agony of Parents," *Jennifer Schwind-Pawlak* (2)

"Delicate Friend," *Lauren Jackson* (3)

"The Front Porch," *Chester McCovey* (4)

"Black Like I Thought I Was," *Erin Aubry Kaplan* (5)

"An Imperfect Reality," *Rebecca Hollingsworth* (6)

"*The Andy Griffith Show:* Return to Normal," *Ed Bell* (9)

"Throwing Up Childhood," *Leonard Kress* (10)

"American Consumerism," *Jamie Bentley* (10)

"An Apology to Future Generations," *Simon Benlow* (12)

"Unemployed and Working Hard," *Simon Wykoff* (12)

# Popular Culture

What is the relationship between the individual and his or her popular culture? In what ways are we products of our own pop culture? From beauty pageants to theme parks, these readings allow you to consider the world that surrounds you from a fresh perspective. You can explore the *why* of your own behavior, considering how you and others are influenced by pressures of which you are both very aware and barely aware.

# Technology

We cannot overlook technology. How does it influence the way we live? Through reading, writing, and discussion, you can explore beyond your initial thoughts and perceptions to consider the complex relationship in today's world between the individual and technology—or between one individual and another *because of technology*. What idea about technology might you discover and share with others, helping them to think or act differently?

# Note to Instructors

Like most college writing instructors, we see English composition as a vital component of an academic career. Without a transformative composition experience, many college students will struggle, fumble, or worse. And beyond the college classroom, we see writing instruction as intimately connected to students' everyday lives. We believe that composition courses are not only preparation for more academic work but also a genuine study of one's own rhetorical situations. More specifically, we assume that student writing should do two things:

1. It should emerge from the discursive entanglements of students' everyday lives. Student writing is often stiffened by the popular-but-distant topics of the day: gun control, abortion, cloning, cell phone use, and so on. Of course, for some students, these topics intersect with everyday life, but for the vast majority, they are glorified encyclopedic preformulations. They offer no possibility for new connections, no possibility for radical rethinking, no hope for discovery, and no exigence whatsoever. They are dead. Therefore, we hope to offer a pedagogy that genuinely guides students into the tensions, cracks, and un-seen notches of their own lives. Perhaps, then, they will see that this whole enterprise is worthy of the immense intellectual energy it requires.

2. It should prompt students to think more adeptly, to invent a better way of knowing. We believe the only reason to write an essay is to generate a better way of thinking about a topic. In professional academic work, essays are not written to prove grammatical prowess or syntactic proficiency, but to share an important new insight, to contribute to an ongoing conversation, to reveal an otherwise hidden position or viewpoint. In the composition course, it should be no different. And it's been our experience that classroom engagement increases dramatically when students understand this rhetorical mission.

Over the editions of this book, we've been asked: why such focus on invention? What led us to place invention at the center of the pedagogy? Initially, this focus came from understanding our own students—from witnessing how they struggle, succeed, and fail. We asked ourselves some basic questions: What do we value but fail to teach explicitly? What do other writing instructors value and assess? What are the gaps between proficient high school writing and proficient college writing? What we discovered was a type of hidden curriculum. Instructors want revelation, discovery, depth, rigor, intellectual richness. But such qualities are not taught explicitly and consistently at the high school level. Students entering college often lack the discursive tools for generating the richness and complexity that college composition instructors hope to see. Our conclusion: students need specific guidance in developing that complexity.

As we looked closely at our students, we noticed that successful writers tend to:

- Start thinking about their topics and their own responses early on
- Turn ideas and positions around—investigating intellectual possibilities
- Re-think based on the values, assumptions, and claims of others
- Address and even envelop opposing ideas

In short, successful writers invent. They do what the classical rhetoricians taught: use language to explore what's possible.

Contrarily, unsuccessful writers skip invention. Their relationship with language is at best tentative . . . at worst, antagonistic. And they often carry some counterproductive notions about thinking and writing: ideas emerge fully formed from an individual's head; good writers do not struggle or re-think; the only way to develop an idea is by adding facts; an essay is good if it's properly arranged and grammatically correct. Such assumptions work against writers—even more than their unfamiliarity with grammatical conventions or other "basics." Before they even begin a course or an assignment, these quiet notions stymie many students' foray into an intensive writerly experience.

With *The Composition of Everyday Life,* we hope to vitalize students' assumptions about writing, and to dramatize a simple but crucial point: language is not merely a conduit for expression but a tool for developing ideas. We hope that students imagine writing as an act of public exploration, a process of inventing and sharing what can be thought, what can be said, what can be known. This book, then, is grounded in and driven by a set of principles that we've deemed *invention pedagogy.* It emerges not only from our understanding of students but also from the pre-Socratic Greek sophists—those folks who invented rhetoric (and the practice of democracy). The broader goal is to get students using language in public writing to develop increasingly sophisticated ideas. More specific goals are tied up in the sections of each chapter:

**Point of Contact** sections encourage students to slow down and notice the nuances of life around them while considering possibilities for writing topics. The questions pull students away from stiff and distant topics and toward the real entanglements of their own lives.

**Analysis** sections help students develop meaning and significance while prompting them to explore their topics with questions and dialogic activities.

**Public Resonance** sections draw attention to the rhetorical situation—to the assumptions, values, and beliefs of others. Writers are prompted to explore what others believe and how the particular writing project can influence common belief.

**Thesis** sections in each invention chapter help students to hone their ideas to a fine edge. Each section contains prompts, sample thesis statements, common thesis problems, and an Evolution of a Thesis chart, which illustrates the gradual development of an idea.

**Rhetorical Tools** sections explain the support strategies that are most applicable and appropriate to the writing situation. The sections teach students that all rhetorical tools (such as narration, argumentative appeals, allusions, and so on) can be applied according to the writer's particular needs.

**Organizational Strategies** sections give students options for arranging their ideas—options beyond rigid structures they may have learned for essay exams or placement tests. These sections are driven by common questions about arrangement, for example, How should I begin? How should I conclude? Where should I deal with counterarguments?

**Writer's Voice** sections prompt students to experiment with voice—with the broad range of strategies for projecting character or mood in writing. These sections illustrate each strategy with passages from the chapter readings.

**Vitality** sections explain and illustrate particular strategies for pruning, weeding, trimming, and vitalizing the writing. With this section, students can see that deliberate and repeatable strategies can make sentences more intense and lively. (We hoped to diffuse the mystery and fog created by "awk" and other such codes.)

**Revision** sections suggest ways to work back through essay drafts, applying even more invention strategies. Each section also features chapter-specific questions for peer reviewers.

**Reflection** sections ask students to articulate ideas about how their essays work. These prompts get students writing about writing, dealing metacognitively with the particular intellectual maneuvers required/prompted in that chapter. Many of the Reflection sections also invite students to go "Beyond the Essay"—to take their ideas from the chapter and re-cast them in some other format: a poster, a cartoon, and so on.

As they work through the sections, students may feel their ideas getting more complex, even unwieldy. That's okay. In fact, if we are doing our jobs well, our students' thinking will likely get messier. But if we walk through the entire intellectual journey (i.e. assignment) with them, students may see their ideas re-gain focus. They may see assignments as intellectual pathways.

As all writers know, good ideas require intellectual grappling, occasional cognitive slippage, and plenty of revision. We think students at this particular point in history, in these particular economic and cultural times, must learn how to grapple and re-think. We cannot assume that such critical and nuanced skills will seep into student consciousness—that some lucky students will "pick up on" the most crucial discursive moves. If writing instructors value rigorous (*inventive, rich, deep, intensive, analytical, critical*) thinking, and if we reward it with a grade, then we owe students the tools for making it happen. We cannot simply provide interesting samples and expect them to extract the epistemology. If we value invention, we must teach students how to explore, how to unpack their initial thoughts, and how to persist beyond the commonplaces.

A quick glance at the economy, labor relationships, world politics, and demographic shifts portends a new kind of literacy: People will need intellectual agility; they will have to think around topics, beyond themselves, beyond their initial assumptions, to simply get along in a fast-changing cultural landscape. Having an opinion and writing it neatly in five coherent paragraphs will be its own kind of illiteracy. Those who can only say what they think will get left behind. Those who can invent new intellectual postures for themselves and others will thrive.

# New to This Edition

**New Information Literacy Chapter:** In this era of information overload, students need help understanding how texts speak to and within disciplinary debates and cultural trends. They need to understand how information works, where it comes from, whom it is designed for. In short, students need help understanding the din of voices. New Chapter 14, "Analyzing, Synthesizing, and Evaluating Sources," guides students through specific intellectual moves necessary for better understanding the rhetoric of secondary sources.

**Thinking Critically about Statistics and Facts:** Many first-year college students suffer under the statistic and fact myths——that numbers are inherently truer than opinions and that facts are inherently better than theories. These notions can undermine students' understanding of argument, information, and the inventive acts of writing. Contained in Chapter 14, this section explains how facts come to be——how they come to be accepted in a community, how they function in debate, how they reinforce perspectives. Once students learn to value statistics appropriately and consider them critically, they will be better able to enter into argument.

**New Reflection activities:** In each writing project chapter (Chapters 2–12) students are asked to articulate ideas about how their essays work. These Reflection prompts get students writing about writing and move them towards self-assessment. When students develop this sort of meta-language, they are better prepared to enter into a dialog, instead of monolog, with instructors grading/responding to their writing.

**New reading selections:** Eleven new readings from such writers as Nicholas Carr and Kathleen Norris illustrate the intellectual moves essential to inventive writing.

**Unique images:** The fourth edition features additional images for several readings, the same kind of intriguing and unexpected images that reviewers have told us are useful for invention and class discussion.

# Key Features

**Emphasis on invention:** Unlike any other writing guide, *The Composition of Everyday Life* offers twelve invention chapters, guiding students to be inventive thinkers and writers. In addition, "Point of Contact" sections encourage students to slow down and notice the nuances of life around them while considering possibilities for writing topics, thus promoting the union of invention and everyday life.

**Three Sample Essays Per Chapter:** Each invention chapter features a carefully selected triad: a professional writer, a student writer, and a commissioned writer. While students are comforted at seeing another student's approach to the chapter, the student essays illustrate only one approach. So we asked writers, many of them composition instructors themselves, to work through the chapter invention sections and to develop a project of their own that addresses the audience (students and instructors of college composition) and illustrates "what's possible" in each particular situation. The result is a compelling range of essay projects that illustrate key moves and increase the continuum of possibility.

**Clean design:** Instructors and students tell us the design of *The Composition of Everyday Life* helps students focus easily on the key ideas and activities in each chapter. With each edition, we strive to make the layout and design both more powerful and less noticeable.

# Instructor Resources

### *The Composition of Everyday Life: A Guide to Writing*, Brief Fourth Edition

A brief edition of *The Composition of Everyday Life* includes sixteen chapters, omitting the handbook.

### Instructor's Manual and Survival Guide for Teachers

John Mauk and John Metz have revised the instructor's manual alongside the fourth edition of *The Composition of Everyday Life,* updating its numerous resources to help you prepare for class. Teaching tips, syllabus planning, and lesson organization are all included.

### Enhanced InSite™ for *The Composition of Everyday Life*, Concise Fourth Edition

You can easily create, assign, and grade writing assignments with Enhanced InSite™ for *The Composition of Everyday Life,* Concise Fourth Edition. From a single, easy-to-navigate site, you and your students can manage the flow of papers online, check for originality, and conduct peer reviews. Students can access a multimedia eBook that offers a text-specific workbook, private tutoring options, and resources for writers, including anti-plagiarism tutorials and download-able grammar podcasts. Enhanced InSite™ provides the tools and resources you and your students need, plus the training and support you want. Learn more at www.cengage.com/insite.

### CourseMate for *The Composition of Everyday Life*, Concise Fourth Edition

Printed Access Card | ISBN-13: 9781133230878
Instant Access Card | ISBN-13: 9781133230885
Cengage Learning's English CourseMate brings course concepts to life with interactive learning, study, and exam preparation tools that support the printed textbook. Students' comprehension will soar as your class works with the printed textbook and the textbook-specific Website. English CourseMate goes beyond the book to deliver what you need! Learn more at cengage.com/coursemate.

### Interactive eBook for *The Composition of Everyday Life*, Concise Fourth Edition

Students can do all of their reading online or use the eBook as a handy reference while they're completing coursework. The eBook includes the full text of the print version with interactive exercises; an integrated text-specific workbook; user-friendly navigation, search, and highlight tools; and links to videos that enhance the text content.

# Acknowledgments

A textbook is a big invention workshop, and we are fortunate to have extremely savvy collaborators. We offer our humble gratitude: to our development editor, Stephanie Pelkowski Carpenter, for her powerhouse clarity, nuanced decision-making, and persistent wisdom; to Margaret Leslie for supporting our vision; to Leslie Taggart for supporting all the layers of the development process; to Lyn Uhl for reinforcing the company's commitment to our work; to Danielle Warchol for expertly managing a range of things on the inside; to Corinna Dibble for overseeing production and keeping her hands in the mix; to Lisa Koehler for checking the soundness and accuracy of every assertion; to Matthew Orgovan (Lachina Publishing Services) for deftly steering us through each intensive phase of production; to the marketing crew at Cengage, particularly Stacey Purviance, who deals with our sensitivities and hopes; to Sara Golden (PreMediaGlobal) for tracking down rights and permissions; and as always, to the intensive sales folks throughout the country who give arms and legs to our books.

Thanks also to our students and colleagues who graciously stumble along with us in our efforts to transcend what is and to invent what could be. Thanks to our families and friends for enduring yet another project—who have stopped saying, "I thought you were done."

Any textbook project requires hearty professionals who give up their time and energy to help steer the pedagogy in valuable directions. We relied heavily on the insights of our reviewers and were often humbled at their prowess. We are indebted to the following teachers, theorists, rhetoricians, and scholars:

Susan Achziger, *Community College of Aurora*

Belinda Adams, *Navarro College*

Andrew Andermatt, *Clinton Community College*

Sonja Andrus, *Collin College*

Thomas Barthel, *Herkimer County Community College*

Larry Beason, *University of South Alabama*

Goretti Benca, *SUNY New Paltz*

Russell Bodi, *Owens State Community College*

Robert Bonds, *New England Institute of Art*

Jim Bosinger, *University of Toledo*

Jon Brooks, *Okaloosa-Walton College*

Ron Brooks, *Oklahoma State University*

Bessie Brown, *Hinds Community College*

Harryette Brown, *Eastfield College*

Patricia Buck, *East Tennessee State University*

Jolene Buehrer, *Bowling Green State University-Firelands*

Walter Cannon, *Central College*

Peter Caster, *University of South Carolina Upstate*

Carole Chapman, *Ivy Tech Community College of Indiana*

Colin Charlton, *University of Texas-Pan American*

Kirk Colvin, *American River College*

Lucinda Coombs, *Central Maine Community College*

Sheilah Craft, *University of Indianapolis*

Bryan Davis, *Georgia Southwestern State University*

Martha Dede, *California State University, Long Beach*

Dominique Dieffenbach, *Florida Community College at Jacksonville*

Mariellen Dietz, *Wartburg College*

Lori Doddy, *Texas Woman's University*

Steve Edgehouse, *Bowling Green State University*

Dianne Fallon, *York County Community College*

Daniel Fitzstephens, *University of Colorado*

Saundra Foderick, *Argosy University Twin Cities and Online*

Erwin Ford, *Albany State University*

Luisa Forrest, *El Centro College*

Anne Marie Fowler, *Keiser University*

Todd Fox, *California State University, Long Beach*

Christina Francis, *Bloomsburg University*

Linda Fricker, *North Dakota State University*

Jackie Garfat, *Dakota High School*

Sharon George, *College of Charleston*

Patricia Golder, *Victor Valley College*

Nate Gordon, *Kishwaukee College*

Rebecca Gorman, *Metropolitan State College of Denver*

Jack Grier, *Wilkes University*

Susan Grimland, *Collin County Community College*

Eduard C. Hanganu, *University of Southern Indiana*

Robin Hanson, *Minnesota State Community and Technical College*

Betty Hart, *The University of Southern Indiana*

Jennifer Hazel, *Owens Community College*

Anne Helms, *Alamance Community College*

Michael Hill, *Henry Ford Community College*

Valerie Hockert, *TESC, Axia*

Dedria Humphries, *Lansing Community College*

William Hutchings, *University of Alabama at Birmingham*

Tammy Jabin, *Chemeketa Community College*

Lowell Jaeger, *Flathead Valley Community College*

Hershman John, *Phoenix College*

Darlene Johnston, *Ohio Northern University*

Peggy Jolly, *University of Alabama at Birmingham*

Peggy Karsten, *Ridgewater College*

Mark Kessler, *Washington State Community College*

Elizabeth Kleinfeld, *Red Rocks Community College*

David Konitzer, *Art Institute of Tampa*

Elizabeth Kuipers, *Georgia Southwestern State University*

Jane Lasarenko, *Slippery Rock University of Pennsylvania*

Jeanette Lugo, *Valdosta State University*

Criostoir MacSuibhne, *SUNY Canton*

Mercedes Martinez, *Global Language Institute*

Sean Mathews, *Adirondack Community College*

Diane Matza, *Utica College*

Sheila McAvey, *Becker College*

Jim McKeown, *McLennan Community College*

Pat McQueeney, *Johnson County Community College*

Robert Mellin, *Purdue University North Central*

Neil Michaels, *Saginaw Valley State University*

Mutiara Mohamad, *Fairleigh Dickinson University*

Missy-Marie Montgomery, *Springfield College*

Cleatta Morris, *Louisiana State University in Shreveport*

Mary Ellen Muesing, *UNC Charlotte*

Beverly Neiderman, *Kent State University*

Julie Nichols, *Okaloosa-Walton College*

Pam Nichols, *Alma High School*

Deborah Noonan, *University of South Florida*

Shelley Palmer, *Rowan-Cabarrus Community College*

James Pangborn, *SUNY at Oswego*

Carolyn Perry, *Westminster College*

Mary Peterson, *Avon Unit Community Schools*

Robert Petersen, *Middle Tennessee State University*

Andrew Preslar, *Lamar State College-Orange*

Arthur Rankin, *Louisiana State University at Alexandria*

Robin Reid, *Texas A&M University-Commerce*

Diane Reuszer, *Northeastern Junior College*

Andrey Reznikov, *Black Hills State University*

Katherine Riegel, *SUNY Potsdam*

Rebekah Rios-Harris, *Cedar Valley College*

Danielle Saad, *Alvernia College*

Linda Sacks, *Monmouth University*

Michael Schanhals, *North Muskegon High School*

Lisette Schillig, *Lock Haven University of Pennsylvania*

Summer Serpas, *Orange Coast College*

Elizabeth Shannon, *West Allegheny*

Beverly Slavens, *Arkadelphia High School*

Helen Szymanski, *College of DuPage*

Jeff Tate, *Northern Oklahoma College*

Luke Tesdal, *University of Texas Arlington*

Donna Townsend, *Baker College of Clinton Township*

Rita Treutel, *University of Alabama at Birmingham*

John Wegner, *Angelo State University*

Vernetta Williams, *Southwest Florida College*

Robert Wilson, *Cedar Crest College*

Carmen Wong, *John Tyler Community College*

Kristy Wooten, *Catawba Valley Community College*

Elizabeth Wurz, *Columbus State University*

# 1 Inventing Ideas

# Chapter Contents

# "Writing is not simply a one-way flow of information from the brain to the hand. Quite the opposite . . ."

Thousands of students across the country are required to take introductory college writing courses. These courses are nearly universal requirements, and it seems reasonable to ask, Why? What's the purpose of these courses, and more specifically, what's the purpose of writing? How does writing well relate to engineering, nursing, photography, business management, or aviation? Why do business and governmental leaders throughout the country want all students to take more, not less, writing? If students will not be writing essays in their jobs, why should they write essays in college?

When asked such questions, people tend to respond that writing is important for two reasons: because it helps to *express* thoughts and *communicate* ideas. However, they often forget a third point. Beyond expression and communication, there is another, perhaps far more powerful, reason:

Writing is an invention tool. It helps us to generate new ideas and add dimension to the ideas we already have. Writing is not merely the performance or expression of something we know or believe. It's also an *act of inventing, developing, and reinventing what can be known.*

Writing is not simply a one-way flow of information from the brain to the hand. Quite the opposite—it actually produces new thoughts, changes everyday life, and vitalizes the consciousness of the writer, the reader(s), and the people who interact with them both. These are the reasons that writing is nearly a universal requirement. And it is not simply because our culture needs better communicators, but because we will always need better ideas and better ways of thinking about the situations we face every day.

Have you ever asked yourself where ideas come from? Do they pop out of thin air? Do they come from divine beings whispering in our ears? Do they come from lab experiments? From chemical reactions in beakers and test tubes? From someone's heart? Another organ? Most scholars who wrestle with such questions believe that ideas come from language, that people build, refine, pull apart, and rebuild ideas with words. And while we can use words silently in our heads, the act of writing dramatizes and amps up the whole idea-making process. In other words, writing is like an idea calculator. It allows us to put ideas "out there" on a page or a screen and then process them—adding, subtracting, multiplying, and dividing. Writing allows us to put an idea into a formula, add exponents, and radicalize. It allows us to keep several abstractions floating around at once, to link thoughts, to collapse them, to evaluate them, and even to cancel them out.

At the individual level, inside one's own head, writing is the act of developing a better relationship with ideas. (That's an important relationship!) When we develop a point in writing, we can get distance from it and see it in front of us. Like a painter, a writer cannot simply hold his or her ideas in the mind. They must be drawn out (in language). Then the writer can add color, shading, sky, ground, background—or even redraw from a different perspective.

At a social level, writing can be an invitation, a convergence of many minds. In fact, in academia, writing is seen as a tool for creating social and institutional momentum: for directing people's energies, for guiding policies, for urging on new and better enterprises. Writing changes the way people act, spend, vote, teach, think, and even hope—which means this is all pretty serious and heavy business.

# Asking Questions

One of the most powerful ways to invent ideas is to ask questions. For instance, let's explore a basic or common concept such as *freedom.* We might ask, *What is it?* First, we might write out some initial thoughts:

### What is freedom?
Freedom is the ability to do whatever one wants. It's the feeling we get when we know that we can do whatever we want.

But can we go further? What else can be known or thought about freedom? Let's apply more questions:

### What particular behaviors are associated with freedom?
Politically speaking, voting, protesting, speaking one's mind, worshipping whatever or whomever one desires— or not worshipping at all. Personally, free people do what they want whenever they want. They make their own choices: what they want to buy or drive or eat, how they want to spend their time, where they want to go, what they want to read, whom they want to love or marry.

### What responsibilities come with freedom?
Maybe none. If people are free, they do what they want and let others clean up the mess or worry about the consequences. That sounds somehow wrong or bad, but that's what true freedom is. There's no impending rule that says one must do something or think something. Put this way, freedom—true freedom—might be pretty messy. People would get away with murder. Literally.

### What hidden role does freedom play in people's lives?
Most people are always trying to get free—from work, duty, homework, etc. They want to be "done" with the things other people assign to them. They want Saturday afternoon—when no one is saying, "Be here and do this." And politically (again), people throughout the world are dying for it. They stand in front of tanks, blow up government buildings, or pack their families onto wagons and trudge for hundreds of miles so they can experience freedom. So those are the obvious ways freedom works. But "a hidden role"? Is freedom hidden? Do we hide it from ourselves? Why would we do that? Don't we want it? I think most Americans spend their time in some kind of duty—work, school, both. When they're not working under someone else's guidelines, they look to fill up the freedom-time. They schedule it. I wonder if people know what to do with freedom . . . with time not gobbled up by duty. Skateboard? Listen to music? Read? Watch TV? Is that what freedom is? What about retirement? Isn't that supposed to be total freedom? If so, why do people get lonely? Why do senior citizens want something to do? Why do they volunteer? (They're always the ones at voting booths, libraries, bake sales, etc.) Maybe people want to be given things to do. Maybe they want to be a part of something. Beyond having the right to speak, marry, vote, work, and travel at will, people want to feel commissioned—to be of some good use. And in some way, that's the opposite of freedom. People yearn for freedom but suffer when they experience it in the extreme.

When the writer applies more Invention Questions, the concept grows. The writer's thinking gets richer, more complex. After the third question here, the writer gets past the obvious, taken-for-granted layer and digs up some truly interesting ideas, for instance, that unmitigated freedom could be ugly.

> **Obvious Layer:** freedom is about escaping duty.
> **Deeper Layer:** escaping all duty comes with a price.

This intellectual process is invention. Asking questions and writing responses makes writers go from an obvious idea (*freedom is doing whatever one wants*) to something less obvious (*freedom is the sometimes spiritually hollow lack of duty*). And in academic writing, readers are hoping for something less obvious. The goal isn't to state what most people, or even some people, already think. Rather, it is to bring hidden layers to the surface.

This is no easy task. The process requires a certain degree of endurance—a willingness and ability to continue thinking through intellectual walls and past "answers." In other words, inventive writers do not imagine having answers stored up inside their heads. Instead, they imagine the questions as highways, roads, alleys, and hidden trails to more complex thoughts. Offering a quick answer to an Invention question is like stopping at, and never leaving, the first rest area at the start of a cross-country trip.

## Activity

With a small group, take a concept (such as education, individuality, authority, crime, or art) and try to dig up something new—some hidden layer or less obvious quality, something that others in your class may not imagine. Use the following questions:

▶ What is it?

▶ What particular behaviors are associated with it?

▶ What responsibilities come with it?

▶ What hidden role does it play in people's lives?

# Re-inventing Education

Some may ask, *Why go through all this work? Why not just write a draft of the first idea that comes into our heads? Why twist and turn the ideas and potentially get confused?* These are fair questions. The answers again may lie in the broader goals of higher education and of writing courses. In the twentieth century, public education in the United States emphasized getting things in the right order. It was the age of factory thinking. Education adopted the industrial model of cranking out products (students) who fit a mold, who all knew the same kinds of things about the same topics. In writing classrooms, students wrote essays to demonstrate their mastery of a format. They mimicked the correct order of ideas. They were given formulas for making things look right: *Put your thesis, no matter what it is, at the end of the first paragraph; make sure your paragraphs are five to seven sentences long;* and so on. But such thinking, such assignments, such assumptions about learning and work are fading into history.

We are often reminded that the world is changing at an exponential pace. Much of the information that you learn this year will be outdated, or completely irrelevant, in two to three years. Most current college students will change careers, not simply jobs, several times. Many of you will have jobs that do not exist today in industries or services that are not even imagined. You will deal with problems that have no label yet. In this shifting professional life, workers, leaders, employees, and employers who can invent new ways to think, new ways to reach people, new ways to serve and connect people will thrive. Those who cannot will fall behind. More than any other time in human history, new ideas will matter. Because so many people will grasp for the same resources, good thinkers will be in high demand in every profession. And in this environment, the "correct" placement of your thesis is not as important as the development of a good idea.

Imagine that you're an employer. Your company is about to go global. In fact, in an indirect way, you're already global because similar companies from India, China, Canada, and Germany are putting offices in your state. Two essays walk into a job interview. (That's right. The candidates are essays—and they can walk.) You carefully review the candidates:

## Essay A

- Gives three reasons why X is bad. (You've heard all three reasons many times before because the topic has been debated publicly for years.)
- Has a clearly worded thesis at the end of the first paragraph.
- Includes a few statistics from an online encyclopedia.
- Has okay grammar and contains proficient sentences all about the same length.
- Has a title: Three Reasons Why X Is Bad.

## Essay B

- Offers a new perspective about an unusual topic.
- Addresses unstated assumptions of potential readers.
- Engages potentially opposing claims (fears and doubts about this new perspective).
- Explains a hidden complexity in the topic, something that people may otherwise ignore.
- Develops a careful line of reasoning.
- Has okay grammar and contains a variety of sentence patterns to dramatize the thinking.

Now, considering your company's situation, which essay would you rather hire? Which one will help contribute something in the shifting and complex global economy? Which one will add vitality?

If it's not clear already, we believe that the students who can invent ideas, who can develop an inventive intellectual posture, will thrive in their academic and professional lives. Those who can recalculate old formulas and feel comfortable writing their way to new ideas will fare far better than those who can only master conventional formats. But we must also admit that invention is difficult work. In fact, the act of writing is an intellectual struggle to shape thoughts and make connections that seem, at first, totally impossible. Good writers do not look for easy topics; they understand that valuable ideas are not those that simply fall out of their brains and onto the page. And in the most difficult moments, they remember that difficulty is an essential part of the process. Because the human brain is not a *linear* machine (it does not necessarily produce thoughts that go from left to right and then down a page), writers understand that their ideas have to be formed and re-formed. And in that long, and sometimes exhausting, process, they turn frustration to inquiry. They hope to find valuable insights in moments of uncertainty.

And we should also note that invention—all the intellectual practices that work to develop increasingly focused insights—does not belong only to academic and professional life. It is, or can be, a vital practice in everyday life. After all, our domestic and social affairs often (maybe on an hourly basis!) call for good thinking, not just intellectual habit. An inventive thinker learns to ask productive questions and crack open possibilities:

- How can I calm my mother-in-law's anger about my religious views?
- Why does my roommate think I'm against her?
- How do we get out of this constant battle with the neighbor's teenage kids?
- Which candidate will really change the economy for the better?

What we call *invention* was not created for schoolwork, for essay assignments, or even for business. It was conceived 2,400 years ago by the ancient Greeks as a tool for analyzing and debating everyday issues. Invention was the first part of a bigger practice called *rhetoric*—the study or art of persuasion.

The Greeks had the radical notion that common people, not holy or military leaders, could think for themselves and even make policies best suited for their own affairs. In other words, the Greeks invented the thing we now call democracy. And when they started to solve problems and debate issues publicly, some people realized that successful thinkers and speakers employed certain moves; they weren't just the loudest talkers or the most charming personalities. It didn't take them long to realize that good thinking was about inventing new insights, not simply rephrasing a common opinion in fancy words. Good thinkers could ask hard questions. They could use language to show complexity and possibility. It was soon obvious to the Greeks that everyday life in a democracy requires good thinking—inventive thinking.

Colin Dixon/Arcaid/Corbis

# Considering the Essay

Why do all of these introductory college courses assign essays? What's so important about an essay? After all, most people will not spend their post-college lives writing in essay format. So there must be something besides the format that people in higher education find valuable.

If the goals of college writing were only expression and communication, instructors could assign all kinds of texts, from posters to letters, that are much better at announcing opinions than the traditional academic essay. But college writing courses go far beyond the act of announcing an idea. These courses focus on the processes of refining and developing ideas—on inventing new ways to think about familiar issues. And to those ends, the essay still serves well. Perhaps more than any other kind of text, the essay is an open invitation for readers to think differently. Every academic essay, no matter what the topic, says to readers, "Come into this space for the time being, and let us work through an idea. In fact, let us think differently about X." The essay is fundamentally different from other texts:

- Posters and fliers announce ideas to readers.
- Letters share ideas with a specific readership.
- Reports communicate previously compiled information.
- Memos communicate the status of some situation or bit of news.
- Essays work through the complexity of a new or developing idea.

Of course, the distinctions are not quite this clean. Letters can work through complexity, and memos can share ideas and communicate information. And the goals of announcing and communicating are often reached through much thought and invention. But the driving force of an academic essay is somewhat different from that of other texts. Its goal is to help both writers and readers walk carefully through unfamiliar complexity.

But what about electronic texts? Technology has generated a range of new texts and new ways of dealing with ideas. Blogs, tweets, chat rooms, Facebook status updates, and wikis, to name a few, have blended traditional types of writing to accommodate various communicative needs and desires of the information age. Blogs, for instance, borrow a great deal from the essay tradition, and, like the essay, they vary tremendously in their degree of formality and complexity. (Some blogs are unfocused political rants, some are daily personal expressions, and some are sophisticated examinations of current issues.)

Also, consider the significant role of the essay in academic life. The essay has become the most common tool in most fields for publicly working through new ideas. When engineers, philosophers, nurses, physicians, and scholars in all disciplines develop something helpful, some new way of practicing their trade, they do not simply announce it to their peers in an ad or a memo. (A quick announcement is not likely to change how people think; it will not uproot common disciplinary practices or alter the flow of daily life.) Instead, they explain the new idea in a professional essay and publish it in a scholarly journal (*Journal of the American Medical Association, Social Psychology Quarterly, Rhetoric Review, Critical Care Nursing Quarterly,* and so on). These essays carefully walk readers through a new concept. They show the assumptions, previously held beliefs, conventional wisdom, and the writer's new contribution to the field. The essay is a tool for intellectual climate change.

In college classes, most instructors hope for the same: They hope that students will make some new contribution to conventional wisdom. They hope that essays will do more than announce a common opinion (that guns are dangerous, that abortion kills babies, that marijuana could solve a host of physical ailments if only Congress would awaken from the medicinal dark ages), and instead help readers to see those topics, or any topic, in a slightly different light. They hope your essay will help you and your peers to think differently. And they probably hope that your essay will change their own thinking for the better. (Believe it or not, most college instructors are waiting to be influenced by the essays they assign!)

This may be different from what you've been taught. Unfortunately, standardized tests and proficiency exams suggest that essays are proving grounds, places where students show they can properly perform good textual manners by arranging thoughts in the right order and punctuating correctly. While grammatical and stylistic conventions are important because they help with communication, they are not the sole features of an academic essay. As you will see by samples and readings in this book, an essay must, first and foremost, invite readers to think differently about a topic.

## Activity

Find an academic journal article that corresponds to your major or a major that you've considered. Most college or university libraries have databases with long lists of academic journals. You might find them under *Periodicals* or *Journals.* Read the introduction to one of the essays. How does the essay relate to or speak to common practice or wisdom in the field?

# Reading for Intellectual Agility and Rhetoric

If your situation is like that of nearly every other college student, instructors will ask you to read essays that have little or no obvious connection to your life. You may be interested in football, and your college English instructor may assign an essay about the punk movement in Europe or vineyards in Washington. Why? Why should urban students read about agricultural practices, rivers, or forests? Why should rural students read about the streets of Chicago, the Manhattan subway, or the opera? Why should twenty-year-olds read about the role of the World War II generation in shaping the suburbs? Is it because the instructors want students to get specific information on those topics? Probably not. In fact, reading assignments in college English courses are often connected to a larger academic goal: to broaden students' perspectives.

Most readers ask themselves questions. Two questions seem to arise consistently:

Do I like this essay?

Can I relate to this information?

But those questions can limit readers. In fact, if they're the *only* questions available, they put the reader at a big disadvantage by limiting what he or she can learn. Most instructors want students to think about topics from different angles, and to examine life outside of their own spheres. In other words, instructors hope that students gain some *intellectual agility*—the ability to move from position to position without tremendous difficulty, to imagine a realm of experience and perspective beyond their own biases and reflexes.

If readers have some other questions in mind, some other reasons to continue (besides liking something or relating to it), they might discover something and gain intellectual agility. Imagine, for instance, how the following questions might take a reader somewhere more valuable than the two preceding questions:

How does this essay prompt me to think?

What new idea does it offer?

What new connections does it make?

Why am I resisting the point? Why do I agree with the point?

Where is this essay taking me? How far will it go?

With such questions swirling in their heads, good readers are more apt to push onward through foreign ideas, to examine new assumptions, to carry away something significant.

Good readers do more than read. They read and monitor their own thinking as they move through the text, and they allow themselves to go further than their personal likes or ability to relate. They tolerate (maybe even bask in) intellectual discomfort. They consider ideas and assumptions that might seem foreign, weird, abstract, or unnecessarily provocative.

So the purpose of reading in college goes far beyond the two most common questions readers may ask themselves. In an academic setting, we do not read merely to relate or associate with the information. We read to rethink issues, to discover positions we had not previously imagined, to revise common perceptions. And to fulfill such goals, we must expect to work through ideas, even struggle at times. Most importantly, we must expect to be surprised, to have our tidy mental rooms messed up occasionally. Reading in academia means being intellectually adventurous and expecting something new or radically different.

In the world beyond college, employers are not looking for people who are deeply self-interested, those who can be excited only about their own interests, who can think well only about their favorite topics. They want people who can think well beyond their favorite talking points, who can shift perspectives and see an issue from another point of view. And shifting perspectives takes practice. It's not easy. One powerful way to warm up the intellectual muscles—to stretch how our minds work—is to read about people, places, and perspectives that are foreign to our experiences.

Another goal of reading assignments involves the *rhetorical* layer: Behind the obvious content of an essay, there lurks a complex set of *rhetorical tools*—strategies that persuade the reader to accept the writer's ideas. Even though an essay may be about pollution, cats, childhood obesity, or any other topic, it has another dimension, a rhetorical dimension. You might think of this as the machinery of the essay, the stuff that makes it go. And most often, that rhetorical dimension is the reason instructors assign particular essays. It's not the "information" that instructors want students to focus on, but the way information is dealt with (analyzed, revised, dramatized, even radicalized). For example, in Chapter 4, Anne-Marie Oomen's essay focuses on a sand dune. If you are asked to read Oomen's essay, it's probably not because your instructor loves sand, nature, or hiking. So the essay must have some other value. It must be up to something other than celebrating sand dunes. And that something must be important to college writing—and to higher education. What is that something?

The answer lies in Oomen's rhetorical prowess: her ability to help readers to think differently, to yank readers' attention away from the mundane aspects of everyday life and conventional ways of thinking:

I have come to love the wind here, the power it has to erase through its insistent presence. Just as it has blown out the hilltop, the very place that represented the great mother, Michimokwa, the wind has fragmented the story itself, altered what the place means. The meaning shifts, catches in the wind, lifts and transforms until there will be nothing left of even her heart. This is not sad, but rather the wind waking the imagination and simultaneously, paradoxically, waking us to emptiness, to the limits of story. To mystery. This is the wind making the place where story meets void, the opposite of meaning. The hollow bowl that also shapes our being.

It wouldn't matter if the essay were about canyons, skyscrapers, or subways; what's important are her strategies for nudging readers to think—to re-see themselves, their lives, their mysteries, their stories. So when you do get to the Oomen essay, don't be fooled. *It ain't about sand.*

## Activity

When we see only the obvious content (or information) of the essay and miss the rhetorical dimension, we miss the most transferable and usable part. It is like going for a drive and seeing only the windshield of your car; like seeing a movie and remembering only the names of the actors; like walking through a town and seeing only the street signs. To illustrate your understanding of this point, generate another analogy and share it with the class. *When we see only the obvious content of the essay and miss the rhetorical dimension, it's like _____.*

# Applying Rhetoric to Your Own Writing

The rhetorical dimension of an essay is the layer of strategies that prompt readers to accept its ideas. When we read an essay, we get not only the information but also the set of intellectual moves and rhetorical strategies the writer employs. We can learn from and use these strategies in our own writing. In the following passage from "How I Lost the Junior Miss Pageant" (page 31), Cindy Bosley makes a sophisticated rhetorical move. She focuses on her own misunderstanding or naïvety but then quickly pulls the reader outward and focuses on the town of her childhood—a hard-knuckled town that seemed out of sync with the idea of beauty contests:

> Clearly, I lacked the save-the-whales-and-rainforest civic-mindedness required not only of Miss America, but of Junior Miss America, too. Even, although one wouldn't think it, in Ottumwa, Iowa, where my mother would go on to work in a bathtub factory, and then a glue factory, and then an electrical connectors factory (the factory worker's version of upward mobility), and finally, a watch factory where they shipped and received not just watches but cocaine in our town that at that time had more FBI agents in it than railroad engineers. And even in this town where my sister would go to work the kill floor of the pork plant where, for fun, the workers shot inspection dye at each other and threatened each other's throats with hackknives. And even in this town where my cousin, age 13, would bring a bomb to seventh grade for show-and-tell, and get caught and evacuated, and be given community service to do because the public-school-as-terrorist-ground phenomena hadn't yet been born.

Bosley's passage holds some valuable lessons for writers. At the grammatical level, she takes significant risks (such as some intentional sentence fragments) that parallel some of the essay's insights. At the rhetorical level, she lines up particular details about her hometown. These details are intensely specific and even gruesome, and more importantly, they add up to a feeling about the place, about Bosley's childhood, which was completely at odds with the notion of a beauty contest.

If we remove specific content (information about beauty contests, pork plants, and bombs for show-and-tell), what do we have left? We have some rhetorical moves that we can transport to other topics:

- Personal testimony works if the details are riveting.
- Grotesque details can be highly engaging, even necessary.
- If the details are specific enough and lined up together, they can add up to an undeniable conclusion about a place or an event.
- As writers, we're allowed to wonder ourselves.

In an essay from Chapter 4: Observing, Chester McCovey contrasts the past and the present. Like Bosley, he does not simply say that something happened. He imagines how it happened and what it means:

> My grandparents' garages were small, just enough for one car and a few tools—not much of a garage for today's homeowner. In those days the garage kept a car and a small lawnmower, some rakes, and so on. The garage today must keep much more. One can see, then, how the exchange occurred. Like an old-fashioned trade in baseball, gone is the home team's beloved front porch, replaced by a big, new garage. Of

course the trade is much more interesting than that. And a look at how it occurred enlightens us a little about the world in which we live. More importantly, it tells us not so much about how life is now but about how it came to be. And, I would argue, it shows us the way in which things will continue to change.

After making the simple contrast between the past and present, McCovey offers an analogy (a comparison to trading in baseball). And then he suggests some hidden complexity—some "interesting" dynamics going on behind the shift from porch to garage. (He later deals with these dynamics in the essay.) For both Bosley and McCovey, meaning lies beyond the facts of the case. The writer must probe behind the physical things and events.

In his essay, "Americans and the Land," John Steinbeck describes how early Americans ravaged the continent, and he laments that modern Americans carry on those early traditions. In the following passage, he notes how carefully scientists work to avoid polluting outer space:

> Since the river-polluters and the air-poisoners are not criminal or even bad people, we must presume that they are heirs to the early conviction that sky and water are unowned and that they are limitless. In the light of our practices here at home it is very interesting to me to read of the care taken with the carriers of our probes into space, to make utterly sure that they are free of pollution of any kind. We would not think of doing to the moon what we do every day to our own dear country.

Steinbeck reveals the absurdity of common practice—a standard yet critical move for writers. His point is not simply "don't pollute," a common sentiment. Instead, he shows the blindness and hypocrisy of polluting one's own country. He references one behavior (being careful not to pollute the moon, where no one lives) and juxtaposes it to a common behavior (openly poisoning our land, where all humans live). From this passage, we might carry away a single powerful question: What act do we allow or even defend in one situation that we forbid in another?

Good reading leads to good writing. If we keep our radar on and look at the content and the rhetorical dimension of essays, we are more apt to see the moves, questions, and strategies that can be used for any topic.

## Activity

Read the following passage from Jayme Stayer's essay, "Whales R Us" (page 213), an argument about Sea World. Behind the specific information about Sea World, what is Stayer *doing*? What kinds of rhetorical moves does he make? How might a writer use those moves for another topic?

> I'm an educator, and I pay close attention when someone is trying to teach me something. So on my way out of Sea World, I asked myself what I had learned. Like a student who has crammed for an exam, I was able to recall lots of idiocies, but could only say I had truly learned two things. (1) Thanks to the film, I learned that sharks attack humans only when provoked, and, (2) thanks to their anthropomorphizing skits, I learned that sea otters are *cute* little buggers. Even if these elements were judicious pedagogical objectives (which they are not), they still don't add up to anything resembling education. In fact, the entire experience of Sea World is suspiciously similar to the exact opposite of education: mind-control.

# How to Use *The Composition of Everyday Life*

As is probably clear, this book is about discovering and developing ideas through reading, inventing, and writing. Each of the main chapters (2–12) begins with three sample essays that illustrate key rhetorical moves. The Invention sections follow the sample essays and constitute the majority of each chapter.

## Sample Essays

The essays in this book were written for fellow scientists, philosophers, economists, business leaders, politicians, family members, students, and public citizens. They show the real writing that gets done in the public sphere—how professionals in all walks of life talk to their colleagues and to the public. Despite their individual discipline or career field, the writers all seek to develop ideas that involve and impact the world around them.

Each chapter features a professional writer (someone whose writing was published prior to this textbook), a commissioned writer (a writer or teacher who used the chapter to develop an essay), and a student writer (a college student who used an earlier version of the textbook to create a successful project). Each type of writer (professional, commissioned, student) brings something unique to the chapter and shows a set of qualities that you might adopt in your own projects. And while some of the writing techniques and personal styles differ, some qualities are constant: valuable insights, well-supported ideas, and engaging voices.

To help you reach beyond the obvious content of each essay and get at the rhetorical dimension, each reading is followed by Writing Strategies and Exploring Ideas questions. Also, each chapter features an *annotated* essay (an essay with comments and analysis in the margins). These annotations show a reader stopping at certain places, noticing particular claims and strategies, and speaking back to ideas.

## Writing Topics

*The Composition of Everyday Life* offers several possibilities for inventing and developing writing topics. You can (1) read the essays in a designated chapter and then use the Ideas for Writing after one or more of the essays; (2) use the Point of Contact section, which will help generate topics from everyday life; or (3) read several content-related essays, according to the thematic table of contents at the front of the book, and then develop topics that emerge from the readings. For all three options, the Invention section of each chapter can be used to develop writing projects.

As you consider your own writing projects, imagine that topics are not pre-packaged issues—as though writers simply choose something they like and start drafting. Instead, imagine topics as ideas that emerge slowly through an invention process. If you imagine topics as something to *develop,* rather than something to *choose,* your intellectual experience and your writing will likely be more intense.

## Invention

**"Invention is the mother of necessities."**
—*Marshall McLuhan*

As we explain at the beginning of this chapter, invention is the process of discovering some new idea and developing that idea through focused exploration. It is often associated with one particular activity: coming up with an idea to write about. However, invention is a complex activity that extends far beyond the initial topic idea. It involves committing to an idea, exploring it in depth, and discovering its worth.

When writers take the time to explore topics, they discover something worth sharing, something that is not already floating around in everyone's minds. In short, invention makes all the difference between powerful, engaging writing that introduces new ideas and dull, lifeless writing that offers nothing but a writer's attempt to fulfill an assignment.

Because invention is the most difficult but most reward-ing part of academic writing, this book devotes several sec-tions per chapter to it. The following sections appear in each chapter and are designed to help you through the invention process:

- **Point of Contact** will help you discover a topic from everyday life.
- **Analysis** will launch you beyond initial thoughts and help you explore the topic.
- **Public Resonance** will help you extend the topic out-ward, to make the topic relevant to a community of readers.
- **Thesis** will help you focus your thinking and develop a revelatory point.
- **Rhetorical Tools** will help you support your point with a variety of common strategies.

The questions in each section, those marked by green arrows, are not meant to be answered directly in a final essay. Instead, they are meant to generate ideas, focus, and support strategies for your writing.

## Invention Workshops

Throughout the Invention sections in the chapters, you will see Invention Workshops—prompts to enlist the help of others in the development of your projects. Rather than answer the Invention Questions alone, you can gather in a small group and take turns explaining your topic to others. The whole group then can explore your topic with you by focusing on a single question or set of questions.

Invention Workshops can be the most powerful ele-ment in a composition course. If all parties are invested in the struggle to focus and vitalize ideas, the process can dra-matically improve the thinking and writing for each project. But be warned! If approached uncritically or lackadaisically, workshops can decrease energy and deflate ideas. For exam-ple, in the first four workshop transcriptions that follow, the ideas get derailed. One of the participants shuts down the thinking or diffuses it somehow. But in the fifth workshop, the participants take Linda's topic to a compelling place. By following the ideas put forward, they build to a new insight:

### Workshop 1

LINDA:     What is the significance of a tattoo?
MARCUS:   The significance is just whatever people think it is.

### Workshop 2

LINDA:     What is the significance of a tattoo?
DIANA:     Well, it depends on the actual tattoo, doesn't it? A flower has a different significance than a skull.
LINDA:     Maybe. But why do people get any tattoos?
DIANA:     They just want to. Everybody has their own reasons.

### Workshop 3

LINDA:     What is the significance of a tattoo?
JACK:      What do you mean?
LINDA:     What do tattoos mean? What's the meaning behind inscribing ink permanently onto the skin?
JACK:      My cousin has this huge tattoo on his back.

### Workshop 4

LINDA:     What is the significance of a tattoo?
MARCUS:   What do you mean, "significance"?
LINDA:     You know, what's the fundamental meaning of a tattoo? What's the *meaning* behind inscribing ink permanently onto the skin?
DIANA:     I think it's gross, myself. I mean, don't get me wrong, people can do whatever they want with their own bodies, but it's really disgusting to me.

### Workshop 5

LINDA:     What is the significance of a tattoo?
MARCUS:   What do you mean, "significance"?
LINDA:     You know, what's the fundamental meaning of a tattoo? What's the *meaning* behind inscribing ink permanently onto the skin?
DIANA:     Well, when people get a tattoo, they're doing something permanent to themselves—or at least they assume they are.
MARCUS:   They're making a statement of some kind.
DIANA:     A statement that has permanence.
JACK:      Yeah, that's gotta mean something. People must want to have something about themselves, on themselves, that is not going to go away. It must feel . . . sorta . . . important, ritualistic, big, you know . . .

LINDA: So, people long for permanence. That's interesting. And a tattoo is a little (maybe tiny) way of establishing that . . . on their own bodies.

MARCUS: It's also something that is totally personal. I mean, you can have a tattoo of anything, and it's all your own.

DIANA: Yeah, that's why people get tattoos of their loved ones' names.

JACK: My brother has a tattoo of his old girlfriend's name.

DIANA: Yeah, my dad has a tattoo of some kind that doesn't really mean anything, and he won't even tell us what it's from. He got it when he was a teenager.

LINDA: OK. But what do those examples show? Tattoos are still there, but the people's lives go on.

MARCUS: Well, life is change. You can't escape change.

LINDA: And tattoos are a way of resisting change? A way of marking the present on one's body—storing it, keeping it with you.

MARCUS: Right! That's the significance.

## Activity

1. What rhetorical decisions derail the first four discussions?

2. What rhetorical decisions propel the discussion in number 5?

3. Conduct your own invention workshop on the significance of tattoos. What other insight can you develop about the topic?

## Point of Contact

The Point of Contact section, the first part of the Invention section in each chapter, invites the writer to slow down, to stop, to notice common and not-so-common aspects of life. The point of contact refers to the writer's moment of awareness. It is where the writer's vision collides with issues, events, situations, behaviors, and other people. The idea in this section is that writing begins with a discovery—a real-

ization about something that might otherwise go unnoticed. Therefore, writers have to be ready; their radar has to be on.

As you go through the Point of Contact sections, you will notice lists of questions that are designed to generate possibilities for writing topics. Think of the questions as exploration tools; they raise possible points of interest for writing. However, the lists are by no means exhaustive; they are simply examples of what can be asked. Follow up (in peer groups or alone) to generate more questions. (And if you are outside of an academic setting, it is certainly fair play to borrow a family member or friend to help with the invention process.)

## Analysis

We are all familiar with analysis. We participate in it constantly. We see auto mechanics analyze our cars to discover the cause of the knocking sound. We see our doctors analyze conditions to understand why we feel sick. Basically put, such analysis is a process of discovering why and/or how something occurs. But analysis also involves discovering meaning. Writers are not content to simply see a person, situation, or object. They explore the significance; that is, they imagine what ideas a thing might suggest. For instance, a writer sees an empty storefront in a strip mall and imagines that it suggests corporate irresponsibility or a declining economic system or even the end of an era when businesses lasted for several years before leaving a community. In other words, the storefront has potential meaning when analyzed (and often that analysis, as we will make clear in the next section, can make a topic relevant to a broader community).

Analysis leads to the complexities of issues, and revealing those complexities, rather than avoiding them, is at the heart of college writing. The Invention Questions in each Analysis section are designed to help you reveal the complexities of your topic. (See the questions and responses about *freedom* on page 6.) As in all the Invention sections, the goal of the questions is to help generate some idea that is distinct, surprising . . . even weird.

## Public Resonance

Perhaps the most important feature of writing is that it matters to a reader. This may sound obvious, but topics are not necessarily intrinsically relevant to people's lives. They need to be made relevant. They need to be expressed in a way that involves readers. Consider capital punishment: It is not, in itself, a relevant topic to the average college student, or even the average American citizen. Most people have not had a personal experience with the death penalty, but many people still have much to say about it. Why? The answer is rather simple: Capital punishment has been made relevant. Human rights activists, civil liberties groups, and religious groups have spoken or written the relevance of capital punishment into being. They have made the life of a death row inmate in Texas relevant to a suburban schoolteacher in Minnesota or a biology major at UCLA.

Good writers can make an issue resonate with their readers' feelings, thoughts, and situations. They can transform a bad day at the office into an important efficiency issue for all workers. Or they can make a seemingly distant event, like the destruction of rainforests or the death of a prison inmate, real and immediate. They make a connection between two things: (1) what they see, know, do, believe, and feel; and (2) how that matters to other people. It may not matter to every other person, but generally, it *resonates* with the public. It speaks to and engages the members of a community who, like the writer, are able to look beyond themselves (the "me") and into the public arena (the "we").

The assumption behind public resonance is that we are deeply connected to others in our communities, and even beyond those communities. Our very identities are bound to a complex system of relationships that extend into all different realms of social life. We are tied by economic, social, institutional, political, familial, religious, and even physiological connections. We share laws, fears, dreams, and hopes. And when writers tap into those connections, when they make topics part of that large social network, they achieve public resonance.

Finally, consider the Public Resonance sections as Analysis. In these sections, we're not simply analyzing the topic; we're analyzing how people tend to think about the topic.

**Analysis:** Focuses on the topic itself.
**Public Resonance:** Focuses on how people think.

Writers cannot simply consider their topic. They must consider the values, assumptions, beliefs, and opinions that people have about the topic. Only then can they understand what to emphasize, what to minimize, what to insist upon, what to dramatize. Generally, writers can do this even without extensive research. By asking key questions, however, they can discover a great deal about the social realm. The following questions (taken from Chapter 5: Analyzing Concepts) might help us to discover some important layers to freedom:

### Is the concept generally agreed upon?

Not really. People in the U.S. talk about freedom, but there are many disputes about it. Should people have the freedom to burn the flag, marry the person they love, get an abortion, own a machine gun or two, stockpile hand grenades, stage a protest at a funeral, or hold the majority of a company's stock and be the CEO at the same time? The answers to such questions are wrapped up with one's political beliefs.

### What is the possible connection between the topic and some public concern?

People are deeply concerned about not simply their own freedom but other people's freedom. In the 2004 election, millions of people voted to make sure that other people didn't have the freedom to marry whom they want. In this sense, personal freedom is a kind of misnomer. It's not personal at all. An individual's freedom in the U.S. depends entirely on what everyone else thinks! I'm only free as far as others allow me to be.

Here, we're beginning to explore how complex freedom gets when it's analyzed against a backdrop of human affairs. This is the spirit of the Public Resonance sections throughout this book. The goal is to seek out the most resonant layers of the topic—the most powerful way the topic embeds itself into the deep structure of public life. This is no easy task. Often, the most resonant layer is the most hidden. For example, we can easily discover how freedom comes up in everyday life in songs, anthems, and public documents, but it's more difficult to discover how freedom works in public thinking, beneath those songs and anthems.

## Activity

Public resonance is about extending a topic outward—pulling it into social, political, cultural layers beyond the individual writer and reader. Consider one of the following topics: your pet, college loans, *American Idol.* What is the possible connection between the topic and some public concern?

Try to discover how the topic wraps around the deep structure of public life—how it clings to some quiet values, ways of thinking, ways of believing.

## Thesis

A thesis statement is more than a one-sentence summary of an essay. It represents an essay's most pointed and dense idea, the one that gives everything else in the essay purpose. Whether the essay project is observing, arguing, or problem solving, thesis statements focus writer and reader on some new insight.

Throughout the chapters, we make a distinction between flat and revelatory thesis statements—between statements that announce an obvious opinion and those that provoke a new way of thinking. Revelatory statements contribute something; they prompt readers to imagine topics differently; they pose alternative notions, reveal hidden sides.

> **Flat Statements:** obvious, plain
> **Revelatory Statements:** provocative, insightful, contributive

For example, in the following sentences, the first statement is flat, a simple announcement of common thinking. But the follow-up sentences dig up something new. The last three statements are ripe for a powerful essay on an otherwise typical topic:

> Cell phones can make people behave rudely.
>
> Cell phones enable teenagers to perform their social lives for an audience.
>
> Cell phones reinforce the quiet notion that everyone is starring in his or her own reality show.
>
> Cell phone calls crowd out time for the most important dialogue in life—the one in our own heads.

Creating revelatory statements is not magic. In fact, language drives the process. When writers replace words with other words in a sentence, they replace patterns for thinking. The revelatory statements about cell phones were created by trading out the main verb in the original sentence. The writer removed *can make* and started dropping in other verbs: *enable, reinforce, crowd out.* These verbs actually made the writer think differently: What acts or attitudes do cell phones enable? What ideas, behaviors, assumptions do cell phones reinforce? What voices do cell phones crowd out?

Thesis statements do not emerge out of thin air. They come from an intensive evolution in which writers develop ideas with hard questions, focused dialogue, and reflective writing. Therefore, each chapter of *The Composition of Everyday Life* includes a Thesis section with prompts, sample thesis statements, and common thesis problems. Each section also shows the Evolution of a Thesis, the gradual development of one writer's idea. (The section comes after the Analysis and Public Resonance sections to allow writers the opportunity to think through and around their topics, to imagine a range of possible positions and perspectives, before committing to a particular statement.)

## Rhetorical Tools

As we mentioned, a rhetorical tool is a persuasion technique, a strategy for making people believe or accept an idea. Throughout the book, we will often refer to writers' rhetorical strategies—the techniques they use to convey their ideas and attempt to convince others to accept their positions. Good writers use good rhetorical tools. They come in many forms:

*Narration* is the act of storytelling. Stories are often used to persuade people, to help them appreciate the value of an idea.

*Description* involves giving specific details to the reader. Sensory details (sounds, smells, sights, tastes, touches) prompt a reader to experience a topic and so accept the ideas that the writer offers.

*Illustration* is the graphic depiction of an idea. While illustration certainly suggests pictures and charts, it can also be accomplished with words.

*Allusions* are references to some bit of public knowledge such as a historical event, a news event, a popular culture icon, or a literary text.

*Scenarios* are hypothetical situations.

*Testimony* is an eyewitness account of a particular scene or situation.

The operating assumption is that these tools can be used for any topic, that writers can apply them according to their specific needs. For example, allusions function for a huge number of writing situations. Imagine that we're developing an analytical essay about freedom. We might refer to various moments in history: the Revolutionary War, the Emancipation Proclamation, women's suffrage, Woodstock, the Patriot Act, civil unions, medical marijuana legislation, and so on. These are well-known situations that writers can reference as a way to make meaning about the idea of freedom.

The Rhetorical Tools section in each chapter explains the strategies that are most applicable and appropriate to that writing situation. However, no strategy is exclusive to any particular kind of writing. (The tools depend on the task at hand—the purpose, the audience, the topic.) The strategies introduced throughout the book can be used for unlimited writing situations. In Chapter 7: Making Arguments, the rhetorical tools become a bit more complicated. They involve *appeals, counterarguments,* and *concessions.* As you will see, the latter chapters of the book (from Chapter 7 on) all involve argumentative rhetorical tools; however, those introduced earlier in the book (such as narration and allusion) can also apply to argumentative writing. As you move through the book, think of your collection of rhetorical tools growing.

## Organizational Strategies

Writers must decide when and where they will use different rhetorical tools. Whether narrating an event, describing a scene, offering evidence, or making an allusion, writers can arrange rhetorical tools in an unlimited number of ways. If a writer has succeeded, a completed text should read like a coherent journey: The reader begins with some sense of direction (a good introduction) and passes through various locations and over different terrain (separate paragraphs), which are all connected with road signs (transitions). Finally, having traveled an intellectual route, the reader should feel as though he or she has arrived somewhere unique and valuable (a good conclusion).

The Organizational Strategies sections suggest possible ways ideas might be arranged. They present common (and sometimes less-common) options for shaping essays, ordering points, and connecting ideas.

## Writer's Voice

When we talk, we project a character or mood, not only by choosing certain words but also by changing the sound, pitch, and pace of our voices. (Some people talk with dramatic ups and downs; others blab at us in a single-note dirge.) Also, when we talk, we have the added tool of physical gestures. We can swing our hands around wildly, bow our heads, or open our eyes very wide at different moments of a sentence, simply to project an attitude. As writers, we have just as many strategies at our disposal. We may not be able to use our hands and eyes to gesture to the reader, but we have plenty of writerly strategies.

Every writer, for each writing event, creates a voice—the character that is projected by the language and style of the essay. Writers use a vast array of techniques to create voices. Sometimes those voices are very sober and formal. Other voices are comedic, even hilarious. This does not mean that the topic itself is funny; it means that the writer's presentation of ideas is humorous. Some of the best writers can make a potentially dull topic feel quirky, or a light topic have depth and profound significance. Of course, most writers fall somewhere in the middle between serious and comic, between utterly stiff and totally untamed.

Ultimately, you will create a voice, whether you know it or not. By simply writing a sentence, you create a voice in some small way. And since a writerly voice will emerge from your essays, it's certainly better to be crafty; otherwise, your voice might very well come off as . . . well . . . boring.

The Writer's Voice section in each chapter will help you to shape an appropriate voice or to explore different voices. While it is valuable to develop a personal voice (a style that feels unique or somehow genuinely more *you*), it is more valuable to experiment with voices. Because we often have to write in various contexts, for various audiences, and on various occasions, we need to be flexible, able to fit into audiences' conventions and expectations. Learning how to stylize voice according to the audience and situation is one of the most valuable skills for a writer.

## Vitality

Vitalized writing is lively. It yanks on readers' awareness. Vitality sometimes calls for winding sentence patterns that bring the reader through important intellectual curves and into nuanced, layered thoughts. And it sometimes calls for brief statements—short pops to the brain. The important principle is that sentences are the only interaction between a reader and writer. If the sentences are full of empty phrases, stiffened by repetitious patterns, or slowed by jumbled clauses, the reading experience will be lifeless.

Creating vitality in writing requires close attention to sentence patterns as well as a commitment to shaping and reshaping the language. To that end, each chapter in *The Composition of Everyday Life* includes a section that explains and illustrates particular vitality strategies. Like rhetorical tools, vitality strategies are not exclusive to any one chapter or writing situation. They can be applied across the board, according to the writer's discretion.

## Revision and Peer Review

Revision is about re-approaching ideas. As academic writers work, they constantly rethink their original ideas. To some degree, revision is fused into every act of the writing process. Writers are constantly asking questions: "Is this the best way to do this? Is there a better way to engage my reader?" Writers also benefit from a holistic rereading of their work: a process that involves first stepping away from the text for a period of time, and then reexamining everything (the main ideas, the supporting points, the organization, and even the voice). This probably sounds intimidating—rethinking everything after a significant amount of work has already gone into a draft. But revision is often where writers finally have a grasp on the whole, where they can make the ideas cohere, tighten, and come to life.

Each chapter provides a variety of revision prompts. They appear throughout the Invention sections and invite you to stop, refocus on the ideas you've created and to investigate the value and complexity of those ideas, with the hope that everything can be more intense, more focused, more engaging. Each chapter also includes a final Revision section with Peer Review questions so that writers can share their projects with others and receive focused and helpful feedback.

## Reflection

We often need time and distance from daily events before we understand them. As our brains and bodies rush onward and process information, we rarely have time to think about our own thinking—to get metacognitive. But when we're lying down at night, we can review the day and realize causes, effects, and nuances that we ignored in the moment. And it's often weeks, months, or years after an event that we begin to understand it.

The same goes with academic work. Often, the real intellectual benefit occurs after we are done writing. Only when we are in the fumes of the chaos, in the cerebral aftermath, do we understand what happened, what we had thought, what we now think. For this reason, writers often write about their own work after it is completed, submitted, put to rest. They look back on what they said and re-create something. In fact, much of the work that we now call scientific discovery was written as a kind of reflection on a previous study.

When writers look back on their projects, they can also see what worked and what didn't. If they look honestly, they may see strategies to use in the future and moves they'll never use again. This kind of reflection is critical to improvement. Without a formal and explicit step that requires us to examine our work, writers may leap to the next project with no wisdom gained.

Each chapter of this book offers an opportunity to reflect—to look back on your own writing and understand it from the vantage point that completion allows. Each Reflection section gives specific questions. Some sections also include an opportunity to go "beyond the essay" and re-create ideas in some other genre.

## A Final Note

As you work through the chapters, remember that writing is not merely a tool for expressing opinions; rather, it is a tool for making new ideas, and for adding new dimensions to old ideas. Our purpose in writing is not merely to express what we think, but to shape what can be known. We are hoping to explore intellectual possibilities. In this light, the college essay can be seen as a record of intellectual exploration—a writer's attempt and invitation to figure out something new.

# Inventing Ideas Assignment

Remember that invention is the engine behind good writing. Picture yourself as a creator of ideas rather than a writer of essays. In fact, rather than write a traditional essay for this assignment, imagine that your objective is to generate an increasingly focused and revelatory idea about the topic.

1. Choose one of the following topics: college writing assignments, high school sports programs, public art in the United States, the status of hip-hop music, teacher salaries, ghosts, trees in your neighborhood, leash laws, UFOs, a local coffee shop, a local grocery store, live music in your town or city.
2. Use the following Invention Questions, those marked by green arrows, as springboards for thinking about your topic. Write out your responses. Like the passages about freedom (pages 6 and 19), try to seek new dimensions to the idea.
3. After working through the questions, review your invention work. Where did you reveal something? In other words, which statements or passages pose alternative notions or reveal hidden sides? Describe those statements or passages, and explain why you think they are the most revelatory.

## Invention Questions

▶ Specifically, how does the concept influence or change people's lives?

▶ What particular emotions, behaviors, or ideas are associated with it?

▶ What hidden role does it play in everyday life?

▶ Are there complexities to the concept that people overlook?

▶ Is it generally agreed upon?

▶ Why is it important that people have an appropriate understanding of this concept? ■

# 2 Remembering Who You Were

# Chapter Contents

# "Those who fail to learn the lessons of history are doomed to repeat them."

—George Santayana

You have probably heard this famous statement—perhaps when someone in a history class asked plaintively, "Why do we have to learn this stuff?" Santayana's point, of course, is that the past is filled with situations that teach us about ourselves, and that ignoring the past results in blindness to the present and future. While Santayana's statement is most often applied to a collective history (e.g., American or world history), it also suggests something for the individual. In the same way that countries learn from their pasts, individuals come to new insights because of their own experiences. Obviously, we learn basic *dos* and *don'ts* from experience (not to ride a bike over the icy patch in the driveway, not to talk during math class, not to indulge too much the night before an exam). But our pasts are filled with more opportunity for insight beyond simple I'll-never-do-that-again situations. A vast array of moments lurks in the past,

moments that may mean far more than what we have always assumed.

Writers looking into their pasts attempt to learn something new, to understand the importance of some moment, or to understand the significance of a situation. They are retrieving an event or situation, uncovering a moment, and examining it from their present perspective. The hope is that the writer will see more about the situation than he or she possibly could have seen in the past. Imagine an adult writer looking back at a childhood baseball game: As a child, he fretted over striking out in the last inning. But as an adult, he can see how important that moment of failure was to his life, to his intellectual and spiritual growth. The present (adult) writer is able to see this because the elapsed time has allowed him emotional and intellectual distance.

In academia, writers often look to their own pasts for insight:

- In a sociology course, students recall their childhood communities; they pay close attention to the institutions (churches and schools) they attended and include their memories in a theory about institutional affiliation.

- A psychology professor prompts students to recall their early experiences with nonparental authority (such as teachers, extended family, and babysitters) and form a theory of authority based on those experiences.

- In a Western civilization course, students recall their early experiences with organized religion. They include their experiences in their collective examination of religious principles.

Memories do not, in themselves, teach us anything. We must create the lesson. We must look back at the past with a certain perspective: one of curiosity and possibility. Although we have lived through the past, we must entirely rediscover it if we are to learn.

This chapter will help you rediscover a specific situation or event from your past, explore it in depth, develop a particular point about it, and communicate your ideas in writing. The following essays will provide insight into various writing strategies. After you read the essays, you can find a topic in one of two ways:

1. Go to the Point of Contact section to find a topic from your everyday life, or
2. Choose one of the Ideas for Writing that follow the essays.

After you find a topic, go to the Analysis section to begin developing your ideas.

# Selling Manure

## Bonnie Jo Campbell

Writers try to see beyond the obvious—beyond simple reflexes and common associations. As they reach beyond the usual responses to everyday life, they may discover vulgarity in nice places and beauty where others least expect it. In this essay, Bonnie Jo Campbell, a celebrated short story writer and novelist, helps the reader to see value in a dirty and potentially menial job—selling manure. Obviously, such work would stink. But Campbell helps us to consider the quiet honor and honesty of the job.

Mid-May, after school was out, I found myself staring six weeks of unemployment in the face. This bothered me only until I began to envision myself reading novels in the shade of my favorite hickory tree, or making and eating entire batches of chocolate fudge, staying up late to watch black and white movies. How long had it been, I tried to recall, since I spent an entire day on my horse or in the treehouse? My mother, however, had no patience for such idleness, and she lined up myriad farm chores to occupy me—including mucking out her big horse barn. The manure was so deep in places that the horses were scraping their heads on the ceilings.

"How are we going to get rid of this stuff?" I asked.

"You're going to load it in the back of the truck," said Mom, who was conveniently under doctor's orders to refrain from activities such as scooping, lifting, and flinging. "And then we're going to sell it."

She placed ads in the *Kalamazoo Gazette* and *The Kalamazoo Shopper,* offering manure for 35 dollars a truckload. My portion for doing the physical work was a generous 20 bucks; Mom got 15 for providing the truck and the product. Right away we got calls. A surprising number of people wanted the stuff we were so anxious to get rid of.

I spent much of that unseasonably hot May and June sweating inside the barn, moving layer after layer of manure and urine-soaked straw. Periodically, Mom brought me quart jars of iced tea to keep up my spirits and electrolytes—I could tell she was even feeling a little guilty about my working so hard. I didn't tell her that, far from feeling wretched as I loaded the truck, I was feeling revived. For one thing, I was in good company. The horses and donkeys wandered through and sniffed at me; the dogs lay in holes they'd dug outside the barn door and chewed on chunks of manure; a little garter snake who lived in a hole in the dirt floor slithered in and out of the barn under the wall. And I was enjoying letting my thoughts wander. After months of sitting in class, focusing on the drone of professors and poring over books and notes, I finally had rejoined the world of the living.

Delivering the manure was a little embarrassing at first. The body of my mother's pick-up truck was rusting away and the two sides of the bed were held together with shock cords. Most of our deliveries were to west side neighborhoods, and it was problematic that construction crews had narrowed West Main to one lane in each direction. Stuck in a traffic jam, in ninety-five degree heat with a half a ton of manure in the back, we made quite a sensation. In the beginning, I put my hand over my face and hoped that I wouldn't see anyone I knew.

Within about a week, however, I began to see the absurdity of our situation as liberating. As we rattled through well-kept neighborhoods in a pickup full of stinking manure, I loosened the safety belt and hung my leg out the passenger side window, and I felt like master of all I surveyed. Perhaps this was how a prostitute felt toward a wealthy, respectable client; I might be dirty, but I have something you need.

Mom and I provided an excellent quality product at a fair price to decent folks. The people who bought our product were nice—after all, only very earthy people would order manure from the farm rather than buying it deodorized and sterilized in bags from the store. Customers often tried to help me shovel, but after I rebuffed their advances they stood back and smiled at the cascading dung. Hands on hips, eyes sparkling, they might have been fantasizing about late-summer gardens brimming with tomatoes and squash.

One man who lived just off Stadium Drive was planting a full acre of garden on land he'd rented from the utility company. After I unloaded the truck under the power lines, he took Mom and me to admire a mound across the way. "Do you know what that is?" he asked. "That's llama manure. And this pile over here, that's pig manure. And that's chicken." The pig pile was so fragrant that I figured he'd soon have trouble with his neighbors in the nearby apartment complex, but his enthusiasm was touching. I felt proud that our manure was out in the world, mingling with other manures, making things grow.

There is no vocation more honest than selling manure. Consider what most people do for a living. They go to work where they build crap, or sell crap, or move crap, or spin a line of bull over the telephone, all the while trying to convince the customer that their product is something other than crap. When I deliver a load of manure to someone's garden, the customer and I are both upfront about what we were dealing with. All I have to ask is, "Where do you want this shit?"

This experience has made me reflect on the idea of work in general. Any job is an important job, whether it is selling manure or selling insurance. People should take pride in what they do, and not assume that a low-paying job or a dirty job makes them second class citizens. And even the smelliest job has its rewards.

My darling Christopher works second shift at a paper converting plant in Parchment. "What are you doing today?" he asked me, as I walked him out to his truck. I told him I was going to spend the afternoon shoveling manure.

"Aren't we all," he said, nodding. "Aren't we all."

Peter Burnett/istockphoto.com

# Writing Strategies

1. What is the main idea of Campbell's essay? And how is it something beyond the obvious?

2. Explain how detailed description works in the essay. For instance, how do the details about the barn, the dogs, and the heat figure into her main idea?

3. How does Campbell support the notion that her work was *liberating?*

4. How does Campbell create public resonance? Point to a particular passage in which Campbell makes her own experience relevant to others.

5. Explain how the customers' responses work in the essay (in ¶8 and ¶9). Focus on specific sentences or descriptions, and explain how they relate to Campbell's main idea.

# Exploring Ideas

1. Campbell boldly states, "There is no vocation more honest than selling manure." How is that true?

2. Campbell says that the absurdity of her situation made it liberating. How does that work? Explain how absurd predicaments free us from something—from our usual routines, from the oppression of our daily concerns.

3. In ¶7, Campbell compares herself to a prostitute. What makes that an appropriate or inappropriate comparison?

4. This essay suggests something about socioeconomic status—working-class, middle-class, and upper-class jobs. How is this essay a defense or celebration of working-class life?

# Ideas for Writing

1. What experience was a little (or a lot) embarrassing at first but later became liberating? Help the reader understand how you came to feel differently about the experience. (Avoid making obvious points, such as it was no longer embarrassing because you were better at doing it.)

2. What job of yours was either very honest or very dishonest? Help the reader see the less obvious value the work had for you and for others.

If responding to one of these ideas, go to the Analysis section of this chapter to begin developing ideas for your essay.

# How I Lost the Junior Miss Pageant

## Cindy Bosley

Most people have never participated in a beauty pageant. But nearly everyone has experienced the angst associated with the quiet pageantry of everyday life—the constant pressure to perform well in public, to look the part of a happy, stable, well-to-do member of society. Cindy Bosley, a teacher and published poet, is brave enough to share her early attempts at dealing with this pressure. On one hand, this essay is an examination of beauty pageants and the awkward system of values and beliefs that surround them; on the other, it is an intimate look at a mother/daughter relationship defined by the social goings-on of a small city in the middle of America.

Every evening of the annual broadcast of the Miss America Pageant, I, from the age of seven or so, carefully laid out an elaborate chart so that I might also participate as an independent judge of the most important beauty contest in the world. From my viewing seat on a green striped couch in my parents' smoky living room where the carpet, a collage of white, brown, and black mixed-shag, contrasted so loudly with the cheap 70s furnishings that it threatened my attention to the television set, I sat with popcorn and soda, pen in hand, thrilled at the oncoming parade of the most beautiful women in the world.

In the hours before the show began, I'd carefully written out in ink, sometimes over and over, names of all 50 states, Washington, D.C., and Puerto Rico along the *y* axis of my paper. And my categories of evaluation of the contestants ribbed themselves along the *x* axis—beauty, poise, swimsuit, evening gown—plus categories of my own—hair, likability, teeth. Over the years, an increasingly complex system of points and penalties evolved: an extra point for being tan, a loss of points for sucking up, more points for breasts, more points for unpainted nails, fewer points for big noses, fewer points for skinny lips, an extra point for smartness, subtraction of a point for playing the piano. Who wants to hear a sonata? Dance for me, bounce your bootie.

My mother had secret hopes. Finally divorced for the second time from the same man, my father, she sat with me and gave her own running commentary about who was cute, who smiled too much, who would find a handsome husband. My mother, having always been a little to a lot overweight, excelled at swimming, and she told me much later that she chose swimming because she didn't feel fat in the water. Her sister was the cheerleader, but she was a swimmer, too heavy for a short skirt of her own, she said. My mother's secret was that she wanted the winner to be her daughter. Sitting with me on the couch at 137 North Willard Street, she already knew I wasn't tall enough or pretty enough in the way of models and movie stars to ever stand a chance, but her real fear, which I only became aware of as an older teen, was that I would always be too chubby and too backward and too different and too poor, for which she blamed herself, to win a beauty pageant. Still, there were always those surprises of the contests—Miss Utah? She was no good! Why did she win? What were those judges thinking! It should have been Miss Alabama, anyone can see that. Who would have guessed Miss Utah, with that mole on her shoulder?

After my mother's never-subtle hints that if I'd just lose 20 pounds boys would like me and I might even win a beauty contest, it was my friend Bridget who wanted us to enter the Ottumwa (pronounced Uh-TUM-wuh) Junior Miss Pageant together. I secretly believed that I stood a better chance than Bridget did, though she had the right name and the right body, though she wore the right clothes and was more magazine-beautiful than I. I had *some* hope for the contest: I had *some* talents and a kind of baby-cute innocence complete with blond hair and blue eyes that I was sure the judges would find "charming and fresh." Yeah, okay, so I was already engaged to be married—so what—I was still on my way to college, and Bridget was not. And Judy was funny but had a flat face. Marcy was smart but had no breasts or hips. Carol was pretty but totally uncoordinated and her knees came together when she jumped. Desirea had enviable boobs, almost as nice as mine and probably firmer, but her chin did weird things when she smiled and her eyes were brown.

We practiced, all of us together, several times a week with a lithe woman—somebody's mom with good hair and body—getting us into form for the stage. This was the era of *Flashdance,* so we all wore our own leg warmers and torn sweatclothes and fancy headband scarves. If you were

---

Cindy Bosley, "How I Lost the Junior Miss Pageant." Reprinted with permission of the author.

one of the north-side girls (that meant your daddy was a businessman or doctor), you had gotten your leg warmers from Marshall Field's in Chicago. If you were Bridget, your dad worked at John Deere like mine but was in management and not out in the factory threading bolts on a greasy, noisy machine, so you got your leg warmers from the mall in Des Moines. If you were me, with a factory dad who didn't even live in the same house, you got your leg warmers from Kmart down the road because Target was all the way across town and too expensive, and Wal-Mart hadn't yet been born as far as we knew. The fancy mom-lady made sure everyone had a brochure about her charm school (this is small-town Iowa, mind you, so anyone operating a charm school and modeling agency in this town was kidding themselves. But making lots of money.).

So 14 of us, nervous, jealous, ears ringing with Mirror-Mirror-on-the-Wall, met daily for two weeks prior to the pageant to go over our choreographed group fitness routine to be performed, not in swimsuits, but in short-shorts and white T-shirts, Hooters-style (also not invented yet as far as we knew), and to discuss such techniques as Vaseline along the teeth and gum lines to promote smooth smiles, lest our lips dry out and get stuck in a grin during discussions with the judges of the agonies of world hunger. We were each responsible for our own talent routines and props, and each one of us had to provide a 5×7 black-and-white photo for the spread in the town paper.

The photographs were a problem. My father did not believe in such things for girls as shoes, clothes, haircuts, college, or photographs for Junior Miss, and so there was no way he was going to give a penny for a pageant-worthy dress or a professional photographer's 10-minutes-plus-proofs. I believe my mother even humiliated herself enough to ask. This was hard for her, since he'd admitted before leaving to a five-year affair with a woman who looked surprisingly like my mother but heavier. So Mom and I tried some Polaroid headshots against the side of the house, but me dressed up in my prettiest sailor blouse couldn't counteract the hospital green of the aluminum siding. We moved up to our only other option, which was my mother's flash camera with Instamatic film, and still nothing suitable (I could have agreed on one of the Polaroid shots, but my mother knew it would knock me out of the contest for sure even before the night itself).

I don't know who she borrowed the money from or what she did to get the favor, but my mother had me down at Lee's Photography the very next afternoon, and he took one shot and offered us the one proof. Abracadabra, there was my face among all the other faces as a contestant in the Uh-TUM-wuh Junior Miss Pageant. From the layout in the paper, it looked to me, and to my flushed mother, as though I had as good a shot as any.

The contest night went quickly: my foot, couched, pinched, and Band-Aided uncomfortably in a neighbor's hand-me-down high heels, slipped (hear the auditorium's quick and loud intake of breath in horror!) as I walked forward to say my name with a strong, vibrant hello just like I'd been coached by the fancy-mom; my dress was last year's prom dress, which earned me no cool points with my peers but didn't lose me any either since I had none to subtract; I managed not to land on my bottom (as I had in every practice before the contest) in my gymnastics routine, self-choreographed with my own robot-style moves to the synthesizer-heavy tune "Electricity," by a band that was popular in Sacramento, California, in that year, 1985, but not yet in my hometown. (The cassette tape had been given to me by my Hispanic, juvenile delinquent, just-released-from-young-boy-prison-in-California ex-boyfriend Jim.)

My exercise routine went off very well in front of the crowd, and I don't think anyone could even tell that my shorts were soaking wet from having been dropped by me into the toilet just an hour before as I arranged my items for quick-change. My mother and fiancé were actually sitting together, their mutual hatred of each other squeezed like a child between them. I'd even kept myself from leaving my mother behind when, backstage after the contest as I hugged and cried in joy for the co-winners and out of desperate relief that it was over now, my mother, beside herself with embarrassment for me and disappointment for herself, and misunderstanding my tears, hissed loudly enough for the benefit of everyone, "STOP your crying, they'll think you're not a nice LOSER!"

So I had done it: I had been a contestant in the Junior Miss Pageant and my mother had the snapshots to prove it.

I'd lost the contest because I didn't yet know how to tell people what they wanted to hear. The small girl that boys secretly liked but wouldn't date doesn't win Miss

America. The girl hiding in her room reading and writing poetry doesn't win Miss America. The girl playing violin despite her mother's anxiousness that other people will think she's weird doesn't win Miss America. The girl on Willard Street doesn't ever win Miss America.

But the truth is that I'd lost the contest when I told the judges, when they asked, that my most personal concern was my mother's loneliness, and if I could change anything at all, I would give her something—a man, God, anything to free her from that loneliness.

Clearly, I lacked the save-the-whales-and-rainforest civic-mindedness required not only of Miss America, but of Junior Miss America, too. Even, although one wouldn't think it, in Ottumwa, Iowa, where my mother would go on to work in a bathtub factory, and then a glue factory, and then an electrical connectors factory (the factory worker's version of upward mobility), and finally, a watch factory where they shipped and received not just watches but cocaine in our town that at that time had more FBI agents in it than railroad engineers. And even in this town where my sister would go to work the kill floor of the pork plant where, for fun, the workers shot inspection dye at each other and threatened each other's throats with hack-knives. And even in this town where my cousin, age 13, would bring a bomb to seventh grade for show-and-tell, and get caught and evacuated, and be given community service to do because the public-school-as-terrorist-ground phenomena hadn't yet been born. And even in this town where if you want to go to college, you better know someone who knows how to get you there because otherwise it's too far away and too much money and too much trouble and way, way, way beyond your own intellect and sense of self to do it alone. How scary (get married). How wasteful (get married). How expensive (get married). How strange (get married). How pretentious (get married). How escapist (get married).

If your parents are crazy and poor, and if you can't win the Junior Miss Pageant, and if it's the kind of town where you stay or they don't ever want you coming back, you get married, you move to Texas where your husband sells drugs, you hide away from the world until your self grows enough to break you out, and then you leave and you pray for your mother's loneliness and you spend your life learning to come to terms with your own, and you are smart and willful and strong, and you don't ever have to draw another chart before the pageant begins.

My mother told me later that she was just sure I would have won the Junior Miss contest if I hadn't made that awful mistake in my gymnastics routine (I don't know what mistake she was talking about—it was the least flawed part of the evening), but I knew the truth about why I'd lost, and I knew I'd lost even before the contest or the practices began. I'd lost this contest at birth, probably, to be born to my father who had a date that night, and to my mother who believed some girls—girls like me, and girls like her—had to try very hard to catch and keep a boy's attention. I'd lost the contest in borrowed shoes and an out-of-date dress. I'd lost the contest with the engagement ring on my seventeen-year-old finger. I'd lost the contest with wet shorts and too funky music. I'd lost the contest with a bargain photograph and Kmart leg warmers. I'd lost the contest with an orange Honda Express moped parked between the other girls' cars. I'd lost the contest in a falling-down green house. I'd lost the contest in the grease on my father's hands and hair and the taste of grease in his lunchbox leftovers. I'd lost the contest in my growingly cynical evaluation of Miss America as I'd gotten older—"chubby thighs touching, minus five points," "big hair, minus three points," "too small nipples, minus two," "flabby arms, minus five," and subtract and subtract and subtract. It's a contest no one should want to win. Our mothers should not have such dreams for us. Our mothers should not have such loneliness.

# Writing Strategies

1. Complete the following sentence: The main idea of Bosley's essay is that _____.

2. Bosley uses details to hold the reader's interest. Select three details that got your attention and explain how they help the reader understand and accept Bosley's main idea.

3. How does Bosley make her essay matter to someone who doesn't care about pageants?

4. Describe Bosley's writer's voice. For example, would you say it is angry, comedic, intense, dark, professional, light? Come up with your own descriptive term (or terms) and explain how three sentences from the essay support your description.

5. Divide Bosley's essay into at least four parts and briefly summarize the purpose of each part.

# Exploring Ideas

1. What basic value or belief drives the way Bosley now thinks about pageants?

2. Explain how Bosley's point about pageants speaks to one of the following issues: competition, class, tradition, media. To what other issue does the essay speak? What point does it make about the issue?

3. Interview several people to find out how they view pageants. Record their responses, then explain what viewpoints are the most common, most unusual, and most thought provoking.

# Ideas for Writing

1. Discover the significance of an experience or activity in which you participated with disappointing results.

2. Discover the significance of an experience or activity at which you exceeded your own expectations.

If responding to one of these ideas, go to the Analysis section of this chapter to begin developing ideas for your essay.

# The Thrill of Victory . . .
# The Agony of Parents

## Jennifer Schwind-Pawlak

We often get caught up in the moment. As children—and as adults—we first react to situations one way, and then later make better sense of what happened. Jennifer Schwind-Pawlak, who wrote the following essay for a college writing course, explores one of these moments from her past. As you read the essay, notice how Schwind-Pawlak uses her own particular experience to tap into a more universal one. From a new perspective, allowed for by the distance of time, she finds the positive value of what appeared back then to be a negative experience. In this essay, she stands back and talks about the experience, engaging the reader with key details, a mature writer's voice, and an important lesson.

**Writing Strategies**

**Exploring Ideas**

Parents—one word that can strike many emotions in children when said aloud. Some children will smile and think about how silly their dad looked when he put carrot sticks up his nose that very morning, while others will cringe when they think about how their mother picked them up from school last week wearing orange polyester pants and a green shirt, oblivious to the hard work that some fellow went through to create the color wheel. My own emotional state of mind seemed to run the gamut throughout childhood. I chose to blame my parents for all of the traumatic events that unfolded but took pride in my obvious independence during the successes. One of the most heinous crimes that my parents committed was "the soccer foul." If I could have ejected them from the game of life at that point, I would have.

The relationship between parents and children. Parents commit "fouls" or "crimes."

Ironically, I was not particularly fond of soccer. Being the youngest of four children, I often chose to run around the field with friends while my brothers and sisters performed feats of soccer, the likes of which had only been seen during the World Cup. I would happily contort my fingers into chubby pretzels while singing "The Itsy Bitsy Spider" as the game's events were recounted on the drives home. Still, whether by guilt or by the need to belong, I joined the team when I became of age.

The team that I played on was designed to turn the young and awkward into the swans of the soccer field. My father (a one-time soccer coach) explained several times that this was the time that I would learn the rules and workings of the game and that

*Introduces general subject matter leading up to the main idea: parent/child dynamics.*

*Develops essay through narration and description.*

"The Thrill of Victory, The Agony of Parents," by Jennifer Schwind-Pawlak. Reprinted with permission of author.

I shouldn't expect much more than that. Since it was a child's league, learning and the team experience were the focuses. Winning was a pleasant bonus but should not be achieved at the cost of the main objectives. This litany was taken and stored somewhere in the recesses of my brain. For me, however, the main objective was looking cool while running down the field chasing a spotted ball. Everything else seemed secondary.

Due to the family history, I attended every Tuesday and Thursday practice and managed to make each a social occasion while going through the motions of the game. I succeeded in understanding the game and, though not the most skilled of players, began to enjoy the half game of playing time that was required by the league for each player. Though I was far from a star player, I felt that my contribution mattered to the overall outcomes of the games, all of which had been lost to this point.

Sunday, the morning of the fifth game of the season, came with no warning. I got up, went to church with the family, then came home to suit up for the game. Upon arrival at the field, I was greeted by the coach and went to take my place along the sidelines with the rest of my team. There was a buzz of excitement that left me with the feeling that I would get when my brother would poke me with his fingertip after dragging his stocking feet across the carpet. The team that we were playing had a record identical to ours. We could win this game. I didn't care what the parents said. Winning would be a blast.

The coach kept me on the sidelines the entire first half of the game, which my pre-adolescent mind attributed to my obviously increasing skill at the game. He was saving his trump card, me, for the last half of the game. I knew this was rare, but I was sure that his reason was to bedazzle the crowd and the other team with my pure firepower on the field. The other players, except one other girl, continued to cycle in and out of the game. While I was excited because we were winning the game, I was concerned that the coach had forgotten about me. I inched, ever so slowly, toward him and started mindless conversation to let him know that I was there. He spoke to me, so I knew that he could not have forgotten about me. As the game was winding down, I was sure that he must have decided to put me in for the last play of the game.

The game ended.

I was horrified to realize that I had not played one moment of the first win of the season. After all of that practice and the ugly uniform, I was deemed such a poor player that I was not even good enough to play one moment of that game. How would I ever live this down at school? How would I face all of my classmates on Monday? My stomach began to churn, the way

**Side notes (left margin):**

Details are carefully selected: father's explanation becomes key later in the essay.

Sums up practice and games thus far.

Sets up the fifth game. Excitement, suspense are building.

Description of the fifth game.

Three-word paragraph has dramatic effect.

**Side notes (right margin):**

We have all participated in these childhood activities that were supposed to teach us lessons, about sportsmanship, teamwork, etc.

Her relationship with soccer seems to be developing, changing.

We all—most of us—have not gotten to play at some point: common experience?

She is "horrified" not to play.

that it does when you are going down the first hill of any great roller coaster. I looked to my parents for support, which only added to the horror of that day.

Joann (the name I call my mother when she does something embarrassing) was screaming at the coach. In a voice so screeching that it rivaled fingernails on a blackboard, she told him that he was a disgraceful coach and that he should be ashamed of himself. She continued to point out the error of his ways by reminding him that I had not played at all in the game. How could she do this to me? My mother had managed to enlighten the few people that hadn't noticed on their own that I had not played at all. What was she thinking? She might as well have rented billboard space saying, "So what if Jeni sucks at soccer? The coach wouldn't let her play." My only thought was, "I don't want to go to school tomorrow!"

Looking back, I realize that it wasn't so bad the next day at school. I walked out to recess and talked about how nuts my mother was and everyone seemed to agree, sympathize, and get on with the important task of freeze tag. At that moment I wasn't sure that I would ever be able to forgive my mother for what happened that day, but, as far as I can recall, I began loving her again within the week. I am sure that she either cooked my favorite dinner, told a corny joke, or told me how much she loved me to make that lump of anger fade away.

I never went to soccer again. As a matter of fact, I never played another organized sport again. Maybe it was the fear of rejection. Maybe it was the uncertainty of my talent. Maybe I was just too busy with other things. I never really felt the urge to compete on that level after that day.

The relationship that I have with my parents has changed very much throughout the years. The polyester pants don't bother me anymore, but the carrot sticks still make me laugh. While their "soccer foul" embarrassed and angered me at the time, I understand and appreciate it now. My mother was angry *FOR* me. She was hurt *FOR* me. Through the pages of time, I can look back and see that, more often than not, I embarrassed her. She never stopped feeling for me, loving me, or protecting me. I have grown enough to realize that, though I often pointed out my parents' fouls, they scored countless goals that I didn't even notice.

---

Description of "the foul."

Reflects on her experience—what "looking back" means.

She gives possible reasons for never playing another organized sport again.

Finds meaning through reflection.

---

She is "horrified" and looks to her mother for help. Turns out, her mother is "horrified" too, and reacts in a way that makes things worse. What does she learn about her mother, parents, and relationships from her mother's reaction—and from her reaction to it?

She sees the experience differently now. Sometimes—many times—we see differently when something's happening than we do later on.

One consequence is that she quit soccer, sports. She's not sure why? Complexity.

She sees the experience differently now. Parents and children embarrass each other sometimes. This is part of the relationship. In this situation, though, her mother was angry/hurt FOR her.

## Writing Strategies

1. Explain why Schwind-Pawlak's opening paragraph makes the reader want to continue reading.

2. Why does Schwind-Pawlak tell us that her father "explained several times that this was the time that [she] would learn the rules and workings of the game and that [she] shouldn't expect much more than that" (¶3)?

3. Is Schwind-Pawlak's writer's voice funny, serious, pensive, silly? Describe it in your own words and then refer to three sentences that support your decision.

4. What subject would you say Schwind-Pawlak's essay is about: parents, soccer, life, growing up, or something else? What is Schwind-Pawlak's main point about the topic?

5. What details does Schwind-Pawlak use to help the reader understand and accept her main idea?

## Exploring Ideas

1. In groups or on your own through writing, discuss experiences like Schwind-Pawlak's. Can you recall a similar embarrassing experience of your own? Are such experiences inevitable? What makes them valuable? What can make them harmful?

2. What activity did you have the ability, opportunity, and interest to do again, but only did once? What is it, or was it, about yourself that kept you from doing it again?

## Ideas for Writing

1. What is the significance of a big game or event from your past?

2. What emotional or intellectual experience has prevented you from ever doing something again? How has the experience influenced your later decisions?

If responding to one of these ideas, go to the Analysis section of this chapter to begin developing ideas for your essay.

Julie Elliot/StockXchng

# INVENTION

"I'm digging in the dirt / To find the places I got hurt / To open up the places I got hurt."

—"Digging in the Dirt," Peter Gabriel

Invention is not simply about finding a topic. It also involves exploring and analyzing that topic, examining your thoughts, and developing points. For a remembering essay, the process will be self-reflective. It will begin with a personal exploration, but the broader goal is to discover something that others can share. The following three sections are designed to help you through invention—specifically, to discover a particular topic, situation, or event from your past (in Point of Contact), to develop points about the topic (in Analysis), and to make it relevant to a community of readers (in Public Resonance). The Invention Questions in each section are not meant to be answered directly in your final written assignment, but using them to explore ideas will help you begin writing and keep intensive ideas flowing.

# Point of Contact

You might think that nothing interesting has ever happened to you, but even if you have never won the lottery, wrestled an alligator, or been on a first date, your life is filled with thousands of situations that can reveal something to you and to your audience. Use the following questions to help find a specific situation, event, or set of events from your life.

- **Call or Write Someone from Your Past** Ask him or her about your shared history.
  - —What do you remember most about our lives back then?
  - —What was the best part of our lives? The worst?
  - —How have we both changed since then? Why did we change?
  - —What forces, feelings, or situations kept us together?

- **Do Something that You Have Not Done for Many Years** Go fishing, play baseball, listen to a particular song, reread a particular book. Then consider the following: How was doing the activity now different from doing it in the past?

- **Visit a Place from Your Past** A schoolyard, a house, an apartment building, an old neighborhood, a workplace, etc.
  - —What memories or feelings are most prominent?
  - —How have my feelings about the place changed?

- **Look through a Photo Album or Yearbook**
  - —What do I remember thinking or feeling at the time of the photograph?
  - —How is that different from what I feel now looking at the photograph?

- **Recall an Event from Your Past Life**
  - —**School** Did I ever get beat up? Did I ever beat up someone else? Was I ever embarrassed by a teacher or classmate? Did I ever win or lose a big sporting event? Was I popular or unpopular? Did I fit into a particular clique (jocks, hoods, hippies, punks, nerds)? When did I come out of my shell?
  - —**Work** What was my first job? Did I like or dislike it? Why did I leave? How did I get along with my peers? My boss? Did the job put me in any weird situations?
  - —**Social Life** When was my first date? When did I first stay out late? Did I have a lot of friends? No friends? What situation led to my first friendship? When did I first learn about the differences between girls and boys? Was I asked to drink or try drugs? When did I first drive a car (illegally or legally)? Did I ever change my hair or image drastically?
  - —**Family Life** Did I experience a sibling being born? Have I experienced a child of my own being born? Did we have a pet? Did we take any family vacations? Have I ever embarrassed my family? Has my family embarrassed me? What did we do on weekends? Did we eat dinner, watch television, or attend religious services together?

## Activity

The questions above only hint at the many possible topics. In a group or alone, generate more questions until one has triggered something for you.

# Analysis

Analysis is an art and a science. It involves intellectual free-dom and careful, deliberate probing. Good analysis calls for writers to venture into possibilities while monitoring their thinking. This difficult intellectual work yields insight and meaning. As you examine a particular event or situation from your past, try to find the *significance* (why something is important for both the writer and the reader).

## Invention Questions

▶ How did I change? (Who was I before and after the situation?)

▶ Why did the event or situation occur? What forces were at work?

▶ Did I realize the significance of the event at the time? Why or why not?

▶ What do I see now that I didn't see then? What did that younger person not understand?

▶ Why was the event or situation important to me?
  —Did it help me to understand myself as a man or woman?
  —Did it help me to grow intellectually? Spiritually? Socially?
  —Did it help me to see myself in a different way? ∎

As you analyze, remember that the goal is not simply to tell a story about your past, but to discover something meaningful—something that can be shared with and valued by others. Avoid moving too quickly through your thoughts. Imagine a writer, Jack, who visited his old elementary school:

**What do I see now that I didn't see then?**
I see that school is important, and back then I didn't.

Jack answers the question and *begins* walking the path of analysis, but his brief answer does not go far enough. It does not reveal the real complexity of his experience. He says that "school is important," but such a phrase is broad and hollow. What particular aspect of school, we might ask, is impor-tant? What specific moments or situations are valuable to a growing individual? Struggling through impossibly diffi-cult classes? The reward of a good grade? Being prompted to read material one would otherwise ignore? Or maybe what's important is the slow and charted evolution of one's iden-tity through various classes, teachers, friends, and hallways. Jack's answer blankets such rich possibilities, covering them up with a broad, sweeping phrase.

Another writer, Diana, goes further in her thinking:

**What do I see now that I didn't see then?**
When I was younger, I didn't see the big picture, how my life in school connected to anything outside of school. I went, did the work, and came home, but mostly day-dreamed about the time I'd spend away from schoolwork. For me, and probably most of my friends, life was sepa-rate from schoolwork. Every day, the goal was to get it done so we could be away from it. I remember the feeling of freedom in running out the door after school or during recess, but what I was running toward was a bunch of silly games, posing, and meaningless searches for excitement. I never thought, maybe I was never taught, that learning is really what makes life worth anything, that an intellectual challenge is real excitement. When I was a teenager, I was focused on the surface—the shallow giddiness of thrills and "parties." I thought school was a drag—and I looked for every possible excuse to be bored. I actually *convinced* myself to be bored. But now that I am older, I realize that school is the only place where people actually care about your mind—where they want you to grow, imagine, and experience new ideas. These are the things that make life outside of school worth living. I see that now.

All the jobs I had after high school just wanted me to perform a certain duty. No one wanted me to explore my intellectual potential. And unfortunately, I see a lot of younger college students still thinking the way I did in high school. They moan at challenging assignments; they just want to duck out of everything. Today, a boy said to me, "Can you believe how long that reading took?" as though the goal were to get through it. What's that about? Well, I know what it's about—blindness to the big picture.

Diana's thoughts are developing. She is making specific dis-tinctions between her present and her past understanding. In the past, she did not question her own boredom. But in the present she has distance from her old self and can see false assumptions and misplaced values.

# Thinking Further

Although Diana has already analyzed further than Jack did, she should not stop yet. Through analysis she has unearthed some interesting new ideas. Now she can review her invention writing and identify her best ideas, using them not as final conclusions but as springboards into further exploration. Now she can seek out some insight that lurks even further below the surface of her previous discoveries.

For example, if Diana's goal is to share the significance of a memory, she could say that she realized *school is where people care about your mind—where they want you to grow, imagine, and experience new ideas—and that these are the things that make life outside of school worth living.* And she could illustrate her thesis by discussing how certain teachers encouraged her to grow and imagine while she scorned their encouragement. But what if Diana sought out the underlying reasons for her childhood behavior? She could quickly claim that she was a wild and typical adolescent. Or, she could think past that assumption, returning to the Invention Questions on the previous page. Now that she has generated some new thinking, the same questions (and new ones that Diana comes up with on her own) can lead to even further insights. For example,

**Why did the event or situation occur? What forces were at work?**

Why didn't I see the big picture? Who or what is to blame? It isn't as if everybody in high school failed to take advantage of it. Many students were highly motivated. (Although even students who seemed motivated might have had misplaced priorities.) Still, had I known then what I know now, I might have worked harder and learned more, perhaps gone to a better college, and excelled in all kinds of ways. Perhaps my parents should have forced me to study harder, or helped me to better understand the importance of high school. Perhaps—probably—they didn't understand it themselves. But couldn't my teachers have gotten through to me? So many of them seemed disinterested. Others tried, but what could they do? And what about the media, pop culture, sports, the mall? All these factors competed and, in my case, won out over education.

By analyzing further, Diana is getting closer to the root of a complex issue: She is discovering that her attitude toward high school was impacted by competing factors, such as the media, pop culture, sports, and the mall. However, the writing above does not provide final answers. Diana has even more exploring to do, which might include additional invention writing, discussion with others, and secondary research.

To go further with your own thinking, focus on a key issue in your invention writing. Then return to the Invention Questions on page 42 and create probing questions on your own. Use them to reveal something deeper, more hidden, more complex, about the situation. For example:

- What other forces were at play?
- Why were they hidden from my view back then?
- What makes people blind to such forces in their lives?

In her response to the Invention questions on page 45, Cindy Bosley hones in and finds meaning in a "small moment." Bosley's notes are exploratory. They are not simple answers to questions. Much of the language in her response does not appear in her final essay, but she is willing to explore and stretch her reasoning:

**Why did the event or situation occur?**

If I isolate the event or situation as the gulf between my own grasp of fun and happiness and my mother's severe disappointment and embarrassment, her concern that others would think I was not a "nice loser" in that small moment, I think it clearly speaks so much more about my mother—as though I saw her, her disappointments and worries about image and desirability in herself through me. She was no stage mother, not at all, but she must have had these fears about how people in the town looked at her, and at us, her three children, because of my father to a certain extent, but also just because she herself was a woman who'd grown up to some degree "unacceptable" in her and her family's eyes because she was heavy, or because she liked lots of boys, or because she got pregnant and married, or because she moved so far away. My mother was and is a creative, talented, vibrant woman and she worked very hard, and very successfully, sacrificing so much for herself so my sister, brother, and I could have the things that we wanted like the other kids, things that might help us break out of our own family's economic situation. Things like acrobat lessons, and cheerleading camp, and swimming lessons, and overnight birthday parties. I have absolutely no idea how she pulled all those things off.

Bosley does not focus only on the beauty pageant but on the layers of emotions beneath it—those tied to her mother. She discovers a fresh perspective about the pageant by looking closely at the life that led up to and surrounded it. And from these notes, the ideas evolve in her essay:

> But the truth is that I'd lost the contest when I told the judges, when they asked, that my most personal concern was my mother's loneliness, and if I could change anything at all, I would give her something—a man, God, anything to free her from that loneliness.

Discovering the significance of the past can be tricky because it is not obvious. In fact, the most significant events might be those that seem totally normal or insignificant. For example, a single soccer game spent standing on the sidelines would seem to have no meaning, other than frustration, for the younger Schwind-Pawlak; but to the older writer looking back, the game reveals something about her relationship with her parents.

## Invention Workshop

After exploring the past on your own, you might hit a wall. Here's where an invention partner can help you break through and discover a focused insight worth sharing with the reader. Review your invention writing thus far, and with your invention partner, or several partners, discuss: *What could I now tell that younger version of me?* In your discussion, explore, discover, and develop possibilities, then ask: *What hidden forces were at work? Why didn't I understand things differently back then?* Remember that the goal of this invention workshop is to reveal something new.

# The goal is to reveal some idea that is hiding in the past—to offer a revelatory insight to readers.

# Public Resonance

What you discover about your past should suggest something for the lives of your readers. Dealing with public resonance means addressing the connection between your particular memory and a public or shared issue. You may have already found public resonance by answering the Invention Questions. If not, closely consider your response to the following:

▶ What public issue is related to my memory and how?

▶ What does my memory reveal or show about the nature of _____? (Childhood? Teenagers? Towns? Families? Schools? Teachers? Religious institutions? Education? Parenthood? Growing up? Failing? Succeeding? Suffering? Dying? Healing?)

▶ Who might relate to my memory? ■

In this excerpt from Cindy Bosley's invention notes, she does not merely reinforce her early feelings of confusion; she discovers "the truth of" her confusion:

> **What public issue is related to my memory?**
> This isn't about my mother so much as it is about women more generally, and the images we're given through history at birth and before and never ever really break. I always felt shame after what I told the judges about wanting my mother to not have to be so lonely—how narrow of me, how far I missed the point—and yet, now I feel the truth of it, and I hope if I could go back, I'd still tell them that's the one thing I'd want to be able to change— for my mother to be able to feel beautiful and free and lovely and bright, overweight or not, advanced education or not, and with or without a man.
> I remember my joy in graduate school when my friend Karen hosted a Miss America party the night of the pageant, and maybe my essay began to grow here. It was that night that I discovered I wasn't the ONLY little girl making up my own score sheets for the contest, hoping to predict who would win, and always imagining, because we thought it was the thing to wish for, that we could someday be Miss America. And all the usual stuff about

women's narrow, "perfected" images in the media, Barbie dolls, fairy tales, all of it comes to bear here. There's such a feeling of shame and degradation (I don't think it is too big a word to describe it) in allowing oneself to be judged in this way, whether literally in a contest, or even just by agreeing to play, which we all do, by all the ancient rules of "fitting in," whether you're male or female. And there seems to be this desperate hole of loneliness and fear that seems anchored to it all. We often recognize it first in other people.

Your answers to the Invention Questions may not appear word-for-word in your final writing. However, they should generate focused thinking that finds its way into the final draft. For example, in her notes, Bosley discovers that her situation (and her mother's loneliness) is not unique. And in the conclusion of her essay, she makes this evident by changing the personal pronoun from *I* to *our,* thereby including others in her thinking. This links her realization about pageants and mother/daughter relationships to others so that her essay is not simply about herself, but about people who grew up in similar conditions. Bosley shows us how an unusual memory can resonate with readers: the importance and meaning of the memory translates into something beyond her personal feelings.

## Activity

Before you write a thesis and begin drafting an essay, imagine how the significance of your memory might have meaning for the reader. Doing this will help you develop a thesis that can guide your essay. With others or on your own through writing, explore: What might readers learn about themselves from my memory? How can I connect the significance of my memory to the readers' interests?

# Thesis

Like any essay, one that is based on a personal experience should have a main point or *thesis*. And that point should reveal something to the writer and reader. It may be tempting to offer an overly broad statement about life, but more valuable statements will narrow in on a particular quality, situation, relationship, or layer of everyday life. The first broad statement in each set can be developed into more revelatory possibilities:

1. People are deeply influenced by their friends.
   - Friends develop our sense of ambition—what we want for ourselves.
   - Friends create the intellectual terrain of our past and present.
   - Friends mirror our own worldviews back to us.
2. Family is all that matters.
   - Our early struggles with brothers and sisters create the limitations we place on ourselves later in life.
   - As we grow into adulthood, our siblings keep alive the memory of our childhood selves.
   - Fathers create a sense of place, a sense of location that looms throughout our lives, even when we are spinning far out of control.
3. Teenage years are wild.
   - During adolescence, the world makes sense, even though that sense is a complete illusion.
   - A fourteen-year-old boy can barely contain all the energy coursing through his veins. He spends most of his time struggling to tame instincts that he cannot even name.
   - Before leaving our formative years, we might glimpse the best and worst habits we have acquired from our families . . . if we are lucky.

So how does someone go from a broad, flat statement to a revelatory idea? Intensive analysis! More intensive analysis always (not sometimes, but *always!*) leads to more intensive and focused statements. But when writers have difficulty expressing an intensive single statement, they can re-tool the specific words—the key verbs and nouns. Notice how the more intensive and revelatory statements often avoid linking verbs (*is, am, are, was, were,* and so on). Instead, they rely on active verbs (*develop, create, mirror, keep, glimpse*) to pull the reader's mind through ideas. So changing the verb in a sentence can actually prompt the writer to think differently, in more intensive ways.

## Activity

Create a broad, flat sentence, something that offers very little new insight. Then, from that sentence, develop three or more intense, focused, and insightful statements. In these more insightful statements, try to reveal something that normally goes ignored or that rarely gets considered. To create more insightful statements:

1. replace broad nouns with more specific nouns;
2. replace linking verbs with active verbs. Use adventurous or unusual verbs . . . and see where your mind goes.

## Evolution of a Thesis

The thesis of a remembering essay suggests the *significance of the memory.* Notice how the following statement evolves from a description of what happened to an explanation of its significance:

- I remember as a kid sitting in my grandparents' backyard listening to them and my parents tell boring family stories.
- I realize now that I learned a lot about my family history from sitting around as a kid listening to my grandparents and parents tell family stories.
- We learn important things about who we are and where we came from by listening to family stories.
- Though we might prefer not to hear them, we can better understand who we are and why by taking in family stories as children.

An *explicit* thesis is stated directly in the essay; an *implied* thesis is suggested by the details in the essay but is not directly stated. Having an implied thesis does not mean a writer can simply wander through many different ideas. The details throughout the essay must be focused and coherent enough to suggest a main point, both for the writer and the reader.

Because you have already explored the significance and public resonance of your memory, you may already have a thesis. Ask yourself: *What is the most important point about this memory that should be communicated?* Try to express that point in one statement. (Even if you have an implied thesis, stating the main idea will help you develop the essay.)

## Common Thesis Problems

When it comes time to craft a focused statement, writers also should avoid the temptation to flatten out their experiences into an overused phrase, or *cliché*. Clichés have a comfortable ring to them, but they rarely prompt new insight or reveal complexities. In fact, clichés often *cover up* complexities because they are applied as blanket statements to many different situations:

- You don't know what you've got until it's gone.
- Blood is thicker than water.
- What doesn't kill you only makes you stronger.
- Home is where the heart is.

Such statements may be true and worth considering, but academic writing seeks to reveal something new. Clichés are worn-out expressions. They might sound like profound statements, but when a thesis is a cliché, the main idea of the essay doesn't reveal something new. Instead, it restates an old, worn-out idea.

### Revising Your Thesis

Share your thesis statement with a group of peers:

- What general words can be replaced with specific ones?
- What clichés can be replaced with intense, revelatory language?
- How can the thesis better express the significance of the memory?
- What is the most important point about this memory?

# What is the most important point about this memory?

# Rhetorical Tools

Even though the writing for this chapter is personal in nature, it needs to involve the audience, developing a point that connects to the public. As author Joan Didion said, "Quite often you want to tell somebody your dream, your nightmare. Well, nobody wants to hear about someone else's dream, good or bad; nobody wants to walk around with it. The writer is always tricking the reader into listening to the dream." To do this, writers can explore various tools.

## Narration

Narration is a retelling of events, a story. As Joan Didion argues, we must do more than tell a story. We must trick the reader into listening to the story and accepting its significance. The art of storytelling involves pace, or the movement of events. At important points in a narrative, the amount of detail tends to increase, and so the reader slows down and experiences each moment. But good storytellers move quickly through unimportant events. It might be helpful to think of this strategy as it works in movies: At the climax of an adventure movie, the events slow down (we see the lead character's hand grasping for the light saber; we hear each breath of the character as she runs down the hallway and toward the open window), but during less important moments, an entire day or week can flash by in a second.

In her narrative, Jennifer Schwind-Pawlak moves quickly through unimportant events. She quickly relates the pregame events (going to church, suiting up) because they do not have a significant impact on the main idea of the essay:

> Sunday, the morning of the fifth game of the season, came with no warning. I got up, went to church with the family, then came home to suit up for the game. Upon arrival at the field, I was greeted by the coach and went to take my place along the sidelines with the rest of my team.

However, the narrative slows down (and offers more details) at important moments:

> Joann (the name I call my mother when she does something embarrassing) was screaming at the coach. In a voice so screeching that it rivaled fingernails on a blackboard, she told him that he was a disgraceful coach and that he should be ashamed of himself. She continued to point out the error of his ways by reminding him that I had not played at all in the game. How could she do this to me? My mother had managed to enlighten the few people that hadn't noticed on their own that I had not played at all. What was she thinking? She might as well have rented billboard space saying, "So what if Jeni sucks at soccer? The coach wouldn't let her play." My only thought was, "I don't want to go to school tomorrow!"

As you consider your own narrative, slow the pace when relaying events that are directly related to your main idea.

## Allusions

Allusions are references to some public bit of knowledge (such as a historical event, a political situation, or a popular culture figure). An allusion can give a personal essay a more public and broader feeling; that is, it can make the ideas and events of a personal situation relate to the reader through a shared culture. Because the allusion is shared knowledge, it communicates this broader, public feeling more quickly than a longer explanation would. This helps to keep the essay moving along. For example, Bosley's allusion to the Hooters restaurant chain ("to be performed, not in swimsuits, but in short-shorts and white T-shirts, Hooters-style . . .") quickly creates an image in the reader's mind because of the shared knowledge about the Hooters uniform. Later, when Bosley refers to "the save-the-whales-and-rainforest civic-mindedness required not only of Miss America, but of Junior Miss America, too," she quickly communicates an idea that without the allusion would take much longer to explain. Because the allusion is public knowledge, the writer connects with the reader because the reader feels that she, too, is *in on it*.

# Dialogue

Dialogue, discussion between two or more people, can make an event or memory more real and engaging to the reader. It is most valuable when used to emphasize a main point and show something significant rather than simply to convey events. Conveying general events is better left to narration. Formatting for dialogue involves several steps:

- Use quotation marks before and after the actual spoken words.
- Put end punctuation (such as a period) inside the end quotation marks.
- Indent when a new speaker begins.

Integrating a speaker's words can be accomplished in several ways:

- Use a comma between the quotation and the speaking verb (*explained, asked, said, yelled, proclaimed*, etc.).

   Louisa asked, "What are we going to do now?"

- Use a colon before the speaker's words. In this case, the narrator usually forecasts the ideas or mood of the speaker in the sentence preceding the colon.

   I was clearly agitated by her accusation: "What the heck are you talking about?"

- Work the speaker's words directly into the grammar of your sentence.

   But Louisa was convinced that our decision would "hurt us either way."

   See all of these rules operating in the following exchange:

   "Come on in," Mr. Smith said.

   "Hey, something smells great," I said as I walked into his lamp-lit living room. The small terrier looked up out of its lazy place on the sofa as Mr. Smith reached to get his wallet.

"Yep, I've been cookin' my chili again. It's Max's favorite." He gestured at the complacent blurry-eyed dog. "So, is the price of papers still the same?"

"Well, as far as I know, it's still $4.25 for the month." And then without considering the consequences, I asked the wrong question: "How have you been, Mr. Smith?" It took him 45 minutes to explain his "return to normal" after a long spell of stomach flu.

In this example, notice how attributive phrases (such as *he said*), which give ownership to the spoken words, are absent after the second indentation. Generally, after the dialogue pattern is established and the reader can easily tell who is speaking at each indentation, attributive phrases are unnecessary.

## Activity

Before drafting your essay, use writing to plan.

- Write down your thesis.
- What narrative events will you move through quickly, and what narrative events will you slow down for?
- What historical, popular, or fictional situations, events, or characters relate to your situation?
- If you are considering dialogue, how will that dialogue help show the significance of the main idea?

# Organizational Strategies

## What Details Should I Include?

Sometimes when we tell stories (especially our own), they take over, and we wander through irrelevant details. To prevent this, consider two strategies: (1) leave out irrelevant details that distract the reader, and (2) emphasize details that help illustrate the main idea. For instance, Schwind-Pawlak is selectively specific as she details her youth soccer experience. In her second paragraph, she provides a few precise details to illustrate that playing soccer was not important to her:

> "I often chose to run around the field with friends while my brothers and sisters performed feats of soccer, the likes of which had only been seen during the World Cup. I would happily contort my fingers into chubby pretzels while singing 'The Itsy Bitsy Spider' as the game's events were recounted on the drives home."

Then she summarizes the early part of the season. She made practice "a social occasion while going through the motions of the game"; she "began to enjoy the half game of playing time that was required by the league for each player"; and all the games "had been lost to this point." Sharing particulars about her socializing, about plays she made (or didn't make), and detailing how each game had been lost could bog down the essay and distract the reader from the main point. As the fifth game of the season arrives (¶5), she slows down and focuses on the details.

Details should add up to the main point. As readers work through the text, gathering details along the way, they should be led to the main idea; they should experience the deep complexity of living in a particular moment. Without those details, the reader will merely experience being told something about a distant time and place.

As you consider your own narrative, think of the details that can help illustrate your point. If the moment is important, provide details. For example, if you were sitting in an alley, explain the color of the empty bottles and the smell of the damp brick. If you were standing in a classroom at the end of a day, explain the placement of the desks and the dying fern by the window. If you were swimming in a pond, explain how the weeds waved back and forth from the impact of your movements. But only provide details that take your reader closer to the main idea. Ask yourself: what details from the past will help the reader to fully understand my point?

## How Should I Begin?

One strategy is to begin in the past, taking readers back in time from the first sentence:

> Every evening of the annual broadcast of the Miss America Pageant, I, from the age of seven or so, carefully laid out an elaborate chart so that I might also participate as an independent judge of the most important beauty contest in the world.

Bosley begins narrating and waits until later in her essay to characterize or give meaning to the events. Another strategy is to make a general statement about the subject, and then begin narrating events:

> Parents—one word that can strike many emotions in children when said aloud. Some children will smile and think about how silly their dad looked when he put carrot sticks up his nose that very morning, while others will cringe when they think about how their mother picked them up from school last week wearing orange polyester pants and a green shirt, oblivious to the hard work that some fellow went through to create the color wheel. My own emotional state of mind seemed to run the gamut throughout childhood. I chose to blame my parents for all of the traumatic events that unfolded but took pride in my obvious independence during the successes. One of the most heinous crimes that my parents committed was "the soccer foul." If I could have ejected them from the game of life at that point, I would have.

Here Schwind-Pawlak begins with a statement that has public resonance, then she narrates her particular experience.

# How Should I Conclude?

One strategy for concluding a remembering essay is to explain the significance or public resonance. Bosley ends her essay by explaining the significance of her memory, even suggesting that others can share the personal significance:

> It's a contest no one should want to win. Our mothers should not have such dreams for us. Our mothers should not have such loneliness.

Schwind-Pawlak also explains the significance of her memory in her conclusion:

> The relationship that I have with my parents has changed very much throughout the years. The polyester pants don't bother me anymore, but the carrot sticks still make me laugh. While their "soccer foul" embarrassed and angered me at the time, I understand and appreciate it now. My mother was angry *FOR* me. She was hurt *FOR* me. Through the pages of time, I can look back and see that, more often than not, I embarrassed her. She never stopped feeling for me, loving me, or protecting me. I have grown enough to realize that, though I often pointed out my parents' fouls, they scored countless goals that I didn't even notice.

Campbell, too, concludes her essay by emphasizing the significance of her memory:

> This experience has made me reflect on the idea of work in general. Any job is an important job, whether it is selling manure or selling insurance. People should take pride in what they do, and not assume that a low paying job or a dirty job makes them second class citizens. And even the smelliest job has its rewards.
>
> My darling Christopher works second shift at a paper converting plant in Parchment. "What are you doing today?" he asked me, as I walked him out to his truck. I told him I was going to spend the afternoon shoveling manure.
>
> "Aren't we all," he said, nodding. "Aren't we all."

## Activity

1. Share the introduction to your essay with two peers. Each peer should write an alternative introduction, using an entirely different strategy. Discuss the pros and cons of each introduction.

2. Discuss your conclusion with a group of peers. How does the conclusion explain the significance or public resonance of the essay? How might the significance or public resonance be made more clear?

# Details should add up to the main point.

# Writer's Voice

A writer's voice characterizes the ideas in a text. It creates the mood. Imagine you walk into a party and the host greets you at the door: "Hey! Look what the cat dragged in!" Her interaction would prompt you to assume that the party is fairly informal and festive. But the host could also greet you more soberly: "Hello. Please come in. May I take your coat?" In this case, her voice would lend formality to the affair. In other words, the host creates a particular mood for the incoming guests. Likewise, a writer creates the mood in which readers will enter the text. And this can be accomplished in a variety of ways.

## Using Figurative Language

Figurative language is nonliteral. It goes beyond basic definitions and suggests imaginative connections between ideas. Consider incorporating the following types of figurate language into your writing: metaphor, simile, understatement, and hyperbole.

> **Metaphor** A comparison in which one thing is made to share the characteristics of another: Her home was a sanctuary where we felt healed spiritually and psychologically.

> **Simile** A comparison of two seemingly unrelated things using *like* or *as:* Life is like a box of chocolates.

Similes and metaphors help create voice. For example, Forrest Gump's simile in the previous example fits with his uncomplicated and easygoing character. A box of chocolates is a simple, pleasant surprise, and so it equates with his character. (It certainly would not be fitting for Gump to say, "Life is like a raging volcanic explosion bursting forth from the fires of the earth.")

Jennifer Schwind-Pawlak's metaphors help create her voice:

> At that moment I wasn't sure that I would ever be able to forgive my mother for what happened that day, but, as far as I can recall, I began loving her again within the week. I am sure that she either cooked my

favorite dinner, told a corny joke, or told me how much she loved me to make that lump of anger fade away.

Her anger is "a lump," not a mountain or a raging river. The smaller, more manageable, lump fits the mood of a child. We get the sense from her language that she is effectively over her childhood emotions.

> **Understatement** A claim that is deliberately less forceful or dramatic than reality: Hurricanes tend to create a little wind.

> **Hyperbole** A deliberate exaggeration: I'm so hungry, I could eat a horse.

These strategies lend a certain layer of informality to writing. That is, writers who are attempting to lay low, to remain seemingly invisible, or to write formally usually refrain from hyperbole and understatement.

**A writer's voice characterizes the idea in a text. It creates the mood in which the reader will approach the ideas.**

# Choosing Details

Details help create voice. Both Bosley and Schwind-Pawlak focus on their mothers, but they give different details. While Schwind-Pawlak's details are comedic and overtly appeal to universal traits, Bosley's are darker and more specific. The details alone make the reader experience the memories and the writers differently:

**Schwind-Pawlak:**

Some children will smile and think about how silly their dad looked when he put carrot sticks up his nose that very morning, while others will cringe when they think about how their mother picked them up from school last week wearing orange polyester pants and a green shirt, oblivious to the hard work that some fellow went through to create the color wheel.

**Bosley:**

My mother had secret hopes. Finally divorced for the second time from the same man, my father, she sat with me and gave her own running commentary about who was cute, who smiled too much, who would find a handsome husband. My mother, having always been a little to a lot overweight, excelled at swimming, and she told me much later that she chose swimming because she didn't feel fat in the water. Her sister was the cheerleader, but she was a swimmer, too heavy for a short skirt of her own, she said.

# Using Sentence Length

Sentence length is a powerful tool for creating voice. Long, winding sentences that travel in and out of various ideas before returning the reader to the original path can create a self-reflective and sophisticated voice, one that considers complexities. Short sentences can create a determined voice. Notice the difference between the following:

Childhood was a gas.
Childhood was a raucous journey of twists and turns in which each moment was its own forever and every day a monument.

While the metaphors help create distinct voices, the sentence length also helps characterize the writer's voice. Notice how the sentence length in Bosley's passage tugs and pulls at the reader. The first sentence is short, and because of the content, it is almost a whisper. The second, longer sentence takes the reader further into the idea. The back and forth movement between long and short sentences creates the sensation of a living person telling a story, and the content of those sentences helps communicate the feelings and emotional complexities of that human.

## Activity

How do you want to appear to the reader? This decision will determine other writing decisions you make. So that your writer's voice isn't an accident or a mistake, make a deliberate decision about your voice for this essay and describe it: is it darkly reflective, comfortable, learned, free-spirited, urgent, passionate? Come up with your own descriptive term, then use it to help you make other writing decisions:

- Will I use figurative language? What types? How often?

- What details will I provide? What moments will I emphasize? How will these details not only convey ideas but shape how people feel about those ideas?

- Where should I vary sentence length?

# Vitality

Vitalized writing keeps readers' minds awake and moving. When readers encounter lively writing, they may not know exactly what's happening, but they find themselves gliding along, almost disappearing into the text. There are many strategies for sentence vitality, but techniques such as combining sentences, repeating structures, and intensifying verbs can make a dramatic difference.

## Combine Sentences

Sentences cue the reader. A period says, "Stop." A new sentence says, "Go." This stopping and starting helps create life. (Readers, like all humans, are drawn to pulsating movement.) But too many starts and stops keep readers from settling into ideas, so writers combine sentences to keep readers gliding along.

Sentences can be combined with *coordination* (adding together clauses of equal importance):

> My father did not believe in such things for girls as shoes, clothes, haircuts, college, or photographs for Junior Miss, <u>and</u> so there was no way he was going to give a penny for a pageant-worthy dress or a professional photographer's 10-minutes-plus-proofs.

> I was starving for adult conversation, <u>but</u> with family and friends scattered across the country, I didn't feel like I could call back the troops.

> Mrs. Rath had an ability to recognize the kids that actually wanted to read and learn and, often times, would send a few of us down to the library where it was quiet <u>and</u> we could have some sanctuary from the usual classroom shenanigans.

The underlined conjunctions in these sentences show where the writers joined ideas together. The ideas before and after the conjunctions are grammatically equal; the grammar cues the reader to give them equal intellectual weight.

Sentences also can be combined with *subordination* (making an idea less important than the main part of a sentence). Subordination involves tucking some ideas into others, creating the critical overlapping quality of good writing:

> For years <u>it sat empty</u>, the massive entrance looking out on Upton Avenue with no expression.

> As hoped for and expected, <u>a figure appeared out of nowhere</u>.

> Almost half a day later, around midnight, <u>the train crunched into Chicago</u>, where I hopped off, exhausted and exhilarated.

These examples of subordination show a variety of possibilities. Each sentence has a main clause (underlined), and other parts attached, or subordinated, to it. Notice how the third sentence, from Leonard Kress's "A Beat Education," would read differently if the ideas were separated into full sentences:

> Almost half a day later, around midnight, the train crunched into Chicago. I hopped off, and I felt exhausted and exhilarated.

Although the difference is small, this version creates more stops and starts for the reader. Those shorter, separated ideas sometimes are valuable, but good writers subordinate less important information. Hopping off the train is necessary information for Kress's narrative, but it is not something readers need at the front of their minds. Kress thus subordinates the fact to other details.

## Activity

Combine the following ideas using either coordination, subordination, or a combination of the two:

1. George worked on his truck. He crawled up into the engine. I saw him out the kitchen window.

2. I was busy. I went over and helped George. He might have been hurt. He couldn't see. He was shaky.

3. I worked at a restaurant in Texas. The customers were very nice. I left in the summer. It was too hot. I went back to Leadville.

## Repeat Structures

Although readers need a variety in length and structure, vitalized writing sometimes repeats key phrases or clauses. It is the writerly equivalent of pounding on a podium, driving a set of ideas at the audience:

> I never went to soccer again. As a matter of fact, I never played another organized sport again. Maybe it was the fear of rejection. Maybe it was the uncertainty of my talent. Maybe I was just too busy with other things.

> I'd lost the contest because I didn't yet know how to tell people what they wanted to hear. The small girl that boys secretly liked but wouldn't date doesn't win Miss America. The girl hiding in her room reading and writing poetry doesn't win Miss America. The girl playing the violin despite her mother's anxiousness that other people will think she's weird doesn't win Miss America. The girl on Willard Street doesn't ever win Miss America.

The repeating patterns create a cyclical feel, making the reader return to the same feeling established at the start of each passage.

## Intensify Verbs

Readers like intense verbs that create specific images of movement. It is easy to use weaker verbs, such as <u>is</u>, <u>are</u>, <u>was</u>, and <u>were</u>. But such verbs do little to propel the reader's mind through ideas. Notice the verb use in the following passages:

> I couldn't open the can of beans I'd brought along, and the slices of bread I'd <u>stuffed</u> into my rucksack <u>fell</u> onto the floor and <u>coated</u> themselves in rust-flecked grease. The freight did, however, <u>grant</u> me a spectacular view of the setting sun as it <u>ambled</u> ever so slowly along the banks of Lake Michigan.

> I would happily <u>contort</u> my fingers into chubby pretzels while singing "The Itsy Bitsy Spider" as the game's events <u>were recounted</u> on the drives home.

> I <u>checked out</u> Tortilla Flat and The Wayward Bus from the library and <u>asked</u> Mrs. Rath what else he <u>wrote</u> and where I <u>could get</u> it. She <u>loaned</u> me her copy of "In Dubious Battle." Soon, I <u>wanted</u> to own all of Steinbeck's books. I <u>scoured</u> the bookstores to complete the collection, a collection that <u>has traveled</u> with me for 25 years.

The verbs in these sentences do more than point out the action of the world. They portray that action—a necessary quality of vital writing.

### Activity

With a group of peers, identify the verbs *is, are, was, were, have, has,* and *had* in your essay and try rewriting sentences so that they rely on lively action verbs instead. Remember, *is, are, was, were, have, has,* and *had* function as linking verbs (the verbs you will try to replace), but they also function as helping verbs with participles (for example, *is running, was sailing, has concentrated*). If you can make a helping verb and participle livelier, you should; but these verb forms, because of the participles (*running, sailing, concentrated*), may already be lively enough.

# Vital writing does not merely describe action. It portrays the movement of the world.

# Revision

Revision is a necessary part of good writing and of one's development as a writer and thinker. Revision is when you step back and analyze your own rhetorical decisions, and perhaps even your own mind. Writers can revise alone or with others.

## Peer Review

Peer review, revising with the help of others, can be done in various ways. Your instructor may provide specific guidelines and, of course, you are free to try different approaches outside the classroom. If your instructor asks you to exchange essays with a peer or form small groups and read your essays aloud, the following advice can help you work efficiently and get results:

- Provide peer reviewers with a readable copy of your draft.
- Help focus the reviewers by writing down your carefully worded questions about your draft.
- If you read your essay aloud, don't read too fast.
- Be specific when responding. In addition to saying what you think, say why you think it.
- Be honest and encouraging. Providing only praise will not help the writer, yet phrasing your comments too negatively might be discouraging.
- Do not defend your essay, but instead view it as a work in progress. Be open to all ideas.
- Consider all comments, then make the changes you think are appropriate.

After you exchange drafts with another writer, use the following questions to guide your review:

1. How does the essay prompt you to think differently? (For instance, do you see something with more complexity, more beauty, more ugliness, or more intensity than you did before?) Explain what the essay helps you see differently. If you have a difficult time answering this question, perhaps the essay has not yet gone far enough.

2. What clichés should the writer replace with a new, revelatory idea? (Look closely. Clichés sometimes masquerade as profound thoughts.)

3. Which details best illustrate the main idea? (Which details reinforce the main idea and make you picture something specific?)

4. Which details could be added to illustrate the main idea? What particular behaviors or events could be further dramatized with details? For instance, the essay probably has a focused moment—a specific event that holds intense meaning. Could that moment use more detail?

5. Which details do not seem related to the thesis of the essay? Why not?

6. How could the writer create more public resonance?

7. Do any paragraphs lack coherence? Do they ramble or wander pointlessly through the past? Look for details that may hold meaning for the writer but don't develop the point of the essay.

8. How could the essay begin with more intensity? (For instance, if the essay begins with a broad statement such as *Children are curious creatures,* could it instead begin with a specific narrative or a more focused or surprising statement?)

9. Describe the writer's voice. Is it appropriate and consistent? Could the writer use figurative language or details that are more fitting? Where could sentence length be varied?

10. What sentences could be rewritten to create more vitality?
    - Where can the writer combine sentences with coordination?
    - Where can the writer combine with subordination?
    - What verbs can be more intense?
    - Where do basic grammatical issues (such as run-on sentences, sentence fragments, or pronoun/antecedent agreement) distract the reader?

# Peer Review Truisms

- **The process can make writers think differently about their own work.** Humans are great modelers. We model our behavior after others, and we make all kinds of subtle changes to our thinking when we read others' work. As modelers, peer reviewers can discover new approaches to an assignment, new writerly moves, new patterns of thinking, or new strategies for creating an engaging voice. (Reviewers can also discover qualities that they want to avoid in their own writing. They might discover some sentence or organization patterns and try to avoid them!)

- **Even the most inexperienced writer can offer valuable comments.** Some people believe that they have little to offer: "I'm not the teacher!" they'll announce. However, peer review is not about pointing out wrongs and rights. It's about reading closely and responding as a thoughtful human in a shared situation. If you can read and focus your attention, you can be a valuable reviewer. In fact, fellow students may even have more to offer one another because they're in a similar situation—faced with a similar task, experiencing the same pressures, at the same moment, in the same place.

- **Chat is the great enemy of good analysis.** Some instructors may set up sessions so that writers can converse about their drafts. Such sessions can be valuable and engaging—even intense and animated. But the danger is that they can devolve into chat sessions about the topics (or something else!). While chatting about one's topic is helpful (and can be worked into a class), a focused and intensive peer review session has its own kind of value.

- **Peer review can be the most valuable component of a writing class.** Writing in college is a social occasion. An academic essay (or any writing assignment) is an intersection of writers, instructors, and students. Peer review brings that to life. It makes the interaction of thinkers real and dramatic. When reviewers take the process seriously, it increases the value of the experience.

- **All writers need help.** Even the best of the best writers rely on the insights and assistance of others. Name a great writer from the past or the present (Steinbeck? Tolkien? Morrison? Dillard?). All of them used the ideas and thoughts of others to help shape their projects and even their sentences.

- **Done carelessly, peer review can be a terrible thing.** If peer reviewers read drafts quickly and only point to small, surface-level issues, they waste their partners' time. It is a similar waste if they read for "agreement" and "disagreement"—simply looking for passages they agree or disagree with—and then announce their approval or disapproval of certain points.

# An act of writing is an act of creation.

# Reflection

Students develop as writers and thinkers not just by writing an essay but also by reflecting on an essay *after* it has been written. The work of a college student is not just to write, but to write *about* writing (and to think *about* thinking). Now that you have written a Remembering essay, step back and explain it.

1. Even though your essay focuses primarily on *your* past, how does it have meaning for others? What passages from the essay connect your particular memory to a public concern?
2. What focused insight does your essay express?
3. Before you wrote your essay, how did you discover and develop your essay's insightful point? Your response to this question should trace the specific development of your insight throughout the writing process. Rather than give a general statement, try to give a detailed description of your process.
4. When used effectively, narration helps readers understand a writer's insight about a topic. When used ineffectively, it can take over the essay, drowning out the insight. Explain how narration in your essay helps the reader understand your insight without overshadowing it. Explain how the insight shines through.
5. The best writers work hard at saying more in fewer words. They are concise, using only the words necessary to make a point. Find a sentence in your essay that is concise, and then find one that is wordy. Rewrite the wordy sentence.

As you reflect on your essay, write complete sentences that are concise and carefully edited. If you try to write well each time you write, you will develop the habit of good writing. When you develop the habit, you will become a good writer.

## Beyond the Essay

An *autobiography* is an account of a person's life told by that person. A *biography* is an account of a person's life told by someone else. Autobiographies and biographies are like Remembering essays in that they do not merely report what happened; instead, they present certain events in a particular light to tell a story or make a point. Consider one autobiography or biography you have read or watched. How did it make a particular point by presenting certain events or details of a person's life?

 For additional resources including instructional videos and links to helpful websites, access your English CourseMate through cengagebrain.com.

# 3 Explaining Relationships

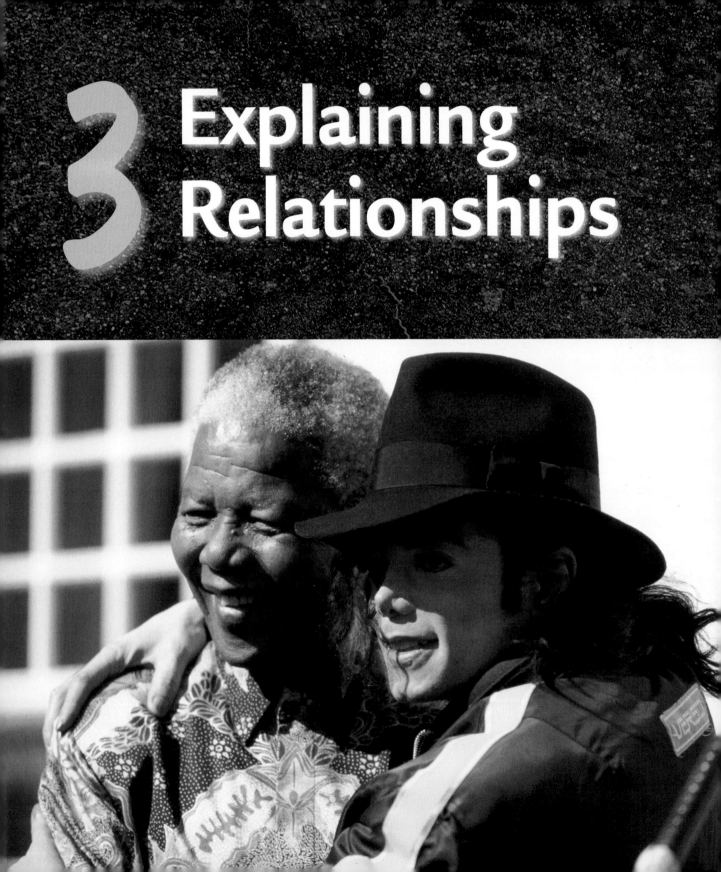

# Chapter Contents

**"It is little wonder that [the American settlers] went land-mad, because there was so much of it. They cut and burned the forests to make room for crops; they abandoned their knowledge of kindness to the land in order to maintain its usefulness. When they had cropped out a piece they moved on, raping the country like invaders. The topsoil, held by roots and freshened by leaf-fall, was left helpless to the spring freshets, stripped and eroded with the naked bones of clay and rock exposed. The destruction of the forests changed the rainfall, for the searching clouds could find no green and beckoning woods to draw them on and milk them."**

—John Steinbeck

In the above passage, from "Americans and the Land," John Steinbeck characterizes the relationship between early European settlers and the North American continent. Contrary to the conventional view of settlers as brave frontiersmen, Steinbeck describes them as land-mad invaders. Later in his essay, he describes them as "overindulged children."

Explaining relationships is common daily work: people on city councils explore the relationship between neighborhoods to help their cities better understand ethnic diversity; corporate executives try to understand the relationship between their own companies and their competitors; and certainly everyone is aware of the ongoing attempts by political leaders to explain the relationships between countries or regions. In a shrinking world, in which people of vastly different value systems attempt to coexist, explaining relationships is more than an exercise. It is an act of survival. To understand our place in the world, in a culture, in a family, in any system, we have to understand relationships.

One might even argue that the greatest discoveries have involved the discovery of relationships—between, for example, atomic elements, religious practices, geological events, historical figures, or heavenly bodies. Albert Einstein spent his life exploring the relationship between the impossibly small and the seemingly infinite; Carl Jung explored the relationship between the conscious and unconscious; Helene Cixous explored the relationship between sexuality and language. And we might see the history of science as a series of questions about relationships: How does the sun relate to Earth? How does matter relate to energy? How do particles relate to waves? How do fish relate to mammals? How does climate relate to the atmosphere? The same goes for philosophy. From ancient civilizations to modern institutions, people have asked, for instance, how language relates to thought, how ethics relate to religion, and how the individual relates to the community.

In all academic disciplines, people work to understand and communicate the nature of relationships:

- In a computer technology course, students study the
  relationship between an individual computer and a
  network of computers, or between a group of users
  and the Internet.

- In an anthropology course, students explore the
  relationship between a particular waterway and the
  ruins of a past civilization.

- In a biology course, students and faculty work to see
  the relationship between two forms of bacteria.

- In an interior design course, students examine the
  relationship between a large interior office space and
  a front entrance to a particular building.

This chapter explores relationships—among places,
things, events, people, and even ideas. The goal here is
to investigate, to seek out some of the hidden dynamics
of relationships, to discover the nature of a relationship,
or to discover a relationship where one is not necessarily
seen.

This chapter will help you discover a topic (a
particular relationship), explore that relationship in depth, and explain the nature of the
relationship in writing. The following essays will
provide valuable insight and necessary strategies for
exploring relationships. After reading the essays, you
can begin looking for a particular relationship in
one of two ways:

1. Go to the Point of Contact section to find a
   relationship from everyday life.
2. Choose one of the Ideas for Writing questions that follow the essays.

After finding a topic, go to the Analysis section to
begin developing the evaluation.

# Americans and the Land

## John Steinbeck

In John Steinbeck's novels, such as *The Grapes of Wrath* and *Of Mice and Men,* the setting is a vital element of the stories. Steinbeck often draws attention to the ways in which the land influences people's lives. In this essay, from *America and Americans,* Steinbeck focuses on the American settlers' impact on the land. Notice that the land, here, is not something to simply live *on* or even *from*. Instead, it is something to live *with*—or, in the case of many early Americans, to live *against*. As with so many of his novels and stories, Steinbeck's essay invites readers to see the relationship that people cultivate with the world around them.

I have often wondered at the savagery and thoughtlessness with which our early settlers approached this rich continent. They came at it as though it were an enemy, which of course it was. They burned the forests and changed the rainfall; they swept the buffalo from the plains, blasted the streams, set fire to the grass, and ran a reckless scythe through the virgin and noble timber. Perhaps they felt that it was limitless and could never be exhausted and that a man could move on to new wonders endlessly. Certainly there are many examples to the contrary, but to a large extent the early people pillaged the country as though they hated it, as though they held it temporarily and might be driven off at any time.

This tendency toward irresponsibility persists in very many of us today; our rivers are poisoned by reckless dumping of sewage and toxic industrial wastes, the air of our cities is filthy and dangerous to breathe from the belching of uncontrolled products from combustion of coal, coke, oil, and gasoline. Our towns are girdled with wreckage and the debris of our toys—our automobiles and our packaged pleasures. Through uninhibited spraying against one enemy we have destroyed the natural balances our survival requires. All these evils can and must be overcome if America and Americans are to survive; but many of us still conduct ourselves as our ancestors did, stealing from the future for our clear and present profit.

Since the river-polluters and the air-poisoners are not criminal or even bad people, we must presume that they are heirs to the early conviction that sky and water are unowned and that they are limitless. In the light of our practices here at home it is very interesting to me to read of the care taken with the carriers of our probes into space, to make utterly sure that they are free of pollution of any kind. We would not think of doing to the moon what we do every day to our own dear country.

When the first settlers came to America and dug in on the coast, they huddled in defending villages hemmed in by the sea on one side and by endless forests on the other, by Red Indians and, most frightening, the mystery of an unknown land extending nobody knew how far. And for a time very few cared or dared to find out. Our first Americans organized themselves and lived in a state of military alertness; every community built its blockhouse for defense. By law the men went armed and were required to keep their weapons ready and available. Many of them wore armor, made here or imported; on the East Coast, they wore the cuirass and helmet, and the Spaniards on the West Coast wore both steel armor and heavy leather to turn arrows.

On the East Coast, and particularly in New England, the colonists farmed meager lands close to their communities and to safety. Every man was permanently on duty for the defense of his family and his village; even the hunting parties went into the forest in force, rather like raiders than hunters, and their subsequent quarrels with the Indians, resulting in forays and even massacres, remind us that the danger was very real. A man took his gun along when he worked the land, and the women stayed close to their thick-walled houses and listened day and night for the signal of alarm. The towns they settled were permanent, and most of them exist today with their records of Indian raids, of slaughter, of scalpings, and of punitive counter-raids. The military leader of the community became the chief authority in time of trouble, and it was a long time before danger receded and the mystery could be explored.

After a time, however, brave and forest-wise men drifted westward to hunt, to trap, and eventually to bargain for the furs which were the first precious negotiable wealth America produced for trade and export. Then trading posts were set up as centers of collection and the exploring men moved up and down the rivers and crossed the mountains, made friends for mutual profit with the

Indians, learned the wilderness techniques, so that these explorer-traders soon dressed, ate, and generally acted like the indigenous people around them. Suspicion lasted a long time, and was fed by clashes sometimes amounting to full-fledged warfare; but by now these Americans attacked and defended as the Indians did.

For a goodly time the Americans were travelers, moving about the country collecting its valuables, but with little idea of permanence; their roots and their hearts were in the towns and the growing cities along the eastern edge. The few who stayed, who lived among the Indians, adopted their customs and some took Indian wives and were regarded as strange and somehow treasonable creatures. As for their half-breed children, while the tribe sometimes adopted them they were unacceptable as equals in the eastern settlements.

Then the trickle of immigrants became a stream, and the population began to move westward—not to grab and leave but to settle and live, they thought. The newcomers were of peasant stock, and they had their roots in a Europe where they had been landless, for the possession of land was the requirement and the proof of a higher social class than they had known. In America they found beautiful and boundless land for the taking—and they took it.

It is little wonder that they went land-mad, because there was so much of it. They cut and burned the forests to make room for crops; they abandoned their knowledge of kindness to the land in order to maintain its usefulness. When they had cropped out a piece they moved on, raping the country like invaders. The topsoil, held by roots and freshened by leaf-fall, was left helpless to the spring freshets, stripped and eroded with the naked bones of clay and rock exposed. The destruction of the forests changed the rainfall, for the searching clouds could find no green and beckoning woods to draw them on and milk them. The merciless nineteenth century was like a hostile expedition for loot that seemed limitless. Uncountable buffalo were killed, stripped of their hides, and left to rot, a reservoir of permanent food supply eliminated. More than that, the land of the Great Plains was robbed of the manure of the herds. Then the plows went in and ripped off the protection of the buffalo grass and opened the helpless soil to quick water and slow drought and the mischievous winds that roamed through the Great Central Plains. There has always been more than enough desert in America; the new settlers, like overindulged children, created even more.

The railroads brought new hordes of land-crazy people, and the new Americans moved like locusts across the continent until the western sea put a boundary to their movements. Coal and copper and gold drew them on; they savaged the land, gold-dredged the rivers to skeletons of pebbles and debris. An aroused and fearful government

"Logging in the Everglades" Photo courtesy of HistoryMiami Archives and Research Center

made laws for the distribution of public lands—a quarter section, one hundred and sixty acres, per person—and a claim had to be proved and improved; but there were ways of getting around this, and legally. My own grandfather proved out a quarter section for himself, one for his wife, one for each of his children, and, I suspect, acreage for children he hoped and expected to have. Marginal lands, of course, suitable only for grazing, went in larger pieces. One of the largest land-holding families in California took its richest holdings by a trick: By law a man could take up all the swamp or water-covered land he wanted. The founder of this great holding mounted a scow on wheels and drove his horses over thousands of acres of the best bottomland, then reported that he had explored it in a boat, which was true, and confirmed his title. I need not mention his name; his descendants will remember.

Another joker with a name still remembered in the West worked out a scheme copied many times in after years. Proving a quarter section required a year of residence and some kind of improvement—a fence, a shack— but once the land was proved the owner was free to sell it. This particular princely character went to the stews and skid rows of the towns and found a small army of hopeless alcoholics who lived for whisky and nothing else. He put these men on land he wanted to own, grubstaked them and kept them in cheap liquor until the acreage was proved, then went through the motions of buying it from his protégés and moved them and their one-room shacks on sled runners on to new quarter sections. Bums of strong constitution might prove out five or six homesteads for this acquisitive hero before they died of drunkenness.

It was full late when we began to realize that the continent did not stretch out to infinity; that there were limits to the indignities to which we could subject it. Engines and heavy mechanical equipment were allowing us to ravage it even more effectively than we had with fire, dynamite, and gang plows. Conservation came to us slowly, and much of it hasn't arrived yet. Having killed the whales and wiped out the sea otters and most of the beavers, the market hunters went to work on game birds; ducks and quail were decimated, and the passenger pigeon eliminated. In my youth I remember seeing a market hunter's gun, a three-gauge shotgun bolted to a frame and loaded to the muzzle with shingle nails. Aimed at a lake and the trigger pulled with a string, it slaughtered every living

thing on the lake. The Pacific Coast pilchards were once the raw material for a great and continuing industry. We hunted them with aircraft far at sea until they were gone and the canneries had to be closed. In some of the valleys of the West, where the climate makes several crops a year available, which the water supply will not justify, wells were driven deeper and deeper for irrigation, so that in one great valley a million acre feet more of water was taken out than rain and melting snow could replace, and the water table went down and a few more years may give us a new desert.

The great redwood forests of the western mountains early attracted attention. These ancient trees, which once grew everywhere, now exist only where the last Ice Age did not wipe them out. And they were found to have value. The Sempervirens and the Gigantea, the two remaining species, make soft, straight-grained timber. They are easy to split into planks, shakes, fenceposts, and railroad ties, and they have a unique virtue: they resist decay, both wet and dry rot, and an inherent acid in them repels termites. The loggers went through the great groves like a barrage, toppling the trees—some of which were two thousand years old—and leaving no maidens, no seedlings or saplings on the denuded hills.

Quite a few years ago when I was living in my little town on the coast of California a stranger came in and bought a small valley where the Sempervirens redwoods grew, some of them three hundred feet high. We used to walk among these trees, and the light colored as though the great glass of the Cathedral at Chartres had strained and sanctified the sunlight. The emotion we felt in this grove was one of awe and humility and joy; and then one day it was gone, slaughtered, and the sad wreckage of boughs and broken saplings left like nonsensical spoilage of the battle-ruined countryside. And I remember that after our rage there was sadness, and when we passed the man who had done this we looked away, because we were ashamed for him.

From early times we were impressed and awed by the fantastic accidents of nature, like the Grand Canyon and Yosemite and Yellowstone Park. The Indians had revered them as holy places, visited by the gods, and all of us came to have somewhat the same feeling about them. Thus we set aside many areas of astonishment as publicly owned parks; and though this may to a certain extent have been because there was no other way to use them, as the feelings of preciousness of the things we had been destroying grew in Americans, more and more areas were set aside as national and state parks, to be looked at but not injured. Many people loved and were in awe of the redwoods; societies and individuals bought groves of these wonderful trees and presented them to the state for preservation.

No longer do we Americans want to destroy wantonly, but our new-found sources of power—to take the burden of work from our shoulders, to warm us, and cool us, and give us light, to transport us quickly, and to make the things we use and wear and eat—these power sources spew pollution on our country, so that the rivers and streams are becoming poisonous and lifeless. The birds die for the lack of food; a noxious cloud hangs over our cities that burns our lungs and reddens our eyes. Our ability to conserve has not grown with our power to create, but this slow and sullen poisoning is no longer ignored or justified. Almost daily, the pressure of outrage among Americans grows. We are no longer content to destroy our beloved country. We are slow to learn; but we learn. When a super-highway was proposed in California which would trample the redwood trees in its path, an outcry arose all over the land, so strident and fierce that the plan was put aside. And we no longer believe that a man, by owning a piece of America, is free to outrage it.

But we are an exuberant people, careless and destructive as active children. We make strong and potent tools and then have to use them to prove that they exist. Under the pressure of war we finally made the atom bomb, and for reasons which seemed justifiable at the time we dropped it on two Japanese cities—and I think we finally frightened ourselves. In such things, one must consult himself because there is no other point of reference. I did not know about the bomb, and certainly I had nothing to do with its use, but I am horrified and ashamed; and nearly everyone I know feels the same thing. And those who loudly and angrily justify Hiroshima and Nagasaki—why, they must be the most ashamed of all.

## Writing Strategies

1. Focus on Steinbeck's opening paragraph. How does it function? Does it state or imply the main idea? How does it establish Steinbeck's voice? Does it invite the reader into the essay? If so, how?

2. Throughout the essay, Steinbeck describes detailed situations (anecdotes) that illustrate his point. Which of these anecdotes best supports his point about the relationship between settlers and the land?

3. In ¶10, Steinbeck describes the people that the railroad brought west as "land-crazy." He says they moved "like locusts." Identify other figurative expressions he uses to describe the people. Explain how these expressions function in the essay. How do they work with his overall point about the relationship between Americans and the land?

4. In ¶16, Steinbeck gives some examples that show contemporary Americans are, perhaps, more thoughtful about the land. How does this paragraph impact your understanding of the essay? How does it impact Steinbeck's voice?

5. In his conclusion, Steinbeck talks about shame. Explain how this passage supports his overall point about Americans' relationship with the land.

## Exploring Ideas

1. What does Steinbeck say about Americans and the land? What is he trying to accomplish in this essay?

2. Imagine Steinbeck as a guest on a current political talk show. What kinds of people would call in? Who would support Steinbeck's point? Who would angrily deny it?

3. What is your relationship with the land? What everyday actions of your own have a positive impact on the land? What everyday actions of your own have a negative impact on the land?

4. How have you been taught to think about American settlers? How does Steinbeck's essay fit into or push against the history you've been taught?

## Ideas for Writing

1. What is the relationship between Americans and the land today?

2. Describe your relationship with your immediate surroundings (your house, bedroom, apartment, dorm, etc.). How is it typical (or not typical) of your broader attitude concerning the relationship of humans to the land?

3. Observe the way land is used in your community. Take field notes. Discuss your observations with others, looking for ways that you might participate in Steinbeck's discussion of Americans and the land. How might you contribute to this discussion? What idea, for example, could use further explanation or clarification?

If responding to one of these ideas, go to the Analysis section of this chapter to begin developing ideas for your essay.

# Mugged

## Jim Crockett

Jim Crockett, a Spanish instructor, songwriter, farmer, and carpenter, has been drinking coffee for fifty years. As with millions of other Americans, coffee is fused to his everyday life. In this essay, Crockett focuses on a particular part of his relationship with coffee. But the essay goes far beyond his personal rituals and habits; it reveals something about the "small behaviors we cling to" and the size and scope of those seemingly simplistic habits that create meaning and familiarity. (Portions of Crockett's invention work appear later in the chapter.)

I have been mugged. Not accosted as I walk to my parked truck across a dark lot; not waylaid by thugs in the night. But mugged, nevertheless. I have been mugged by insinuation, by the insertion into my life of a cylindrical drinking vessel: one that holds coffee. I have been mugged by a to-go cup.

The relationship, or mugging, that has developed with my coffee mug is one-sided and is, because a mug's needs are simple, an easy relationship to maintain. Oh, I rinse and wipe it out every morning, and occasionally wash it with detergent, but these are minimal maintenance requirements, ones easily met. So why, if all this object does is simply hold coffee, would I consider our relationship worthy of the time and effort spent in its exploration and explication? Why would I seek depth of meaning in a seemingly superficial attachment to such a mundane object? Maybe the very mundanity of the object, the very quotidian nature of the relationship, deepens the attachment, suggests that the relationship goes symbolically deeper, symptomatically deeper, than I think.

In exchange for its minimal upkeep, my coffee mug gives back much more than it takes. Its secure lid keeps my mustache drip-free and, therefore, my books, shirts, and papers clean. My mug is insulated so it delivers hot, delicious, organically shade-grown, fair trade coffee for a couple of hours at a time, and in so doing, helps me directly support the small coffee growers and their cooperatives around the world. It is also an environmentally friendly mug. When I buy a cup of coffee, I only buy coffee: the paper cup and insulating sleeve, both little bits of tree, remain in the store. I remain weaned from dependence upon the earth- and human-pillaging multinational coffee cartel.

Wrought in stainless steel and plastic, this bit of industrial-designer paraphernalia (it holds my drug of choice) is every cup holder's dream. Its shape, curvaceous, tapered, slim-waisted and a bit heavier on top, is designed to fit cup holders in most vehicles, while being a natural-feeling extension of the human hand; or, in my case, a necessary adjunct to, a logical appurtenance thereof. My coffee cup is in my hand a lot.

In fact, when it is not in my hand, when I misplace it momentarily, or when, like the other day, I leave it on the bumper of my truck and see a flash in the rearview mirror as my mug goes airborne into the filthy slush of the winter street, I feel a twinge of separation anxiety. When I stop traffic to rescue it from the gutter after a close call with a Chevy Suburban, impatient and angry faces glare through wiper-slapped windshields to remind me that the small choices we make, the small behaviors we cling to, affect the way in which we are perceived in the world.

I worry, at times, when students and colleagues ask how much coffee I drink, or say they've never seen me without my coffee mug, that my attachment to my little friend is symptomatic of some neurosis or other, or that it indicates an obsessive/compulsive disorder. I don't, however, worry for long. Because, even though my mug is always nearby, whether on the lectern or table in front of the classroom, in the cup holder on the dashboard of my truck, on the desk where I am writing this essay, or just dangling from my hand, all it really signifies is an addiction to caffeine and the need, because I am human, for some small and securing daily grounding ritual. In an *econoculture* so far removed from its agrarian and wilderness roots, from its time-worn rituals of life, my coffee mug provides a needed, however tiny, bit of continuity in my daily doings, a small tie to place and home.

## Writing Strategies

1. How does the connotation of *mugged* impact the essay? How does the idea add to Crockett's point about his own relationship with coffee?

2. Although this essay focuses primarily on Crockett's personal relationship, how does it make broader, more public, points? What particular passages or sentences pull the reader beyond Crockett's personal situation?

3. Describe Crockett's voice. How does word choice impact the "sound" of his voice?

4. In his conclusion, Crockett characterizes the society around him as an *econoculture*. What idea is he creating with that term? How does it resonate with other passages or points in this essay?

5. What is Crockett's most compelling rhetorical move?

## Exploring Ideas

1. Crockett claims that humans need "some small and securing daily grounding ritual." What is a grounding ritual? Do you think it is, indeed, a fundamental human need?

2. Some sociologists, psychologists, and writers claim that the small moments in **everyday** life tell us the most about human behavior. Does this seem like a fair claim? In considering your own life, your own habits, is it true?

3. Why do people "cling" to their own habits?

4. Some historians have noted that the arrival of coffee and tea in medieval Europe could have been primary catalyst of the Renaissance. Caffeine, they say, woke up Europe! To what extent does caffeine impact our present culture—or your own ability to participate in the *econoculture?*

## Ideas for Writing

1. What is the most consistent daily ritual in your life? What does it reveal about your identity?

2. What common ritual do you share with millions of others?

3. Crockett says, "Maybe the very mundanity of the object, the very quotidian nature of the relationship, deepens the attachment, suggests that the relationship goes symbolically deeper, symptomatically deeper, than I think." What mundane object is symbolically, symptomatically fused to your identity?

If responding to one of these ideas, go to the Analysis section of this chapter to begin developing ideas for your essay.

Used by permission of the author

# Delicate Friend

## Lauren Jackson

Jackson wrote the following essay for her first-semester college English course. As she wrote drafts, responded to Invention Questions, and participated in Invention workshops, she discovered increasing complexity. Jackson's relationship to cigarettes is not simply a matter of nicotine, personal choice, or even peer pressure. The relationship is instead driven by some basic human needs.

Writing Strategies

Focuses on the main idea immediately—without broad overarching statements.

Exploring Ideas

She watched how a social group worked.

Perched on the white and brass speckled counter of my mother's kitchen is where I found my niche in the social circle. My mother smoked Marlboro Light 100s in a box and only in the kitchen when it was cold. She was courteous to the rest of the house: keeping the children out, always emptying the ashtray right away, and spraying air freshener. I used to sit in the dining room around the corner of the wall, to be out of view, and listen to her gossip and smoke while she danced around the linoleum with the telephone cord. When her girlfriends would come over, they would drink coffee, smoke, and talk about any and everything— usually discourse unsuitable for innocent ears. They would shoo the kids out of the kitchen and explain we couldn't be around the smoke. It seemed to me that smoking was an invitation to the secrets they shared. It was what they had in common, what they did. As I got older, I would sneak in for a glass of water and slink into a corner until they noticed and kicked me out. I wanted desperately to be included in the bond of the adult women and trusted with the whispered character assassinations. I wanted to be an integral part of a whole. I wanted to belong to something exclusive.

Describes the particular desire that drives the relationship.

A public resonance strategy.

This shows how people become attracted to exclusivity. It's the sociology of exclusion!

During middle school, a place when all children loathe themselves, anything and everyone, I decided it was time to define myself. I started stealing an occasional Marlboro Light from my mom. She kept them in a drawer in the kitchen that squeaked, so it took time and skill. There is a system to smoking below the legal age. And I had it perfected. I had a tin box containing various brands of stolen cigarettes, a few pairs of rubber gloves so my hands wouldn't hold the smell, a travel bottle of mouthwash, and dollar store body spray. I felt ingenious living this reticent life. There were safe places throughout the neighborhood. A barbeque pit at a nearby abandoned house was ideal.

The details about place help to ground the broader claims about identity.

A circle of trees hid it from public view. It became my private smoking place.

At school, smoking garnered status. After some bragging and showing off the goods, I quickly joined up with "The Bad Girls." I was someone. We stole cigarettes from our relatives and smoked before and after school. Having the smell on us was impressive and intimidating. The small patch of trees just outside the gym door was our lair. We practiced French inhaling. Instead of chemistry, English, or math, we talked about the cutest boys and who had gone how far with whom. What I found in those tight little rolls of tobacco was acceptance and courage. And when I started college, my initial friends were the smokers. I was relieved to discover them, and our conversations started easily. Smoking did the talking for me. *Hey, got a smoke? A light? Cold out here, isn't it?* Those turned into *Where ya from?* and *Maybe we can get together later.* I was granted a reassuring feeling that whatever the other people in class might think of me, the three smokers approved. I was not alone.

Gradually the media became an enemy to my pal and social crutch. Anti-smoking hysteria dominated televisions. Screens were filled with commercials of men singing out of voice boxes, bodies strewn about the streets depicting actual numbers of deaths from lung cancer. Smoking was banned from within 15 feet of all public entrances, most restaurants, a few bars, and then the entire downtown area. Government programs were issuing free nicotine patches along with information packets about quitting. Many folks, it seemed, were acknowledging the obvious health risks. They either quit or made it their business to make others quit (or both). My associates and I were characterized as irresponsible, reckless addicts. But the fact is that I am more addicted to the social environment of smoking than I am the actual nicotine. That is what enticed me initially. I was not attracted to the strong odor that saturates my clothes and hair, the stain on my hands and teeth, the risk of ruined health or an imminent death. I was attracted to something else. I learned how to be social, intimate, helpful, constant, and rebellious by smoking. Those are possibly not the most ideal values to uphold, but they worked for me.

No one likes to be a social outcast, unless of course you can be involved in a separate society of them. We want validation. We crave belonging and confirmation. Perhaps the Good Samaritans trying to save the world from a chemically enhanced haze are seeking that confirmation themselves. The validation I craved was freely given to me in a box pack of twenty.

Moves from private/secret smoking to public/collective smoking.

Moves from public behavior to the cultural/political issue.

Responds to the cultural/political messages—and reveals the quiet layers of the relationship.

The final insight addresses the tension developed in preceding paragraphs.

Identities have status, power, force.

She admits to the craving for affirmation—for belonging.

Group identity cancels out the fear of being outcast.

# Writing Strategies

1. How does the opening paragraph function in this essay? How does the memory of Jackson's mother help to establish the main idea?

2. Jackson describes the particular places that she smoked. What do these passages do for your understanding of the essay? How do they help you to see her point about smoking?

3. How does Jackson create public resonance? What particular passages seem most important for making her experience relevant to readers?

4. How is Jackson's essay revelatory? Explain how she gets to something more complex than the common sentiments about self, identity, or belonging.

5. This essay is largely narrative, but a college essay should do more than tell a story—more than relay events. It should also analyze how something (like a relationship) works. So how is Jackson's essay doing more than telling a story? Point to specific passages that reveal how the relationship works.

# Exploring Ideas

1. Jackson describes herself as craving connection, belonging, even exclusivity. How is that craving similar to or different from an addiction to nicotine?

2. Jackson explains that she learned to be "social, intimate, helpful, constant, and rebellious" through smoking. But she admits that such qualities may not be valued by her readers. Why might someone object to these qualities? Do you object to any of them?

3. Jackson describes an important distinction: while people don't want to be isolated from the mainstream, they enjoy being part of a rebellious group. What other groups, besides smokers, might consider themselves rebels? How do they illustrate Jackson's point?

4. Jackson describes her desire for validation both as a child and as a college student. This suggests that adults crave validation as much as children do. Describe a situation that supports or refutes this suggestion.

# Ideas for Writing

1. Have you ever been a social outcast? Do you know a social outcast? What is the relationship between the outcast and the culturally accepted?

2. What has the craving for acceptance or validation prompted you to do? Has the craving for validation prompted you into a relationship?

If responding to one of these ideas, go to the Analysis section of this chapter to begin developing ideas for your essay.

# INVENTION

Invention is the activity of discovering ideas, developing points, and thinking through a topic. For academic writers, it is a necessary activity, one that leads to vital and valuable ideas. In this chapter, the invention process will involve focusing on a particular relationship and exploring its possible meaning. The following sections are designed to help you through the process: specifically, to discover a topic (in Point of Contact), to develop particular points about the topic (in Analysis), to make it relevant to a community of readers (in Public Resonance), to develop a focus (in Thesis), and to generate support (in Rhetorical Tools). The Invention Questions in each section are not meant to be answered directly in your final written assignment. Rather, they are meant to help you develop increasingly intense ideas for your project.

# Point of Contact

When you hear the word *relationship,* you may imagine an intimate personal bond between significant others, family members, or friends. But consider the relationships that are less obvious, those that surround or define us but remain hidden by the patterns of everyday life. Imagine the intense, but also subtle, relationships that define life as we know it: between an old man and his backyard, among people in a corporate office, between a lake and a local economy, between pigeons and people in a park.

As you explore possible topics, ask yourself, "What is the nature of this relationship?" If you can't answer the question easily, you may have a good topic—one worthy of continued thinking and writing. Use the following suggestions and questions to begin exploring:

- **Visit a Public Place**
  —How do the people interact or depend on each other?
  —How do the people relate to their surroundings? To objects? To buildings? To nature?
  —How do the objects (buildings, tools, products, shops) relate?
  —How do people or objects influence each other?

- **Examine Your Own Relationships**
  —Consider the groups or allegiances that you claim: are you a smoker, a cyber punk, a metal head, a gamer, a comic book fanatic?
  —What are the tensions, contradictions, or quiet associations that come along with that identity?

- **Examine a Job Site**
  —How do workers relate to their tools or equipment?
  —How must the people relate to each other? (How must they influence or depend on each other?)
  —How do workers relate to their environment?
  —How do workers relate to the public?

- **Examine Everyday Civic Bonds**
  —Between a customer and a sales clerk, a customer and a mail carrier, the public and a city police force, a politician and her constituents, or an artist and the public.

- **Imagine Human/Object Relationships**
  —Between a person and a computer, a person and a musical instrument, a person and a car; or between two objects, such as a college course and a textbook, a book and a computer, an old car and a new one, or a road and a house.

- **Examine Relationships in Your Academic Major**
  —Between the professionals in your field of study and the public (such as nurses and their patients, or business marketing professionals and potential consumers).
  —Between two things in your field of study. Students of criminal justice, for instance, can explore how one case (or one kind of case) relates to another; environmental scientists can explore the relationship between waterways and surrounding land or between trees and animal life.
  —Between your field of study and another field. Most academic disciplines and professional fields define themselves in conjunction with other fields. For instance, biology explores its relationship with ethics, computer technologies involve visual or graphic design, and political science involves religious studies.

Hal Wilson/StockXchng

Valeria Obregon/StockXchng

Cengage Learning

Jonas Jordan, USACE/U.S. Army

Dawn M. Turner/MorgueFile

Norbert Machinke/StockXchng

# Analysis

Analysis is the process of inspecting how or why something works, but analysis also involves discovering connections and meaning. In this chapter, analysis involves investigating all the possible ways entities relate to each other. It means going beyond the obvious relationship and exploring the hidden connections. For example, we might begin with some basic understanding of a relationship:

- Students have a relationship with education.
- Smokers have a relationship with cigarettes.
- Pet owners have a relationship with their pets.
- Athletes have a relationship with their equipment.

Inside of the broad idea, we can look for relational clusters—for more specific relationships that maintain or give meaning to the broader idea. For instance, a student has a relationship with education, but more specifically, a computer sciences student may have a relationship to technology *and* change *and* Generation Y. Or a pet owner may have many specific relationships because of her dog—say, with a certain open field, a leash law, or a neighborhood park. When we begin to see clusters of relationships within the broader idea, we get closer to revealing important connections. Use the following Invention Questions to explore deep layers of the relationship that you will explain in your essay:

## Invention Questions

▶ What relationships exist within the broader relationship? How do those smaller relationships drive the broader relationship?

▶ Is the broader relationship difficult? Why?

▶ What keeps it going?

▶ How does the presence of one entity (person or thing) influence the other? In what hidden or indirect ways do they influence one another?

▶ What would occur to one if the other were gone? ■

If you examine an intimate personal relationship, try to go beyond the initial common thoughts ("it is supportive"; "it is difficult"; "it has ups and downs"; "it is loving") and find some hidden complexity. Use the following Invention Questions to explore the complexities of a human relationship:

▶ In what ways do I communicate with this person?

▶ To what degree do I share in his or her personal crises?

▶ Do I ever feel obligated to do, think, or say something for this person?

▶ Why am I in this relationship?

▶ What kinds of disagreements arise in the relationship? Do they become sources of debate and tension, or do they fade away? ■

As you work through these Invention Questions, use them to develop ideas. For example, in the following excerpt, Jim Crockett's invention writing helped him discover the insights he shares in his essay. In his responses to the Invention Questions, we can see how important concepts emerge and lay the groundwork for his essay:

> **In what hidden or indirect ways do [the persons or things] influence one another?**
>
> At the outset, I'm really wondering why I need to use the same mug every day and not one of the many on the shelf that perform the same function, i.e., keep my mustache dry and drip-free while keeping coffee hot. Maybe it's because I received this mug for my birthday a few years back—received it from good friends. Maybe it's the functional good looks of the stainless steel and plastic—industrialized design good looks. Maybe it's because I have a need to carry a security object (Linus's blanket). What if I have an obsessive/compulsive disorder? What if? Does it really matter? Do I really care? Is this really a big deal? Maybe not, but it's probably worth looking into—probably worth unraveling the thread of the warm blanket (warm sweater?) of my relationship with my coffee mug.

Here, Crockett explores various layers. He raises some questions that later evolve into the essay, and he makes two important discoveries: that any possible psychological "disorder" is less important than some basic human need and that he connects his mug with security.

Now let's look at a different topic and writer. In the following, Marcus uses the Invention Questions to explore the relationship between a police department and the surrounding community. Notice how Marcus's response to the last question (Why am I in this relationship?) takes him further into his own thinking. Although the question seems unrelated to his topic, it actually prompts him to see an essential point: *People can be in a relationship without consciously thinking about it.*

**Is the relationship difficult?**

Yes. My father is a police officer, and he is constantly stressed about the work. Patrolling in some neighborhoods is hard work—and dangerous. And even though many officers face dangerous situations, they are expected by people in the community to be totally passive. It's nearly impossible work.

**What keeps it going?**

People stay in the job for obvious reasons: they need money, they have the training, they get some satisfaction out of the job (most of them still assume that they are "protecting and serving"). But the real question is: what keeps the tension going? And that's a mixture of things: On one side, economic problems in the city create bad neighborhoods where people are desperate. On the other side, every time the news reports anything involving the police, it's going to be bad, so people learn to associate police cars and uniforms with negative feelings.

**Why am I in this relationship?**

Technically, I'm not in it. Or maybe I am. I am "the community." But I guess most people probably don't think they are in the relationship until they see the flashing lights behind them. That's also part of the reason that the tension keeps going. People in the community don't see themselves as part of the relationship—maybe they don't even see a relationship.

# Thinking Further

How do writers identify potentially interesting ideas? Of all the ideas swimming around, how do they decide which to pursue and which to ignore? You might consider two key strategies:

1. **Capitalize on Uncertainty.** If you are uncertain how to answer a question, or you can answer it several ways, explore further. (The uncertainty is a sign of complexity!) For example, Marcus writes, "Technically, I'm not

in it. Or maybe I am." As Marcus reviews his notes, he can focus on this indefinite answer and explore the ambiguity.

2. **Look for Fresh Perspectives.** Occasionally you might see a topic differently than most other people. Because writers are looking for a new perspective, such realizations are vital. For example, when Marcus writes, "the tension keeps going" because "people in the community don't see themselves as part of the relationship," he has discovered an important idea worth pursuing further.

If writers discover some uncertainty or fresh perspective, they can then ask even more questions to pursue their thinking. For example, Marcus might explore further by asking the following questions:

**"Technically, I'm not in it. Or maybe I am."**

- Am I in the relationship or not? What is the nature of the relationship?
- Can I ever get out of the relationship? What would happen if I did?
- How does the relationship influence me in hidden ways? How does it influence law enforcement?

**"People in the community don't see themselves as part of the relationship—maybe they don't even see a relationship."**

- Why don't people in the community see the relationship? How is their not seeing helpful or harmful?
- Who does see the relationship? How do people who see the relationship act differently?
- If more people saw the relationship, would it be less difficult? Would people be influenced differently?

# Invention Workshop

Meet with at least one other writer and use one of the Invention Questions (on page 76) to initiate a focused discussion on your topic. Briefly explain your topic to the other writer(s), and then ask one of the Invention Questions. Try to stay focused on that question until you've reached some new insight about the relationship.

Look into the deep connections, both present and past; look at the consequences of actions; consider the effects of attitudes. And remember two key strategies: (1) capitalize on uncertainty, and (2) look for fresh perspectives.

## Sample Invention Workshop

Writer (explains the topic): I want to write about my relationship with snowboarding. I really like snowboarding. I do it all winter. It's what I do with my friends. I love the snow, the speed, and the excitement. It's expensive though, and risky.

Peer (applies an Invention question): Let's use one of the Invention Questions to probe deeper: What relationships exist within the broader relationship? How do those smaller relationships drive the broader relationship?

Writer: Well, if the broader relationship is me and snowboarding, then some smaller relationship that exists within it might be…

Peer (helps the writer identify smaller relationships): You mentioned speed and excitement and risk. Do you think speed is part of the risk? Is excitement part of the risk? Or vice versa?

Writer: Well, I'd say both. Maybe they're all tangled together. The speed creates a kind of risk—of physical harm, I guess—and that creates excitement. The rush comes from zooming down the hill, not poking along.

Peer (prompts writer to explore uncertainty): So the speed wouldn't be as intense if there weren't some peril involved? Are peril and intensity linked in some way?

Writer: Probably. Well, it's not totally about the potential harm. I mean, you don't go out there looking to get hurt or fall down a mountain. It's also about the skill it takes to avoid crashing—and to go faster, to do more with your own body.

Peer (prompts further thinking): Your own body? Why's that important?

Writer: Well, it's just you and the board—and the hill. Nothing else. You and natural forces. No computers, no monitors, no nothing. And if you move the wrong way, just a little, you feel the consequences.

Peer: And the opposite could also be said, right? That moving just the right way makes you feel something?

Writer: Definitely. You really learn what your body's capable of—split second decisions and reflexes.

Peer: So maybe that's how the speed figures in. It cranks up the need for your body to respond? To rely on reflexes?

Writer: Exactly. And you don't get that anywhere else. I don't anyway. The rest of my life is about sitting, watching, pushing buttons, reading—all eyes, ears, and fingers. I need more than that.

Peer: So snowboarding makes your body wake up to itself—and in a really intense way. Okay. Here's another Invention question. What would occur to one if the other were gone?

Writer: Well, if I didn't have snowboarding, I don't think I'd be aware of my own reflexes. I don't know if I'd understand how my reflexes and body even work.

The writer is now digging into the relationship. From here, she could go into the Public Resonance questions (on the following page) and explore the issue further. For instance, the writer may examine how people need a certain degree of raw intensity—something beyond the digital, clinical, and predictable routine of everyday life. That further exploration might yield a revelatory thesis.

# Public Resonance

Remember that you are not writing entirely for yourself. You are writing to explain something for others. The particular relationship you are explaining may be specific and narrow (perhaps between two people), but it may suggest something beyond the particular—something that is relevant or important to your readers. As you consider your own topic, ask the following questions:

## Invention Questions

▶ Does the relationship reveal something about people's strengths, weaknesses, or needs?

▶ Why is it important that people see the meaning of the relationship?

▶ Is there something unusual or usual about this relationship?

▶ Does this relationship show how difficult, easy, or valuable human relationships can be?

▶ Does this relationship show how rewarding or valuable a particular kind of relationship can be? ■

Exploring public resonance can be hard work. But the process takes writers somewhere important, even vital: to new insights. In his project, Jim Crockett discovers the bigger significance of a relationship—that his simple mug is not merely a personal habit but a representation of human habit and a basic need. He also considers how the specific relationship functions within the broader sphere of relations between humans and their economy, humans and their home, and humans and their past:

> Why is it important that people see the meaning of the relationship? We all need daily ritual in our lives in an increasingly alien world—a culture, econoculture removed from the time-worn agrarian rituals, from the ties to place and home. How much coffee do you drink anyway? The cup/mug is natural—a natural extension of the human hand, a necessary adjunct to, a logical appurtenance thereof. Small choices—these

small behaviors we cling to—affect the way in which we are perceived in the world.

And in further writing, Crockett picks up on an idea that surfaces in the previous passage—the idea of ritual. He realizes that *ritual,* the term itself, has significance, meaning beyond the obvious, so he says more about it. Notice that he finds his way back to the concept, to the word, and thinks about its role in the world. In this sense, Crockett's own language is pulling him further into ideas. He is inventing by exploring the meaning and significance of his words:

> I'm tired of people asking how much coffee I drink. Do they really care? Caffeine or antioxidants? Whose side are you on? They should care where their coffee comes from. They should care about buying coffee in tree-killing paper cups. They should know that the small choices they make affect the world; that the smallest choices have power. !!! Ritual power—the power of small rituals. We are grounded by our rituals—in the wider world—in the econoculture—the world of corporate greed—we (individuals) have no control. My mug ritual gives me some control in the huge arena of coffee trading. My money goes to the small farmer in Chiapas (at least more of my money) not to the national cartels. The ritual grounds me and ties me to the place and affects, as well, the wider world, the world far removed from its agricultural roots, a world where wilderness is a theme park and where the agrarian rituals have been replaced with what? Maybe they haven't been replaced. Maybe just forgotten. Maybe ritual behaviors are no longer deemed important in a society driven by techne—a society enamored of subject only. Who's doing the verbing here? It doesn't matter who's the recipient, the object. That's why this matters. Maybe we should ask—maybe we should be asking: Whom or what do the small behaviors, ones we cling to, affect? How do they affect the way we are perceived in the world?

# Thesis

As you focus your topic, you will also be narrowing in on a thesis statement or main idea. Like many writers, you may write your way to a thesis, or you may try to focus the idea before drafting. Either way, you need to have a single statement that not only gives focus to your topic but also gives your particular insight on that topic. Your project might do one of the following:

- **Explain the significant qualities of a particular kind of relationship.**
  —Human/dog relationships rely on so little understanding and effort from humans and so much work, agility, and determination from the dog.
  —Rock stars and their fans both rely on a sense of urgency and exclusivity.

- **Explain what is sometimes hidden in a particular kind of relationship.**
  —Beneath the obvious authority issues between teachers and students, there exists a mutual kind of awe in which each marvels at the will of the other.
  —Homeowners often forget the powerful underground struggle between plumbing and trees—until they see stems and leaves swimming in the toilet.

- **Explain the difficulties or problems of being a child, friend, parent, or significant other.**
  —Our children's birthdays are a tangle of joy and unutterable sadness that comes with knowing how time will eventually do its work and create absence.
  —College friends are surrogate families, which means they always fall short in some quiet way.

- **Explain how a particular relationship is much like something else.**
  —Presidential candidates and their potential supporters are both authors of fiction, each conjuring visions of what the other will certainly do.
  —If the surrounding neighborhood is a family, the 7-11 is like a bad in-law that has slowly been accepted.

- **Explain how a particular relationship reveals something important about a subject.**
  —The river's color beyond the city shows how water willingly carries the by-products of human endeavor.
  —The association between gun and police officer speaks of our culture's assumption about power.

Regardless of your approach, avoid the fog. Steer clear of unfocused generalizations. A narrower and more particular thesis will create a more intensive experience for both writer and reader. Notice the difference among the following:

| General | Specific | More Specific |
| --- | --- | --- |
| Students | Third-grade girls | The attitudes of third-grade girls |
| Employees | Retail sales associates | Retail sales associates' energy |
| Campus | The new buildings | The look of the new buildings |

The more specific subjects help readers (and writers!) focus on more specific insights. They help readers and writers tune in to intricacies and intimacies. (They actually help sharpen consciousness.) In considering the focus of your project, examine the nouns you use. Can they be more specific?

If nouns (or subjects in sentences) help create focus, then verbs can help create *revelation*. A revelatory thesis statement shows something new—a commonly overlooked layer, connection, or idea. Notice the following statements:

- The attitudes of third-grade girls *depend* upon the number of close friends.
- Retail sales associates' energy *relies* on the number and nature of customers.
- The flat, corporate look of the new buildings on campus *competes* with the traditional stone giants and illustrates the clash between the old academic tradition and the new corporate designs on education.

In these statements, the verbs *(depend, relies, competes)* are active and intensive. They help show how two things or groups of people relate.

# Evolution of a Thesis

Writers should allow their initial ideas to become increasingly more focused and revelatory. Notice how a broad statement can become more intense and sophisticated as it becomes more focused:

- **Runners develop an intense relationship with the road.**

  Here, "intense relationship" can be defined or narrowed. It's potentially interesting, but we need to see the intensity.

- **Runners share space with humans and machines.**

  The writer can keep thinking about that space—what happens in that shared space?

- **Runners must confront the overwhelming presence of both cars and car culture when they take to the road.**

  The writer has helped us to see a kind of difficulty or tension in the relationship. We're examining not only the physical presence of cars, but some set of assumptions or attitudes related to cars.

## Revising Your Thesis

A key part of writing is developing an intellectual rearview mirror—a habit of looking back and redirecting your course. Apply the following questions:

- In my thesis, which nouns could be narrower, more specific?

- In my thesis, which verbs could be intensified to reveal more about the relationship?

- How does the statement offer something beyond a commonsense or simplistic assumption? How is it revelatory?

Other writers can help you with this process. Try exchanging your initial ideas with others and using the preceding questions for peer evaluation.

Avoid the fog. Steer clear of unfocused generalizations.

# Rhetorical Tools

The next step is to develop and support ideas. Remember that a potential reader already knows about relationships in general. (He or she is certainly mired in several.) But in your essay you have the opportunity to shed light, to go beyond ordinary thinking, and to reveal something that most people do not necessarily consider.

## Using Narration

Narration, or storytelling, is appropriate for many kinds of writing. It is not simply relegated to remembering events. You might consider beginning your essay with a brief retelling of a situation regarding the relationship, or using a brief account to illustrate something about the relationship. It will be important to determine how much narration to use. For example, Lauren Jackson relies heavily on narration. Jim Crockett uses narration more sparingly. If you decide to use narration, make good choices:

1. Start the narrative at an appropriate place. That is, limit your story to include only relevant parts of the situation.
2. Focus on only the relevant details of the events.
3. Use consistent verb tense. (In most cases, past or present tense can work in retelling a story. However, you must be consistent throughout the narrative.)
4. At some point, make sure to explain the significance or relevance of the narrative to the reader.
5. Refer to Chapter 2 for other valuable narrative strategies.

## Using Description

Readers like details. The more detailed the images, the more intensely the reader will experience them. In this essay, you might decide to describe the people involved in the relationship—their particular postures, facial expressions, and gestures. Or you might need to detail more abstract qualities—their imaginations, their appetites, their pride, their esteem, their effect on strangers. In the following, a writer is describing the relationship between a coffee shop and the students who frequent the place. The first passage is broad and without detail:

> The coffee shop makes them feel more academic. It is more than a location to do homework and drink caffeine. It is a place where students totally surround themselves in college work.

These are valuable statements, but they remain abstract, general, and ultimately unhelpful to the reader. But the ideas come to life more with details:

> The coffee shop is more than a location for doing homework. It is like a satellite campus where students and professors alike work, talk, reflect. On any given day, several tables will be pushed together while a group of students work together on a project, their papers and notebooks scattered between coffee cups and half-eaten bagels. Invariably, a professor, graduate student, or staff member from the college will sit at one of the corner tables reading a newspaper. Several students will be perched on the windowsill, their backs against the outside world as they read through textbook chapters.

You might need to describe a particular situation in detail. In that case, narration and description will work together. For instance, Steinbeck includes several situations or anecdotes in his essay that dramatize the relationship between American settlers and the land:

> Another joker with a name still remembered in the West worked out a scheme copied many times in after years. Proving a quarter section required a year of residence and some kind of improvement—a fence, a shack—but once the land was proved the owner was free to sell it. This particular princely character went to the stews and skid rows of the towns and found a small army of hopeless alcoholics who lived for whisky and nothing else. He put these men on land he wanted to own, grubstaked them and kept them in cheap liquor until the acreage was proved, then went through the motions of buying it from his

protégés and moved them and their one-room shacks on sled runners on to new quarter sections. Bums of strong constitution might prove out five or six home-steads for this acquisitive hero before they died of drunkenness.

# Using Figurative Language

Any explanatory essay can benefit from figurative language, which is language that goes beyond words' basic definitions and uses them to suggest imaginative connections between ideas. Figurative language does more than just make inter-esting comparisons. It also reveals a new dimension to the topic; it helps writers and their readers to see the topic in a new light.

**Metaphor:** A metaphor is a comparison in which one thing is made to share the characteristics of another. In his essay, Jim Crockett slides in a subtle metaphor that graphi-cally describes most consumers' relationship with big coffee corporations:

> When I buy a cup of coffee, I only buy coffee: the paper cup and insulating sleeve, both little bits of tree, remain in the store. *I remain weaned from dependence* upon the earth  and human-pillaging multinational coffee cartel.

**Simile:** A simile is a comparison that uses *like* or *as*. John Steinbeck's similes help to characterize the nature of the relationship between American settlers and the land:

> I have often wondered at the savagery and thought-lessness with which our early settlers approached this rich continent. They came at it *as though it were an enemy,* which of course it was.

> There has always been more than enough desert in America; the new settlers, *like overindulged children,* created even more.

As you consider your own topic, apply the following questions:

▶ What brief story will help the reader to see my point about the relationship?

▶ What vivid details will help demonstrate the precise nature of the relationship?

▶ Can I compare the relationship (or the entities in the relationship) to an animal? A thing? A place? A person? What new dimension would this comparison reveal? ■

## Activity

Before developing a draft, plan out your writing. A brief plan, in fact, can make all the difference between writerly hiccups and writerly flow. If you have an overall plan, you'll be able to more smoothly move along. Chart out your ideas: What is your thesis? What are your main sup-port strategies? What examples will you use? What stories will you tell? And where will you begin and end those? What comparisons will you make?

# Organizational Strategies

## How Should I Begin?

If a good introduction comes to mind, by all means, write it down. But if one doesn't, don't worry. Go ahead and write the essay without an introduction. Once you have a draft (without the introduction), you'll have a better idea what you are introducing; thus, the introduction should be easier to write.

As we will suggest throughout this book, the possibilities for introductions are boundless. For this particular essay, you might do any of the following:

- Begin with a general statement about the relationship. Steinbeck begins with a general statement about American settlers and the land:

  I have often wondered at the savagery and thought-lessness with which our early settlers approached this rich continent. They came at it as though it were an enemy, which of course it was. They burned the forests and changed the rainfall; they swept the buffalo from the plains, blasted the streams, set fire to the grass, and ran a reckless scythe through the virgin and noble timber.

- Begin with a brief story or anecdote about the relationship. Jackson begins her essay with an anecdote that develops the main idea.
- Begin with a typical belief or stereotype about the relationship, and then turn to your particular insight. For instance, here's how a writer might focus on the relationship between the police and the surrounding community:

  Most people assume they have no relationship with their local police departments. Other than in an emergency situation, most are even reluctant to acknowledge police officers. They often treat them as uniformed specters lurking on the roads of their towns. But the police of any community are deeply connected to the everyday patterns of life. They are serving their communities and participating in daily routines at all levels.

- Begin with a fictional account, or scenario, of a relationship. Imagine the same topic about police and communities beginning differently:

  Imagine a community in which the police only appeared for emergencies, in which people had to make a 911 call simply to get a police car to visit the area. Imagine the streets of a crowded city without the occasional police cruiser. Imagine the downtown stores without the presence of a city officer.

## Where Should My Thesis or Main Point Go?

Remember that a thesis can be either explicitly stated or *implied* (suggested by the content but not stated in the essay). Of course, even if a thesis is implied, the author needs to know the main idea. A thesis for this essay might go in any of these places:

- At the very beginning—the first sentence of the first paragraph
- At the end of the first paragraph
- In the conclusion
- After a brief account that illustrates the main idea

## When Should I Change Paragraphs?

Remember that paragraphs are tools for focusing and refocusing your readers' attention. Paragraph breaks stop readers and signal them to refocus their attention. Particularly for this essay, you might change paragraphs at any of these times:

- When beginning a scenario or narrative
- When offering a memory
- When changing scenes or time in the middle of a longer narrative
- When offering a detailed allusion

# How Should I Make Transitions?

You might think of paragraph transitions in two ways. Sometimes making paragraph transitions is as easy as choosing the right information to come next—that is, choosing the most appropriate information to begin the paragraph. In these cases, the content of the paragraphs works to bridge the gap between them. (See Steinbeck ¶7–9. The content of each paragraph follows logically from the preceding paragraph. Steinbeck uses a time sequence to move from one point to the next, so explicit transitions are unnecessary.) Often, however, the writer needs to create a phrase, sentence, or sentences at the beginning of the new paragraph to clarify the relationship between the old and the new. This sentence or phrase helps to bridge the gap between points. In the following, Jim Crockett provides a very small, but important, bridge between two paragraphs. The small phrase "in fact" carries the reader from an idea to a closer examination of that idea:

> My coffee cup is in my hand a lot.
>
> In fact, when it is not in my hand, when I misplace it momentarily, or when, like the other day, I leave it on the bumper of my truck and see a flash in the rearview mirror as my mug goes airborne into the filthy slush of the winter street, I feel a twinge of separation anxiety.

As you consider transitions, do not be deterred. If you cannot see the relationship between paragraphs as you are drafting, continue onward. (Don't get held up trying to imagine one perfectly crafted phrase!) Writers often come back through their drafts and fill in the cracks—adding transitional phrases, sentences, or entire paragraphs. After they have developed all the nuances of their thinking, they can then ask questions: How do the paragraphs relate? Are they contrary? Is one an extension of the other? Is the second paragraph more particular than the first? Or is the second more broad?

# How Should I Conclude?

As with introductions, the possibilities for conclusions are limitless. Short explanatory essays (such as those under 1,000 words) usually do not need to summarize main points. Instead, writers often use conclusions to suggest the significance of the ideas expressed in the body of the essay. For this essay, you might consider concluding in one of the following ways:

- The overall statement on, and particular meaning of, the relationship (the thesis).
- An allusion that best illustrates your points about the relationship. An allusion can be a powerful conclusion strategy because it projects the point of the essay onto some other subject or idea. It extends the essay's reach outward. Notice Steinbeck's use of a historical allusion:

> But we are an exuberant people, careless and destructive as active children. We make strong and potent tools and then have to use them to prove that they exist. Under the pressure of war we finally made the atom bomb, and for reasons which seemed justifiable at the time we dropped it on two Japanese cities— and I think we finally frightened ourselves. In such things, one must consult himself because there is no other point of reference. I did not know about the bomb, and certainly I had nothing to do with its use, but I am horrified and ashamed; and nearly everyone I know feels the same thing. And those who loudly and angrily justify Hiroshima and Nagasaki—why, they must be the most ashamed of all.

- A return to an introductory image or scene that reveals something significant about that image. This strategy is often called "framing." Having gone through the complexities of the essay, the readers now know something special and different about the opening image. Returning to it does not merely recap the point but helps the readers understand just how far they've gone. They understand a new poignancy, a new sticking point, about the topic.

# Writer's Voice

Some writers create very serious, sober voices. They offer claims with the utmost formality. Sentences may be consistent in length and structure. Slang words and contractions are often absent, as in this passage from John Steinbeck's essay:

> This tendency toward irresponsibility persists in very many of us today; our rivers are poisoned by reckless dumping of sewage and toxic industrial wastes, the air of our cities is filthy and dangerous to breathe from the belching of uncontrolled products from combustion of coal, coke, oil, and gasoline.

Other writers create more relaxed or even humorous voices; they offer asides (in parenthetical statements) and fun metaphors. Their allusions also might be informal. For example, in an essay about his relationship with his dog, David Hawes alludes to the Beatles:

> I realize this is an odd paraphrase of the Beatles, but it certainly seems fitting: I have a dog, or should I say, my dog has me? Often it seems unclear which of us is in charge in this arrangement.

As you write, decide how you want to come off to the reader, how you want to posture yourself. The following strategies can be used for various kinds of voices, whether formal, comedic, or somewhere in between. These strategies help make any voice more engaging.

## Writerly Whispers (Ways to Draw Readers in Closer)

- Parenthetical statements can offer gentle asides, as in Jennifer Schwind-Pawlak's essay in Chapter 2:

> Joann (the name I call my mother when she does something embarrassing) was screaming at the coach. In a voice so screeching that it rivaled fingernails on a blackboard, she told him that he was a disgraceful coach and that he should be ashamed of himself.

Or in Jim Crockett's essay:

> Wrought in stainless steel and plastic, this bit of industrial-designer paraphernalia (it holds my drug of choice) is every cup holder's dream.

- Longer sentences with long phrases can create a sense of delicacy and can bring the reader into the subtleties of a thought. In Jim Crockett's concluding paragraph, the intricacy of his long sentences brings the reader into the quiet complexities of the relationship:

> Because, even though my mug is always nearby, whether on the lectern or table in front of the classroom, in the cup holder on the dashboard of my truck, on the desk where I am writing this essay, or just dangling from my hand, all it really signifies is an addiction to caffeine and the need, because I am human, for some small and securing daily grounding ritual.

## Writerly Yells (Ways to Give Emphasis)

- Interrupting the natural flow of a sentence with a phrase or clause can draw attention to an idea. This does not mean that the writer is angry or shouting at the reader; rather, it allows the writer to guide the reader's attention to particular ideas. This is often done, as in Jim Crockett's essay, with interrupting words, phrases, or even clauses set off by commas:

> The relationship, or mugging, that has developed with my coffee mug is one-sided and is, because a mug's needs are simple, an easy relationship to maintain.

- Repeating words, phrases, or clauses can highlight an idea. John Steinbeck repeats *us* to highlight the collective nature of the issue:

> No longer do we Americans want to destroy wantonly, but our new-found sources of power—to take

the burden of work from our shoulders, to warm us, and cool us, and give us light, to transport us quickly, and to make the things we use and wear and eat— these power sources spew pollution on our country, so that the rivers and streams are becoming poisonous and lifeless.

- Short sentences can work many ways. Paradoxically, they can work as whispers or as yells, depending on the content and the context. They sometimes create emphasis because of their placement after longer sentences or after questions, such as in Lauren Jackson's essay:

    At school, smoking garnered status. After some bragging and showing off the goods, I quickly joined up with "The Bad Girls." I was someone.

- Exclamation points . . . of course!

# Writerly Pace (Ways to Control Speed and Time)

- Having more details slows down time for the reader. Like in a film, time slows down when a writer (or producer) focuses in on many particular details. Steinbeck uses details throughout his essay to focus on particular moments in history:

    Quite a few years ago when I was living in my little town on the coast of California a stranger came in and bought a small valley where the Sempervirens redwoods grew, some of them three hundred feet high. We used to walk among these trees, and the light colored as though the great glass of the Cathedral at Chartres had strained and sanctified the sunlight. The emotion we felt in this grove was one of awe and humility and joy; and then one day it was gone, slaughtered, and the sad wreckage of boughs and broken saplings left like nonsensical spoilage of the battle-ruined countryside.

- Having fewer details speeds up time for the reader. The fewer details a reader gets, the more quickly he or she moves through the events or thoughts in a text. Certainly, it is important to decide which ideas you want the reader to slow down for—and which ideas you want the reader to move through quickly. For instance, Lauren Jackson wants us to linger in a particular memory from her childhood, so she gives details to the scene, but she moves quickly out of the situation (in one final sentence), which shoos readers (along with the kids) to the next idea:

    My mother smoked Marlboro Light 100s in a box and only in the kitchen when it was cold. She was courteous to the rest of the house: keeping the children out, always emptying the ashtray right away, and spraying air freshener. I used to sit in the dining room around the corner of the wall, to be out of view, and listen to her gossip and smoke while she danced around the linoleum with the telephone cord. When her girlfriends would come over, they would drink coffee, smoke, and talk about any and everything—usually discourse unsuitable for innocent ears. They would shoo the kids out of the kitchen and explain we couldn't be around the smoke.

# Vitality

The delete key is perhaps the most underused key in college writing (and college textbooks!). Deleting anything often seems like a burden, like working against our own goals as writers. But good writers face their own sentences and willingly cast away clauses and phrases that dull the ideas, slow down the reader, and lessen the intensity.

## Avoid *Be* Verbs When Possible

*Be* verbs are also called linking verbs: *is, am, are, was, were, being, been,* etc. They link the subject of a sentence to a quality or other noun.

> The kittens are cute.
>
> The government is out of control.
>
> Sentences are cues for the reader.

Although such verbs are often necessary and valuable, they are often overused—hanging around in a sentence that would benefit from a more active verb. With a small, but important, change to the final example sentence above, we can make the verb active—and shorten the sentence:

> Sentences cue the reader.

This may not mean much for one sentence, but changing *be* verbs to active verbs throughout an essay can have dramatic effects. For instance, in the following passage, John Steinbeck's verbs pull the reader through the ideas:

> The great redwood forests of the western mountains early attracted attention. These ancient trees, which once grew everywhere, now exist only where the last Ice Age did not wipe them out. And they were found to have value. The Sempervirens and the Gigantea, the two remaining species, make soft, straight-grained timber. They are easy to split into planks, shakes, fenceposts, and railroad ties, and they have a unique virtue: they resist decay, both wet and dry rot, and an inherent acid in them repels termites. The loggers went through the great groves like a barrage, toppling the trees—some of which were two thousand years old—and leaving no maidens, no seedlings or saplings on the denuded hills.

## Activities

1. Rewrite Steinbeck's passage using *be* verbs instead of active verbs. For instance, replace *resist decay* with *are resistant to decay.* How do these changes impact the nature of the passage?

2. Examine a paragraph from your current draft. Rewrite the paragraph by simply changing any *be* verbs (*is, am, are, was, were,* and so on) to more active verbs. How do those changes impact the nature of the passage?

## Turn Clauses to Phrases

Clauses (elements that include both a subject and verb) can often be shortened to phrases so that sentences become more concise and concentrated. The following two sentences represent a common opportunity for collapsing a clause into a phrase, thereby combining the sentences. The second sentence, from John Steinbeck's essay, avoids the unnecessary "that were":

> On the East coast, and particularly in New England, the colonists farmed lands *that were* meager and close to their communities and to safety.

> On the East coast, particularly in New England, colonists farmed meager lands close to their communities and to safety.

The same goes for the following sentence. Notice how the second version, from John Steinbeck's essay, trims the clauses into phrases:

> When a super-highway was proposed in California which would trample the redwood trees in its path, an outcry arose all over the land *that was* so strident and fierce that the plan was put aside. And we no longer believe that a man, *because he owns* a piece of America, is free to outrage it.

> When a super-highway was proposed in California which would trample the redwood trees in its path,

an outcry arose all over the land, so strident and fierce that the plan was put aside. And we no longer believe that a man, by owning a piece of America, is free to outrage it.

Although these differences are slight, the phrases increase the sentences' vitality. And if the strategy is spread out over several pages of text, the essay reads more smoothly, more intensively. (Often, when students are concerned about "the flow" of their essays, this is exactly the type of strategy that can be applied. It is one of many tools for creating a more sophisticated-sounding text.)

# Turn Phrases to Words

The same principle can be applied to phrases; they can often be boiled down into single words. Consider the following two sentences. The second, also from Steinbeck's essay, boils down a common phrase to a more succinct word:

> Almost every day, the pressure of outrage among Americans grows.

> Almost daily, the pressure of outrage among Americans grows.

Although the differences are slight, such small transformations can build up throughout an essay, creating the difference between slower, droopier writing and intensive, vitalized writing. The process also makes writers search for thicker, more concentrated words—as in the following:

> The decision was not very smart.
> The decision was illogical.

> Back in the day, people did not assume that all communication should be instantaneous.
> Historically, people have not assumed that all communication should be instantaneous.

## Are Sentence Fragments Legal?

You may have seen well-known writers break important sentence rules. You may have thought, "Why can they do that when I cannot?" Is it a special privilege? Do the laws vary from state to state, school to school? Not exactly.

Many writers intentionally massage the conventions—and their readers allow it, even revel in it. For example, you may have seen fragments, often called *stylistic fragments,* that create an informal voice. Jim Crockett's introduction includes a stylistic fragment:

> I have been mugged. Not accosted as I walk to my parked truck across a dark lot; not waylaid by thugs in the night. But mugged, nevertheless.

The fragment does something significant, and many would say helpful, to the movement of the passage. If this seems like an attractive move, ask your instructor his or her thoughts about the strategy. Is it in or out of bounds? Is it valued? Under what circumstances?

# Revision

Revision is the most difficult intellectual step in writing. It requires a commitment to rethink some basics, to step back and ask if the writing does, at its most basic level, what it should. For instance, does the draft, as it stands, offer a revelatory insight about a relationship? Does it go beyond describing a relationship and, instead, offer a focused insight beyond what readers already know? Does it help readers to rethink the nature of the relationship?

Before you get a peer review, go back through the main sections of the chapter and ask some basic questions: How well does my draft explain the hidden complexities of a relationship? Does the draft connect to or involve issues or relationships beyond my personal relationship? Is the thesis sufficiently focused and revelatory? Does the draft provide details, narration, and explanation that support the thesis? Is it organized so that readers can follow the ideas? How does the voice engage readers? How does it do more than fulfill an assignment? Which sentences can be vitalized? How can the draft be woken up, turned up, or intensified?

## Peer Review

Exchange drafts with at least one other writer. Before passing your draft to others, underline the thesis, or write it on the top of your essay. This way, reviewers will get traction as they read.

As a reviewer, use the following questions to guide your response.

1. Point out any phrases in the thesis that could be more specific. (See the Thesis section for more guidance.)
2. Where can the writer do more analysis and reveal more about the relationship? (Point to passages that seem most obvious to you.) As you read, look for claims that anyone could immediately offer without intensive analysis.
3. Help the writer illustrate his or her claims with details. As you read, look for broad characterizations. If you see phrases such as "influence one another" or "depend on one another," ask yourself: Could this be more specific?

Can we *really* see the influence or dependence? Suggest further details to the writer. Explain what you would like to see.

4. Offer some figurative language to help characterize the relationship. After you have read the entire draft, offer your own metaphor or simile about the relationship. Make sure it is something that fits the writer's voice—something that he or she could use.
5. Are the paragraphs coherent? Do you ever get the sense that a paragraph is wandering? Mark any passages or details that seem unrelated to the point of the essay.
6. Help the writer kick-start the essay. The writer might begin with a broad statement about the relationship—or about something even broader. But the most focused statement possible often makes for a better introduction. Suggest a surprisingly focused opening statement.
7. Consider the writer's voice. Where could the writer employ a whisper or a yell (see page 86) to better engage the reader?
8. Point to particular sentences and phrases that could gain vitality and intensity. Use the following questions:
   - Where can the writer change *be* verbs to active verbs?
   - Look for clauses (especially those that begin with *which are, which is, that are, that is,* etc.). Suggest a strategy for boiling down the clause to a phrase.
   - Look for phrases (especially prepositional phrases that begin with *about* or *of*). Suggest a strategy for boiling down the phrase to a word.
   - Consider vitality strategies from the previous chapter:
     —Combine sentences.
     —Repeat structures.
     —Intensify verbs.
     —Help the writer avoid common grammatical errors: comma splices, sentence fragments, or lack of pronoun/antecedent agreement.

# Reflection

For writers, the big insights come after they have completed a project—after they have thought through an idea, developed an essay or article, revised, edited, and given it to the world beyond them. Only then, after all of these steps, do writers sometimes have a sense of what they've accomplished, what they've discovered.

Look back on your project—from the invention to the final draft—and develop some reflective writing based on the following questions:

1. How is the main insight revelatory? (How does it go beyond what people normally imagine about this kind of relationship? How might it have even taken you, as a writer, to a new intellectual place?)
2. What support strategies were the most important? If you used narrative, what made you focus on particular scenes or situations?
3. What would you say is the public resonance of the essay? How does your main insight resonate with some broader issue, idea, tension, trend, or behavior?
4. Describe your voice. If every essay has a voice, what does yours sound like? Is it sober? Formal? Lazy? Intense? Meditative? Forceful? Earnest? What particular passages best show the character of your voice?

## Beyond the Essay

The ideas generated in writing courses do not belong exclusively to essays. Those ideas can take many forms or extend to various media. Find an image that relates to your essay. If you can't find one, or if you prefer, create an original image: a drawing, painting, photograph, sculpture, and so on.

1. After you have found or created an image, explain how the image reveals something about the nature of the relationship. How does it, for instance, reveal some complexity in the relationship between dogs and people, between alcohol and people, between prescription drugs and people, between people and the land they inhabit?
2. Present the image to others in your class. Explain how the image reinforces ideas in your essay. Also explain how the image and essay differ: What complexities does the image suggest beyond your essay? What does your essay reveal that the image conceals? Does your essay go further than the image? How?

 For additional resources including instructional videos and links to helpful websites, access your English CourseMate through cengagebrain.com.

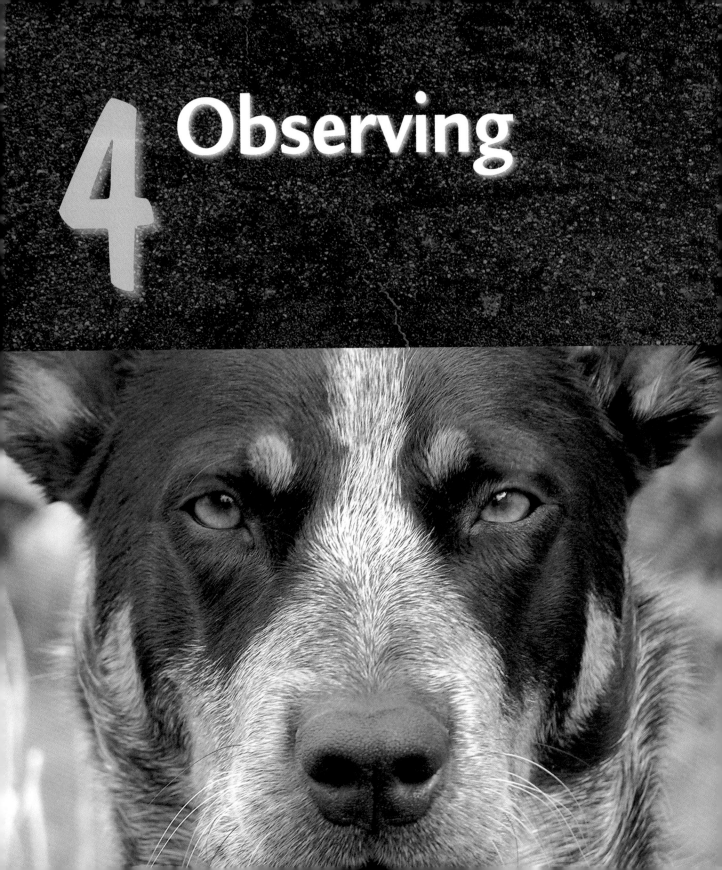

# 4 Observing

# Chapter Contents

# "As I sat there I felt the expectant thrill that, for me, always precedes a day with the chimpanzees, a day roaming the forests and mountains of Gombe, a day for new discoveries, new insights."

—Jane Goodall

Jane Goodall, world-renowned ethologist, has made a life of observing. She has shown the academic community what can be learned through close attention to the living world. As Goodall suggests in the preceding passage, observing is about discovery—about finding something unique and particular about a subject. It involves more than simple description. Careful observers go beyond the casual glance; they study their subjects and learn something by seeing them in a particular way. In some ways, then, learning how to observe involves learning how to see things, how to notice what is beneath the surface.

We casually observe our daily lives constantly. We watch our communities carrying on with life; we watch our coworkers, friends, children, and families. Occasionally, we take time to study, to focus on subjects and take in something beyond surface meanings: at those times we go beyond what something means to us and discover something outside of our expectations and biases. We see, for instance, how a man sitting on a street corner means something to the city that surrounds him; we suddenly see the systematic design in the movements of a seemingly chaotic crowd of people. Such seeing involves more than open eyes; it involves an open consciousness.

Observation is an essential strategy in academic life:

- Child psychology students observe the behaviors of young teens at a video arcade.
- Education students observe the interaction between high school teachers and their students.

•

- Biology students study the growth of bacteria over a 24-hour period.
- Chemistry students observe the effects of mixing different compounds.
- Sociology graduate students and faculty observe the language habits of a small island town.

Observers find the hidden meaning, the significant issues, and the important aspects of a particular subject. They point out how and why a particular subject is of interest to a broader public. We experience this kind of observing and reporting when we watch documentaries or nature specials. Writers and researchers for such programs first make general observations. Then they focus their perspective on a particular issue or subject. They analyze that issue or subject to find the most important or valuable thing to say. Throughout this process, the observing writer is always looking to discover, to find and communicate a fresh and interesting idea.

This chapter will help you choose a subject to observe, discover something particular about that subject, and develop a focused essay about your discovery. The following essays will provide insight to various strategies for observing. After reading the essays, you can find a topic in one of two ways.

1. Go to the Point of Contact section to find a topic from everyday life, or
2. Choose one of the Ideas for Writing that follow each essay.

After you find a topic, go to the Analysis section to begin developing your observation.

# Heart of Sand

## Anne-Marie Oomen

In "Heart of Sand," Anne-Marie Oomen takes the reader to
a place, a massive sand dune. Through careful observation she explores the meaning of that place and the legend
about it. Oomen is author of *An American Map,* a collection
of essays; two memoirs, *Pulling Down the Barn* and *House
of Fields;* and a collection of poetry, *Uncoded Woman.* She
teaches creative writing at Interlochen Arts Academy and
in the Solstice MFA program of Pine Manor College.

Before the legend of the Sleeping Bear became Michigan's state story, I was struck by its sad contradictions.
It is the tale of the great she-bear, Michimokwa, who,
to escape a Wisconsin forest fire, swam with her cubs
across Lake Michigan to a new peninsula. Though she
reached the open sand on the Michigan side, her young
cubs drowned a short way from the Michigan shore.

In the story, the great spirit, Gitche Manitou, transformed the cubs into the two islands we call the Manitous, but it is that west-facing dune on the shore that is
the pivot point for the legend, the one that represents the
great she-bear watching those two islands. She is said to
watch from the dunes for her cubs to make it to shore. She
is said to call for them. She is said to sleep in peace under
the sand. I know how stories twist, how they must mean
many things in order to last, but how could she sleep in
peace and be ever watchful at the same time?

Would I understand it better if I went there?

In the autumn, I decide to visit Sleeping Bear Dunes
National Lakeshore and walk to the Sleeping Bear, the
single dune identified by sailors among the seventy thousand acres of dune and forest and islands that are named
for her. I decide to go on my birthday, to mark the moment
with a look at the great mother.

5    I drive the park's forested scenic road to the point
where it opens to the light and sand of the dunes. I park,
hike the boardwalk to a lookout with benches offering
a view of the Bear to the north. This civilized platform
is where most people stop, read the story printed on the
signs, and then return to their cars. From here I can see the
rough rise and darkness of the dune in the distance.

A mile? Two?

Cold and bluster bully me as I squeeze under the railings and step off the lookout, cutting directly across the
dunes, trudging through this northern desert. From the
lookout, the dune seemed close enough, but when I leave
the deck and start walking through sand so soft it leaves a
clean print only after rain, I realize there is a good reason
not many people visit the specific dune I have chosen. The
hard walk up and down the crumbling slopes dampens my
determination to find a place I have never been.

But it is my birthday.

I stumble along the shoreline bluff, walking slowly
through varied soil, sometimes soft sand, sometimes
coarse gravel or crusty silt—all of it light. The wind
gusts fiercely along these bluffs, and even though the
dunes are still snowless, winter is already pushing its way
toward these arid places. As I move over the drifts of
glacial debris, walking absorbs my attention. I watch my
feet, notice snail shells in abundance, along with small
stony fossils. Here and there are scattered rust-colored
beer cans leftover from the days when the dunes were
privately owned and dune buggies carrying thrill-seekers
tore across the fragile dune ecosystem. There are tracks
everywhere in this part of the dunes—though I see no
animals and hear little except the alarm of the crows, the
distant roar of waves below the bluffs. The wind picks up,
slams sand against my jeans.

10    I think I may be lost.

Deep swales. I cannot see the lake or the distant reference point of the dune. I stop, disoriented, pull my hood
back to let the wind cool my face, and then start again, but
without a clear sense of direction. I am out here alone, and
even my husband does not know I have decided on this
birthday sojourn. I wonder if I have lost my bearings and
study the slopes for landmarks, just as I think I should turn
back before my tracks are obliterated by wind, a slow rise
carries me up a low ridge and there, across the distance,
high green foliage marking the Bear. I keep going, fighting wind and poor footing and now, colder air.

Half an hour later, having spanned the final mile—
and struggled up through rough scrub, I crest the rim—
gasping for breath, and look down into what is the bowl of
the bear. I had expected something else, a plateau marked
with thick and tattered shrubbery. But this dune is decep-

tive, secretive. What from a distance looks like a hilltop and rises like a rough upturned dish, like some solid and long-standing pedernal, is instead something in motion. Open space. Instead of the flat-topped mound that would have been the geological metaphor for the bear, a hollow. The Bear is a huge basin, winnowed out and case empty by wind, an immense sink of sand.

It has become a blowout.

A blowout is a dune summit or ridge that may have once looked like a lush foliage-covered hilltop. But because of the lightness and fragility of the soil—almost dust—and the death, due to drought or other weather conditions, of that vegetation, plus exposure to the constant westerlies, the dune sand erodes away from the roots, especially at the crest of these hills. After years of enduring this relentless wind, the vegetation blows away, and the dune begins to hollow itself out, like a bowl, weathered down from the high point, leaving the lower, less exposed sides to rise like a rim. Dune walkers commonly

John Mauk

stumble on blowouts all over the open duneland, but this one is startling for its immensity and grandeur, a huge basin carved by wind.

15    And then, there is the beauty of her bones.

From the crater of sand where her body would have rested, ghost trees rise, scattered and leaning and awful. The remnants of this spirit forest are scattered like ribs and femurs and spine. They shimmer silver gray, smoothed by the gales, their grain polished to gleam against the half-lit day.

I stand there for a long time, asking quietly if I may enter, and when the wind drops, I take it as acceptance and climb inside, where the wind drops but never ceases.

How long can one explore a void? The inside of the word *hollow?* I wander, spiraling lower, touching the driftwood trees that were once green and are now an uncanny architecture, shards of some immense being. I sniff cold air, dryness, dune dust. Wind mutes and huffs through this place, and over the years, it has not only hollowed the bowl but shaped a broad opening at the west side of the blowout—as though the sand that once made the mound was poured out of a wide spigot. But this is the opposite of the truth. The broad opening is where the constant westerlies enter the blowout and lift sand particles up and carry them east and farther into the dunes—shifting the landscape every season.

Finally, I do what I have been avoiding. There is here a place within a place. I look to the center of the blowout, which contains a smaller mound, still intact, around which the wind has worked all these years. It is perhaps two stories high, and despite the fact that all else around it is hollowed out and left to bones, it stands over this desert and the skeletal trees, a rough, grass-pocked cone with its top sheered off. I have been circling its irregular slopes cautiously because I feel the anomaly. This entire rise has been blown away, but this core has remained, grasses still clinging to its surface. I choose the least steep slope on the backside, the slope protected from the lake winds, and scramble up, slipping with every step. Finally I am perched on this upturned funnel in the middle of windy emptiness. Breathless, I lie down and watch the rush of combed skies.

20    Is this place within a place what's left of her mammoth heart? Is this heart of sand the stalwart core of emptiness?

It is a place that simply resists. Resists just enough to hold, even against the force of the west winds. Resists a bit longer than the rest of the earth against the inevitable wearing down. A symbol of the Bear, who waits—held in the paradox of eternal sleep and eternal watchfulness—for her cubs, those distant islands of Manitou.

Before I climbed the interior mound, I had been imagining that her bones would someday rise and gather themselves into body, whole and muscled and covered with the mat of her great hide. I saw her walk on water, raise up her startled cubs, cuff them into motion, and then lumber over the land to call us all out of sleep. This is how I hoped the legend would wake us, wake me. As something fierce and alive, resurrected in power. But now, sitting on the mound, staring out, I imagine her heart defined by a will to stay, to endure a little longer the inevitable winds.

What does a thousand years mean to a mother waiting?

Since then, I have tried to make the trek once a year, usually in the fall when the isolation is more remarkable. I know better ways to get there now. I have learned to go quietly, with reverence, and not to move anything, not to touch much. I always climb the mound, sit in what I perceive as the center of not just this dune, but of all the shifting acres for miles around.

I have come to love the wind here, the power it has to erase through its insistent presence. Just as it has blown out the hilltop, the very place that represented the great mother, Michimokwa, the wind has fragmented the story itself, altered what the place means. The meaning shifts, catches in the wind, lifts and transforms until there will be nothing left of even her heart. This is not sad, but rather the wind waking the imagination and simultaneously, paradoxically, waking us to emptiness, to the limits of story. To mystery. This is the wind making the place where story meets void, the opposite of meaning. The hollow bowl that also shapes our being.

## Writing Strategies

1. Observing involves going beyond the casual glance to discover something new. What does Oomen discover, or learn, about her subject?

2. How does Oomen go beyond "simple description" and communicate a new way of seeing? Provide excerpts of description from the essay to develop your response.

3. Good description appeals to the senses. To which senses (hearing, sight, touch, smell, taste) does Oomen appeal? What appeal is especially evocative because of the detail Oomen provides?

4. Complete the following sentence: Oomen's main point is that _____.

5. Oomen uses several one-sentence paragraphs. How do these paragraphs function and why? (Are they main ideas, support strategies, miscellaneous information, headings, or what?)

## Exploring Ideas

1. With a group of peers, discuss the feeling created by Oomen's essay. How was the essay more than informational or informative? What passages stirred your feelings and why?

2. How does Oomen resolve the "sad contradictions" she originally had about the legend of the Sleeping Bear?

3. When have you carefully observed or studied a subject as carefully as Oomen did the Sleeping Bear dune? Why did you observe it? What did you discover?

## Ideas for Writing

1. In ¶20, Oomen describes "a place within a place." Observe a place so closely that you discover a new way of seeing it and can take the reader to "a place within a place."

2. As part of Oomen's observing state of mind, she even observes herself: "As I move over the drifts of glacial debris, walking absorbs my attention." As you observe a subject, also observe yourself observing it.

3. In ¶18 Oomen asks, "How long can one explore a void?" Find a void, or what you might at first imagine to be a void, and explore it. For example, you might explore an empty gym, a field, or an abandoned part of town.

If responding to one of these ideas, go to the Analysis section of this chapter to begin developing ideas for your essay.

# The Front Porch

## Chester McCovey

Chester McCovey's observing essay illustrates how one can use an observation as a point of contact and then, through analysis, explore why the observation matters. McCovey makes a simple observation: that people don't sit out on their front porches like they did when he was a kid. Then he explores and determines that the loss of the front porch equals a loss of community. Through analysis, he goes from a specific observation (about garages and porches) to a general insight (about a loss of community).

**Writing Strategies**

The essay begins with a personal observation and connects with the reader.

States the main observation: porch replaced by garage.

The writer uses personal details to develop the observation.

The essay moves toward analysis. Why did this happen, and what does it mean?

If you walk through my neighborhood, you won't see many porches, at least not the kind people sit on in the evenings. Those days are gone where I live, and likely where you live, too.

The front porch has been replaced—by the two-car garage. Both sets of my grandparents, who lived in the same small town, had big front porches, and summer visits often meant sitting on the porch, talking, and watching cars and people out walking. After a while someone might have suggested getting some ice cream. The adult conversation was often dull, sometimes painfully so for a child, but sometimes it was interesting. The everyday people a child sees in church or at the Little League field in a small town have a few years behind them, and what person who has lived a little doesn't have a story to tell—or a story to be told about them? Sometimes those stories would come out and bring to life a previously uninteresting Frank or Gretchen. Small towns are full of life's everyday dramas. A child hears and figures out many things on a place like a front porch on a thing like a warm summer night.

My grandparents' garages were small, just enough for one car and a few tools—not much of a garage for today's homeowner. In those days the garage kept a car and a small lawnmower, some rakes, and so on. The garage today must keep much more. One can see, then, how the exchange occurred. Like an old-fashioned trade in baseball, gone is the home team's beloved front porch, replaced by a big, new garage. Of course the trade is much more interesting than that. And a look at how it occurred enlightens us a little about the world in which we live. More importantly, it tells us not so much about how life is now but about how it came to be. And, I would argue, it shows us the way in which things will continue to change.

**Exploring Ideas**

The front porch was a place where people used to talk (pass the time, shoot the breeze).

The shift from porch to garage tells us about the world in which we live, how it came to be and how it will continue to change.

From Chester McCovey, "The Front Porch." Reprinted with permission of the author.

Back then, our own garage held two cars, a riding lawn-mower, a push mower, bicycles, and lots of tools. We had a front porch and sat on it, but mostly just when we had company. Our house, then, represents the transition between two generations: my grandparents' generation that traveled less, received only three television stations (*sans* remote control), and didn't have air conditioning and my own generation that is more likely to be on the go (driving from one place to another) or sitting inside, on the computer or watching TV.

The front porch fell victim to its two natural enemies: the internal-combustion engine (automobiles) and electricity (air conditioning, lights, and TV). Now, instead of gathering on our front porch as our grandparents did, we are either gone somewhere thanks to our transportation or we are at home but indoors.

The writer's own childhood house illustrates the transition from porch to garage.

Main Ideas: What happened to the front porch and why: automobile and electricity. What happened because of that: we are either gone or indoors.

how life must have splashed

out of the cup

on warm summer nights

before the cool air

of electricity

urged us all to relax

in the fluttering glow

of color tv

Because of automobiles and electricity, we spend more time driving alone or watching TV than we do talking with our friends and neighbors. Is this a problem? A loss of community?

We have traded sitting on the front porch for sitting in traffic, or to be more positive about it, for sitting in our automobile as we speed along to some very important place to be. The shift from porch to garage is beautifully simple. It goes like this: I need a place to park my transportation machine (car, truck, SUV) and I don't need a large, outdoor room for sitting. The reasoning (the reality of the situation) is just as simple: There's not as much action on the sidewalk as there once was (the neighbors are indoors or driving somewhere) and I don't need to sit outdoors to stay cool on muggy nights (the air conditioning indoors takes care of that). So, a need or desire—to stay cool, to be entertained, to keep up with what's going on—is replaced not by a different need or desire but instead by a new way of meeting it.

Explanation: how/why the shift occurred.

Need or Desire—To Stay Cool

Previously met by evening breeze; now

met by air conditioning

Need or Desire—To Be Entertained

Previously met by conversation with
neighbors; now met by TV, computer,
shopping at the mall, conversation with
friends who we drive to see
Need or Desire—To Keep Up with What's
Going On
Previously met by discussion with
neighbors and friends; now met through
national media (TV and Internet)

I am not saying there are no front porches. Obviously there are.
And I am not saying everyone has a two-car garage instead. In
my neighborhood, small garages not connected to the house still
reign. But obviously, their days are numbered. The new houses
sometimes look as much like a house attached to a garage as a
garage attached to a house. Today's garage often dominates the
house.

Finally, the careful reader is insisting that I deal with the
backyard patio deck. What about *it?* When we do sit outdoors,
we choose to do it out back, away from the rest of the world.
This is interesting. We need a break, I would suggest, from the
hustle and bustle of daily life, so we retreat to our own backyard
to be left alone with our families. But that hustle and bustle is
mostly the hustle and bustle of traffic, radio, television, and a
few quick transactions with total strangers. Of course another
reason for opting to relax in the backyard is that, as previously
mentioned, there just isn't that much going on out front these
days. (If there were, I wonder if we would sit on the front porch
and watch it . . . *and* contribute to it.) I am arguing that we lose
something very basic—very fundamental—when we lose the
front porch culture.

On Sunday drives through the country, I see big new houses
with big new porches. As Americans we can have it all—the
house with the big front porch *and* the big garage. But I never
(I am tempted to qualify this statement and say "almost never"
or "rarely" but I have been thinking about it and I do mean
"never")—I never see anyone out sitting on those porches. I
am not prepared here to argue that we are a civilization in deep
trouble because of this, though it does seem to me appropriate
that we should lament, at least a little, the loss of the front porch.

Imagine: Being entertained by sitting on a porch and talking.

---

To avoid oversimplifying, the writer qualifies the point and concedes that there are still front porches, *but* that their days are numbered.

Anticipates a potential concern of the reader: what about the back deck?

Main point: we lose something very basic—very fundamental—when we lose the front porch culture. Leaves the reader to consider the cost of this change.

Concludes by asking the reader to imagine.

The back deck takes us out back, away from community.

Sunday drives in the country bring to mind an earlier time, when people hung out on the front porch talking with neighbors.

Ironically, McCovey is *driving around.*

Where do people talk like they used to on a front porch: the kitchen table, the student lounge, Facebook, Twitter?

# Writing Strategies

1. What is the essay's thesis?

2. What details help the reader value the thesis and why?

3. In a paragraph, summarize McCovey's explanation of *how* the shift from porch to garage occurred and *why* it matters.

4. Why is it important that McCovey writes about the backyard patio deck? How does this paragraph help the reader accept the main claim?

5. Where does McCovey use a metaphor or simile (comparing two unlike things: *The clerk was a bear* [metaphor]; *The clerk was like a bear* [simile])? Where else does he use figurative language?

# Exploring Ideas

1. Based on this essay, what does McCovey value? To what degree do you value the same thing?

2. In your own words, summarize McCovey's main idea. Then share your summary with several classmates who have also read the essay. Discuss your understanding of McCovey's main idea, and then reread his essay and revise your summary as necessary.

3. To further explore this issue, share your summary with people of various age groups, asking them to respond to McCovey's ideas. Describe how their views are similar to or different from McCovey's.

4. Think of a metaphor or simile of your own that might work well in this essay.

# Ideas for Writing

1. Besides the move from porch to garage, what other change has taken place? How has that change impacted everyday life?

2. Observe some difference in a way of living, whether it be the result of time (your grandparents and you, for example) or location (Southern Californians and Midwesterners). Do not be afraid to generalize, as long as you do it thoughtfully and are mindful of exceptions.

If responding to one of these ideas, go to the Analysis section of this chapter to begin developing ideas for your essay.

# Corpse Colloquy

## Justin Scott

Justin Scott, a biology major at Western Michigan University, uses the Invention Questions in this chapter to look beneath the surface and find new meaning in a familiar place, the graveyard. "Corpse Colloquy" is an example of how an observation essay goes beyond mere description. Through careful observation and analysis, Scott helps the reader see cemeteries differently, as "the key to a more exposed and fulfilling life."

The cemetery nestles within the confines of the city. "Oakwood," the sign announces. One can hardly help but wonder if the name is meant to reference the now-sparse trees, or if perhaps it refers to the dense forest of tombstones laden with a 6-foot-shallow bone root system. One must battle traffic and stoplights to gain entrance rather than multi-headed dogs and demanding ferry captains. The other thing that separates this still world of the dead from the busy world of the living is the winter skeleton of a hedge.

One thing is immediately obvious in this cemetery: Those laden with the gifts of life often choose to utilize them in death, and those less fortunate make do with what they must. Class warfare spills into the afterworld: Business owner is segregated from bricklayer, clergy is separated from atheist. There are large domineering crypts bearing the surnames of the wealthy dead inside, branch-scraping obelisks with ornate script, tombs carefully sculpted to resemble tree stumps, small temples dedicated to their dead in ancient Greek style, and, inevitably, the sunken, flat, and nondescript markers of the poor or humble. Some of the dead have even had exclusive gated communities constructed; large, elegant gravestones are surrounded with walls of iron or marble to keep the pauper corpses at a proper distance. The military and various secret societies have also their own niches; war memories, ranks carved into stones, and Mason symbols can be found throughout the cemetery, often placed more prominently than the name of the dead or when they were alive. Did people value their association with a group more than their own identity?

Toward the center of the field is an open plot with a marker denoting a common grave. Here lie the forgotten. Time will not remember their names any more readily than they were remembered while alive, for here are the mentally ill, the locked away and the vagrants. One large marker bids us to forget identity entirely.

Religion separates the dead as surely as the living. While in the living world the borders are less physically concrete, here signs announce the religious preference of those buried underneath. A walking tour reveals that here lie the Catholics, there the Jews, and over yonder are sundry reformists. Crosses, six-pointed stars and IHS[1] are distributed freely.

Neatly shorn trees line the carefully built roads. Were they interred there to keep the bony remains underneath from warring over wealth and religion as they would in life? Were it not for the snow, one would surely find grass cared for with the precision of a golf course and symmetrically trimmed bushes. The roads inside are paved but do not bear names; only the dead have that privilege here.

Modern society has a calculated and placated feel to it. Most things are carefully contrived in order to generate the most profit, and we are medicated to be placid and unfeeling; in the end, we are dedicated consumers in all things. Our deaths are as sterile and distant from us as the cemeteries in which our remains rest forever; manicured nails and laws make way for manicured plots of land and stones and preservation via formaldehyde. We supposedly live in *post-ironic* times. "Irony is dead," some would say. But irony is alive and well and can unmistakably be found among the dead in cemeteries worldwide.

It is said that only two things are certain in life: death and taxes. The cemetery, despite pomp, segregation, and sundry other shows for the living, does not belie that old aphorism. Everyone resting in that place, under or above earth, Catholic, Protestant, or Jew, poor or rich, remembered or forgotten, has succumbed to the scythe. Everyone

"Corpse Colloquy," by Justin Scott. Reprinted with permission of the author.

1. An abbreviation for the name of Jesus in Greek letters.

dies. Yet in the frenzied pace of modern life this truth is lost, and we as ever fall into the patterns of exclusivity, neglect, bigotry, and *schadenfreude*.

More time should be spent learning the dead. Their testament is spoken to us from within the maelstrom of coffins and gravestones. Their ghosts bade us not to be concerned with materialism, creed, or race; through them and the past they represent is the key to a more exposed and fulfilling life. *Graveyards are the doppelganger of the living world.* Seeing and recognizing the shadow-self of the graveyard allows us to enrich our lives and live beyond the lessons it presents. The cemetery, above all, tells us of acceptance and judgment: to embrace the former and neglect the latter. Life is finite, precious, and far too short to waste on arrogant trappings already so thoroughly explored by those entombed under earth.

*Dona eis requiem sepiternam.*

John Metz photo

# Writing Strategies

1. In Scott's essay, what does a cemetery reveal about life?

2. What details are most effective in helping the reader understand and accept Scott's main point?

3. Describe Scott's writer's voice. Refer to three sentences to support your description.

4. What other paragraph in the essay could Scott have used as the opening paragraph? Why would or wouldn't that paragraph be an effective new beginning?

5. How is Scott's essay a call to action?

# Exploring Ideas

1. What does Scott value? How might his essay connect with a reader because he or she values the same thing?

2. How is the way you see a cemetery different from the way Scott sees one? Go beyond the casual glance. What else might a cemetery symbolize or reveal?

3. Talk to several people to find out their views on cemeteries. Do they visit cemeteries often? What word would they use to describe a cemetery: *peaceful, spiritual, creepy?* Why do people view cemeteries differently?

4. Research the modern cemetery. When did cemeteries become park-like, and why?

# Ideas for Writing

1. Spend several hours observing a cemetery. How can your observations help a reader see something about cemeteries and life differently?

2. Observe your college's campus or a particular building. Take notes and make connections among details. What new idea can you share about college, your college campus, education, life?

If responding to one of these ideas, go to the Analysis section of this chapter to begin developing ideas for your essay.

# INVENTION

Observation requires a good deal of analysis and planning. It goes far beyond simply choosing a subject and writing down details. Writers usually go through a cyclical invention process, in which they return repeatedly to their original notes to find patterns and significant points. The following sections are designed to help you through this process: specifically, to discover a topic (in Point of Contact), develop particular points about the topic (in Analysis), make it relevant to a community of readers (in Public Resonance), focus your ideas (in Thesis), and develop them into an essay (in Rhetorical Tools). The Invention Questions in each section are not meant to be answered directly in your final written assignment. They are designed to help generate ideas—to guide you through an intellectual process.

# Point of Contact

The goal here is to see something in a new way, to see beyond the casual glance. You may choose to visit places and do things you have never done before, or you may visit the usual places but with focused attention. Use the following as possible starting points for your observation.

## Observing a Place

Job site, family restaurant, factory, office, break room, playground, park, movie theater, shopping mall, video arcade, college hall, college club, campground, woods. Gather details about the place. In addition to obvious details, consider the less obvious:

- What subtle behavior patterns do you detect?
- Is there a hidden competition or collaboration going on?
- What mood might the creatures (people, animals, plants) share? How do they unknowingly maintain that mood?
- Are people free to do as they please, or does something restrain them? (Do they know that something is restraining them?)
- What is the unstated, normal mode of behavior?
- Does anyone or anything break out of the norm? What are the hidden consequences?
- What is missing?

## Observing People

Supervisor, manager, line worker, server, religious leader, teacher or professor, principal, athlete, bingo player, student. Use notes, audio and video recorders, and/or photographs to gather details about the person. You might also interview the subject. (See the section on interviews in Chapter 13.)

- In what hidden ways is the subject working with or against the surroundings?
- Does the subject reinforce or work against rules?
- How do others treat the subject (with respect, disdain, indifference, or something else)?
- If the subject is a group, how do the individuals maintain harmony or unity? How do they conflict?
- What explicit or hidden rules do they follow?

## Observing an Animal

Family pet, friend's or neighborhood pet, stray cat or dog, birds, animals at a park or zoo, wild animals, farm animals. Gather basic information about the animal's behavior, but also look beyond the simple glance:

- What does it know?
- What secrets does it have?
- How does it signal its mood?
- Does it have dramatic mood changes?
- How does it get along with humans? With the world around it?
- What habits does it have?
- Is it a public or private creature?
- Does it compromise or alter its behavior to accommodate others?

## Observing a Person or Event Involved in Your Major

Use the questions in this section to help gather information about a subject related to your major, but also develop more questions. By observing a particular person or event, what can you discover about the nature of your major?

## Activity

Choose a category (a place, person, animal) and develop ten more questions that will reveal something interesting about a subject.

# Analysis

Details do not have their own meaning. It is up to people to *make* meaning from details. As we analyze, we move from observation notes to focused ideas, from a collection of potentially unrelated details to a set of particular points. Analysis prompts us to see patterns, connections, and paths within the particulars. The following questions can help you to make meaning out of your observation notes and look at the subject as something more than its physical characteristics.

## Invention Questions

▶ What is unique about the subject?

▶ What is ordinary about this subject? (How are its qualities common to other places, people, or animals?) What does that quality show?

▶ Is this subject symbolic of something? (Does it stand for some idea or ideal?)

▶ Does the subject seem different after the observation (more complicated, less intimidating, more human, less human, more predictable, and so on)?

▶ What does the subject "say" about life (about human interaction, social behavior, institutions, nature, and so on) in this place and time? ■

While focusing on and gathering details may be a challenging aspect of observation, analyzing those details poses a difficulty of its own. Because a list of details offers so many options and no obvious path for making meaning, the process can be uncertain and confusing. However, it can be an intensive and valuable process. Imagine a student, Linda, who observed people at her place of work, a small factory. Her observation notes include long lists of details about the environment, the lighting, the physical actions of the workers, and their interaction with the machines and with each other. But as she begins to analyze, using one of the Invention Questions, she finds connections in those details. Notice how she goes beyond her first simplistic answer to a more complex idea:

**What does the subject "say" about life (about human interaction, social behavior, institutions, nature, and so on) in this place and time?**

At first, I thought that my coworkers were just miserable people at a job. They work at their individual stations, occasionally interact to communicate something about a machine part or materials, and then go to breaks—or home. But outside of that, I couldn't see anything important. But the more I looked over my notes, I realized something was going on in those small and infrequent interactions between people. While they might seem miserable and disconnected at times (maybe even most of the time), they all offer some support to one another: a small glance, a shared roll of the eyes when the supervisor inspects one person's work, the way Rob, the oldest in the shop, actually runs over to someone who needs help with something, the extra cup of coffee Bob got Maria because she didn't have time during break. All these things mean something—the underground, almost secretive, strategies to keep each other afloat in their shared situation. After I realized this, I went back over all my notes and remembered things I had not written down. The days are actually filled with these little gestures; they happen at all times: at breaks, on the way into the shop in the morning, while the machines are operating.

Linda could then develop this point in her writing. The idea may even develop into a thesis statement. This would mean that many other details (about physical structure, about the machines themselves) might be abandoned unless they have some significance for worker interaction. In this way, Linda's observation goes from a list of seemingly unrelated details to a focused idea.

## Activity

Observe the activities in your classroom. Consider actions and behaviors among work groups, among demographic groups, before the instructor arrives, or as the class ends. As a class or in a group, discuss the possible meaning or significance of particular events, behaviors, or interactions.

Chester McCovey's invention notes explore the meaning of the garage—not simply what it does for people (store their cars) but how it works in their lives, how it says something about the way people live.

> **Is this subject symbolic of something? (Does it stand for some idea or ideal?)**
>
> It is, perhaps. These big garages are obviously a necessity for today's homeowner. I mean, most of these homes are not within walking distance of where the owner works. Many, I suspect, can only be afforded if both husband and wife work—two cars! Now, fill the garage up with all the other machinery you need to maintain the yard. The garage quite simply says "go," "drive," "automobile," "transportation." I am at home, but not for long. No doubt the cars have air conditioning, as does the house. One need never be hot (or cold). The garage has replaced the porch. You pull into the garage and go inside and stay inside the house. Then get in the air-conditioned space bubble car when you want to leave. Of course there is recreation, but recreation is getting away from life and not a part of it. Let's take a break in our day and burn some calories, not let's burn some calories in the natural course of our day. The garage symbolizes driving, moving, loss of neighborhood, community, wealth, poverty . . .

# Thinking Further

In the previous paragraph, McCovey uses invention writing to seek out the significance of today's big garage. His exploration leads him to write, "The garage symbolizes driving, moving, loss of neighborhood, community, wealth, poverty . . . ." Now McCovey, alone or with others, could explore this idea further, digging deeper and uncovering new details and complexity. (Or he might choose a different idea from his invention writing to explore further.)

## Activity A

Use the following questions to explore McCovey's invention writing:

- Using McCovey's paragraph and your own ideas, explain how the big garage might be symbolic of or stand for driving. For moving. For loss of neighborhood. For wealth and poverty. Develop your responses in the spirit of exploration.
- Of the six ideas McCovey mentions, which one is the least obvious and why? Which one is the most important and why? Which one is the most interesting and why? (Consider focusing on the least obvious, most important, or most interesting.)

Remember, your purpose in this writing is not just to say what you think or know. Your purpose is to explore and figure out what can be thought about the topic.

## Activity B

Consider your own invention writing, as you just considered McCovey's. For help, explore ideas further through discussion.

- What new way of thinking (what insight, what revelation) did you discover?
- How might you explore the complexities of that idea further? For example:
  —How might that thinking be wrong?
  —How can you probe more deeply by asking why, how, or so what?
  —What contradictions or inconsistencies must be explained?

# Public Resonance

Writers do more than focus on a subject, such as a sand dune, porch, or cemetery. They make the subject resonate with the lives of others. The following Invention Questions will help broaden your subject's perspective and make it resonate with a potential audience.

## Invention Questions

▶ Why is this subject important to people? (Why is its uniqueness important?)

▶ Why should your peers know about this subject?

▶ What do people normally experience, understand, or assume about the subject?

▶ Does the presence or action of this subject teach people something—about themselves, about life, about work, about happiness, about materialism, about sincerity, about identity, about relationships, about the past, about the future, about death? ■

Notice how McCovey explores the breadth of his subject—how the question helps him to see the broad implications of porches and garages:

> **Does the presence or action of this subject teach people something—about themselves, about life, about work, about happiness, about materialism, about sincerity, about identity, about relationships, about the past, about the future, about death?**
>
> What we see is a loss of community. The big garage shows us we're leaving our own neighborhood a lot. The fact that the garage is connected to the living space shows us that we go from our living area directly, by pushing a button that opens the door, into the street and to another community far enough away that we drive to it. We don't interact with our neighbors (we might not even know their names). We drive past them with our windows rolled up. We maybe don't even smell or feel our neighborhood (I guess that's an exaggeration, but there's something there). Remember, we're not talking about all houses. We're talking about the ones built today. Is loss of neighborhood a loss to the people who live in those

neighborhoods? Does big garage/no front porch mean loss of neighborliness? Yes, these relationships—or ones like them—can exist outside one's own neighborhood. But what is the effect of this? What is a neighbor anymore?

Here McCovey explores connections to broader cultural trends. While some subjects have more automatic public resonance, others need to be *made* relevant to the audience, and it is up to a writer to make the connection.

# Invention Workshop

An essay does not just relay information; it invites readers to see something new in a familiar world. If you think a topic is boring, you have an opportunity to unpack the boredom, finding something new and worth sharing with others. Instead of allowing a dull topic to stop one's thinking, a good observer uses analysis to make the topic interesting.

1. Share your observation with others and discuss what the subject shows about the way people live, about the way people see the world around them. The goal is to develop new insights for your project.

2. After exploring the public resonance of your topic with others and writing down any new insights, return to the Analysis questions on page 108. Respond in writing to these questions again, now that you have focused on the public resonance of the subject. See what else you can find. As you write, think about how you can re-approach the questions from a new, more informed perspective. For example, how might you see something else unique about the subject now? Does the subject now seem unique in some less obvious way?

• What new insights emerged from your second round with the Analysis questions?

• What new questions emerged?

# Thesis

The thesis, whether stated directly or implied, reveals a specific insight on a subject. The more narrow the insight, the more focused and intensive the writing will be. Although it is easy to offer a first-glance statement, try to narrow in on a particular quality. Notice how the following bulleted statements offer broad and predictable ideas. But the purple statements reveal something unique and specific:

- The people at the local tavern keep to themselves.

     In the dark, smoky quiet of Timothy's Pub, the regulars face straight ahead but share intimate crises in their quick coded exchanges.

- The neighborhood is a quiet place.

     The disappearing porches in the neighborhood signal a shift to a more disconnected, isolating, but technologically advanced time.

- The Fun Factory has a spirit of competition.

     Once the games begin at The Fun Factory, the players shift radically: from unfocused adolescent "dorks" to focused competitive intellectuals.

The more specific theses focus on more particular subjects: people vs. regulars; neighborhood vs. disappearing porches; Fun Factory vs. players. These specific sentences bring the reader up close. (We can even imagine a television camera literally zooming in to the more particular subjects.) Also, the purple sentences have stronger verbs: *keep* vs. *face/share; is* vs. *signal; has* vs. *shift.* The stronger verbs do more than create action; they enrich the content, making the nouns work harder. As a result, the sentences push the reader through the sentence with more energy.

## Revising Your Thesis

Before drafting your essay, develop a thesis to guide you. Then, in groups, discuss your working thesis statements. For each noun, suggest a more specific word. Suggest stronger verbs.

## Evolution of a Thesis

Imagine a writer is observing students at a community college. She notices many things about the students: their clothes, their ages, and so on. But she decides to focus on a particular point: *The students at Beach Community College spend their time coming and going primarily alone.* Such a statement offers a particular idea about the college students. The essay then would focus on the solitary nature of the students. The point might grow and develop layers throughout the invention process:

**Point of Contact:**

- The majority of the students coming in and out of the buildings are alone; they do not talk together or in groups. If people are talking, they are talking on cell phones.

**Analysis:**

- Although I have always associated college with social life, the students at Beach Community College show that college is often a solitary experience.

**Public Resonance:**

- When most people talk about college, they inevitably bring up campus life: the parties, the Greek system, the study groups, etc. They think of all the movies and stories about those crazy college years, but the reality may be fundamentally different for many students.

**Working Thesis:**

- Despite the popular notions of social life on college campuses, the students at Beach Community College show that higher education can be a solitary experience.

# Rhetorical Tools

An observing essay shares an insight about a particular sub-ject. While writers discover and develop this insight through careful observation, they communicate it to the reader through a variety of rhetorical tools.

## Using Details

The details of an essay are what paint the writer's point, giv-ing the essay focus and value. When Anne-Marie Oomen details her walk to the Sleeping Bear dune, she says, "The hard walk up and down the crumbling slopes dampens my determination to find a place I have never been." Oomen has never been to the Sleeping Bear dune, nor has she sorted out the contradictions of the Sleeping Bear legend. The details that follow contribute to both explorations:

- I stumble along the shoreline bluff, walking slowly through varied soil, sometimes soft sand, sometimes coarse gravel or crusty silt—all of it light. (¶7)
- I stop disoriented, pull my hood back to let the wind cool my face, and then start again, but without a clear sense of direction. (¶9)
- I choose the least steep slope on the backside, the slope protected from the lake winds, and scramble up, slipping with every step. (¶17)

Throughout her narrative, Oomen provides details of sight, sound, and touch that not only describe the scene but express the significance. To choose details for your writing, consider:

▶ What details will not only describe your observation but also help to focus the reader on its significance? ■

## Using Narrative

Some writers narrate an observation, explaining the events leading up to a particular moment of discovery. When nar-rating, writers avoid unnecessary events and details, limiting the narration to key events and details that help convey the significance of the observation. Oomen's essay is a narra-tive beginning with her decision to visit the Sleeping Bear Dunes National Lakeshore. She tells how she "drive[s] the park's forested scenic road," "squeeze[s] under the railings and step[s] off the lookout," "stumble[s] along the shore-line bluff," and "crest[s] the rim—gasping for breath, and look[ing] down into what is the bowl of the bear." While narration is a savvy rhetorical move for Oomen's observation (she narrates her physical trek as well as her intellectual one), narrating an observation is not necessary: neither McCovey nor Scott relies on narration to communicate his insights. If you are considering using narration in your writing, ask yourself the following questions:

▶ Would narrating the events leading up to the obser-vation help engage the reader?

▶ Would narrating part of the observation help to engage the reader? ■

## Using Allusions

Allusions are references to bits of public knowledge, things, events, or people outside of the main subject being observed. Writers use allusions to help illustrate a point or create a feel-ing. For instance, McCovey alludes to baseball when discuss-ing the front porch:

> One can see, then, how the exchange occurred. Like an old-fashioned trade in baseball, gone is the home team's beloved front porch, replaced by a big, new garage.

McCovey's allusion calls the reader back to an earlier time when people sat outside on front porches and talked to neighbors passing by. The allusion to baseball helps to cre-ate the feeling of which McCovey speaks in his conclusion: "I am not prepared here to argue that we are a civilization in deep trouble because of this, though it does seem to me appropriate that we should lament, at least a little, the loss of the front porch." Some (not all) readers will immediately identify with the feeling the allusion conjures, of a time in baseball before free agency when many players began and ended their careers with the same team, when fans became more attached to their hometown players and were more likely to lament their departure, when life was simpler, the pace was slower, and baseball was the national pastime.

McCovey's allusion to the old-fashioned trade in baseball illustrates both the value of and the concern with using allusions. Some readers won't pick up on the baseball allusion. McCovey decides to use it anyway, understanding this. The allusion adds texture and depth of meaning for some readers, but McCovey does not allow the overall meaning of his essay to be lost on a reader who doesn't understand the allusion. (A reader would not say: I didn't understand his main idea because I don't know what an old-fashioned trade in baseball is.) The following questions will help you develop allusions for your own writing:

▶ Does my subject relate to any political event or situation?

▶ Does my subject relate to any social or cultural event or situation?

▶ Does my subject relate to any person or event in history? In literature? In popular culture (movies, television, music)? ■

# Using Figurative Language

Figurative language makes an imaginative connection between ideas, creating pictures for readers and making points more intense. For example, Oomen uses figurative language to help the reader imagine the bowl of the Sleeping Bear dune: "Wind mutes and huffs through this place, and over the years, it has not only hollowed the bowl but shaped a broad opening at the west side of the blowout—as though the sand that once made the mound was poured out of a wide spigot." To help the reader experience the dune, Oomen creates a visual image. By describing the shape of the dune as "sand pouring out of wide spigot," she even creates a sort of motion picture, an image of the sand moving.

While figurative language can be bold and dramatic, it is frequently quiet, quick, and effective—creating a clarifying image in few words. In the following examples, Oomen uses a type of figurative language called *simile*, which compares two things using *like* or *as.*

• After years of enduring the relentless wind, the vegetation blows away, and the dune begins to hollow itself out, like a bowl, weathered down from the high point, leaving the lower, less exposed side to rise like a rim.
• The remnants of this spirit forest are scattered like ribs and femurs and spine.

For your own writing, remember that figurative language should be used to help the reader understand main insights. Apply the following questions:

▶ A thing? A place? A person?
▶ What purpose would this comparison serve? ■

## Activity

As writers develop, they learn to insert intellectual space between the writing instructions and their essay. Where the inexperienced writer might read the instructions and then write an essay, the more experienced writer inserts space by first using writing to plan, to ask questions, to invent, and to reflect. Before you draft your essay for this chapter, write down a working thesis and several supporting ideas. For example, how might you use narration, allusions, dialogue, or some other strategy to help the reader understand and accept your thesis? Then share your sketch with others to get feedback before you draft an entire essay.

# Organizational Strategies

## When Should I Change Paragraphs?

You might think of paragraph changes as camera shifts. You can change paragraphs when you want to create a new field of vision, when you want the reader to see a new thing or imagine a new scene. Notice how these opening sentences from Ooman's paragraphs shift the scene, moving readers through the sand dunes and the points Oomen makes about them:

- Before the legend of the Sleeping Bear became Michigan's state story, I was struck by its sad contradictions.
- In the story, the great spirit, Gitche Manitou, transformed the cubs into the two islands we call the Manitous, but it is that west-facing dune on the shore that is the pivot point for the legend, the one that represents the great she-bear watching those two islands.
- I drive the park's forested scenic road to the point where it opens to the light and sand of the dunes.
- Cold and bluster bully me as I squeeze under the railings and step off the lookout, cutting directly across the dunes, trudging through this northern desert.
- I stumble along the shoreline bluff, walking slowly through varied soil, sometimes soft sand, sometimes coarse gravel or crusty silt—all of it light.
- Deep swales, I cannot see the lake or the distant reference point of the dune.
- Half an hour later, having spanned the final mile and struggled up through rough scrub, I crest the rim—gasping for breath, and look down into what is the bowl of the bear.
- A blowout is a dune summit or ridge that may have once looked like a lush foliage-covered hilltop.
- From that crater of sand where her body would have rested, ghost trees rise, scattered and leaning and awful.
- How long can one explore a void?

- Finally I do what I have been avoiding. There is here a place within a place. I look to the center of the blowout. . . .
- Since then, I have tried to make the trek once a year, usually in the fall when the isolation is more remarkable.
- I have come to love the wind here, the power it has to erase through its insistent presence.

Since her essay has a central point and is not simply moving chronologically through events, Oomen sometimes begins paragraphs when she develops particular kinds of support for her central observation. For example, when she comes to a blowout in her narrative, she begins a paragraph defining *blowout:*

> A blowout is a dune summit or ridge that may have once looked like a lush foliage-covered hilltop. But because of the lightness and fragility of the soil— almost dust—and the death, due to drought or other weather conditions, of that vegetation, plus exposure to the constant westerlies, the dune sand erodes away from the roots, especially at the crest of these hills. After years of enduring this relentless wind. . .

Later, Oomen uses a paragraph to take the reader to a place within a place. After creating the scene with carefully selected details, she begins a new paragraph that reflects on and makes sense of the place:

> Finally, I do what I have been avoiding. There is here a place within a place. I look to the center of the blowout, which contains a smaller mound, still intact, around which the wind has worked all these years. It is perhaps two stories high, and despite the fact that all else around it is hollowed out and left to bones, it stands over this desert and the skeletal trees, a rough, grass-pocked cone with its top sheered off. I have been circling its irregular slopes cautiously because I feel the anomaly. This entire rise has been blown away, but this core has remained, grasses still clinging to its surface. I choose the least steep slope on the backside, the slope protected from the lake winds, and scramble up,

slipping with every step. Finally I am perched on this upturned funnel in the middle of windy emptiness. Breathless, I lie down and watch the rush of combed skies.

Is this place within a place what's left of her mammoth heart? Is this heart of sand the stalwart core of emptiness? It is a place that simply resists. Resists just enough to hold, even against the force of the west winds. Resists a bit longer than the rest of the earth against the inevitable wearing down. A symbol of the Bear, who waits—held in the paradox of eternal sleep and eternal watchfulness—for her cubs, those distant islands of Manitou.

# How Should I Deal with Public Resonance?

The questions on page 110 relating to public resonance might simply help the writer develop a sense of mission. However, writers sometimes choose to make a direct appeal to the audience; that is, they invite the reader directly into the issue. For example, McCovey extends his observation to the reader's situation. This is an explicit strategy to make the subject relate to the reader:

> If you walk through my neighborhood, you won't see many porches, at least not the kind people sit on in the evenings. Those days are gone where I live, and likely where you live, too.

As his essay develops, McCovey makes his observation a public concern, and by the concluding paragraph suggests something about the nature of American public life:

> On Sunday drives through the country, I see big new houses with big new porches. As Americans we can have it all—the house with the big front porch *and* the big garage. But I never (I am tempted to qualify this statement and say "almost never" or "rarely" but I have been thinking about it and I do mean "never")— I never see anyone out sitting on those porches. I am not prepared here to argue that we are as a civilization in deep trouble because of this, though it does seem to me appropriate that we should lament, at least a little, the loss of the front porch.

After describing the cemetery throughout his essay, Justin Scott makes sure the reader knows what his carefully selected details should mean to the reader:

> More time should be spent learning the dead. Their testament is spoken to us from within the maelstrom of coffins and gravestones. Their ghosts bade us not to be concerned with materialism, creed, or race; through them and the past they represent is the key to a more exposed and fulfilling life. *Graveyards are the doppelganger of the living world.* Seeing and recognizing the shadow-self of the graveyard allows us to enrich our lives and live beyond the lessons it presents. The cemetery, above all, tells us of acceptance and judgment: to embrace the former and neglect the latter. Life is finite, precious, and far too short to waste on arrogant trappings already so thoroughly explored by those entombed under earth.

# Writer's Voice

## The Present "I"

Some writers make themselves visible in the text. They refer to themselves and their interactions with the subject. McCovey includes himself in his observations and refers to his own presence in the scenes or situations. But he does not simply inject the "I" without good cause. His presence helps to show the lack of front porches in a particular area, and his recollections of his grandparents help make a point about changes that have occurred in American society. His use of "I" gives support to his more general claims.

Oomen's present "I" is even more important to her observation. Her own quest to understand the Sleeping Bear legend is part of her observation, and she shares observations of herself: "As I move over the drifts of glacial debris, walking absorbs my attention. I watch my feet, notice snail shells in abundance, along with small stony fossils."

## The Invisible "I"

In observation, the writer is sometimes invisible. That is, the writerly "I" never appears; instead, the text focuses entirely on the subject. Justin Scott remains invisible in his observation, yet his essay still projects a particular voice:

> One thing is immediately obvious in this cemetery: Those laden with the gifts of life often choose to utilize them in death, and those less fortunate make do with what they must. Class warfare spills into the afterworld: Business owner is segregated from bricklayer, clergy is separated from atheist. There are large domineering crypts bearing the surnames of the wealthy dead inside, branch-scraping obelisks with ornate script, tombs carefully sculpted to resemble tree stumps, small temples dedicated to their dead in ancient Greek style, and inevitably, the sunken, flat, and nondescript markers of the poor or humble. . . .

Scott's passage illustrates how a writer's voice can be projected not through "I" but through careful word choice and sentence structure.

You might ask your instructor if he or she finds the writerly "I" valuable, but every writer should also ask some basic questions:

▶ Should I put myself in the observation?

▶ If "I" am in the observation, what purpose does it serve? ■

## Level of Formality

Formality is the adherence to an established convention. A formal text follows certain expectations and avoids slipping out of conventional language and organizational patterns. Because essays are used in a number of situations and academic disciplines, the conventions vary, and so does the expected level of formality. Generally, writing that draws no attention to the writer's presence or writing style is considered more formal, while writing that draws attention to the writer's presence and style is considered less formal. (Of course, this is a general rule, and it does not apply to all writing situations.) As you consider your own writing, ask yourself:

▶ Should I break some academic conventions? What might be the consequences?

▶ Should I appear formal? Why? What good will it do?

▶ Should I put myself in the observation?

▶ Will my presence help communicate the main idea or distract the reader from experiencing the subject? ■

# Vitality

Sentences are the writer's only connection to readers. Engaging sentences lead to engaged readers. Flat, safe, unvaried sentences lead to disinterested readers. In short, sentence structure can make all the difference. Consider the following strategies.

## Experiment with Length

If writers aren't careful, they can slip into monotone, in which every sentence has generally the same number of words, the same number of clauses, and the same types of phrases. Just as good speakers vary the sound of their voices, good writers vary the length of sentences. Notice how Scott varies sentence length in the following passage:

> One thing is immediately obvious in this cemetery: those laden with the gifts of life often choose to utilize them in death, and those less fortunate make do with what they must. Class warfare spills into the afterworld: business owner is segregated from bricklayer, clergy is separated from atheist. There are large overbearing crypts bearing the surnames of the wealthy dead inside, branch-scraping obelisks with ornate script, tombs carefully sculpted to resemble tree stumps, small temples dedicated to their dead in ancient Greek style, and inevitably the sunken, flat and nondescript markers of the poor or humble.

In his first two sentences, Scott uses a colon to connect an explanation to the preceding sentence part, an independent clause. The colons help to break up the ideas for the reader and create a rhythm and voice. By following these shorter sentences with a longer one that expresses the different ways people are segregated in a cemetery, Scott helps give the reader a sense that many ways exist. While Scott's final sentence is lengthy, because it is grammatically correct the reader will not become lost in the ideas.

## Experiment with Brevity

Short sentences keep readers alert and moving—but only when they are interspersed with longer ones. Short sentences can also help dramatize thought, as in this passage from McCovey:

> I am not saying there are no front porches. Obviously there are. And I am not saying everyone has a two-car garage instead. In my neighborhood, small garages not connected to the house still reign.

Oomen uses short sentences as well, even as single paragraphs:

> [. . .] There are tracks everywhere in this part of the dunes—deer, raccoon, mice, gulls and small birds—though I see no animals and hear little except the alarm of the crows, the distant roar of waves below the bluffs. The wind picks up, slams sand against my jeans.
>
> I think I may be lost.
>
> Deep swales. I cannot see the lake or the distant reference point of the dune. I stop disoriented, pull my hood back . . .

## Change Out Vague Nouns

Vague nouns refer to nothing in particular: *people, society, things, everyone,* and so on. It is often tempting to rely on vague nouns to float ideas past readers, but vague nouns have at least two negative effects: (1) they keep the reader from focusing, and (2) they signal that the writer has not committed to a statement. Vague nouns plague college writing (and instructors everywhere dislike them). While they are not inherently evil (sometimes writers need to use words such as *things* and *people*), they generally make for vague statements.

## Invention Workshop

With one or two peers, inject more vitality into your writing. Point to particular sentences and phrases that could be more intense.

1. **Help the writer experiment with length and brevity.** Take one paragraph and rewrite its sentences. Combine some sentences, weaving together several interconnected ideas. Shorten other sentences so that the passage tugs and pulls, varying long and short sentences for a dramatic effect.
2. **Change out vague nouns.** Underline vague nouns (such as *people, society,* and *things*) and suggest more specific words.

# Revision

Writers create essays through invention, drafting, and revision. A draft is very much a work in progress, and it must be viewed that way. Writers don't just buff a draft—correcting spelling, punctuation, grammar—instead, they ask hard questions about their basic approach: Does my thesis and essay *really* express a focused insight about the subject? Drafts often express a variety of general ideas, so revision can involve making brutal, sometimes painful cuts to focus entirely on the single most important, most valuable insight. Another tough question is whether the thesis and essay are *really* revelatory. Many drafts have not yet revealed something unique and particular enough to make the essay stand out, so revision involves examining the supporting points, returning to the Analysis and Public Resonance questions, and exploring *one* less-obvious, potentially interesting point more deeply. Before exchanging drafts with a peer, ask yourself hard questions about your essay's focus and insight.

## Peer Review

Exchange drafts with at least one other writer. Before passing your draft to others, underline the thesis, or write it above your essay. This way, reviewers will get traction as they read. As a reviewer, use the following questions to guide your response.

1. Point out any words or phrases in the thesis that could be more specific. (See the Thesis section, page 111 for more guidance.)
2. Where can the writer do more analysis and reveal more about the subject in the observation? (Point to passages that seem most obvious to you. As you read, look for claims that anyone could immediately offer without intensive analysis. Beside these passages, write "more analysis?" If you can suggest an interesting idea, explain it on the back of the writer's draft.)
3. Help the writer to illustrate his or her claims with details. As you read, look for broad characterizations —those that anyone could imagine without a close observation. Ask yourself: Could this be more specific? Can we *really* see the particular nuances of the subject?

In the margin, write "more details" where the writer could more intensely show the points.
4. Offer some figurative language to help characterize the subject. After you have read the entire draft, offer your own metaphor or simile about the subject. Give your suggestion on the back of the draft. Make sure it is something that fits the writer's voice, something that he or she could use.
5. If the writer uses narrative, does it help support the main idea of the observation? How? (If you have difficulty explaining how it supports the main point, perhaps the writer should rethink its use in the essay!)
6. Are the paragraphs coherent? Do you ever get the sense that a paragraph is wandering—giving you details that seem unrelated to one another or unrelated to the point of the essay? If so, write in the margin "check paragraph coherence."
7. The most focused statement possible often makes for a better introduction. Suggest a surprisingly focused opening statement. (The writer might decide to use it.)
8. Consider the writer's voice.
   - If the writer is present (using "I"), is this necessary? Explain how the presence of the writer helps make the point of the observation.
   - If the writer is invisible (no "I"), how is that beneficial?
   - Where could the writer be more informal (breaking some conventions) or more formal?
9. Help the writer avoid common grammatical errors: comma splices, sentence fragments, or pronoun/ antecedent agreement.
10. Write down the specific subject of the observation: a sand dune, porches, cemeteries, for example. Then complete the following statement: Ultimately, this essay is not about [the specific subject: a sand dune, for example]. It is about _____ _____.

# Reflection

As a developing writer and thinker, you should be able to not just write an essay but articulate ideas about your essay. Now that you have written an Observing essay, step back from it and answer the following questions:

- What does your observation say about life in this place and time?
- What do people normally experience, understand, or assume about the subject, and how does your essay present a new way of thinking about it?
- List three rhetorical tools you used in the essay and explain specifically how each one helps the reader understand and accept the thesis.
- Identify several sentences that are especially lively and well written. What is it about the nouns, verbs, sentence length, word order, and other sentence particulars that make the sentences lively and well written?

As you respond, remember to practice good writing. Invent, draft, and revise your responses. Write carefully edited complete sentences, not fragments.

## Beyond the Essay

Our fundamental values and beliefs dictate how we see and what conclusions we come to. For example, someone looking at a car lot full of shiny SUVs might see ridiculous and costly waste, while someone else might see opportunity and signs of success.

### Person A
- Values moderation, health, conserving resources, family comfort
- Believes that people should tread carefully upon the Earth
- Believes most people are victims of materialist propaganda
- Hopes for a future with cleaner air, better health, less poverty, and less international strife
- Sees a lot full of SUVs as a shiny, attractive waste of resources, a nicely structured delusion about the present and the future

### Person B
- Values financial success, health, nice neighborhoods, family comfort
- Believes that people should reap the benefits of their hard work, that human desire is good for the economy, that material things support the pursuit of happiness
- Believes most people do not work hard enough for what they want
- Hopes for a future of more economic stability, upward mobility, and less international strife
- Sees a lot full of SUVs as a sign of America's economic success and people's individual hopes for a more stable and secure life

Consider the essay you wrote for this chapter and the conclusions you came to about the subject:

- What values lie beneath your conclusions?
- What beliefs (about people, the past, the present, the future, comfort, animals, cities, etc.) lie beneath your conclusions?
- What hopes for yourself, for the future, for all people might have influenced the way you see the subject of the observation?
- More than anything else, what value or belief controlled the way you saw the subject?

 For additional resources including instructional videos and links to helpful websites, access your English CourseMate through cengagebrain.com.

# 5 Analyzing Concepts

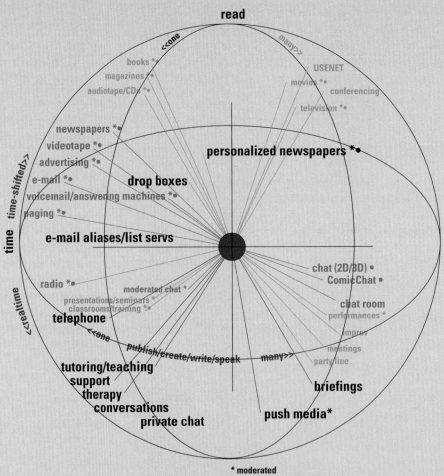

read

<<one          many>>

books *•
magazines *•
audiotape/CDs *•

USENET
movies *•          conferencing
television *•

newspapers *•
videotape *•
advertising *•
e-mail *•
voicemail/answering machines *•
paging *•

personalized newspapers *•

drop boxes

time          time-shifted>>

e-mail aliases/list servs

chat (2D/3D) •
ComicChat •

radio *•

moderated chat *

presentations/seminars *
classrooms/training *•

<realtime

telephone

chat room
performances *

<<one

improv
meetings
party line

publish/create/write/speak          many>>

tutoring/teaching
support
therapy
conversations
private chat

briefings

push media*

* moderated
• captured record/archive

# Chapter Contents

# "Concepts have no 'real' definitions; instead, they have uses. They are our ways of coming to understand the world and deciding how to behave within it."

—Susan R. Horton

Concepts are ideas or abstract formulations. They are generalized notions beyond specifics. For example, we have concepts of *college, marriage, friendship,* or *technology* that go beyond any particular college, spouse, friend, or piece of equipment. And when our colleges, spouses, friends, and machines do not measure up to our concepts, we get frustrated, and we may even alter our concepts.

Within a particular culture, concepts change, sometimes drastically. Consider how the concept of *president* has changed for many people. Before the Watergate scandal (involving President Nixon), the Iran Contra scandal (involving President Reagan), the Monica Lewinsky scandal (involving President Clinton), or the invasion of Iraq (involving President Bush), most Americans' concept of *president* probably did not include scandal. But in the wake of such events, the concept has changed. Or consider how the idea of *America* changed after September 11, 2001. Before that date, most Americans probably did not consider how their country related to the concerns of people in the Middle East; however, after the terrorist attacks, Americans' concept shifted to accommodate our role in global politics.

Of course, people do not always agree on concepts. A dispute over a concept is often the catalyst for major conflict between people, cultures, and countries. Think about the intense and extended battles brought on by differing notions of *God* or the political struggles brought on by differing concepts of *woman, man, family, life, torture,* or *freedom.* Analyzing concepts turns out to be a rather important and sticky business.

In academia, students and professors are mired in the process of analyzing, discussing, and arguing about concepts. Consider, for example, *sex:*

- In a biology course, students discuss sex as reproduction. The concept in biology involves the study of hormones and reproductive systems (egg, sperm, gestation periods, embryo, and so on).

- In psychology, sex might be understood as a complex of drives. Students explore it using Freud's understanding of sexual development, repression, and parental affiliation.

- In sociology, students might approach sex as socially patterned behavior. A sociological understanding of sex may involve the study of social customs (such as dancing, choosing clothing, dating, and marriage).

These concepts are obviously different; in fact, many people claim that a discipline's take on a concept partly defines that discipline. (In other words, part of what defines a sociologist is how he or she understands *sex* or *community* or *family.*) Disciplines also focus on and develop their own concepts. *Ego,* for instance, is a concept developed by psychology. And much of your college career will involve exploring and analyzing the main concepts of different disciplines and your chosen field.

This chapter will help you analyze a particular concept, develop a focused explanation, and communicate your ideas in writing. The following essays will provide valuable insight into various analytical strategies. After reading the essays, you can find a concept in one of two ways:

1. Go to the Point of Contact section to find a topic from everyday life, or
2. Choose one of the Ideas for Writing that follow the essays.

After finding a subject, go to the Analysis section to begin developing the analysis.

# World Gone Mad

## Derrick Jensen

Derrick Jensen is a writer and an activist. He holds degrees in mineral engineering physics and creative writing. He has published fifteen books including *End Game, The Land of Make Believe,* and *Resistance Against Empire.* His work consistently questions the collective actions of mainstream American culture. In this essay, published in the September/October 2010 issue of *Orion* magazine, Jensen analyzes the concept of sociopathic behavior—and shows how the concept applies to our way of life.

I don't know about you, but whenever I attend some "green" conference, I know I'm supposed to leave feeling inspired and energized, but instead I feel heartbroken, discouraged, defeated, and lied to. It's not the inevitable talk about farmers (re)discovering organic farming; about plastic forks made from cornstarch; about solar photovoltaics; about relocalizing; about the joys of simple living; about grieving the murder of the planet; about "changing our stories"; and most especially about maintaining a positive attitude that gets me down. It's that no one, and I mean no one, ever mentions psychopathology.

Why is this important? Because those in power destroy sustainable communities—and not just sustainable indigenous communities. If people develop new ways to live on their land more sustainably, and those in power decide that land is needed for roads and shopping malls and parking lots, those in power will seize that land. This is how the dominant culture works. Everything and everyone must be sacrificed to economic production, to economic growth, to the continuation of this culture.

A few months ago I was watching a documentary on David Parker Ray, a serial killer from Truth or Consequences, New Mexico, who is suspected of killing up to sixty women. He kidnapped women and held them as rape slaves. He turned an entire tractor-trailer into a well-stocked torture chamber, where he videotaped what he did to them. In the documentary, an FBI profiler compared Ray's attitudes toward his victims to those most people have toward tissues: Once you use them, are you concerned about what happens to them? Of course not, she said. And that was how Ray perceived—or rather didn't

perceive—his victims: simply as something to use and throw away.

When the profiler said this, my first thought was *passenger pigeons.* Then *chinook salmon.* Then *oceans.* How deeply do most members of this culture mourn passenger pigeons? Salmon? Oceans? This culture as a whole, and most of its members, gives no more consideration to the victims of this way of life than David Parker Ray gave to his victims. Blindness to suffering is one of this culture's central defining characteristics. And it is a central defining characteristic of sociopathology.

*The New Columbia Encyclopedia* states that a sociopath can be defined as one who willfully does harm without remorse: "Such individuals are impulsive, insensitive to others' needs, and unable to anticipate the consequences of their behavior, to follow long-term goals, or to tolerate frustration. The psychopathic individual is characterized by absence of the guilt feelings and anxiety that normally accompany an antisocial act."

Um, how sensitive are members of this culture, on the whole, to the needs of native forests (98 percent gone), native grasslands (99 percent gone), ocean life (90 percent of the large fish gone)? How sensitive is this culture to indigenous land claims? How clearly are members of this culture able to anticipate the consequences of destroying forests, grasslands, oceans, or denying indigenous land claims? With sea level already rising and glaciers already disappearing, how capable are this culture's decision makers of anticipating the consequences of global warming?

Dr. Robert Hare, an expert on sociopaths, states that "among the most devastating features of psychopathy are a callous disregard for the rights of others and a propensity for predatory and violent behaviors. Without remorse, psychopaths charm and exploit others for their own gain. They lack empathy and a sense of responsibility, and they manipulate, lie and con others with no regard for anyone's feelings." I'm reminded of something Red Cloud said: "They made us many promises, more than I can remember. They only kept but one. They promised they would take our land, and they took it."

Hare also says, "Too many people hold the idea that psychopaths are essentially killers or convicts. The general public hasn't been educated to see beyond the social stereotypes to understand that psychopaths can be entrepreneurs, politicians, CEOs and other successful individuals who may never see the inside of a prison." They can be the president, a boss, a neighbor.

Let's now consider the dominant culture in relation to the characteristics of sociopaths as listed in section F60.2 of *The ICD-10 Classification of Mental and Behavioural Disorders,* published by the World Health Organization, Geneva, 1992:

a) *callous unconcern for the feelings of others.* Where to start? Have members of this culture shown any concern for the feelings of the indigenous as they've stolen their land? How about the feelings of nonhumans being driven from their homes, or those being driven out of existence? Further, doesn't the mainstream scientific community demand that emotion be removed from all scientific study? Aren't we also told that emotions must not interfere with business decisions and economic policy? Do chickens in battery cages have feelings? What about dogs in vivisection labs? What about trees? Rain? Stones? The culture goes beyond "callous unconcern" for the feelings of these others to deny that their feelings even exist.

b) *gross and persistent attitude of irresponsibility and disregard for social norms, rules and obligations.* Is there an action more irresponsible than killing the planet? Now consider the norms, rules, and obligations of this culture. Norms: rape, abuse, destruction. Rules: a legal system created by the powerful to maintain their power. Obligations: to get as much money and power as possible.

c) *incapacity to maintain enduring relationships, though having no difficulty in establishing them.* I live on Tolowa land. The Tolowa had enduring relationships with their human and nonhuman neighbors for at least 12,500 years. When the dominant culture arrived here about 180 years ago, the place was a paradise; now the place is trashed. Exploitation is not an enduring relationship—whether with another animal or a landbase.

d) *very low tolerance to frustration and a low threshold for discharge of aggression, including violence.* The civilized have been eradicating the indigenous for ten thousand years. The United States is constantly "discharging aggression" against (i.e., invading) other countries. Individuals and corporations and governments discharge aggression daily toward coyotes, prairie dogs, sea lions, wetlands, coal-bearing mountaintops, and oil-bearing coastal plains.

e) *incapacity to experience guilt and to profit from experience, particularly punishment.* How much guilt do you believe timber company CEOs experience over the destruction of ancient forests? And the word *profit* here does not mean the financial profit they derive from killing forests, oceans, and so on, but profit in terms of hindsight. After deforesting the Middle East, all of Europe, much of the Americas, Africa, and Asia, does it seem at all plausible that those in charge are learning from their past mistakes? Are they learning anything from their decisions and policies that are altering the climate through unrestrained burning of coal, oil, and natural gas?

f) *marked proneness to blame others, or to offer plausible rationalizations, for the behaviour.* Do CEOs take responsibility for their violence? The average rapist for his? George Bush blamed forest fires for his urge to deforest. Clinton said it was all the beetles' fault. And many still rationalize their denial of our rapidly warming planet every time a winter storm slams the East Coast.

Of course we don't all act this way. But those of us who are not sociopaths, who are trying to live differently, need to step up and call out the larger culture for the way it behaves.

Sharing our finite planet with this culture is like being stuck in a room with a psychopath. There is no exit. Although the psychopath may choose other targets first, eventually it will turn to us. Eventually we'll have to fight for our lives. And so if we want access to a landbase we can inhabit, and want our descendants to be able to live there long into the future, we need to organize politically to stop this lethal culture in its tracks.

# Writing Strategies

1. Analysis involves breaking something down into constituent parts. How does Jensen break down sociopathic behavior?

2. Explain how Jensen connects sociopathic traits to an entire civilization. Point to specific passages or sentences.

3. Sometimes an analytical process feeds a broader argumentative purpose. What passages in this essay seem more argumentative? In other words, where do you most sense Jensen's argument?

4. Jensen refers to a range of psychological experts and disciplinary texts. Describe how those sources help to support his point about sociopathic behavior.

5. Jensen also refers to Red Cloud, an American Indian (Oglala Lakota Chief) who fought against the advancement of military troops in the 1860s. How do Red Cloud's words support Jensen's point?

## Exploring Ideas

1. Jensen seems to use psychopath and sociopath interchangeably. Briefly research these terms. Can you discover any consistent differences in the concepts?

2. No doubt, many Americans would be offended by Jensen's ideas. Why? Why are many not offended? (Are you offended?)

3. Jensen's comparison assumes that a culture can function as a whole—as a coherent identity. This is a common move for historians, sociologists, politicians, anthropologists, and literary writers. Give examples of times you've heard about cultures or countries being characterized as a unified whole.

4. Considering the specific behaviors listed in the *Classification of Mental and Behavioural Disorders* (items a–f in Jensen's essay), how are you a sociopath?

5. What does Jensen mean by "the dominant culture"?

## Ideas for Writing

1. Focus on another psychological condition. Compare its specific behaviors or symptoms to an institution or public body.

2. What is *dominant culture?*

If responding to one of these ideas, go to the Analysis section of this chapter to begin developing ideas for your essay.

woraput chawalitphon/istockphoto.com

# Black Like I Thought I Was

## Erin Aubry Kaplan

Over the centuries, Americans have struggled with race and ethnicity. We have built laws, institutions, and schools of thought around widely held categories. But collectively, we have not made up our minds about difference, diversity, or sameness. As with many concepts, the more we explore, the more we re-discover our own misconceptions. In short, it seems that the concept of race keeps escaping us. In this essay, originally printed in the *LA Weekly,* Erin Aubry Kaplan shows how some deeply grounded assumptions about race may be shattering.

Wayne Joseph is a 51-year-old high school principal in Chino whose family emigrated from the segregated parishes of Louisiana to central Los Angeles in the 1950s, as did mine. Like me, he is of Creole stock and is therefore on the lighter end of the black color spectrum, a common enough circumstance in the South that predates the multicultural movement by centuries. And like most other black folk, Joseph grew up with an unequivocal sense of his heritage and of himself; he tends toward black advocacy and has published thoughtful opinion pieces on racial issues in magazines like *Newsweek.* When Joseph decided on a whim to take a new ethnic DNA test he saw described on a 60 Minutes segment last year, it was only to indulge a casual curiosity about the exact percentage of black blood; virtually all black Americans are mixed with something, he knew, but he figured it would be interesting to make himself a guinea pig for this new testing process, which is offered by a Florida-based company called DNA Print Genomics Inc. The experience would at least be fodder for another essay for *Newsweek.* He got his kit in the mail, swabbed his mouth per the instructions and sent off the DNA samples for analysis.

Now, I have always believed that what is now widely considered one of slavery's worst legacies—the Southern "one-drop" rule that indicted anyone with black blood as a nigger and cleaved American society into black and white with a single stroke—was also slavery's only upside. Of course I deplore the motive behind the law, which was rooted not only in white paranoia about miscegenation, but in a more practical need to maintain social order by keeping privilege and property in the hands of whites. But by forcing blacks of all complexions and blood percentages into the same boat, the law ironically laid a foundation of black unity that remains in place today. It's a foundation that allows us to talk abstractly about a "black community" as concretely as we talk about a black community in Harlem or Chicago or South-Central (a liberty that's often abused or lazily applied in modern discussions of race). And it gives the lightest-skinned among us the assurance of identity that everybody needs in order to feel grounded and psychologically whole—even whites, whose public non-ethnicity is really ethnicity writ so large and influential it needs no name. Being black may still not be the most advantageous thing in the world, but being nothing or being neutral—the rallying cry of modern-day multiculturalists—has never made any emotional or real-world sense. Color marks you, but your membership in black society also gives you an indestructible house to live in and a bed to rest on. I can't imagine growing up any other way.

Wayne Joseph can't, either. But when the results of his DNA test came back, he found himself staggered by the idea that though he still qualified as a person of color, it was not the color he was raised to think he was, one with a distinct culture and definitive place in the American struggle for social equality that he'd taken for granted. Here was the unexpected and rather unwelcome truth: Joseph was 57 percent Indo-European, 39 percent Native American, 4 percent East Asian—and zero percent African. After a lifetime of assuming blackness, he was now being told that he lacked even a single drop of black blood to qualify.

"My son was flabbergasted by the results," says Joseph. "He said, 'Dad, you mean for 50 years you've been passing for black?'" Joseph admits that, strictly speaking, he has. But he's not sure if he can or wants to do anything about that at this point. For all the lingering effects of institutional racism, he's been perfectly content being a black man; it has shaped his worldview and the course of his life in ways that cannot, and probably should not, be altered. Yet Joseph struggles to balance the intellectual dishonesty of saying he's black with the unimpeachable honesty of a lifelong experience of *being* black. "What do I do with this information?" he says, sounding more than a little exasperated. "It was like finding out you're adopted. I don't want to be disingenuous with myself. But I can't conceive of living any other way. It's a question of what's logical and what's visceral."

Race, of course, has always been a far more visceral matter than a logical one. We now know that there is no such thing as race, that humans are biologically one species; we know that an African is likely to have more in common genetically with a European thousands of miles away than with a neighboring African. Yet this knowledge has not deterred the racism many Europeans continue to harbor toward Africans, nor the wariness Africans harbor toward Europeans. Such feelings may never be deterred. And despite all the loud assertions to the contrary, race is still America's bane, and its fascination; Philip Roth's widely acclaimed last novel set in the 1990s, *The Human Stain,* features a Faustian protagonist whose great moral failing is that he's a black man who's been passing most of his life for white (the book has been made into a movie due in theaters next month).

Joseph recognizes this, and while he argues for a more rational and less emotional view of race for the sake of equity, he also recognizes that rationality is not the same thing as fact. As much as he might want to, he can't simply refute his black past and declare himself white or Native American. He can acknowledge the truth but can't quite apply it, which makes it pretty much useless to other, older members of his family. An aunt whom he told about the test results only said that she wasn't surprised. "When I told my mother about the test, she said to me, 'I'm too old and too tired to be anything else,'" recalls Joseph. "It makes no difference to her. It's an easy issue."

After recovering from the initial shock, Joseph began questioning his mother about their lineage. He discovered that, unbeknownst to him, his grandparents had made a conscious decision back in Louisiana to *not* be white, claiming they didn't want to side with a people who were known oppressors. Joseph says there was another, more practical consideration: Some men in the family routinely courted black women, and they didn't want the very public hassle such a pairing entailed in the South, which included everything from dirty looks to the ignominy of a couple having to separate on buses and streetcars and in restaurants per the Jim Crow laws. I know that the laws also pointedly separated mothers from sons, uncles from nephews, simply because one happened to be lighter than the other or have straighter hair. Determinations of race were entirely subjective and imposed from without, and the one-drop rule was enforced to such divisive and schizophrenic effects that Joseph's family—and mine—fled Louisiana for the presumably less boundary-obsessed West. But we didn't flee ourselves, and didn't expect to; we simply set up a new home in Los Angeles. The South was wrong about its policies but it was right about our color. It had to be.

Joseph remains tortured by the possibility that maybe nobody is right. The essay he thought the DNA test experience would prompt became a book that he's already 150 pages into. He doesn't seem to know how it'll end. He's in a kind of limbo that he doesn't want and that I frankly wouldn't wish on anyone; when I wonder aloud about taking the $600 DNA test myself, Joseph flatly advises against it. "You don't want to know," he says. "It's like a genie coming out of a bottle. You can't put it back in." He has more empathy for the colorblind crowd than he had before, but isn't inclined to believe that the Ward Connerlys and other professed racial conservatives of the world have the best interests of colored people at heart. "I see their point, but race *does* matter, especially with things like medical research and other social trends," he says of Connerly's Proposition 54, the much-derided state measure that seeks to outlaw the collection of ethnic data that will be voted on in the recall election next Tuesday. "Problems like that can't just go away." For the moment, Joseph is compelled to try to judge individually what he knows has always been judged broadly, to reconcile two famously opposed viewpoints of race not for the sake of political argument—he has made those—but for his own peace of mind. He's wrestling with a riddle that will likely outlive him, though he doesn't worry that it will be passed on to the next generation—his ex-wife is black, enough to give his children the firm ethnic identity he had and that he embraced for most of his life. "The question ultimately is, are you who you say you are, or are you who you are genetically?" he muses. The logical—and visceral—answer is that it's not black and white.

# Writing Strategies

1. What is Kaplan's main point about the concept of race?

2. This article relies heavily on the story of Wayne Joseph. Explain how his story works—how it helps Kaplan to make a complex point.

3. In ¶5, Kaplan explains that "Joseph struggles to balance the intellectual dishonesty of saying he's black with the unimpeachable honesty of a lifelong experience of *being* black." Why does Kaplan italicize *being*? What distinction is she making?

4. In ¶6, Kaplan says that race "has always been a far more visceral matter than a logical one." How does this statement work in the essay? What kind of distinction does it help the reader to make?

5. Kaplan's article makes a classic academic move: it reveals the complexity in something that seems simple. In other words, she *complicates* our understanding of a concept. She shakes up common and comfortable ways of thinking. Find a passage in which you see Kaplan complicating an idea. Describe the comfortable way of thinking and how Kaplan shakes it up.

# Exploring Ideas

1. What is the difference among race, ethnicity, nationality, and lineage?

2. White Americans sometimes imagine themselves as non-ethnic—as having no ethnicity. Carefully re-read ¶4 in Kaplan's article. What is her response to this way of thinking?

3. A close examination of identity requires debunking common sentiments or clichés. Consider, for instance, the notion that people should simply *be themselves*. What does this sentiment assume about ethnicity or identity? What does it ignore?

4. Kaplan reports that "Joseph remains tortured by the possibility that maybe nobody is right." In other words, he fears that there is no clear answer about his racial identity—about racial identity in general. Why is such a possibility so frightening?

# Ideas for Writing

1. In what ethnic category have you always seen yourself? How has that category fused to your everyday life? How has it shaped the way you live?

2. Beyond race and ethnicity, what other category has determined your identity? Closely examine that label. Interrogate the assumptions that keep it in place.

If responding to one of these ideas, go to the Analysis section of this chapter to begin developing ideas for your essay.

# "Have It Your Way": Consumerism Invades Education

## Simon Benlow

What is a student? This might sound like a silly question, but *student* can be defined in different ways. So can *education*. And the way a person defines or understands these concepts can make a difference in the way that person—and others—acts. In the following essay, Simon Benlow explores what it means to be a student and to participate in an education. Notice how Benlow narrows his focus. He doesn't talk generally about all the characteristics of education, but instead examines the important role consumerism (another concept) plays in education. (Portions of Benlow's invention work are shown in later sections of this chapter.)

Two weeks ago, the faculty and staff received a memo regarding "National Customer Service Week." We were urged to take special efforts in serving our customers—presumably, our students. Certainly, I have no objections to extending extra efforts in helping students feel comfortable and situated in the college environment. However, I am deeply troubled (as are many, or most, instructors and professors) by use of the term "customer" to refer to students. I am concerned, in general, about the slow and subtle infiltration of consumerism into education (by companies buying access to students' brains), and I am downright hostile to the way "customer" has suddenly replaced the word (and maybe idea of) "student" in higher education. And because my concerns may seem ungrounded, I'd like to offer a brief analysis—a quick examination of the basic, and not-so-basic, differences between "customer" and "student."

"The customer is always right." We hear this hollow phrase resound through (almost) every corridor of our consumerist culture. The motive behind the phrase is painfully clear—to keep customers happy, to keep them from complaining, and most importantly, to keep them coming back. (Of course, the meaninglessness of the phrase is well known, too—for those of us who have had the displeasure of talking with Ameritech operators

or "customer service" tellers at our banks.) The phrase is meant to maintain a climate in which the substance of anyone's concerns or complaints is obfuscated by friendly and diplomatic clichés—"your business means so much to us"; "we'll do everything we can to address the problem." Ultimately, then, the goal of customer service, in this sense, is to lull customers into a sense of complacency—even though their phones may not be working or their washers are throwing sparks.

"Have it your way!" Of course, we all know the song and the friendly fried food establishment associated with this slogan. It's a harmless phrase, in and of itself, and one that works particularly well for the franchise. It suggests to customers that their particular appetites can be catered to, that their specific tastes, no matter how eccentric (within the continuum of dip n' serve fried food) can be easily satisfied. It promotes the idea that the institution will shift its entire set of processes to meet the desires of the individual.

The meal deal bargain. Recently, in our hyper-drive-thru culture, we've been given a new ticket to ride—a quicker and easier way to get fast food (and a host of other things as well): the combo or meal deal. In the old days, we had to pull up to the drive-thru board, search under "Sandwiches" and THEN go through the labor of exploring "Sides" and "Beverages." It was all too much. Now, we can simply pull up, and say a number. We don't even have to trouble ourselves with uttering all the stuff we want to eat. We just say, "#1 with a diet." The meal deal craze is, of course, not limited to fast food; it is, simply, most explicitly manifested in the fast food industry. That is, in the fast food world, we can clearly see the motives of an increasingly consumerized culture: (1) to limit the interaction between the provider and the customer, (2) to limit the time the customer has to reflect on his/her wants, and (3) to limit the energy the customer has to exert.

Passivity. Customers are encouraged to be passive. We are prompted in a variety of ways not to be agents of our own making. Our needs and desires are met by the work of others. As customers, we pay for someone else's work, for someone else's acts of invention, creation, and production. And we not only hire out our activities (painting our homes, cooking our dinners); we also hire out our imaginations. We don't even have to imagine what is possible. Others have already done the imagining, created a product or service and have told us how we can use it. (They've even taken the extra step of telling us what NOT to do: "Women who are pregnant or who may become pregnant should not take, or even handle, these pills.") In short, *the world of the customer is based on intellectual inactivity;* we merely have to dial the phone, get online, say a number. We don't have to reflect, invent, produce, or research (*Consumer's Reports* has done it already). Nor do we have to shop: they will deliver. Being a customer means being driven by simple and personal desires . . . and ultimately demanding that those desires be met.

Contrary to the passive, personalizing, self-perpetuating, desire-driven customer, students are encouraged to be active. In college, students cannot simply consume knowledge. Even in its most packaged form, the textbook, knowledge must be regenerated, revised, reinterpreted, and remembered in order to be anything beyond an answer on a multiple-choice test. Students who read textbooks, literature, and articles passively will get nothing from them—it is a kind of paralyzing higher education illiteracy. Certainly, they will be able to read something aloud, or even to themselves, and maybe summarize a main point; however, they will not know how to imagine the implications or significance of a textbook chapter. (And this is what academics mean when they say, "Our students don't know how to *make meaning*.")

Students who come to college with a consumerist attitude are lost. Because they are anticipating their most basic desires will be stimulated (because that's how people are massaged into buying stuff they don't need), consumerist students come to college waiting to be tickled, waiting to see the big boom, waiting for the car chase or the sex scene, waiting for the french fry, waiting for the Cherry Coke. What they encounter, however, are rooms filled with ingredients. They see only black and white words—where they anticipate smashy colors and extravagant tools for getting their attention. In the face of pure ingredients (the stuff for making meaning), they will be confused . . . and ultimately, terribly bored.

Consumerist students (or those who have been tricked into thinking like consumers) will also have a difficult time understanding principles. Principles, established doctrines which are to be followed, or evaluated, in the processes of making knowledge, don't really exist in consumer culture (unless you count slogans as doctrines). Because everything is based on the eccentricities of the individual ("hold the pickle, hold the lettuce"), the individual need not ever think outside of his/her own desires and the reality that is created from projecting those desires onto everything and everyone in view. In higher education, principles establish how a discipline works. Physics works on principles of matter and energy. The goal of a physicist is to discover the principles and understand how they can be used. Composition works on principles—conventions of grammar and persuasion. This is not to say that all knowledge is prescribed. On the contrary, students in such classes are encouraged to invent, to break rules, to go beyond. But in order to do so, they need certain ground rules; they need to understand that certain principles exist in the world outside of their own desires. (One cannot do chemistry and simply dismiss algebra because it is distasteful.)

When I think back to the best teachers and professors in my education, I recall those who demanded everything contrary to the consumerist mentality. They insisted on active students; they made us read staggering amounts of material and then actively put that material to use; they prompted us into confusion and disorientation; they made us uncomfortable, and then, sometimes, offered paths to clarity. In short, they made us into critical, reflective agents of our own becoming, rather than passive bags of desire. Everything valuable about my education came from instructors and professors who were free from the ridiculous tyranny of consumerism.

There is no way higher education can counter the incredible momentum of consumerist culture. It is far more pervasive than the discourses of physics or composition studies. However, if we continue to allow the term "customer" to replace "student," I fear that students will become increasingly blind to the difference between consumerist culture and college culture. I fear they will become increasingly more confused by the expectations of college, and that in the nightmarish long run, colleges will become simply another extension of the consumerist machine in which everyone is encouraged to pre-package knowledge, to super-size grades, and to "hold" anything even slightly distasteful.

# Writing Strategies

1. According to Benlow, what is the essential difference between *student* and *customer?* How does Benlow make this difference clear?

2. Explain how Benlow uses personal testimony. How does it help to support his point about students and customers?

3. Throughout his essay, Benlow alludes to pop culture. Find several allusions that you think are successful and explain why. Which, if any, of his allusions do you think fail?

4. Explain how Benlow prompts readers to consider the importance of the distinction between student and customer.

5. Explain how Benlow's use of the fast food slogan functions in his analysis. What does the slogan (and the accompanying song) help him to do in this essay?

# Exploring Ideas

1. Analysis involves investigating particular parts, elements, or ideas within the whole. What are the particular parts, elements, or ideas within *consumerism?*

2. Benlow claims that consumerism "is far more pervasive than the discourses of physics or composition studies." Offer some support for this claim. How are the discourses of consumerism more dominant in your life than those of academic disciplines?

3. Benlow explains that consumerist students have difficulty with principles. Explain how a consumerist mind-set might be a hindrance to learning a particular principle that you've learned.

4. In what ways have you been addressed or labeled as a customer? Has your college tried to make you into a customer rather than a student? In what particular ways? Do you think it has worked against you?

# Ideas for Writing

1. Spend the next 24 hours noticing terms used in conversation, on television, in junk mail, and so on. Are any terms defined or applied incorrectly?

2. Do members of some other group define themselves incorrectly?

If responding to one of these ideas, go to the Analysis section of this chapter to begin developing ideas for your essay.

Used by permission of the author

# The Real, the Bad, and the Ugly

## Cassie Heidecker

Cassie Heidecker is an art student at Northwestern Michigan College. She developed the following essay about reality television. At first, she struggled not to defend these guilty pleasures but to analyze the concept itself. In this essay, she manages to avoid an explicit argument about the programs, instead revealing how they work on viewers. In her analysis, she discovers key differences among reality, realism, and realistic. And she discovers that reality shows contain a hint of viewers' everyday lives. (Portions of Heidecker's invention work are shown in later sections of this chapter.)

**Writing Strategies**

Describes the obvious tension or apparent contradiction in the concept.

**Exploring Ideas**

Shows aren't real like life. Life is contradictory—dumb, boring, beautiful.

Reality television is a unique form of reality. It's not really real. (Everyone knows that, right?) After all, reality shows have theme music, background sounds, engaging hosts, narrators, sizzling graphics, and makeup artists. The shows are edited so that dialogue is framed and situated for maximum effect. Whatever the contestants say seems snappy, targeted, deliberate, or perfectly stupid. The shows have scenes with pitch-perfect tension, climax, and resolution. But real life has none of these. Real life is mostly boring, uselessly noisy, stagnant, uncertain, ill-defined, repetitive, hopelessly dumb, and sometimes it's quietly and privately beautiful. Such things can't be filmed and put on television for mass viewing. In short, it only takes a moment (or paragraph) to underscore some major differences between reality television and the mundane reality of everyday life.

Alludes to specific shows.

Normal prime-time shows feel soulless and manufactured—to Heidecker and plenty of others!

But reality TV contains something. It draws millions of people away from the Internet and toward their television screens every night. The attraction might simply amount to what it's not: Shows like *Survivor, the Real World, Big Brother, Hell's Kitchen* are not the traditional television fakery where beautiful and two-dimensional humans live two-dimensional lives. These shows are not the plastic, soulless, and formulaic fiction of most prime-time sit-coms and dramas. They are something else.

Hints at the complexity in the concept—at this "something else."

Personal testimony—and a detailed confession.

They are self-aware reality TV junkies.

My husband and I watch culinary reality shows like *Hell's Kitchen* and *Top Chef.* We're embarrassed about it. We don't tell our friends. These shows are trash TV and we don't think of ourselves as trash TV people. But when

Cassie Heidecker, "The Good, the Bad, the Real." Reprinted with permission of the author.

we watch (when we literally run down from our respective work or domestic duties and avoid the phone for that ridiculous hour), we stay glued to the situation. We laugh in all the places we're supposed to laugh. We holler at all the appropriate moments. We laugh at ourselves laughing. We are the unapologetic groundlings at a Shakespearean drama. We yell at the lecherous old men, the conniving women, the smug adolescents, the deceit, the flawed personalities, the near misses, and the moments of predictable victory. We talk about the obvious low-brow appeals of *Hell's Kitchen* and how the quick-fire editing makes the show totally gripping, hilarious, and winky. We discuss the intricate appeals that *Top Chef* makes on our sympathies and the complex character development that works over an entire season.

And we're not alone. Despite the results of a Pew Research Center poll indicating that 63% of the American public thinks that reality TV shows signal our cultural decline, the ratings continue to climb. In fact, "What viewers say they want and what they really watch are not the same" (Carter). So what's the appeal? My husband and I know the shows aren't real. We know we're not watching realism. But we wouldn't be caught dead watching these shows if they featured actors pretending to hope they're going to win the next prize. (Imagine someone like Jennifer Aniston or Zach Braff playing socially awkward but earnest fry cooks.)

What then is the *reality* of reality TV?

Hoping to nail down *reality,* I made the risky move of consulting our unabridged *Webster's* dictionary. As I expected, the definition of reality is tricky—maddening even. The first definition: "The quality or state of being real." The definitions go on in a similar fashion until definition 2c, which states, "What actually exists: what has objective existence: what is not a mere idea: what is not imaginary, fictitious, or pretend." This definition clinches something important. While conventional television dramas are entirely pretend—mere ideas—the people on reality TV shows are real in the sense that they (probably) haven't spent years training to be on stage or behind a camera. In short, they're not actors in the artistic sense. They haven't studied moods and posture and tonality and craft and the thousands of other things that actors study. Instead, they've (probably) spent most of their lives like the rest of us—working day-to-day in some "objective existence" at some job we'd rather not have. They are folks who (probably) want another life—who are taking a momentary swing at something beyond their everyday lives. At least, that's the implied story of so many reality television shows. The con-

---

*Side notes (left margin):*

Allusions and explanations show a complexity to the shows.

Outside source gives public resonance to the previous testimony.

Specific allusions intensify the public resonance—and support the point about reality shows' unique quality.

A single crucial question!

Refers to the most complex aspect of the definition and explains how it sheds light on the concept.

*Side notes (right margin):*

They understand the rhetoric of the shows.

Like Heidecker, most people are ambivalent. They watch but don't want to?

A breakthrough point: The contestants are not practiced at being contestants. They are not imagined people.

testants are from the world we occupy. And they'll most likely return to it when the season ends, when the show gets canceled, when they get kicked off, sent home, chopped, voted out, fired, or whatever the case may be.

The heaviest analytical passage—which also contains the thesis of the essay.

Despite the ridiculous situations, the dopey and overcomplicated rules (that flash by us at the end of the show), reality television has something that viewers automatically sympathize with: the reality behind the characters—not the show itself but the world that the contestants belong to, the world that is unscripted, the world that will surround the contestants again. Maybe the reality part of reality shows is the unfilmed everyday life that bookends the episodes themselves. This reality lingers in the air each week and becomes increasingly palpable, increasingly real, as the season draws to a close.

So viewers always know, quietly, that real life awaits the contestants.

Alludes to the most popular example to support the point.

*American Idol* is the reigning champion of reality television. Every season, millions of callers dial in to make sure that the winners keep on winning, that losers keep on losing. The sheer number of calls gets at something critical about these shows: they're participatory. The shows are imbued with the life outside of them. Pop culture critic James Poniewozik explains, "Reality is more than a TV genre now. . . . It's everywhere. When Scott Brown won an upset Senate victory in Massachusetts, he was joined onstage by his daughter Ayla, an *American Idol* semifinalist from Season 5." He goes on to trace the trajectory of reality TV from mere entertainment to a kind of reality in itself: "In 1992, reality TV was a novelty. In 2000, it was a fad. In 2010, it's a way of life."

Reality TV is part of everyday life. It's as real as this building.

Uses the source to underscore the point made at the start of the passage.

Contrary examples (allusions to novels) show the particular nature of these shows and how they work on viewers (see page 146 for more on "contrary examples").

In the world of high art, such as literary fiction, the writer works to create a fictive dream—a coherent and impenetrable fantasy. The hope is that readers enter the dream and forget the real world. When we read a novel, for instance, our hopes become tied to Gatsby, Frodo, Ishmael, Antonia, Anna, and so on. We suspend our disbelief. And in turn, we are suspended in an ornate web of un-reality. But in reality television, part of the experience is the interplay between the fabricated scene (the kooky kitchen challenge limited to rutabagas and pig liver) and the invisible everyday lives of the contestants. We know that Angelo, if that is his real name, has a life beyond the one in *Top Chef.* And we know that he's probably, at least a little, like the guy we're watching. We know that the same dude making dim sum will be out on the highways, at the grocery store, at the local coffee shop, at the bar, and late to work right along with us. That's a captivating idea. The real and the fabricated are dancing together in our heads.

Reality TV isn't high art, but it's not simply trash either.

A more figurative way of expressing the thesis.

For viewers, this is a powerful aesthetic experience. We know that the contestants are from our world. Most likely, just before shooting the show and being told how to stand, whom to complain about, and what to wear, they were living normal lives. And when the show is over, they'll come back to the non-limelight, to this side of the screen. They'll go back to their own couches and watch their fabricated and edited selves. Maybe this is the appeal. Maybe reality TV attracts so many viewers because of its crafty intermingling of fiction and reality, its tug on the distinctly American belief "that everybody should have a shot. That sometimes being real is better than being polite. That no matter where you started out, you can hit it big, get lucky and reinvent yourself" (Poniewozik), or even that you can temporarily play the game and then go home again.

Some people proclaim self-righteously that reality television is a big hoax—that the winners are hand-selected, that the contestants have been carefully chosen to maximize viewing pleasure, and so on. But these spoilers are focused on the obvious. They're saying, "Look! It can't possibly be real!" And they're right—of course! *Hell's Kitchen, Top Chef, American Idol,* and all their cousins are not real*istic.* They're not real*ism.* They are reality television—a unique and weird phenomenon that is as much about the viewers and our world as anything.

*Yet another figurative way of expressing the complexity of the thesis.*

*Acknowledges and then counters those who might dismiss the complexity of the concept.*

*In fact, it's an aesthetic experience—not just a guilty pleasure.*

*We are the reality of reality TV.*

### Works Cited

Carter, Bill. "Tired of Reality TV, but Still Tuning In." *New York Times.* New York Times, 13 Sept. 2010. Web. 8 Jan. 2011.

Pew Research Center for the People & the Press. *Public Looks Back at Worst Decade in 50 Years: Internet, Cell Phones Are Changes for the Better.* Washington, 2009. Pew Research Center for the People & the Press. Web. 8 Jan. 2011.

Poniewozik, James. "Reality TV at 10: How It's Changed Television—and Us." *Time.* Time, 22 Feb. 2010. Web. 8 Jan. 2011.

"Reality." *Webster's Third International Unabridged Dictionary.* 3rd ed. 1993. Print.

# Writing Strategies

1. Explain what Heidecker reveals about reality television. What aspect of these shows does she help us understand?

2. How does Heidecker's personal testimony function in this essay?

3. Consider the paragraph about novels. How does Heidecker's point about literary fiction figure into the broader point about reality television?

4. In ¶8, Heidecker integrates a quotation by Poniewozik. Explain how the quotation helps support Heidecker's point about the "reality" of reality television.

# Exploring Ideas

1. Heidecker nudges readers beyond an easy judgment of reality television shows. Instead, she prompts us to consider the nature of their appeal. What else can be said about the nature of the appeal? Why else do you think millions of viewers tune in to reality television?

2. Heidecker explains that in reality television, "the real and the fabricated are dancing together in our heads." In your own words, how does this work? How does reality "dance with" the un-real aspects of the shows?

3. Heidecker explains that she and her husband "discuss the intricate appeals that *Top Chef* makes on our sympathies and the complex character development that works over an entire season." Do you have a program that works in a similar fashion on you? What show appeals to your sympathies? How does it work?

4. Given Heidecker's points, what do you think are the differences between realism, realistic, and reality television?

5. Do you have any guilty pleasures? Why do you feel guilty about them?

# Ideas for Writing

1. What concept is at the root of your favorite television show?

2. What do current reality television programs suggest about the concept *competition*?

If responding to one of these ideas, go to the Analysis section of this chapter to begin developing ideas for your essay.

# Outside Reading

Analyzing concepts is common work across academic disciplines. Writers in philosophy, education, psychology, history, sociology, economics, engineering, law, and even practical fields such as nursing explore shared concepts. They break down the layers or dimensions of concepts such as *self*, *community*, *learning*, *anxiety*, *pathology*, *currency*, *trade*, *balance*, *fairness*, *equality*, *individual right*, *assistance*, *power*, and so on. The discoveries writers make about such concepts help to define the purpose of their fields.

Focus on your academic major, or one you are considering, and find a journal or magazine article that analyzes a basic disciplinary concept. To conduct an electronic search of journals and magazines, go to your library's periodical database or to InfoTrac College Edition (available through your English CourseMate at www.cengagebrain.com). For your library database, perform a keyword search, or for InfoTrac College Edition, go to the main search box and choose "keywords." Experiment by typing in various concepts related to your chosen field.

Avoid using phrases or articles such as *a*, *an*, *the*; instead, use nouns separated by *and*. The results will yield lists of journal and magazine articles. After you find an article, apply the following questions:

1. What is the thesis, or main insight, of the article? Try to narrow in on the most revealing point the writer offers.

2. Describe how the writer goes beyond the obvious, beyond a cursory understanding of the concept. Point to passages in which the writer tries to reveal some complexity that wouldn't otherwise be seen.

3. Identify the major rhetorical strategies (such as narration, description, or figurative language). In other words, describe how the writer defends or supports the thesis.

4. Identify any passages in which the writer attempts to create public resonance. The writer might, for instance, try to connect the concept to some broader understanding or some broader social issue.

5. Finally, consider the audience. Who reads the particular publication? Why? Does the audience know certain things or care about certain issues? How does the writer tap into or connect with that knowledge or set of concerns?

# INVENTION

"What does it mean that success is as dangerous as failure? Whether you go up the ladder or down it, your position is shaky."

—Tao Te Ching

For the writing in this chapter, you must seek out meaning beyond your initial thoughts about a concept. The following sections are designed to help you through this process; specifically, to find a particular concept (in Point of Contact), to examine the concept closely (in Analysis), to make it relevant to a community of readers (in Public Resonance), to develop a focused point (in Thesis), and to develop support for that point (in Rhetorical Tools). The Invention questions in each section are not meant to be answered directly in your final essay. They are meant to prompt inventive thinking and intensive writing.

# Point of Contact

We carry concepts around with us and, for the most part, do not question them. But writers are willing to get underneath concepts that would otherwise go unquestioned. As you consider a possible topic, imagine the concepts that go unnoticed in your everyday life. To find a concept, investigate the world around you. Take a concept that goes unchallenged, uninspected. The following may prompt a possible topic:

- **Work:** Success, employment, boss, customer, profit, hours, wage, honesty, freedom, career, experience
- **School:** Education, study, discipline, learning, science, humanities, grade, teacher, student, intelligence
- **Home:** Parent, mother, father, pet, living room, divorce, values, God, marriage, privacy, faith
- **Public Life:** Friend, recreation, commitment, travel, woman, man, patriotism, romance, trash, environment
- **Sports:** Team, entertainment, audience, fan, loser, victory, competition
- **Your Major:** Someone majoring in education could analyze a concept such as learning, success, assessment, or high school. Your major itself might be seen as a concept. For example, engineering is a concept, and how one works in that field depends upon one's concept of it.

- **Television:** What does a local news program that devotes sixty seconds to world news and several minutes to sports suggest about news? What does *American Idol* suggest about America or idolatry? What does *The Real World* suggest about reality? What does *The Late Show* suggest about entertainment? What does a cell phone commercial suggest about freedom? What does an insurance commercial suggest about neighbors?

As you reflect on the program or commercial, ask yourself if the concept is somehow oversimplified or misrepresented. Or does the program or commercial fairly represent the concept? Remember that you are not evaluating the television program but rather using it to prompt an idea, to discover a concept that may need analysis and explanation.

## Activity

Imagine more concepts that define your everyday life. If this can be done in a small group, take turns offering concepts until each participant has chosen a potential topic.

# Do not limit yourself to familiar concepts. You might, in fact, choose a concept that is somewhat foreign to your experiences.

Museum: Phestus/MorgueFile; Clock: Caio Cassoli/StockXchng; Aeroplane: Library of Congress; African Mask: Laura Kennedy/StockXchng; "I Love You!" Paper: Cengage Learning

# Analysis

Analysis involves investigating particular parts, elements, or ideas within the whole. If we were to analyze an object, we might take it apart and look inside. We might, for instance, analyze a computer by opening the case and looking at the internal wires, the cards, and the connections. But when examining a concept, we cannot take off its cover and simply look inside—at least, not physically. Instead, we have to depend on intellectual inquiry. Rather than physical tools (screwdrivers or wrenches), we have to develop questions that get inside the abstraction. We have to ask questions that point to the particular elements of the concept. And the more particular we get, the more we're apt to discover. In other words, if we should try to understand the concept in the most narrow terms possible. For example, consider *college*. To analyze the concept, we must break it down and look at particular issues: What does college suggest for people's lives? Is it a time and place for learning specific skills or for exploring boundless ideas? Is it a place for making choices or for generating options? Such questions are analytical; they help to shed light on specific issues inside the broader, more abstract idea. As you look closely at the concept you have chosen, use the following Invention Questions to break it down:

▶ Specifically, how does your chosen concept influence or change people's lives?

▶ What particular emotions, behaviors, or ideas are associated with it?

▶ What hidden role does it play in everyday life?

▶ Are there complexities to the concept that people overlook? ■

In his invention writing, Simon Benlow looks closely at the particular qualities that define student and customer. He attempts to get at root behaviors and attitudes:

**How does it influence or change people's lives?**

I'm dealing with two concepts: "student" and "customer." "Customer" influences people to buy things and ideas, but the concept also makes people believe certain things about themselves—that they are better off only when they have obtained some thing or some service. It makes people lazy. When people totally buy into the consumer mentality, they feel as though they should be waited on, catered to, and dealt with, no matter what the circumstances. Being a student is the opposite—or at least, being a good student is the opposite. Students have to discover meaning and to struggle through their own biases, while customers hope to have their biases fed.

**What particular emotions, behaviors, or ideas are associated with it?**

When consumerist students come to college, they get angry and frustrated. Their expectations about institutions have been created, in large part, from their interactions with retail. They've been advertised and sold to for most of their lives. In college when the tables are turned, when they have to do all the discovering, all the inventing, all the developing, they are often freaked out.

Benlow then develops these ideas in his essay. (See the particular development in the first half of his essay on page 130.)

# Invention Workshop

As you consider the Invention Questions, avoid skimming the surface of broad ideas. Enlist the help of at least two other writers. Use one of the Invention questions to launch a focused discussion. As you address the question, try to avoid chatting aimlessly about the topic (which is always tempting!). Instead, follow new ideas that surface. For example, in the discussion below, Cassie discovers an important complexity to the concept *reality television:*

**Are there complexities to the concept that people overlook?**

DIANA:     Yeah, those shows aren't real. They're not reality at all. Everything is scripted and the characters are all predictable. There's the quiet, good-looking guy, the mean bitch that no one likes, the bully with big muscles, the ditz. It's like a cast of stereotypes.

CASSIE:     And it's great entertainment. People love watching. I think it's because the contestants are often rough around the edges. Some are rough in the middle too. But it's the lack of refinement that I like.

MICHAEL:   And because the contestants aren't actors. They're people. They have day jobs and families back home.

CASSIE:     You think people watch *American Idol* because the contestants have real lives?

MICHAEL:   Exactly. That's part of it. They have real lives. That's why they show the small hometown once they start whittling down the contestants. They show the bedroom, the street, the place waiting for them at the end of the season. The point is, these people have real lives.

DIANA:     Real lives. That's pretty funny. The reality is supposed to refer to the show, not the contestants.

CASSIE:     Well, maybe it's like Michael says. The reality of their lives—outside of the show itself—might be the key. That's the big attraction.

# Thinking Further

To explore further, writers look and listen for statements that bend away from the obvious. For example, in an Invention Workshop, Cassie begins to realize something beyond the simple distinction, realistic versus unrealistic. She can pursue the idea further by asking more questions:

- How are reality television shows different from scripted dramas?
- If reality television is still scripted and edited heavily, why do the shows feel so different from conventional programs?

Watch what happens when Cassie takes these questions and runs. She begins to discover something.

> **If reality television is still scripted and edited heavily, why do the shows feel essentially different from conventional programs?**
>
> On one hand, it feels like anything could happen. One of the characters might freak out or leave the show or cut her finger off. But realistically, viewers know that only a certain kind of anything will happen. Does that make sense? I mean, the shows we watch were likely filmed months beforehand and edited and tweaked. And I guess we know that at some level of thinking. (I'm trying to imagine myself watching *Top Chef* and thinking this way.) I know that a winner will be announced at a particular point, that a car chase isn't going to start up, that Jennifer isn't going to run into the room naked. In other words, the shows really are very predictable. But here's the thing: inside of that overall script are these contestants who could be the person next door. And as I'm watching the show (months after filming), most of those people have returned to their lives. They're real again. That's the catch. The people I'm watching are temporary celebrities and then full-time non-celebrities afterward. That's the weird attraction to it all. That's the "reality" of it.

Cassie is thinking further; she's doing the work of academic writing. She avoids simple answers and easy responses. Her thinking is increasingly complex—and it yields a sophisticated analysis essay. (See page 133.) As you consider your own topic, explore your Invention Writing. Look for statements that seem unusual, that bend away from the obvious, and then generate probing questions of your own.

# Public Resonance

It is up to the writer to make a concept relevant to readers. At some level, your concept already resonates with others, because a concept is, by definition, beyond particulars. Whether it is *reality, college,* or *student,* a concept necessarily involves others. Still, a concept is not always entirely understood—even by those who would, presumably, understand it. Consider *freedom:* As Americans, we often speak of it, sing about it, and even go to war over it, but do most Americans really understand the concept? Even though freedom is part of our collective language, we might not realize its complexities and meaning. As you consider the social significance of your own topic, use the following questions:

▶ Is the concept generally agreed upon?

▶ Why is it important that people have an appropriate understanding of this concept?

▶ Does the concept need to be rethought? Why?

▶ What is the possible connection between the topic and some public concern? ∎

If you choose not to directly state the public resonance of your concept, answering these questions serves another goal—to help you envision the relationship between your audience and your topic. In thinking about the public resonance of your chosen concept, you may come across your *purpose*—the reason you are writing. If you believe that the concept is often misunderstood, then the purpose of your analysis might be to educate your audience. Or if your concept is overlooked, the purpose may be to elevate the status of the concept in your reader's mind.

In the following excerpt, Simon Benlow discovers why *student,* as a concept, is necessary and why people should rethink it. Benlow could have given up early in his exploration. He could have merely stopped with "education will suffer." Instead, he tries to imagine specific effects, and in doing

so, he further draws out the difference between customer and student:

**Is the concept generally agreed upon?**
No! That's the whole problem. Many students don't know what it means to be a student.

**Why is it important that people have an appropriate understanding of this concept?**
If college students really understand what it means to be a student (and not a consumerist student), their experience at college will be defined by self-discovery and enlightenment rather than petty frustration and grumbling. If colleges across America continue to confuse "student" with "consumer," education will suffer. Much of the time spent in college will be on customer service (keeping students happy) rather than challenging their beliefs, developing their minds, and broadening their horizons. Customers ultimately do not want their ideas about themselves to change; they want products and services to support what they think. If college continues down the present path, it is not hard to imagine colleges being devoid of genuinely new ideas.

Benlow's essay grows out of this thinking—out of concern for the potential harm to students and higher education.

We can see Benlow's initial thoughts most directly in the essay's conclusion (page 131):

There is no way higher education can counter the incredible momentum of consumerist culture. It is far more pervasive than the discourses of physics or composition studies. However, if we continue to allow the term "customer" to replace "student," I fear that students will become increasingly blind to the difference between consumerist culture and college culture.

# Thesis

You probably have many different things to say about your topic, but your project will gain focus and intensity with a thesis statement, a single claim that expresses your particular view on the concept. Look over your notes from the Analysis and Public Resonance sections. Find a theme or pattern running through those notes and try to articulate that idea in a sentence. Your project might:

- **Explain how particular parts or qualities make up a concept.**
  —Maturity involves both recognition of past failures and attempts to retune behavior with those failures in mind.
  —Punk rock involves an explicit and dramatic disdain for common wisdom, popular aesthetic, and accepted manners.

- **Reveal a side or layer of a concept that normally goes unnoticed.**
  —Health is not simply an internal condition but a sound relationship between body and an immediate environment.
  —Behind the common image of trees, lakes, and loose critters, *nature* is a verb—an unyielding cyclical process.

- **Show a quality that distinguishes one concept from another.**
  —Contrary to the passive, personalizing, self-perpetuating, desire-driven customer, students are encouraged to be active. (Benlow)
  —Childhood is not pre-adulthood but an existence fundamentally distinct and characterized by a peculiar mixture of wonder and fear.

- **Explain the inner workings of a concept.**
  —Formal education and therefore educators function as one of the primary authorities in defining proper intellectual behavior and the path to work. (Petra Pepellashi)
  —In today's use of the term, *patriotism* demands a persistent turning away from self-evaluation.

## Evolution of a Thesis

Remember that a thesis does not materialize out of thin air. It develops over time. It may involve a long process of reflection and discussion. And often, a good thesis emerges only after a writer has thoroughly analyzed the topic. Consider the example from the Analysis section, in which Cassie's topic, reality television, is developed through a discussion. Her thesis evolves slowly as she tries to get a handle on the complexity of the idea:

- Reality television is not real in the sense that anything could happen.
- Reality television contains both highly edited fiction and some unscripted reality.
- We watch reality television because we understand that the contestants are, for the most part, real people.
- The reality part of reality shows is the unfilmed everyday life that bookends the episodes themselves.

As you consider your own thesis, remember that narrower statements yield more interesting writing. At first, you might think, "I can't possibly write more than a paragraph about something so narrow." However, the process of developing the ideas will generate content for your writing. And the more focused thesis will help you illustrate particular points rather than listing many marginally related issues.

### Revising Your Thesis

After you have developed a single statement, take time to reconsider: What do people normally say or assume about the concept? How have you complicated or enriched the common way of thinking?

# Rhetorical Tools

## Examples

Each writer in this chapter puts forth a particular way of seeing a concept, and each must support that way of seeing with scenarios (hypothetical accounts), allusions (references to bits of public knowledge), and examples. Because analyzing concepts requires abstract thinking, writers must be extra careful to illustrate points with concrete examples. In his essay, Benlow uses a detailed scenario to illustrate his concept of *student:*

> In higher education, principles establish how a discipline works. Physics works on principles of matter and energy. The goal of a physicist is to discover the principles and understand how they can be used. Composition works on principles—conventions of grammar and persuasion. This is not to say that all knowledge is prescribed. On the contrary, students in such classes are encouraged to invent, to break rules, to go beyond. But in order to do so, they need certain ground rules; they need to understand that certain principles exist in the world outside of their own desires. (One cannot do chemistry and simply dismiss algebra because it is distasteful.)

In some cases, writers may use details to illustrate how *not* to conceptualize an idea. They use **contrary examples** (situations or accounts that show the opposite of the writer's point). For example, Benlow uses contrary examples in several paragraphs to show consumerist mentality—the opposite of his way of conceptualizing *student.* And Cassie Heidecker uses contrary examples to help her distinguish between genuine fiction and reality television:

> In the world of high art, such as literary fiction, the writer works to create a fictive dream—a coherent and impenetrable fantasy. The hope is that readers enter the dream and forget the real world. When we read a novel, for instance, our hopes become tied to Gatsby, Frodo, Ishmael, Antonia, Anna, and so on. We suspend our disbelief. And in turn, we are suspended in an ornate web of un-reality. But in reality television, part of the experience is the interplay between the fabricated scene (the kooky kitchen challenge limited to rutabagas and pig liver) and the invisible everyday lives of the contestants.

The contrary examples (which are actually allusions to literature) help her to narrow in on particular elements about her topic. They allow Heidecker to draw clear intellectual lines—to demarcate what something is and what it is not.

Often it is not enough to simply mention an example. A powerful and convincing strategy is to explain in detail *how* an example or allusion reveals something relevant. For example, Benlow does not simply mention consumerist slogans; he gives detailed explanations of their significance:

> "The customer is always right." We hear this hollow phrase resound through (almost) every corridor of our consumerist culture. The motive behind the phrase is painfully clear—to keep customers happy, to keep them from complaining, and most importantly, to keep them coming back. . . . The phrase is meant to maintain a climate in which the substance of anyone's concerns or complaints is obfuscated by friendly and diplomatic clichés. . . . Ultimately, then, the goal of customer service, in this sense, is to lull customers into a sense of complacency—even though their phones may not be working or their washers are throwing sparks.

## Definitions and References

Sometimes a dictionary definition supports a writer's take on a concept. Or in Heidecker's case, a definition actually helps to make an important distinction:

> **What then is the *reality* of reality TV?**
> Hoping to nail down reality, I made the risky move of consulting our big Webster's dictionary. As I expected, the definition of *reality* is tricky—maddening even. The first definition: "The quality or state of being real." The definitions go on in a similar fashion until definition 2c, which states: "What actually exists: what has objective existence: what is not a mere idea: what is not imaginary, fictitious, or pretend." This definition clinches something important. While conventional television dramas are

entirely pretend—ideas only—the identities on reality TV shows are real in the sense that they (probably) haven't spent years training to be on stage or behind a camera.

Derrick Jensen does not consult a common dictionary but, instead, goes to a specialized reference book, which gives him a list of particular qualities and behaviors for his topic. In fact, it is the "*Classification of Mental and Behavioural Disorders,* published by the World Health Organization," that helps Jensen explain the real complexity of his topic. For both Heidecker and Jensen, the official definitions (of *reality* and *sociopath*) help to open up the ideas and reveal important dimensions.

As you consider your topic, apply the following rhetorical tools to help show increasingly complex dimensions of the concept.

- ▶ **Examples:** What specific examples in everyday life illustrate my point about the concept?
- ▶ **Contrary Examples:** What programs, ads, or other examples from everyday life illustrate an inappropriate or oversimplified way of understanding the concept?
- ▶ **Scenarios:** What hypothetical account could demonstrate the concept?
- ▶ **Allusions:** What person or event from history, current events, popular culture, or literature illustrates the point about the concept? ■

## Invention Workshop

In small groups, collectively develop support for one another's projects. Each writer should announce his or her thesis to the group. Each group member then should offer at least one response to each of the following questions:

1. What specific examples in everyday life illustrate the writer's point?
2. Name something from popular culture (such as a television show, a movie, an advertising campaign) that illustrates the writer's point. Explain how the writer could allude to it.
3. Name something from history (a person, an event, a trend) that reveals or supports something about the writer's point.

4. Explain how the writer's point is different from how people normally think about the concept.

As the group members offer ideas, the writer should record the group members' responses so they can be integrated later.

## Outside Sources

Writers are often surprised to find how many others have addressed their topics and explored the same intellectual pathways. On one hand, outside sources can help a writer substantiate points, and on the other, can help to add dimension—create intellectual twists and turns. Notice how Cassie Heidecker uses sources in both ways. In the first passage, she cites a Pew poll that adds public resonance to her personal reaction to reality television. In the second, she uses a quotation from a cultural critic who supports her own sophisticated claim:

> And we're not alone. Despite the results of a Pew Research Center poll indicating that 63% of the American public thinks that reality TV shows signal our cultural decline, the ratings continue to climb. In fact, "What viewers say they want and what they really watch are not the same" (Carter).
>
> The sheer number of calls gets at something critical about these shows: they're participatory. The shows are imbued with the life outside of them. Pop culture critic James Poniewozik explains, "Reality is more than a TV genre now. . . . It's everywhere. When Scott Brown won an upset Senate victory in Massachusetts, he was joined onstage by his daughter Ayla, an *American Idol* semifinalist from Season 5." He goes on to trace the trajectory of reality TV from mere entertainment to a kind of reality in itself: "In 1992, reality TV was a novelty. In 2000, it was a fad. In 2010, it's a way of life."

Heidecker illustrates a common move when using outside sources. She begins her paragraphs with her own assertion—her own understanding of the topic. She brings in the outside source, then, to reinforce a complex idea that she has already begun describing. (For more guidance on integrating ideas from sources, see Chapter 15: Integrating and Documenting Sources.)

# Organizational Strategies

## How Should I Begin?

Introductions depend on the tone or level of formality of the writing situation. (See more on level of formality on page 116.) An analytical text written for a government agency or a corporate entity would begin formally, perhaps with a general discussion about the concept. In less formal situations, introductions vary widely, and the primary goal is to capture the reader's attention, to provoke a sense of curiosity. Among many others, here are three consistent and effective strategies:

**Describe the common view,** which you later correct or oppose. Heidecker begins with a common view and then spends the rest of her essay dealing with and complicating that view:

> Reality television is a unique form of reality. It's not really real. (Everyone knows that, right?) After all, reality shows have theme music, background sounds, an engaging host, a narrator, sizzling graphics, and makeup artists. The shows are edited so that dialogue is framed and situated for maximum effect. Whatever the contestants say seems snappy, targeted, deliberate, or perfectly stupid. The shows have scenes with pitch-perfect tension, climax, and resolution. But real life has none of these. Real life is mostly boring, uselessly noisy, stagnant, uncertain, ill-defined, repetitive, hopelessly dumb, and sometimes it's quietly and privately beautiful. Such things can't be filmed and put on television for mass viewing.

**Re-create the point of contact.** Explain how you first encountered the idea. This is often more informal, since it requires some personal narration, as in Derrick Jensen's introduction:

> I don't know about you, but whenever I attend some "green" conference, I know I'm supposed to leave feeling inspired and energized, but instead I feel heartbroken, discouraged, defeated, and lied to. It's not the inevitable talk about farmers (re)discovering organic farming; about plastic forks made from cornstarch; about solar photovoltaics; about relocalizing; about the joys of simple living; about grieving the murder of the planet; about "changing our stories"; and most especially about maintaining a positive attitude that gets me down. It's that no one, and I mean no one, ever mentions psychopathology. Why is this important? Because those in power destroy sustainable communities—and not just sustainable indigenous communities.

Benlow makes a similar move. His essay begins with the event that provoked his need to write:

> Two weeks ago, the faculty and staff received a memo regarding "National Customer Service Week." We were urged to take special efforts in serving our customers—presumably, our students.

**Begin with a popular reference.** Writers often invite readers into their ideas by alluding to something in popular culture, such as a television program, an advertisement, a song, or a current event. This strategy instantly creates public resonance. It allows readers to enter the world of the essay through a familiar door. In an essay about conspiracy, for instance, a writer might begin with an allusion to a popular show from the 1990s, *The X-Files:*

> The popular program *The X-Files* stokes our suspicions of and paranoia about the government. It invites us to imagine a vast network of officials, heads of state, military groups, and secret agencies making deals with aliens. Doctors, scientists, politicians, FBI agents, and numbers of spies all share covert plans, meet in smoky, quiet rooms, and plan the future of all humans. It's great entertainment. But conspiracies are often more nuanced, less concocted, less dramatic than what *The X-Files* suggests.

## When Should I Change Paragraphs?

Remember that paragraphs are tools for directing a reader's progress. Paragraphs stop the reader and refocus his or her attention on the next point. Jensen uses paragraphs to clearly separate different aspects of sociopathic behavior. In his case, the different aspects lend themselves well to separate development. But some topics are not so easily parsed out. Some topics, or some insights about some topics, have not been delineated. Paragraphs, then, become an organizational tool for the writer's thinking. Heidecker, for instance, uses paragraphs to slowly move readers further into the concept—explaining with each step (paragraph) the differences between reality television and other types of entertainment.

Paragraphs can also be used to separate specific support strategies. A writer might use paragraphs to separate several examples. Simon Benlow, for instance, dedicates four of his first five paragraphs to a particular element of the consumerist culture. These writers all use paragraphs to refocus the reader on a new ingredient or element in the discussion.

Paragraph breaks generally accomplish the following:

- Change from analyzing one element or quality to another.
- Shift from a common view to a new or uncommon view of the topic.
- Move from one support strategy (such as allusion) to another (such as scenario).
- Transfer from the past to the present.

# How Should I Conclude?

As with introductions, the possibilities for conclusions are limitless. Short explanatory essays (under 1,000 words) usually do not need to summarize main points. Instead, writers often use conclusions to suggest the significance of the ideas expressed in the body of the essay. Consider the strategies used by the authors in this chapter. Jensen ends with public resonance—and even a kind of argumentative call to action:

> Sharing our finite planet with this culture is like being stuck in a room with a psychopath. There is no exit. Although the psychopath may choose other targets first, eventually it will turn to us. Eventually we'll have to fight for our lives. And so if we want access to a landbase we can inhabit, and want our descendants to be able to live there long into the future, we need to organize politically to stop this lethal culture in its tracks.

Benlow makes a similar, but slightly more subtle, move:

> However, if we continue to allow the term "customer" to replace "student," I fear that students will become increasingly blind to the difference between consumerist culture and college culture. I fear they will become increasingly more confused by the expectations of college, and that in the nightmarish long run, colleges will become simply another extension of the consumerist machine in which everyone is encouraged to pre-package knowledge, to super-size grades, and to "hold" anything even slightly distasteful.

Caution: The explicit call to action—or fear of not acting, in Benlow's case—can move the project away from analysis and toward overt argumentation. And when the argumentative quality gets too heated, the analytical thinking can, sometimes, suffer. But Jensen's and Benlow's essays are primarily focused on analysis. The concluding passages emerge from an intense analytical inspection.

Heidecker also veers toward argument at the beginning of her conclusion. She takes on an opposing view, but then pulls the focus back toward her main insight. (Beginning in Chapter 7, we will call this move counterargument.)

> Some people proclaim self-righteously that reality television is a big hoax—that the winners are hand-selected, that the contestants have been carefully chosen to maximize viewing pleasure, and so on. But these spoilers are focused on the obvious. They're saying, "Look! It can't possibly be real!" And they're right—of course! *Hell's Kitchen, Top Chef, American Idol,* and all their cousins are not real*istic.* They're not real*ism.* They are reality television—a unique and weird phenomenon that is as much about the viewers and our world as anything.

Each strategy is different but effective. None of the writers in this chapter wastes time summarizing or "wrapping up" points that have already been made. Instead, they use their conclusions to extend their points into the reader's world (by scenarios, direct appeals, or examples).

# Writer's Voice

A writer's voice can make the reading experience formal or relaxed, rigorous or casual. Remember that a casual voice does not necessarily mean casual thinking. A very sophisticated analysis can be presented in a casual manner. For instance, Benlow approaches the fast food, customer service issue on its own terms. He borrows the phrases and the lowbrow tone of drive-through culture:

> In the old days, we had to pull up to the drive-thru board, search under "Sandwiches" and THEN go through the labor of exploring "Sides" and "Beverages." It was all too much. Now, we can simply pull up, and say a number. We don't even have to trouble ourselves with uttering all the stuff we want to eat. We just say, "#1 with a diet." The meal deal craze is, of course, not limited to fast food; it is, simply, most explicitly manifested in the fast food industry.

You may detect a slight shift in the last sentence—where Benlow pulls away from the drive-through language and makes a broader point about society. In this sense, Benlow's voice ebbs and flows. It adopts the casual language of consumption and then snaps, in some respects, at those same casual-sounding phrases.

This raises an important aspect of voice, or voicing: it is far more complex than discovering a single, personal, or genuine sound. In our everyday lives, as in speech, we often shift in subtle ways, borrowing tones and phrases from popular culture, academic culture, business, entertainment, and politics. We fuse those elements into our own tongues—and it all ends up sounding like us, like the single person speaking. (But don't be fooled! Voice is often, or always, filled with the subtle tones of others.)

## Activity

Closely examine the following passage from Heidecker's essay. How would you describe the voice?

> My husband and I watch culinary reality shows like *Hell's Kitchen* and *Top Chef.* We're embarrassed about it. We don't tell our friends. These shows are trash TV and we don't think of ourselves as trash TV people. But when we watch (when we literally run down from our respective work or domestic duties and avoid the phone for that ridiculous hour), we stay glued to the situation. We laugh in all the places we're supposed to laugh. We holler at all the appropriate moments. We laugh at ourselves laughing. We are the unapologetic groundlings at a Shakespearean drama. We yell at the lecherous old men, the conniving women, the smug adolescents, the deceit, the flawed personalities, the near misses, and the moments of predictable victory.

## Using Figurative Language

Figurative language, such as similes and metaphors, does more than support an idea. It also adds tonality to a writer's voice. Because figurative language transforms or bends the usual meaning of words and phrases, it should bend toward the nature of the writer's voice: sobering, comic, condemning, hopeful, absurd. In other words, the nature of a simile or metaphor directly impacts how the voice sounds to readers. For instance, the first simile below would likely create a casual or even slightly humorous tone and the second, a more sophisticated or lofty tone:

> Hardcore punk singers are like public belchers—guys, primarily, with digestion problems and microphones.

> Hardcore punk singers are like angry court jesters, calling attention to their own raucous behavior while slipping in serious social commentary.

# Using Allusions

Allusions are references to some public bit of knowledge (such as a historical event, a political situation, or a popular culture figure). An allusion can give a personal essay a broader and more public feeling while developing its ideas. But allusions can also help create voice. The allusions one chooses contribute to the voice created in the essay.

For example, the following allusion helps to characterize Benlow's voice—especially early in the essay when he sounds intolerant of customer life. The nature of the allusion (to a fairly unimportant matter like fast food) helps Benlow to trivialize consumer culture and appear slightly above it.

> "Have it your way!" Of course, we all know the song and the friendly fried food establishment associated with this slogan. It's a harmless phrase, in and of itself, and one that works particularly well for the franchise. It suggests to customers that their particular appetites can be catered to, that their specific tastes, no matter how eccentric (within the continuum of dip n' serve fried food) can be easily satisfied.

Heidecker uses a range of allusions. The references to popular (and low-brow) television programs impact how readers hear her voice. But Heidecker complicates things a bit when she alludes to a series of novels—such as *The Great Gatsby, Lord of the Rings, Moby Dick, My Antonia,* and *Anna Karenina:*

> In the world of high art, such as literary fiction, the writer works to create a fictive dream—a coherent and impenetrable fantasy. The hope is that readers enter the dream and forget the real world. When we read a novel, for instance, our hopes become tied to Gatsby, Frodo, Ishmael, Antonia, Anna, and so on. We suspend our disbelief. And in turn, we are suspended in an ornate web of un-reality. But in reality television, part of the experience is the interplay between the fabricated scene (the kooky kitchen challenge limited to rutabagas and pig liver) and the invisible everyday lives of the contestants.

# Promoting Curiosity

One of the primary jobs of a writer is to pique curiosity in readers. Very rarely does a writer (in any situation) seek only to tell readers what they are already thinking. Instead, writers seek to light a small fire in readers' minds, to make them want to *consider* an issue. Perhaps the most important strategy for promoting curiosity is to embody it, that is, to be curious as a writer. Curious writers make curious readers. In the following passage, from a well-known essay by Pico Iyer, the writer's own curiosity about the world drives the analysis. Iyer himself seems curious about—even awed by—language. He seems to be totally unafraid of his own imagination:

> Punctuation is the notation in the sheet music of our own words, telling us when to rest, or when to raise our voices; it acknowledges that the meaning of our discourse, as of any symphonic composition, lies not in the units but in the pauses, the pacing, and the phrasing.

The person we detect through the language seems full of wonder. And it is not only the content of the passage; notice also the sentence structure. He uses long sentences to keep the reader in his perspective (as though he is holding us underwater without a breath). As you consider your voice, ask yourself the following:

▶ What uncommon details reveal my point about the concept?

▶ Can I avoid telling the reader that something is "interesting," "exciting," and so on, and instead create images or use examples that show it?

▶ Can I use metaphors to make the reader see the intensity or scope or depth of the concept?

▶ Can I show the reader a new way to see an everyday phenomenon? ■

# Vitality

Filling up pages is easy. But good writers avoid filling. They are careful with their readers' minds. (Sentences, after all, are the only conduit between a writer's thoughts and a reader's life.) Consider the following strategies for making your final text more lively and intense.

## Avoid Clichés

Clichés are tired, worn-out phrases. We hear them constantly in everyday life. We use them when there is nothing else left to say—or to make it seem like there is nothing else left to say. We read them on greeting cards, hear them in popular songs or political speeches, and even share them in casual conversations. Think of all the times you have heard these phrases:

> You don't know what you have until it's gone.
>
> We should expand our horizons.
>
> Follow your dreams.
>
> Anything is possible.
>
> Children are the future.
>
> I believe in my heart that . . .
>
> Hang in there.
>
> Discover who you are as a person.
>
> People are entitled to their own opinions.
>
> Whatever will be will be.
>
> Reach for the stars.
>
> Think outside the box.
>
> Everyone is different.
>
> Different strokes for different folks.
>
> It's all just water under the bridge.
>
> Fight the good fight.

Or even consider smaller phrases that get plugged into sentences but rarely get inspected:

> the real world
>
> hard work
>
> the good life
>
> family values
>
> the American people
>
> today's society
>
> common sense

The list goes on and on. Such common phrases are not tools for thinking—they are substitutes for thinking. Because they have been used repeatedly and in so many different contexts, their meaning has been emptied.

Clichés blur complex thinking. They actually hide the possibility of further thought and block genuine analysis. For instance, notice the thinking that might go on behind this cliché: We should expand our horizons.

> What are horizons? How do they form? Are horizons imposed on us, or do we adopt them ourselves? If they are imposed by others, can we simply choose to expand them or do we have to break some rule? How do we know when a horizon expands? What experiences or voices or situations make them expand? Are we just as likely to shrink our horizons? Isn't that human nature? What kind of action broadens our understanding? Is it just a new experience or something else?

All of these questions suggest the complexity behind the idea. But rather than promote hard thinking, clichés invite writers and readers (both!) into quiet, unreflective agreement. In a sense, clichés are strategies for quieting the mind—the opposite goal of academic writing.

## Activity

In a small group, develop a list of clichés. Share this list with the whole class to create a comprehensive list of phrases to avoid.

# Avoid Stilted Language

If clichés are the common, overused phrases of the day, stilted language is the opposite—an overly elaborate jungle of clauses and phrases. Stilted language is unnecessarily elevated—and like a person walking on stilts, it makes the ideas slow and wobbly. For example:

*Writer A:*

People, in every walk of this big life, should query themselves about the direction of their occupational goals. And they should do this persistently, both before entering into a projected career path and while enduring the veritable ins and outs of said career path. Is it not fitting to examine the very essence of such matters, which would otherwise remain beyond our consciousness in the mundane existence of work? Certainly, we should endeavor to explore the cracks and folds of our lives and thereby free ourselves of any unknown shackles.

Here, the ideas are vague because they are stretched out over unnecessary, but pretty, phrases. The writer injects strings of needless constructions ("in every walk of this big life," "the very essence of such matters") and elaborate language ("their occupational goals," "mundane existence of work") that inflate the importance of the ideas. Writer A also mingles two competing metaphors at the end of the passage. As readers, we are left exploring the "cracks and folds" while

also freeing ourselves from "unknown shackles." Notice a less stilted approach:

*Writer B:*

Before entering a job, people should ask themselves if it fits their broader career plans. Even after working at a job for months or years, people should return to this question. Otherwise, the workaday lifestyle can prompt us to believe that a present career path is the best—the one that we should continue to walk.

Writer B does use a metaphor at the end, but it works here because it does not compete with other figurative language in the same sentence. Now that the ideas are less ornate, they seem less overwhelming. In fact, stated more plainly, the ideas appear rather ordinary (and this might even prompt a writer to explore the ideas further).

These passages reveal two major problems with stilted language: (1) It jumbles ideas so that readers are left guessing or wondering, and (2) it inflates ideas so that they seem beyond exploration. Writers and readers should not be impressed with ornate language but rather with intense ideas.

## Activity

Who can conjure the most stilted passage? Write a stilted paragraph, one that dresses up an idea in ornate wordiness, competing metaphors, and lofty sentences. And then write a more tame, less ornate version. Share both versions with the class.

# Revision

Revision is the most difficult step for many writers. We have to genuinely face what we've said and analyze rigorously. We have to take apart what feels complete, finished, and sealed up. If we analyze well, we may find passages that work better than others—those that better support the thesis and those that veer away or simply repeat a bland point. Also, the closer we look, the less apt we are to make generalizations: *It all works. The whole thing is terrible.* Before you pass your draft to review, give it one last read and decide for yourself which passages are the most supportive, which are the most focused and intense, which are the least focused, the least vitalized.

## Peer Review

Exchange drafts with at least one other writer. Before passing your draft to others, underline the thesis, or write it above your essay. This way, reviewers will get traction as they read.

As a reviewer, use the following questions to guide your response.

1. Which words or phrases in the thesis could be more focused?
2. Point out passages or sentences that could use more specific illustration. Suggest an example from everyday life that illustrates the writer's point. For example, in an essay about athletics, you might read:

   Athletics are the great motivator of many students. Without sports, many would not feel compelled to attend school at all.

   You might suggest that "the great motivator" could be illustrated more specifically.

3. Suggest an allusion (to popular culture, literature, or history) that illustrates the writer's point. Rather than accept claims as they are, help the writer make a connection to some other time, place, or text so that the concept (whatever it is) connects to a broader set of ideas.

4. The writer might rely on a dictionary to get started, but the ideas should extend beyond that definition. (Hopefully, the essay takes you beyond a definition that you could easily look up yourself.) Where do you feel that "liftoff" away from a standard definition? If there is no liftoff, where might the writer concentrate attention? If you can, offer a path beyond the definition.
5. Consider the paragraphs: Do they focus on one specific point? Point to any paragraphs that seem to stray into several ideas.
6. In which passages does the writer's voice seem most engaging? (Where do you feel yourself, as a reader, most inspired by the ideas?) Why?
7. Referring to the Vitality section in this chapter, and previous chapters, point to particular sentences and phrases that could gain intensity.

## Questions for Research

If the writer used outside sources,

- Where must he or she include in-text citations? (See pages 470–471.)
- Are quotations blended smoothly into the argument and punctuated correctly? (See pages 456–468.)
- Where could more direct textual cues or transitions help the reader? (See pages 466–467.)
- Is the Works Cited page formatted properly? (See pages 469–480.)

# Reflection

As we say in the chapter introduction, "Writers are willing to get underneath concepts that would otherwise go unquestioned." In this sense, academic writers are not simply reporting information or expressing personal opinions. They are excavating, digging, sneaking into intellectual alleys and exploring the cultural trash bins. They are revealing the quiet, sometimes loud and obnoxious, complexities of everyday life.

Now that you've invented, written, revised, and edited a project, you probably have a much deeper understanding of the concept. To draw out that understanding, write a final reflective essay that addresses the following questions:

- How did you get beneath a concept?
- What was the most revelatory insight? Was it your thesis?
- What was your most powerful supporting passage? What does it accomplish?
- How does your project explore the intellectual back roads and alleys? How does it go behind the conventional, obvious ways of thinking about the concept?
- Given what you've written, will readers think or behave differently?
- What might be the benefits to others? How might others be impacted?

## Beyond the Essay: Conceptual Mapping

A conceptual map is a graphic presentation of ideas. Using words, shapes, lines, even photographs, the creator of a conceptual map attempts to depict the complexity of ideas—how they relate, what they mean in relation to other ideas. This strategy is well suited for illustrating the various layers of a concept. For instance, in the image that opens this chapter, a conceptual map depicts cyberspace.

Now that you have taken a concept, broken it down, examined its parts and layers, and explored how it works, draw your understanding.

- Try to depict the complexity of your ideas using only key words or phrases from your essay.
- Graphically show how those words and phrases relate.
- Use lines, arrows, and other shapes to depict the relationship between ideas.
- Use colors (if possible) to group ideas or to distinguish between types of ideas.

Present your conceptual map to others. Explain how the map represents the complexity of the ideas in your essay. Also explain how the map reinforces or falls short of the essay.

---

See the opening image for this chapter. This conceptual map, designed by Nathan Shedroff for Cyber Geography, represents the relationships in cyberspace: With the placement of each term, line, and graphic, the designer suggests particular connections. Notice, for instance, that one of the outer spheres is "time," and it turns in tandem with "read." This suggests that time, in cyberspace, is dependent on the act of reading. This interesting relationship is part of Shedroff's particular conceptualization.

 For additional resources including instructional videos and links to helpful websites, access your English CourseMate through cengagebrain.com.

# 6 Analyzing Images

# Chapter Contents

# "At the speed of light, policies and political parties yield place to the charismatic images."

—Marshall McLuhan

Mainstream life in the United States is deluged with images—not random pictures and photographs, but carefully selected images designed to influence what we think and how we feel. Drawings, computer graphics, digitized photos, and airbrushed faces surround us. The minute details of each appeal to our values, desires, needs, and assumptions. And even after the image itself is gone and its immediate appeal is behind us, it still influences how we see the rest of the world.

There is no doubt about it: The barrage of images in our culture dramatically influences how we think, how we live, what we value, what we believe. But are we victims of everything we see? Is each advertisement, poster, graphic, and illustration another intellectual demand? Can we do more than see and accept? What value is gained from seeing inside the workings of images? Living in an image-soaked culture prompts such questions. Especially since most of the images we encounter were designed to influence our thinking, such questions may be vital.

As images in consumer society become increasingly sophisticated, consumers need to become more sophisticated seers. We'll then be more able to see what things are about—and what else they are about. When we break down an image, we can better understand how it works, how it conveys meaning, how it conceals values and beliefs. And we can also better understand how that image relates to the world around it. In short, the more analytical we become, the more we see.

Analysis is the act of breaking down something to its basic elements and attempting to understand something of value in the process. Therefore, analyzing images involves breaking down the elements of an image and understanding how those elements convey ideas and feelings, how they work on the consciousness of the viewer, how they speak to a surrounding culture, and how they resonate with surrounding values and beliefs.

At first glance, images might seem simple, coherent, and impenetrable. However, even the most simplistic image has rhetorical tools, strategies

Used by permission of the author

for persuading readers of some idea. For example, the advertisements above were displayed in the window of a health food store.

The poster on the far left relies on the image of a young woman. She is sassy and vibrant. She asserts herself outward. The image connects the product and health with youth, vitality, and even a fashionable hairstyle and makeup. The poster on the right features a sunflower, a symbol of nature and purity. The sunflower, along with the promotion for a "new look," sits on a green background, which helps convey newness and freshness.

Such details are no accidents. They are closely scrutinized and are meant to impact consciousness in particular ways. But even if they were accidents, the particular elements impact readers. The particulars help convey ideas, assumptions, and values. Any detail, a streak of sunlight through an image or the reflection of a passing car, may also create an effect—whether the artist intended it or not. Regardless of the intent, we should be cognizant of the way details, the minute and the marginal, figure into the meaning of the image.

This chapter will help you analyze a particular image, develop focused explanation, and communicate your ideas in writing. Specifically, the goal is to explain how the elements of an image work to impact the feelings and consciousness of viewers. The following essays will provide valuable insight into various analytical strategies. After reading the essays, you can find an image in one of two ways:

1. Go to the Point of Contact section to find a topic from your everyday life, or
2. Choose one of the Ideas for Writing that follow the essays.

After finding a subject, go to the Analysis section to begin developing the evaluation.

# Rise of the Image Culture: Re-Imagining the American Dream

**Elizabeth Thoman**

Americans are so used to watching TV that they take the commercials for granted and don't consider the impact these images have on their lives. As Elizabeth Thoman, founder of *Media & Values* magazine, says, "Each commercial plays its part in selling an overall consumer lifestyle." Throughout her essay, Thoman explains how television commercials have become fused with the patterns and habits of everyday life and how that fusion might be staved off with a new critical awareness.

Like most middle-class children of the '50s, I grew up looking for the American Dream. In those days there were no cartoons in my Saturday viewing, but I distinctly remember watching, with some awe, *Industry on Parade.* I felt both pride and eager anticipation as I watched tail-finned cars rolling off assembly lines, massive dams taming mighty rivers and sleek chrome appliances making life more convenient for all.

When I heard the mellifluous voice of Ronald Reagan announce on *GE Theatre* that "Progress is our most important product," little did I realize that the big box in our living room was not just entertaining me. At a deeper level, it was stimulating an "image" in my head of how the world should work: that anything new was better than something old; that science and technology were the greatest of all human achievements and that in the near future—and certainly by the time I grew up—the power of technology would make it possible for everyone to live and work in a world free of war, poverty, drudgery, and ignorance.

I believed it because I could see it—right there on television.

The American Dream, however, was around long before television. Some believe the idea of "progress" goes back to when humankind first conceived of time as linear rather than cyclical. Certainly the Judeo-Christian heritage of a Messiah leading us to a Promised Land

inspired millions to strive for a better world for generations to come.

Indeed, it was the search for the "City on the Hill" that brought the Puritans to the American colonies and two centuries later sent covered wagons across the prairies. In 1835, Alexis de Tocqueville observed that Americans "never stop thinking of the good things they have not got," creating a "restlessness in the midst of prosperity" that drives them ever onward.

Even the U.S. Constitution, remember, only promises the pursuit of happiness. It doesn't guarantee that any of us will actually achieve it.

It is this search for "something-more-than-what-we've-got-now" that is at the heart of the consumer culture we struggle with today. But the consumer culture as we know it could never have emerged without the invention of the camera and the eventual mass-production of media images it made possible.

## Reproducing Pictures

In 1859 Oliver Wendell Holmes described photography as the most remarkable achievement of his time because it allowed human beings to separate an experience or a texture or an emotion or a likeness from a particular time and place—and still remain real, visible, and permanent. He described it as a "conquest over matter" and predicted it would alter the physics of perception, changing forever the way people would see and understand the world around them. Holmes precisely observed that the emergence of this new technology marked the beginning of a time when the "image would become more important than the object itself and would in fact make the object disposable." Contemporary advertising critic Stuart Ewen describes the photographic process as "skinning" the world of its visible images, then marketing those images inexpensively to the public.

But successive waves of what might be called reality-freezing technology—first the photograph, followed by the phonograph and the motion picture camera—were only some of many 19th-century transformations that paved the way to our present image culture. As the wheels of industrialization began to mass-produce more and more consumer goods, they also increased the leisure time available to use these products and the disposable income required to buy them. Soon the well-being of the economy itself became dependent on an ever-expanding cornucopia of products, goods, and services. The Sears-Roebuck catalogue and the department store emerged to showcase America's new abundance and by the turn of the century, as media critic Todd Gitlin notes, "production, packaging, marketing, advertising, and sales became functionally inseparable." The flood of commercial images also served as a rough-and-ready consumer education course for the waves of immigrants to America's shores and the thousands of rural folk lured to the city by visions of wealth. Advertising was seen as a way of educating the masses "to the cycle of the marketplace and to the imperatives of factory work and mechanized labor"—teaching them "how to behave like human beings in the machine age," according to the Boston department store magnate Edward A. Filene. In a work world where skill meant less and less, obedience and appearance took on greater importance. In a city full of strangers, advertising offered instructions on how to dress, how to behave, how to *appear* to others in order to gain approval and avoid rejection.

Granted, the American "standard of living" brought an end to drudgery for some, but it demanded a price for all: consumerism. Divorced from craft standards, work became merely the means to acquire the money to buy the goods and lifestyle that supposedly signified social acceptance, respect, even prestige. "Ads spoke less and less about the quality of the products being sold," notes Stuart Ewen, "and more about the lives of the people being addressed."

In 1934, when the Federal Communications Commission approved advertising as the economic basis of the country's fledgling radio broadcasting system, the die was cast. Even though early broadcasters pledged to provide free time for educational programs, for coverage of religion, and for news (creating the famous phrase: the "public interest, convenience, and necessity"), it wasn't long before the industry realized that time was money—and every minute counted. Since free enterprise dictates that it's better to make money than to lose it, the American commercial broadcasting system was born. But it was not until the 1950s that the image culture came into full flower. The reason? Television.

Television was invented in the 1930s, but for many years no one thought it had any practical use. Everyone had a radio, even two or three, which brought news and

sports and great entertainment right into your living room. And if you tired of the antics of *Fibber McGee and Molly* or the adventures of *Sergeant Preston of the Yukon,* you could always go to the movies, which was what most people did at least once a week.

So who needed television? No one, really. What needed television, in 1950, was the economy. The post-war economy needed television to deliver first to America—and then to the rest of the world—the vision, the image, of life in a consumer society. We didn't object because we thought it was, well, just "progress."

## What Price Progress?

Kalle Lasn, a co-founder of the Canadian media criticism and environmentalist magazine *Adbusters,* explains how dependence on television first occurred and continues today each time we turn on our sets: "In the privacy of our living rooms we made a devil's bargain with the advertising industry: Give us an endless flow of free programs and we'll let you spend 12 minutes of every hour promoting consumption. For a long time, it seemed to work. The ads grated on our nerves but it was a small price to pay for 'free' television. . . . What we didn't realize when we made our pact with the advertisers was that their agenda would eventually become the heart and soul of television. We have allowed the most powerful communications tool ever invented to become the *command center of a consumer society* defining our lives and culture the way family, community and spiritual values once did."

This does not mean that when we see a new toilet paper commercial we're destined to rush down to the store to buy its new or improved brand. Most single commercials do not have such a direct impact. What happens instead is a cumulative effect. Each commercial plays its part in selling an overall *consumer lifestyle.* As advertising executive Stephen Garey noted in a recent issue of *Media & Values,* when an ad for toilet paper reaches us in combination with other TV commercials, magazine ads, radio spots, and billboards for detergents and designer jeans, new cars and cigarettes, and soft drinks and cereals and computers, the collective effect is that they all *teach us to buy.* And to feel somehow dissatisfied and inadequate unless we have the newest, the latest, the best.

Just like our relatives at the turn of the century, we learned quickly to yearn for "what we have not got" and to take our identities from what we own and purchase rather than from who we are or how we interact with others. Through consuming things, through buying more and more, we continue the quest for meaning which earlier generations sought in other ways—conquering the oceans, settling the land, building the modern society, even searching for transcendence through religious belief and action. With few places on earth left to conquer today, the one endless expanse of exploration open to us is the local shopping mall.

### Transcending Materialism

Thus the modern dilemma: While few of us would turn in our automatic washing machines for a scrub board or exchange our computers for a slide rule, neither can we expect the images of the past to provide the vision for the future. We must recognize the trade-offs we have made and take responsibility for the society we have created.

For many today, the myth of "progress" is stuttering to a stop. The economic slowdown of the early '90s presents only the most recent example of the human suffering created by the boom and bust cycles of the consumer economy. But even if some magic formula could make steady economic growth attainable, we can no longer afford it. Material limits have been set by the Earth itself. Unlimited exploitation in the name of "progress" is no longer sustainable.

True progress, in fact, would be toward a materially renewable lifestyle that would fulfill the physical, spiritual and emotional needs of all—not just some—of the world's people, while allowing them to live in peace and freedom. Under such a system, communication's most important aim would be to bring people together. Selling things would be a part of its function, but not the whole.

Disasters like Chernobyl and the Alaskan oil spill raise hard questions about the long-term social impact of technological innovation. In the U.S., the loss of whole communities to the ravages of drugs, crime, and homelessness threatens the very principles which allow any humane society to flourish.

At the same time, the global events of 1991—the breakup of the Soviet Empire, the struggles for national identity, even the rise of fundamentalist governments in many parts of the Third World—bear witness to a growing desire for meaningful connections as well as material and political progress.

In many ways we are living in a new world, and around that world hungry eyes are turning toward the Western democracies' longstanding promises of freedom and abundance—the promises the media has so tantalizingly presented.

Yet behind the media culture's constantly beckoning shop window lies an ever-widening gap. West or East, North or South, the flickering images of the media remain our window on the world, but they bear less and less relationship to the circumstances of our day-to-day lives. Reality has fallen out of sync with the pictures, but still the image culture continues.

We'll never stop living in a world of images. But we can recognize and deal with the image culture's actual state, which might be characterized as a kind of mid-life crisis—a crisis of identity. As with any such personal event, three responses are typical:

1. *Denial.* Hoping that a problem will go away if we ignore it is a natural response, but business as usual is no solution.
2. *Rejection.* Some critics believe they can use their television dials to make the image culture go away, and urge others to turn it off, too. But it's impossible to turn off an entire culture. Others check out emotionally by using drugs, alcohol, addictions of all kinds to vainly mask the hunger for meaning that comes when reality and images don't converge.
3. *Resistance.* A surprisingly active counterculture exists and is working hard to point out the dangers of overreliance on the image culture. But such criticism is negative by its very nature, and critics tend to remain voices crying in the wilderness.

A positive alternative is needed. What I have called *media awareness*—the recognition of media's role in shaping our lives and molding our deepest thoughts and feelings—is an important step. The three steps I have outlined above provide simple but effective tools for beginning to work through this process. Although they seem basic, they have their roots in the profound state of being that Buddhism calls *mindfulness:* being aware, carefully examining, asking questions, being conscious.

Even a minimal effort to be conscious can make day-to-day media use more meaningful. Being conscious allows us to appreciate the pleasure of a new CD album and then later turn it off to read a bedtime story to a child. Being conscious means enjoying a TV sitcom while challenging the commercials that bait us to buy. Being conscious allows us to turn even weekend sports events into an intergenerational get-together.

But however achieved, media awareness is only a first step. Ultimately, any truly meaningful attempt to move beyond the image culture will recognize the spiritual and emotional emptiness that the material objects it sells cannot fill.

By convincing us that happiness lies at the other end of the cash register, our society has sold us a bill of goods. To move beyond the illusions of the image culture we must begin to grapple with some deeper questions: Where is the fine line between what I want and what all in society should have? What is the common good for all?

Or to rephrase Gandhi: "How do we create a society in which there is enough for everyone's need but not everyone's greed?"

Thousands of years ago a philosopher wrote of a cave of illusion in which captive humans were enraptured by a flood of images that appeared before them while they ignored the reality outside the cave. This prophetic metaphor contained its own solutions. Once again we are summoned into the light.

# Writing Strategies

1. What is Thoman's thesis?

2. How does Thoman use history to develop the main idea? What other strategies does she use?

3. What connection does Thoman make between images and lifestyle?

4. How is Thoman's essay a call to action?

# Exploring Ideas

1. In ¶8, Thoman quotes Oliver Wendell Holmes as saying the "image would become more important than the object itself and would in fact make the object disposable." With others or alone, think of examples to support Holmes's point.

2. Interview others to find out how they think advertising influences them. Based on the interviews, to what degree would you say others have media awareness? (See ¶25.)

3. In her conclusion, Thoman references Plato's Allegory of the Cave. Read Plato's allegory, which can easily be found on the Internet. How does Plato's point about image and reality support Thoman's insight?

4. What is the difference between advertising and education?

# Ideas for Writing

1. Explore the relationship between advertising images and the economy, education, family, health, or the environment.

2. Thoman says, "Most single commercials do not have such a direct impact. What happens instead is a cumulative effect." (¶5) Use a certain type of image to support or refute this theory.

If responding to one of these ideas, go to the Analysis section of this chapter to begin developing ideas for your essay.

# The Mighty Image

## Cameron Johnson

Although exposed to advertising every day, most Americans are unaware of how advertisements and commercials work in their everyday lives. While ads and commercials seem harmless—or even absurd, as Cameron Johnson explains in the following essay—companies spend millions on advertising because it works. Johnson also explains the logic that keeps most people from seeing the effects of advertising in their lives. (Portions of Johnson's invention work are shown in later sections of this chapter.)

**Writing Strategies**

Begins with public resonance: by addressing a flawed way of thinking among many Americans.

Introduces the issue of images.

Claims that most Americans don't realize the influence images have.

Brief analysis of images and their role in public behavior.

Develops a line of reasoning: millions of products get purchased after a slick marketing campaign; mainstream thinking is that images don't make people buy things; we should explore this logic further.

By the time we Americans are old enough to make hard choices (what to buy, what to wear, what to drive, where to shop, where to buy our degrees, and the like), we imagine ourselves as independent, free, separate, and in control. We like to see ourselves making our own decisions. And because we are attracted to such a self-image, we believe in it. We believe it is *true*. This belief requires us to dismiss the rhetorical power of images in our lives. In fact, most people argue adamantly that they are not influenced by advertising images, that what they purchase is the choice of their own coherent and impenetrable consciousness. Some may concede that images conjure up certain feelings. They may admit, "Those images really moved me" or "That picture brought out lots of feelings in me." But other than the occasional emotional poke, images, say most Americans, have no effect on their reasoning powers—and absolutely no effect on their behaviors.

This is a peculiar stance in a culture that is submerged in advertising images—ones that are highly successful at getting millions of people to wear, drive, buy, and even fight over the same things at the same time. A quick glance at America's spending habits (millions of products suddenly get purchased directly after a slick marketing campaign) reveals the tremendous power of a finely wrought image. Still, the mainstream argument against the power of advertising goes something like this: *Images do not make people buy things. They do not make kids do drugs. They do not make people buy blue jeans or tennis shoes. They do not make adults smoke cigarettes or buy cars or jewelry.* Such statements have an obvious logical ring to them. Of course images do not *make* anyone buy anything. Pictures alone do not *make* people do things. But wait. We should explore this logic a bit further.

**Exploring Ideas**

To what degree are we independent, free, separate, in control?

How do images influence our thinking?

Spending habits suggest that images influence the way we think.

Pictures alone don't make people buy things. So, how does it work?

In the mainstream perspective, humans are *either* driven by media images or they are entirely independent thinkers. They *either* see something and buy a car or they decide not to buy a car. They *either* want a certain pair of blue jeans or they don't even imagine themselves wanting them. Such a perspective ignores the complexities of desire and the power of images. Of course, people do not simply run to the car lot and buy an SUV after seeing an ad in *Time.* But they consume the image and *the apparent value of the image.* When we see an image (whether it be a hairdo, a body type, or a vehicle), we also get an assumption about its worth in the culture. And this assumption stays with us. It molds into our sense of daily life. (This is, of course, why corporations spend millions of dollars to place images everywhere—so that our ideas about daily life naturally come to include the product or the image.)

Contrary to popular belief, humans are gregarious. We think and act in groups, according to historical trends. About every five years in America, kids laugh at what came five years earlier: "Look at that guy's jeans!" "Hey, check out the hairdo on her!" About every decade or so, certain social behaviors become extinct or come into favor: wearing hats, not wearing hats, getting married at 18, waiting to get married, having multiple sexual partners, being monogamous, and so on. And in the bigger spectrum of history, political consciousness changes: from thinking Indians should die to forgetting they exist, from thinking women should stay home and breed to celebrating female CEOs. How do these trends occur? How can a population make such tremendous shifts in belief in relatively short periods of time? Again, human beings don't think or make decisions in isolation. They decide on their hair, clothing, cars, homes, favorite colors, favorite body types, favorite drinks, and favorite pastimes according to the huge cultural menu of their time. Every important psychologist, anthropologist, and philosopher of the twentieth century taught us this: People do make free choices only insofar as they are free from overt oppression, *but they do not make choices that are free of culture.*

Take, for example, the SUV craze in the United States. Certainly, we can point to various causes for the increased sales of SUVs over the past decade: more disposable income, cheap gas prices (relative to other industrialized nations). But given the tremendous escalation of SUV sales, we might assume that significant changes have occurred: dramatic increases in snow throughout the nation, the general depletion of the highway system, rampant mudslides from coast to coast, a sudden migration

---

*Marginal notes:*

Further analyzes the way images work in everyday life—explaining the complexity of how images influence thinking (debunking the oversimplistic view).

Broad cultural allusions help make connections for the reader.

Uses questions (*How do . . . ? How can . . . ?*) to lead the reader to the next point.

Sharp analytical points help make distinctions and reveal the role of images in everyday life.

An extended example about SUVs to illustrate the previous point.

Consuming an image means consuming "the apparent value of the image."

Why do certain behaviors become extinct or come into favor?

People choose from a cultural menu.

Reasons why people should want to buy an SUV.

from cities to mountain hideaways, a dramatic increase in family size, a sudden discovery of free and accessible oil reserves, a sudden realization that SUVs save lives.

Develops the extended example about SUVs.

None of these occurred. But the opposite in each case has: People are generally moving to warmer climates and to cities; snowfall amounts are diminishing even in "snow belts"; family size is shrinking; oil is increasingly more expensive and coated in political stickiness; SUVs are involved in deadly rollover accidents; the nation is increasingly paved—perhaps the smoothest it's ever been in its paleontological history. And more roads go more places. Generally speaking, people have fewer reasons than ever to drive trucks, fewer reasons than ever to drive big people haulers, fewer reasons than ever to have four-wheel drive, fewer reasons than ever to own humungous, extra-large carrying capacity, super-low-gas-mileage vehicles. But the average suburban family is *more* likely to drive such a vehicle—one originally conceived as a tool for ranches or military operations.

Why SUVs aren't a logical choice.

Specific examples help to influence the reader's way of thinking.

Given the facts, we have to look at the mighty image. Given all the issues at hand (the history, the economics, the politics, the geography, the climate, the demographics), we must analyze what's most prevalent and powerful in our culture: advertising. Take, for example, a typical SUV ad, one for a Toyota 4Runner. The 4Runner descends a rocky cliff—a near-vertical drop—and rocky terrain stretches for miles into the background. The main text proclaims: "No intelligent life out here. Just you." (One wonders if Toyota's marketing executives are terribly ironic or terribly shortsighted.) At the bottom of the ad, a smaller message says, "Daily stops to the middle of nowhere." Certainly, most Americans live nowhere close to the middle of nowhere. Very few people will ever get to a place where they are surrounded by nothing but rocks, and even fewer will ever aim a truck down a cliff.

With the groundwork laid in the previous two paragraphs, Johnson emphasizes the role of the advertising image.

How prevalent is advertising in our culture? To what extent does it overcome rational thinking?

Specific details from Toyota 4Runner ad help drive home the idea.

Points out the logical absurdity of the Toyota 4Runner ad, while acknowledging that the ad works.

If we were to examine this ad and then assess the demographics of the buying public, we might guess that it's a joke—or an attempt to ruin Toyota. But the ad obviously works. It conjures up an attractive un-reality for potential consumers. We also might guess that the ad appears in an outdoors magazine—perhaps *Ranchers Quarterly, Mountain Lion News,* or *Rock Slide Specialist.* But the ad appears in *Time*—a decidedly mainstream, middle-class periodical. The vast majority of its readers commute to work on urban streets and suburban highways—and descend the gradual paved slopes of parking garages. Given the distance between readers' actual lives and the ad's imagery, Toyota may have just as logically featured the landscape of Mars.

What other ads work by conjuring up "an attractive un-reality for potential customers"?

Reference to Mars points out logical absurdity.

By appealing to under-
lying values, logically
absurd images leave an
impression.

Further analysis: the
repetition of advertising
images has an impact on
people's consciousness.

Makes final connection
between image and a set
of ideas (values, beliefs,
assumptions).

But such an image leaves an impression. It resonates with our songs (". . . purple mountains' majesty . . ."); it appeals to our longing for escape; it captures our desire for solitude and security; it fits into our drive to scoff at nature. And when such imagery pounds the average citizen relentlessly, it begins to reside in the consciousness. It becomes familiar. Even though most Americans will never see the top of a mountain or career down a cliff (on purpose), they can buy (into) the vehicle attached to the impression.

Advertising images appeal
to our values, desires, and
underlying beliefs—not
our logical reasoning.

The image creates an *allure,* that is, an attractive association of the thing (ridiculously large truck) with a set of ideas (escape, individualism, America, majesty, power, etc.). That set of ideas can be entirely divorced from reality, entirely separate from the needs of everyday life. But everyday life doesn't matter, nor does the logic that it might yield. The mighty advertising image makes it all irrelevant.

## Writing Strategies

1. Describe Johnson's voice as a writer, and refer to several passages for support.

2. How does Johnson's introduction effectively lead into the rest of his essay?

3. Identify one concession Johnson makes and explain how he uses it to further his own argument.

4. What does Johnson imagine his readers think, and how would he like to change their thinking?

5. Johnson concludes ¶8 by saying, "Given the distance between readers' actual lives and the ad's imagery, Toyota may have just as logically featured the landscape of Mars." How does (or doesn't) Johnson earn the right to make such a claim?

## Exploring Ideas

1. Provide support for Johnson's claim that advertisements mold our sense of daily life.

2. In his opening sentence, Johnson lists several "hard choices" Americans have to make. What do such choices say about American culture? What do they say about Johnson?

3. In a group, explore what images Americans consume, settling on several key images. What do those images say about America?

## Ideas for Writing

1. What popular image contradicts the facts (medical, scientific, historical, and so on)? What are the consequences of the contradiction?

2. How is a particular advertising image effective despite its illogical appeal?

If responding to one of these ideas, go to the Analysis section of this chapter to begin developing ideas for your essay.

# An Imperfect Reality

## Rebecca Hollingsworth

In the following essay, Rebecca Hollingsworth, who studies art at Northwestern Michigan College, goes beyond the first glance and shows the reader how an image (an autism-awareness magazine ad) works on the consciousness of the viewer. Through analysis, Hollingsworth breaks down the particulars of an image to show how the overall ad conveys ideas, assumptions, and values, and thus influences the viewer's thinking.

Every day we hear more and more about developmental disorders that afflict children in the United States, disorders that have been misunderstood, downplayed, or ignored. With recent advances in child development and behavior studies, and, perhaps to a large extent, with the explosion of pop psychology personalities like Dr. Phil, Americans are paying more attention than ever to children's mental health. Of course, the general public isn't necessarily any more educated about developmental disorders than it was in the past, but experts and non-experts alike are now insisting that it's okay, even fashionable, to acknowledge and address the ways in which our children aren't "perfect."

One health epidemic at the forefront of public consciousness is autism, a brain disorder that impairs a person's ability to communicate, socialize, and participate in group behavior. Often surfacing by the time a child is three years old, the symptoms of autism include stifled speech and difficulty in displaying joy or affection. According to a 2007 study by the U.S. Centers for Disease Control and Prevention, about 1 in 150 American children are autistic—a staggering number that makes autism the fastest-growing developmental disorder in the United States. Since the release of these findings, nonprofit organizations across the country have been working to raise public awareness of this national health crisis. The largest of these organizations, Autism Speaks, recently launched a multimedia campaign aimed at parents of autistic, or potentially autistic, children.

The 2006 autism awareness campaign sponsored by Autism Speaks challenges common notions of the "perfect kid" by revealing how the reality of autism crushes

Odds of a child becoming a top fashion designer: 1 in 7,000

Odds of a child being diagnosed with autism: 1 in 150

Some signs to look for:

| No big smiles or other joyful expressions by 6 months. | No babbling by 12 months. | No words by 16 months. |

Ad Council

To learn more of the signs of autism, visit autismspeaks.org

AUTISM SPEAKS"
It's time to listen.

Autism Speaks

unrealistic ideals of young American girls and boys. The campaign features a series of television, radio, online, magazine, and billboard advertisements that emphasize the prevalence of the disorder. The campaign's magazine ads show kids doing "kid things"—that is, playing dress-up for girls and playing sports for boys. In one ad (see previous page), a young girl adorns herself with brightly colored clothes and jewelry as proud mom looks on.

The girl wears a cropped, short-sleeved, light pink jacket unzipped to reveal a billowing fuchsia-and-black striped tie and matching fuchsia beaded necklace. She commands the attention of her mother and of us; she stands in a fashionable pose with one leg slightly bent as she looks down to tie a light pink belt around her waist. She towers above her mother, who sits in the lower-left corner of the ad, watching her daughter from the sidelines. The mother's gaze creates a direct line of vision to the young girl, drawing the viewer's eye to this fashionable focal point. Like mom, we look on as the young girl tries on one piece of clothing after another, suggested by the pink, white, and blue clothes draped over furniture in the background. The girl's jewelry—the chunky necklace and the dangly charm bracelet—and her sophisticated tie clash with her long, stringy pigtail braids and big white teddy bear in the background. The pink-and-white washed walls covered in a busy pastel pattern remind us that this is a child's room and that we are witnessing child's play.

The text of the ad jolts us into a reality that is discordant with the idealistic image. Bannered text across the bottom of the image reads, "Odds of a child becoming a top fashion designer: 1 in 7,000. Odds of a child being diagnosed with autism: 1 in 150." This startling statistic of the likelihood that this young girl—any young girl—is autistic turns our viewing experience upside down. As we watch the young girl over her mother's shoulder, we must confront the prevalence of this developmental disability in American children—and the very real possibility that our own child may be that 1 in 150.

The text of the ad goes on to educate parents about the warning signs of autism: a child's inability to show joy by six months, to babble by twelve months, and to talk by sixteen months. And all this text, along with the sobering 1 in 150 statistic, fences us off from the image. In fact, the text separates us from the scene. It's behind the mother's shoulder, but in front of our eyes. We know something she doesn't. In classic dramatic irony, we see the looming, or probable, reality that neither child nor mother can imagine in the ideal bedroom.

The sponsor's logo (a puzzle piece in the shape of a child) and slogan ("Autism Speaks: It's time to listen") appeal to a parent's responsibility to pay attention to her child's behavior, to monitor each developmental step or lack thereof, to hope for the best, to fear the worst. And like all such ads—those that appeal to the complex tangle of parent responsibility and fear—the message begs many questions: Does autism really speak, or does it whisper? How will I know? Once I hear it, what do I do? How could autism affect my child's chances in the world? Is it curable? Is it deadly?

In this sense, the ad does what numerous other campaigns do: it scares us. But this one aims at a particularly vulnerable place: the intersection of our idealism and our fear. It contrasts deluded notions of success—defined here as becoming a top fashion designer—with a statistically harsh truth. We can no longer bask in the old *one in a million* cliché. Like the pretty imagery in the fictional bedroom, that number has been upstaged by a more demanding probability.

### Work Cited

United States. Centers for Disease Control and Prevention. Dept. of Health and Human Services. *Prevalence of Autism Spectrum Disorders: Autism and Developmental Disabilities Monitoring Network, Six Sites, United States, 2000.* By Catherine Rice. 2007. *Centers for Disease Control and Prevention.* Web. 3 Mar. 2011.

# Writing Strategies

1. According to Hollingsworth, what does the Autism Speaks advertisement encourage us to think?

2. Hollingsworth breaks the ad down into its basic elements. Which specific elements are most important to her analysis? How, according to Hollingsworth, do the elements work on the consciousness of the reader?

3. Identify three places where Hollingsworth connects ideas for the reader, where she leads the reader from one idea to the next. Why is or isn't her strategy effective?

4. Hollingsworth generally avoids first-person pronouns in her essay. When she uses them (such as in her opening sentence and in ¶5), she uses the plural *we* and *us* instead of the singular *I* and *me*. What is the effect of these plural pronouns on the reader? Why might Hollingsworth have decided to use the plural instead of the singular? What is the effect created when she does use the singular *I* in ¶7?

5. Study Hollingsworth's use of subjects and verbs. Choose two sentences in which the verbs are especially lively, and explain how they communicate an idea that is important to the main point.

# Exploring Ideas

1. In groups or alone, decide which additional detail of the image Hollingsworth could discuss. How would the additional detail strengthen her analysis?

2. Look up "dramatic irony" and explain Hollingsworth's statement, "In classic dramatic irony, we see the looming, or prob-

able, reality that neither child nor mother can imagine in the bedroom." How is this irony important to Hollingsworth's main point?

3. With a group of peers, examine all the details of an ad, and then decide: What is the main idea of the ad? How does it encourage the viewer to think or act? How do images help the reader understand and accept the ad's main idea? How do text and image work together? Seek out and explain the importance of one hidden, or less obvious, detail.

4. How are you like an ad? What visual details have you created about yourself, and what main idea do you want these details to communicate?

# Ideas for Writing

1. Hollingsworth says, "In this sense, the ad does what numerous other campaigns do: It scares us." Find a particular ad and explain how it scares us. What vulnerability does it take aim at? How does it strike fear? What does the ad achieve beyond scaring the viewer?

2. Find an ad that you consider to be educational. How does the ad connect with the reader beyond providing educational information? How does it get the reader's attention? How does it appeal to the reader's basic values or beliefs?

If responding to one of these ideas, go to the Analysis section of this chapter to begin developing ideas for your essay.

# INVENTION

Most of the images that constitute everyday life are meant to prompt an idea or emotion—not to be analyzed. (This, say many scholars, is all the more reason to analyze them.) In developing ideas for this project, we have to work against what most images ask of us. We have to see into them, into how they work. We have to break down the parts, and then reassemble them in our own minds to understand how they impact viewers. The following sections are designed to help you through this process; specifically, to find a particular image (in Point of Contact), to examine the image closely and understand its relationship to viewers (in Analysis), to develop a focused point (in Thesis), and to develop support for that point (in Rhetorical Tools). The Invention Questions in each section are not meant to be answered directly in your final essay, but to prompt inventive thinking and intensive writing.

# Point of Contact

Images are everywhere. And every image contains more meaning than we might initially imagine. Explore the following possibilities to find a specific image for your own analysis. Consider all the elements of the image: the pictures, text, colors, placement, models, clothing, blank space, audience, and even the surrounding materials such as stories and columns.

## Print Advertisements

Print ads range from dense collages of pictures and words to a single image with one slogan. Browse any magazine or newspaper. Also consider print advertisements that lurk in more inconspicuous places, such as your credit card bill, a public bathroom, a phone book, a calendar, and so on.

Images Courtesy of The Advertising Archives

## Posters

Most often, posters work like billboards. They are designed to catch a passing eye—to shout loudly enough so that anyone in the vicinity will notice the message.

David Pollack/K.J. Historical/Corbis

Blue Lantern Studio/Corbis

## Internet Images

Images found on the Internet range from shocking photos of war to wondrous shots of outer space.

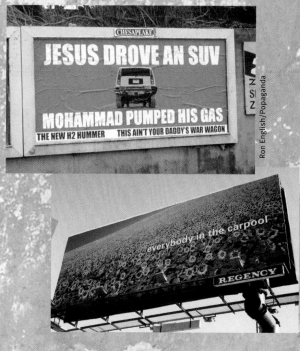

2005 Chin Music Press. Used with permission

Consider sites such as Newsmap (newsmap.jp) or Buzztracker.org in which stories of the world are represented graphically.

## Billboards

Billboards are made to distract people, to yank attention away from the road. Examine one closely to understand how it works toward that goal.

Ron English/Popaganda

Bill Aron/PhotoEdit

**173**

# Analysis

Analyzing an image involves looking at the content (the subject matter) of the image, and then considering the particular visual elements, such as shapes, lines, and colors. Since any image consists of various elements, it can be helpful to remember four main layers: those elements accounting for the image's visual effect, the text, the subtext, and the context. Then consider how the layers work together.

## Image

Even the simplest image contains the following elements:

**Content** The subject, information, or objects that are pictured. Everything within an image is important—from the largest to the tiniest object or detail. They all figure into the nature of the image; they all impact the consciousness of the viewer.

**Framing** What has been placed within the boundaries of the image. Whether by choice, by accident, or by necessity, certain objects are included in the image while other objects are left out. Whether a photographer's (or designer's) deliberate move or pure accident, the framing impacts what is seen. It closes in a particular range of objects and closes out the rest of the world.

**Composition** The way the visual elements of the image are arranged within the frame. Some objects stand in the foreground, others in the background or off to the side. Objects may be crowded, touching, overlapping, far apart. The spatial relationships can be both aesthetic—that is, pleasing to the eye—and meaningful. Composition also includes matters of light and darkness, lines, shapes, focus, and so on.

**Focus** The degree to which some areas of the image are sharp (or clear) and other areas are blurry. The focus impacts the movement of the eye. Sharper objects automatically attract attention away from blurry or fuzzy objects, thereby prompting the viewer to see and understand the image in a particular way.

**Lighting** The degree to which some areas of the image are brightly lit and other areas are in low light or in shadows. An entire image may be dark or light, or some parts of the image may be in shadows or in bright light. While shadows and light may be a natural consequence of a sunny day or a tall building blocking a photographer's light, the way the elements are lit creates an effect. Like careful planning, accidents also can produce strong images.

**Texture** How the image, or certain objects in the image, looks like it would feel if you could touch it. Images can suggest, or appear to have, texture. Just as tree bark and a marble countertop have different textures, visual images can suggest how they might feel if touched. Even if content, framing, composition, and such are all the same in two images, a smooth or rough texture may suggest a different idea about what is being pictured.

**Angle and Vantage Point** The angle at which the image is presented, or the vantage point or perspective from which a photograph, for example, is taken. Every image suggests a perspective. A photograph of a politician speaking with a crowd of supporters behind him suggests one meaning, while a shot of the same politician from behind and speaking to a mere handful of people suggests something else. A low-angle shot of the politician might suggest power; a high-angle shot looking down on the politician might suggest weakness.

**Significance** The collective meaning or impact of all the elements. Our ultimate goal is to figure out how all these elements work together to express ideas, just as the elements of an essay, novel, poem, or movie work together. When analyzing, we focus on one element at a time, but we are always looking at more than one element. For example, when we consider how an image is framed or composed, we are also considering the image's content. When we talk about composition, we are looking at how these various formal elements work together. All elements of an image must be considered, yet some elements will have more impact than others.

Consider the following photo: A man, presumably a farmer, plays an acoustic guitar in an open field. The background is nearly empty except for the lower part of a distant building. The distance behind the man matters—perhaps as much as the man himself. Directly beside him sits a small electric amplifier. The man and the amplifier—adjacent, focused, well lit, in the foreground—seem like a mixed pair,

like they do not belong together, especially surrounded by an open field of dirt. But all the elements of the image insist that we see them together. Even the angle—seeing both of them from the front—makes us (the viewers) feel like an audience. What do all these elements prompt us to think, to imagine, to assume? What feelings are conjured by the interplay of the elements?

## Activity

In a small group, analyze the preceding image. Consider content, framing, composition, focus, lighting, texture, angle and vantage point, and the significance of all the elements.

Dawn M. Turner/MorgueFile

## Invention Questions

Examine the image you have chosen for your project. The following questions will help you analyze how the image works to affect viewers.

▶ **Content**

What content—subject or information—is presented in the image? What are the main objects in the image? Of the main elements, which appear to be most prominent? Which are less prominent?

▶ **Framing**

How is the image framed? What has been placed within the boundaries of the image? What has not been included? How do the boundaries influence your focus?

▶ **Composition**

How are the elements of the image arranged? Are visual elements symmetrical (distributed evenly) or asymmetrical (not distributed evenly)? Are elements touching, overlapping, close together, or far apart? Are elements above or below each other, or to the left or the right of each other? What is in the background? What might the relationship of elements encourage someone to think?

▶ **Focus**

How is the image focused? That is, what objects or areas appear most clear or sharp? What objects or areas are not clear? Is anything unusual or striking about the focus? How does the focus draw your attention? How does it affect the relationship of certain elements?

▶ **Lighting**

How is the image lit? That is, what objects or areas are well lit? What areas are dark, or in shadow? Is the light harsh or soft? Is there a contrast of tones from light to dark? What is darkest, and what is lightest? How does the lighting affect what is pictured? How might different lighting change the image?

▶ **Texture**

What is the texture of the image? If you could touch what is pictured, how would it feel? How does the photograph's texture relate to its content?

▶ **Angle and Vantage Point**

From what angle is the photograph taken? Is it straight-on? Is it exaggerated? How does the angle affect the composition of the image? That is, are some elements more in the foreground or background? Are some more prominent?

You may, in your analysis, consider other elements as well. Colors, for example, may be subdued or bright and splashy. Such details may have significance. ■

# Text

Images—such as photographs, diagrams, and charts—often work in conjunction with written text. In advertising or on posters, meaning is often generated by an interaction of image and text. When text accompanies an image, the two fuse into a single idea. But we can pull them apart and see how they work. For instance, Cameron Johnson examines the way text gives meaning to the image of an SUV:

> The 4Runner descends a rocky cliff—a near-vertical drop—and rocky terrain stretches for miles into the background. The main text proclaims: "No intelligent life out here. Just you." (One wonders if Toyota's marketing executives are terribly ironic or terribly shortsighted.) At the bottom of the ad, a smaller message says, "Daily stops to the middle of nowhere." Certainly, most Americans live nowhere close to the middle of nowhere. Very few people will ever get to a place where they are surrounded by nothing but rocks, and even fewer will ever aim a truck down a cliff.

Holy Cross Family Ministries

Many texts speak back to or depend on other texts to make meaning. That is, they exist in dialogue with other texts—a quality called *intertextuality.* Consider the following bumper sticker:

InternetBumperStickers.com

This sticker makes sense alone but has more impact if the reader knows about *The Sixth Sense,* a movie in which a young boy eerily announces, "I see dead people." If we know the original statement and its context, we are likely to see more significance in the sticker. The same goes with the "Got Faith" ad campaign. It echoes the famous "Got Milk" ads that came several years before. Or imagine an advertising campaign that includes the statement, "You *Can* Always Get What You Want." While the statement makes sense, it has even more significance if we know the Rolling Stones's song, "You Can't Always Get What You Want." With the Stones's song in the background of our consciousness, the advertising slogan would have even more force. It would speak back to something that we had heard many times before.

Intertextuality adds layers of meaning to any text. When designers and advertisers make a text speak to other familiar texts, they tap into the public domain. They create public resonance.

## Invention Questions

Examine the image you have chosen for your project. If the image has accompanying text, answer the following questions:

▶ How does the text correlate with the significance of the image?

▶ How do content, framing, composition, focus, lighting, texture, angle, and vantage point help to convey the ideas?

▶ Does the text echo other texts? (How does the language depend on our familiarity with other texts?) ■

Actually,
he's my
boyfriend.

My son
is slightly
older.

INTRODUCING PREVAGE® Eye
Anti-aging Moisturizing Treatment

Co-created by Elizabeth Arden and the geniuses at Allergan
Dermatology,™ who brought us Botox.® It's the moisturizing
eye treatment with Idebenone, the single most powerful
antioxidant money can buy. So basically, it's Anti-crow's
feet. Anti-dark circles. Anti-puffy skin. Anti-everything.
Proof...not promises.™ prevageskin.com

ALLERGAN
DERMATOLOGY

Sephora

*Image Courtesy of The Advertising Archives*

# Subtext

Not all the meaning that comes from a text is stated. Some meaning is *implied*—suggested but not clearly stated. This layer of *implication* is sometimes called *subtext*—meaning that it is under the more visible and obvious layers. Subtext might also be thought of as a collection of assumptions and hidden values, messages that are not obvious but are present nonetheless. For example, when someone asks what you do for a living, the question is about more than your actual job. It implies questions about your status, your identity, your economic situation, your schedule, even your personality. And even if you offer a short answer ("I'm in marketing"), that answer has a subtext.

Images also have subtext. Even if they have no written text, they still imply ideas. In advertising, images and text

often work together to suggest a layer of subtext. The ad on this page relies on a layer of implication (about age, appearance, and relationships between men and women).

Subtext is invisible, so finding it is hard work. We have to look closely at all the elements of image and text and connect them with common values and assumptions. Notice Cameron Johnson's exploration of subtext:

> **Besides the obvious statements or ideas, what subtle assumptions or beliefs are suggested by (or lurking in) the image?**
>
> To accept anything in the ad as attractive, viewers must believe they are independent—that they have lives of rugged off-road exploration. Maybe it isn't so literal. That is, people might not see themselves driving a truck down a cliff, but they have to believe in the value of rugged self-determination—let's add physical in there: rugged, physical self-determination. The ad relies on that. It only makes sense (especially within the pages of *Time* magazine!) if readers are caught up in that set of beliefs. The ad implies: "Hey . . . you're the type to bust loose and you need a vehicle to get you where you're going." (Of course, most people don't bust loose—especially the people who can afford such vehicles. Funny.)

Examine the image you have chosen for your project and answer the following questions:

▶ What seems to be the main idea of the image?

▶ Besides the obvious statements or ideas, what subtle assumptions or beliefs are suggested by (or lurking in) the image?

▶ How do content, framing, composition, focus, lighting, texture, angle, or vantage point suggest subtle assumptions or beliefs? ■

## Activity

With a group of peers, examine the Elizabeth Arden ad on this page. What seems to be the main idea of the image? Besides the obvious statements or ideas, what subtle assumptions or beliefs are suggested by (or lurking in) the image? How do content, framing, focus, lighting, texture, angle, and vantage point help to convey the ideas?

# Context

Analyzing an image involves examining how the image relates to its context—the things and people surrounding it.

We have all seen an image of the *Mona Lisa,* but how might our response to the painting change if we saw it in the Louvre, as shown in the top image below?

**Specific Context** The specific context is the real physical space that surrounds the image—the building, the magazine, the neighborhood, the campus, the wall, and so on. Every image is affected by the specific context in which it appears. In these images, da Vinci's *Mona Lisa* (the world's most reproduced work of art) is surrounded by different contexts. In the first image, the crowded room at the Louvre influences how the *Mona Lisa* is viewed and what it means. In the other images, the *Mona Lisa* has been recontextualized (recast in different graphic surroundings, even different clothes!). The contexts change how da Vinci's original image works.

**Cultural Context** Nothing exists without culture. Beyond the physical space surrounding an image, the broader culture provides meaning. The values and beliefs that shape everyday life also impact the way an image works—why it gets made, how it gets received.

In his analysis of an SUV ad, Cameron Johnson relies on the specific context (the magazine that published the ad) and the cultural context (the lifestyle of *Time* readers):

> If we were to examine this ad and then assess the demographics of the buying public, we might guess that it's a joke—or an attempt to ruin Toyota. But the ad obviously works. It conjures up an attractive unreality for potential consumers. We also might guess that the ad appears in an outdoors magazine—perhaps *Ranchers Quarterly, Mountain Lion News,* or *Rock Slide Specialist.* But the ad appears in *Time*—a decidedly mainstream, middle-class periodical. The vast majority of its readers commute to work on urban streets and suburban highways—and descend the gradual paved slopes of parking garages. Given the distance between readers' actual lives and the ad's imagery, Toyota may have just as logically featured the landscape of Mars.

## Invention Questions

Examine the image you have chosen for your project and answer the following questions:

▶ What beliefs, attitudes, or morals does it support or appeal to?

▶ What beliefs, attitudes, values, or morals does it chafe against?

▶ What public concern does the image speak to?

▶ How might people benefit by exploring the possible meanings of the image? ∎

In his response to the Invention Questions, Cameron Johnson comes to an easy conclusion about his image, a Toyota 4Runner.

> **What beliefs, attitudes, values, or morals does it support or appeal to?**
>
> That's easy. The image [for Toyota 4Runner] appeals to the value of independence, individualism. Americans like to think of themselves "out there" alone—doing it on the edge of the frontier. It's in our history. And . . . still . . . we're all caught up in that thinking. Many of our goods are sold to us with this basic belief in mind. We are enamored with the idea of ourselves driving across the open majesty of the country with no rules, no road, no official place to be. In the ad, the truck is aiming down a cliff (a flippin' cliff!) and no sign of civilization ruins the moment. (Apparently, that's a fun thing . . . a sign of one's independence, aiming an expensive truck down a cliff.) The print in the ad says, "No intelligent life out here. Just you." Besides that being pretty funny, it reinforces the appeal to independence. Apparently independence = off the road, off the beaten path.

Johnson is just beginning to get traction with his point. He discovers the main appeal in the ad, and the particular elements that drive the appeal.

# Thinking Further

Whenever a question is easy to answer, writers should use that momentum and explore further. They should revel in the ease of the answer and then keep developing nuances, asking more questions. Notice, for instance, what happens when Cameron Johnson continues thinking. He goes beyond the initial answer (that the ad appeals to the idea of independence) and discovers the irony or absurdity of the image:

> What's weird about the appeal is this: Most people aren't at all independent. They follow rules, go to work every day, drive in the correct lanes, park in garages or metered spaces or yellow-lined areas. They trim their lawns to the exact length (about 1/2 inch within the presumed correct length for the neighborhood). They dress according to the rules of their generation. They certainly don't drive their expensive (and very clean) new trucks down cliffs. This ad (and every ad like it) is totally divorced from the real life most people lead. Most Americans are rule followers. We think what the media commentators (or government propaganda) tell us. We do what we can to stay in the lines. But the world of advertising makes it seem like we're all careening down cliffs, splashing through rivers, rockin' it out on the banks of some lake. It ain't true.

This paragraph of invention writing shows Johnson exploring ideas and discovering an insight that will drive the analysis for his essay. This is not Johnson's only invention writing though. Earlier invention helped him think his way up to this discovery. Just one paragraph or page of invention writing won't usually strike gold. Exploring, discovering, and developing ideas takes time and lots of thinking.

One trick to invention writing is to make sure you write in the spirit of invention. Your purpose is to explore, discover, and develop ideas. It is not to just write down what you think, report what you know, ask (but not answer) questions, or make an outline—these are some of the mistakes students make when they are trying to figure out what their invention writing is supposed to do. Invention writing is not when you write to communicate what you think or know to the reader; instead, it is when you write to explore deeper into an idea, to figure out what else you might think.

# Invention Workshop

In a small group, use the Invention Questions to explore your image in depth. First, share your image with others in your group. Then apply one of the Invention Questions. Once someone in the group offers a possible answer, record the response. Someone else in the group should then continue that thinking by asking how the first responder arrived at his or her point. Remember, your goal is to examine the image closely to discover insights about how particular elements impact the viewer.

# Thesis

The purpose of this project is to analyze how an image (or set of images) works to impact viewers. The analysis should reveal something that readers would not otherwise see or imagine. It should show the insides, the mechanics, of the image. Consider the following examples:

- In trendy music videos, the camera looks up from the ground at the performers, which reinforces the notion that the performers have power over, and speak down to, their audiences.
- Beyond the main image of the Cadillac, the sophisticated background elements make the pitch to potential consumers.
- Presidential campaign commercials rely on the imagery of middle-class America so that candidates will be seen as normal working Joes.

Notice that each statement explains the significance, the meaning or impact, of a particular element of the image. Take, for example, the third statement. It explains how *the imagery of middle-class America* (a particular element) casts the candidates as normal working Joes (the element's significance; its meaning or impact). A good thesis for this project has two important qualities:

1. A focus on a particular element, and
2. An explanation of its significance

Look over your invention notes and focus on a particular element (something in the content, the composition, the framing, etc.). Then explain its significance—how that element works to convey meaning or impact the viewer.

## Common Thesis Problems

As in most writing projects, the more specific the claims, the more intensive the ideas will be. If you can point to a particular element in an image and explain how that element works, then you are probably on your way to a focused thesis. Notice the problems in the following statement:

> Many *Sports Illustrated* ads use women as the main focus.

It lacks significance and focus. It targets "many" ads and offers a sweeping statement about them—they use women. The statement does not explain how something in those ads works, how they influence people, or how the individual elements create messages.

The following statement also lacks focus:

> *Rolling Stone* magazine makes one thing clear: sex sells.

*Rolling Stone* is a good-sized magazine—with a table of contents, album lists, pictures, ads, articles about politics, music reviews, movie reviews, and so on. Of course, someone could associate all those elements with sex, but the project would probably lack serious analysis of particular elements. A writer with such a statement needs to look more closely at something specific in *Rolling Stone*.

## Activity

Rewrite the preceding two statements so they are more focused. Consider the two important qualities:

1. A focus on a particular element, and
2. An explanation of its significance

# Evolution of a Thesis

Thesis statements do not always evolve in a neat fashion, progressing from a broader to a more focused insight. Sometimes (maybe most times), they wander, circle back, and jump around as the writer tries to get traction. Below, we can see Johnson searching out meaning through single sentences. He is trying to connect two things: a particular element of the ad and the meaning of that element for viewers. All of the following statements are attempts, some better than others, at forging that connection.

- SUV ads, like that for the Toyota 4Runner, appeal to Americans through natural imagery.
- Ads like the one for Toyota 4Runner give a vision of life that many Americans strive for.
- Even though most Americans' lives do not resemble the natural imagery of SUV ads, that imagery appeals to what many people imagine about themselves.
- The scenic imagery of SUV ads appeals to a lifestyle that most Americans imagine for themselves but rarely realize.
- The ad for Toyota 4Runner relies on natural imagery that is far outside the experience of most Americans, but the ads still have strong appeal.
- The ad for Toyota 4Runner reveals a trend in SUV advertising: the background imagery connects to an illusive vision of American life—one that is contrary to the situation or needs of most potential consumers.

## Revising Your Thesis

Develop a working thesis statement that includes attention to a specific element of an image and explains its significance. Then in a small group, discuss each person's statement. Apply the following:

- Does the statement focus on a specific element (something in the content, composition, framing, angle, focus, etc.)? How could the specific element be narrower?
- Beyond the writer's statement, what is the significance (possible meaning or impact) of that specific element? (What else might it suggest about people, lifestyles, nature, America, clothing, social class, race, gender, politics, domestic life, art, music, and so on?) Be creative. Imagine that the significance is not what people initially assume!
- Make a case for the most surprising or hidden significance in the image. Make a connection that seems, at first, outrageous. Try to convince others in the group that your point is valid.

# The more specific claims, the more intensive ideas.

# Rhetorical Tools

For analyzing images, support comes in two general categories: (1) details from the image, and (2) evidence outside of the image. The first is essential. Readers will need to see how specific claims correspond to the image itself. The second category includes a wide variety of strategies and will help provide meaningful context to your points.

## Using Details from the Image

Any close analysis relies on specific details of the subject. For instance, if you are analyzing an advertisement, readers would expect to see particular features of that ad and an explanation that connects those features to your main point. In her analysis, Rebecca Hollingsworth shows the reader how details make meaning:

> Like mom, we look on as the young girl tries on one piece of clothing after another, suggested by the pink, white, and blue clothes draped over furniture in the background. The girl's jewelry—the chunky necklace and the dangly charm bracelet—and her sophisticated tie clash with her long, stringy pigtail braids and big white teddy bear in the background. The pink-and-white washed walls covered in a busy pastel pattern remind us that this is a child's room and that we are witnessing child's play.

Hollingsworth's analysis shows the power of subtle details that might get overlooked:

> As we watch the young girl over her mother's shoulder, we must confront the prevalence of this developmental disability in American children—and the very real possibility that our own child may be that 1 in 150.

Because we are looking over the mother's shoulder (at the girl from her mother's vantage point), the image confronts us with a real possibility—about American children and about *our own child*. Hollingsworth's careful analysis adds up to a main point:

In this sense, the ad does what numerous other campaigns do: It scares us. But this one aims at a particularly vulnerable place: the intersection of our idealism and our fear. It contrasts deluded notions of success—defined here as becoming a top fashion designer—with a statistically harsh truth. We can no longer bask in the old *one in a million* cliché. Like the pretty imagery in the fictional bedroom, that number has been upstaged by a more demanding probability.

Likewise, Cameron Johnson uses the details of a specific magazine ad to illustrate his thesis that advertising images are out of sync with the reality of everyday life. Notice that he does not merely mention the details; he also explains how those details illustrate his point:

> Take, for example, a typical SUV ad, one for a Toyota 4Runner. The 4Runner descends a rocky cliff—a near-vertical drop—and rocky terrain stretches for miles into the background. The main text proclaims: "No intelligent life out here. Just you." (One wonders if Toyota's marketing executives are terribly ironic or terribly shortsighted.) At the bottom of the ad, a smaller message says, "Daily stops to the middle of nowhere." Certainly, most Americans live nowhere close to the middle of nowhere. Very few people will ever get to a place where they are surrounded by nothing but rocks, and even fewer will ever aim a truck down a cliff.

Return to any notes you generated from the Analysis section of this chapter. Ask yourself the following questions about the image:

▶ What details (about the content, focus, composition, framing, lighting, texture, angle, and significance) best illustrate my main point?

▶ What specific text best illustrates my main point?

▶ Does subtext help to support my main point?

▶ Does the context help to support my main point? ∎

# Using Other Evidence

In some ways, you are attempting to convince readers that your understanding of the image is reasonable. To this end, you can go beyond the image itself and allude to any related events, images, people, or behaviors in the present or past. Some of the readings in this chapter use cultural allusions (references to other well-known texts, films, pictures, photos, or events). For example, in his analysis of ad images, Cameron Johnson refers to broader cultural trends to support the claim that people are influenced deeply by the messages around them:

> Contrary to popular belief, humans are gregarious. We think and act in groups, according to historical trends. About every five years in America, kids laugh at what came five years earlier: "Look at that guy's jeans!" "Hey, check out the hairdo on her!" About every decade or so, certain social behaviors become extinct or come into favor: wearing hats, not wearing hats, getting married at 18, waiting to get married, having multiple sexual partners, being monogamous, and so on. And in the bigger spectrum of history, political consciousness changes: from thinking Indians should die to forgetting they exist, from thinking women should stay home and breed to celebrating female CEOs. How do these trends occur?

Consider the following questions:

▶ How do cultural trends or events relate to the image I am analyzing?

▶ Does anything in history show how the image (or type of image) has influenced people?

▶ Can I create a scenario (a hypothetical situation) to illustrate my point about the image?

▶ Can I narrate a personal experience to show something important about the image? ■

## Research

Using a periodical database (such as InfoTrac® College Edition) or an Internet search engine (such as Google), explore how others have discussed the image you are analyzing. Most likely, you won't find sources about the specific image (unless you are analyzing a historic piece of art or popular culture). However, you'll likely find sources about the type of image—whether an automobile ad, a billboard, a rural photo, and so on. For instance, if Cameron Johnson were exploring for outside sources, he might begin a keyword search with the following combinations:

sport utility vehicle *and* advertisement

sport and utility *and* vehicles *and* advertising

automobile *and* advertisements *and* nature

Of course, keyword searches are not an exact science. (They're not a science at all.) They are always attempts—and sometimes require several restarts with substitutions and small changes. For instance, changing automobile to car or ad to advertisement may yield significantly different results.

For more assistance with using databases and online catalogs for research, see Chapter 13: Finding Sources.

## Activity

Before drafting your essay, write out your thesis and main support in one paragraph. Then discuss your paragraph with several peers. How could the thesis be more focused and intense? What additional support strategies could help?

# Organizational Strategies

## How Should I Begin?

A common and effective opening strategy is to begin with the personal and then move to the public. For example, notice how Elizabeth Thoman begins her essay with personal reflection but moves steadily toward the public relevance of her topic:

> Like most middle-class children of the '50s, I grew up looking for the American Dream. In those days there were no cartoons in my Saturday viewing, but I distinctly remember watching, with some awe, *Industry on Parade*. I felt both pride and eager anticipation as I watched tail-finned cars rolling off assembly lines, massive dams taming mighty rivers and sleek chrome appliances making life more convenient for all.
>
> When I heard the mellifluous voice of Ronald Reagan announce on *GE Theatre* that "Progress is our most important product," little did I realize that the big box in our living room was not just entertaining me. At a deeper level, it was stimulating an "image" in my head of how the world should work: that anything new was better than something old; that science and technology were the greatest of all human achievements and that in the near future—and certainly by the time I grew up—the power of technology would make it possible for everyone to live and work in a world free of war, poverty, drudgery and ignorance.

While Thoman is relating her own personal memories, those memories are moving the reader into a public discussion—about the rise of the image culture and the American Dream. The personal memories she selects are directly relevant to the public concern she will develop throughout her essay.

On the other hand, Hollingsworth and Johnson avoid the personal. Instead of taking the first-person ("I") approach, each starts by focusing the reader on the public ("we") nature of their topics:

> Every day we hear more and more about developmental disorders that afflict children in the United States, disorders that have been misunderstood, downplayed, or ignored.
>
> By the time we Americans are old enough to make hard choices (what to buy, what to wear, what to drive, where to shop, where to buy our degrees, and the like), we imagine ourselves as independent, free, separate, and in control.

## Should I Use Headings?

Since many college writing assignments are brief (1,000–2,000 words), headings are not always necessary. But longer essays can be more inviting when the writer breaks the text into sections and uses headings to indicate the general focus of a section of text. This heading strategy is the same as breaking up even longer writings into chapters.

Chapters and headings help the reader organize major units of thought, and they give the reader a break or a light at the end of the tunnel. Elizabeth Thoman provides the reader with three headings:

**Reproducing Pictures**

**What Price Progress?**

**Transcending Materialism**

While headings should not be used indiscriminately, they can be helpful to both writer and reader. Of course, headings are like topic sentences, which clearly state the main idea of a paragraph. And in shorter essays, clear topic sentences at the beginning of paragraphs effectively serve the same purpose that headings do in longer essays.

## Activity

With a group of peers, break "The Mighty Image" into at least three sections and write a heading for each section.

# How Should I Integrate Outside Sources?

Writers can integrate outside sources by paraphrasing (expressing the ideas of the source in one's own words), summarizing (compacting the ideas of the source and expressing them in one's own words), or quoting (using the exact wording of the source within quotation marks). In an academic essay, all three strategies require documentation: an in-text citation and a bibliographic citation at the end of the essay.

Outside research should be carefully woven into the fabric of your own ideas. It should not be dropped into a paragraph. Passages from research communicate more clearly when the idea has first been set up. In other words, the writer establishes the momentum of the point and brings in an outside source for reinforcement. Then, after a paraphrase, summary, or quotation, the writer may further explain the significance or meaning.

In the following passage, Elizabeth Thoman first explains how commercials influenced consumerism. Then she reinforces the point with a quotation, and finally further explains the idea in the quotation:

> The flood of commercial images also served as a rough-and-ready consumer education course for the waves of immigrants to America's shores and the thousands of rural folk lured to the city by visions of wealth. Advertising was seen as a way of educating the masses "to the cycle of the marketplace and to the imperatives of factory work and mechanized labor"—teaching them "how to behave like human beings in the machine age," according to the Boston department store magnate Edward A. Filene. In a work world where skill meant less and less, obedience and appearance took on greater importance. In a city full of strangers, advertising offered instructions on how to dress, how to behave, how to *appear* to others in order to gain approval and avoid rejection.

These three steps are not required with every use of an outside source. Sometimes, the third step is unnecessary and the writer only sets up the point. In the following passage,

Thoman sets up the point about commercials' power then brings in an outside source (Stephen Garey), to reinforce the point:

> This does not mean that when we see a new toilet paper commercial we're destined to rush down to the store to buy its new or improved brand. Most single commercials do not have such a direct impact. What happens instead is a cumulative effect. Each commercial plays its part in selling an overall *consumer lifestyle.* As advertising executive Stephen Garey noted in a recent issue of *Media & Values,* when an ad for toilet paper reaches us in combination with other TV commercials, magazine ads, radio spots, and billboards for detergents and designer jeans, new cars and cigarettes, and soft drinks and cereals and computers, the collective effect is that they all *teach us to buy.* And to feel somehow dissatisfied and inadequate unless we have the newest, the latest, the best.

Notice how Hollingsworth begins with a main idea, then introduces the source, paraphrases the supporting information, provides in-text documentation, and then comments on the paraphrased information:

> One health epidemic at the forefront of public consciousness is autism, a brain disorder that impairs a person's ability to communicate, socialize, and participate in group behavior. Often surfacing by the time a child is three years old, the symptoms of autism include stifled speech and difficulty in displaying joy or affection. According to a 2007 study by the U.S. Centers for Disease Control and Prevention, about 1 in 150 American children are autistic—a staggering number that makes autism the fastest-growing developmental disorder in the United States (Rice). Since the release of these findings, nonprofit organizations across the country have been working to raise public awareness of this national health crisis. The largest of these organizations, Autism Speaks, recently launched a multimedia campaign aimed at parents of autistic, or potentially autistic, children.

For more on integrating sources and documentation, see Chapters 13 and 14.

# Writer's Voice

## Creating Intensity

Analysis requires intellectual commitment from both readers and writers. When writers intensify their voices, they bring readers into that commitment. But what does it mean to intensify a voice? What does it mean to make the voice you've fashioned into something more engaging and insistent? What features create intensity?

The following Cameron Johnson passage insists that the reader pay attention. Johnson creates intensity with repetition, parenthetical phrases, and word choice:

> But such an image leaves an impression. It resonates with our songs (". . . purple mountains' majesty . . ."); it appeals to our longing for escape; it captures our desire for solitude and security; it fits into our drive to scoff at nature. And when such imagery pounds the average citizen relentlessly, it begins to reside in the consciousness. It becomes familiar. Even though most Americans will never see the top of a mountain or careen down a cliff (on purpose), they can buy (into) the vehicle attached to the impression.

What if Johnson's passage were slightly different? Notice how the subtle changes in the following passage influence the voice:

> But such an image leaves an impression. Even if you think it does not, it does. The image resonates with common songs (". . . purple mountains' majesty . . ."); it appeals to the longing for escape and captures the desire for solitude and security. Also, such an image supports the idea that we are not slowed down by the perils of nature. When such an image consistently shows up in our magazines and television screens, it begins to take over the consciousness and create familiarity. Even though most Americans will never see the top of a mountain or drive down a cliff in a truck, they can buy the vehicle attached to the impression.

Not all passages in an essay can be intense. Some passages, even in the most ferocious and passionate essays, are more relaxed. They let the reader move along without a fierce intellectual commitment and build a foundation of thought. In the following passage from her essay "Addiction as a Relationship," Jean Kilbourne analyzes the relationship between alcoholism and alcohol advertising:

> An important part of the denial so necessary to maintain alcoholism or any other addiction is the belief that one's alcohol use isn't affecting one's relationships. The truth, of course, is that addictions shatter relationships. Ads like the one for B and B (a brand of alcohol) help support the denial and go one step further by telling us that the alcohol is, in fact, an enhancement to relationships.

While this passage is direct, clean, and highly analytical, it is not necessarily insistent. But notice the next paragraph in Kilbourne's essay. Something changes:

> "In life there are many loves, but one Grande Passion," says an ad featuring a couple in a passionate embrace. Is the passion enhanced by the liqueur or is the passion for the liqueur? For many years I described my drinking as a love affair, joking that Jack Daniels was my most constant lover.

Kilbourne's voice changes pitch. It invites us to ask questions, to enter her life. It becomes slightly more informal and intimate. (But it is no less analytical.) Because reading (like all human activity) depends on a tug and pull, an ebb and flow of consciousness, these subtle changes in pitch help make Kilbourne's writing seem more intense and alive.

## Activities

What else does intensity look like? What does it sound like?

1. In a small group, choose one passage from another chapter's reading. As a group, choose specific features of the sentences that help to create an intensive analytical voice. Also, point to features that seem less intense. How do the more intense and less intense passages affect you as readers?

2. Examine any passage you've drafted for this project. How could it be more intense? What statements work against an intensive analytical voice? What words or phrases seem most intense to you? Rewrite the passage while trying to achieve more intensity. Try to abandon the original passage completely. Do something foreign to your habits.

## Using the Personal to Analyze

Analysis does not have to be dry, sterile, or impersonal. It can involve, even rely on, the intimate experiences of the writer. In her essay, Elizabeth Thoman uses the personal to bolster a close examination of images. She uses her experience as a springboard, to take us to a deeper level:

> When I heard the mellifluous voice of Ronald Reagan announce on *GE Theatre* that "Progress is our most important product," little did I realize that the big box in our living room was not just entertaining me. At a deeper level, it was stimulating an "image" in my head of how the world should work: that anything new was better than something old; that science and technology were the greatest of all human achievements and that in the near future—and certainly by the time I grew up—the power of technology would make it possible for everyone to live and work in a world free of war, poverty, drudgery, and ignorance.

## Communicating with Action Verbs

The best writing relies on action verbs that create images in the reader's mind. Notice how action verbs bring a controlled intensity to Hollingsworth's writing:

- Every day we **hear** more and more about developmental disorders that **afflict** children . . .

- The largest of these organizations, Autism Speaks, recently **launched** a multimedia campaign **aimed** at parents of autistic, or potentially autistic, children.

- The girl **wears** a cropped, short-sleeved, light pink jacket . . .

- She **commands** the attention of her mother and of us; she **stands** in a fashionable pose . . .

- The text of the ad **jolts** us into a reality . . .

- This startling statistic . . . **turns** our viewing experience upside down . . .

- And this text . . . **fences us off** from the image.

- We can no longer **bask** in the old *one in a million* cliché.

## Activity

With a group of peers, highlight other action verbs in Hollingsworth's essay. Then rewrite a paragraph from a group member's essay by replacing less expressive linking verbs with more vivid action verbs.

# Vitality

And now for the hard part: pruning your own language. Once an essay is drafted, it is easy to walk away from it. Returning to your own sentences with a willingness to trim and vitalize takes a combination of writerly humility and courage. (One has to be humble enough to recognize shortcomings and courageous enough to address them!) Consider the following common issues.

## Avoid Blueprinting

Sometimes writers draw attention to their own plans. That is, they tell the reader what they are doing or what they are about to do. This strategy can be called *blueprinting* because it gives the reader a rough plan (like the blueprints for a house). Blueprinting is not inherently wrong, but it does draw attention away from the ideas and toward the writer's processes, which can be distracting. Most readers would rather stay focused on the ideas themselves. Rather than announcing plans, writers can simply state the points.

Consider this blueprinting passage: In the following pages, I will explain how the advertising images on MTV influence the present generation.

Removing the blueprinting leaves a relatively vague sentence: Advertising images on MTV influence the present generation.

So the writer might develop a more focused point: *Advertising images on MTV promote the belief that clothes create identity.*

When the blueprinting is removed, sentences have more potential because important content can be added. In fact, it must be added. As the previous example shows, blueprinting can fool a writer into thinking that sentences are saying more than they are.

There are also more subtle forms of blueprinting:

Next is the composition.

Now, after examining the content, we should explore composition.

These more subtle forms are fairly common because writers use them as paragraph transitions. While they are generally more accepted, there are still better ways to connect ideas:

Closely related to content, composition influences how viewers come to an image.

With the blueprinting removed, a sentence can hold more information. Even when the blueprinting is subtle, it diminishes the vitality and intensity of sentences.

---

### Activity

Consider the following blueprinting sentence:

Next, I will examine the specific framing strategies in the photograph.

To remove the blueprinting, you might write:

The specific framing strategies in the photograph . . .

The idea now requires more information. Complete the revised sentence by providing important information that relies on an action verb. (For example, you could write, The specific framing strategies in the paragraph *help convey the feeling of panic.*)

---

**Blueprinting diminishes the vitality and intensity of sentences.**

# Subordinate Less Important Ideas

Pruning sentences also involves subordinating less important ideas to more important ones. This relationship of *main idea to subordinating idea* is essential to the vitality of any piece of writing:

> One health epidemic at the forefront of public consciousness is autism, a brain disorder that impairs a person's ability to communicate, socialize, and participate in group behavior.

This sentence conveys two ideas: a main idea (that autism is a health epidemic at the forefront of public consciousness) and a subordinate idea (the definition of autism). Consider another example:

> Often surfacing by the time a child is three years old, the symptoms of autism include stifled speech and difficulty in displaying joy or affection.

Here the writer conveys two important ideas (when autism surfaces and what its symptoms are). The first idea is subordinate to the second one, because the second idea is expressed in the main, or independent, clause. Subordinating one idea to the other helps to keep the essay moving along. Notice how the pace would slow if neither of the previous two sentences included subordination:

> One health epidemic at the forefront of public consciousness is autism. Autism is a brain disorder that impairs a person's ability to communicate, socialize, and participate in group behavior. It often surfaces by the time a child is three years old. The symptoms of autism include stifled speech and difficulty in displaying joy or affection.

## Activity

With a partner, rewrite several sentences in your essay by subordinating one idea to another.

# Avoid Vague Pronouns

Pronouns help create coherence in and between paragraphs. Pronouns such as *these, this, those,* and *it* are often used to refer back to previous ideas so readers feel a sense of familiarity as they move forward. Notice how *this* works in the following example to keep the reader connected to information in a previous paragraph:

> Even the U.S. Constitution, remember, only promises the pursuit of happiness. It doesn't guarantee that any of us will actually achieve it.
>
> It is this search for "something-more-than-what-we've-got-now" that is at the heart of the consumer culture we struggle with today.

Elizabeth Thoman uses the pronoun to bring the reader from one paragraph to another while maintaining her key point ("this search"). But she also gives us more information, so the transition between paragraphs is smooth: "this search for 'something-more-than-what-we've-got-now.'" The additional information keeps the reader in tow. In such a passage, the pronoun offers extra glue between ideas. But imagine if the pronoun had to act alone:

> Even the U.S. Constitution, remember, only promises the pursuit of happiness. It doesn't guarantee that any of us will actually achieve it.
>
> This is at the heart of the consumer culture we struggle with today.

Now the pronoun carries all the burden of the transition between paragraphs. If the reader is not entirely certain what *this* is, the transition is unsuccessful. For better vitality and coherence, make certain that pronouns refer directly to, or accompany, specific nouns. (Don't let them go it alone!)

# Revision

Your analysis should reveal something readers would not otherwise see or imagine. This involves inventing your way to a focused and insightful thesis and then using rhetorical tools to help the reader understand and accept that thesis. Before exchanging your draft for peer review, return to the questions in the Analysis, Public Resonance, and Rhetorical Tools sections, and explore further from your new perspective (the perspective you developed last time you worked through those questions). See how you can improve your focus, insight, and support before getting feedback from a peer.

If you have analyzed an image for your project, what detail of the image have you overlooked? How might some quiet detail strengthen your analysis? Return to your image and the Analysis section of this chapter for help.

## Peer Review

Your analysis should reveal something that readers would not otherwise see or imagine. Write down what you think your analysis reveals, and then exchange drafts with at least one other writer. After reading your draft, the other writer should write responses to the following questions:

1. What did the analysis reveal? That is, what didn't you see or imagine about the image until you read the essay?
2. How might the thesis be more specific and revealing? Offer particular rewording, or a whole new direction, even if you think the thesis is good as is.
3. What additional details from the image might be used to strengthen or refocus the analysis?
4. Are there any blueprinting passages? Can they be eliminated? Suggest a strategy that keeps the reader focused on the ideas rather than on the structure of the essay.
5. What sentences can be combined through subordination? Combine two sentences in the opening paragraph, subordinating one idea to the other. Combine at least two sentences elsewhere in the essay.
6. What strategies from other chapters can make sentences more vital?
   —Mark any clichés. Explain how the cliché conceals or blurs thinking, and then suggest an alternative to the cliché.
   —Note any stilted language. Suggest an alternative approach to the passage.
   —Help the writer experiment with sentence length and brevity. Reconstruct one paragraph, extending some sentences and abbreviating others. Try to create intensity with shorter sentences.
   —Change vague nouns to specific nouns.
   —Change *be* verbs (*is, are, was, were*) to active verbs.
   —Change clauses to phrases.
   —Change phrases to words.
   —Combine sentences.
   —Repeat structures.
   —Intensify verbs.
7. What grammatical or proofreading issues make reading difficult or create small distractions for a reader?

# Reflection

Before moving on to another writing project, reflect on this one. The following questions ask you to think about how you used rhetoric to create and deliver your essay. The writing you do in response to these questions is sometimes called *meta-writing*, which is when you take a step back and think and write about your writing. Getting this distance can help you see and learn new things, even after you've written your essay.

1. What is the essay's thesis?
2. How does your analysis of a particular visual element (or several elements) reveal a new way of understanding the image?
3. How does a particular reference to evidence from outside the image help the reader understand and accept your thesis? If you didn't use any outside evidence, what outside evidence might you have used and why?
4. What is the essay's most intense passage and why?
5. How did the essay evolve through the process of inventing, drafting, and revising?
6. How did writing this essay help you develop as a writer and thinker?

## Beyond the Essay

"What was your Analyzing Images essay about?" We are often asked such questions, not only about the essays we have written, but also about other aspects of our lives. A boss may ask, "What happened last night with the customer who called this morning to complain?" A professor may ask, "How is your writing project coming along?" A family member may ask, "How'd Cindy's softball game go?" In some cases we can simply answer, "Not much" or "Fine." But sometimes we must give a briefing on an important situation. Some of these briefings are impromptu: we don't have time to prepare and must answer on the spot. Other briefings are more formal: for example, each day the president's press secretary briefs the press on important issues.

Giving a focused, organized, and concise briefing is a valuable skill. For practice, prepare a one-minute briefing of your Analyzing Images essay. Your briefing should include your main idea (thesis), your main supporting ideas, and the most important details. Write out your briefing and practice your verbal delivery. Be prepared to brief a group of peers.

 For additional resources including instructional videos and links to helpful websites, access your English CourseMate through cengagebrain.com.

# 7 Making Arguments

# Chapter Contents

# "Someone who makes an assertion puts forward a claim—a claim on our attention and to our belief."

—Stephen Toulmin

Argument is the art of persuading people how to think. This may sound absurd since most people, we hope, already know how to think, or at least *what* to think about particular issues. But with argument, we can change how people view things, even slightly, and so affect how they approach and process ideas.

Arguments come to us in different forms. We hear them given in speeches, debates, and informal discussions. We hear them every day on talk shows, in break rooms, college hallways, and public meeting places like restaurants and pubs. Arguments get delivered through action. They come explicitly in protests, parades, sit-ins, labor strikes, and elections. They also come in more subtle forms: people donate to charities (thereby expressing their favor of a particular cause); they patronize or boycott a particular store; they choose not to vote (thereby expressing their stance against the entire political process). Arguments get made through art in all media: sculpture, painting, music, and so on. And arguments are major elements of literature. For example, it has been said that Aldous Huxley's book *Brave New World* argues against the extremes of materialism and industrialization and that Kate Chopin's *The Awakening* argues for a new vision of women's identity. Even poems offer arguments: Walt Whitman's masterpiece *Leaves of Grass* argues for the value of common American workers and their common language.

People in all occupations make or deal with arguments. For example: a human resources manager for a packaging company argues in a report that more supervisors should be hired in the coming fiscal year; several department store sales associates collectively write a letter to store and regional managers in which they claim current scheduling practices minimize sales commissions; the public affairs director of a major automobile company argues that a new advertising campaign should not be offensive to a particular demographic group; the lawyers for a major computer software company argue in a district court that the company's business practices comply with federal antitrust laws. In academia, argument is everywhere:

- The biology faculty at a state university argues for the need to study cloning and petition the administration for more leeway to do research.

- A historian argues about the number of Native Americans on the continent before European settlers so that people more deeply understand history.

- A psychologist argues that Freudian analysis is overused and that new strategies for exploring patients' psychological makeup should be further developed.

- College administrators argue for more state funds for their schools.

- Students in an architecture class argue that a particular structural design is more sound than competing designs.

- Students in a nursing program must convince others that a new staff management technique is valuable for large hospitals.

In any situation, those who can deliver the most sophisticated and engaging arguments tend to have the most influence. Of course, a sophisticated and engaging argument involves a great deal of strategy. For instance, in academic argument, blatant personal attacks, outright aggression, and sugar-coated language are not valued, nor are empty phrases ("don't question what's in my heart") and mean-spiritedness ("your ideas are simply idiotic"). But while academic writers are not out to squash an opponent or cuddle up to audiences, they do more than simply present their opinions. In providing a new way of thinking about a particular topic, academic writers must also analyze others' ideas and explain how their own claims relate to those of others.

This chapter will help you discover an argumentative topic, explore that topic in depth, develop a sophisticated argument, and communicate your argument in writing. The following essays will provide insight into various argumentative strategies. After reading the essays, you can find a topic in one of two ways:

1. Go to the Point of Contact section to find a topic from everyday life, or
2. Choose one of the Ideas for Writing that follow the essays.

After you find a topic, go to the Analysis section to begin developing your argument.

# The Dog Delusion

## April Pedersen

Sometimes writers examine the behaviors and reflexes
that seem most harmless. When a trend seems uncritically accepted in everyday life, writers step forward. In
this essay, April Pedersen, a writer and illustrator living in
Reno, Nevada, goes after a seemingly innocent behavior:
dog idolization. As the argument develops, Pedersen deals
with a range of opposing positions and assumptions.

There was a time when "Dog is my co-pilot" was merely a
fun slap at the "God is my co-pilot" bumper sticker, and it
was funny precisely *because* nobody would ever think to
elevate their dog to such a height. Within the past decade,
however, pets—primarily dogs—have soared in importance. ("Dog is my co-pilot" is now the slogan of *Bark,* a
magazine of dog culture, and the title of an anthology—
published by *Bark*'s editors—billed as essays, short stories, and expert commentaries that explore "every aspect
of our life with dogs.") Canines, with their pack instincts
and trainability, are by far the most likely pet to be anthro-
pomorphized as a family member, a best friend, or a "fur
baby," treated accordingly with gourmet meals, designer
apparel, orthopedic beds, expensive therapy, and catered
birthday parties. Some people even feel (and in some
cases, demonstrate) that their dogs are worth dying for.
Others say the animal lovers are going too far.

In a Pew Research Center study, 85 percent of dog owners
said they consider their pet to be a member of their family. However the latest trend is to take that a step further
in seeing the animal as a child. A company that sells pet
health insurance policies has dubbed the last Sunday in
April as "Pet Parents Day." Glance through magazines
like *Bark, Cesar's Way* (courtesy of "Dog Whisperer"
Cesar Millan), and other mainstream publications, and the
term "pet parent" crops up regularly. The "my-dogs-are-
my-kids" crowd isn't being tongue-in-cheek, either. They
act on their beliefs, buying Christmas presents, photos
with Santa, cosmetic surgery, and whatever-it-takes medical care for their animal. In fact having a puppy, claimed
one "mother," is "exactly the same in all ways as having
a baby." And while pushing a dog around in a stroller
would have gotten you directions to a mental health facil-
ity twenty years ago, today it's de rigueur to see a canine
in a stroller (or a papoose), and some passersby are downright disappointed to discover a human infant inside.

Who's to say what a pet's value is (aside from the
purchase price)? Shouldn't people be free to spend whatever they want on things for their dog? What real harm
is there in believing one's schnauzer is a "child who
never grows up?" The implications are more ridiculous
and far reaching than you might expect. Take the widely
held notion that dogs give us unconditional love and non-
judgmental loyalty. Praising dogs for being incapable of
acting like bad people is not only junk logic, it turns the
animal into an idealized (godlike?) version of ourselves,

MASTER DOG   OWNER BEST FRIEND   GUARDIAN   4-LEGGED FAMILY MEMBER   PARENT CHILD   WORSHIPER GOD

April Pedersen, "The Dog Delusion," from *The Humanist Magazine*, November/December 2009. Reprinted with permission.

to be rewarded with all manner of pampering. How can the comparatively complex human being compete with creatures said to exude unwavering faithfulness, forgiveness, trust, love, and innocence? Pets are pegged as more loving, more pure, more giving, more devoted. They are implied to be our moral superiors for not stealing money, starting wars, or judging people by their physical appearance. They accept us for who we are, while we come across as scheming, judgmental malcontents who love on condition only. I have quite a collection of misanthropic utterances from dog lovers, most along the lines of "I'll take dogs over humans any day," and "dogs love without having an agenda!" It's no surprise that many dog lovers would rather be stranded on an island with a dog than with their spouse (or with any other person for that matter). Then there's the CEO who said he doesn't trust clients who don't have pets. How sadly similar to the religious who say they don't trust nonbelievers.

Further undermining humans, dogs trained for various tasks are routinely referred to as soldiers, officers, actors, therapists, heroes, or athletes. But a police dog simply can't know the moral difference between a stash of cocaine and an old sock. One of the most absurd examples of anthropomorphism I've seen was a funeral for a drug-sniffing dog. The sheriff's department went all out with a motorcade, flag-draped casket, bag pipers playing "Amazing Grace," a eulogy from a pastor, and a rose-adorned easel on which the dog's portrait rested. Officers from all across the Western United States paid their respects, and the service received heavy local media coverage. All this for an animal that couldn't even grasp what a "law" was.

"Dogs are for people who can't have kids," a gay newspaper columnist told me recently. It's true that homosexual (and straight) couples who can't or don't want children of their own often migrate towards dogs as child substitutes and view the arrangement as a different kind of family, but a family nonetheless. Such dog-based "families" may at first blush seem benign or even beneficial. After all, people with a family mentality are more likely to form stable, safe neighborhoods and have a vested interest in the community. Those without children may benefit from nurturing a living creature and learning to be less self-centered. But doesn't it make more evolu-

tionary sense to want to care for the young of your own species over another species? Couples without kids for whatever reason could still opt to be foster parents, mentors, or Big Brothers/Sisters to make a positive difference in a child's life instead of funneling all their concerns into dogs. And what about devoting one's time to saving endangered species of animals (whose survival also affects that of humans)?

Yet each day dogs gain more and more importance, protection, and access to realms once reserved for humans. Michigan is considering a bill that would allow pet care as a tax write-off. What's next? Dogs counted as residents in the U.S. Census?

This shift in the status of dogs hasn't gone unnoticed by animal rights advocates. Already thirteen U.S. cities have ordinances that ditch "pet owner" for "pet guardian." The change is intended to be merely symbolic, its fans claim. If so, why make the effort? I worry it's a foot in the door to gradually desensitize society to the outlandish idea of pets being the equals of minor children. Allowing ourselves to glance down the slippery slope, we might foresee absurd lawsuits over injuries to pets, murder charges for those suspected of negligence in a pet's death, and laws requiring guardians to strap their fur kids into car seats, or to walk them twice a day, or giving any number of rights to the animals. Recently dog owners have begun to demand off-leash beaches and trails, under the premise that dogs have a "right" to run free. What's next, making spaying or neutering a crime, because pets should have the right to reproduce? Or allowing dogs to bite people or chase livestock in order to fulfill their right to behave as predators? Where would the "pet" line for special status be drawn? At gerbils? Ferrets? Canaries? Hermit crabs? The funny part is, not even the pet industry can decide if pets are children or property. In ads hawking pet supplies, dogs and cats are promoted as family members, loved ones, and babies. Yet the defense strategy, if sued over, say tainted pet food or a defective squeaky toy, is to focus only on the economic aspect of the pet.

Viewing dogs as our children extends to risking life and limb to save them as well. What would evolutionary psychologists make of healthy people of reproductive age leaping to their deaths into scalding hot springs, icy rivers, or smoke-filled infernos in an attempt to rescue a possibly neutered animal? Among surveyed pet owners, 93 percent, which includes the young and childless, would do just that. Of course, most dog owners fully expect their pet to save them, Lassie style, should the need arise. But if not trained for rescue work, most dogs would simply stare, hide, or eat the contents of their owner's picnic basket as their master sinks under the lake's surface. Cases abound where pets happen to save people from perilous situations, but they, the pets, were acting as animals, not as humans.

One can always argue that, from an environmental perspective, the pets-as-kids thing makes sense. With the human population reaching unsustainable numbers, pets can fill our desire to nurture without adding to the surplus of humans. Even so, dogs still eat a lot and produce a lot of waste (which has to be cleaned up unless the status lift requires potty training). And don't forget that dogs have to come from somewhere, and parents will show preferences for certain breeds. Puppy mills would be happy to meet the increased demand for dogs, if it can be considered ethical in the best of circumstances to take puppies away from their mothers and litter mates and give them to another species to raise them. Interestingly, our popular pets such as the domestic dog play no balancing role in any ecosystem; they are human-developed and human-maintained. Even feral dogs prefer to hang around our vil-

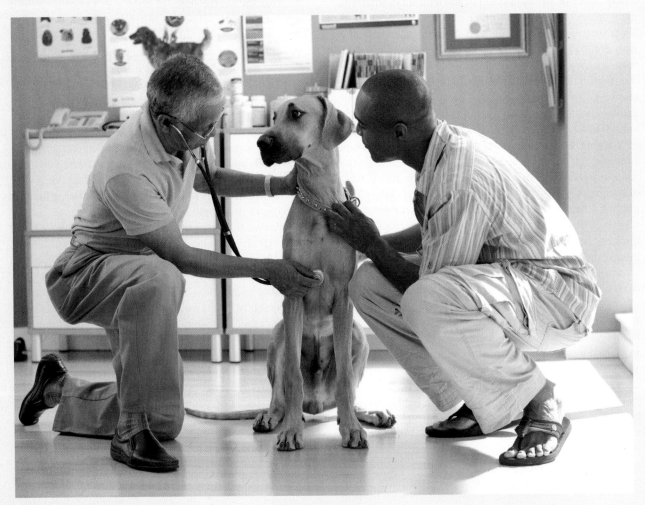

LWA-Dann Tardif/Corbis

lages, urban areas, and garbage dumps instead of returning to the woods to dance with wolves. And if too many people opted against having children in favor of pets, the result couldn't be good for economies; children are the future workforce, consumers, voters, tax payers, innovators, you name it.

Let's outsmart dogs a little by cutting back on the over-the-top stuff. The dogs won't notice. Funds spent on a dog's blueberry facial or in-room canine massage at a swanky hotel ($130 an hour) are about as close to setting a pile of cash on fire in front of a destitute person as I can imagine. Ditto on buying a sweater for an animal covered in fur, or a carob-coated eclair for a scat eater, or personalized cookies for the species that can't read (that would be all species except us). Certainly dogs can't visualize themselves as Homo sapiens of any age, and are becoming obese and even ill-mannered at the hands of their besotted owners. It makes no sense whatsoever to pour so much time, money, and emotion into an animal whose main "goal" in life is to leave its scent on a tree. Think about it—how would you like to be a dog? To be unable to talk, write, or question. To look upon a masterpiece of art without an ounce of admiration, to gaze at the starry night without an iota of wonder, to see a book and have not the slightest inclination to open it, or stare without comprehension at a voting booth.

It's fine to enjoy a pet. I've had several myself, including a cat that lived eighteen years. When his kidneys failed, a $12,000 kidney transplant was off the radar (a case can be made that such surgery on an animal is unethical anyway), and I didn't consider him to be my son. This need not diminish pets. We can enjoy them for what they are, without the anthropomorphic delusion.

## Writing Strategies

1. Plenty of pet owners would disagree with Pedersen's claims. Explain how Pedersen takes on opposing views. Describe a particular passage and explain how she pushes back or refutes the opposition.

2. How does Pedersen concede to the opposition or qualify her points? Describe particular passages. (For information on concessions and qualifiers, see pages 232–233.)

3. Explain how Pedersen uses appeals to logic. (See pages 229–231 for an understanding of appeals.)

4. Read about logical fallacies on pages 234–235. How does Pedersen's use of *slippery slope* impact her argument?

5. Pedersen appeals to values throughout her argument. What particular appeals to value do you detect?

## Exploring Ideas

1. Pedersen explains that "our popular pets such as the domestic dog play no balancing role in any ecosystem; they are human-developed and human-maintained." Why is this point important to her argument?

2. Explain why it would be wrong to characterize Pedersen as "anti-dog."

3. Pedersen compares some pet owners to "the religious who say they don't trust nonbelievers." Consider this comparison. How might dog ownership resemble religious belief or practice?

4. Even if you disagree vehemently with Pedersen, why might she have a sound position?

## Ideas for Writing

1. Consider some other widely accepted form of ownership. How might it be undermining human development?

2. What particular aspect of dog ownership makes people more humane?

If responding to one of these ideas, go to the Analysis section of this chapter to begin developing ideas for your essay.

# Cruelty, Civility, and Other Weighty Matters

## Ann Marie Paulin

As with most engaging essays, Paulin's originates in personal circumstance. (See her Invention Writing on page 222.) Also, as with most engaging essays, the writer extends her thinking into the public sphere. As you read "Cruelty, Civility, and Other Weighty Matters," notice how Paulin puts forth an argument while keeping herself in the background, only briefly referring to herself in the essay's introduction and conclusion. As you will see, Paulin goes beyond the increasingly common argument against the media's portrayal of women; she reveals something about the subtle effects of that portrayal. Paulin, who teaches English and gender studies at Owens Community College in Toledo, Ohio, shows that a writer's voice matters—that savvy use of voice actually creates layers to an argument. That is, her voice re-humanizes the issue and the people involved. If the media have dehumanized "fat people," Paulin does more than argue against the media; she strikes back with an intense, multifaceted presence.

I swear, if I have to sit through one more ad proclaiming that life is not worth living if you aren't thin, I'll slug somebody. So much for the theory that fat people are jolly. But, contrary to what magazines, talk shows, movies, and advertisements proclaim, we aren't all a bunch of sorrowful, empty losers with no friends and no self-esteem, either. As with most complex issues—religion, politics, human relationships—most of what we see in mass media is hugely oversimplified and, therefore, wrong. So, if many of us recognize the media are notorious for getting things less than accurate, you might wonder why I let these images bother me so much. Well, if you were one of the millions of fat Americans living in a culture where you are constantly depicted as some sort of weepy loser, ill-dressed buffoon, or neutered sidekick, your good nature might wear a bit thin as well. But far more important than my ill temper is a creepy sense that these inaccurate images have shifted our vision of what is important in life way out of whack, so far out that people are being hurt. What I'm proposing here is that we need to get some perspective on this issue.

First of all, let me make it clear that I'm not advocating that everyone in America go out and get fat. According to the news media, we are doing that very handily on our own, in spite of all the messages to the contrary and the shelves of diet food in every supermarket. (One of my colleagues came by today with a newspaper article on the Krispy Kreme Donut chain; evidently, Americans eat three million Krispy Kreme donuts each day. We may talk tofu, but we gobble glazed.) Americans all need to work on eating healthier and getting some exercise. Of course, the thin fanatics claim to advocate a healthy lifestyle as well, but I question how healthy people are when they are living on low-calorie chocolate milk drinks, or taking herbal supplements containing goodness knows what, or loading up on the latest wonder diet pill. Remember Fen-phen?

And most diets don't work. An essay by Rebecca Puhl, Ph.D., and Chelsea Heuer, MPH, in the *American Journal of Public Health,* cites studies which found:

> Most weight losses are not maintained and individuals regain weight after completing treatment. Patients who have lost weight through lifestyle modification typically regain 30% to 35% of their lost weight during the year following treatment, and regain most (if not all) of their lost weight within five years. ("Obesity Stigma: Important Considerations" 1021)

The authors go on to quote from a study by Mann, et al: "Dieters who gain back more weight than they lost may very well be the norm, rather than an unlucky minority" (qtd. in Puhl and Heuer 1021). My point here is not to argue that overweight people should not try to lose weight for health reasons. Indeed, even a modest weight loss of ten percent of a person's body weight is beneficial to one's health (Puhl and Heuer, "Obesity Stigma: Important Consideration" 1021). But such modest weight loss, while healthy, is rarely enough to earn a person fashionably thin status. And despite what the cultural messages suggest, most of us fat folks are trying to eat more sensibly, but the environment does play a role. In a culture where most of us are rushed from work to classes to other activities, the temptation to grab fast food is huge. Sugary or fatty foods are often available in grab and go packages that are so much easier to take to work or eat in the car than making a healthy snack. And, there is evidence to suggest we may even be wired to prefer junk food. Brownell and colleagues, in an essay in *Health Affairs,* cite studies which show: "Animals given access to food high in sugar and fat—even when healthy food is freely available—consume calorie-dense, nutrient-poor food in abundance, gain a great deal of weight, and exhibit deteriorating health" (379). I know, I know. We aren't rats. We are thinking beings, but this article goes on to point out that it is not so different for people: "Research has shown consistently that people moving from less to more obese countries gain weight, and those moving to less obese countries lose weight" (379).

So we are surrounded by a culture, even an infrastructure, that encourages obesity, yet the culture also

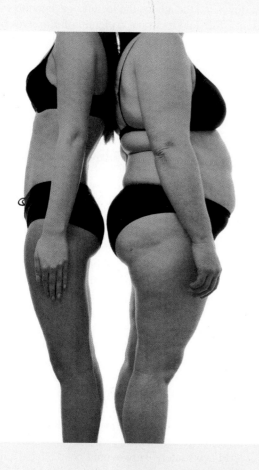

hartphotography/istockphoto.com

breeds a prejudice against fat people. Various articles and news magazine programs have reported that Americans of all sizes make far more than simple aesthetic judgments when they look at a fat person. Fat people are assumed to be lazy, stupid, ugly, lacking in self-esteem and pride, devoid of self-control, and stuffed full of a host of other unpleasant qualities that have nothing to do with the size of a person's belly or thighs. But, as anyone who has ever been the victim of such prejudice can tell you, the impact such foolish notions have is real and harmful. For example, Marilyn Wann, in her book *Fat! So?,* cites an experiment in which "[r]esearchers placed two fake personal ads, one for a woman described as '50 pounds overweight' and the other for a woman described as a drug addict. The drug addict received 79 percent of the responses" (59). So, in spite of the agony addiction can cause to the addict and those who love her, people would rather get romantically involved with an addict than a fat person. And not much has changed. In a 2008 article, "The Stigma of Obesity: A Review and Update," Puhl and Heuer report:

> One study asked college students (N=449) to rank order six pictures of hypothetical sexual partners, including an obese partner, a healthy partner, and partners with various disabilities (including a partner in a wheelchair, missing an arm, with a mental illness, or described as having a history of sexually transmitted diseases. Both men and women ranked the obese person as the least desirable sexual partner compared to the others. (10)

While it is certainly good news to see that people can look beyond disabilities, such as a wheelchair or a missing arm, and see the value of the whole human being, it is distressing that Americans refuse to do the same for a person's weight. Why would anyone want to date someone who will land them in the STD clinic? How dangerous is that? And yet, such a person is clearly seen as a better romantic choice than a heavy person. Here is a case where weight prejudice is certainly more dangerous to the person with the prejudice than it is to the fat person.

5     Another area of discrimination based on weight is in employment, both in getting hired in the first place and in receiving equal pay for equal work. In 1998, Wann pointed out that the average fat woman earns about $7000

less per year than her thinner sisters (80). Today, things are still not improving. As of 2004, a study from the National Longitudinal Survey of Youth found that obese men and women suffered a "wage penalty" for their excess weight. For men, wages ranged from 0.7–3.4% less than their slimmer coworkers, while for women the wage losses ranged from 2.3 to 6.1% (qtd. in Puhl and Heuer, "The Stigma of Obesity" 10). Here, as in other areas, we find that obese women are penalized more by society than obese men. Either way, in many jobs, a person's weight has nothing to do with the quality of their performance. In my case, I teach English at a community college. Jobs in academia require an advanced degree, so I happen to have a Ph.D., which has nothing to do with my body size, unless you want to count the weight I gained from thousands of hours sitting reading, sitting at a keyboard, sitting grading papers.

At the least, given the reports and studies, we can conclude that weight prejudice is not merely aesthetic judgment. It's an alarming trend, just like obesity itself, that hurts real people. When people are denied a place to live or a means of support not because of any bad behavior or lack of character or talent on their part but because of someone else's wrongheaded notions, then we need to get our minds straightened out.

The messages are particularly insidious when they suggest that being thin is more important than a man's or, more often, a woman's relationships with her loved ones or even than her health. The media churn the images out, but the public too often internalizes them. For example, in one commercial for Slim Fast, the woman on the ad is prattling on about how she had gained weight when she was pregnant (seems to me, if you make a person, you ought to be entitled to an extra ten pounds) and how awful she felt. Then there is a shot of this woman months later as a thin person with her toddler in her yard. She joyously proclaims that Slim Fast is "the best thing that ever happened to me!" The best thing that ever happened to her?! I thought I heard wrong. What about that little child romping by her heels? Presumably, there is a daddy somewhere for that little cherub. What about his role in her life? The thought that losing that weight is the most important thing that ever occurred in her life is sad and terrifying. It's even worse for the folks who share that life with her. I kept hoping that was not what she meant. I'm sure her

family is really most important. But she didn't say, "Next to my baby, Slim Fast is the best thing that ever happened to me." Advertisers don't spend millions of dollars creating ads that don't say what they intend them to; this message was deliberate. Granted, this is only one ad, but the message is clear: The consumer is the center of the universe, and being thin is the only way to ensure that universe remains a fun place to live. The constant repetition of this message in various forms does the damage to the humans who watch and learn.

While we can shrug off advertisements as silly, when we see these attitudes reflected among real people, the hurt is far less easy to brush away. For instance, in her essay, "Bubbie, Mommy, Weight Watchers and Me," Barbara Noreen Dinnerstein recalls a time in her childhood when her mother took her to Weight Watchers to slim down and the advice the lecturer gave to the women present: "She told us to put a picture of ourselves on the 'fridgerator of us eating and looking really fat and ugly. She said remember what you look like. Remember how ugly you are" (347).

I have a problem with this advice. First, of course, it is too darn common. Fat people are constantly being told they should be ashamed of themselves, of their bodies. And here we see another of those misconceptions I mentioned earlier: the assumption that being fat is the same as being ugly. There are plenty of attractive fat people in the world, as well as a few butt-ugly thin ones, I might add. Honestly, though, the real tragedy is that while few people in this world are truly ugly, many agonize over the belief that they are. Dr. Pipher reported: "I see clients who say they would rather kill themselves than be overweight" (91). Pipher wrote of these attitudes in 1995, but there is not much evidence to suggest we have become any more reasonable or sensible. In fact, in the article "Stigma and Discrimination in Weight Management and Obesity," Brownell and Puhl cite a 2001 study which showed that "28% of teachers in one study said that becoming obese is the worst thing that can happen to a person" (21). Statements like this make me despair for my profession. We are supposed to encourage critical thinking, not mindlessly parrot nonsense and pass it on to the younger generation. And if people think being fat is the worst thing that can happen, they have not watched the world news lately. How would people feel if the attitude was reversed: *The worst thing you can be is thin. All those skinny students must be lazy and stupid. They haven't got enough sense to eat enough or to look the way we want them to. Why bother with them?* And don't think that idea doesn't apply to fat prejudice. Brownell and Puhl cite another study that shows "controlling for income and grades, parents provide less college support for their overweight children than for their thin children" (21). What is up with that? A person's weight certainly has nothing to do with his or her intellect or curiosity about the world. Plus, based on the data I've reported so far, we plus size folks need all the education we can get just to struggle up to a living wage.

10    And don't think teachers are the only educated people with crazy ideas about overweight folks. Based on my research, the medical profession is full of people who despise us. "Stigma and Discrimination in Weight Management and Obesity" reports that "24% of nurses say they are 'repulsed' by obese persons" (21). That's a virulently negative attitude to get from someone upon whom your life may depend. And according to Puhl and Heuer, things are just as depressing with the doctors: "In a study of over 620 primary care physicians, .50% viewed obese patients as awkward, unattractive, ugly, and noncompliant" (The Stigma of Obesity 4). But how many people are willing to be compliant with someone who makes them feel awkward, unattractive, and ugly? The article goes on to explain that "one-third of the sample [of doctors] further characterized obese patients as weak-willed, sloppy, and lazy" (4). That's a lot of judgments to make after a ten-minute office visit. Shoot, my doctor is a republican, and if I'm willing to overlook that, the least he can do is overlook a few extra pounds. But, all kidding aside, this prejudice may have real and dangerous effects. Overweight people often do not seek medical care, especially preventive care. Puhl and Heuer go on to report:

> Several studies show that obese persons are less likely to undergo age-appropriate screenings for breast, cervical, and colorectal cancer. Furthermore, research shows that lower rates of preventive care exist independently of factors that are typically associated with reduced health care use, such as less education, lower income, lack of health insurance, and

greater illness burden. ("The Stigma of Obesity: A Review and Update" 7)

This bullying of the overweight is not only coming from professional and public life. Sadly many people face the cruelest ridicule from family, those we count on most for love and support. Another example of this bullying comes from Pipher's book *Hunger Pains: The Modern Woman's Tragic Quest for Thinness*. Pipher recounts a conversation she overheard one day in a dress shop:

> I overheard a mother talking to her daughter, who was trying on party dresses. She put on each dress and then asked her mother how she looked. Time after time, her mother responded by saying, "You look just awful in that, Kathy. You're so fat nothing fits you right." The mother's voice dripped with disgust and soon Kathy was crying. (89)

Pipher goes on to suggest that Kathy's mother is a victim of the culture, too, because she realizes how hard the world will be on her fat daughter. Unfortunately, what she doesn't realize is how much better her daughter's quality of life would be if she felt loved by her mother. Puhl and Heuer cite the results of a 2006 study of 2,449 overweight and obese women. "Participants were provided with a list of 22 different individuals and asked how often each individual had stigmatized them because of their weight. Family members were the most frequent source of weight stigma, reported by 72% of participants" (qtd. in "The Stigma of Obesity: A Review and Update" 10).

And the familial insensitivity doesn't stop at adulthood. In Camryn Manheim's book *Wake Up! I'm Fat,* the actress discusses her battle with her weight. She expected many of the difficulties she encountered from people in the entertainment industry, which is notorious for its inhuman standards of thinness for women. But when she gained some weight after giving up smoking, she was stunned when her father told her she should start smoking again until she lost the weight (78). In *The Invisible Woman: Confronting Weight Prejudice in America,* W. Charisse Goodman cites a 1987 study that concluded: "When good health practices and appearance norms coincide, women benefit; but if current fashion dictated poor health practices, women might then engage in those practices for the sake of attractiveness" (30). Like taking up smoking to stay slim.

Certainly everyone is entitled to his or her own opinion of what is attractive, but no one has the right to damage another human being for fun or profit. The media and the diet industry often do just that. While no one can change an entire culture overnight, people, especially parents, need to think about what they really value in the humans they share their lives with and what values they want to pass on to their children. We need to realize that being thin will not fix all our problems, though advertisements for diets and weight loss aids suggest this. Losing weight may, indeed, give a man or woman more confidence, but it will not make a person smarter, more generous, more loving, or more nurturing. It won't automatically attract the dream job or the ideal lover. On the contrary, people who allow the drive to be thin to control them may find that many other areas of their lives suffer: They may avoid some celebrations or get-togethers because of fear they may be tempted to eat too much or the "wrong" foods. They may cut back on intellectual activities like reading or enjoying concerts or art museums because those activities cut into their exercise time too much. The mania for thinness can cause a person to lose all perspective and balance in life. I know. It happened to me. My moment of revelation came about twelve years ago. I was a size ten, dieting constantly and faithfully keeping lists of every bite I ate, trying to lose fifteen more pounds. While I was watching the evening news, a story came on about a young woman who was run over by a bus. I vividly recall that as the station played the footage of the paramedics wheeling the woman away on a stretcher, I said to myself, "Yeah, but at least she's thin." I've been lucky enough to have gained some wisdom (as well as weight) with age: I may be fat, but I'm no longer crazy. There are some things more important than being thin.

## Works Cited

Brownell, Kelly D, et al. "Personal Responsibility and Obesity: A Constructive Approach to a Controversial Issue." *Health Affairs* 29.3 (2010):378–86. Yaleruddcenter.org. Web. 6 Jan. 2011.

Brownell, Kelly D., and Rebecca Puhl. "Stigma and Discrimination in Weight Management and Obesity." *The Permanente Journal* 7.3 (2003):21–23. Yaleruddcenter.org. Web. 6 Jan. 2011.

Dinnerstein, Barbara Noreen. "Bubbie, Mommy, Weight Watchers and Me." *Worlds in Our Words: Contemporary American Women Writers.* Ed. Marilyn Kallet and Patricia Clark. Upper Saddle River: Prentice, 1997. 347–49. Print.

Goodman, W. Charisse. *The Invisible Woman: Confronting Weight Prejudice in America.* Carlsbad: Gurze, 1995. Print.

Manheim, Camryn. *Wake Up! I'm Fat.* New York: Broadway, 1999. Print.

Pipher, Mary. *Hunger Pains: The Modern Woman's Tragic Quest for Thinness.* New York: Ballantine, 1995. Print.

Puhl, Rebecca, and Chelsea Heuer. "Obesity Stigma: Important Considerations for Public Health." *American Journal of Public Health* 100.6 (2010):1019–28. Yaleruddcenter.org. Web. 6 Jan. 2011.

—. "The Stigma of Obesity: A Review and Update." *www.ObesityJournal.Org* (Jan. 2009):1–23. Yaleruddcenter.org. Web. 6 Jan. 2011.

Wann, Marilyn. *Fat! So? Because You Don't Have to Apologize for Your Size.* Berkeley: Ten Speed, 1998. Print.

# Writing Strategies

1. Why do you think Paulin refers to "overweight" people as "fat"? What is the effect of this word on the reader?

2. Paulin helps the reader to understand her main ideas by stating them at the beginning of paragraphs. Find three paragraphs in this essay that begin with the main idea. Do those sentences also connect the paragraph to the previous paragraph? If so, describe how.

3. Paulin uses written sources to support her argument. In some places she directly quotes the sources; in others she paraphrases or summarizes (that is, she puts what the source says in her own words). Find an example of each (quote, paraphrase, summary). How do you know the information is from a source? Does Paulin make that clear? Notice how Paulin introduces the information and punctuates it.

4. Paulin's conclusion does not merely summarize points she has already made. Reread the conclusion and describe how it goes beyond mere summary. What does it try to do?

5. Paulin seems to know that her audience needs to be nudged along to accept her point. In your view, what particular rhetorical strategy is most effective at nudging readers to see the real harm of the media's portrayal of weight?

# Exploring Ideas

1. How is weight a public issue?

2. In her opening paragraph, Paulin says that inaccurate images about weight "have shifted our vision of what is important in life way out of whack, so far out that people are being hurt." Then she calls for perspective. What support can you provide for her claim that our vision of what is important is out of whack? What support can you provide that people are being hurt?

3. Why should or shouldn't comedians refrain from making fat jokes about specific individuals?

4. In her conclusion, Paulin says, "[P]eople who allow the drive to be thin to control them may find that many other areas of their lives suffer." Apply her thinking to some other situation besides body weight and explain how a particular drive has led to suffering.

# Ideas for Writing

1. In what subtle ways are short people marginalized or dismissed in everyday life?

2. What are the quiet hardships of beauty? Focus on one particular struggle that traditionally attractive girls, boys, men, or women encounter.

If responding to one of these ideas, go to the Analysis section of this chapter to begin developing ideas for your essay.

# Floppy Disk Fallacies

## Elizabeth Bohnhorst

As computers become increasingly fused to everyday life, students and teachers may struggle to ask hard questions about the proper role of technology in the classroom. In 2005, Elizabeth Bohnhorst wrote this essay for a college class. Since then, computers have, no doubt, become more normalized in classroom teaching. As you read, consider how Bohnhorst's argument resonates with the current educational climate—if her argument has become more or less significant in recent years.

**Writing Strategies**

The personal testimony feeds into the main idea.

"Another boring PowerPoint," responds Jennifer when I ask about her day at school. I might not find these words so discouraging coming from a company executive after a long meeting or even a college student leaving an informative lecture. But these words of an eleven-year-old elementary school student leave me feeling slightly uneasy. PowerPoint presentations are intended to compel students to become more interested in the subject with the use of neon colors and moving graphic images. But these flashy additions to current educational strategies haven't fooled everyone. The text and material covered is still the same boring grammar and spelling lessons, but the educator has altered: It is a screen.

This final flat statement reinforces an obvious problem with flashy technology.

A thorough concession to the educational power of technology.

Computers can undoubtedly contribute wonders to the field of education. In fact, computer education is a must if children intend to thrive in modern society. The possibilities are endless when it comes to surfing the Web or using the thousands of educational programs currently available. These programs are capable of reading text on a computer with icons beside words that take students to a galaxy of options, icons to learn more about the era in which the text was written, fascinating facts about the author, and helpful notes about the morals of the story. But computers are being used more and more frequently as a substitute for books, blackboards, and in some cases, the teachers themselves.

A turnabout paragraph—ending with a counterargument.

America leads the world in the amount and density of computers in our public schools. In 1992, the typical high school had one computer for every ten students, while elementary and middle schools averaged thirteen students per computer ("Computers"). Compared to current numbers, the early 1990s were a time of deprivation. Some schools, such as Kent Central School in rural Connecticut, are considering funding for each student to have his or her own laptop. After visiting the school, Anne

The evidence shows the scope of the issue—that computer technology has become a widespread and conventional classroom tool.

**Exploring Ideas**

Even young children can see past the techno mania. The colors have fooled plenty of educators but not all the kids.

Computers link kids to more and more information, more options, more data.

We lead the world in computer use, but aren't we far behind most industrialized countries in student performance?

Guignon reports that "students use the computers in school, take them home each night, use the computers for homework, and soon will be able to tap into the Internet." In such situations, traditional school lingo such as "Take out a piece of paper and a number two pencil" might be replaced with "Take out your floppies and boot up your Toshibas." Unfortunately for some students, dogs cannot digest discs.

> More evidence that administrative bodies across the country celebrate computers as a primary educational tool.

And the Texas Board of Education is only steps behind the Kent Central School. "The Texas Board of Education now has state officials seriously examining whether to give all public school students laptops instead of textbooks," states a *New York Times* investigator. The Board "is looking at $1.8 billion in projected costs for textbooks over the next six years, and . . . given technology improvements that have lowered the price of computers, it may be cheaper, to say nothing of innovative, to lease a laptop for each of the state's 3.7 million students" (Guignon).

> So much of the school budget will go to computer retailers.

5  Now, what could possibly be wrong with such a sophisticated device for learning? In reality, "thirty years of research on educational technology has produced almost no evidence of a clear link between using computers in the early grades and improving learning," states Michael Dertouzus, director of the MIT Laboratory for Computer Science. In fact, evidence of hazardous effects of frequent use of computers in young children is overwhelming. They do little to promote a healthy childhood. "Computers are perhaps the most acute symptom of the rush to end childhood. The national drive to computerize schools, from kindergarten on up, emphasizes only one of the many human capacities, one that naturally develops quite late—analytic, abstract thinking—and aims to jump start it prematurely," continues Dertouzus.

> Evidence shows no causal connection between computers and better learning.

> What many people have been saying for years: a screen may not be the most interactive or nurturing form of education. In fact, it might be the opposite.

> The "national drive" refers back to her previous paragraphs.

Elementary schools are not only responsible for teaching children reading, writing, mathematics, and other basic skills; they also reinforce and indirectly establish guidelines for everyday behavior. Therefore, consistent use of computers in schools ultimately plants the idea in the developing mind that computers are safe, educational, and perhaps one of the most important tools of modern society. Thus, a child returns home from school after hours of staring into an illuminated box, flips through the channels of yet another illuminated box, and then proceeds to play "Final Fantasy Four" on the Macintosh for three more hours. A 1999 study by the Kaiser Family Foundation showed that children ages two to eighteen spent an average of four hours and forty-five minutes per day plugged into electronic media of

> This gets into more complex, but less obvious, injuries—into the quiet layers of harm that computers do to young students.

> All these illuminated boxes!

all kinds. These numbers are excluding the time spent with such machinery during school hours (Dertouzus).

Here, we walk even further into those layers of harm. The writer keeps moving us into deeper dimensions.

The emotional and social values learned during childhood are also disrupted by computerized education in elementary and middle schools. Students learn more than state capitals and multiplication; they develop a sense of social importance and are taught values of friendship and other relationships. Through interaction with peers, intimacy and companionship are only a few of the many principles computers are unable to relay to children. Dr. Stanley I. Greenspan, former director of the Clinical Infant Development Program, is concerned that the impersonal culture formulated by computerization has serious detrimental effects on children's emotional development: "So-called interactive, computer-based instruction that does not provide true interaction but merely a mechanistic response to the student's efforts," states Greenspan, can be directly linked to "the increasingly impersonal quality that suffuses the experience of more and more American children" (qtd. in Dertouzos). He also adds that lack of nurturing for children at home and at school can likely result in "increasing levels of violence and extremism and less collaboration and empathy" (qtd. in Dertouzos).

Computers don't teach socialization—unless we count the quick blurbs and self- promotion of Facebook.

We're definitely seeing increased violence.

To go yet further into the harm and past the common assumptions, she analyzes the concept of *creativity*.

Besides affecting emotional and social development in primary students, computers can also disrupt creative thinking. Like all other electronic viewing systems (television and video games), computers leave little or no room for imagination. Of course, the virtual reality computers create is often full of fantastic images. However, because imagination involves generating one's own images and ideas, consistent exposure to ready-made images only makes it more difficult for children to summon their own creativity. The intensity of the images squashes the need for intensive creativity.

Another turnabout paragraph: a concession followed by a counterargument.

Computer software is often, then, anti-imagination. It does the imagining for students.

Educational psychologist and former school principal Jane Healy has observed that "teachers find that today's video-immersed children can't form original pictures in their mind or develop an imaginative representation. Teachers of young children lament the fact that many now have to be taught to play symbolically or pretend—previously a symptom only of mentally or emotionally disordered youngsters" (qtd. in Dertouzus). Not only do these images affect creativity and imagination; they also have potential to diffuse the sparks of curiosity. For example, if a class is learning about regional watersheds, computerized classrooms will most likely turn to the handy diagrams so conveniently laid out on the screens before the students. In a classroom that values hands-on learning techniques, a school field trip to a local stream or swamp may be an effective strategy. In short, a successful education should not replace children's curiosity to explore the world around them with Internet Explorer.

Explore is a verb. Explorer is a product. Big difference!

10   On the other hand, technology is an effective way to get kids interested in learning, considering "that there is a passionate love affair between children and computers" (Setzer). A colorful computer screen is obviously more attractive to a child than an old novel or a textbook. But this attraction is more likely a fascination with animation and sound effects rather than a genuine exploration of ideas. Dr. Valdemar W. Setzer, a professor of computer science, wonders, "What happens to a student who gets used to learning with computers? Will she be able to tolerate a normal class without all those cosmetic and video game effects?"

Computers are another form of cosmetic!

As technology's role in American society grows, we should observe its influence in public education. It is easy to consider the benefits of computerization: simplicity, standardization, and elimination of other physical controversies. But in the same light we must also consider the hazards and how important traditional education is to children. The obvious concern with traditional education is the students being "left behind" in the rush toward increasing technological advancements.

Educating students in computer skills is and should be a priority in all schools. But when it comes to teaching basic skills and allowing for intellectual development, human interaction and exploration of the real world should never come second to electronic devices. In an effort to preserve the qualities of education, we should not allow ourselves to become mesmerized by teachers that require an electrical outlet and textbooks that require a point-and-click to turn the page.

The difference between computer skills and other skills.

A call for pause: for thinking through the implications, that have been offered throughout the essay.

She gives a qualifier: the distinction between teaching computer skills and more complex dimensions of human development.

## Works Cited

"Computers in American Schools, 1992: An Overview." *IEA Computers in Education*. U of Minnesota, 12 July 1995. Web. 20 July 2005.

Dertouzos, Michael. "Developmental Risks: The Hazards of Computers in Childhood." *The Alliance for Childhood*. Alliance for Childhood, n.d. Web. 20 July 2005.

Guignon, Anne. "Laptop Computers for Every Student!" *Education World*. Education World, 19 Jan. 1998. Web. 20 July 2005.

Setzer, Valdemar W. "A Review of Arguments for the Use of Computers in Elementary Education." *Southern Cross Review* 4 (2000): n. pag. Web. 20 July 2005.

# Writing Strategies

1. Bohnhorst begins with some personal testimony. How does that impact her argument? What is the effect?

2. Why does Bohnhorst's reference to PowerPoint strengthen her argument about computers?

3. Bohnhorst is tackling a common assumption in education: that more technology is inherently good. Describe her strategy for confronting and overturning this assumption. How does she do it?

4. How does Bohnhorst apply appeals to value in her argument?

5. How does Bohnhorst deal with specific opposing ideas? Where does she reveal the shortcomings of other positions? Where does she acknowledge the value of other positions?

# Exploring Ideas

1. Consider the following claims made by Bohnhorst:

   Computers can undoubtedly contribute wonders to the field of education. (¶2)

   In fact, computer education is a must if children intend to thrive in modern society. (¶2)

   With others, explore these claims further, trying to discover new ways of thinking about them. Begin by discussing whether you think the claims are true, and then pinpoint and explore why people might disagree.

2. Bohnhorst explains that "the intensity of the [computer] images squashes the need for intensive creativity." Explore how this might work. Consider a specific video game or website and describe how its intensity squashes a need for creativity.

3. How might computers in the classroom prevent learning?

4. How do you define learning? How does popular educational software fit into or oppose your definition of learning?

# Ideas for Writing

1. What argument might you make by taking a more extreme stance on the role of computers in education?

2. To develop your own argument, research some claim Bohnhorst makes, such as "teachers find that today's video-immersed children can't form original pictures in their mind or develop an imaginative representation." (¶8)

If responding to one of these ideas, go to the Analysis section of this chapter to begin developing ideas for your essay.

# Whales R Us

## Jayme Stayer

Good writers often invite, and sometimes force, us to confront ideas we would rather not examine. In his argument
about Sea World, Jayme Stayer sheds new light on the
park. His points might seem unreasonable at first. After
all, why should someone target a theme park? But Stayer's
essay illustrates an important move in academic writing:
uncovering the layers of meaning behind the propaganda
of everyday life. Stayer, a professional musician and T.S.
Eliot scholar, is a Jesuit, an order of priests and brothers
in the Catholic tradition. He has taught at Texas A&M–
Commerce, Universidad Centroamericana in El Salvador,
and John Carroll University.

Mickey Mouse scares the bejesus out of me. Shamu, on
the other hand, simply makes me queasy. I'm not the first
to express loathing for Mickey & Co.: a giggling rodent as
mascot for a nasty, litigious, multimedia *Über*-corporation.
But you don't hear too many people railing against Sea
World, though Shamu has a dark side too.

One of the first things to irk me at a Sea World park
happened during a bird show. A perky blonde was displaying a few parrots, and she kept up a stream of banter about
their feeding habits and origins. "When our ancestors came
to this continent," she breezily explained to an audience
chock full of non-Europeans, "they brought with them this
breed of parrot from Africa." Since I'm almost certain that
slaves brutally shipped to the Americas were not allowed
bird cages as carry-on luggage, what she should have said
was that European—not "our"—ancestors stopped off in
Africa and loaded up with parrots and slaves. One needn't
be a fanatical multiculturalist to be ruffled by inaccurate
history and specious assumptions about an audience's
makeup.

In America, unexamined notions of history and the
coercive politics of majority identity go hand in hand with
boorish nationalism. (See, for example, the debate over
the Confederate flag and its supposed status as symbol
of a unitary "Southern" culture.) Oddly, the bird show at
Sea World confirmed this. Her parrots now retired, the
perky woman waltzed around the stage with a bald eagle
while the audience was subjected to a chummy patriotic

tune. So the eagle was presented not as the largest or most
impressive of birds, or as indigenous to Canada, or even
as another instance of the marvels of creation, but as the
Bird of American Democracy—this, in spite of the fact
that eagles' politics tend to the monarchist side and that
their feeding habits indicate a predisposition for brutal
dictatorship. The bird becomes valued, in other words,
for the cultural associations "we" Americans slapped
onto it, not for any of its intrinsic properties. The eagle, in
Sea World's monistic version of the world, becomes just
another happy commodity—like parrots, slaves, designer
clothes sweatshops—that makes America the Great
Nation It Has Always Been.

But not all employees were as chipper as the bird
show people. There are two types of teenagers who work
at Sea World: the aggressively happy and the sullenly
aggrieved. These two opposed mentalities are as old as
the summer job itself: namely, the optimism of youths
who want to change the world vs. the cynicism of kids
who despise their jobs, resent their pay, and wouldn't give
a hooey if they were fired because some enraged Yuppie
did not get good service with a grovelling smile when he
bought his Sno-Cone. I personally sided with the disaf-
fected and wished I had brought copies of *The Communist
Manifesto* to slip into their pockets.

5    The most important job at Sea World—and teenagers
are particularly good at it—is making lots of noise. Since
most Americans are terrified of being alone in a store
without Muzak, Sea World willingly obliges its customers with rock-concert levels of decibels. All of the shows
keep up a noxious patter complete with ear-splitting sound
effects; the walkways have abrasively loud music piped
over them; and even the exhibits have teenagers chained
there with microphones in hand, droning their mantra of
dull facts.

It is ironic that a park putatively designed to extol the
wonders of nature is obsessed with high-tech wizardry
and mega-voltage noise, noise, noise—even when it is
extolling the wonders of nature's silence. Another talking
point of the bird show featured how silently an owl could
fly. The bird's flight began in blissful silence, but half-
way through its flight the soundtrack faded back in with
a shimmer of violins, followed by a cymbal crash when
the owl landed. Even the absence of noise is packaged

Jayme Stayer, "Whales R Us." Reprinted with permission of the author.

with noise: The owl's silence is first framed with amplified yakking (noise), then underlined as it happens (quiet noise), then punctuated (big noise) so the audience knows when to clap (make more noise).

One of the most ludicrous moments of the Shamu show was an assertion by another relentlessly cheerful teenager: "We here at Sea World believe we have the greatest jobs in the world." With its overtones of Orwellian party-speak, it was only slightly risible until she added: "We get to work with nature's most wonderful animals and contribute to the world's knowledge about them." Her jejune assumption that "world knowledge" exists as some kind of huge, accumulative spittoon—rather than a set of competing claims and shifting paradigms—was hilarious enough, particularly coming from a kid who is probably still struggling with basic algebra and who wouldn't recognize "world knowledge" if it landed on her in a heap. I imagined her logging on to a marine biology chat group and making an announcement—in all caps, no doubt—followed by an emoticon: "SHAMU DID A BACK FLIP TO-DAY!!! : )" Thus does the world's cup of knowledge runneth over.

And that insistent refrain of "We here at Sea World believe" was another thing that rankled me, because it was usually followed by patronizing flimflam. Some prime examples: "We here at Sea World believe that animals should not be taken from their natural habitat." Or: "We here at Sea World believe only in the use of positive reinforcement in the training of animals." The audience is supposed to believe that these are lovely sentiments. How noble that they try to find injured or orphaned animals to "befriend." How comforting to know Shamu isn't being shocked with electricity or poked in the eye when he's tired or just damned fed up with giving piggyback rides. Most disturbing was that these credos came mostly out of the mouths of the teenage staff, whose inexperience made their We-Believe proclamations ring even more hollowly.

Taken individually, some of these moments were only mildly unnerving, but there was one occurrence that stood out as gratuitous. Situated on a lake, the Sea World I visited featured a water show with ski jumps and corny skits. The theme of that year's show was *Baywatch,* which involved—predictably enough—nubile bodies in poorly choreographed dance routines, the bold rescue of

Kamal Sellehuddin/ZUMA Press/Corbis

someone in the water, and the odd appearances of two buffoons (fat old man with hysterical wife), all of which was irritatingly narrated by an emcee's we-havin'-fun-yet? voice-over. At one point, the old man and his wife were "accidentally" pulled into view: the man (vertical) on skis, the woman (horizontal) with her legs wrapped around his torso. They were in the unmistakable position of sex, the two actors in a flurry of feigned embarrassment at having been "caught." (Whut in tarnation cud be more funny than ol' fat folks havin' sex? Har dee har har.) The emcee and other characters on stage slyly absolved themselves of complicity in this vulgarity by shrugging their shoulders, as if to say: "Golly, what was that all about?" Sea World, by the way, bills itself as a place for the whole family.

10   You might think that a park that sponsors PG-13 shows would divest itself of prudishness.

Alas, there was more self-righteousness there than at a revival. Case in point: the shark exhibit. Before we could enter, we were forced to watch a short film about sharks; the doors to the exhibit were pointedly barred until after the film was over. The film gave us a hellfire-and-damnation scolding: you thought that sharks were human predators? WRONG. You thought sharks were abundant in the ocean? WRONG AGAIN. After airing its grievances with us—the ill-informed public—it asserted that much damage had been inflicted on these misunderstood fishies. Because we've all been shark-haters at heart, fishermen have felt free to kill them. Quivering with virtue, the film called "intolerable" the fishermen who "senselessly" destroyed the sharks, either because the sharks got caught in the nets or because the sharks fed on prized fish. With vast self-contentment Sea World then relayed how they had successfully worked to stop this great evil.

While I'm pleased to have my horror-film notions of sharks corrected, the film's smugness was unbearable. And in spite of Sea World's professed vigilance, I'm not convinced that sharks aren't still being arbitrarily killed somewhere in the world. Even so, I wonder if sharks, given the choice, would prefer to stay in a Sea World bathtub for the rest of their lives or take a chance with those fishnets.

Of the many inanities hurled at me, my favorite was an emcee's sign-off: "And remember," she intoned

from a precipitously high moral ground, "before we can have peace *on* the Earth, we have to make peace *with* the Earth." Indeed. As if, in the interest of world peace, the United Nations agenda should be scuttled in favor of dotting the globe with Sea Worlds to promote feel-good vibes between humans and dolphins. Here's more glib reasoning: to make peace *with* the Earth implies the Earth was a peaceful place before we humans mucked things up. Yet the last time I looked, the Earth was full of viruses, earthquakes, predatory animals, and a survival-of-the-fittest mentality that Sea World has apparently never heard of.

And maybe it was petty of me to be irked when the woman narrating Shamu's activities insisted that whales scratch their backs on the pebbled shores when they're contented. There was captive Shamu scratching his back on the simulated shore. The audience oohed and aahed. Never mind that Shamu had been explicitly directed to scratch his back, and that to have disobeyed would have resulted not in a whack on the head (lucky for him) but in the withholding of food (not so lucky). Is that contentment then? With the help of an extraordinarily costly visual aid, the audience was expected to "learn" a fact of whale behavior that could be shown only at the cost of candor.

15   Sea World, I realized after an afternoon of learning very little, was a place that was desperately trying to present itself as a place where education occurs. And for twenty-some bucks, your educational experience goes roughly like this: You can give up an afternoon of watching vapid TV shows and take your whole family to watch a skit based on a vapid TV show. You get to ogle busty women and hirsute men. You get to have constant noise crowd out any independent thoughts that might be percolating to the surface of your brain. You get to harbor the illusion that America is a happy, white, European family, as well as a leading maker of world knowledge, and that Sea World is largely responsible for such happiness and abundance. You get to imagine you hold the key to world peace (remember to give the dog a kiss when you get home). You get to indulge in patriotic goosebumps ("the *American* eagle!"), have your heart-strings jolted ("Ah—Shamu's happy to be here!"), get your sluggish sense of morality jump-started ("*baaaad* fishermen, *gooood* sharkie"). And if you're willing to invest another three bucks, you can fling a sardine

at dolphins that have been petted to within an inch of their lives. Best of all, at the end of the day you get to go home with the vaguely self-congratulatory feeling that you've *learned* something, by God.

I'm an educator, and I pay close attention when someone is trying to teach me something. So on my way out of Sea World, I asked myself what I had learned. Like a student who has crammed for an exam, I was able to recall lots of idiocies, but could only say I had truly learned two things. (1) Thanks to the film, I learned that sharks attack humans only when provoked, and, (2) thanks to their anthropomorphizing skits, I learned that sea otters are cute little buggers. Even if these elements were judicious pedagogical objectives (which they are not), they still don't add up to anything resembling education. In fact, the entire experience of Sea World is suspiciously similar to the exact opposite of education: mind control.

It was only in retrospect that I realized that these annoyances were related: the high-pitched entertainment and trivial sexual jokes, the shut-up-and-listen attitude, the constant noise and verbal presence, the Big Brotherly refrains of exactly what "We here at Sea World believe." These are all rhetorical strategies of a government diverting its citizens, masking something it doesn't want the public to know. And what is it that Sea World doesn't want its customers to think about?

In a review lambasting Disney World, an author hilariously describes the ideology of the place as "benign fascism": The streets are immaculately clean; the worker bees wear impossibly happy smiles; the rides and trains run on time; and every day, the gloved hero appears on parade, where the hordes worship him and his lickspittles with songs and fireworks. The author's comparison of Mickey to Mussolini is more than just amusing: He ties it into his critique of how history is portrayed at the Epcot center. Because Disney does not want to offend any of its ethnically and racially diverse customers (Sea World: take note), their film on American history carefully controls the emotional barometer of its vacationers. The Disney film of American history is whitewashed to the point of banality, and such central topics as the atomic bomb, racial conflict, and imperialist genocide are entirely avoided. The point is that fascists, benign or not, always

have political and economic reasons for telling history the way they do. And like Disney World and other fascist operations, Sea World likes to keep a tight grip on what and how its visitors think.

Take, for example, the "we-believe-animals-should-be-treated-in-this-way" gestures that continually crop up. These assertions pose as facts the audience ought to memorize in preparation for an exit quiz. Yet the nervous tic of emphasizing the politically correct means of treating animals in captivity belies Sea World's uneasiness with the larger, unasked question: Should we even have animals in captivity for our bourgeois amusement? Nowhere in their literature, exhibit signs, or rehearsed prattle of their miked minions is this basic question broached or answered.

[20] Part of the way Sea World can get away with ignoring the obvious fact that these animals are there for our entertainment is that it nervously insists that it is a place of science and research, and disingenuously implies that entertainment easily meshes with education and research. While I scoff at the idea that important research gets done at Sea World, the problem isn't really with what kinds of knowledge Sea World makes, or how much, or how important it is. Rather, the problem is Sea World's communication of that knowledge, or to be more explicit, their refusal to level with its visitors about its real cultural role and worth. If they would fess up to the fact that Sea World is essentially a playground and not a classroom, that might be a start towards a real educational experience.

Sea World keeps up its image of itself as a classroom by propagating signs with facts and statistics on them. These factoids—and their Post-it Note ubiquity—are a peculiar manifestation of "textbook knowledge": boring chunks of data unconnected to any larger, compelling theme. There were a plethora of facts swimming around at Sea World and a dearth of ideas, which is why I couldn't remember anything at the end of my day. Like the eager student who has a bad teacher, I was given no complex or interesting framework inside of which ideas jostled about; so I was reduced to cramming lists of unconnected information in preparation for a never-to-be-taken exam.

I'm not suggesting that Sea World become a place that sponsors round-table discussions of animal rights and lets biology students present their theses during Shamu intermissions. But I do think that instead of slavishly subscribing to popular notions of science, Sea World might call them into question. This is what real education does.

As it stands, none of our deeply rooted cultural beliefs are explored or challenged at Sea World. After a trip there the visitor is likely to keep thinking that facts are equivalent to knowledge; that America is synonymous with Europe; that science and technology are the greatest goods imaginable; that education means being fed a list of facts in a condescending manner; and that sated, docile fish—who decorously eat buckets of non-cute sardines—are practically vegetarians.

A skit in which a lovably frisky sea otter has its head chomped off by a hungry predator is not the kind of bloody epiphany Sea World is likely to promote. Imagine the screams of the unsuspecting children. Imagine the lawsuits of offended suburbanites who like their nature sanitized and safe. But imagine, too, how such a moment would educate an audience about the dangers of humanizing certain animals at the expense of others. Such a skit might end with a question to the audience about why its government enacts laws to protect the habitat of owls but not of insects or low-income humans.

25 The only cultural assumption that was seriously challenged at Sea World was the premise of *Jaws*—and that was much too heavy-handed, not to mention incorrect, as events in Florida have shown. It turns out that sharks *will* attack idle swimmers. It should come as no surprise that a capitalist venture like Sea World can't even get its basic facts straight. Neither can the tobacco industry seem to grasp what everyone else knows about nicotine addiction. Nor is Disney equipped to navigate the treacherous waters of American history.

Surely the most real moments at Sea World occurred when the fascists lost control, for example, when the staff had trouble getting the animals to obey their directions. Such glitches in the program put their slapstick routines and canned jokes on hold, and forced them to talk to the audience about fixing this problem. It also gave the teenage apparatchiks an opportunity for some inspired ad-libbing, disburdening them from their less endearing lecture notes.

If the ideology of Disney is benign fascism, then the ideology of Sea World is exploitative spectacle masquerading as education. Too occupied with obscuring the real moral, environmental, and scientific issues at stake, Sea World is constitutionally incapable of teaching respect for nature. Love of nature is spiritually informed and politically assertive. It is not the kind of passive, sentimental quackery Sea World prefers, and it cannot be taught with the crude tools in Sea World's lesson plans: glib moralizing, base pandering, and clichés masquerading as insights.

But in the last analysis, Sea World—to paraphrase Auden—makes nothing happen. Sea World is a reflection of American culture: a consequence, not a cause; a mirror of consumerist desires, not a promoter of political change via education. The American traits Sea World reflects most clearly are its gullibility and irrationality. It's a consolation, albeit a small one, to consider that Americans are likewise gullible to the very real beauty of nature. It's that kind of openness—and not Sea World's preaching—that makes the connection between humans and dolphins seem worth investigating. It's less of a comfort to consider another analogy between Americans and marine life that Sea World leaves unexplored: America's exorbitant arms race, its rape of the environment, its valorization of guns and violence, its giddy, media-fueled acclamation of the death sentence that disproportionately murders minorities: Are these not strikingly similar to the fierce logic of the food chain? Screw the little guy; I'm hungry and more powerful.

So my advice is to go to Sea World anyway. Even inside the ideological frame where they are forced, the creatures there—including the teenagers—are amazing, hilarious, and terrifying. Who can remain unimpressed when a mammal the size of a Mack truck lifts itself out of the water? As for Sea World itself: If, aided by earplugs and skepticism, you can ignore what they're trying to teach you, you just might learn something.

**Work Cited**
Alexander, Maxwell. "Promise Redeemed: At Long Last Mickey." *Johns Hopkins Magazine* Apr. 1995: 5. Print.

# Writing Strategies

1. What word would you use to describe the voice of this essay—humorous, serious, urgent, angry, light, or something else? Identify several passages to support your description.

2. Stayer is trying to call Sea World out—to reveal something disingenuous or fake about the park's rhetoric. In your own words, what is Stayer trying to reveal?

3. How does counterargument function in this essay? Point to particular passages in which Stayer is countering some opposing claim and explain how that passage figures into the overall point of the essay.

4. How does Stayer use Sea World to make broader points about American culture?

5. How does Stayer's conclusion work on the audience? Describe what the conclusion does for readers—how it reinforces or develops a kind of relationship between Stayer and the reader.

# Exploring Ideas

1. What new way of thinking does Stayer introduce? (Consider his points about education, entertainment, theme parks, even American popular culture.)

2. Based on this essay, how are Stayer's thoughts, values, beliefs, or feelings similar to or different from yours?

3. Stayer argues, "If the ideology of Disney is benign fascism, then the ideology of Sea World is exploitative spectacle masquerading as education." In small groups, paraphrase this sentence. How does this point work in Stayer's overall argument?

4. How does Stayer's thinking go beyond one's initial ideas about entertainment parks?

# Ideas for Writing

1. What public place—such as Sea World—presents itself in a way that is different from what you know (or suspect) about that place?

2. What public place presents itself honestly and accurately?

If responding to one of these ideas, go to the Analysis section of this chapter to begin developing ideas for your essay.

# INVENTION

Academic audiences demand more than "three reasons why I believe X" arguments. They want to experience more in an argument than a writer's personal beliefs; they want to learn a new way of thinking. So academic writers often look for a way to make people rethink an issue. They try to create a new position on a familiar topic or assert a position on an entirely fresh topic. And good writers do not merely *choose* topics; instead, they *build* topics from the novel and surprising moments of everyday life.

The following sections are designed to help you develop ideas for your argument: specifically, to discover a topic (in Point of Contact), develop particular points about the topic (in Analysis), make it relevant to a community of readers (in Public Resonance), focus your position (in Thesis), and create support for that position (in Rhetorical Tools). The questions in each section will help you generate intense ideas and start writing. Your responses to the Invention Questions may take you in various directions, and some of your responses may get left behind. That is to be expected in academic work—or in any work that seeks to discover something valuable.

# Point of Contact

Some situations in everyday life are obviously significant—what they mean for our lives, or for the lives of others, is apparent. When our country goes to war or when a new president is elected, for example, most Americans understand the significance. Many situations, however, are far more subtle; their potential meaning is hidden by life's hustle and bustle. To understand their meaning, we must stop in our tracks and focus on them. Use the following suggestions and questions to explore possible topics. If a question seems engaging to you, or if you associate some emotion or idea with the question, start writing. Ask yourself: "Can I change someone's mind about this situation or issue?"

**School**   What lurking attitude is ruining the learning process? If we're a country of progress, why should history be taught anyway? How is mainstream fashion brainwashing even the smart kids? Will football be the end of serious public education? How was *Napoleon Dynamite*'s portrayal of high school right on target? How are high schools destroying students' ability to cope with the first year of college? How is high school its own form of religion?

**Work**   What doesn't the public understand or appreciate about my work? Are the work expectations fair? Are the hours fair to workers? What hidden forces or assumptions work against productivity? Why don't people in my line of work get paid more? Are they paid way too much?

**Home**   What does my neighborhood layout suggest about being a human? How does the layout of my house or apartment or dorm help me to be a better person? What is the central appliance in my living space and how does that affect my thought process? Should more people have gardens? What do cathedral ceilings (or some other architectural feature of our homes) make people think about themselves?

**Community**   Does my town know what to do with teenagers? Does the water taste funny? Does my town offer ample mass transit? How does the police force function—as keepers of the peace or something else? How important are trees?

**Pop Culture**   How does *American Idol* impact popular music? Can a democracy seriously thrive without a good punk scene? What is a culture without a vibrant funk subculture? Should we be leery or supportive of a whole channel dedicated to food? What does the Discovery Channel do for science? Should there be a fun show about language and writing? Calculus?

**Your Major**   Look through a current journal in your field to find controversial issues: Are entry-level personnel in my field treated fairly? Is some research in my field or major controversial? Is my field undervalued by the public? Has my field changed any of its practices, for better or worse, in recent years? Should my field be more diverse (in gender and/or ethnicity)?

## Activity

Make a list of other questions that draw attention to troubling situations in the world around you. What attitude or basic assumption lies beneath some troubling behavior or policy?

# Analysis

Analysis cracks open the layers of a topic—and helps a writer to see more than his or her initial thoughts about it. Without analysis, writers may find themselves with little new to say. As you answer the Invention Questions, avoid answering too quickly. Instead, use the questions to search for deeper understanding, which will then translate into more intensive writing. Allow time and space for your own thinking to develop.

## Invention Questions

▶ What is the particular point of crisis or tension?

▶ How has the situation (or condition, behavior, policy) come about, and why does it continue?

▶ What are the effects of the situation (or condition, behavior, policy)?

▶ Why do I have an opinion on this topic?

▶ Why is my belief valuable? ■

Ann Marie Paulin looks beneath the initial tension or problem and discovers a hidden layer. She goes beyond being "angry" and discovers that media trends indirectly support, even "encourage," mistreatment and incivility:

### Why do I have an opinion on this topic?

I have been fat since I was a kid. For about two days in my twenties I starved my way down to a size ten, thereby earning this head-turning compliment from the guy I was then dating: "You'd be a real fox if you'd just lose a few more pounds." I've had complete strangers say the most astonishing things to me on the street. For example, on my way through a parking lot to get to my car, I passed a young man who looked over at me and shouted: "I don't !,#$ fat chicks!" Who was asking? While these behaviors have sometimes hurt me, they mostly make me angry. And when I look around at the society in which I live, I don't see any signs that this kind of behavior is discouraged. Indeed, the media seems to suggest that fat people, by their very existence, seem to deserve contempt and abuse.

### How has this situation come about?

Where it gets tricky is that by the media's definition, damn near everyone is fat. How has this situation come about? I'm not sure, but I've watched it develop. When my mother was young, a size ten or twelve was a respectable dress size. When I was in my twenties, a size eight was a respectable size. Now, you must be a size four, two, or even better, a zero to be considered thin. Now, a six-foot-tall model who wears a size twelve dress is considered plus size. She only gets her photo in Lane Bryant ads and such. It's as if society has completely forgotten the concept of "normal size," and so a person is either thin (if you can count all her bones when she appears in a bathing suit) or she's fat. And that leaves the majority of women believing they are fat and hating themselves for it.

Paulin's thinking shows how writers work: In the process of analyzing ideas, they create various possible writing directions. However, as they begin to develop their projects, they become more focused and revelatory; they grab onto one point and take it somewhere. They go beyond the common complaints and reveal a particular quality, effect, or layer of the issue.

# Invention Workshop

Enlist the help of another writer in answering one of the Invention Questions. Use the question to initiate a discussion. Explore further by questioning one another's responses to the questions. For example, Jack is focusing on his high school education. Notice how the discussion with Marcus goes beyond Jack's initial response:

### What is the particular point of crisis or tension?

JACK:      My high school education was inadequate. I graduated with a B average, and I came to college having to take developmental courses before I could even begin taking credit courses.

MARCUS:   But is that the high school's fault?

JACK:      Well, if I couldn't cut the mustard in entry-level college courses, why did I get mostly Bs

MARCUS:   in high school? It seems like something's out of whack.

MARCUS:   OK. So the standards are too low in high school?

JACK:   Yeah, I think so.

MARCUS:   Were you ever warned about the standards in college?

JACK:   Sure. All the time, teachers would scare us with things like, "Wait 'til you get in college; you've got to work constantly to keep your grades up."

MARCUS:   But did anyone ever share specifics with you? Did you know what kinds of writing, for instance, you would be doing in college?

JACK:   Not really. It's all been a big surprise.

MARCUS:   Maybe that's the issue: high school students (and maybe teachers and administrators) don't really know what kinds of things go on in entry-level college courses.

JACK:   Yes—and so there's this huge gap in between, and some students fall right into it.

It would be easy to reinforce Jack's initial idea—the inadequacy of high school—by sharing examples of bad teachers or rotten classes, but Marcus and Jack do better. They develop the initial idea into something more specific and revealing: the gap between high school and college standards.

# Thinking Further

Analysis is not about answering a question and finding an answer. The real insights lie beneath the answers. Return to your responses to the Invention Questions and try to find the most valuable ideas:

- What statements reveal something specific?
- Which statements or phrases seem new to you?
- Which statements or phrases make a new connection, one that you had not considered before?

Now, you can take the statements or phrases forward and use them to develop increasingly intense ideas for your argument. If nothing stands out at this point, consider re-approaching the Invention Questions and invite another person to join your exploration. And this time, deliberately take the ideas further:

- What behavior, policy, or quality is at the heart of the topic? (What is beneath the tension you initially discovered?)
- What attitude, value system, or assumption rests beneath the actions of people who are involved?

# Public Resonance

Writers transform issues or personal concerns into arguable topics, issues that matter in some way to other people. Making a personal concern resonate with a public issue is simply a process of extension. To this end, the following Invention Questions can be used as springboards from personal concerns to public issues. For example, examine the following question: *Is my living situation conducive to my goals as a student?* You may have answered: "Yes. I live at home with my parents and commute to school." Your situation is not unique. Many college students struggle with their living situations—with the decision of living on campus, in a nearby apartment complex, or at home with their parents, away from the campus altogether. This decision involves more than a simple personal choice. It has something to do with college funding, with the success of college students, with the entire college experience. In this sense, your situation resonates with a more public issue. The initial (more personal) question might evolve into a more public question: *Is it beneficial for college students to live at home while going to school?* As you consider your own topic, use the following questions to move from a personal concern to a public issue.

▶ Who might care about this issue? Why?

▶ Who *should* care about this issue? Why?

▶ How are my readers involved in this issue? How *could* they be involved?

▶ What group of people might understand or sympathize with my situation?

▶ Is this issue an example of some trend?

▶ Why is it important that others hear my opinion about this issue?

▶ What else has been said about this issue, and how are my ideas different? ■

Public resonance is key in Ann Marie Paulin's project. Her essay shows that the more a topic affects people, the more attention it may deserve. In her responses to the Invention Questions, she explores the hidden messages in ads and the unstated assumptions lurking in the public domain. Paulin's responses show her making connections between her own situation and many others. By extending her thinking outward, she is developing the public dimensions of her idea:

**Who might care about this issue? Why?**

This is certainly a very public issue because it is almost impossible to escape the media: magazines, newspaper ads, billboards, radio, TV, movies, ads plastered in public restrooms and on the walls of buses, ads in your e-mail every day. And every one of those images that deals with weight or beauty makes it clear that to be fat is completely unacceptable and completely fixable if only a person tries hard enough and buys the right products.

Now, if this were just an issue of vanity, it might be something that could be shrugged off. But it goes much deeper than that. If you really pay attention to those ads, their real message is often that if you are fat, no one will love you. Your husband will leave you (if you ever manage to get one to begin with). Your children will be ashamed of you. Your friends will give up on you. You will be alone and unloved because you are fat. That is the message that really hits us where we live. Who wants to be some lonely outcast? We must conform to whatever it takes.

And so, most of us try the diets, the pills, the exercise classes, the wonder machines, and sometimes even more extreme measures like stomach stapling surgery. But in spite of all the time, money, and effort we expend, most of us are still fat. If you look at the studies done, the results are all about the same: Anywhere from 90% to 98% of the people who lose weight gain it all back within five years.

Sometimes writers need to go beyond the *actual* effects or consequences of an issue and *imagine* the possible ways others are involved. Consider the following: A writer is arguing about college students living at home. The issue seemingly affects only college students, and maybe their parents. But the writer makes the issue resonate with many other potential readers by transforming a personal issue into a more public one:

> How college students live is not simply a matter of personal choice and comfort. It is a public issue, a public education issue. At the federal, state, and local levels, Americans are increasingly focused on the out-of-school living conditions of elementary and secondary students. Whenever people talk about the quality of education, invariably they end up discussing the living situation of students—the stability of their homes, the qualities of the neighborhoods. Why? Because people are beginning to realize that education does not occur in a vacuum, that how and where students live impact how they learn. But for some reason, we don't seem to be concerned once students are in college. Consequently, millions of college students swarm off to school every fall, often without deeply considering the implications of where they will live. And when millions of dollars of loans and grants go down the drain when students fail out their first year, we don't seem to ask the same questions we ask about elementary and secondary students.

## Research

Consider using outside sources to help you invent—to help you imagine the hidden values, assumptions, and attitudes people have about the topic. Discover what has been said about your topic, what people have argued, why they have taken certain positions, or why they have ignored it altogether. (See Chapter 13 for help with finding sources for help with finding sources.)

## Going from Private to Public

### Private Concern:

Where should I live during my first year in college?

### Public Concern:

What is the relationship between college failure rates and student living conditions?

# Thesis

An argumentative thesis invites debate or suggests that opposing claims exist. For example:

> But far more important than my ill temper is a creepy sense that these inaccurate images [about body type] have shifted our vision of what is important in life way out of whack, so far out that people are being hurt.

The process of narrowing down an argument to an intensive single sentence helps writers to understand the heart of their idea. At an early stage in your project, you need not settle into an exact wording, but trying to generate a focused statement can help your ideas gain intensity.

An argumentative thesis should have four qualities:

**Arguability**  It should be arguable. That is, an arguable thesis should take a stand on an issue that has two or more possible positions. If you can conceive of other possible positions on the topic, you are probably in arguable territory.

**Scope**  It should be appropriately narrow. Scope can be addressed by asking narrow enough questions. Be careful of broad questions: *Is my town boring?* To answer such a question, one would have to consider all of the town's complexities, all of its goings-on, all of its people, all of its places, and so on. However, the question *Does my town offer sufficient activities for teens?* is more easily answerable—and ultimately arguable.

**Public Resonance**  It should address an issue that resonates with the readers. A good argument addresses a concern that others have *or that a writer thinks they should have.* In other words, a thesis should express something that matters (that has some significance) to readers. It should involve others.

**Revelation**  Academic writers attempt to do more than argue for their own opinions. They try to *reveal* an unfamiliar topic or reveal a new layer to a familiar topic. *Revelatory* thesis statements change readers' (and the writer's) thinking

because they show something new. They clear away the mundane thinking and reveal the roots of an issue. Often, revelatory thesis statements:

- Include a reference to the opposition.
- Overturn or contradict popular opinion.
- Show a particular effect or relationship.
- Uncover a hidden layer.

## Activities

1. Transform the following into revelatory thesis statements:

   - The Internet has changed the world.
   - Video games are bad for kids.
   - Sixteen-year-olds who commit crimes should be punished as adults.

2. In a small group, choose one of the following topics and develop at least one revelatory argumentative statement:

   - Leash laws in your town
   - The process for choosing presidential nominees
   - Product placement in movies
   - The cost of college textbooks
   - High school English courses

# Evolution of a Thesis

A writer can always increase the focus and revelation of a thesis. The following idea evolves into an increasingly sophisticated point:

- College students benefit from living at home.
- Traditional college students still need the support structure of their home lives to deal with the new challenges of college.
- Because college culture demands intense intellectual and social change from high school culture, traditional college students need the support structure of home.

The first statement announces a simple opinion. The second narrows in on a specific tension: "the new challenges of college." But the statement is still a bit vague, and the idea will intensify with even more focus on that tension. The third statement brings us up close to the primary tension and shows us something that might otherwise escape our awareness: the "intense intellectual and social change" between high school and college culture. The reader of the last two theses, especially the third, has been given a novel insight about schooling. In this way, revelatory thesis statements are more than personal opinion; they are particular and persuasive insights.

# Common Thesis Problems

**The Question Problem** A question is not a thesis, because it offers no stance. People sometimes use questions to imply a stance: *Isn't that the point of college? Why can't you be like your sister?* But this is generally an informal strategy—something people do in everyday talk. A formal argumentative stance should suggest a particular position amidst a realm of many others.

**The Obvious Fact Problem** An argument that simply announces a commonly known condition is no argument at all. Imagine someone arguing: *Many people go to college for their futures; Americans love cars;* or *Space exploration is expensive.* Such statements do not invite opposition because they are widely held beliefs. They are safe statements about the condition of our civilization. But the statement *Space exploration is too expensive to continue at its present pace* invites opposition.

**The Personal Response Problem** Argument depends upon the presence of several other perspectives peering at the same topic. However, when people proclaim a personal response (about their tastes, likes, dislikes, or desires), they merely make public their own state of mind. "I really liked the movie" is not an argumentative stance. It is a statement about a person's tastes. But the statement, "Johnny Depp's portrayal of a wayward pirate illustrates his superior range as an actor" invites opposition. Other positions can engage the point critically.

## Revising Your Thesis

Before moving on, try to express the main point of your argument in a single sentence. Then evaluate the statement using the following questions:

- How is the statement arguable? (What other positions might be taken?)
- Can the statement be narrower? (What words are too vague or broad?)
- With what public issue or concern does the statement resonate?
- How does the statement reveal a unique insight or hidden layer of the issue?

You might also exchange your working thesis statement with two or three peers and use these questions to generate helpful responses.

# Rhetorical Tools

Crafting an essay, or any written text, is a recursive process: Writers move back and forth, drafting, rethinking, redrafting. It is not a simple step-by-step journey that looks the same for everyone. But all writers benefit from a large collection of strategies, various tools they can use according to their particular needs, situations, and voices. The strategies in this section will help you build a sophisticated and engaging text—one that emerges from your particular ideas.

Academic argument involves four basic ingredients or elements:

- Main claim/Thesis
- Support
- Counterargument
- Concession

Cengage Learning

# Support

Support gives substance and legitimacy to an argumentative claim and comes in a variety of forms. Consider the following as a collection of usable support strategies, a toolbox for persuading readers of your position, despite the particular topic.

**Examples**  Specific cases or illustrations of a phenomenon. (See Pedersen ¶4 and 6, Paulin ¶7, Stayer ¶6 and 7.)

**Allusions**  References to history, science, nature, news events, films, television shows, or literary texts. (See Paulin ¶2, Stayer ¶1–4 and 9.)

**Personal Testimonies/Anecdotes**  Individual accounts or experiences. (See Pedersen ¶11, Paulin ¶1 and 2, Bohnhorst ¶1.)

**Scenarios**  Hypothetical or fictionalized accounts. (See Pedersen ¶7.)

**Statistics**  Information (often given as numerical value) collected through experimentation, surveys, polls, and research. (See Pedersen ¶2, Paulin ¶4, Bohnhorst ¶3.)

**Authorities**  References to published (most often written) sources. When using authorities, writers must formally document the use of any information, ideas, and expressions taken from sources. For an extended explanation of formal documentation and integration of sources, see Chapter 14: Integrating and Documenting Sources. (See Paulin ¶2, Bohnhorst ¶5.)

**Facts**  Agreed-upon events or truths, or conclusions drawn from investigation. (See Stayer ¶1 and 2, Bohnhort ¶2.)

Additionally, arguments depend on appeals, which make a connection between the topic and the audience's thought process. In fact, appeals have such rhetorical force that they give meaning to and can even dominate over other forms of evidence. The first three appeals that follow (to logic, emotion, and character) are often discussed using three classical Greek terms: *logos* (for logic), *pathos* (for emotion), and *ethos* (for character). These are sometimes referred to as the Classical appeals.

**Appeal to Logic**  Relates the argument to the audience's sense of reason or creates a line of reasoning for the audience to follow. (See Pedersen ¶7, Paulin's conclusion, Stayer ¶14 and 15 and 19, Bohnhorst ¶10 and 11.)

**Appeal to Emotion**  Relates the argument to an emotional state of the audience, or attempts to create a particular emotional state in the audience. (See Paulin ¶1 and conclusion.)

**Appeal of Character**  Relates the argument to a quality of the author/speaker. (See Pedersen ¶11, Stayer ¶15.)

**Appeal to Need**  Relates the argument to people's needs (spiritual, economic, physical, sexual, familial, political, etc.). (See Bohnhorst ¶8 and 9.)

**Appeal to Value**  Relates the argument to people's values (judgments about right/wrong, success, discipline, selflessness, moderation, honesty, chastity, modesty, self-expression, etc.). (See, Bohnhorst ¶7 and 8.)

> The appeal to logic, or *logos,* is the most valued appeal in formal argument. It requires the arguer to establish premises—claims that must be accepted in order for the main claim (or conclusion) to be acceptable. One example is the *syllogism,* which asserts two premises and a conclusion: A is true and B is true; therefore, C must also be true.

Too often, writers limit themselves by assuming that facts and statistics are the primary support tools for a good argument, when the truth is that facts and statistics are merely a fragment of what's possible—and what's most valuable. Writers have the whole world of culture and history within reach. They can make connections (allusions) to historical or current events, literary texts, science, nature, and their personal lives. For example, perhaps you see a connection between your topic and a recent news event. You could briefly explain details of the event and then describe what it means for your topic—how it reveals something significant and ultimately validates your opinion. The same thing goes for a movie, an ad, or a historical event. For instance, imagine a writer developing the argument about college residence policies. He might bring popular culture to his aid:

> In movies and popular television shows, college is nearly always portrayed as a raucous social engagement. The typical movie college student (like those in *American Pie* or *Animal House*) is a dormitory, apartment, or frat or sorority house dweller who thrives or suffers in the family-free environment. The whole point of college in mainstream movies is to create a living situation in which the students just tread the line between responsible participation in society and utter immersion in bohemian life. It's no wonder that going to college seems synonymous with "going away" to college. When students long to avoid living in the chaotic social climate of campus life, they are working against more than some college policies. They are working against popular culture.

If you see a connection, especially one that others might not see, it can create a new way of thinking about the topic. Use the following questions to develop allusions, testimony, and scenarios for your argument:

▶ Does a historical situation or trend (say, the rise of a particular fashion, organization, or individual) illustrate something about my topic?

▶ How has popular culture treated my topic? Does it show up in television shows, movies, or commercials? If so, how is it characterized, mishandled, or celebrated?

▶ Have fictional characters illustrated something important about the topic or some behavior related to it?

▶ How does nature (animals, life cycles, plants, biological processes, and so on) demonstrate something about my topic?

▶ What has science taught people about my topic?

▶ Do any news events illustrate my point or stance?

▶ What have I witnessed or experienced that illustrates my point?

▶ What hypothetical situation could illustrate my point?

▶ What do other writers or authorities on the matter say about the topic? ■

Now, imagine how using appeals can help your argument. The various appeals can be applied to nearly any topic. Notice how a writer might tie an argument about college students to broader values—family intimacy and self-determination:

> Going to college should not have to mean going away to college. The intellectual commitment required of a student should not necessarily require a domestic commitment. Coming into an institution should not necessarily mean abandoning the intimacy of family. And entering college should not mean entering a compulsory social climate. But policies that require first-year students to live on campus impose a domestic and social arrangement onto students.

The most valued strategy in formal academic argument is the appeal to logic—or what is often called a *line of reasoning*. When writers create a line of reasoning, they create an intellectual path for readers—several steps (sometimes called premises) that lead to the writer's thesis. Consider the topic from the previous section: college students living at home. If we want to convince readers to believe that colleges should not require students to live on campus, we might create the following line of reasoning:

**a.** The shift from high school to college culture is significant.

**b.** Many students experience a kind of culture shock in the transition.

**c.** This culture shock negatively impacts their academic performance.

Each of these statements requires further explanation, examples, illustration, evidence, and appeal. In other words, this line of reasoning might require several lengthy passages of text. But if the readers could accept each claim, then they would be led directly to the main point—that college policies should not require on-campus residence for all first-year students.

As you consider your own topic, use the following questions to develop appeals:

▶ What line of reasoning can I create for the reader to follow? What premises do readers have to accept before they accept my thesis?

▶ How can I connect the topic to people's values (sense of right and wrong, success, discipline, selflessness, moderation, honesty, chastity, modesty, self-expression, etc.)?

▶ How can I connect the topic to people's basic needs (spiritual, economic, physical, sexual, familial, political, etc.)?

▶ How can I connect the topic to people's emotions (fear, hope, sadness, happiness, etc.)?

▶ Does my life (my role in a relationship, on a job, in school, on a team, etc.) lend credibility to my position on this topic? ■

## Activity

Generate a variety of appeals for each of the following claims:

• Although war illustrates human cruelty and malice, it also illustrates human compassion and sympathy.

• Most proponents of capital punishment fail to consider the impact on the executed person's loved ones.

• Democracy cannot thrive in a two-party system.

• Excessive marketing leads to a lack of civility and respect among citizens.

# Counterargument

Counterarguments anticipate and refute claims or positions that oppose those being forwarded by the writer. Writers must anticipate and account for positions outside of or opposed to their own claims(s) and include reasoning to offset that potential opposition. For example, a savvy teenager who wants to attend a party will imagine his parents' concerns and work them into his argument about why he should be allowed to go. A politician will anticipate her opponent's position on an issue and formulate her speech accordingly.

The most successful arguers are good counterarguers. They address and even dismantle the specifics of opposing claims. In her essay, Ann Marie Paulin counterargues by summing up advice given to Barbara Dinnerstein: "She told us to put a picture of ourselves on the 'fridgerator of us eating and looking really fat and ugly. She said remember what you look like. Remember how ugly you are." In the paragraph that follows this advice, Paulin explains why she disagrees:

> I have a problem with this advice. First, of course, it is too darn common. Fat people are constantly being told they should be ashamed of themselves, of their bodies. And here we see another of those misconceptions I mentioned earlier: the assumption that being fat is the same as being ugly. There are plenty of attractive fat people in the world, as well as a few butt-ugly thin ones, I might add. Honestly, though, the real tragedy is that while few people in this world are truly ugly, many agonize over the belief that they are. Dr. Pipher reported: "I see clients who say they would rather kill themselves than be overweight" (91). I never have figured out how trashing a fellow being's self-esteem is going to help that person be healthier.

In academic argument, opposing claims are vital. Instead of ignoring or fearing them, good writers *use* them to develop points. In developing your argument, try to address opposing claims. Doing so will make your own argument more complex, more developed, and more persuasive.

In fact, some writers anticipate the opposition and integrate a counterargument directly into their thesis statements. For example, let's examine the working thesis: *College students benefit from living at home while attending school*. This thesis is somewhat focused, but it could better if we imagine the opposition: Someone might argue that the college experience depends on moving away from home, that intellectual growth requires leaving one's family and familiar turf. This opposing position might be supported with personal testimony and stories in literature that tell of heroes leaving their homeland to seek knowledge or wisdom in the world. We would do well to consider these points, and perhaps work against some of them directly. We might even work part of the logic into our own thesis: *Despite the attraction of living away from home and experiencing life in unfamiliar territory, college students benefit from living at home while attending school.* This thesis now contains a counterargument. It is both an assertion and a response to a primary opposing point.

## Invention Workshop

This activity is designed to generate counterarguments. The process involves an intensive group exchange. Follow these steps:

- Assemble writers into small groups (three or four per group works best).
- Each writer should have his or her thesis statement (main argumentative claim) written down.
- The first writer should read his or her thesis statement aloud to the group.
- Taking turns, each group member then should attempt to refute the position given in the statement. The idea is to play devil's advocate, to complicate the writer's ideas.
- The writer should record each opposing claim that is offered.
- After everyone in the group has given an opposing claim to the first writer, the second writer should recite his or her thesis, and the process begins again.

## Concession and Qualifier

While counterarguments refute objections, concessions acknowledge the value of others' claims. Put another way, if the writer says that an objection or alternative is wrong, the response is a counterargument; but if the writer says that the objection or alternative is right, that response is a concession.

Concession is a vital aspect of academic argument. In her argument, Elizabeth Bohnhorst offers a thorough concession to the value of computers before she begins her powerful argument against their role in the classroom:

> Computers can undoubtedly contribute wonders to the field of education. In fact, computer education is a must if children intend to thrive in modern society. The possibilities are endless when it comes to surfing the Web or using the thousands of educational programs currently available. These programs are capable of reading text on a computer with icons beside words that take students to a galaxy of options, icons to learn more about the era in which the text was written, fascinating facts about the author, and helpful notes about the morals of the story.

Conceding in academic argument does not make an argument wishy-washy. In fact, a good concession, such as Bohnhorst's, shows that a writer understands the broader context—other opinions, values, hopes, and perspectives. A good writer might discuss the logic of another position and show, *to some degree,* how that position has validity. This does not mean that the writer's own point is weak; on the contrary, it means that his or her point is so strong and valid that it can even acknowledge the soundness of other positions. (See more on this in the Writer's Voice section.)

*Qualifiers* are closely related to concessions. They acknowledge the limitations of, or make clear boundaries for, the writer's own argument. For example, when giving a speech on the evils of corporate tax evasion, a senator qualifies her statements: "Granted, most companies in America pay taxes responsibly, but we must focus on those few rogue and politically powerful companies." When arguing for a salary increase, a union leader acknowledges a point made by the opposition: "We understand that economic times ahead could be perilous and that a salary increase could make the company more financially vulnerable to outside forces, but the future of the company certainly depends upon the well-being of its loyal employees." And in her argument, Paulin makes an explicit qualifier, which may keep readers from mischaracterizing her position:

> First of all, let me make it clear that I'm not advocating that everyone in America go out and get fat. According to the news media, we are doing that very handily on our own, in spite of all the messages to the contrary and the shelves of diet food in every supermarket.

### Activity

Before drafting an essay, plan out your main elements. Write out your working thesis and then, below it, create five headings:

- Personal testimony
- Examples, allusions, or scenarios
- Evidence from sources or reference to authorities
- Opposing positions
- Counterarguments, concessions, or qualifiers

Under each heading, list the ideas or information you've generated so far. This plan, or informal outline, can help you to move forward.

# Concessions and qualifiers show that a writer understands the broader context of the argument.

# Caution: Logical Fallacies

Logical fallacies are flaws in the structure of an argument that make the claims invalid. A fallacy is a falsehood, so a logical fallacy is a logical falsehood that makes no sense within a given situation. For example, consider this familiar line:

> If you break a mirror, you'll have seven years of bad luck.

We may recognize this as superstition. In academic terms, it is called *faulty cause/effect*. That is, the broken mirror does not actually cause misfortune in one's life. The statement seems categorically faulty. However, the success (or logic) of any argument depends on the particular situation. All argumentative statements exist in situations that give those statements credibility. (If someone's entire fortune were tied to a mirror, then the previous statement would be more logical!) Statements are logical or illogical based on the situation.

In academia, recognizing logical fallacies is part of being a critical thinker in all disciplines. There is no quicker way to make readers of your own work suspicious than committing any of the following fallacies when making an argument.

## Ad hominem (Latin for *to the person*) Attacks a person directly rather than examining the logic of the argument.

- We cannot possibly consider Ms. Smith's proposal because she is a Catholic.
- Mr. Mann's argument is suspicious because he is a socialist.

## Strawperson Exaggerates a characteristic of a person or group of people and then uses the exaggeration to dismiss an argument.

- Islamic fundamentalists are crazy. They only want to destroy Americans. We cannot accept their claims about imperialism.
- Environmentalists are radical. They want to end everyone's fun by taking cars and boats away.

## Faulty Cause/Effect Confuses a sequential relationship with a causal one. Assumes that event A caused event B because A occurred first.

- Since the construction of the new baseball stadium, homelessness in the downtown area has decreased.
- The tax cut made energy rates drop.

## Either/or Reasoning Offers only two choices when more exist.

- Either we destroy Russia or it will destroy us.
- The American people will choose to control their own lives or give away their wills to socialist candidates.

## Hasty Generalization Draws a conclusion about a group of people, events, or things based on insufficient examples (often, the logical flaw behind racist, sexist, or bigoted statements).

- Men are too possessive. My ex-boyfriend would never let me go out alone.
- French people are rude. When I went to France, the civilians grunted French statements when I asked for help.

## Non sequitur (Latin for *it does not follow*) Skips several logical steps in drawing a conclusion.

- If we do not trash the entire tax code, the downtown area will slowly deteriorate.
- A new baseball stadium downtown will help with the homelessness problem.

## Oversimplification Does not acknowledge the true complexity of a situation or offers easy solutions to complicated problems.

- If we could give kids something to do, they wouldn't get depressed.
- This credit card will end all of my financial problems.

**Slippery Slope** Assumes that a certain way of thinking or acting will necessarily continue or extend in that direction (like a domino effect). Such an argument suggests that once we begin down a path, we will inevitably slip all the way down, and so the effects of a particular action or idea are exaggerated.

- If the college makes students take more mathematics, the next thing we know, advanced calculus and quantum physics will be requirements for all graduates.
- If North Vietnam succeeds in making South Vietnam communist, it will eventually threaten the shores of the United States of America.

**False Analogy** Makes a comparison between two things that are ultimately more unlike than alike. The differences between the things make the comparison ineffective or unfair, or the comparison misrepresents one or both of the things involved.

- Writing is like breathing: you just do what comes naturally.
- Like Galileo, Bill Clinton was breaking new ground, but no one understood him.

**Begging the Question** Attempts to prove a claim by using an alternative wording of the claim itself.

- Girls should not be allowed into the Boys' Military Academy because it is for boys only.
- I believe that all cigarette smoking should be banned from public places because I truly believe in smoking bans.

## Activities

**A.** What logical fallacies might you overhear in everyday situations? Consider the following scenarios: a customer trying to return an item; a store clerk trying to sell an extended warranty; a teacher explaining why a student cannot receive credit for a late assignment; a student arguing that he or she should receive a better grade; two politicians debating a tax cut; a husband explaining why he should go fishing with his cousin all weekend.

**B.** In groups, write an example for each of the fallacies listed in this chapter.

**C.** In groups, write short argumentative essays loaded with logical blunders. Someone in each group should read the completed essay aloud, and the class should attempt to point out and name the fallacies.

# Organizational Strategies

## How Should I Begin?

As with all essays, the sky is the limit. Remember some of the basic introductory tools (anecdote, provocative question, shocking statement). Remember, too, that introductions not only create focus for the topic but also establish the tone of the essay. They are the invitation to *start* thinking. But if an introduction is flat, typical or vague, it is an invitation to *stop* thinking. Notice this typical, vague introduction:

> There are many critical issues facing today's public schools. They have to consider violence, financial constraints, teacher training, drugs, and student apathy, just to name a few. But in this difficult era, educators have become enamored with a saving grace: technology. Computers are everywhere in our public schools. But the problem is that the technology isn't the saving grace that it seems. Schools should rethink their allegiance to computers.

This introduction illustrates a few critical mistakes. First, the writer begins with a statement that nearly everyone knows. It is not an invitation to think rigorously or explore an issue. Second, it is far too broad for the reader to get traction. Third, because the introduction begins so broadly, it makes at least two large intellectual leaps in the goal of getting to the writer's thesis at the end. Fourth, the attempt to place the thesis at the end of the paragraph makes all the other information seem contrived and formulaic.

To the contrary, in her essay Elizabeth Bohnhorst takes us directly to the critical issue, showing a specific example. She does not need to rush through several vague statements to suggest her position on the issue. She makes it indirectly from the outset:

> "Another boring PowerPoint," responds Jennifer when I ask about her day at school. I might not find these words so discouraging coming from a company executive after a long meeting or even a college student leaving an informative lecture. But these words of an eleven-year-old elementary school student leave me feeling slightly uneasy. PowerPoint presentations are intended to compel students to become more interested in the subject with the use of neon colors and moving graphic images. But these flashy additions to current educational strategies haven't fooled everyone. The text and material covered is still the same boring grammar and spelling lessons but the educator has altered: It is a screen.

Bohnhorst does go on in her essay to speak about computer technology in general, but here she focuses on a specific program, PowerPoint, which gives her argument, and her readers, a focal point.

### Activity

Reread the introductions to the essays in this chapter. Notice the difference among strategies. Do the introductions help to establish the tone in each essay?

## Where Should I Put Counterarguments?

Counterarguments can be tricky, but they need not be. First, they can be placed anywhere in a paper: at the beginning, throughout the body, and even at the conclusion. You might explain an opposing point and then counter, explain another opposing point and then counter. (Depending on the amount of detail given to each counter, each point might be an entire paragraph, or more, with supporting evidence.)

> Opposing Point A
> Your counterargument
> Opposing Point B
> Your counterargument
> Opposing Point C
> Your counterargument

Some writers use a turnabout paragraph for counterarguments. A turnabout paragraph begins with one point and then shifts to an opposing or alternative point while giving the reader a clear sign of the shift. For example, you might begin a paragraph explaining an opposing position, and then counterargue in that same paragraph. In the following example, the opposing claim (that global warming is not a real problem) is addressed within the paragraph. The paragraph also includes the change of direction ("This argument, however . . ."):

> Some people argue that global warming is not a problem at all. They suggest that all the discussion about the ozone layer is merely fear-mongering by left-wing political activists. This argument, however, ignores the volumes of evidence compiled by scientists (many of whom are Nobel Prize winners) from around the world—scientists from different cultures, from different religious contexts, from different political systems, and with different political agendas. The amount of data they have collected and the sheer din of their collective voices ought to be enough to convince people that global warming is much more than the delusions of a few environmental groups.

You might decide that the opposing viewpoint(s) require significant explanation, and that it would be best to keep them grouped together. Therefore, you might devote a chunk of space at the beginning of your paper before countering:

Opposing Point A

Opposing Point B

Opposing Point C

Your counterargument to A

Your counterargument to B

Your counterargument to C

You also might decide that your argument only needs a single main counterargument. That counter might come after you have given your supporting evidence and appeals, or it might even begin the argument. Or several opposing claims might be discussed, and addressed, in one paragraph. (See Paulin ¶2.)

# How Should I Make Transitions?

Regardless of your general organization strategy, make certain to cue the reader when giving a counterargument. It is important that the reader understand when the focus is shifting from counter- to main argument. You might begin a paragraph with an opposing viewpoint: "Some opponents might argue that. . . ." If so, you will need to shift the reader back to your logic: "But they do not understand that. . . ." Here is a list of some strategic transitions when doing counterargument:

On the other hand,

Contrary to this idea,

Although many people take this stance,

However, (; however,)

Despite the evidence for this position,

But

Also, remember that transitions can wait. While developing rough drafts, writers often wait to add the glue between paragraphs. Rather than fret over difficult transition statements, they move ahead with their arguments and return later to fill in gaps. (For more on transitions, see page 85.)

# Writer's Voice

Argument need not be cast as an act of aggression or belligerence. While arguments are sometimes heated and intense, they need not attempt to belittle their opponents. In fact, the fastest way to alienate, or turn off, a reader is to sound narrow-minded, mean, arrogant, or intimidating. A good argument attracts readers and engages those who might oppose the claims being made; a bad or unsuccessful argument loses readers. Here are some strategies for maintaining a cool tone—one that invites readers rather than alienates them.

## Conceding and Qualifying

Conceding or qualifying a point can make an argument seem more controlled and more inviting; therefore, even when writers have a very strong conviction, they will often acknowledge the value of some other point or the limits of their own argument. Imagine the following argument:

> First-year college students are not mature enough to live on their own, without the guidance of parents and the familiarity of home turf. Dorm life is a celebration of self-destruction and disorientation. The social distractions draw students away from the real purpose of college and defeat even the most focused and determined students. Colleges should rethink the requirements for first-year students to live on campus.

While these claims unfairly generalize college students (see *logical fallacies*) and threaten the logical soundness of the argument, they also project a hasty or pushy voice. Such unqualified claims create a certain character in readers' minds—someone who is overly anxious and forceful. But the same argument can be cast with a different voice (which uses concession). The following paragraph acknowledges some value in dorm life and, as a result, seems fairer and less alienating:

> Dorm life does hold some value for young students. It can create a climate of inquiry and academic engagement. However, many young college students are overcome by the utter freedom, lack of genuine guidance, and constant social distractions. And too many

students who would otherwise succeed in their first years at college are suffering or failing because they are forced to live on campus. Colleges should, at least, begin to reevaluate requirements for on-campus living.

While conceding can create a more engaging voice, conceding unnecessarily, or too often, can have negative results. Imagine the same argument, but with a distracting degree of concession:

> Living in dorms can be the best thing possible for a college student; however, dorm life can also defeat many students. Sometimes, even the brightest and most determined students can be overcome by the social distractions. Although it all depends on the individual student's personality and upbringing, college dorm life can actually work against the whole purpose of going to college. Certainly, each college should consider the characteristics of its own student body, but policies that require students to live on campus should be reevaluated.

All the concessions and qualifiers undermine the importance of the argument. The voice behind the text seems concerned about offending potential readers. But, ironically, such writing makes readers feel distant or detached from the ideas. Because the writer seems uncommitted, readers have no reason to engage the ideas. (Be cautious not to concede away your argument—and your level of commitment.)

## Avoiding Harsh Description

It is often easy to use the most emotionally loaded terms to describe something or someone, to proclaim an opposing view as "dumb" or "evil." Such description, however, is most often exaggerated and suggests that the writer has not fully investigated the subject. In the following, Paulin does not attack the media and the diet industry with aggressive adjectives, but argues that they damage people's lives. This is a far more sophisticated and useful strategy than merely dismissing them with a simple negative word or phrase:

Certainly everyone is entitled to his or her own opinions of what is attractive, but no one has the right to damage another human being for fun or profit. The media and the diet industry often do just that. While no one can change an entire culture overnight, people, especially parents, need to think about what they really value in the humans they share their lives with and what values they want to pass on to their children.

# Talking with, Not Arguing at, Readers

An academic argument is not an argument with readers. It is a *conversation with readers about an argumentative position.* And if that conversation is compelling, the reader may find that position valuable. In other words, argumentative writing speaks with the reader about a particular position or set of positions and attempts to make one position more logical and/or valuable than others.

To help visualize the role of the writer and reader, imagine the following: The writer sits beside the reader, pointing at and directing attention to a set of claims. The writer does not sit in front of and point his or her finger at the reader. This may seem like a subtle difference, but notice how it may change a passage. In the following example, Elizabeth Bohnhorst urges readers to consider computers in the classroom:

> Educating students in computer skills is and should be a priority in all schools. But when it comes to teaching basic skills and allowing for intellectual development, human interaction and exploration of the real world

should never come second to electronic devices. In an effort to preserve the qualities of education, we should not allow ourselves to become mesmerized by teachers that require an electrical outlet and textbooks that require a point-and-click to turn the page.

But imagine if Bohnhorst had talked at us directly. In the following, the writer tries to convince the reader ("you") to change his or her behavior:

> Educating students in computer skills is and should be a priority in all schools. But when it comes to teaching basic skills and allowing for intellectual development, you cannot put human interaction and exploration of the real world second to electronic devices. In an effort to preserve the qualities of education, do not allow yourself to become mesmerized by electrical wizardry.

## You, We, or One?

Writers often struggle with this issue: Should we refer to readers directly (*you*)? Should we refer to ourselves along with readers (*we*)? Or should we refer to the general nondescript human (*one*)? One way to make the decision is to consider the desired level of formality: *You* is considered least formal. *We* is considered more formal. *One* is most formal.

# Vitality

While the editing strategies in other chapters can be applied here, argumentative writing has potential difficulties of its own. Because argument is such a common everyday practice, writers have to be especially mindful of some informal habits that can make formal written argument less intense and vital.

## Avoid Unnecessary Attention to I

In argumentative writing, it is especially tempting to use the first-person pronouns *I, me,* and *my*. As in the following two sentences, personal pronouns can distract the reader from the argument itself and bog down the sentences:

> I think that social security ought to be tied to the marketplace.
> It is my personal belief that social security should not be a gamble.

In each of these sentences, the main idea is subordinated in a *that* clause. *I* statements such as these are unnecessary in argumentative writing because the claims are already attributed to the writer. By simply attaching his or her name to an essay, the writer has already implied "I believe." Saying it again is redundant.

However, writers do occasionally choose to insert personal pronouns. When dealing with several claims or outside sources, writers may insert the first-person pronoun to make a clear distinction between their own thoughts and others', as Paulin does:

> For instance, in her essay, "Bubbie, Mommy, Weight Watchers and Me," Barbara Noreen Dinnerstein recalls a time in her childhood when her mother took her to Weight Watchers to slim down and the advice the lecturer gave to the women present: "She told us to put a picture of ourselves on the 'fridgerator of us eating and looking really fat and ugly. She said remember what you look like. Remember how ugly you are."
> I have a problem with this advice. First, of course, it is too darn common.

Paulin could also have avoided the first-person pronoun:

> But this advice is dangerous to young women.

But she chose the first-person pronoun, perhaps because it is less formal and coincides with the personal voice she has established in her essay. While it is good practice to avoid unnecessary use of first-person pronouns, writers like Paulin can make effective, occasional use of it.

Writers also use *I* for personal narratives—telling a story or anecdote involving their own experiences. Such uses are legitimate and important. Narratives draw attention to the relevant experience of the writer, which requires use of the first-person pronoun.

### Unnecessary I Statement
I think that history should be taught with more attention to the lives of everyday people.

### Appropriate Personal Narrative
When I was in high school, my history courses focused almost exclusively on big battles and big governmental moments.

## Avoid Unnecessary Attention to You

The second-person pronoun *you* refers directly to the reader—the person holding your text and reading from it. And because academic essays are invitations to a broad audience (to instructors, peers, and even the broader community of thinkers that they represent), *you* is generally avoided. Like the first-person singular pronouns (*I, me, my*), *you* distracts the reader from the issue at hand. But *you* is especially hazardous in academic writing because it makes writers shift into the imperative mood—the mood of commands. Here, the writer shifts focus and mood:

> Political parties do their best to keep people from closely examining issues. Instead, they wash over complexities and invite voters to stand on one side or another. You should consider your allegiance to any political party.

The first two sentences focus on political parties, people, and voters. But the final sentence shifts and suddenly speaks at the reader. To most academic audiences, this shift is unacceptable. (See more about speaking *with* versus *at* the reader in Writer's Voice.)

# Vitalize with Verbs

Verbs are the engine of a sentence. And they are the agent of motion for the reader's mind: they move the reader's thoughts. Weak verbs make for little movement. In the following, the first sentence depends on a weak verb:

> Handheld video games are bad for kids to have in the car.
> Handheld video games have destroyed the family road trip.

The verb of the first sentence, *are,* is often called a *linking verb.* When linking verbs act as the main engine of a sentence, they limit what's possible. Often, they corner the writer into using a vague adjective, in this case *bad.* The second sentence uses an active and more intensive verb: *destroyed.* The second sentence creates a more engaging image. In the following sentences, linking verbs actually create unnecessary layers and clauses. Notice how each can be tightened and vitalized with an *active verb:*

> The problem with this *is* that the house is too expensive for our budget.

> *Vitalized:* Here's the problem: the cost of the house *exceeds* our budget.

> The committee *is* not prone to allowing everyone *to be* as free with their money as they want.
> *Vitalized:* The committee will probably not *allow* everyone to *spend* resources freely.

Using active verbs rather than linking verbs vitalizes writing. This is not to say that using linking verbs is always a mistake. (Sometimes, they are necessary.) However, changing to more active verbs can dramatically impact your writing, creating more focused statements, more intensive ideas, and more revelatory thinking.

## Activity

Revise and vitalize the following sentences. Try replacing the linking verb first and see how that impacts your decision about other parts of the sentence:

1. Energy drinks may give you wings, but they are not helping students to focus.

2. It's going to be a long time before that cat is home again.

3. The arguments against global warming are often full of strawperson fallacies, which are fallacies that unfairly characterize a person or group of people.

4. Presidential candidates seem to be getting more mean-spirited as time goes by, but elections early in American history were often deeply hostile as well.

# Revision

Sometimes, argumentative essays take on too much. Their focus is too broad. A broad thesis prompts writers to make vague, often unsupportable, points. Take one last look at your thesis—the main argumentative assertion of your essay. Does it focus on a particular tension, a particular aspect of an issue, a specific element or dimension of a broader topic? What words or phrases (*things, people, society*) can be substituted for something more specific? How might you focus on one aspect of an issue rather than the whole issue?

## Peer Review

Underline your thesis, or write it at the top of your essay so that reviewers will get traction as they read. Then, exchange drafts with at least one other writer. Reviewers should use the following questions to guide a helpful response:

1. How well can you follow the writer's line of reasoning? (See appeal to logic, pages 229–231.) Imagine the line of reasoning as though it is a stone path. If the path is well laid out, you should feel a stone at every step. If it is not, you might miss a step; you might feel like some intellectual step is missing.
2. Can you think of another cultural, literary, historical, or political allusion that relates to the writer's position?
3. Suggest specific points that the writer should concede or qualify. For instance, the writer's position might seem too extreme; the claims might include too many people or a large, diverse group without making any distinctions. Point out such claims, and help the writer to see the need to acknowledge subtlety, complexity, and exceptions.
4. Can you imagine another opposing point that the writer could address in a counterargument? While the writer may have dealt with several opposing positions, you might think of an additional issue that should be addressed.
5. Consider the writer's voice. Circle passages or sentences that shift mood and speak *at,* rather than *with,* the reader. Suggest an alternative strategy or phrasing.

6. Do paragraphs focus on one main point? Point to sentences in paragraphs that stray from the initial idea put forth in the paragraph.
7. What is the most engaging passage in the draft so far? Why?
8. Check for sentence vitality.
   - Where can the writer change linking verbs to active verbs?
   - Where can the writer avoid drawing attention to *I* and *you?*
   - Consider vitality strategies from other chapters:
     —Help the writer change unnecessary clauses to phrases.
     —Help the writer change unnecessary phrases to words.
     —Point to expletives (such as *there are* and *it is).*
     —Help the writer change passive verbs to active verbs for more vitality.
     —Help the writer avoid common grammatical errors: comma splices, sentence fragments, or pronoun/antecedent agreement.

## Questions for Research

**If the writer used outside sources,**

- Where must he or she include in-text citations? (See pages 470–471.)
- Are quotations blended smoothly into the argument and punctuated correctly? (See pages 456–468.)
- Where could more direct textual cues or transitions help the reader? (See pages 466–467.)
- Is the Works Cited page formatted properly? (See pages 469–480.)

# Reflection

Academic essays are not merely vehicles for communicating thought. They are intellectual playing fields—places for writers and readers to discover something. Those discoveries do not exist in the vacuum of an essay; they resonate outward through the lives of the writers and readers. An argument essay in particular sets out to assert something about the world, and that assertion is bound to impact reality—because people live according to the arguments they accept. Now that you have written an argumentative essay, respond to the following:

- How does your thesis reveal something about everyday life?
- How does your essay challenge something about the way most people live and think?
- How important are appeals to your argument?
- How do you engage opposing positions? How do they make your argument more complex?
- How do you concede or qualify?

## Beyond the Essay: The Open Letter

Argumentative essays have changed the world. They've started revolutions, supported religious movements, initiated new scientific organizations, spotlighted atrocities, and prompted a broad range of political events. But sophisticated arguments can impact the world through other genres.

The open letter is closely related to the essay. It is aimed at a particular audience, a particular reader or set of readers, but it also resonates with a broader audience. An open letter draws both writer and reader, and an otherwise private discussion, into a public setting—a powerful move! For example, Martin Luther King, Jr.'s "Letter from Birmingham Jail" was originally aimed at nine fellow clergy members, but the letter also speaks to millions of others. In effect, King performs his response to a particular audience for a broader audience. The conversation occurs among a few particular people, but the issues and claims involve many. Or consider the apostle Paul's letters to the Romans that now constitute part of the New Testament. They have become known to millions of readers, but they were originally aimed at a particular group of people. Or more currently, newspapers and magazines often print open letters to the president, to an editor, or to corporate heads.

Because letters are written with a particular audience in mind, they may draw attention to specifics about the readers' lives, such as specific behaviors, policies, attitudes, or events. The writer may then draw out the significance, explaining the impact on or meaning for others.

Return to your essay and imagine a particular person or group of people who should read and accept your claims. Then develop an open letter addressed to that particular audience. The following questions may help shape your ideas:

- ▶ Who has the power or authority over the issue?
- ▶ How can you make a specific connection between them and the issue?
- ▶ To what specific behavior, attitude, event, or policy can you draw attention?
- ▶ What is the public significance of that behavior?

 For additional resources including instructional videos and links to helpful websites, access your English CourseMate through cengagebrain.com.

# 8 Responding to Arguments

# Chapter Contents

The border between Tijuana Beach, Mexico and the U.S. is marked by the wall shown here.

Carlos Cazalis/Corbis

# "We hold these truths to be self-evident, that all men are created equal, that they are endowed by their Creator with certain inalienable rights, that among these are life, liberty, and the pursuit of happiness."

—The Declaration of Independence

Arguments are all around us. They lurk in nearly every behavior and event of our lives, and we often respond to arguments that hover but are not stated directly. Imagine an American citizen protesting nuclear energy; she carries a sign that says, "Nuclear energy ≠ clean energy!" Her sign is a response to the argument that nuclear energy is cleaner than energy from oil and coal. The protester is not responding to a particular text or person, but to an argument made by many people (such as politicians) in many different contexts. The sign actually evokes (or brings to mind) this argument and directly refutes it. Someone might also respond to an advertiser's argument that cigarettes promote social and physical pleasures. Such an ad argues that a certain brand of cigarette provides pleasure beyond inhaling the smoke and feeling the nicotine, and a writer might (quite easily) argue the opposite.

In academia, writers most often respond to arguments that are formally delivered (in an essay or editorial). They respond to a particular text or person and to particular statements or claims:

- A psychologist responds to Freud's theory of ego development, explaining that such a theory is not valuable in treating female patients.

- A political science student supports a revised historical account of U.S. foreign policy that holds Henry Kissinger partly responsible for atrocities in Chile during the 1970s.

- Law students respond to a Supreme Court ruling that upholds the rights of law enforcement officers to detain citizens for traffic violations. They argue that the ruling erodes protections against "unreasonable search and seizure."

- An English professor reviews a controversial new book and defends its claims against rampant consumerism.

As these examples suggest, responding to an argument does not necessarily mean disagreement. The initial argument (whether a court ruling, a book, an essay, or a historical account) provides the position on a topic. A writer has many options beyond agreement or disagreement. For instance, he or she might agree with the initial argument and extend the ideas with additional points, disagree with a particular point, redefine the issue, or point out some logical flaws.

As you can imagine, this is a somewhat more sophisticated task than what we examined in Chapter 7, Making Arguments. However, responding to arguments is an engaging activity, one that is not only vital to and valued in academia, but also necessary for maintaining a democracy.

Although a writer can respond to many different kinds of argument, this chapter focuses primarily on arguments that are formally delivered. The chapter will help you discover and analyze an argument, develop a sophisticated argumentative response, and communicate your position in writing. Read the following essays, which illustrate a variety of arguing strategies. After reading the essays, you can find an argument in one of several ways:

1. Go to the Point of Contact section to find an argument from everyday life,
2. Choose one of the Ideas for Writing that follow the essays, or
3. Respond to any argumentative essay from another chapter in this book.

After you find a topic, go to the Analysis section to begin developing your response.

# What Orwell Didn't Know

## George Lakoff

George Orwell, the pen name of Eric Arthur Blair (1903–1950), was a journalist, novelist, and political commentator famous for his most popular works, *Animal Farm* (1945) and *1984* (1949), two influential novels that have been required reading in many high school and college courses. Like *Animal Farm* and *1984,* Orwell's essay "Politics and the English Language" (1946) has been required reading for many college students. As George Lakoff (1941–), a professor of cognitive linguistics at the University of California, Berkeley, explains in the following essay, Orwell argues that inaccurate language leads to "political propaganda and its effects." While Lakoff commends Orwell's essay for its important contribution, his response labels it an anachronism because, as Lakoff explains, those in his profession have "learned a lot about the brain, the mind, and language since then."

George Orwell will forever be a hero of mine. When I read *1984* in high school, I became sensitized to the workings of propaganda. After more than forty years as a linguist and cognitive scientist, I remain sensitized.

When I first read "Politics and the English Language" as an undergraduate in the late 1950s, I loved it. Nearly fifty years later I find it an anachronism. Why? I, and those in my profession, have learned a lot about the brain, the mind and language since then. Orwell's essay belongs to an earlier time, a time that lacked our deepening understanding of how the human brain works.

Orwell suffered from what we might now call the "Editor's Fallacy": Bad habits of "foolish thought" and inaccurate, slovenly, dull, pretentious, ungraceful, and meaningless language—the "decay of language"—lead to political propaganda and its effects. If we just "let the meaning choose the word," he claimed, we would all be saved. This is not only false, it is dangerously naïve.

Orwell fell into traps—false views of language: *Meanings are truth conditions. Words have unitary meanings. If people are told the truth, they will reason to the right conclusions—unless they are stupid or ignorant. And ignorance can be cured by truths conveyed in good prose.*

All of that is false. Yet progressives still fall into those traps. Even you, dear reader, may have fallen into them. And even *I* am trying to cure ignorance via truths conveyed in good prose. I am banking on cognitive dissonance—yours! Dissonance between the real brain and the apparent mind. Intellectuals are confident they know their own minds, though they realize they don't know their own brains. But their brains betray their confidence in their minds. Neuroscience and cognitive science reveal a far more interesting picture than Orwell could have guessed.

Probably 98 percent of your reasoning is *un*conscious—what your brain is doing behind the scenes. Reason is inherently emotional. You can't even choose a goal, much less form a plan and carry it out, without a sense that it will satisfy you, not disgust you. Fear and anxiety will affect your plans and your actions. You act differently, and plan differently, out of hope and joy than out of fear and anxiety.

Thought is physical. Learning requires a physical brain change: Receptors for neurotransmitters change at the synapses, which changes neural circuitry. Since thinking is the activation of such circuitry, somewhat different thinking requires a somewhat different brain. Brains change as you use them—even unconsciously. It's as if your car changed as you drove it, say from a stick shift gradually to an automatic.

Thought is physical in another way. It uses the brain's sensory-motor system. Imagining moving uses the same regions of the brain as moving; imagining seeing uses the same regions of the brain as seeing. Meaning is mental simulation, activating those regions of the brain. Reasoning from A to B is the neural activation of the mental simulation of B, given the mental simulation of A. Mental simulation, like most thought, is mostly unconscious.

Thought is structured, in large measure, in terms of "frames"—brain structures that control mental simulation and hence reasoning.

You think metaphorically, perhaps most of the time. Just by functioning with your body in the world as a child, you learn at least hundreds of simple "conceptual metaphors"—metaphors you think with and live by. For example, Quantity is understood in terms of Verticality (More is Up), and the words follow along: *prices rise and*

George Lakoff, "What Orwell Didn't Know," from *What Orwell Didn't Know About the Brain, the Mind, and Language*. Reprinted by permission.

*fall, skyrocket and hit bottom.* Why? Because every day of your life, if you pour water into a glass, the level rises. You experience a correlation between quantity and verticality. In your brain, regions for registering verticality and quantity are activated together during such experiences. As a result, activation spreads, and circuits linking Verticality to Quantity are formed. Those circuits constitute the metaphor More is Up in your brain. As a child lives in the world, his or her brain acquires hundreds of such "primary" conceptual metaphors that are just there waiting to be used in everyday thought.

We have high-level moral worldviews—modes of reasoning about what's right and wrong—that govern whole areas of reason, both conscious and unconscious, and link up whole networks of frames and metaphors.

Cultural narratives are special cases of such frames. They stretch over time and define protagonists and antagonists—and heroes, victims, and villains. They define right and wrong, and come with emotional content. And most important, we all live out cultural narratives—with all their emotionality and moral sensibility. We even define our identities by the narratives we live by.

What are words? Words are neural links between spoken and written expressions and frames, metaphors, and narratives. When we hear the words, not only their immediate frames and metaphors are activated, but also all the high-level worldviews and associated narratives—with their emotions—are activated. Words are not just words—they activate a huge range of brain mechanisms. Moreover, words don't just activate neutral meanings; they are often defined relative to conservative framings. And our most important political words—*freedom, equality, fairness, opportunity, security, accountability*—name "contested concepts," concepts with a common shared core that is unspecified, which is then extended to most of its cases based on your values. Thus conservative "freedom" is utterly different than progressive "freedom," as I showed in detail in *Whose Freedom.* Liberals such as Paul Starr, in *Freedom's Power,* unselfconsciously use their own version of freedom, as if there were no other version. Not understanding conservative "freedom" and pointing out its problematic nature greatly weakens one's effect.

A few words in political language can activate large portions of the brain: *War on Terror, tax relief, illegal immigration, entitlements* (turned to conservative use by Ronald Reagan), *death tax, property rights, abortion on demand, cut and run, flip-flop, school choice, intelligent design, spending programs, partial birth abortion, surge, spreading freedom, private accounts, individual responsibility, energy independence.*

When they are repeated every day, extensive areas of the brain are activated over and over, and this leads to brain change. Unerasable brain change. Once learned, the new neural structure cannot just be erased: *War on Terror* be gone! It doesn't work. And every time the words are repeated, all the frames and metaphors and worldview structures are activated again and strengthened—because recurring activation strengthens neural connections. Negation doesn't help. "I'm against the War on Terror" just activates the *War on Terror* metaphor and strengthens what you're against. Accepting the language of issue and arguing the other side just hurts your own cause.

Can you counter such brain change? There are two possibilities. First, you can try to mark the idea—as silly, immoral, stupid, and so on—by having lots of people say so over a long period of time. That's what conservatives did with "liberal," starting back in the 1960s when most people wanted to be liberals. *Tax and spend liberal, liberal elite, liberal media, limousine liberal,* and so on repeated over and over slowly got across the idea to lower- and middle-class Republicans that liberals were elite, financially irresponsible, and oppressing poor conservatives. And it undermined liberals' confidence in themselves.

The second strategy is to provide an alternative honest framing—either by inhibiting what is in the brain or by bypassing it. Done honestly, it is righting history. Done dishonestly, it is "rewriting history." Conservatives have done this with the Vietnam War: We lost because we didn't use enough force—"*We had one hand tied behind our backs.*"

Neither is quick or easy.

Today, sophisticated right-wing propaganda is very well-written—the editor in Orwell would love David Brooks's prose. Mind control works via brain change, through the effective use of well-written language to activate not just frames, conceptual metaphors, and emotions, but whole worldviews. When the language is repeated and the words become just "the normal way you express the idea," then even the best people in the media get sucked in. Journalists have to use words people understand, and they have to use the words most people normally use to express the ideas they are writing about. As a result, they often have no idea that they are using conservative language, which activates a conservative view of the world as well as the conservative perspective on the given issue. They are rarely aware that in doing so, they are helping conservatives by strengthening the conservative worldview in the public's mind, and thereby accelerating brain change.

Once a member of the public has undergone brain change, he or she then thinks as a conservative on the issue. Not convinced rationally, just subject to the techniques every marketer uses. Is free will being exercised? The very idea of "free will" has been changed.

Orwell wasn't aware of how brains, minds, and language really work, nor was anyone else in 1947. But we don't have that excuse today. Yet even the very best of our news media are stuck in the same traps. Every now and then a result about the brain will leak out into the *Science Times* or *Discover,* only to be forgotten the next week. But what we know about the brain, the mind, and language barely ever makes it to the front page or opinion pages where politics is discussed. The ghost of Orwell still haunts our very best news and political opinion media.

Orwell's old-fashioned views about reason and language also haunt the Democratic Party. But there are promising developments. Presidential candidate John Edwards has rejected the very term *War on Terror* as an inappropriate metaphor and a means to grab power. In the Democratic debate in New Hampshire in June 2007, the questions Wolf Blitzer of CNN asked were all framed from a conservative viewpoint. Democratic candidate Barack Obama stepped forward and rejected *one* of the conservatively framed questions as "specifically designed to divide us."

In another positive development, progressives have been saying out loud that conservatism itself is the problem. Robert Borosage, in the *The American Prospect,* staunchly argues from a progressive worldview, "Conservatives cannot be trusted to guide the government they scorn. Not because they are incompetent or corrupt (although corruption and incompetence abound), but because they get the world wrong."

This is half right. But it ignores the thousands of conservative "successes" from *their* point of view, which Borosage cites as "failures." In hundreds of cases (excepting Iraq—a big exception), conservatives would say that George W. Bush got the world right—because he changed the world as he wanted to.

If Democrats think that those who voted for Bush will consider all those "successes" as failures, they might just find a way to lose the next election. Moral: To counter conservatism, you have to understand, and publicly discuss the problems with, the conservative moral worldview. And to do that, you need to know how largely unconscious worldviews work.

Conservatives think tanks, over thirty-five years, started with the conservative worldview and showed how to apply it everywhere on every issue, and even beyond issues in the acts of governance—cutting regulating budgets, reassigning regulators, using the courts to redefine the laws, changing the facts on Web sites, eliminating libraries. New Democratic think tanks haven't helped much. The problem is that they are *policy* think tanks. They mistakenly think that "rational" programs and policies constitute political ideas. They don't understand unconscious thought. It's the unspoken ideas behind the programs and the policies—the worldviews, deep frames, metaphors, and cultural narratives—that need to be changed in the public mind. Only one progressive think tank, the Rockridge Institute, is even working in this direction. Its handbook for progressives, *Thinking Points,* applies the study of mind to the cause of truth.

Is it legitimate to use the real mechanisms of mind—worldviews, frames, metaphors, emotions, images, personal stories, and cultural narratives—to tell important truths? Hell, yes! It is usually the only way that works. Al Gore's movie, *An Inconvenient Truth,* uses all those mechanisms of mind and heart—and it works. Had it just given facts and figures unframed, it would have flopped.

It is time to exorcise Orwell's ghost. We all need to understand how the brain, mind, and language really work. We need to apply that knowledge effectively to make truths meaningful and give *truths* the power to change brains. Our democracy depends on a clear and open understanding of the political mind.

# Writing Strategies

1. Describe Lakoff's opening strategy. How does it set the tone for the essay?

2. What does Lakoff disagree with George Orwell about? To Lakoff, why is the disagreement important?

3. Lakoff says, "Thought is physical." Summarize his explanation and then explain how this idea is important to Lakoff's main point.

4. As part of his response, Lakoff defines *words*. How is his definition important in helping the reader understand and accept his main idea?

5. According to Lakoff, what are the real mechanisms of mind, and why should they be used to tell important truths?

# Exploring Ideas

1. Lakoff says, "You think metaphorically, perhaps most of the time." Summarize Lakoff's explanation, and then come up with an original example of metaphorical thinking that supports Lakoff's point.

2. Explain Lakoff's idea that cultural narratives are frames.

3. With a group of classmates, come up with an original example to illustrate Lakoff's claim that "[a]ccepting the language of issue and arguing the other side just hurts your own cause."

4. Why does Lakoff think "[o]nce a member of the public has undergone brain change, he or she then thinks as a conservative on the issue"?

5. Do some research on think tanks to become more informed about what they are. What is the purpose of a think tank? Why are think tanks important to Lakoff's response?

# Ideas for Writing

1. Respond to an older way of thinking that has played an important role in your development, but that now needs to be revised in some important way.

2. In groups or alone, generate ideas for an essay by creating five titles, filling in the blanks: What _____ Didn't Know About _____.

If responding to one of these ideas, go to the Analysis section of this chapter to begin developing ideas for your essay.

# Entitlement Education

## Daniel Bruno

We often respond to the people (and arguments) that we agree with the most. In the following essay, Daniel Bruno agrees with most of Peter Sacks's original argument. His introduction explains: "But he fails, it seems, to emphasize enough a most harmful effect of this sense of entitlement." Bruno's response does not disagree but rather *emphasizes* a crucial point in an attempt to make the reader more aware of it. (Portions of Bruno's invention work are shown in later sections of this chapter.)

**Writing Strategies**

Overall summary of original argument.

Main response to the original argument.

(Attention to "I") Bruno's thesis, and distinction between his argument and the original.

Turnabout paragraph.

Analysis of several possible arguments about the results of student entitlement.

In his book *Generation X Goes to College,* Peter Sacks describes, among other things, the sense of entitlement that some students in today's consumerist culture have toward a college education. One entire chapter explores this issue alone, providing examples of this "sense" and looking into its "humble beginnings." Sacks shows how consumerism has invaded education, leading some students to expect good grades for little effort. But he fails, it seems, to emphasize enough a most harmful effect of this sense of entitlement. The biggest problem, as I see it, is that although students are able to graduate from high school (and even some colleges) with minimal effort, those students may find themselves cheated in the long run.

How might they be cheated? One might argue that students get cheated because entitlement doesn't go on forever. At some point it stops. For example, a college graduate with a marketing degree, but especially weak thinking or writing skills, may find himself disadvantaged on the job. It is not that his boss puts her foot down; instead, the job does. Our student finds himself not well prepared for it. He gets cheated because he is disadvantaged at his job—a job that he paid money to learn how to do. Of course the point isn't about marketing majors. The same is true of students in any field. (Marketing is just what came to mind.)

One might also claim that students will be cheated because their lives will somehow *be less*. This argument claims that a person's intelligence contributes to his quality of life. Here we must remember that "intelligence" is not just "knowledge." Instead, it is being able to use knowledge, to make connections and figure things out, to see causes and solve problems. A person may have much knowledge—that is, he may have accumulated a lot of facts—but not have much intelligence . . . or so the argument goes. As one goes from first grade to twelfth, from twelfth grade to college, and from freshman to senior, education shifts focus

**Exploring Ideas**

Entitlement: expecting to get good grades for little effort.

Cheated out of adequate job preparation.

Cheated out of quality of life.

From Daniel Bruno, "Entitlement Education." Reprinted with permission of the author.

from mere accumulation of information (knowledge) to application of information (intelligence). And while we may accumulate more knowledge as a senior in college than we did as a senior in high school, the focus in college has (or should have) shifted from mere knowledge to intelligence—that is, to the ability to make good use of one's knowledge.

Other standard arguments claim other ways students might be cheated. For example, we might feel sorry for someone who doesn't get a joke—or a reference. Allusions to literature, history, philosophy, and so on allow us to say much in few words. But does the listener understand? If a person is unaware of common references—the Battle of the Bulge, Normandy, Existentialism, T. S. Eliot, World War I, Rasputin, John the Baptist, Gandhi, apartheid, Jonas Salk, Johnny Appleseed, Lewis and Clark, the Trail of Tears, slavery, the Donner Party, and so on— he misses out on conversations, on meaning, on *connecting with his fellow inmates*. Of course, here one might counter that you don't need to know all of these things. And, I agree, you don't. People tend to hang out with people who have similar interests and tastes.

One more argument claims that because we live in a democracy, we must be well-educated. Since all the citizens are responsible for the government, our forefathers promoted public education so that all citizens—not just the wealthy and elite— would know how to read and write. Thomas Jefferson wrote,

> I know no safe depository of the ultimate powers of society but the people themselves; and if we think them not enlightened enough to exercise their control with a wholesome discretion, the remedy is not to take it from them, but to inform their discretion by education. This is the true corrective of abuses of constitutional power. (278)

In what ways can educated citizens correct abuses in a democracy? A person's way of life, his purchases and activities— not just a person's vote or protest march—is part of the responsibility. Thus, consumers and neighbors and co-workers and so on should behave responsibly and think intelligently. It is our responsibility as citizens of a democracy.

True enough, these are all ways that students who are allowed to just slide by end up getting cheated. But another way (and one less talked about) strikes me as being far more offensive. This reason hinges on the fact that many students are not just sliding by.

Return to the original
argument.

In *Generation X Goes to College,* Peter Sacks illustrates that all of today's college students cannot just be thrown in the same big barrel. In describing the modern/post modern clash in education, he spends the majority of his time talking about those students who are underprepared, who lack the basic study skills required in academic work, and who demonstrate little real commitment to their own education. Yet, he does not discuss this problem in isolation. He also mentions another type of student. For example, he introduces the reader to Marissa and Carol: "As very good students, [their views] were virtually excluded by The College in order to accommodate the whiners and complainers" (61). And he says they "suffered not only educationally" (63). In addition to discussing specific good students, an entire chapter presents survey results about students' attitudes toward education. While he makes claims such as "nearly a quarter of the students . . . harbored a disproportionate sense of entitlement," this very statement tells the reader that a full three-quarters (that is, three out of four) students *do not* "harbor a disproportionate sense of entitlement" (54–59). He wraps up the book by focusing on another student, Andie, who he describes as "a good student, constantly picking [his] brain for information and feedback on her work" (186–87). His final paragraph, before the Epilogue, says, "Let's create a system that encourages people like Andie at least as much as the ones who don't give a damn" (187). Thus, Sacks shows that today's students are a more diverse group—in skill level, background, and attitude toward education—than has ever before been gathered together in the college classroom.

Modern = marked by distinctions between lowbrow and highbrow thought. Postmodern = marked by chaos and blurring of boundaries.

Quotations illustrate particular points of the original. A properly used colon—to introduce a quote with words that could be punctuated as a sentence—provides coherence. The reader knows immediately the relationship of the words on the left and right of the colon. Quotation marks provide coherence by making clear that the words inside them are from a source.

1/4 students feel entitled.

3/4 students do not.

More summary of the original argument.

Diversity in skill and attitude.

Transition paragraph.

Now when we connect two things—the present grade-inflated, entitlement-driven education system that has got a foot-hold in most of America's high schools and colleges AND the diversity in skill and attitude toward education of today's college students—two problems appear.

One problem is that the motivated students are not being as challenged as they could be. Although their situation is not ideal, it is far from hopeless. They have at least three options: (1) take advantage of the easy system and learn a little along the way; (2) motivate themselves, working harder (and learning more) than the system requires them to; and (3) attend a more academically rigorous school (of course such schools still exist, though they are likely to cost more to attend).

Motivated students are cheated.

Sacks's quotation supports Bruno's argument.

While motivated students suffer in our too-lax system, so do the un- (or under-) motivated ones. And these students, who need our help the most, are the ones most cheated. As Sacks says, "I now believe the students are the real victims of this sys-

Under-motivated students are cheated.

tematic failure of the entitlement mindset" (189). The students who are allowed to slide by, who are content to slide by, who perhaps don't even realize that they are sliding by because sliding by is all they know—those students find themselves arriving at college less prepared and less motivated than the "better students." And what happens next? Sadly, the gap between these two groups grows even wider.

Gap between students
grows bigger.

The motivated student with good study skills (the one who has had at least an adequate high school education) attends class, takes notes, understands reading assignments, follows instructions, develops even better habits of mind, gains even more knowledge, and learns ways of making that knowledge work for her and her fellow humans. But in a system where B's are average and C's might indicate that although a student "tried" she did not demonstrate understanding or skill, the poorer students continue to advance through the system while remaining trapped at the bottom. Their level of thinking does not change much, while that of their better-prepared peers does.

Scenarios are the main
support tool.

The injustice, then, has been done to the students (as Sacks says, the students are the victims). While the student has happily skipped (or unhappily slogged) along through sixteen years of formal education, she is allowed, if she wants, to come away with very little in terms of education. She is allowed, unfortunately, to escape practically unscathed by learning. The problem, of course, is that the two students have entered college on different academic levels and the one on the higher level has graduated on an *even higher* level while the one on the lower level has remained pretty much the same.

Sacks and Bruno argue
the same point.

Students would do well to look around them, at the room full of fellow classmates. They should imagine that many of those students will be graduating one day. And they should imagine the students in the classroom next door and across the hall and in all the other buildings on campus. They will be graduating, too. They should also imagine all those students at the more than 4,000 other colleges throughout the country: Ohio State, Michigan, Michigan State, Findlay College, Iowa State, Oklahoma A&M, The University of Utah, California This or That. (*The Chronicle of Higher Education*'s 2000–2001 "Almanac" lists 4,096 colleges in the United States.) Many of those students are well-prepared, working hard, and developing even better habits and thinking skills.

They do not even realize
they are being cheated.

The statistic creates some
alarm for student readers.

In our competitive world, the sad truth is that even some of the very good students, though their college dreams were to be doctors and lawyers and pharmacists and engineers, will be

Competition for jobs and
status.

Qualifier.

The "I" draws attention to Bruno's personal concern.

waiting tables. Don't get me wrong: There is no shame in that. The point is, that's not why they went to college. The truth is that for some students, college will be a tough uphill climb (a climb that could have been avoided with a more adequate high school education). A sadder truth, I am afraid, is that because of skills and attitudes developed in high school, for some students the reality of genuine learning (as opposed to just getting by) might already be too late.

It's too late for many!

## Works Cited

"Almanac." *The Chronicle of Higher Education.* Chronicle of Higher Education, 2000. Web. 18 Oct. 2001.

Sacks, Peter. *Generation X Goes to College.* Chicago: Open Court, 1996. Print.

# Writing Strategies

1. Are you able to understand Bruno's response to Peter Sacks, even if you have not read *Generation X Goes to College?* What helpful background information does Bruno provide? What other information might have been helpful?

2. Bruno defines "intelligence" in his essay. How is this definition important? Might he have deleted this definition without damaging his essay?

3. What is Bruno's thesis?

4. Explain how Bruno's essay has public resonance. That is, how is what he says important to others besides himself?

5. What evidence does Bruno provide to support his thesis? What other kind of evidence might he have provided?

# Exploring Ideas

1. With a group of peers, explore how the education system you have experienced is or is not "too lax." Provide specific examples.

2. What is the purpose of education in elementary school? High school? College? After you write out responses, explore further with a group of peers: what else might be the purpose, or *a* purpose, of education?

3. How might high school better prepare students for college? How might it better prepare them for life?

4. Bruno says, "[academically] poorer students continue to advance through the system while remaining trapped at the bottom" (¶12). Explore Bruno's claim further: Is it true? Can you provide examples for support? Why do some students get trapped at the bottom? Is it okay for them to be trapped there? What, if anything, should be done about this?

# Ideas for Writing

1. What does Bruno get wrong?

2. If you agree with Bruno, what new and important point might you add?

If responding to one of these ideas, go to the Analysis section of this chapter to begin developing ideas for your essay.

# Reality Check

## Alison Hester

While some responses point out how an argument is wrong, others spotlight the particular value of an argument. Do Americans ignore reality? In the following essay, Alison Hester, an English major at Northern Michigan University, illuminates Jayme Stayer's claim that they do. Stayer's challenging essay (217–221) uncovers layers of meaning that a reader at first might have difficulty accepting. Our initial response might be, Why criticize an amusement park? How can such criticism be worthwhile? Shaping an essay from her responses to the Invention Questions in this chapter, Hester helps the reader understand and accept Stayer's claims.

Sea World is a place where humans can come to a better understanding of animals and experience the tranquility and magnificence of nature. To some, this is a valid and heartfelt statement about Sea World. But to others, such as author Jayme Stayer, it is not only a false statement, but one that masks a perilous underscoring issue of American culture. In his essay "Whales R Us," Jayme Stayer bravely exposes the truth behind Sea World's lofty statements and divulges the well-hidden realities of Sea World. Stayer steps apart from the crowd to reveal that what is deemed normal and satisfactory in society is actually the opposite, which, in turn, compels his readers to come to terms with reality.

In America we have produced a society that allows its citizens to ignore reality. We buy designer clothing made by children in sweatshops, drive cars that are impractical but stylish and status-setting, and permit the majority of the our population to pay little to no attention to other countries' governments or issues. Living in a country without reality is easy and pleasant and upholds our American way of life. Stayer discusses ignoring reality, shows us its destructiveness, and divulges underlying dangers in his darkly humorous analysis of Sea World.

Jayme Stayer reveals the multitude of falsehoods in Sea World. He shows how Sea World is not a representation of nature's tranquility but a bombardment of noise and underdeveloped factoid presentations. Throughout his essay, Stayer accuses Sea World of a plethora of inexcusable blunders. He turns their lofty statements about contributing to "world knowledge" (218) and making "peace with the earth" (219) against themselves to expose their blatant hypocrisy and lack of knowledgeable statements. Stayer chuckles at the idea of world knowledge being something fixed, an "accumulative spittoon" (218), and corrects this hasty, generalized outlook by explaining that world knowledge is in actuality "a set of competing claims and shifting paradigms" (218). Stayer challenges the idea that we can prospectively make peace with the earth by reminding us the world isn't innately peaceful but a place of "viruses, earthquakes, predatory animals, and a survival-of-the-fittest mentality" (219). He criticizes their mindless skits while suggesting that sex is a reality that family viewers should not have to face at Sea World. As the essay continues, it takes on a more serious nature. Stayer decides to dig even deeper into the design of Sea World to reveal its true intentions.

Stayer brings his reader's attention to the issue of Sea World's focus on education. After a thorough analysis and discussion of Sea World's "education," Stayer concludes that what takes place isn't education at all, but a form of "mind control" (220). Stayer has discovered that all of the microphones, manipulated applauding, and silly skits are there for no other purpose than to distract viewers from the reality of what they are witnessing. Sea World has decided what their audience needs to see, hear, and think in order to enjoy their visit. They make sure to keep bad thoughts out by replacing them with noise, "heartfelt" slogans, and the conjured proof of the captive animal's happiness and contentment. Sea World carefully sidesteps another harsh reality, which Stayer brings to the surface.

5     The animals at Sea World are there solely for our entertainment. In order for Sea World to hide this reality, they inform their audience of all the education that occurs at Sea World. The problem is, as Stayer points out, that "Sea World's communication of that knowledge, or to be more explicit, their refusal to level with its visitors about its real cultural role and worth" (220) is the most pressing issue of all. Sea World has decided for the better of the audience's entertainment to conceal the truth behind

why Sea World even exists and instead base everything on education that doesn't even take place. What does this say about Americans and entertainment?

Through all of his examples, clever quips, and harsh accusations, Stayer's essay evolves into the real issue at hand. Stayer has discovered that Sea World is a "consequence" (221) of American culture: a result of Americans creating a world where a person may never have to face reality. Sea World is a perfect example of an ever-increasing problem in America. At Sea World, Americans are privileged to enjoy a show while avoiding harsh realities of potentially miserable animals or our abuse of nature in general. We have placed our entertainment above accepting reality and being able to believe what we see and hear. Those who believe that Sea World truly does support education and living harmoniously with the

earth's creatures inevitably disagree with Stayer's arguments and disdainful outlook on Sea World.

Some might argue that Sea World is really a place of education. This would mean that there is no mind control and Stayer's argument falls. If Sea World really is based around teaching, learning, and the transfer of knowledge, then Stayer must have made countless inaccurate observations. That would mean that all the whale's back flips and the dolphin's synchronized jumps were not the point of the show, but rather the actual facts about the whales and dolphins were. This is obviously not so. People go to Sea World to see these sea creatures perform magnificent shows and create presumed warm connections between humans and nature. Sea World is not about the animal's vanishing habitats, or their family dynamics, or even how we can help these animals. Although these subjects might

Mike Theiss/Ultimate Chase/Corbis

be footnotes at Sea World, the real purpose is undeniably entertainment.

We would like to believe that Sea World is simply a fabulous way to learn. But after reading Stayer's essay, having the realities of Sea World revealed, one cannot deny that he makes a strong case. Stayer daringly commits the unspeakable crime of exposing a carefully masked reality of American culture. Stayer suggests that perhaps Sea World is another product of American desires, that we place our hunger for agreeable entertainment above individual opinion and being able to realize the truth behind something. A world has been created where animals are in synthetic environments, are hassled all day long, and if they could, would trade the security and comfort for true freedom. Acknowledging the truth of these creatures' existence at Sea World makes one realize that there can be no true education or productivity at the expense of captive creatures. But there is no reason to face these realities at Sea World if you don't wish to.

Yes, it's true, reality is an ugly portrait. It's no wonder, as advanced as our culture is, that we would create a world without reality. A world without reality is undeniably more pleasant and unrestrained. But to ignore reality is like ignoring a covered pot full of boiling water. Eventually the water will spill over the sides and create an unnecessary mess. That is exactly what reality is in America. We cover and ignore it, but it still exists. Hopefully, as a collective culture we can come to terms with the danger of denial and face the ugliness of reality. It's frightening to realize that continuing to live in a bubble without reality will eventually lead to a boiling-over that at one point was controllable.

### Work Cited

Stayer, Jayme. "Whales R Us." *The Composition of Everyday Life,* 4th ed. Ed. John Mauk and John Metz. Boston: Wadsworth, 2013. 217–221. Print.

# Writing Strategies

1. To what argument does Hester respond? Based on Hester's response, summarize Jayme Stayer's argument.

2. How does Hester respond to those who think Sea World might be a place of education? What specific support strategies are important in her response?

3. Notice how Hester guides the reader through her response. Identify several sentences in which she uses pronouns or introductory phrases to connect one idea to the next.

4. What support does Hester provide for the claim that "there can be no true education or productivity at the expense of captive creatures?"

5. Describe Hester's voice as a writer. Refer to two sentences as support for your description.

# Exploring Ideas

1. Hester says, "Stayer steps apart from the crowd to reveal [that] what is deemed normal and satisfactory in society is actually the opposite, which, in turn, compels his readers to come to terms with reality." What about Sea World is deemed normal and satisfactory? Why isn't this normal or satisfactory? According to Hester, how does Stayer compel readers to come to terms with reality?

2. In your view, what, like Sea World, claims to be a place of education but isn't?

3. Based on Hester's thinking, how might reality spill over and create an unnecessary mess, as Hester suggests in her conclusion? Do you agree or disagree with her fears?

4. What other reality of American culture is masked?

5. How does the image on this page support or refute Stayer's argument?

# Ideas for Writing

1. Write an argument that further develops Hester's claim that "there can be no true education . . . at the expense of captive creatures."

2. Respond by providing more and stronger support that American culture creates "a world without reality."

If responding to one of these ideas, go to the Analysis section of this chapter to begin developing ideas for your essay.

# INVENTION

Responding to an argument involves sophisticated thinking and planning. In a sense, this project is an argument², an argument to the second power. You are not only taking on another argument (with its own layers and nuances), but you are also developing a layered argument of your own. The following sections are designed to help you through the invention process; specifically, to find an argument (in Point of Contact), to discover the mechanics of that argument (in Analysis), to understand how the points relate to a community of readers (in Public Resonance), to invent a focused stance of your own (in Thesis), and to develop your own support (in Rhetorical Tools).

# Point of Contact

In this chapter, the point of contact is an actual argument. You will be responding to an explicit argument that someone else has formulated or to an argument expressed by many people. Remember that an argument need not be an essay; arguments are also made by advertisements, posters, and billboards. To find an argument that may relate directly to the goings-on of your life and community, examine the following options:

- **Local/City/Campus Newspapers:** Search the editorial pages and letters to the editor for arguments.
- **National Newspapers:** Publications such as the *New York Times, USA Today,* and *The Wall Street Journal* have editorial pages and columnists who offer arguments on various political and social issues.
- **Magazines:** Popular weeklies (such as *Newsweek, The Nation, Time,* and *US News and World Report*) and monthly or quarterly magazines (such as *Utne Reader* or *The New Republic*) are filled with argumentative articles and personal columns on social and political issues.
- **A Publication from Your Major** (such as *Education Journal, Nursing, Applied Science and Engineering*): Examine not only main articles but also reviews and personal columns.
- **Disciplinary Databases** (databases that focus on specific disciplines): Go to your library and check the electronic databases for your major or a closely related one.

- **Websites:** Go to your favorite search engine and enter topical keywords (*dogs, skateboards, economy,* etc.). You might find argumentative sites or pages more quickly if you combine potential topics with words such as *law, policy, argument, crisis,* or *debate*.

You can also focus your search on arguments made by bloggers by using blog searchers such as Google Blog Search (blogsearch.google.com), or a blog directory such as the one found at technorati.com.

Choose an argument that interests you and that you can address with some authority. Once you have found a potentially interesting argument, answer the following question:

- Why does the argument interest me?
  —Because something or someone has been omitted?
  —Because something or someone has been misrepresented?
  —Because I disagree or agree with it?
  —Because it raises an important issue that should be further discussed?
  —Because it changed my mind on a topic?
  —Because it is potentially important (helpful or dangerous)?

# A powerful response can come from a slight disagreement.

# Analysis

To analyze the argument in front of you, it may help to think of that argument as having two layers: (1) the four elements of argument and (2) the underlying warranting assumptions.

## The First Layer: The Four Elements of Argument

**Thesis**  Before we can respond to an argument, we must know *exactly* what is being argued. That is, we must figure out the thesis, the particular stance the writer takes on the topic. Finding the thesis for a written argument can be trickier than it seems. While some essays have explicit theses (stated directly), others are implied (not stated, but suggested by the supporting points). Once we locate the thesis (or understand it based on the details of the argument), we can then see how it is supported.

**Support**  Initially, the thesis might seem outlandish, but good support strategies will invite readers to accept even the most extreme thesis statements. Remember that support comes in a variety of forms:

| | |
|---|---|
| Statistics | Scenarios |
| Authorities | Appeal to Logic |
| Facts | Appeal to Emotion |
| Examples | Appeal of Character |
| Allusions | Appeal to Need |
| Personal Testimonies/Anecdotes | Appeal to Value |

Depending on the medium of the argument (essay, poster, etc.), the support may be varied. Or the writer may depend on a single key support strategy. We might ask: *How well does the support strategy connect to the thesis?* Or, *Given this argument, how appropriate is the support strategy?* For a detailed explanation of support strategies, see pages 229–231 in Chapter 7.

**Counterargument**  Sophisticated arguments anticipate and refute opposing claims. In fact, the success of an argument may depend on its counterarguments—on the ability of the writer to fend off opposing claims. A key counterargument strategy is the turnabout paragraph, in which a writer explains an opposing perspective and then responds directly.

**Concession**  Concessions acknowledge the value of opposing claims. Writers who concede acknowledge that others' positions may offer some insight outside of the writers' own claims. When writers concede points, their arguments do not lose force; instead, they appear more fair-minded. A writer who concedes shows that he or she has considered a range of other ideas.

To fully understand the first layer of the argument, answer the following questions for the argument to which you are responding.

### Invention Questions

▶ What is the main claim/thesis?

▶ What are the means of support for the main claim?

▶ Do the support strategies sufficiently prove the thesis?

▶ How does the argument address opposing claims? Are those claims sufficiently refuted?

▶ Does the argument concede to outside positions? What is the effect of those concessions?

▶ Does the writer define the issue correctly? ■

Daniel Bruno uses one of these Invention Questions as a springboard to discover a specific shortcoming in Sacks's book:

> **Does the writer define the issue correctly?**
> Sacks defines the issue correctly as far as he defines it. Entitlement education has the negative effect that he says it does, but he fails, it seems, to discuss or focus on an important aspect of the issue, which is that some students, who don't have an entitlement mentality, learn a great deal in school while others, who do, don't learn a great deal, or very much at all. The students who have

the entitlement mentality slide by while their classmates are learning more and more. The gap between the two groups widens. So, what does this mean to those students who feel entitled to good grades because they showed up (high school) or paid the tuition (college)? They get grades, but did they learn anything? Did they get an education?

## Rogerian Argument

Rogerian argument is based on the work of Carl Rogers (1902–1987), who is best known for his contributions to clinical psychology and psychotherapy. Rogers's ideas about mutual understanding, trust, and supportive rather than competitive rhetoric have become key concepts in argument.

According to Rogerian argument, arguers should first try to understand opposing views. In "Communication: Its Blocking and Its Facilitation" (1952), he writes, "The next time you get into an argument . . . stop the discussion for a moment and for an experiment, institute this rule. 'Each person can speak up for himself only after he has first restated the ideas and feelings of the previous speaker accurately, and to that speaker's satisfaction.'" This means that "before presenting your own point of view, it would be necessary for you to really achieve the other speaker's frame of reference—to understand his thoughts and feelings so well that you could summarize them for him."

This sounds simple, but it isn't. Rogers says, "But if you try it you will discover it one of the most difficult things you have ever tried to do. However, once you have been able to see the other's point view, your own comments will have to be drastically revised." According to Rogers, doing this takes courage: "If I enter, as fully as I am able, into the private world of a neurotic or psychotic individual, isn't there a risk that I might become lost in that world?"

As you respond to an argument for this chapter, first accurately summarize it. For help, ask a group of classmates to suggest where you might be misrepresenting the original argument.

# The Second Layer: Warranting Assumptions

Beneath the first, most visible, layer of an argument lurk warranting assumptions: the beliefs that connect points in an argument. Warranting assumptions are the root system of an argument; although they most often go unstated, they are as important as the most directly worded points. When we dig up warranting assumptions and investigate them closely, we can decide for ourselves if they are reasonable.

Philosopher Stephen Toulmin developed a powerful analytical system for digging up assumptions. In his perspective, every argument has a structure with interrelated parts. Using this, we can see how those parts relate and how well they function. Here are the three basic elements:

**Claim:** The main argumentative position (or thesis) being put forward

**Grounds:** The support for the position (evidence, examples, illustrations, etc.)

**Warranting Assumption:** The idea, often unstated, that connects the claim and the grounds—or that justifies the use of the grounds for the claim

The warranting assumption lies (often hidden) between the claim and the grounds. See how the elements work in the following example:

| | |
|---|---|
| Claim: | Sport utility vehicles are dangerous. |
| Grounds: | Many models roll over easily. |
| Warranting Assumption: | **Vehicles that roll over easily are dangerous.** |

The assumption lies between the claim and the grounds, connecting them logically.

In this example, the rollover frequency of SUVs supports the claim that they are dangerous. The warranting assumption (vehicles that roll over easily are dangerous) lies between the claim and the grounds. The assumption is entirely acceptable; few people would challenge it. But consider a different argument:

| Claim: | Sport utility vehicles are valuable to the average American driver. |
|---|---|
| Grounds: | The extra-large carrying capacity and four-wheel drive capability meet traveling needs. |
| Warranting Assumption: | Extra-large carrying capacity and four-wheel drive are valuable for the average American driver's traveling needs. |

The assumption here is less acceptable. Someone might argue against this warranting assumption on the grounds that the average American driver does not need extra-large carrying capacity and four-wheel drive, and that these aspects are actually unnecessary for most drivers. Stating the assumption thus reveals a particular weakness in the argument and provides an opportunity to respond.

Dissecting arguments in this fashion allows for various critical opportunities. Writers can focus attention on (take exception or agree with) two different layers of an argument: grounds and/or assumptions. Consider, for example, the first claim: *Sport utility vehicles are dangerous.* Although the assumption *vehicles that roll over easily are dangerous* is acceptable, the grounds for the claim *many models roll over easily* can be challenged. Someone might agree with the assumption but cite statistics showing that only a few models are prone to rollover accidents.

| Claim: | Sport utility vehicles are dangerous. | |
|---|---|---|
| Grounds: | Many models roll over easily. | (Questionable) |
| Warranting Assumption: | Vehicles that roll over easily are dangerous. | (Acceptable) |

Responding with such statistics could help a writer challenge the original argument. In this case, the responding writer would be challenging the grounds. For other arguments, both the grounds and assumption might be arguable:

| Claim: | The environment is not in danger from human influence. | |
|---|---|---|
| Grounds: | The environment is supporting the Earth's population today. | (Questionable) |
| Warranting Assumption: | The present human population directly illustrates the health of the environment. | (Questionable) |

Here, both the grounds and the warranting assumption are questionable. While the grounds could be refuted on their own terms (by illustrating the vast numbers of people starving throughout the world), the more interesting response might point to the warranting assumption. The mere presence of people, of course, does not indicate the health of the environment. Someone, for instance, might point to dramatic increases in skin and other cancers to illustrate the effects of greenhouse gases and environmental contamination. In this case, discovering the warranting assumption would allow a responding writer to point out a flaw in the logic.

The following questions can help you develop a response to the argument you have chosen to examine.

## Invention Questions

▶ What is the warranting assumption?

▶ Is the assumption acceptable or arguable?

▶ Can I prove that the assumption is incorrect?

▶ What else does the author of the argument assume (about life, identity, society, people's behavior, time, politics, human nature, etc.)? ■

# Public Resonance

Public resonance refers to the way in which a topic (or argument) relates to a community. In most cases, any published argument that you find will already have public resonance, especially if it comes from a newspaper, magazine, or journal. Your job, however, is not complete. As a responding writer, you can draw attention to the effects of the original argument on its readers and on the community at large.

To develop public resonance, examine the argument to which you will respond, and answer the following questions:

- Has the argument had an impact on readers? Any specific person or people?
- How *could* the argument affect people (negatively or positively)?
- What other issues or situations does the argument relate to or address?
- How can I relate the argument to the needs/wants of my audience (or anyone who is involved in the topic)?

## Invention Workshop

In a small group of writers, use one of the Invention Questions to start a discussion about your topic. First, briefly explain the original argument (the argument to which you are responding) to your group members. Then pose the question. (It may be helpful to write the question on a board or have all group members focus on this page so the question does not get lost in the discussion.)

In the following excerpt, Daniel Bruno explores *what* and *how* people might think about the topic of student entitlement. Here, Bruno has narrowed in on a particular issue from the original argument (Peter Sacks's book about college students). It's not merely that students shouldn't feel entitled to high grades. Bruno goes further and discovers the double jeopardy of entitlement: Those who feel entitled are "missing out" on their own educations:

**How can I relate the argument to the needs/wants of my audience (or anyone who is involved in the topic)?**

Some students feel entitled, which means expecting a good grade automatically, without working or learning anything. Some don't. The wants of the entitlement students are different than their needs. They want a grade or degree but need to learn and work. Interestingly, the students who feel entitled are the ones missing out, while the ones who don't feel entitled benefit. Maybe the students who believe they are entitled would benefit from thinking about the students who think differently, the ones who they will be competing against in the future, the ones who perhaps will be better prepared and have a better work ethic. The entitlement-minded students may find out too late that others are working hard and developing good skills and attitudes.

## Research

What have others said about your topic? If you are responding to a specific text (like an article or a book), go beyond that author's views and seek out other perspectives. Examine your invention writing and seek out keywords. Enter them into a periodical database search. (Remember that periodical databases, such as InfoTrac® College Edition, rely on keywords rather than phrases.) Enter main nouns linked together with *and*. If you have no luck, keep changing the nouns; try replacing them with synonyms. For instance, Bruno might enter: *students and college and entitlement.* Then, he might try: *students and college and attitude.* He might replace *attitude* with *achievement, success, study skills, apathy,* or a combination of these.

# Thesis

Responding to arguments is complicated because another set of claims must be engaged. But do not let those other claims confuse you. Resist chasing ideas throughout the original argument, and instead focus on a particular issue and then springboard into your own reasoning. Your argument might do one or more of the following:

- Redefine the issue according to your understanding.

   Sacks shows how consumerism has invaded education, leading some students to expect good grades for little effort. But he fails, it seems, to emphasize enough a most harmful effect of this sense of entitlement. (page 252)

- Argue for the value of a particular point or assumption in the original text.

   In "Technology, Movement, and Sound," Ed Bell argues against our culture's increasing love affair with technology. The real value of his argument is its focus on the relationship between personal technology and public effects.

- Argue against a particular point or assumption in the original text.

   Simon Benlow insists that students are increasingly more consumerist in their approach to education, but consumption is not inherently passive or anti-educational.

- Extend the original argument to include a broader set of ideas.

   April Pedersen concludes, "When his kidneys failed, a $12,000 kidney transplant was off the radar (a case can be made that surgery on an animal is unethical anyway), and I didn't consider him to be my son."

   While it might be hard to argue that $12,000 is too much to spend on saving a human life, Pedersen's point can be applied to humans as well as dogs: Far too many receive medical care that is unnecessary and arguably unethical, even if it is life-saving.

- Narrow the argument and suggest an important emphasis.

   As Jayme Stayer argues in "Whales R Us," theme parks such as Sea World are a "reflection of American culture . . . not a promoter of political change." His argument shows us that mainstream American culture may entirely lack a language for political change.

As you can see in these statements, it is not enough to say "I disagree" or "I agree." Instead, a project such as this benefits from a more focused point—one that shows something (important, harmful, inaccurate, valuable, etc.) in the original argument. The following questions can help generate the thesis of your argumentative response.

▶ With what *particular* point do I agree or disagree?

▶ How are my assumptions different from or similar to those of the writer?

▶ How is the original argument too narrow or too exclusive?

▶ What particular point in the original argument might readers fail to see? Why is it so important?

▶ How can I extend or broaden the original argument? ■

# Resist chasing various ideas; instead, focus on a particular issue.

# Evolution of a Thesis

Notice how the following idea evolves from summary, to gut reaction, to analytical insight:

- In "Crimes Against Humanity," Ward Churchill argues that the use of Native American symbols for sports teams is racist.    **Summary**

- Churchill's argument made me mad, and I think it may do the same to a lot of people. It basically suggests that everyone who supports certain professional sports teams is somehow tied to genocide.    **Gut reaction**

- Mainstream America might need to be pushed before it will accept new ideas.    **Analytical insight**

- Churchill's "Crimes Against Humanity" reminds us that mainstream opinions often do not change unless people encounter shocking, even offensive, claims.    **Focused statement**

Throughout this intellectual journey, the writer, by discovering something specific about Churchill's argument and its potential effect on readers, moves from dismissing the argument to revealing a quality in it.

# Thinking Further

While gut reactions can get a writer started, they are often too vague. The following statements show what someone might feel directly after reading an argument. While these initial feelings are valuable, they are only the beginning:

- Ann Marie Paulin's argument is right on target.
- April Pedersen's argument is important for dog lovers to hear.
- In "Crimes Against Humanity," Ward Churchill is just making a mountain out of a molehill.

These initial reactions must be explored. The writers might ask:

- What particular idea or assumption of Paulin's argument is insightful or valuable? Why is it insightful or valuable?
- Why is Pedersen's argument important? What particular aspect is valuable to animal lovers?
- Why might the issue really be a mountain?

In asking such questions, the writers can take their gut reaction to the next level—to more focused ideas:

- Ann Marie Paulin reveals the quiet everyday prejudices against overweight people.
- April Pedersen's argument correctly challenges the common misconception that caring for pets as one would care for humans is harmless.
- Churchill describes a view of American history and sports that most people do not consider.

## Revising Your Thesis

With a group of peers, explore your thesis statements. Each group member should share his or her thesis. Then the group should collectively attempt to narrow it by asking questions such as the preceding ones. Go after broad adjectives (*valuable, wrong, irresponsible, good, intense,* etc.). Prompt the writer to give specific descriptors or explanations. Also, check out the Common Thesis Problems in Chapter 7 on page 227. The same problems may lurk in this project as well.

# Rhetorical Tools

Even though you are responding to someone else's argument, you are still creating your own argument. Consider all the argumentative strategies introduced in Chapter 7.

## Using Support

Remember you have the whole world beyond the original argument to support your points. You can use various forms of evidence (such as personal testimony, examples, and facts, as well as allusions to history, popular culture, and news events) and appeals.

▶ What particular examples from everyday life show my point?

▶ Does a historical situation or trend (say, the rise of a particular fashion, organization, or individual) illustrate something about my topic?

▶ How has popular culture treated my topic? Does it show up in television shows, movies, or commercials? If so, how is it characterized, mishandled, or celebrated?

▶ How has literature (novels, poetry, drama, short stories) dealt with my topic? Have fictional characters illustrated something important about the topic or some behavior related to it?

▶ How does nature (animals, life cycles, plants, biological processes, and so on) demonstrate something about my topic?

▶ How can this topic relate to people's sense of logic? What line of reasoning can I create for the reader to follow?

(See pages 229–231 in Chapter 7: Making Arguments, for more help in developing evidence and appeals for your argument.) ■

## Counterarguing

Good writers address opposing claims. Notice how Alison Hester responds to an opposing position:

> Those who believe that Sea World truly does support education and living harmoniously with the earth's creatures inevitably disagree with Stayer's arguments and disdainful outlook on Sea World.
>
> Some might argue that Sea World is really a place of education. This would mean that there is no mind control and Stayer's argument falls. If Sea World really is based around teaching, learning, and the transfer of knowledge then Stayer must have made countless inaccurate observations. That would mean that all the whale's back flips and the dolphin's synchronized jumps were not the point of the show, but rather the actual facts about the whales and the dolphins were. This is obviously not so. People go to Sea World to see these sea creatures perform magnificent shows and create presumed warm connections between humans and nature. Sea World is not about the animal's vanishing habitats, or their family dynamics, or even how we can help these animals. Although these subjects might be footnotes at Sea World, the real purpose is undeniably entertainment.

As you develop your own argument, ask yourself the following questions:

▶ Apart from the author of the original argument, who might disagree with my position? Why?

▶ What reasons do people have for disagreeing with me?

▶ What evidence would support an opposing argument? ■

# Conceding and Qualifying Points

When responding to an argument, a writer should be especially mindful of giving credit to others' points. For example, in Bruno's response to Peter Sacks's book, he acknowledges several important elements of Sacks's argument:

> His final paragraph, before the Epilogue, says, "Let's create a system that encourages people like Andie at least as much as the ones who don't give a damn" (187). Thus, Sacks shows that today's students are a more diverse group—in skill level, background, and attitude toward education—than has ever before been gathered together in the college classroom.

Exploring the following questions will help you to see possible concessions for your own argument.

▶ Does the original argument make any valid points?

▶ Does my argument make any large, but necessary, leaps? (Should I acknowledge them?)

▶ Do I ask my audience to imagine a fictional situation? (Should I acknowledge the potential shortcomings of a fictional or hypothetical situation?)

▶ Do I ask my audience to accept generalizations? (Should I acknowledge those generalizations?) ■

## Activity

After responding to the preceding questions, discuss with peers the extent to which you should concede and qualify each point you discovered. For example, if you discovered that your argument made a large but necessary leap, should you acknowledge the leap in a phrase, a sentence, or an entire paragraph?

# Remembering Logical Fallacies

Logical fallacies are logical stumbles—gaps or shortcomings in reasoning. Examine the original argument closely to determine if it is free of fallacies. Finding logical fallacies in an argument can help you generate a response. For example, in the following passage, the writer points to a logical shortcoming in the original argument:

> Smith argues that incoming college students cannot handle the intellectual rigors of academia. He characterizes an entire generation as "undisciplined and whimsical." But like all arguments about entire generations, Smith's depends upon a hasty generalization. The truth about today's college students is far more complex than Smith's assertions, and any statement that seeks to characterize them as a whole should be looked upon with suspicion.

See a list and examples of logical fallacies in Chapter 7, pages 234–235.

## Activity

Write a one-paragraph summary of the essay you plan to write, stating your thesis and main supporting ideas. Share your summary with several peers and look for logical fallacies such as ad hominem, strawperson, faulty cause/effect, either/or reasoning, hasty generalization, non sequitur, oversimplification, slippery slope, false analogy, and begging the question. (See pages 234–235.) Although such fallacies are common in one's early thinking about an issue, they can be hard to spot. To find them, you may have to discuss the summaries and examine ideas carefully.

# Organizational Strategies

## Should I Quote the Original Argument?

Quoting is like putting a spotlight on a key passage. Responding writers sometimes want to draw attention not only to a point but also to the particular way the author delivered it. A quote can flag the shortcoming in the original text:

> In her argument, Ross claims banks "only share customers' personal information with affiliated companies" (43). However, an "affiliated company" in the present economic environment can be any company with which a bank does business. [. . .]

Sometimes writers quote the original argument to illustrate the importance or value of a particular point, or to extend an idea. Notice Bruno's quotation of Peter Sacks:

> While motivated students suffer in our too-lax system, so do the un- (or under-) motivated ones. And these students, who need our help the most, are the ones most cheated. As Sacks says, "I now believe the students are the real victims of this systematic failure of the entitlement mindset" (189). The students who are allowed to slide by, who are content to slide by, who perhaps don't even realize that they are sliding by because sliding by is all they know—those students find themselves arriving at college less prepared and less motivated than the "better students." And what happens next? Sadly, the gap between these two groups grows even wider.

Here, Bruno builds his argument from Sacks's point. That is, he begins with Sacks's idea, and then goes further to show the greater extent of the problem.

Rather than quote the original argument (or any outside source), you may choose to summarize or paraphrase. The exact language of a source is often unnecessary and can be a distraction. Notice how Hester restates information from Stayer's original argument in her own words by summarizing or paraphrasing, but quotes a few key words:

> Jayme Stayer reveals the multitude of falsehoods in Sea World. He shows how Sea World is not a representation of nature's tranquility but a bombardment of noise and underdeveloped factoid presentations. Throughout his article, Stayer accuses Sea World of a plethora of inexcusable blunders. He turns their lofty statements about contributing to "world knowledge" (329) and making "peace with the earth" (330) against themselves to expose their blatant hypocrisy and lack of knowledgeable statements. [. . .]

**Quotation**, using the exact words of a source, puts a spotlight on another writer's language. It allows writers to integrate especially important phrasing or passages. Quotes match the source word for word and are placed within quotation marks.

**Summary**, like paraphrasing, involves expressing a source's idea in your own words instead of the source's words, but unlike paraphrasing, summary removes much of the detail. Summarized information is not placed within quotation marks.

**Paraphrase** is a detailed rewording of the original source using your own words and expressions and conveying the detail and complexity of the original text. Although different from the source in organization, sentence structure, and wording, paraphrase matches the meaning of the original passage. Paraphrased information is not placed within quotation marks.

For more information on quoting, summary, and paraphrase, see Chapter 15, Integrating and Documenting Sources.

# How Should I Structure My Response?

The structure of your essay largely depends on what you intend to address from the original argument. You can use some standard organization strategies, such as

> Point A (from original argument)
> Your evaluation and response
>
> Point B (from original argument)
> Your evaluation and response
>
> Point C (from the original argument)
> Your evaluation and response

Of course, you also might have points D, E, F, and so on. And each of your evaluations and responses can vary in length from a sentence to several paragraphs. You might decide that the opposing viewpoint requires significant explanation, and that it would be best to keep all your points grouped together rather than separating them with passages from the original:

> Point A (from original argument)
>
> Point B (from original argument)
>
> Point C (from original argument)
>
> Your evaluation and response to A
>
> Your evaluation and response to B
>
> Your evaluation and response to C

Remember that the turnabout paragraph (see page 237) is a good strategy for counterargument. A turnabout paragraph begins with one point, and then changes directions, giving the reader a clear indication of that change.

# Invention Workshop

**A.** With a group of peers, examine the argument to which each group member is responding.
  1. What specific language from the argument might the writer quote and why?
  2. What ideas should be summarized in a sentence or two and why?
  3. What ideas should be paraphrased and why?

**B.** With a group of peers, imagine possible structures for each group member's response essay.
  1. What idea or ideas from the original argument will the essay develop responses to? List each idea.
  2. What are the advantages and disadvantages of a Point A/Your response, Point B/Your response, Point C/Your response structure?
  3. What are the advantages and disadvantages of a Point A, B, C/Your response structure?
  4. How might the reader use a hybrid structure (combining 2 and 3 above)?

> **Whether information is quoted, summarized, or paraphrased, it should blend smoothly into the text. (See Chapter 13.)**

# Writer's Voice

## Rogerian Argument

Because argument can potentially create hostility and turn people away from each other, Carl Rogers developed an argumentative perspective that emphasizes building connections between different positions (as shown on page 265). People who use Rogerian argument look for similarities rather than differences between arguments. Such a strategy creates an engaging voice—one that invites exploration of ideas rather than harsh dismissals. All the writers in this chapter establish common ground with the argument to which they are responding.

> George Orwell will forever be a hero of mine. When I read *1984* in high school, I became sensitized to the workings of propaganda. After more than forty years as a linguist and cognitive scientist, I remain sensitized.
>
> When I first read "Politics and the English Language" as an undergraduate in the late 1950s, I loved it. Nearly fifty years later I find it an anachronism. Why? I, and those in my profession, have learned a lot about the brain, the mind, and language since then. Orwell's essay belongs to an earlier time, a time that lacked our deepening understanding of how the human brain works.

Even though his essay will show how Orwell was wrong, George Lakoff begins by acknowledging the value of Orwell's ideas and explaining that they are understandably flawed, because since Orwell's time we have developed a "deepening understanding of how the human brain works." Bruno takes a similar approach:

> In his book *Generation X Goes to College*, Peter Sacks describes, among other things, the sense of entitlement that some students in today's consumerist culture have toward a college education. One entire chapter explores this issue alone, providing examples of this "sense" and looking into its "humble beginnings."
>
> Sacks shows how consumerism has invaded education, leading some students to expect good grades for little effort. But he fails, it seems, to emphasize enough a most harmful effect of this entitlement. The biggest problem, as I see it, is that although students are able to graduate from high school (and even some colleges) with minimal effort, those students may find themselves cheated in the long run.

Rogers suggests that before responding, one should accurately restate the ideas being responded to. Notice how Bruno establishes common ground by summing up and acknowledging the value of the idea to which he is responding.

## Invention Workshop

With a group of classmates, seek out the common ground between your argument and the argument to which you are responding. How might you use similarities in thinking as a way of getting at the key difference?

## The Invisible/Present "I"

Many academic disciplines favor writing that does not draw attention to the writer (to the *I*). Writing for English courses, which often focuses on personal insights and reflection, avoids unnecessary attention to *I* as well. This is because argumentative writing implies or assumes the presence of the writer. In other words, every claim or position in a paper that is not attributed to some other source belongs to the writer; therefore, phrases such as "I think that," "In my opinion," or "I believe" are often unnecessary.

However, the first-person pronoun occasionally can be used to make a distinction between an outside argument and the writer's own opinion. If the writer is dealing with several ideas or outside opinions, he or she might decide that using the first-person pronoun refocuses attention on the main argument:

> The biggest problem, as I see it, is that although students are able to graduate from high school (and even some colleges) with minimal effort, those students may find themselves cheated in the long run.

## Activity

If you are enrolled in multiple courses, ask each instructor about his or her stance on first-person pronouns in writing. You might also ask about the standard practice of your major, or examine a professional journal in your field of study to see how (and how often) first-person pronouns are used.

## Consider Tone

If you are responding to a specific argument, you are encountering a tone (the color or mood of a writer's voice). Sometimes writers who are responding to an argument choose to mimic the tone of the original argument. In other words, if you are responding to a very sober and formal argument, you might do well to respond in kind. On the other hand, changing the tone of a discussion can be a powerful rhetorical tool. When writers want to challenge an argument, they may not only argue against the ideas but also shift the tone to their own particular liking. For example, imagine a politician arguing against the comedic rants of Howard Stern. The politician might put forth a very sober argument against Stern—thereby arguing on her own ground rather than on Stern's comedic turf. The opposite is often done: Many writers (and public figures) argue informally to challenge a seemingly formal argument. Consider programs such as *The Daily Show with Jon Stewart* and *Saturday Night Live* or Michael Moore's film *Roger & Me*. They respond to "serious" political arguments by spoofing them—by revealing their flaws and deliberately changing their tone.

As you examine your chosen argument (the one to which you are responding) and your own position, consider tone. Ask yourself the following questions:

▶ Has the tone been established by someone else's argument?

▶ Do I want to change the tone slightly or dramatically?

▶ What effect would a change in tone have on the argument? ■

# Changing the tone of a discussion can be a powerful rhetorical tool.

# Vitality

For any essay project, boiling down text is a key strategy. When writers approach a final draft, they benefit from taking time away and then returning to the draft with one goal in mind: to make it more concise and intensive. This requires the willingness to boil away unnecessary phrases, clauses, and sentences. To help you make decisions at the sentence level, consider the following guidelines.

## Avoid Over-Embedding

Sometimes sentences can be hard to read because of too many overlapping clauses. In the following sentence, notice how two overlapping dependent clauses (that Thoreau has with the government that depends upon the majority) get between the subject (The problem) and the verb (is), thus causing interference and making the sentence less vital and less readable.

> The problem that Thoreau has with the government that depends upon the majority is that the majority often fails to think of what is right and what is wrong.

For better vitality, the sentence might be rewritten:

> According to Thoreau, a government of the majority has a key problem: Majorities often fail to distinguish between right and wrong.

While a well-placed clause between the subject and verb can help create a clear and lively sentence, a string of loose clauses can zap a sentence's strength and clarity. Strings of overlapping clauses naturally occur in the drafting stage. Writers must learn to notice these clauses and then revise to create a more clear and concise sentence.

## Break Bad Habits

Developing as a writer involves identifying and breaking bad habits. Some writers are surprised to learn that they have picked up their worst habits from previous writing courses. For example, instead of working to boil down text, they try to stretch it out. This raises the question: if I am supposed to delete unnecessary phrases, clauses, and sentences, how can I make my essay long enough? The answer is: invention!

The parts of the writing process are not entirely separate from each other; they are all connected. Vitality, for example, relates to invention. As writers work to make their writing more lively, they delete not only phrases, clauses, and sentences, but examples, paragraphs, and entire sections when possible. Good writing packs a punch: instead of taking longer to say less, good writing says more in fewer words. To reach the required length, writers don't simply dig up a lot of facts, statistics, or examples; instead, they complicate their thinking through analysis. As you boil down your essay, complicate your thinking by revisiting the Invention Questions in this chapter.

Good writing packs a punch: Instead of taking longer to say less, good writing says more in fewer words.

# Clean Up Attributive Phrases

Attributive phrases connect an author and his or her ideas: *According to Biff Harrison; in Jergerson's argument; as Jacobs points out;* and so on. Because you are dealing with another text, you may need to draw consistent attention to the author's words and use attributive phrases. But be cautious of clumsy phrasing such as the following:

1. In "Letter from Birmingham Jail," by Martin Luther King, Jr., King writes about how society can be unjust.
2. In Jayme Stayer's perspective, Sea World reveals the shallowest qualities of American culture. He believes that "[t]he American traits that Sea World reflects most clearly are its gullibility and irrationality."
3. Ann Marie Paulin wrote an essay about incivility and obesity. It is called "Cruelty, Civility, and Other Weighty Matters."

Each of these sentences makes a similar error: Each draws an unnecessary degree of attention to the act of writing or to the author's thoughts. Each could be boiled down.

1. In "Letter from Birmingham Jail," Martin Luther King Jr. writes about injustice.
2. In Jayme Stayer's perspective, Sea World reveals the shallowest qualities of American culture: "The American traits that Sea World reflects most clearly are its gullibility and irrationality."
3. Ann Marie Paulin's essay "Cruelty, Civility, and Other Weighty Matters" shows the deeply personal impact of media images.

# Try Absolutes!

Absolute phrases—which consist of a noun, modifiers, and often a participle—modify an entire clause or sentence, not just a word or phrase. Absolutes can help intensify ideas—weaving them together to create a more sophisticated, yet concise, sentence. Consider the following two sentences:

> The beauty pageant had finally concluded and the whole ordeal had finally come to an end. Cindy Bosley could now escape the desperate feelings around her.

Although these sentences are correct and functional, they can be combined with an absolute phrase. The verbs of the first sentence will be omitted, the ideas slightly compressed into an absolute phrase and attached to the clause:

> The beauty pageant concluded and the whole ordeal finally over, Cindy Bosley could escape the desperate feelings around her.

If used sparingly, absolute phrases can add subtle variety to an essay, helping readers escape the march of subject/verb, subject/verb, subject/verb sentence patterns.

---

## Activity

Read through your essay to identify and revise:

- an over-embedded clause
- text that is stretched out (to make it longer) instead of boiled down (so it packs a punch)
- a clumsy attributive phrase
- two sentences that could be one sentence with an absolute phrase.

# Revision

The Invention Questions in this chapter are not meant to be answered just once. The value of these questions is in responding to them as a way of discovering and developing new ideas, then returning to them and exploring further from your new perspective. Before you exchange drafts with a peer, revisit the questions in the Analysis, Public Resonance, Thesis, and Rhetorical Tools sections of this chapter. Try to ratchet up your thinking even further.

## Peer Review

Exchange drafts with at least one other writer. Before exchanging, underline your thesis (or write it at the top of the first page) so that others will more quickly get a sense of your main idea. Use the following questions to respond to specific issues in the drafts:

1. Can any phrases or terms in the thesis be narrowed? If so, circle them and make some suggestions for more focus.
2. Is the main idea of the original argument sufficiently summarized? (Could the summary be shorter? How?)
3. Where could the writer support broad statements with specific evidence (allusions, examples, facts, personal testimony, scenario)? Writers often fall into the habit of making broad claims that should be illustrated. For instance, someone might argue, "All students learn differently." But such a statement needs to be supported with specifics. Otherwise, a reader has no reason to accept it, no reason to see it as true.
4. Where might the writer oversimplify the original argument/issue or mischaracterize the original author's position? (Look especially for ad hominem or strawperson logical fallacies. See page 234.)
5. What paragraphs shift focus? Where do you sense gaps in the lines of reasoning? How could the writer fill those gaps?
6. Circle any clichés or overly broad statements that could be transformed into specific and revelatory insights.

7. Consider sentence vitality:
   - What sentences are over-embedded? (Point to any clauses that overlap with other clauses, causing a disconnect between ideas.)
   - Examine attributive phrases. Point out unnecessary phrases or sentences that could be boiled down.
   - Consider vitality strategies from other chapters:
     —Where can the writer change linking verbs to active verbs?
     —Where can the writer avoid drawing attention to *I* and *you*?
     —Help the writer change unnecessary clauses to phrases.
     —Help the writer change unnecessary phrases to words.
     —Point to expletives (such as *there are* and *it is*).
     —Help the writer change passive verbs to active verbs for more vitality.
     —Help the writer avoid common grammatical errors: comma splices, sentence fragments, or pronoun/ antecedent agreement.

## Questions for Research

**If the writer used outside sources,**

- Where must he or she include in-text citations? (See pages 470–471.)
- Are quotations blended smoothly into the argument and punctuated correctly? (See pages 456–468.)
- Where could more direct textual cues or transitions help the reader? (See pages 466–467.)
- Is the Works Cited page formatted properly? (See pages 469–480.)

# Reflection

Now that you have responded to an argument, reflect on how you invented your response. Consider this: Just as we discuss ideas with others as part of the invention process, we also play out discussions in our own minds. We have both external and internal dialogues. For example, to invent for this essay, you may have written responses to Invention Questions, discussed publicly (with others), and created internal dialogues (imaginary discussions between you and others inside your head). We create internal dialogues while driving, walking the dog, working out, and so on.

1. Which did you rely on most for invention: written responses to Invention Questions, public dialogue, or internal dialogue? Which might you have utilized more and why?
2. List at least two key points in your essay.
   a. For each point, did you invent the point through written responses to Invention Questions in the text, public dialogue, internal dialogue, a combination of the three, or some other way? Explain.
   b. How did each key point function in the essay? Was it the thesis? A support strategy? An opening (introduction) strategy? Part of the conclusion?

3. If you can recall any internal dialogue from your invention process, describe how it worked:
   a. Who was your imaginary discussion partner?
   b. What was the nature of the discussion? Was it cooperative, combative, or something else?
4. How was your essay a response to an ongoing public discussion? What specific ideas from that public discussion was your invention (writing as well as public and private dialogues) a response to?

## Beyond the Essay

Find or create an image that responds to the argument you made in your essay for this chapter.

- What response does the image make?
- How do particular visual elements make the response clear to the audience?

Share the image with a peer, and ask him or her to respond to the preceding questions. Then discuss the similarities and differences in your responses.

For additional resources including instructional videos and links to helpful websites, access your English CourseMate through cengagebrain.com.

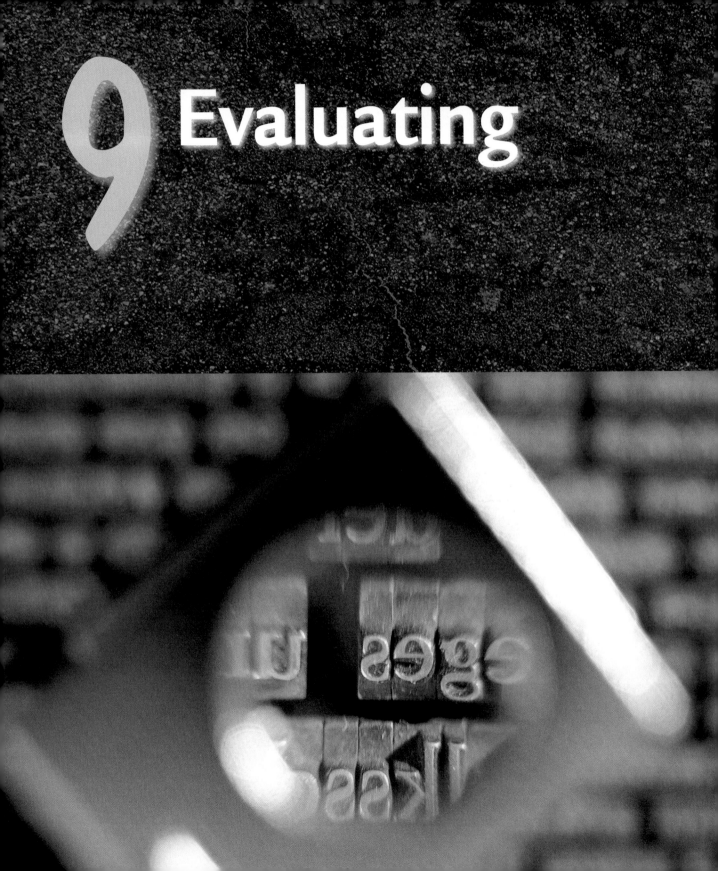

# 9 Evaluating

# Chapter Contents

# "The trouble with normal is it always gets worse."

—Bruce Cockburn

Evaluating is the act of judging the value or worth of a given subject. We make informal judgments constantly throughout our daily lives: we decide that we like a particular car more than another, or that one song on the radio is better than another. Such evaluations are informal because they involve little analysis; that is, we do not usually take the time to thoroughly analyze each song we hear on the radio as we are sweeping through stations. We also take part in formal evaluation, a process that goes beyond an expression of likes and dislikes: teachers must evaluate student performance; jury members must evaluate events, people, and testimony; voters must evaluate political candidates; members of unions must evaluate contracts; managers must evaluate employees; executives must evaluate business proposals; citizens must evaluate laws and lawmakers. In such situations, mere personal tastes cannot dictate evaluative decisions. Instead, a formal process—sometimes entirely intellectual, sometimes organized in visible steps—is necessary for sound evaluation.

The ability to make formal evaluations is essential to academic thinking and writing:

- Biologists at a national conference evaluate the success of a particular molecular research process.
- Law enforcement students are assigned to evaluate a new highway safety program.
- Crime lab scientists evaluate a particular procedure for gathering evidence.
- University civil engineers evaluate a downtown rezoning plan.
- English professors evaluate a new textbook for the department literature courses.
- Education faculty members and graduate students evaluate the state's controversial new standardized tests.
- Art students evaluate a set of paintings from the early Modernist era.

Much literary work is also evaluative. Barbara Kingsolver's *Poisonwood Bible,* for example, condemns twentieth-century missionary work in Africa. Yann

Martel's *Life of Pi* critiques scientific rationality. Ralph Ellison's *Invisible Man* reveals a range of racist assumptions and practices. And Jonathan Swift's *Gulliver's Travels,* perhaps one of the most famous examples of evaluative literature, critiques (or satirizes) political and economic institutions of eighteenth-century England.

Whether one is an author, jury member, civil engineer, or voting citizen, the person who can evaluate well and make judgments outside of his or her personal tastes is able to make valuable decisions, to help distinguish the best course of action, to clarify options when many seem available. And in a culture that is increasingly filled with choices (among political candidates, retirement plans, religious paths, and lifestyles, to name just a few), it is increasingly important for the literate citizen to evaluate well.

The essays in this chapter all make judgments and, in doing so, present their subjects to the reader in a particular light. In other words, each writer gives an opinion about a subject (be it a video game, a television show, etc.) and then supports that opinion by showing selected details of the subject. While the writers give some form of overview (some general summary about the subject),

they also focus the reader's attention on the details that support their judgments. This is fair play. In drawing attention to certain details (and ignoring others), they are simply creating argumentative positions—the positions they want the reader to accept. Notice, also, that the writers tend to draw on support outside their subjects; that is, they refer to other similar subjects to show particular points, which gives credibility to their judgments.

This chapter will help you develop a formal evaluation of a particular subject and communicate your evaluation in writing. The following essays will provide valuable insight to various evaluation strategies. After reading the essays, you can find a subject in one of two ways:

1. Go to the Point of Contact section to find a topic from your everyday life, or
2. Choose one of the Ideas for Writing that follow the essays.

After finding a subject, go to the Analysis section to begin developing the evaluation.

# Talibanned

## Benjamin Busch

Benjamin Busch is an actor, poet, essayist, photographer, film producer, and former Marine major. As an actor, he played memorable characters on programs such as *Homicide, The Wire,* and *Generation Kill.* As a Marine, he served two tours in Iraq and was awarded the Bronze Star. He has, then, an acute understanding of the tension between reality and fiction. In this essay, Busch uses one particular criterion to evaluate a video game: realism. This essay was recorded in an edited form as "A Video Game Does Not a Soldier Make" on National Public Radio's *All Things Considered.*

My Grandfather fought the Nazis and was wounded. For years afterward, my father recreated that war in games in his Brooklyn neighborhood, where some of the children playing had lost their fathers overseas. But war games require two sides, and someone in Brooklyn always had to play the Germans.

When I was a boy, I was given plastic army men. They were posed already fighting. I arranged them in the sandbox behind our house, and I killed them. I voiced their commands and made the sounds of their suffering. I was every one of them, and I was their enemy. I imagined their war—and I controlled it. I was a child. But I lost those magical powers as a Marine in Iraq.

We know children are immersed in digital interactivity now, and the soldier of today has grown up on video games. It is becoming a new literacy of sorts. Playing and risking your life are different things, of course. In the video war, there may be some manipulation of anxiety, some adrenaline to the heart, but absolutely nothing is at stake.

The military has recognized the attraction of trigger based combat games and has incorporated them into recruitment and training. There is an official U. S. Army Game called *America's Army.* Gamers are encouraged to download a free video game where they can "play *America's Army 3* on Steam and earn Steam Achievements, ranking up among your friends as you earn distinguished status, badges, medals, and ribbons." Without leaving home, players can comfortably attain rank and recognition

online as imaginary soldiers on a game platform designed to transform their entertainment into military service. On the same site the U.S. Army places ads picturing members in uniform. One says:

> Meet PVT Alaniz. He joined the Army to pay for a college education and is proud to follow in his grandfather's footsteps. Free room, board and laundry allow him to put money toward some of the important things in life: like treating his girlfriend and buying a plasma TV to play Xbox 360. Check out the opportunities the Army created for PVT Alaniz.

There is something disingenuous about this interactive advertising. Player characters cannot be killed in *America's Army 3.* As their "avatars" become distinguished soldiers, players can more easily see themselves in uniform. Video game training continues after enlistment. The Army now uses games like *Full Spectrum Warrior* and *Full Spectrum Command* to develop leadership skills in virtual combat environments.

Electronic Arts (EA) developed a modern combat game with members of the U. S. Special Forces. It is called *Medal of Honor* after the highest American military decoration for heroism, and it is based in the current Afghanistan war. *Medal of Honor* allows gamers to play as the Taliban as well as U.S. Forces in multi-player contests. This brought immediate outrage from members of allied leadership in England, where Defense Secretary Dr. Liam Fox called for a ban on the sale of the game because players choosing to play as Taliban could "kill" allied soldiers. Pressured by this objection, the U.S. military followed suit, banning the sale on its bases. Despite the controversy, AE did nothing more than change the name of "the enemy" from "Taliban" to "Opposing Forces." Changing the name of the enemy doesn't change who it is.

I honestly don't like that *Medal of Honor* depicts the war that is happening in Afghanistan right now because— even as fiction—it equates war with the leisure of games. Hundreds of combat games use historical conflicts, especially World War II, as their subject but there is a great deal of psychological separation from these events. There has been time to recover from loss, and to mourn. A game that claims "authenticity" played during the same conflict it depicts is not emotionally distant from it but is, instead, emotionally parallel. Furthermore, the age of the game's target audience is the same as that of the soldiers fighting so the line between casual entertainment and traumatic reality blurs.

But what nation or military has the right to govern fiction? Banning the representation of an enemy is imposing nationalism on entertainment. The game cannot train its players to be actual skilled special operations soldiers, nor is it likely to lure anyone into Islamic fundamentalism. It can grant neither heroism nor martyrdom. What it does do is make modern war into participatory cinema. That is its business.

Despite my objections to certain aspects of the video war game, I don't know that game makers have any particular responsibilities to any of us. They are a market based entertainment business. Their sales are subject to mature audience restrictions like film and pornography, but game ratings are not enforced by any government agency in the United States. We can only hope that business values social decency, and respects essential humanism but a gaming company is only truly concerned with market reception in the form of product sales. The responsibility is placed on the consumer and parents. At the age of 18, an American citizen can vote, and can enlist in the armed services without parental consent. We should assume that they can also choose their entertainment for better or for worse. Issues of responsibility arise when our military develops war games with private companies and then allows them to be sold publicly. The game then partially becomes a governmental, even military, product and its messages are unable to speak free of politics or real war.

The more our imagination is disengaged from our environment, the more we detach from visceral experience, and that is a problem if soldiers are being trained on video games for artificial wars. Part of their comprehension of the real war may be based on this manufactured fantasy of it.

But imagine how frustrating this game would be if, just as you began to play it, an invisible sniper shot you dead every time. The game would not be popular because being killed that way isn't fair—just like war. Reality has a way of correcting misconceptions.

The power of controlling your situation, to be able to stop the war and rest, is something that our soldiers are quietly desperate for. For those who patrol the valleys of Helmand, it is a way to impose limits on the uncertainty of war, and the constancy of vulnerability. A video game can produce no wounds, and take no friends away. The soldier understands the difference.

The games of my youth seem more innocent than the fully articulated violence delivered for the modern day boy, but so did the films, news, and books. There is a truth common to all, and that is that playing war in any medium is not combat, and for a gamer, it's not even political. It's just sedentary adventurism in need of a subject. In the real "war gaming" of the invasion and occupation of Afghanistan, perhaps the Pentagon should have allowed someone to play as the Taliban.

The truth is that there are two ways out of Afghanistan: wounds or luck. Proficiency is only part of surviving the randomness of death, and playing games will not protect or endanger soldiers or governments. If gamers are inspired to join the Taliban, they should talk to John Walker Lindh first. And for those who truly want to play for a Medal of Honor, recruiters are standing by. Only eight have been awarded since we invaded Afghanistan. All but one have been posthumous.

## Writing Strategies

1. Busch begins his essay with some family history and personal testimony. Explain how these two introductory paragraphs help to launch his evaluation.

2. What is the essay's most powerful statement against *Medal of Honor?*

3. In ¶9, Busch says, "We can only hope that business values social decency, and respects essential humanism but a gaming company is only truly concerned with market reception in the form of product sales." How does this subtle appeal to decency help with his evaluation of the video game?

4. How does Busch counterargue or concede to opposing positions? Describe particular passages.

5. Explain how Busch's conclusion reinforces his position on *Medal of Honor.*

## Exploring Ideas

1. Consider Busch's point: that *Medal of Honor* "equates war with the leisure of games." Why might that equation be something to evaluate, even if (or especially if) you are an avid gamer?

2. Busch explains that the U.S. military works closely with private corporations to develop software. Why might that interaction be a concern for both soldiers and citizens?

3. Busch describes gaming as "sedentary adventurism in need of a subject." How is this phrase an indictment of gaming? How is *sedentary adventurism* negative?

4. In his conclusion, Busch alludes to John Walker Lindh—a U.S. citizen who traveled to Afghanistan in 2001, trained with Taliban forces, and fought against the U.S. military. He was captured that year, detained as an enemy combatant, and is currently serving a twenty-year prison sentence. How does Lindh's story figure into the argument about games such as *Medal of Honor?*

## Ideas for Writing

1. Video games are often condemned for their levels of violence. Choose a particular game and develop an evaluation. Avoid simply attacking or defending the portrayal of violence. Consider other criteria.

2. Focus on an advertisement for military recruiting. Evaluate its moves, its strategies, its realism, or even its parallels to popular video games.

If responding to one of these ideas, go to the Analysis section of this chapter to begin developing ideas for your essay.

# *The Andy Griffith Show:* Return to Normal

## Ed Bell

Evaluations invite readers to see why something is valuable or deficient. To do this, a writer may propose a new standard of judgment (a criterion) upon which the evaluation is based. For example, a writer might suggest that a television show should not only entertain but also *comfort* its audience. In this essay, Ed Bell, a writing instructor, does just that, first establishing comfort as a potential criterion for a prime-time television sitcom, then arguing how well *The Andy Griffith Show* meets that criterion. Portions of Bell's invention work are shown later in this chapter.

**Writing Strategies**

Introduction discusses what sitcoms do (their purpose): instruct, entertain, comfort. Evaluation of show can be based on how well the shows do this.

Main claim: "More than any other sitcom . . ."

Criteria for evaluation. How *Andy Griffith* differs from other shows—it's more comforting because things return to normal.

Develops argument by discussing what happens in other shows: things work out okay, but we can tell a new crisis will loom.

From those early days of Lucy and Ricky to our own Dharma and Greg, situation comedies have been part of American culture. And for all the advancements, it still seems like the plots of most of them are something cooked up by Lucy who dragged along Ethel and got caught (and ultimately forgiven) by Fred and Barney . . . uh . . . Fred and Ricky, I mean. Whether or not these shows instruct is, I suppose, debatable. But what is not debatable is that over the past 50 years they have entertained millions. And, I would suggest, through that very act of entertaining us, they have comforted us—the most comforting of them all being *The Andy Griffith Show.*

More than any other sitcom, *The Andy Griffith Show* leaves its viewers with a sense that everything is all right. While *Three's Company* or *Dharma and Greg* or *MASH* may also wind things up happily after 30 minutes, there is—even though the complication of that particular week's crisis has been worked out—always a sense on those shows that things are not quite right. Yet *The Andy Griffith Show* leaves us with the feeling that, even though our friends sometimes get big-headed ideas or strangers from Raleigh come driving or dancing or swindling their mixed-up way into our peacefulness, life will eventually return to normal, all warm and wonderful.

On *Three's Company* or *Seinfeld* or *Friends,* things work out in the end. The friends are getting along just fine, but we can see that they are bound for another conflict in a week or so. Though this week's crisis has worked itself out, the pace of their lives or their natural temperaments or their complicated living conditions are still spinning wildly and we know next week they're in for trouble again. On *Dharma and Greg* or *Green Acres* or *I Love*

**Exploring Ideas**

Connects to life of viewer: Do sitcoms instruct? How?

Okay, but there must be "other" shows like *Andy*— such as *Leave It to Beaver.*

From Ed Bell, "*The Andy Griffith Show*: Return to Normal." Reprinted with permission of the author.

*Lucy* (even on *The Dick Van Dyke Show*), the family has once again survived, but as with the shows about friends, on the shows about families there seems to be only temporary comfort in the happy ending. Dharma and Greg are still bound for a divorce. Lisa, on *Green Acres,* is only putting up with the farm life a little while longer and Oliver loves it so much that he is never going back to the city. Though she is ironically more suited to the place than he is, she longs always to live elsewhere. No one could possibly put up with all Lucy's scheming. And as for Richard and Laura Petrie, the most stable of our sample couples, to the average American they seem only a step away from falling into the New York swinger crowd. On *MASH* or *Hogan's Heroes* or *Gomer Pyle,* they are either at war or could be. There's little real and lasting comfort in these folks who are gathered together out of necessity so far from home. Yes, they're buddies and that's nice, but it's all so temporary.

This seems to go beyond initial thinking. (I've never thought about it.)

Author concedes that there are other sitcoms and other types of sitcoms.

This doesn't exhaust all the sitcoms or all the types, but it does set up the reasons that *The Andy Griffith Show* comforts us more than the others. The show's main character, Andy, is full of southern wisdom. He is quiet and listens and makes better decisions in the midst of all the madness than we could have. That is comfort number one: Someone—the general, the man in charge, *the sheriff*—has things under control. All the madness results

Goes beyond initial thinking here. Gets specific. Show provides comfort because someone's wise. Madness because of (1) intruders; (2) natural growing up; (3) ego, ambition, pride.

CBS/Landov

from one of three things: either intruders, but Andy gets rid of them after they have caused only a little trouble; or just boys (Opie and sometimes his friends) going through what is natural to go through growing up, but Andy deals with this expertly, too; or ego, ambition, and pride—usually Barney is having the trouble here, though it could be Aunt Bea or one of the others. Andy understands all of this, though not so well or right away that the show isn't a little bit interesting. The plot is better than most sitcoms: There is always a solution that takes a little while to get to, and we believe it when we finally do.

What's most comforting about this show, however, is that things return to normal. That is, *The Andy Griffith Show* offers us a normal that can be returned to. With *Andy Griffith* we get a sense that the complication has blown through like a summer thunderstorm, instead of us getting the sense that a little blue sky has blown through a place where it is otherwise always thunderstorming. The characters are at home. They're not strangers thrown together, and they haven't been transplanted in some strange land (such as Hooterville, New York City, or Postmodern America). They are familiar with their surroundings and like (both "similar to" and "fond of") each other. The zaniness on *Andy Griffith* could just as well not ensue . . . but it does. On all those other shows, it must ensue. How couldn't it?

The situation itself—small-town people in a small town—is comforting. The show develops this sense with Andy's quiet wisdom, but also with the integrity of the wacky supporting characters. All of them to some degree are like Barney—a liability and an asset all at once. They are, like us, good people flawed. We are all familiar with the show's gentle theme song, whistled as Andy and Opie walk along with fishing poles. And the black and white camera shots are always perfectly composed, like a photo we'd see in *Life* magazine. The dialog is quiet, engaging, funny, real. For 30 minutes we are practically back in the womb of Mayberry—a place that doesn't exist, but does. It is a place that, whether we ever felt it as a child or not, as adults we feel that we once knew. We can feel it now, and *The Andy Griffith Show* captures what we all now think that we once felt back then.

Not all sitcoms set out to comfort, though all do set out to entertain. Some, such as *All in the Family* or *Soap* or *Will and Grace,* might even set out to challenge us, to make us think. But *The Andy Griffith Show,* I believe, sets out to entertain and comfort and it succeeds as no other show ever has . . . or ever will. *The Cosby Show* could only circle in *Andy's* orbit. The reason is, I suppose, because the times have changed. Today an

---

**Margin notes (left):**

Develops argument through specific analysis of *The Andy Griffith Show.* Shows specifically why/how *Andy Griffith* comforts us.

Main idea: says what is most comforting about the show (relates to title of essay).

Connects to reader (public resonance): they are, like *us,* good people flawed. The use of "we" (though not required) helps make this connection.

Concession/Qualifier: Not all sitcoms set out to comfort. Some may even do the opposite.

**Margin notes (right):**

This seems to go beyond initial thinking: things are normal and get wacky, instead of things generally just being wacky.

Is this true? Doesn't it have to ensue because of Barney, etc.?

The situation itself (small-town life) contributes to comforting.

The show captures something. What is it?

attempt to create the comfort of Mayberry (an attempt to say your small-town life is idyllic) would somehow fail. It would seem a lie without any of the twenty-first-century issues (drugs, pregnancy, homosexual kissing), without any of the edgy technology, the music, the rapid-fire slick wit, the self-aware writing and directing. Mayberry exists, cliché as it sounds, in our hearts. The show, like no other, captured what we want to remember, whether it happened or not. It tells us that blue skies are normal.

*Concludes by providing a possible reason why The Andy Griffith Show is more comforting than today's shows.*

*Connects to viewers because it is comforting. Assures viewer that blue skies, not storms, are normal. (Even if this is not true? Is it?)*

## Writing Strategies

1. What criteria (standards of judgment) does Bell use to evaluate *The Andy Griffith Show?*

2. Highlight any background or summary information necessary to understand Bell's evaluation. Where does such information appear? Why is it helpful?

3. Evaluations are forms of argument. Describe how Bell makes some conventional argumentative moves: How does he use appeals? How does he counterargue?

4. Describe how Bell's allusions to other television shows support his main idea. How are those other shows used?

## Exploring Ideas

1. How does Bell's essay encourage the reader to think differently about TV sitcoms—or entertainment in general?

2. *The Andy Griffith Show* originally aired through the 1960s—over forty years ago. How is Bell's evaluation still relevant? How does he work to make it relevant?

3. Think of three television shows that might impact the quality of the viewer's life. Explain how each show might influence the way that people think or act.

4. How do popular television shows relate to popular sentiments or values? Do they, for instance, reflect what we imagine about ourselves, what we hope for, what we fear? Explain the relationship between what we watch and who we are.

## Ideas for Writing

1. What television show is overestimated or underestimated? Why do audiences have the wrong take on it?

2. Examine a popular website and try to discover an element of the design that people may not usually consider—font use, spatial arrangement, color scheme, and so on. How does that particular aspect positively or negatively impact the overall effect of the site?

If responding to one of these ideas, go to the Analysis section of this chapter to begin developing ideas for your essay.

# *Star Trek:* Where No Man Has Gone Before

## Jaren Provo

Most people have a favorite television program, but few of us consider how that program resonates with broader cultural trends—how it speaks to, addresses, or challenges common biases and prejudices. In this essay, Jaren Provo takes a close look at *Star Trek.* She goes beyond merely celebrating its attributes; she evaluates *Star Trek* according to the role it has played in shaping attitudes about and within popular culture. Provo wrote this essay for her first-semester college writing course. Now an English major at Arizona State University, she plans to study English literature and history in graduate school.

"The greatest danger facing us is ourselves, and irrational fear of the unknown. But there's no such thing as 'the unknown,' only things temporarily hidden, temporarily not understood." —Captain James T. Kirk

Since its stunning and innovative debut in 1966, *Star Trek* has given modern culture a new promise for the future, one of peace, cooperation, and tolerance not seen in such tenacity or splendor before or since. Yet, despite the significant cultural contribution *Star Trek* has made, many see this legendary universe as unreachable, non-applicable, influencing only the stereotypical Klingon-quoting, uniform-donning, convention-going fan. However, this view is false. *Star Trek* empowers mainstream America to imagine a future of hope-filled opportunity rather than horrific obliteration.

Each of us is familiar with *Star Trek* in some manner, whether it be the phrase "Beam me up, Scotty" (which, actually, was never said verbatim in the series), the *USS Enterprise,* the . . . very . . . long pauses . . . of William Shatner's portrayal of Captain Kirk, or its groovy theme music. *Star Trek* is best described, by Roddenberry himself, as the 1960's television show set "close enough to our own time for continuing characters to be fully identifiable as people like us, but far enough into the future for galaxy travel to be fully established" ("*Star Trek* Is"). It

is not until much later in the franchise that we realize *Star Trek* is set in the 2260s AD, focusing on the crew and voyages of the starship *Enterprise* as it carries out its five-year mission of peaceful exploration. As the *Enterprise* travels through space, it encounters various worlds with attributes reminiscent of Earth, and discusses numerous issues of political, social, and human nature. *Star Trek* shows us, through a cast of recurring dynamic characters and a space-oriented view, a reflection of humanity and its possibilities.

The specific focus here is Roddenberry's first series, the original series (or what Trekkies refer to as TOS). There have been five television spin-off series and ten movies deriving their roots from TOS, but each successive reiteration of *Star Trek* brings an even more commercialized version of Roddenberry's standard-defying innovation. In these new series, special effects have replaced meaningful plots; de rigueur characters have replaced dynamic ones. Roddenberry's vision rose above the need for believable explosions, unrecognizable aliens, and shoot-em-up alien-invader plots, such that *Star Trek* struggled to remain on the air during its short (but syndicate-able) three-year stint; it was a vision that broadcasting officials placed little promise in, as it was most certainly not a mainstream science fiction show.

But this vision was so powerful and so magnificent that it opened an avenue to engage humans in their own universe. While popular culture at the time focused on the individual and his or her worldly place in society, *Star Trek* expanded the horizons of the human mind toward the furthermost reaches of space. In the *Star Trek* future, there are no physical boundaries or burdens, for the greatest, most inaccessible reaches of the universe are merely a warp speed away, the unknown cultures of a million worlds much like Earth are open for communication and exploration. Indeed, one of the core principles of *Star Trek* is the "parallel worlds concept"—that there are billions of planets with conditions comparable to Earth that could harbor similar social, ecological, and humanlike development ("*Star Trek* Is"). It is this principle that shapes the core mission of the *USS Enterprise* herself: "to boldly go where no man has gone before."

And in so doing, the humans of the twenty-third century do not have to face a decimated, physically and

"*Star Trek*: Where No Man Has Gone Before," by Jaren Provo. Reprinted with permission of the author.

culturally broken world similar to those in many recognizable pop culture realms, such as *Terminator* or *The Matrix*. Instead, they are a functioning global culture. These individuals are able to realize their own humanity by exploring and relating to alien cultures in the depths of the universe, offering aid and relief to struggling civilizations, but willing to observe and maintain the customs of the native peoples. This core idea constitutes the Prime Directive, a predominant theme throughout *Star Trek*. The Prime Directive advocates involvement with, but not indoctrination of, other cultures (unless there is a lack of a progressing, stable culture). To each world the *Enterprise* travels, it promotes a mission of peace and negotiation, rather than conquest.

Through this process, humans become increasingly tolerant of groups within their own species. Bigotry or intolerance in any form is seen as a horrendous trait and a mark of low character. On the bridge of the *Enterprise,* such individuals as an African woman, Asian American man, Scottish engineer, pointed-eared alien without emotions, nationalistic Russian youngster, and even an Iowan hunk with a rhythmically related speech deficiency are regular residents, each respected for his or her own talents and merit as a member of the crew. Even representatives of such backgrounds as German, French, Irish, Indian, British, Native American, and more are seen frequently on the *Enterprise.* Jeff Greenwald, author of *Future Perfect: How "Star Trek" Conquered Planet Earth,* echoes this idea: "[*Star Trek*] has given us a model of a truly multicultural world, where all races and creeds are afforded equal respect and rights" (qtd. in Schrof 8). Together, this diverse and accepting group explores the human condition, such items as the role of good and evil (in such episodes as "The Savage Curtain" and "The Enemy Within"), maturity and age (in the episodes "Miri," "Charlie X," and "The Deadly Years"), and an ambition-free life ("This Side of Paradise").

However, some feel that *Star Trek*'s diverse cast is not as accepting and multicultural as it appears. In his piece, "Carved From the Rock Experiences of Our Daily Lives: Reality and *Star Trek*'s Multiple Histories," Lincoln Geraghty concedes that TOS casts "token" minority members as crew and is deficient because of its lack of an openly homosexual crewmember (161). In this way,

he argues, *Star Trek* repeats the "mistakes other popular television series made" (161). However, it is important to observe the cultural climate of the 1960s, especially in popular media. If indeed minority groups were portrayed, they were often playing roles of servants (Asian Americans), slaves (African Americans), or senseless and vicious warriors on the Western plains (Native Americans). The latter was not often represented by those from this culture; often, individuals of Italian descent were given the roles of Native Americans. Though perhaps not main characters with substantial parts (with the exception of Spock, who is an alien and would in a sense be considered a member of a "minority" group), these individuals are not degraded, but are respected on the merit of their performance and contributions to the ship itself. These individuals also took on a more active role as *Star Trek* progressed; in the third season, *Star Trek* was even so bold as to portray the first interracial kiss on television ("Plato's Stepchildren"). Given the exclusive nature of the times, *Star Trek*'s role was an advanced platform (unlike other pop culture outlets) upon which racial, ethnic, and gender acceptance could be built.

Together, these humans learn from past mistakes, attempting to avoid their occurrence in other cultures developing in similar manners (as in the episodes "Patterns of Force" and "A Taste of Armageddon"). Indeed, as William Blake Tyrrell states in his 1977 article (around the peak of *Star Trek*'s syndication-led revival), "*Star Trek* creates a future world where the glories of the past are pristine and the failures and doubts of the present have been overcome. It gives us our past as our future, while making our present the past, which . . . is safely over and forgotten" (qtd. in Geraghty 167). But in *Star Trek,* the past is not so much forgotten as it is no longer dwelled upon; it is often revisited for comparative and developmental purposes. Humanity in the future does not degrade; it matures and refines itself toward a more ideal form.

Notably absent from *Star Trek*'s list of qualities is the predominant science fiction theme regarding space aliens: "When they come, they'll destroy us all." This permeated view is reflected in numerous locales, such as *Independence Day, Invasion of the Body Snatchers,* and H.G. Wells' *War of the Worlds.* Yet in *Star Trek,* the first contact with aliens is a diplomatic one, in which logical, peaceful Vulcan representatives come to Earth to note their presence and encourage future technological development. After this contact, more connections are forged with other alien worlds, such that the United Federation of Planets develops (with a flag suspiciously reminiscent of that of the United Nations) to promote peaceable cooperation among these cultures. Alien cultures are not (generally) out to conquer Earth and all of humanity in a blazing inferno of death and destruction, but are civilized, developing worlds willing to forge ties with others in the universe to assure mutual survival.

Also uncharacteristic of *Star Trek* but common in the sci-fi realm is the element portraying humans as slaves of technology, hopelessly existent only in body. This concept is perhaps most prevalent in the *Matrix* trilogy. Yet *Star Trek* foretells humans as harnessing the resources of technology to propel themselves outward into space, to explore, to contact, to impact in a positive way. The transporter and warp drive allow for expedient, efficient movement among planets and realms; the communicator (predecessor to the flip-phone?) and universal translator aid in interpersonal and intercultural contact; the scientific tricorder (a handheld programmable scanning device) and ship's scanners enhance exploration purposes; and medical tricorders and unknown, but apparently technical, whirring devices devised from salt 'n' pepper shakers exist for medical purposes. True, some matters of technology are dangerous and destroy human independence, such as the M-5 Multitronic Computer in the episode "The Ultimate Computer." Essentially, this device is meant to save lives by replacing the human presence on a starship, yet it manages to entirely control the ship and destroy hundreds of innocent lives in the process. However, this technology is not typical, and ends up being destroyed. M-5 reminds us to maintain a fine balance between technology serving and subverting humankind.

Some, however, disagree with the assertion that *Star Trek* promotes a palate of peace, tolerance, and diplomacy, pointing to the predominant enemy throughout the series: the Klingon Empire. They observe the constant conflict between the Klingons and the Federation, between their opposing interests of complete colonization and diplomatic cooperation. Certainly the Federation is not peaceful toward or tolerant of this group of aliens. Yet, the Klingon Empire is an imperialistic, dictatorial force of conquest interested in destroying the diplomatic network of the Federation and its promotion of freedom and democracy. Actions taken against the Klingons are in matters of defense, not of aggression, and peace negotiations between the Klingons and Federation persist throughout and beyond the series. Eventually, internal political movements bring the dictatorial regime to its knees, and even the Klingons themselves are incorporated into the Federation.

Many also claim that *Star Trek* is merely a scripted TV show, unrealistic and inaccessible to all but the most obsessive fans. However, *Star Trek* has reached and influenced some of the leaders of technology and society, including individuals such as Bill Gates, several NASA scientists and engineers, and even the late Dr. Martin Luther King, Jr. The message of *Star Trek* resonates through these and other individuals familiar with *Star Trek*'s ideals, such that all in society are influenced by this series. Many outlets in society and the media also carry *Star Trek*'s concepts into their settings on an entertainment level. Considering entertainment's pivotal role in our society (take, for instance, the large number of individuals who gain current events knowledge from comedy shows such as *The Daily Show, The Tonight Show with Jay Leno,* and *Saturday Night Live),* the sheer entertainment quality of *Star Trek* brings it into our everyday lives. Furthermore, the core concepts of *Star Trek* are not fictional and far-reaching, but are based on events and themes within the Vietnam War era and relating to the human condition.

Imagine a world in which *Star Trek* is absent. We would miss more than the phrases "He's dead, Jim" and "Beam me up, Scotty," more than warp drive and the same men in red shirts dying before the introductory theme each week. Our culture would be void of a revolutionary promise, a promise of tolerance, peace, exploration, and humanity in our future. Without *Star Trek,* modern pop culture would be filled only with bleak visions for tomorrow, of aliens ruthlessly invading and destroying Earth, of a humanity decimated and barely clinging to the edge of existence, of survival depending upon backstabbing and cruelty. *Star Trek* is one of the few (perhaps the only) candles flickering in the darkness of popular apocalypti-cism, a guarantee of a secure future where tomorrow may not be such a horrible thing after all.

We must be sure not to violate the magnitude of *Star Trek* and its whispers of truth for the days ahead. We must not be intolerant of that which heralds a tolerant tomorrow, doubtful of a harbinger of hope, or disparag-ing toward a beacon of peace or humanity. The zeitgeist bestowed upon our culture by *Star Trek* must be appre-ciated for its complexities and considered in its hopeful message to the people of today.

### Works Cited

Geraghty, Lincoln. "Carved from the Rock Experiences of Our Daily Lives: Reality and *Star Trek*'s Multiple Histories." *European Journal of American Culture* 21.3 (2002): 160–177. *Academic Search Elite*. Web. 8 Apr. 2008.

Schrof, Joannie M. "A World of Trekkies." *U.S. News and World Report* 29 June 1998: 8. *Academic Search Elite*. Web. 7 Apr. 2008.

"*Star Trek* Is." *Memory Alpha*. Memory Alpha, n.d. Web. 8 Apr. 2008.

## Writing Strategies

1. How does Provo address the common dismissal about "Trekkies"?

2. Although she does not state them directly in the essay, what can you infer about Provo's criteria (standards of judgment)? In other words, in her view, what makes a good television program? Why does *Star Trek* meet those standards?

3. How does Provo counterargue? Describe how particular counter-arguments add dimension and value to her essay.

4. Provo's points often sound extremely positive—as though she cannot imagine a downside to the topic. Where does Provo qual-ify or concede to some other point of view? Why might she be justified in such glowing praise of the program?

5. How does Provo's sentence structure influence her voice? Focus on a particular paragraph and explain how the sentences impact the "sound" of the argument.

## Exploring Ideas

1. Provo argues that television programs are more than entertain-ment—that they deal with important culture issues within a given era. What current television dramas attempt to deal with the political and cultural tensions of our era? How do they suc-ceed or fail?

2. Provo celebrates *Star Trek* because it challenged racial prejudic-es of the 1960s. Do you think television can genuinely challenge or overturn common assumptions about race or gender? Why or why not?

3. Provo argues that most science fiction in popular culture, other than *Star Trek,* predicts a future of "horrific obliteration." What recent movies or television programs reinforce Provo's point? Do any challenge her notion?

4. From ancient times to the present, civilizations imagine other nations, tribes, people, or species as inherently wicked or debased. Oral stories, religious traditions, novels, and popular movies often characterize some faraway, unknown group as hos-tile, weird, or even corrupt. How does *Star Trek* fit into that long tradition?

## Ideas for Writing

1. What particular program works to break down common preju-dices or stereotypes? How does it succeed or fall short?

2. Consider a current commercial or ad campaign. How does it subtly reinforce negative stereotypes about people? Why don't viewers tend to acknowledge such stereotypes?

If responding to one of these ideas, go to the Analysis section of this chapter to begin developing ideas for your essay.

# INVENTION

**"I criticize by creation . . . not by finding fault."**

—Marcus Tullius Cicero

Invention is the primary strategy for generating new ideas. As you work through the following sections, imagine possibilities beyond your initial thoughts. The Point of Contact section will help you to find a subject for the evaluation; Analysis will help you to develop particular points about the subject; and Public Resonance will help you to make it relevant to a community of readers. The Thesis and Rhetorical Tools sections will help you develop a specific claim and support it appropriately. As in the other chapters, the Invention Questions in each section are not meant to be answered directly in your final written assignment. They are meant to prompt reflection and discovery; however, your answers may translate directly into your drafts.

# Point of Contact

An evaluator needs to have particular insight into his or her subject, so choose something that you can examine carefully. Your instructor may provide subjects, or you can use the following suggestions and questions to seek out and focus on a particular subject. Once you've focused on a subject, take notes. Record as much information about the subject as possible.

**Visit a Place** (a restaurant, movie theater, night club, amusement park, college classroom or campus, shopping mall, grocery store, etc.). Gather information about the place. How do people behave? What behavior is tolerated, supported, ignored? What is on the walls? How does this influence the mood of the place? How much open space is available? Is the place empty, crowded, stuffy, clean, lonely, isolated, intense?

**Attend an Event** (a carnival, circus, beauty pageant, dance, tractor pull, art show, concert, poetry reading, company meeting, college class, etc.). What happens before the event? What is the mood? How are the participants treated during the event? What kinds of interaction occur during the event? Where does the event take place? What impact does the location have on the event?

**Investigate a Person** (a government official, doctor, religious leader, talk show host, roommate, professional athlete, work supervisor or manager, work associate, etc.). Evaluating a person can be tricky because it is easy to fall into an explanation of one's likes and dislikes. Instead, focus on the qualities or actions of the person in terms of his or her particular position or title. Is he or she willing to listen to people? For how long? What does he or she do while listening to someone? How do people respond or react to this person? Are people comfortable around this person? Is this person entertaining, enlightening, engaging, comforting, informative, energizing (or the opposite of any of these)?

**Watch a Movie or Show** (a motion picture, sitcom, documentary, television drama, music video). Gather information and details, going beyond simple likes and dislikes. Does the dialogue reveal something about the characters that their actions do not? What kinds of graphic or sexually explicit images appear? Is the movie/show humorous or frightening in some way? How? What message(s) does the movie/show offer? Does the movie/show have stereotypes (of rich people, poor people, women, men, racial groups, children, the elderly)?

**Read a Text** (a book, article, poster, letter, website, etc.). Consider texts from your major. In this case, go to one of the journals for your major, or to a database in your library. In some ways, evaluating a text is easy because it can be examined closely without having to rewind or travel somewhere. However, a written text can be a complicated mass of elements. What is the main idea or main argument of the text? What kind of evidence or support is used? How formal is the language? What is the tone of the text? If the text is an argument, does it address counterarguments? Does it use concession? What strategies are used to draw the reader into the ideas of the text?

# Like a detective, gather all the information you can. Ask hard questions. Ask weird questions.

# Analysis

Imagine taking your car to a mechanic because you hear a strange knocking sound when you accelerate. As you pull into the garage, the mechanic smiles and exclaims, "Hey, nice car! I love Ford Mustangs! There's nothing wrong with *that* car." Obviously, you'd be a bit disoriented, and maybe a little grumpy. You'd also probably complain: "Hey, I want you to tell me what's wrong with the car—tell me why it's making that sound!" The problem with this scenario is that the mechanic does no analysis and uses no *criteria* (the standards on which judgments are based). The evaluation of the car is based on the mechanic's own likes and dislikes.

Or imagine reading a review of a fine Italian restaurant. While ignoring the wine list, entrees, and presentation of the food, the reviewer gives the restaurant a very low rating because of a limited number of ice cream flavors. In this scenario, the reviewer uses the *wrong* criteria. The reviewer evaluates a fine dining establishment with criteria for judging an ice cream shop. This would be similar to judging a historical drama negatively because it is not funny: historical dramas are not, usually, supposed to be funny, nor are fine Italian restaurants supposed to have wide varieties of ice cream.

## Discovering the Purpose of the Subject

The first analytical step is to discover the subject's purpose or goal—to understand, in other words, what the subject is attempting to achieve. We can only develop criteria and then evaluate a subject if we know the subject's purpose and audience. For example, we can evaluate a movie only if we understand what the movie is attempting to do: to succeed as a comedy for teens, to maintain high action for adults, or to retell a classic fairy tale for children. Evaluating something means understanding what that subject is attempting to do.

## Invention Questions

▶ What does your subject try to achieve? (Be specific. For example, an Italian restaurant may be attempting to provide an elegant dining experience with a particular ethnic cuisine. This is different from the goal of a general chain restaurant such as Denny's, which attempts to provide economically priced food from a general menu.)

▶ What do other like subjects try to achieve? (Think about subjects similar to yours—other teachers, other comedic movies, other restaurants, and so on.)

▶ Who is your subject's audience? (Whom does your subject attempt to engage or attract?) If you have not already considered the audience, imagine who might use, benefit from, and interact with the subject.

▶ What goals *should* your subject, or all subjects like it, have? (It might be argued, for instance, that a restaurant should attempt to elevate the dining experience, to transform the mundane act of eating into a cultural and social event. Once this criterion is established, someone might then use it to judge a particular restaurant.) ■

In Ed Bell's invention writing, he grapples with the idea of entertainment—what it does and should do for its audience:

> **What does this subject try to achieve?**
> *The Andy Griffith Show* is a sitcom (situational comedy). It tries to entertain people. If people are entertained, they will continue watching the show. That's the basic idea. But entertain how? Some shows entertain through violence, others drama, some through sex, and so on. Sitcoms try to entertain through comedy, but not just comedy. There has to be something even more specific than just comedy. Comedy how? What kind of comedy? *The Andy Griffith Show* has a particularly comfortable, slow pace to it. One might say that the show tries to entertain, but in a relaxing, maybe even comforting, way.

**What is the subject's audience?**

The original audience for this show was the general American public in the 1960s, I imagine. Perhaps the show's producers had some more specific demographic in mind. But at the time, most people got three stations—NBC, CBS, and ABC. Americans tuned in to watch one of three shows. Looking back, it may be difficult, yet interesting, to imagine the audience. I imagine it being a simpler time. I wonder if such a show could even be created today, or if it would seem unrealistic, fake, insincere. The audience today is different but still likes the show. For some reason, the show has maintained its appeal (perhaps because it's just pleasant, comforting). Maybe there's something valuable about creations from the past.

# Applying Criteria to the Subject

Now that you have a sense of the subject's purpose, you can begin making specific evaluative points. Refer to your notes from the Point of Contact section and answer the following:

▶ In what particular ways does the subject achieve its goal? What specific parts, tools, or strategies help the subject to achieve its goal?

▶ In what particular ways does the subject fall short of achieving its goal?

▶ What goals does the subject ignore?

▶ How does the subject compare to and contrast with other similar subjects?

▶ What is unique about your subject's approach or strategy to achieving its goal? ■

In his exploration of *The Andy Griffith Show,* Bell discovers the main point of his essay:

**How does the subject compare to and contrast with other similar subjects?**

More recent sitcoms take on issues. *All in the Family* comes to mind. That sitcom changed things a little. It opened up the range of what a situational comedy can be or do. As for shows more like it that do not attempt to take on cultural issues as *All in the Family* did, they are all pretty much the same: standard situations, basic character types, and so on. It seems that these shows always begin with some normal, comfortable scene; then something happens to create confusion or turmoil; then it gets sorted out in the end. If it's different at all, maybe *The Andy Griffith Show* returns to normal. Or, said another way, maybe the normal that it returns to is a different kind of normal—a normal that is more comfortable and lasting. (We might call this type of normal "Mayberry.") That is to say, other sitcoms of the time such as *Hogan's Heroes* or *Gomer Pyle* (and later ones like *MASH* or *Three's Company)* don't really start or end with a "normal" situation. Instead, with those shows you have inevitable trouble always bound to emerge.

# Public Resonance

A meaningful evaluation considers how the subject affects or influences people—how it resonates with people's lives and concerns. For example, a movie critic might argue that children's movies carry the responsibility of developing notions of right and wrong. Or someone might suggest that a restaurant affects the health and well-being of a community and influences the image of a neighborhood. Ultimately, it is up to the writer to reveal the influence of a subject.

Each of the writers featured in this chapter (Busch, Provo, and Bell) develops public resonance by connecting the specific subject to broader social issues. In her essay, Jaren Provo makes an explicit case about *Star Trek*. She, in fact, argues about the show's influence on American pop culture:

> Imagine a world in which *Star Trek* is absent. We would miss more than the phrases "He's dead, Jim" and "Beam me up, Scotty," more than warp drive and the same men in red shirts dying before the introductory theme each week. Our culture would be void of a revolutionary promise, a promise of tolerance, peace, exploration, and humanity in our future. Without *Star Trek*, modern pop culture would be filled only with bleak visions for tomorrow, of aliens ruthlessly invading and destroying Earth, of a humanity decimated and barely clinging to the edge of existence, of survival depending upon backstabbing and cruelty. *Star Trek* is one of the few (perhaps the only) candles flickering in the darkness of popular apocalypticism, a guarantee of a secure future where tomorrow may not be such a horrible thing after all.

In his article, Benjamin Busch also deals explicitly with public resonance. In the following passage, he transitions from his own objections to broader, and murkier, problems associated with video games and the portrayal of war. The paragraph begins with a kind of concession about legal responsibilities but then ends with some larger (social or humanistic) layers of responsibility:

> Despite my objections to certain aspects of the video war game, I don't know that game makers have any particular responsibilities to any of us. They are a market based entertainment business. Their sales are subject to mature audience restrictions like film and pornography, but game ratings are not enforced by any government agency in the United States. We can only hope that business values social decency, and respects essential humanism but a gaming company is only truly concerned with market reception in the form of product sales. The responsibility is placed on the consumer and parents. At the age of 18, an American citizen can vote, and can enlist in the armed services without parental consent. We should assume that they can also choose their entertainment for better or for worse. Issues of responsibility arise when our military develops war games with private companies and then allows them to be sold publicly. The game then partially becomes a governmental, even military, product and its messages are unable to speak free of politics or real war.

As Busch and Provo illustrate, public resonance can become an integral part—maybe the most critical part—of your argument. Use the following questions to help develop public resonance for your own evaluation:

▶ How does the subject influence people's lives (their health, attitudes, living conditions, etc.)?

▶ Why is this subject important in people's lives?

▶ What do people expect from the subject? ■

# Invention Workshop

With at least one other writer, use one of the Invention Questions to launch an intensive and focused discussion about your subject. Try to go beyond your first thoughts on the subject. For example, Linda, who is evaluating a new restaurant in her town, transcends her initial thoughts. Her discussion leads to a more complicated understanding of the subject and its relationship to people's lives:

**Why is this subject important in people's lives?**

LINDA:    That's easy . . . a restaurant serves people food. And people need food.

MARCUS:    But do restaurants just provide food?

JACK:    No, they also provide service—someone bringing you the food. And they also make eating a social event.

LINDA:    But that isn't the important part.

MARCUS:    Well, it isn't the main part, but I'd say people need that social aspect in their lives, and eating is naturally a social activity. That's what's so enjoyable about eating out—you get to feel social.

LINDA:    But eating is also a personal thing, right? It's about the home and family, too.

JACK:    I would say that restaurants are important because they provide a place where people can feel slightly special—like they're somewhere besides their living room with a bowl of cereal. They make eating feel elevated.

LINDA:    If that's the case, what's the deal with all these restaurants saying they're "just like home"?

MARCUS:    Well, that's the goal of those chain restaurants, which really aren't like home at all. They're trying to make people feel close to home.

LINDA:    So these restaurants provide something psychologically to people. I guess that's why restaurants spend so much on atmosphere and advertising.

MARCUS:    So what about the particular restaurant Chunky's? Does it make people feel "at home"?

LINDA:    Not really. It feels like a chain restaurant that's attempting to not feel like a chain restaurant.

Linda has discovered something beyond the obvious about the subject's purpose: Restaurants aren't simply about food; they are also about familiarity. (There's an important psychology to food service!) This discovery could impact how she evaluates the particular restaurant.

In Bell's invention writing, the public resonance is tied to the main discovery he makes in Analysis. In the following excerpt, he narrows in on the actual thesis of the essay:

> **Why is this subject important in people's lives?**
>
> It is some people's favorite TV show, a show that they grew up watching and that gives them a certain feeling. It makes them feel good. It makes them feel at home. The same could be said about *Star Trek* or *Will and Grace* or other shows. Specifically, *The Andy Griffith Show* goes beyond being funny in the way that it presents what people might like to think of as "normal." Life is full of all sorts of characters (some wacky, some annoying) and all sorts of situations or complications arise, and in all sitcoms (maybe not all, but probably) the conflict is resolved. But *The Andy Griffith Show* seems to suggest that the resolution is normal, whereas other shows suggest that conflict or tension is normal.

## Research

Consider using outside sources to help you figure out what others have said about the subject. Do not expect to find writers who share your perspective. Instead, explore for various perspectives. Have people generally found the subject valuable, worthy, deficient, dangerous, helpful? If your subject is very specific (such as a local diner) you might search for evaluations in that general category (local diners). See Chapter 13 for help with finding sources.

# Thesis

An evaluation makes a judgment about a subject. An evaluative thesis statement gives focus to that judgment: the thesis sheds light on a particular element of the subject. For instance, a movie has many elements, such as characters, plot, cinematography, themes, special effects, and dialogue. A thesis can help create focus, telling the reader that the evaluation will deal primarily with plot, not character development and costumes:

> The movie's plot is unnecessarily confusing.

An evaluative thesis need not be completely positive or completely negative. It need not, for example, claim that a particular movie is absolutely great or downright rotten. Many evaluative thesis statements are a mixture of judgments. A statement might concede some value but focus primarily on a shortcoming as in the following:

> While the movie's cinematography is engaging, the plot is unnecessarily confusing.

> Although the student government has been more public than in previous years, it has still failed to address the student body's most significant concerns.

> Even with the new ensemble tricks, which provide an interesting layer of ear candy, Ebenezer Typhoon's new collection of songs still lacks any substantive message.

> The menu at Robinson's Grill may lack diversity, but it does what so many other restaurants cannot: deliver a genuinely local dining experience.

## Evolution of a Thesis

A good thesis gives focus to an entire project. Linda's evaluation of a restaurant (in the Public Resonance section) gains focus as she works to craft a thesis. First, she discovers the subject's purpose. Then, while exploring public resonance, she discovers another, less obvious, layer. From there, she refines the idea into an evaluative claim:

- Chunky's attempts to give people a variety of good food and friendly service.
- People like to feel attached to their surroundings, to the places they shop and eat. Therefore, restaurants such as Chunky's try to create the illusion that diners are patronizing a friendly neighborhood grill.
- Although Chunky's attempts to make people feel comfortable in a small neighborhood grill, it doesn't work very well.
- Although Chunky's attempts to make people feel comfortable in a small neighborhood grill, the atmosphere and food still seem prepared by a distant corporate chef.

Linda's thesis evolved as she worked through the complexities of the subject. She discovered a subtle gap between the restaurant's purpose and the actual dining experience. This insight reveals something that might otherwise go unnoticed.

# Common Thesis Problems

**The blurry focus problem**  A sufficiently narrow focus can mean all the difference between intensive and bland writing. First, a writer needs to home in on a particular subject, such as a particular band, a particular college campus or program. But that is often not enough. As in the following examples, the specific subjects still do not provide intensive points:

- Green Day is a great punk band.
- Big River Community College is a good school.

These statements need more focus. The writers could examine more particular elements (such as the themes of Green Day's songs or the accessible class times at Big River). Or the writers could develop more vital statements by avoiding the broad predicates "is a great . . ." and "is a good. . . ."

**The obvious fact problem**  The goal of evaluative writing is to help readers see the subject in a new light—to help them see some particular value or shortcoming. But writers sometimes fall into the trap of stating the obvious:

- Howard Stern offends people.
- Although some purists did not like it, the *Lord of the Rings* trilogy made a lot of money at the box office.

Both of these statements announce common knowledge, facts about the radio shock jock and the Peter Jackson movies. But neither statement offers an evaluation. The stated facts say nothing about the value or shortcoming of the subjects. Offending people, for instance, may be a good thing. And making lots of money may not mean much about the movies' artistic success.

**The noncommittal problem**  An evaluation is an argument; therefore, the writer should put forth a position. But it may be tempting to back away from the evaluation and to let the reader make up his or her own mind about the subject. The following examples back away; they lack a committed stance:

- The new building will please some and offend others.
- It's up to individual readers to decide whether they appreciate Kingsolver's *Poisonwood Bible* or not.

The noncommittal problem is related to a broader issue: Some writers are afraid of pushing too hard. They want to avoid forcing readers into a perspective. While this seems like a legitimate concern, we should remember that readers need not be *forced* into an opinion or new perspective. Instead, they can be invited, lulled, guided, nudged, or attracted. Writers should seek to make their opinions so attractive, reasonable, enlightened, and compelling that readers feel as though they must adopt them. In short, don't fear commitment! Readers are waiting around for their minds to be changed.

## Revising Your Thesis

Develop a thesis by asking a basic question: On what particular value or shortcoming do I want to focus? Try various wordings for your thesis. Let the idea evolve, tighten, over several attempts. Then, share the thesis statement with two other writers. As you look over their statements, look for all three common problems: blurry focus, obvious fact, and noncommittal. Suggest strategies for narrowing and intensifying the statements.

# Rhetorical Tools

## Using Support

Most of the claims made in evaluations are supported with specific information about the subject itself. The writer points out particular details that illustrate the main idea and show the value or shortcoming of the subject. For example, Ed Bell describes particular features of *The Andy Griffith Show:*

> The show's main character, Andy, is full of southern wisdom. He is quiet and listens and makes better decisions in the midst of all the madness than we could have. That is comfort number one: Someone—the general, the man in charge, *the sheriff*—has things under control. All the madness results from one of three things: either intruders, but Andy gets rid of them after they have caused only a little trouble; or just boys (Opie and sometimes his friends) going through what is natural to go through growing up, but Andy deals with this expertly, too; or ego, ambition, and pride—usually Barney is having the trouble here, though it could be Aunt Bea or one of the others. Andy understands all of this, though not so well or right away that the show isn't a little bit interesting. The plot is better than most sitcoms: There is always a solution that takes a little while to get to, and we believe it when we finally do.

### Beware of Too Much Summary

A writer should present some basic facts about, or summarize, the subject as part of the evaluation. The presentation or summary of the subject should *not* constitute the majority of an evaluation, but should offer only the relevant details about the subject. For example, an evaluation using the thesis *While the movie's cinematography is engaging, the plot is unnecessarily confusing* would not devote long passages to the dress or appearance of the characters. Such information would be unnecessary and irrelevant to the evaluation.

You might also go beyond the subject itself—beyond your particular text, show, person, place. As explained in Chapter 7, writers have the world of history and culture at their disposal. This applies to evaluation as well. To prove a point about the subject, you can borrow from other moments in history, from science, nature, popular culture, or merely point out other like subjects. For example, Jaren Provo goes beyond her topic, *Star Trek,* to reinforce her thesis:

> Many also claim that *Star Trek* is merely a scripted TV show, unrealistic and inaccessible to all but the most obsessive fans. However, *Star Trek* has reached and influenced some of the leaders of technology and society, including individuals such as Bill Gates, several NASA scientists and engineers, and even the late Dr. Martin Luther King, Jr. The message of *Star Trek* resonates through these and other individuals familiar with *Star Trek*'s ideals, such that all in society are influenced by this series. Many outlets in society and the media also carry *Star Trek*'s concepts into their settings on an entertainment level. Considering entertainment's pivotal role in our society (take, for instance, the large number of individuals who gain current events knowledge from comedy shows such as *The Daily Show, The Tonight Show with Jay Leno,* and *Saturday Night Live),* the sheer entertainment quality of Star Trek brings it into our everyday lives. Furthermore, the core concepts of *Star Trek* are not fictional and far-reaching, but are based on events and themes within the Vietnam War era and relating to the human condition.

## Invention Questions

To develop claims using outside support, consider the following questions:

▶ Does a historical situation or trend (such as the rise of a particular fashion, organization, or individual) illustrate something about my topic?

▶ Does my topic or situation appear in any movies or television shows? If so, how is it handled?

▶ Does my topic appear in any works of literature? If so, how is it handled?

▶ Has science taught us anything about my topic?

▶ Have I witnessed or experienced someone or something that illustrates my point?

▶ Can I construct a scenario to illustrate my point? ■

# Counterarguments and Concessions

Evaluations can also involve counterarguments and concessions (see Chapter 7, pages 236–238). Because evaluations are argumentative, they must acknowledge that other opinions (other judgments about the subject) are possible. In another passage from Provo's essay, she explains an opposing position, and then in a classic turnabout paragraph, she counters:

> However, some feel that *Star Trek*'s diverse cast is not as accepting and multicultural as it appears. In his piece, "Carved From the Rock Experiences of Our Daily Lives: Reality and *Star Trek*'s Multiple Histories", Lincoln Geraghty concedes that TOS casts "token" minority members as crew and is deficient because of its lack of an openly homosexual crewmember (161). In this way, he argues, *Star Trek* repeats the "mistakes other popular television series made" (161). However, it is important to observe the cultural climate of the 1960s, especially in popular media. If indeed minority groups were portrayed, they were often playing roles of servants (Asian Americans), slaves (African Americans), or senseless and vicious warriors on the Western plains (Native Americans). The latter was not often represented by those from this culture; often, individuals of Italian descent were given the roles of Native Americans. Though perhaps not main characters with substantial parts (with the exception of Spock, who is an alien and would in a sense be considered a member of a "minority" group), these individuals are not degraded, but are respected on the merit of their performance and contributions to the ship itself.

# Invention Workshop

This activity is designed to generate counterarguments. The process involves an intensive group exchange. Follow these steps:

- Assemble writers into small groups (three or four per group work best).
- Each writer should have his or her thesis statement (main evaluative claim about the subject) written down.
- The first writer should read his or her thesis statement aloud to the group.
- Taking turns, each group member then should attempt to refute the position given in the statement. The idea is to play devil's advocate, to complicate the writer's ideas.
- The writer should record each opposing claim that is offered.
- After everyone in the group has given an opposing claim to the first writer, the second writer should recite his or her thesis, and the process begins again.

# Organizational Strategies

## How Should I Include Outside Support?

Like any support tool, the possibilities are limitless. You might reference another similar subject briefly to help describe something, as Jaren Provo does:

> Also uncharacteristic of *Star Trek* but common in the sci-fi realm is the element portraying humans as slaves of technology, hopefully existent only in body. This concept is perhaps most prevalent in the *Matrix* trilogy.

The reference, or allusion, to the *Matrix* movies is quick. It serves only to describe an alternative view, and so the attention on the original subject, *Star Trek,* is only briefly interrupted or broken. However, sometimes writers, such as Ed Bell, want to put more attention on something other than the original subject, and so develop a new paragraph entirely:

> From those early days of Lucy and Ricky to our own Dharma and Greg, situation comedies have been part of American culture. And for all the advancements, it still seems like the plots of most of them are something cooked up by Lucy who dragged along Ethel and got caught (and ultimately forgiven) by Fred and Barney . . . uh . . . Fred and Ricky, I mean. Whether or not these shows instruct is, I suppose, debatable. But what is not debatable is that over the past 50 years they have entertained millions. And, I would suggest, through that very act of entertaining us, they have comforted us—the most comforting of them all being *The Andy Griffith Show.*

## When Should I Change Paragraphs?

When considering paragraphs, it may be helpful to think of a television documentary of the Civil War: The camera pans across an old battlefield while the host's voice narrates events. Then the scene breaks, and the camera focuses on a city that housed the soldiers; then the scene breaks again to focus on plantations that encircled a key battlefield. And when an in-depth analysis is in order, the camera shifts to a studio where the host sits talking with us about the deeper significance of the scenes; that is, the camera focuses on the speaker, so that she or he can expound on one issue.

Paragraphs in an evaluation can work similarly. They can break when the writer wants the reader to focus on a new aspect of the subject, and they can even shift whenever the writer wants to give an extended analysis of a particular point. For example, Jaren Provo uses paragraphs as mini-analytical sections. Each focuses on a particular attribute of her topic. Notice how the first sentence of three paragraphs helps the reader to tune in on that attribute:

> ¶8  Together, these humans learn from past mistakes, attempting to avoid their occurrence in other cultures developing in similar manners . . .
> ¶9  Notably absent from *Star Trek*'s list of qualities is the predominant science fiction theme regarding space aliens: "When they come, they'll destroy us all."
> ¶10 Also uncharacteristic of *Star Trek* but common in the sci-fi realm is the element portraying humans as slaves of technology, hopelessly existent only in body.

# How Should I Deal with Counterargument?

As in any argument, counterargument can be addressed in an unlimited number of ways. It may depend on the nature of your subject and on your position. If you are taking a relatively controversial stance or one that is not often taken, you should be prepared to counterargue. For example, imagine a writer giving a negative evaluation of *Good Morning America,* a popular and seemingly harmless television program. In this turnabout paragraph, the writer briefly addresses an opposing view ("Certainly, many would argue that . . . ") and then immediately counters ("But the problem is not . . . "):

> *Good Morning America* confuses news with feel-good entertainment. Like an evening sitcom, its primary goal seems to be making the viewer feel that all is right with the world—or, specifically, all is right with the shiny happy middle-class world in America. Certainly, many would argue that feel-good shows are a plus and that a morning show devoted to gloom and doom would be a great disservice. But the problem is not with the feel-good mood. It is that *Good Morning America* postures itself as a quasi-news program, so any "news" that is given is ultimately framed by dimwitted celebrities making gratuitous appearances and exercise tips for the on-the-go lifestyle. The show smears news of the world across the same screen as the movie of the week. It's newstainment.

But you might decide to develop an opposing view for an entire paragraph and then counter in a new paragraph:

- ¶ opposing position
- ¶ your counterargument

And if the topic required attention to more opposing points, the pattern can be repeated:

- ¶ opposing position
- ¶ your counterargument
- ¶ opposing position
- ¶ your counterargument

## Activity

Now that you have the basic elements of your evaluation, map it out. Will you state your main judgment in the introduction? Where and how will you address counterarguments? Do you have to include much support outside the subject? What about allusions? Counterarguments? Concessions? In developing her evaluation of Chunky's (see page 302), Linda might create the following map:

Intro: personal testimony about a dining experience

- ¶ Description of the walls—signs and various "old" artifacts
- ¶ "Fun" wait staff and "Happy Birthday" song
- ¶ Menu, entry names, and their appeal
- ¶ Food, the seasoning
- ¶ What a local restaurant should attempt, what atmosphere it should create

Integrate the Jackson article here.

- ¶ What eating in public means, what people pay for

Integrate the psychology article here.

- ¶ Opposing position: consistency—the "no surprises" value of corporate food.

Counterargument: the need for intimacy and locality. Integrate second quote from psychology article.

- ¶ Opposing position: cost—the corporate restaurant offers more deals for families.

Counterargument: that's an illusion that doesn't work out at the final bill.

- ¶ Concessions: Corporate restaurant chains are not inherently evil.

Conclusion: Nearly everything about public life is defined by corporate slogans, aesthetic, and service. (Add allusions.) People need a break from places like Chunky's. We can swallow only so much before our taste buds are ruined for good.

# Writer's Voice

A productive evaluation, like a good argument, attracts readers and engages those who might oppose the claims being made; a bad or unsuccessful evaluation loses readers with overly harsh description or zealous enthusiasm. Here are some strategies for maintaining a cool but engaging tone.

## Finding the Right Balance

It is often easy to use the most emotionally loaded terms to describe something or someone, to proclaim a subject "ridiculous" or "dumb." Such harsh description, however, is usually exaggerated and suggests that the writer has not fully investigated the subject. Be cautious of dismissing a subject by using especially harsh words. Imagine the following passage in which a writer evaluates a government official:

> Mayor G. is out of his mind. He has no understanding of the political spectrum and no concept of city governance. He is just some crazy, power-hungry man looking for a soapbox to stand on. If the city really understood the depth of his insanity, it would kick him out of office immediately.

This passage echoes some of the combative language in mainstream politics, which keeps voters from looking closely at a subject. Such language is rife with logical fallacies. It performs a writer's unfocused aggression. Our goal, in academic writing, is the opposite: to investigate the subject closely.

On the other hand, be careful of the *enthusiasm crisis:* If a writer comes off too amused or too enthralled with a subject, readers may react with suspicion. Imagine a glowing evaluation of a political candidate:

> Zelda Brown is the best politician the country has seen. She has a perfect record as a community leader. Her insights into state politics are responsible for the American dream we are all living.

Certainly, any conscious and critical reader would recognize such claims as overblown and ungrounded. Too much enthusiasm alienates a reader in the same way as excessive negativity.

Seek out a tonal balance. Even if your position is absolutely firm (negative or positive), your voice can still engage those who do not share your outlook. In the following passage, Benjamin Busch comes down hard against *Medal of Honor.* His voice does not resound with nasty condemnation but sober intensity:

> The power of controlling your situation, to be able to stop the war and rest, is something that our soldiers are quietly desperate for. For those who patrol the valleys of Helmand, it is a way to impose limits on the uncertainty of war, and the constancy of vulnerability. A video game can produce no wounds, and take no friends away. The soldier understands the difference.

## Exploring the Boundaries

Some writers perform. Their language suggests, "Look at what I'm saying and how I'm saying it!" Some writers lay low. Their language says, "I'm here, but only to give you some information." Some writers hide. Their language says, "I hope no one sees me in this essay." Every writer has a comfort zone, the place where he or she feels most at ease. The problem is that our most comfortable voices are not always the most appropriate for the situation, and they do not allow us to explore language. In some situations, the intensely performative writer may need to be invisible and understated. The writer hiding behind sentences may occasionally need to step forward and be noticed.

The best writers in all disciplines, occupations, and walks of life are not locked into a voice. They can work with various voices, depending on the writing situation. As you consider your own voice and your own habits, imagine breaking from your comfort zone. Explore the following:

**Asides**  Writers often use parentheses or dashes to make an aside comment or ask a rhetorical question. The material separated by parentheses or dashes is often a more intimate or personal note (something one might share only with the person sitting closest at the table). These often help create a particular voice because they reveal insights that are less public, or even less directly related to the main idea, than other information. In the following passage, Jaren Provo makes two asides:

> After this contact, more connections are forged with other alien worlds, such that the United Federation of Planets develops (with a flag suspiciously reminiscent of that of the United Nations) to promote peaceable cooperation among these cultures. Alien cultures are not (generally) out to conquer Earth and all of humanity in a blazing inferno of death and destruction, but are civilized, developing worlds willing to forge ties with others in the universe to assure mutual survival.

The first, longer aside effectively winks at the readers. It nudges us in the shoulder as if to say, "On the down-low, we know what that's all about, eh?" The second offers a slight qualifier. Because *generally* is set apart from the main part of the sentence (in parentheses), it slows the reader down a bit and makes Provo's voice feel slightly more cautious, more present, more aware of us—her readers. In fact, we might even say that all asides function in this way: to make the writer feel more in touch, more in cahoots, with readers.

## Intensive description
When writers stay abstract and general, when they do not commit to particulars, their voices remain less visible. Abstraction often hides the writer's voice. But when writers characterize their subjects by using particular and focused words, their voices become recognizable. For instance, throughout her essay, Jaren Provo makes some grand claims about *Star Trek,* but she grounds those abstractions in powerful passages of detail. In the following, Provo's voice becomes more and more pronounced as the details increase:

Also uncharacteristic of *Star Trek* but common in the sci-fi realm is the element portraying humans as slaves of technology, hopelessly existent only in body. This concept is perhaps most prevalent in the *Matrix* trilogy. Yet *Star Trek* foretells humans as harnessing the resources of technology to propel themselves outward into space, to explore, to contact, to impact in a positive way. The transporter and warp drive allow for expedient, efficient movement among planets and realms; the communicator (predecessor to the flip-phone?) and universal translator aid in interpersonal and intercultural contact; the scientific tricorder (a handheld programmable scanning device) and ship's scanners enhance exploration purposes; and medical tricorders and unknown, but apparently technical, whirring devices devised from salt 'n' pepper shakers exist for medical purposes.

Ed Bell's description also impacts his voice in his own essay. The intensive description does more than describe the show; it also develops the tone of the essay:

> Yet *The Andy Griffith Show* leaves us with the feeling that, even though our friends sometimes get big-headed ideas or strangers from Raleigh come driving or dancing or swindling their mixed-up way into our peacefulness, life will eventually return to normal, all warm and wonderful.

## Activity
As you consider your own writing, revise abstract passages and describe your subject with intense details.

# Vitality

Readers experience the writer's world and vision only through sentences. Sentences are the readers' lenses for seeing the subject. If the lenses are filmy, the reader's vision is blurry and vague. Sharp, intense sentences create a clear vision. Consider the following strategies:

## Avoid Unnecessary Interruption

Sometimes writers will inject a phrase or clause between a subject and its verb or between verbs and direct objects—the main parts of a sentence. A modifying clause or phrase, like this one, comes between main parts of a sentence. Interrupting elements can be appropriate when the subject needs explaining. In the following, the interrupting element, *Bart's distempered father,* helps explain the subject. It does not slow down the reading significantly:

> Homer Simpson, <u>Bart's distempered father,</u> consistently leads his family through a campaign of treacherous buffoonery.
>
> **Appropriate interruption**

But writers sometimes interrupt the sentence flow unnecessarily:

> Nothing, <u>in the animated town of Springfield,</u> is worthy of the praise it wants.
> So I asked myself, <u>on my way out of Sea World,</u> what I had learned.
>
> **Unnecessary interruption**

In many cases, the interrupting element can simply move to the front of the sentence, which keeps the main parts of the sentence together. This helps the reader's consciousness move along more quickly and easily:

> <u>In the animated town of Springfield,</u> nothing is worthy of the praise it wants.
> <u>So on my way out of Sea World,</u> I asked myself what I had learned.

## Repeat Clause or Phrase Patterns

Repetition in writing is not always bad. In fact, skillful repetition can add vitality and intensity to sentences. When writers re-create a sentence pattern, they create familiar linguistic territory for readers and drive points home. For example, Jaren Provo repeats modifiers—and even replicates the syllable patterns:

> Yet, despite the significant cultural contribution *Star Trek* has made, many see this legendary universe as unreachable, non-applicable, influencing only the stereotypical Klingon-quoting, uniform-donning, convention-going fan. However, this view is false. *Star Trek* empowers mainstream America to imagine a future of hope-filled opportunity rather than horrific obliteration.

Later in her essay, Provo repeats both clause patterns and verb structure to create a powerful conclusion:

> We must be sure not to violate the magnitude of *Star Trek* and its whispers of truth for the days ahead. We must not be intolerant of that which heralds a tolerant tomorrow, doubtful of a harbinger of hope, or disparaging toward a beacon of peace or humanity. The zeitgeist bestowed upon our culture by *Star Trek* must be appreciated for its complexities and considered in its hopeful message to the people of today.

In his essay, Benjamin Busch uses short declarative sentences to create a rhythm, a beat that leads to a powerful idea:

> When I was a boy, I was given plastic army men. They were posed already fighting. I arranged them in the sandbox behind our house, and I killed them. I voiced their commands and made the sounds of their suffering. I was every one of them, and I was their enemy. I imagined their war—and I controlled it. I was a child. But I lost those magical powers as a Marine in Iraq.

As in these examples, repetition can make sentences feel more deliberate and intense, more dramatic and lively. Readers can actually feel the word patterns insisting on attention.

# Condense Wordy Phrases

In everyday life, we use lots of common wordy phrases—phrases that contain unnecessary words. But in writing, we have an opportunity to clean out the filler:

| | | |
|---|---|---|
| black in color | condense to | black |
| square in shape | condense to | square |
| try and explain | condense to | explain |
| due to the fact that | condense to | because |
| in this day and age | condense to | today (or now) |
| back in the day | condense to | then |
| at the present time | condense to | now |
| for the most part | condense to | mostly (or most) |
| in the final analysis | condense to | finally |
| in the event that | condense to | if |
| frank and honest | condense to | honest |
| revert back to | condense to | revert |

Notice the wordy and condensed phrases in action:

### Wordy

In the event that your sentences are more vital, your grades will likely improve due to the fact that instructors, for the most part, want intense ideas rather than bloated sentences.

### Condensed

If your sentences are more vital, your grades will likely improve because most instructors want intense ideas rather than bloated sentences.

## Activities

1. In a small group, rewrite the following passage. Try to repeat clause or phrase patterns so that ideas become even more intense:

- On *Three's Company* or *Seinfeld* or *Friends,* things work out in the end. The friends are getting along just fine, but we can see that they are bound for another conflict in a week or so. Though this week's crisis has worked itself out, the pace of their lives or their natural temperaments or their complicated living conditions are still spinning wildly and we know next week they're in for trouble again. On *Dharma and Greg* or *Green Acres* or *I Love Lucy* (even on *The Dick Van Dyke Show*), the family has once again survived, but as with the shows about friends, on the shows about families there seems to be only temporary comfort in the happy ending.

2. Rewrite the following passage. Condense wordy phrases:

- The problem with the play was that it was, for the most part, about the past, yet the characters all seemed new, hip, and contemporary. It seems as though a play cannot have it both ways. If the goal is to take the viewing audience back in time, then all the elements of said play should correspond accordingly. The dialogue, the costumes, the scenery, even the postures of the characters themselves must work in tandem and together at all points in the drama.

# Revision

Revision requires sound evaluation. As with all forms of evaluation, writers should judge their work according to particular criteria—standards beyond the writer's own likes and dislikes. In a college writing course, these standard are often made explicit on syllabi, assignment prompts, or rubrics. The criteria often come in some of the following broad categories: *focus, support, depth, development, organization, documentation, grammar,* and *mechanics.* Like the sections of this chapter, common criteria often begin with the more difficult or abstract issues, such as *focus* or *depth,* and work toward more concrete or rule-based issues such as *grammar.* Look carefully through your course materials for these standards so that your revision is guided by shared criteria.

## Peer Review

Exchange drafts with at least one other writer. Use the following questions to respond to specific issues in the drafts:

1. Can any phrases or terms in the thesis be narrowed? If so, circle them and make some suggestions for more focus. Does the thesis avoid the common problems? (See page 303.)
2. Does the evaluation summarize or describe the subject thoroughly? (Where might the summary or description be unnecessary or unrelated to the main idea?)
3. Where could the writer support broad evaluative claims with specific details about the subject? For instance, someone might argue "the plot is unnecessarily complicated" but avoid pointing to specific points in the plot. (This is a critical omission for an evaluative argument, so examine the claims closely.)
4. Where might the writer go beyond the specific subject (the place, text, person, etc.) and allude to some other like subject? How could other like subjects help the reader to see the main idea?

5. What other evaluative claims could be made about the subject? How could the writer address other, perhaps opposing, opinions?
6. Do any paragraphs shift focus from one point about the subject to another? Write "shifts focus" in the margins.
7. Identify any passages of harsh description or the enthusiasm crisis (see page 314).
8. As a reviewer, point to particular sentences and phrases that could gain vitality and intensity. Use the following:
   a. Look for unnecessary interrupting clauses and phrases. Underline them and/or draw an arrow to show where the phrase or clause can be moved.
   b. Rewrite a sentence to create more intensity with a repeating pattern.
   c. Cross out wordy phrases, and write in more concise options.
   d. Consider vitality strategies from other chapters:
      • What sentences are over-embedded? (Point to any clauses that overlap with other clauses, causing a disconnect between ideas.)
      • Examine attributive phrases. Point out unnecessary phrases or sentences that could be boiled down.
      • Where can the writer change linking verbs to active verbs?
      • Where can the writer avoid drawing attention to *I* and *you*?
      • Help the writer change unnecessary clauses to phrases.
      • Help the writer change unnecessary phrases to words.
      • Point to expletives (such as *there are* and *it is*).
      • Help the writer change passive verbs to active verbs for more vitality.
      • Help the reader avoid common grammatical errors: comma splices, sentence fragments, or pronoun/antecedent agreement.

# Reflection

Writers of all stripes struggle to evaluate their own work. We often fall on one side of a perilous fence: either celebrating our ideas too enthusiastically or cutting ourselves down too quickly. Quite often, those extremes (*I did a great job* verses *I'm a terrible writer*) say little about the actual work. Good writers can look honestly at their texts. They can apply some criteria beyond their own likes, fears, and hang-ups. Develop an evaluation of your evaluation. (That's right. Evaluate your performance as an evaluator!) Avoid the extremes: exuberant enthusiasm and self-deprecation. Instead, consider the following questions and let them guide you to an honest look at your work:

- How did you do more than express a personal opinion? How did you help readers to genuinely re-see the subject?
- Could you have better engaged opposing positions? Did you do more than dismiss or refute the opposition? How could you have more genuinely dealt with other perspectives, values, or assumptions?
- How inventive were your allusions? How well did you use support outside of the subject itself?
- How did your voice engage readers? Was it boring? Did it do something other than speak in academic monotone?

## Beyond the Essay: Classroom Evaluations

College administrators and faculty consistently examine student course evaluations, those forms that you fill out at the end of every semester. Administrators and professors alike argue about their effectiveness at measuring the success of courses. Some argue that course evaluations are too prone to bias, that students who do well give good evaluations and students who do poorly give poor evaluations. Others argue that student evaluations are "popularity contests" that encourage professors to inflate grades. All these arguments are evaluating evaluations!

Part of the debate about student evaluations involves the criteria—the standards that should be used. The following are some of the criteria in this debate:

- Rigor of the material
- Convenience for students
- Entertainment quality of the material being presented
- Students' interests
- Instructor's appearance
- Instructor's personality
- Grading policies or standards
- Syllabus/calendar clarity
- Adherence to course objectives
- Adherence to departmental objectives
- Individual student needs
- Acknowledgement of students' personal lives

As a college student, you may have significant insight to this issue. Focus on one of the following activities to explore this issue further:

1. As a class, debate one or more of the following:
   a. Individual student needs should (or should not) be a primary concern of a college course.
   b. The rigor of the material should (or should not) be adjusted to meet students' abilities.
   c. A college class should, above all else, be convenient for the college customer.
2. In small groups, develop a set of questions that could be used to evaluate a college writing course. Ask yourselves: What criteria should be used in a college classroom evaluation? What specific components should be examined for a writing course?

 For additional resources including instructional videos and links to helpful websites, access your English CourseMate through cengagebrain.com.

# 10 Searching for Causes

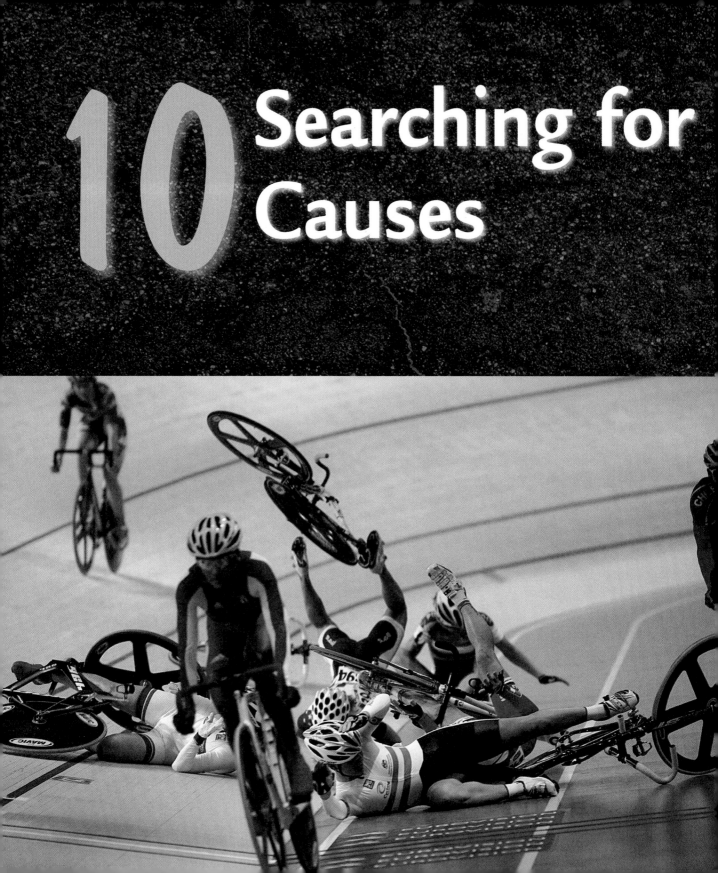

# Chapter Contents

# "All human beings should try to learn before they die what they are running from, and to, and why."

—James Thurber

When something happens in a community, everyone wants to know why. Why did the apartment building catch on fire? Why did the incumbent mayor's campaign lose momentum? Why are so many kids absent from school? What causes the traffic jam on I-95 every day? Why did the stock market suddenly drop? Why did the terrorists attack? Of course, everybody has guesses, but it takes a close analysis to discover the possible causes of such phenomena. Fire officials inspect the ashes of a burned apartment building; political scientists examine candidates' speeches and poll results; civil engineers look closely at travel patterns and highway capacity; economists deliberate over consumption trends and overseas markets. In all these cases, the people searching for causes are detectives attempting to find answers amidst a dizzying array of possibilities.

The search for causes constitutes much of the workload in many occupations. Doctors, of course, diagnose patients (looking for the cause of particular symptoms). Psychologists try to understand the causes of personality disorders or behavioral problems. Business executives hold weekly meetings and discuss the causes of production failures. Education specialists work with children to find the cause of scholastic problems.

As you can imagine (or as you may have witnessed), the search for such causes is not easy. Any number of factors can contribute to an effect. Take, for example, low proficiency test scores in public schools: school administrators might argue that poor teaching is the cause; teachers may point to poor parenting and discipline problems in the classroom; parents may point to bullying on school grounds or drug abuse; others might point to the tests themselves as the cause. The search for this cause, as it turns out, is a heated debate.

In academia, students spend much of their time studying causes:

- In an engineering class, students try to discover what causes one generator to produce more energy than another.

- Educational psychology students discuss why a particular student has lost all motivation.
- In history and economics seminars, students study economic conditions of the nineteenth century and debate the causes of the American Civil War.
- A class of physics students tries to determine the cause of black holes.

It might even be said that academia prepares people to understand causes in different fields—that is, that the study of a particular discipline gives students the critical perspectives necessary for asking the right questions (to find the right answers) within their fields. But despite the particular field or discipline, the process of discovery (of focusing and analyzing) is much the same, and the act of communicating one's discoveries is key in every situation.

This chapter will help you focus on a particular topic (a behavior, event, trend), discover a possible cause, and then develop an argument in favor of that particular cause. The following essays will provide valuable insight to necessary writing strategies. After reading the essays, you can find a topic in one of two ways:

1. Go to the Point of Contact section to find a problem from your everyday life, or
2. Read the following essays and choose one of the Ideas for Writing that follow.

After finding a subject, go to the Analysis section to begin developing the evaluation.

# Is Google Making Us Stupid? What the Internet Is Doing to Our Brains

## Nicholas Carr

The following essay appeared in the July/August 2008 issue of *The Atlantic*. While the title asks if Google is making us stupid, the essay examines how not just Google, but technology (typewriters, clocks, the Internet) changes the way we think. Nicholas Carr is author of *The Shallows: What the Internet Is Doing to Our Brains*.

"Dave, stop. Stop, will you? Stop, Dave. Will you stop, Dave?" So the supercomputer HAL pleads with the implacable astronaut Dave Bowman in a famous and weirdly poignant scene toward the end of Stanley Kubrick's *2001: A Space Odyssey*. Bowman, having nearly been sent to a deep-space death by the malfunctioning machine, is calmly, coldly disconnecting the memory circuits that control its artificial brain. "Dave, my mind is going," HAL says, forlornly. "I can feel it. I can feel it."

I can feel it, too. Over the past few years I've had an uncomfortable sense that someone, or something, has been tinkering with my brain, remapping the neural circuitry, reprogramming the memory. My mind isn't going—so far as I can tell—but it's changing. I'm not thinking the way I used to think. I can feel it most strongly when I'm reading. Immersing myself in a book or a lengthy article used to be easy. My mind would get caught up in the narrative or the turns of the argument, and I'd spend hours strolling through long stretches of prose. That's rarely the case anymore. Now my concentration often starts to drift after two or three pages. I get fidgety, lose the thread, begin looking for something else to do. I feel as if I'm always dragging my wayward brain back to the text. The deep reading that used to come naturally has become a struggle.

I think I know what's going on. For more than a decade now, I've been spending a lot of time online, searching and surfing and sometimes adding to the great databases of the Internet. The Web has been a godsend to me as a writer. Research that once required days in the stacks or periodical rooms of libraries can now be done in minutes. A few Google searches, some quick clicks on hyperlinks, and I've got the telltale fact or pithy quote I was after. Even when I'm not working, I'm as likely as not to be foraging in the Web's info-thickets, reading and writing e-mails, scanning headlines and blog posts, watching videos and listening to podcasts, or just tripping from link to link to link. (Unlike footnotes, to which they're sometimes likened, hyperlinks don't merely point to related works; they propel you toward them.)

For me, as for others, the Net is becoming a universal medium, the conduit for most of the information that flows through my eyes and ears and into my mind. The advantages of having immediate access to such an incredibly rich store of information are many, and they've been widely described and duly applauded. "The perfect recall of silicon memory," *Wired*'s Clive Thompson has written, "can be an enormous boon to thinking." But that boon comes at a price. As the media theorist Marshall McLuhan pointed out in the 1960s, media are not just passive channels of information. They supply the stuff of thought, but they also shape the process of thought. And what the Net seems to be doing is chipping away my capacity for concentration and contemplation. My mind now expects to take in information the way the Net distributes it: in a swiftly moving stream of particles. Once I was a scuba diver in the sea of words. Now I zip along the surface like a guy on a Jet Ski.

I'm not the only one. When I mention my troubles with reading to friends and acquaintances—literary types, most of them—many say they're having similar experiences. The more they use the Web, the more they have to fight to stay focused on long pieces of writing. Some of the bloggers I follow have also begun mentioning the phenomenon. Scott Karp, who writes a blog about online media, recently confessed that he has stopped reading books altogether. "I was a lit major in college, and used to be [a] voracious book reader," he wrote. "What happened?" He speculates on the answer: "What if I do all my reading on the web not so much because the way I read has changed, i.e., I'm just seeking convenience, but because the way I THINK has changed?"

Nicholas Carr    319

Is Google Making Us Stupid? What the Internet Is Doing to Our Brains

Bruce Friedman, who blogs regularly about the use of computers in medicine, also has described how the Internet has altered his mental habits. "I now have almost totally lost the ability to read and absorb a longish article on the web or in print," he wrote earlier this year. A pathologist who has long been on the faculty of the University of Michigan Medical School, Friedman elaborated on his comment in a telephone conversation with me. His thinking, he said, has taken on a "staccato" quality, reflecting the way he quickly scans short passages of text from many sources online. "I can't read *War and Peace* anymore," he admitted. "I've lost the ability to do that. Even a blog post of more than three or four paragraphs is too much to absorb. I skim it."

Anecdotes alone don't prove much. And we still await the long-term neurological and psychological experiments that will provide a definitive picture of how Internet use affects cognition. But a recently published study of online research habits, conducted by scholars from University College London, suggests that we may well be in the midst of a sea change in the way we read and think. As part of the five-year research program, the scholars examined computer logs documenting the behavior of visitors to two popular research sites, one operated by the British Library and one by a U.K. educational consortium, that provide access to journal articles, e-books, and other sources of written information. They found that people using the sites exhibited "a form of skimming activity," hopping from one source to another and rarely returning to any source they'd already visited. They typi-

cally read no more than one or two pages of an article or book before they would "bounce" out to another site. Sometimes they'd save a long article, but there's no evidence that they ever went back and actually read it. The authors of the study report:

> It is clear that users are not reading online in the traditional sense; indeed there are signs that new forms of "reading" are emerging as users "power browse" horizontally through titles, contents pages and abstracts going for quick wins. It almost seems that they go online to avoid reading in the traditional sense.

Thanks to the ubiquity of text on the Internet, not to mention the popularity of text-messaging on cell phones, we may well be reading more today than we did in the 1970s or 1980s, when television was our medium of choice. But it's a different kind of reading, and behind it lies a different kind of thinking—perhaps even a new sense of the self. "We are not only *what* we read," says Maryanne Wolf, a developmental psychologist at Tufts University and the author of *Proust and the Squid: The Story and Science of the Reading Brain,* "We are *how* we read." Wolf worries that the style of reading promoted by the Net, a style that puts "efficiency" and "immediacy" above all else, may be weakening our capacity for the kind of deep reading that emerged when an earlier technology, the printing press, made long and complex works of prose commonplace. When we read online, she says, we tend to become "mere decoders of information." Our ability to interpret text, to make the rich mental connections that form when we read deeply and without distraction, remains largely disengaged.

Reading, explains Wolf, is not an instinctive skill for human beings. It's not etched into our genes the way speech is. We have to teach our minds how to translate the symbolic characters we see into the language we understand. And the media or other technologies we use in learning and practicing the craft of reading play an important part in shaping the neural circuits inside our brains. Experiments demonstrate that readers of ideograms, such as the Chinese, develop a mental circuitry for reading that is very different from the circuitry found in those of us whose written language employs an alphabet. The variations extend across many regions of the brain, including

Christopher Morris/Corbis

those that govern such essential cognitive functions as memory and the interpretation of visual and auditory stimuli. We can expect as well that the circuits woven by our use of the Net will be different from those woven by our reading of books and other printed works.

Sometime in 1882, Friedrich Nietzsche bought a typewriter—a Malling-Hansen Writing Ball, to be precise. His vision was failing, and keeping his eyes focused on a page had become exhausting and painful, often bringing on crushing headaches. He had been forced to curtail his writing, and he feared that he would soon have to give it up. The typewriter rescued him, at least for a time. Once he had mastered touch-typing, he was able to write with his eyes closed, using only the tips of his fingers. Words could once again flow from his mind to the page.

But the machine had a subtler effect on his work. One of Nietzsche's friends, a composer, noticed a change in the style of his writing. His already terse prose had become even tighter, more telegraphic. "Perhaps you will through this instrument even take to a new idiom," the friend wrote in a letter, noting that, in his own work, his "'thoughts' in music and language often depend on the quality of pen and paper."

"You are right," Nietzsche replied, "our writing equipment takes part in the forming of our thoughts." Under the sway of the machine, writes the German media scholar Friedrich A. Kittler, Nietzsche's prose "changed from arguments to aphorisms, from thoughts to puns, from rhetoric to telegram style."

The human brain is almost infinitely malleable. People used to think that our mental meshwork, the dense connections formed among the 100 billion or so neurons inside our skulls, was largely fixed by the time we reached adulthood. But brain researchers have discovered that that's not the case. James Olds, a professor of neuroscience who directs the Krasnow Institute for Advanced Study at George Mason University, says that even the adult mind "is very plastic." Nerve cells routinely break old connections and form new ones. "The brain," according to Olds, "has the ability to reprogram itself on the fly, altering the way it functions."

As we use what the sociologist Daniel Bell has called our "intellectual technologies"—the tools that extend our mental rather than our physical capacities—we inevitably begin to take on the qualities of those technologies. The mechanical clock, which came into common use in the 14th century, provides a compelling example. In *Technics and Civilization,* the historian and cultural critic Lewis Mumford described how the clock "disassociated time from human events and helped create the belief in an independent world of mathematically measurable sequences." The "abstract framework of divided time" became "the point of reference for both action and thought."

The clock's methodical ticking helped bring into being the scientific mind and the scientific man. But it also took something away. As the late MIT computer scientist Joseph Weizenbaum observed in his 1976 book, *Computer Power and Human Reason: From Judgment to Calculation,* the conception of the world that emerged from the widespread use of timekeeping instruments "remains an impoverished version of the older one, for it rests on a rejection of those direct experiences that formed the basis for, and indeed constituted, the old reality." In deciding when to eat, to work, to sleep, to rise, we stopped listening to our senses and started obeying the clock.

The process of adapting to new intellectual technologies is reflected in the changing metaphors we use to explain ourselves to ourselves. When the mechanical clock arrived, people began thinking of their brains as operating "like clockwork." Today, in the age of software, we have come to think of them as operating "like computers." But the changes, neuroscience tells us, go much deeper than metaphor. Thanks to our brain's plasticity, the adaptation occurs also at a biological level.

The Internet promises to have particularly far-reaching effects on cognition. In a paper published in 1936, the British mathematician Alan Turing proved that a digital computer, which at the time existed only as a theoretical machine, could be programmed to perform the function of any other information-processing device. And that's what we're seeing today. The Internet, an immeasurably powerful computing system, is subsuming most of our other intellectual technologies. It's becoming our map and our clock, our printing press and our typewriter, our calculator and our telephone, and our radio and TV.

When the Net absorbs a medium, that medium is recreated in the Net's image. It injects the medium's content with hyperlinks, blinking ads, and other digital gewgaws, and it surrounds the content with the content of all the other media it has absorbed. A new e-mail message, for instance, may announce its arrival as we're glancing over the latest headlines at a newspaper's site. The result is to scatter our attention and diffuse our concentration.

The Net's influence doesn't end at the edges of a computer screen, either. As people's minds become attuned to the crazy quilt of Internet media, traditional media have to adapt to the audience's new expectations. Television programs add text crawls and pop-up ads, and magazines and newspapers shorten their articles, introduce capsule summaries, and crowd their pages with easy-to-browse info-snippets. When, in March of this year, *The New York Times* decided to devote the second and third pages of every edition to article abstracts, its design director, Tom Bodkin, explained that the "shortcuts" would give harried readers a quick "taste" of the day's news, sparing them the "less efficient" method of actually turning the pages and reading the articles. Old media have little choice but to play by the new-media rules.

Never has a communications system played so many roles in our lives—or exerted such broad influence over our thoughts—as the Internet does today. Yet, for all that's been written about the Net, there's been little consideration of how, exactly, it's reprogramming us. The Net's intellectual ethic remains obscure.

About the same time that Nietzsche started using his typewriter, an earnest young man named Frederick Winslow Taylor carried a stopwatch into the Midvale Steel plant in Philadelphia and began a historic series of experiments aimed at improving the efficiency of the plant's machinists. With the approval of Midvale's owners, he recruited a group of factory hands, set them to work on various metalworking machines, and recorded and timed their every movement as well as the operations of the machines. By breaking down every job into a sequence of small, discrete steps and then testing different ways of performing each one, Taylor created a set of precise instructions—an "algorithm," we might say today—for how each worker should work. Midvale's employees grumbled about the strict new regime, claiming that it turned them into little more than automatons, but the factory's productivity soared.

More than a hundred years after the invention of the steam engine, the Industrial Revolution had at last found its philosophy and its philosopher. Taylor's tight industrial choreography—his "system," as he liked to call it—was embraced by manufacturers throughout the country and, in time, around the world. Seeking maximum speed, maximum efficiency, and maximum output, factory owners used time-and-motion studies to organize their work and configure the jobs of their workers. The goal, as Taylor defined it in his celebrated 1911 treatise, *The Principles of Scientific Management,* was to identify and adopt, for every job, the "one best method" of work and thereby to effect "the gradual substitution of science for rule of thumb throughout the mechanic arts." Once his system was applied to all acts of manual labor, Taylor assured his followers, it would bring about a restructuring not only of industry but of society, creating a utopia of perfect efficiency. "In the past the man has been first," he declared; "in the future the system must be first."

Taylor's system is still very much with us; it remains the ethic of industrial manufacturing. And now, thanks to the growing power that computer engineers and software coders wield over our intellectual lives, Taylor's ethic is beginning to govern the realm of the mind as well. The Internet is a machine designed for the efficient and automated collection, transmission, and manipulation of information, and its legions of programmers are intent on finding the "one best method"—the perfect algorithm—to carry out every mental movement of what we've come to describe as "knowledge work."

Google's headquarters, in Mountain View, California—the Googleplex—is the Internet's high church, and the religion practiced inside its walls is Taylorism. Google, says its chief executive, Eric Schmidt, is "a company that's founded around the science of measurement," and it is striving to "systematize everything" it does. Drawing on the terabytes of behavioral data it collects through its search engine and other sites, it carries out thousands of experiments a day, according to the *Harvard Business Review,* and it uses the results to refine the algorithms that increasingly control how people find information and extract meaning from it. What Taylor did for the work of the hand, Google is doing for the work of the mind.

The company has declared that its mission is "to organize the world's information and make it universally accessible and useful." It seeks to develop "the perfect search engine," which it defines as something that "understands exactly what you mean and gives you back exactly what you want." In Google's view, information is a kind of commodity, a utilitarian resource that can be mined and processed with industrial efficiency. The more pieces of information we can "access" and the faster we can extract their gist, the more productive we become as thinkers.

Where does it end? Sergey Brin and Larry Page, the gifted young men who founded Google while pursuing doctoral degrees in computer science at Stanford, speak frequently of their desire to turn their search engine into an artificial intelligence, a HAL-like machine that might be connected directly to our brains. "The ultimate search engine is something as smart as people—or smarter," Page said in a speech a few years back. "For us, working on search is a way to work on artificial intelligence." In a 2004 interview with *Newsweek,* Brin said, "Certainly if you had all the world's information directly attached to your brain, or an artificial brain that was smarter than your brain, you'd be better off." Last year, Page told a convention of scientists that Google is "really trying to build artificial intelligence and to do it on a large scale."

Such an ambition is a natural one, even an admirable one, for a pair of math whizzes with vast quantities of cash at their disposal and a small army of computer scientists in their employ. A fundamentally scientific enterprise, Google is motivated by a desire to use technology, in Eric Schmidt's words, "to solve problems that have never been solved before," and artificial intelligence is the hardest problem out there. Why wouldn't Brin and Page want to be the ones to crack it?

Still, their easy assumption that we'd all "be better off" if our brains were supplemented, or even replaced, by an artificial intelligence is unsettling. It suggests a belief that intelligence is the output of a mechanical process, a series of discrete steps that can be isolated, measured, and optimized. In Google's world, the world we enter when we go online, there's little place for the fuzziness of contemplation. Ambiguity is not an opening for insight but a bug to be fixed. The human brain is just an outdated computer that needs a faster processor and a bigger hard drive.

The idea that our minds should operate as high-speed data-processing machines is not only built into the work-

ings of the Internet, it is the network's reigning business model as well. The faster we surf across the Web—the more links we click and pages we view—the more opportunities Google and other companies gain to collect information about us and to feed us advertisements. Most of the proprietors of the commercial Internet have a financial stake in collecting the crumbs of data we leave behind as we flit from link to link—the more crumbs, the better. The last thing these companies want is to encourage leisurely reading or slow, concentrated thought. It's in their economic interest to drive us to distraction.

Maybe I'm just a worrywart. Just as there's a tendency to glorify technological progress, there's a countertendency to expect the worst of every new tool or machine. In Plato's *Phaedrus,* Socrates bemoaned the development of writing. He feared that, as people came to rely on the written word as a substitute for the knowledge they used to carry inside their heads, they would, in the words of one of the dialogue's characters, "cease to exercise their memory and become forgetful." And because they would be able to "receive a quantity of information without proper instruction," they would "be thought very knowledgeable when they are for the most part quite ignorant." They would be "filled with the conceit of wisdom instead of real wisdom." Socrates wasn't wrong—the new technology did often have the effects he feared—but he was shortsighted. He couldn't foresee the many ways that writing and reading would serve to spread information, spur fresh ideas, and expand human knowledge (if not wisdom).

The arrival of Gutenberg's printing press, in the 15th century, set off another round of teeth gnashing. The Italian humanist Hieronimo Squarciafico worried that the easy availability of books would lead to intellectual laziness, making men "less studious" and weakening their minds. Others argued that cheaply printed books and broadsheets would undermine religious authority, demean the work of scholars and scribes, and spread sedition and debauchery. As New York University professor Clay Shirky notes, "Most of the arguments made against the printing press were correct, even prescient." But, again, the doomsayers were unable to imagine the myriad blessings that the printed word would deliver.

So, yes, you should be skeptical of my skepticism. Perhaps those who dismiss critics of the Internet as Luddites or nostalgists will be proved correct, and from our hyperactive, data-stoked minds will spring a golden age of intellectual discovery and universal wisdom. Then again, the Net isn't the alphabet, and although it may replace the printing press, it produces something altogether different. The kind of deep reading that a sequence of printed pages promotes is valuable not just for the knowledge we acquire from the author's words but for the intellectual vibrations those words set off within our own minds. In the quiet spaces opened up by the sustained, undistracted reading of a book, or by any other act of contemplation, for that matter, we make our own associations, draw our own inferences and analogies, foster our own ideas. Deep reading, as Maryanne Wolf argues, is indistinguishable from deep thinking.

If we lose those quiet spaces, or fill them up with "content," we will sacrifice something important not only in our selves but in our culture. In a recent essay, the playwright Richard Foreman eloquently described what's at stake:

> I come from a tradition of Western culture, in which the ideal (my ideal) was the complex, dense and "cathedral-like" structure of the highly educated and articulate personality—a man or woman who carried inside themselves a personally constructed and unique version of the entire heritage of the West. [But now] I see within us all (myself included) the replacement of complex inner density with a new kind of self—evolving under the pressure of information overload and the technology of the "instantly available."

As we are drained of our "inner repertory of dense cultural inheritance," Foreman concluded, we risk turning into "'pancake people'—spread wide and thin as we connect with that vast network of information accessed by the mere touch of a button."

I'm haunted by that scene in *2001*. What makes it so poignant, and so weird, is the computer's emotional response to the disassembly of its mind: its despair as one circuit after another goes dark, its childlike pleading with the astronaut—"I can feel it. I can feel it. I'm afraid"—and its final reversion to what can only be called a state of innocence. HAL's outpouring of feeling contrasts with the emotionlessness that characterizes the human figures in the film, who go about their business with an

almost robotic efficiency. Their thoughts and actions feel scripted, as if they're following the steps of an algorithm. In the world of *2001,* people have become so machinelike that the most human character turns out to be a machine. That's the essence of Kubrick's dark prophecy: as we come to rely on computers to mediate our understanding of the world, it is our own intelligence that flattens into artificial intelligence.

# Writing Strategies

1. What is the essay's thesis?

2. Explain how Carr uses a combination of support strategies to help the reader understand and accept the thesis.

3. Describe the essay's opening strategy.

4. Carr draws attention to an assumption of Sergey Brin and Larry Page—that we'd all 'be better off' if our brains were supplemented, or even replaced, by an artificial intelligence. Why does Carr think this assumption is unsettling? How is questioning the assumption important to Carr's point?

5. Identify a concession Carr makes and explain how it is important to his argument.

# Exploring Ideas

1. Explain how you have taken on certain qualities of an intellectual technology (a tool that extends one's mental capacities).

2. What is Taylor's ethic, and how is it beginning to govern the mind?

3. What does Carr think we will sacrifice if we lose the "quiet spaces opened up by the sustained, undistracted reading of a book, or by any other act of contemplation . . ."? Do you agree or disagree? What evidence can you provide to support your position?

# Ideas for Writing

1. What besides technology has caused people's minds to function differently?

2. What particular aspect of the media has changed the way people's minds work?

If responding to one of these ideas, go to the Analysis section of this chapter to begin developing ideas for your essay.

# Throwing Up Childhood

## Leonard Kress

The most personal or intimate exploration can have significance for others. Even the contents of one's stomach can have public resonance. Good writers can make a personal search for causes resonate with the lives of others. In this essay, Leonard Kress tries to pinpoint the cause of his bulimic childhood behavior. In that search, he realizes that his own understanding runs contrary to expert opinion and the official positions of published research. But he focuses on, even seeks out, the tension between his own understanding and the answers he finds. In this sense, Kress's essay illustrates thinking further—exploring the cracks and crevices of what he knows and what others know.

**Writing Strategies**

Begins with personal narrative.

Very detailed description.

Allusion to Hansel and Gretel.

More public resonance: the behavior is not new or even that unusual.

New paragraph pulls the reader out of the details.

I remember standing breathless and exhilarated in the hotel lobby, the rest of my family still in the dining room finishing their evening meal. I'm not sure whether or not they can see what I see—the thin gray broken line on the carpet, leading all the way to the back entrance. This time I don't make it out to the patio, the swimming pool, down to the beach, inundated this summer with jellyfish and jelly lichen, Portuguese Man O'War. If only they would leave their table, they could easily find me by following the half-digested dinner rolls and the masticated but intact sirloin morsels, the bitter tomato-broth they soak in. Hansel, whom I imagine to be about my age (seven and a half), couldn't have left a better trail for him and his sister to follow back to their woodland cottage. Even if the birds had pecked it clean, that bile-stain would still remain, like a stripe dividing a country highway. We are here in Miami Beach to visit my grandparents, Ada and Max, and since they live in a tiny apartment, we are staying in this beachfront hotel, more luxurious than we are used to. It occurs to me that only the desk clerk has been following my whole grand performance with any interest. Whatever others there might be carefully and kindly turn away their gaze. But the desk clerk glances over to me and across the lobby, as if surveying both the damage and the cause of it. I recognize that smirk and wonder, was he a vomiter too? I don't have a clue and don't really care; he assiduously computes the cleaning bill.

This isn't the first time. As far back as I can remember, meals out with my parents were capped with similar grand gestures. It didn't matter whether it was a Howard Johnson's, a deli, a steakhouse—sometimes I'd conveniently make it to the bathroom sink or toilet; other times I'd leave a pile on the floor, splat-

**Exploring Ideas**

He is a type of child—a "vomiter."

---

Leonard Kress, "Throwing Up Childhood." Reprinted with permission of the author.

ter the door, the parking lot, the car. I don't know how it happened; I can't make sense of the progression that leads up to it. I ordered from the menu like my brother and sister—appetizer, entrée, dessert. I didn't steal from anyone's plate, stabbing a slab of beef or spearing a soggy fry while they tied a shoe or fidgeted over a response to some parental inquiry. I didn't pick their dregs, dumping half-gnawed bones onto my own fully gnawed pile, I didn't reach across plates and setting to grab a soppy crust of bread or buttered roll. We were all healthy eaters in my family, and we were all well within the recommended weight guidelines. Granted, I was a fast eater; my father and brother were also fast eaters—we lacked the patience to chew, always anxious to move on to something new. I certainly didn't deliberate over the plate like my younger sister did, who always ate like a bird. She'd barely be attending to her main course while the rest of us scraped up the last of our desserts. Compared to her, I wolfed my food, scarfed it, inhaled it, terms I heard over and over again much later. I was a healthy, active second-grader; dinner meant disjuncture, interruption, tactic of delay constructed by mothers to keep their sons from the real work of childhood—hide and seek, wiffle ball, bikes, backyard Olympiad.

  I often wonder now what led me to such disgusting behavior—what might lead any child to such disgusting behavior. Like any good 21st-century questioner/researcher, I go to the Internet, hopeful that a search of current medical literature will provide answers and understanding. So I begin my search, seated in front of my computer. I find a gopher (its name is OVID—aptly named for the ancient Roman writer of *Metamorphoses* or *Transformations),* and it's as versatile as a left-handed shortstop, a triple-threat, able to simultaneously search pediatric, psychology, anthropology, and other allied health databases. I'm confident that with the right *keyword search,* the exact *cross-referencing* or *Boolean limitation,* I will be able to call up some insight. This should be a breeze, I think, *childhood bulimia,* thousands of hits, hundreds of studies from millions of research dollars. After all, anorexia/bulimia was, arguably, *the disease* of the 1990s. I do find something. In *The International Journal of Eating Disorders* (1995) there's an article titled, "Premorbid Onset of Psychopathology in Long-term Recovered Anorexia Patients." And the abstract tells me that 58% of anorexics reported "childhood anxiety disorders at age ten (plus or minus five years)." The most common is childhood depression beginning well before the eating disorder. I also locate "Determinants of Adolescent Obesity: A Comparison with Anorexia Nervosa," in *Adolescence* (1988), which claims that "both anorexics

---

*Marginal notes:*

Intensive details.

Paragraph shift indicates the new focus: from describing the behavior to searching for causes.

An allusion to the writer. Are the titles significant?

Narrating the actual searching process.

Outside source.

No obvious reason for his vomiting.

He was not an overeater. He was not obese or unhealthy.

Active and energetic— otherwise "normal"?

Anorexia and bulimia are the same type of disease? ("the disease of the '90s")

Eating disorders associated with psychological problems.

and the obese are characterized by overprotectedness and enmesh-ment, resulting from a poor sense of identity and effectiveness." After a whole week of research, this seems to be the extent of my findings. I can find nothing to urge me to go beyond the abstracts, nothing at all, though I type in "eating disorder," "vomiting," "obesity," "abnormal psychology," "gluttony," "disgusting and destructive behavior"—always cross-referenced with "childhood."

I was a happy child. I really was. And not only in my par-ents' estimation. I see it now in old snapshots and projected slides. When I was two, the neighbors nicknamed me "Smiley." It stuck. Nothing fazed me—not even the most traumatic inci-dent of my early life, driving my trike over the sides of that same neighbor's screened-in porch, the screens removed for spring cleaning. The tumble left a pus-filled bruise, two weeks in drain-ing. My parents said that I never flinched or lost that smile, even as that neighbor dug and poked and pressed and guiltily reap-plied her expert pity dressings, the whole time boasting inces-santly about her favorite nephew, a fighter pilot almost blasted out of the Korean sky a few years back. "Praise God," I remem-ber her saying, "that he wasn't tortured or starved." Thank God he returned, intact, and (my parents informed me years later) in time to be chosen as one of the original Mercury 7 astronauts. Somehow it seems that this might have been right about the time that I began my career as a public barfer.

Only once do I remember doing it in secret. It was at my grandparents' golden wedding anniversary celebration, a feast my grandmother herself with the help of her Kovno and Litwak sisters, Bronx nieces, and Jersey City daughters prepared. I am not one, however, to gorge on a sumptuous catalogued recita-tion of the feast (more scrumptious than the feast itself?). For the food itself never seemed to matter. For the most part, I ate whatever was cast in front of me. The party took place at my aunt's apartment in Stuyvesant Town on the East Side, where the shouts of roller skaters and stickball players rose up from the playground, mixing with the shrill stab of ambulance, police car, fire truck, and the play-by-play of the Yankees . . . and it is this final detail that I most vividly recall—not the carp swimming all night in the bathtub, walloped against the porcelain rim in the morning, then beheaded and sopped in a bucket of brine. Not the pickled tongue or brisket or pot roast, and kasha, knishes, blin-tzes served up beneath gobs of sour cream, like Chekhov's "crisp bleenies, lacy and plump as the shoulder of a merchant's daugh-ter." There was a full week of food preparation that I gobbled down and then disposed of with great ease and easing. I didn't

---

*Paragraph shifts from the search back to describing the past.*

*Could this be a connection?*

*The details show the culi-nary tradition of his family.*

*The literature does not describe his case.*

*Details to show he was healthy and energetic.*

*Why is this the most vivid detail for him? Is there a connection?*

even have to stick my finger down my throat; I could simply will the partially chewed hearty chunks of meat and potato up from their sour churning stock. It felt so good! *The Encyclopedia of Pediatric Psychology* (1979) reports that children who vomit, farfetched as it sounds, even "those who have learned society's aversions . . . can overcome such scruples and experience vomiting as cathartic, even orgasmic."

I still find it odd that my parents never questioned why I did it. They never seemed to mind, though I'm sure they did, privately. They must have been embarrassed, if not mortified, by my behavior. In spite of that, we went out to dinner often, several times a month. Not once did they ask me to modify my order, limit my portion. They never motioned the waitress aside, and with the promise of a bigger tip, asked her to go easy on the fries. My brother and sister were silent, too, as though my barfing were a perfectly acceptable alternative to an after-dinner mint, a toothpick, a wet-wipe wrapped like a condom. Perhaps they were too busy stashing away the details of the affront, safekeeping for a time of need—like Aesop's despicable, self-righteous ant. I can only imagine the hay they might have later made by simple melodramatic evocations of the sounds of my gagging, as it echoed in tiny bathrooms. The deep, throaty sound of plosively expelling vomit. "Well, whatever I did can't be as gross and disgusting as THAT," I can hear them repeating over and over till they got what they wanted. Or did they have their own equally disgusting but self-customized techniques of catharsis and orgasm back then—I wondered. Does everyone, I still wonder? And how could a "D" in French or a detention or a missed meal or a dent in the car compare with what I did, over and over and over?

It couldn't, of course, it would pale in comparison to that cathartic act of throwing up (knowing that others could hear my retching) that left my face bloodless and pale, my extremities tingling, my chest heaving with giddiness. Perhaps earlier generations of parents and child psychologists had a better understanding of its power and attraction. And that's why older writings on the subject, rare but not unheard of, prescribe such drastic, almost Draconian treatment to stop the behavior. *The Encyclopedia of Pediatric Psychology* (1970) lacks entries for either anorexia or bulimia and refers to it as "psychogenic vomiting." It predates the public and medical concern over the condition, and takes a stern, almost Victorian approach to treatment:

---

*Margin notes (left):*

The outside source integrated (colliding with?) his experiences.

Counterargument?

New paragraph: focus on others around him.

Allusion to the ant and grasshopper story.

Public resonance: does everyone have a technique for releasing tension?

*Margin notes (right):*

Here's the first connection between the search and his experience: it's pleasurable.

Catharsis = relief/release of tension.

The main cause is need for catharsis?

Draconian = code of extreme severity or rigor.

Karo syrup, Phenobarbital, anticonvulsants, chlorpromazine, antihistamines, chin straps, esophageal blocks, thickened feedings, removal of normal appendix, electric shock therapy, and even intensive prayer are all reported to have been used successfully to resolve the problem.

His situation, again, seems slightly different than the literature suggests.

In some cases, and in my case, I suppose, the patient simply outgrows it.

# Writing Strategies

1. How does the essay's introduction grab the reader's interest? How does it establish a tone for the essay?

2. Identify a particular sentence and explain how it helps bring the essay to life.

3. Though Kress deals with a very personal issue, how might his essay resonate with others? What sentences in the essay are most likely to reach out and connect with others, and why?

4. Identify an allusion, using it to explain how allusions convey meaning.

# Exploring Ideas

1. Explore a past behavior of your own, searching for its cause. Research the behavior by reading about it and/or talking to others. Your goal is to arrive not at *the* cause, but at several possible causes. List the possible causes.

2. Evaluate each of the possible causes you discovered for #1. Which ones seem most likely to be the cause of your behavior? Provide convincing evidence to support your conclusion.

3. If you were Kress's parent, what would you do?

4. What does your response to #3 say about your basic values or beliefs?

5. Why is the essay's ending effective? What is its effect?

# Ideas for Writing

1. Reflect as an adult on a puzzling childhood experience. What might be the cause of a certain behavior that you have not yet understood?

2. Kress considers his family's reaction to his vomiting. What is the cause of someone else's puzzling reaction to you?

If responding to one of these ideas, go to the Analysis section of this chapter to begin developing ideas for your essay.

# American Consumerism

## Jamie Bentley

Writers often agree with an argument, yet see value in redirecting attention to some other aspect of the issue *(agree and redirect)*. In the following essay, Jamie Bentley, a first-year student at Umpqua Community College, responds to Simon Benlow's "An Apology to Future Generations" (pages 389–394). First she acknowledges Benlow's idea about the harmful effect a consumerist culture has on the environment, and then she argues about the *more* harmful effect it has on the American family.

Contemporary American culture has a well-documented obsession with consuming things. According to Simon Benlow, "You know how opulently we lived, how we gorged ourselves daily, how we lived beyond the means of ourselves and of the following generations" (577). Benlow states that we have "irreparably harmed the world for those beyond [our time]" (577). There is no doubt that we are harming the environment somewhat; however, more than harming the environment, this consumerist culture is causing individual economic problems and contributes to the breakdown of the family.

While we are individually causing economic distress for ourselves, we are helping to better the economy of the nation. From 1950 to 2000, the gross domestic product (GDP) per capita tripled to $35,970 (Lankford, "Consumerism"). This incredible gain in wealth for our nation supposedly helped us all. Sixty-eight percent of American families own a home, 98% own color televisions, 94% own VCRs, 90% own microwaves, and 83% own washing machines (Lankford, "Consumerism"). I say "supposedly helped" because, while these things greatly increase our comfort and entertainment, they also greatly increase personal debt. The average American household has $18,700 of debt, not including mortgages (Lankford, "Introduction"). In 2000, the average American's consumer debt was 96% of his disposable income; by 2004, that consumer debt increased to 113% of his disposable income (Lankford, "Introduction").

One cause of such increased debt is that "[a]ccording to the *San Antonio Business Journal,* there are over 785 million credit cards currently in circulation, used to charge $1.5 trillion each year" (Lankford, "Introduction"). Jennifer Errick says, "Americans like to shop. We like big stuff and we like lots of it. Everything in our lives is getting bigger, from vehicles and houses to TV screens and bathtubs" (qtd. in Lankford, "Introduction"). Everything is getting bigger, including debt. Credit cards allow instantaneous purchases. Our society is one of instant gratification, and that is part of what makes credit cards so popular. We no longer have to wait to buy something we want until we have enough money; we can just charge it now and pay for it later. In fact, the "[a]verage increase in consumer spending when credit cards are used instead of cash [is] 23%" (New Road Map Foundation). This idea of "buy now, pay later" is largely responsible for our debt. People charge much, much more than they can afford because they think they can always pay later. They do not take into account that all those purchases add up very quickly, and so does the interest that is charged.

Because such massive debt is being accrued by consumers, 1.6 million personal bankruptcy filings took place in the year 2004, up from only 900,000 in 1995 (Lankford, "Introduction"). "'The U.S. Chamber of Commerce estimates businesses lose about $40 billion annually to bankruptcies,' notes the *Arizona Daily Star,* 'passing much of the cost on to consumers'" (Lankford, "Introduction"). This causes a vicious cycle, because when the businesses pass on costs to consumers, they increase prices, which costs the consumer more money, which can lead to more debt, which can lead to more bankruptcy.

American consumerism is not only causing more debt, but it is also causing a sharp decrease in savings. In 1973, the average amount of disposable income put into savings was 8.6%; in 1994 it was 4.2%; by November 2005, it was negative 0.2% (New Road Map Foundation; Lankford, "Introduction").

This consumerist mentality is also contributing to the breakdown of the family unit. When the average family is in debt by $18,700 (Lankford, "Introduction"), it increases the likelihood that both parents will need to work, and work more hours, in order to pay off this debt. With both parents working, the children will need to be in daycare or have some sort of childcare provided for them. When families don't spend time together, they tend to drift apart.

According to a survey done by the New Road Map Foundation, the average parent spends 6 hours a week shopping, but only 40 minutes a week playing with their children. What kind of message does this send to our children? While there is no doubt that these parents love their children, it is subtly sending the message that things are more important than time spent together. This same survey by the New Road Map Foundation showed that "American parents spent 40% less time with their children in 1991 than they did in 1965." That is so incredibly sad, and unfortunately, it will more than likely just get worse. Even sadder still is the fact that only 34% of Americans said they were "willing to forgo raises and promotions to devote more time to their families" (New Road Map Foundation). Children will grow up thinking this is normal, and they will try to provide the same "quality" of life for their children as they had growing up. They will try to accomplish this by working more hours to earn more money so they can buy more things for their families.

The constant shopping and having more material possessions is not making us happier. Ed Diener and Mar-

tin Seligman, psychologists, did more than 150 studies on the links between happiness and wealth and found "that there has been no appreciable rise in life satisfaction over the past decades, despite our increased material wealth" (Lankford, "Materialism"). When parents spend the majority of their time shopping or working, the family unit is placed under stress, and relationships start to suffer (Lankford, "Materialism"). It's very difficult to have a relationship with someone who's never there, and as the New Road Map Foundation study shows, parents are spending less and less time with their children.

Joseph Beckenbach, a software consultant from San Jose, CA, has joined the anti-consumerist movement in order to put less emphasis on consuming (shopping in particular) so that he can "keep . . . focus on what's more important in life, like spending time with my daughter" (qtd. in Emert). The anti-consumerist movement has created what's called Buy Nothing Day in order to encourage more people to put less emphasis on shopping, as

Joseph Beckenbach has. Buy Nothing Day takes place on the day after Thanksgiving, the day that begins the mad rush of holiday shopping for many people. The editor of *Adbusters* magazine thinks that only 1 million people participated in Buy Nothing Day in the year 1999, and that was globally. With 6 billion people on the planet, that was only .0001% (Emert). More people need to take action and get involved with activities such as Buy Nothing Day, or simply just spend more time together as a family.

All of our consuming is also causing damage to the environment. "For packaging (cans, bottles, cartons, etc.) alone, the U.S. uses approximately: 50% of its paper, 75% of its glass, 40% of its aluminum, and 30% of its plastics" (New Road Map Foundation). Every year, the amount of waste in the U.S. is equivalent to filling "a convoy of 10-ton garbage trucks 145,000 miles long" (New Road Map Foundation). If we would just buy less, we would waste less. Most everything we buy comes in some sort of packaging; if our nation as a whole would buy less, manufacturers would produce less, which would equate to less of our resources being used for packaging and ultimately less waste.

A 1991 survey found that "8 out of 10 Americans regarded themselves as 'environmentalists' and half of those said they were 'strong' ones"; 78% of Americans "believed that a 'major national effort' [is] needed to improve the environment" (New Road Map Foundation). However, only 22% of Americans were found to be "actively working toward solutions" (New Road Map Foundation). This seems to be a classic example of the saying "do as I say, not as I do."

Oisin Coghlan, from Friends of the Earth, "believes about 5 per cent of the population are willing to change their behaviour [sic] with minimal pushing, but many more belong to the 'I will if you will' contingent" (qtd. in Cullen). Because our culture is one that is focused on popularity, and what is cool to do at the moment, many people will only do something if "everyone else is doing it." Coghlan also believes that people need incentives in order to become more "green" (Cullen). This plays off of our society's selfish attitude. Many people will only do something if it has something in it for them. Why should they drive out of their way to spend more money on a product that may or may not have an impact on the earth if there is nothing in it for them? Joel Makower, president

of Green Business Network, asks if people will choose the green product over the non-green product, and the answer he comes up with is very true, and a perfect reflection of most people's attitudes:

> . . . if you probe deeper into consumer attitudes, the real answer is that consumers will choose the greener product—IF it doesn't cost more, comes from a brand they know and trust . . . can be purchased at stores where they already shop . . . doesn't require a significant change of habits to use . . . and has at least the same level of quality, performance, and endurance as the less-green alternative.

This just goes to show how selfish most people are. We say we care about the environment, but we don't really want to do anything about saving it if it is inconvenient for us in any way, shape, or form.

People keep saying we need to improve the environment, but we are so focused on consuming things that we would rather keep up our current lifestyle than actually do something to prevent further damage to the environment and further loss of resources. One way to improve the environment would be to start spending less money! "Every time we spend money we consume resources, so saving money links directly to saving forests, other species, mineral resources, water and ultimately the earth. For ourselves, and for all of life, we must return to financial sanity" (New Road Map Foundation). By consuming less, we wouldn't have to work as much with the intent to earn more money in order to pay off our debts. That would free us up to spend more time with our families. By consuming less, we would waste less because there would be less to throw away. By consuming less, manufacturers would be forced to produce less, which would save more resources. By consuming less, we are helping the environment, but we are ultimately helping ourselves by reducing our debts and allowing us to become more family-oriented instead of "stuff"-oriented.

## Works Cited

Benlow, Simon. "Apology to Future Generations." *The Composition of Everyday Life.* Ed. John Mauk and John Metz. 3rd ed. Boston: Wadsworth, 2010. 413–417. Print.

Cullen, Paul. "Landfill and Lightbulbs: Are We Ready to Abandon Our Destructive Past?" *Irish Times* 14 Jan. 2008: n. pag. *Newspaper Source.* Web. 7 Feb. 2008.

Emert, Carol. "Anti-Consumerism Movement Urges Less Shopping/Less Can Be More—Buy Nothing Campaign Gains Strength." *San Francisco Chronicle* 26 Nov. 2000: B1. *Opposing Viewpoints Resource Center.* Web. 7 Feb. 2008.

Lankford, Ronnie D. Jr. "Consumerism Creates a Healthy Economy." *At Issue: Is American Society Too Materialistic?* Detroit: Greenhaven Press, 2006: n. pag. *Opposing Viewpoints Resource Center.* Web. 19 Jan. 2008.

———. Introduction to *At Issue: Is American Society Too Materialistic?* Detroit: Greenhaven Press, 2006: n. pag. *Opposing Viewpoints Resource Center.* Web. 19 Jan. 2008.

———. "Materialism Undermines the Family." *At Issue: Is American Society Too Materialistic?* Detroit: Greenhaven Press, 2006: n. pag. *Opposing Viewpoints Resource Center.* Web. 7 Feb. 2008.

Makower, Joel. "Whatever Happened to Green Consumers?" *New American Dream.* New American Dream, n.d. Web. 7 Feb. 2008.

New Road Map Foundation. "All Consuming Passion: Waking Up from the American Dream." *EcoFuture.* EcoFuture, 17 Jan. 2002. Web. 19 Jan. 2008.

## Writing Strategies

1. According to Bentley, what impact does consumerist culture have on the American family?

2. What support strategies does Bentley use to help the reader understand what she means by "consumerist culture"?

3. Describe Bentley's voice as a writer and provide two sentences that support your description.

4. Based on her essay, what does Bentley value? Provide two ideas from her essay that support your response.

## Exploring Ideas

1. What might be the benefits of people consuming less? What might be the drawbacks?

2. What evidence can you provide that shopping and having more material possessions are not making us happier?

3. Bentley's essay speaks to two issues: the environment and the family. What other issue is seriously impacted by consumerism, and how?

4. With a group of peers, explore some reasons for credit card debt. Generate a list of reasons that people get into debt, and then group the reasons into three to five categories.

## Ideas for Writing

1. Why is American society obsessed with consuming things?

2. What is the root cause of the increase in individual debt?

If responding to one of these ideas, go to the Analysis section of this chapter to begin developing ideas for your essay.

# INVENTION

"One great cause of failure is lack of concentration."

—Bruce Lee

Invention is an act of discovery. It involves opening all the intellectual cases we have closed in everyday life. It involves asking questions where we had assumed we knew the answers. For this chapter, invention involves asking why something occurs (or has occurred) and going beyond the first (and second) guess. In Point of Contact, ask adventurous questions to find a topic. In Analysis, imagine unseen causes. In Public Resonance, consider the ways your topic extends outward and affects the public. In Thesis, focus your ideas to a particular insight, and in Rhetorical Tools, explore a range of possible support strategies. The Invention Questions in each section are not meant to be answered directly in your final written assignment. In fact, as you work through the sections, avoid simply answering them and then moving on. Instead, use them to explore and to develop revelatory ideas.

# Point of Contact

The search for a cause begins with a question: Why did something happen? Why does something continue? What causes some phenomenon? The following questions can help you to explore possible topics. After you have decided on a particular topic, go to the Analysis section to continue your search for causes.

## Work

- Why are some sections/groups/teams more successful than others?
- Why is workplace efficiency up or down?
- Why are profits for the company or organization up or down?
- Why are some workers more content or fulfilled than others?

## Local Events

- Why is urban sprawl taking place in your community?
- Why is a local sports team winning or losing?
- What makes one school perform better than others?
- Why are some areas of town more policed than others?
- Why do so many yards look the same?

## Social Trends

- What causes road rage? Teenage rebellion? Conformity to fashion trends?
- Why are the elderly isolated?
- Why is depression on the rise in the United States?
- Why do Americans love sport utility vehicles?
- Why does the condition of streets change throughout a city?
- Why doesn't anyone care about the future?

## Campus Issues

- Why do college students binge drink?
- Why do some students cheat? Procrastinate?
- What causes boredom?
- Why are some classes more difficult for large numbers of students?

## Politics

- Why do younger generations tend not to vote?
- Why does a certain community consistently vote Democratic or Republican?
- What has made political discourse so uncivil?

## Your Major

- What has caused the field to thrive (or deteriorate) in recent years?
- What has fueled a recent debate in the field? Why has the debate continued?
- Find the cause of a phenomenon in your field, for example:
  —*History:* a revolution, a military victory or loss
  —*Art:* a style (such as impressionism), an artistic revolution
  —*Biology:* an organism's short life span
  —*Criminal Justice:* a jury decision, a Supreme Court decision to hear a case
  —*Business Marketing:* the success or failure of a marketing campaign

## Activity

To create more topic ideas, write down what bothers you, what you do or don't like, what should be different, or what is wrong or unjust. Come up with several different ideas, and then decide on one, using the Analysis section to search for what caused it. For example, if you're bothered by littering, explore what causes people to litter.

# Analysis

Now that you have a topic (any phenomenon from the Point of Contact section), the next step is to begin searching for possible causes. (We use the term *phenomenon* here to refer to anything you are exploring—any behavior, event, situation, attitude, issue, idea, and so on.) You may already have some guesses about the cause. But keep an open mind. Any single phenomenon can be a consequence of many factors, both physical and abstract. Respond to the following questions and refer back to your notes as you continue the process.

## Invention Questions

▶ What events or behaviors led to the phenomenon?

▶ What social conditions or prevailing attitudes led (or could lead) to the phenomenon?

▶ What economic conditions led to the phenomenon?

▶ What state of mind or psychological need may have led to the phenomenon?

▶ What are all the possible reasons someone would carry out this behavior? ■

# Invention Workshop

Use one of the Invention Questions to initiate a discussion about your topic. Stay focused on the responses and keep asking questions so that your initial thoughts evolve. For example, in the following workshop, the participants take on Jack's topic: why people join cults. The conversation progresses because Jack keeps asking questions and others offer focused responses along the way. In the brief exchange, Jack moves from an obvious position to something more complex.

**What state of mind or psychological need may have led to the phenomenon?**

JACK:     These people are obviously sick—mentally ill.

DIANA:    What kind of mental illness?

JACK:     I don't know . . . probably some kind of schizophrenia or something.

DIANA:    But a lot of the people who join cults are otherwise productive members of society—with jobs, families, homes, social responsibilities. I've even heard that some cults attract people who are smarter than average. It doesn't seem like these people are downright mentally ill—at least in the way most people talk about mental illness.

JACK:     So if they aren't sick in some way, why would they possibly leave behind their families and friends, give all their money to a group of strangers, and lose their identities?

MARCUS:   Well, I've heard that a lot of those people don't have friends—they're lonely.

JACK:     How can people be lonely if they have families and jobs?

MARCUS:   Working a job and supporting a family doesn't necessarily make someone truly connected to others. Think about midlife crises—where people run out and have wild flings or buy ridiculously expensive sports cars. They're obviously unfulfilled.

JACK:     But wouldn't you say that joining a cult is a little more extreme than buying a car or having an affair?

DIANA:    Sure, but remember that a lot of people long for something more than sex and fast cars. They wonder what's out there, what their purpose is, what's beyond this life.

JACK:     And religious cults have all those answers—well, at least that's the argument.

DIANA:    Yeah, so the whole issue may be related to loneliness and longing rather than sickness.

## Thinking Further

Invention is not simply answering a few questions. Instead, it is a process of exploring, discovering, and developing ideas. Ideas that emerge from initial responses should be explored even further. For example, in his dialogue with Diana and Marcus, Jack's thinking evolves:

| | |
|---|---|
| Beginning of the dialogue: | Sick people join cults. |
| End of the dialogue: | Loneliness and longing, which run rampant in mainstream culture, drive people to wonder what they're missing. This is where cults come in. |

With this new understanding, Jack might come to more insightful conclusions about the perspective of people who join cults:

> I guess in the eyes of a potential cult member, a cult doesn't look like a cult. I mean, a group doesn't hang a "Cult" sign on the door. They don't say, "Hey!! Join our cult!! We'll all kill ourselves next year! It'll be great!!" No. A cult is merely a group of people who offer a web of relationships and a clear purpose in life. Isn't that why people go to college even though they hate it?! Isn't that why people join the Army?? A clear sense of purpose?!! Is college a kind of cult? Is the Army?!! Here's the message of both institutions: "Leave behind everything—your family, etc. Come here. Stay with us. And . . . you have to follow our strict schedule of events. But in the end, you'll be way better off." Holy crap! We're a culture of . . . cults.

Jack's continued exploration of why people join cults has taken him into new intellectual territory. He is exploring the relationship between something he thinks is dangerous (cults) and something he thinks is normal (college, the army).

Use the following questions to further explore your topic:

▶ How has your understanding of the cause developed? What new idea has entered your thinking?

▶ Why didn't you think about this before? ■

## Research

Find an outside source (a website, article, or book) about your concept. (Consult Chapter 13: Finding Sources to help you explore.) The author(s) of the source may have a different understanding of the causes. Summarize the main points of the source, then answer the following questions:

- Does the source suggest a cause for the phenomenon?
- If not, does the source imply or assume a cause?
- Does the source account for the most direct cause?
- Does the source account for indirect or multiple causes? Hidden causes?

# What caused the cause?

# Public Resonance

Some topics automatically resonate with public concerns. For example, Jamie Bentley's essay discusses how our love of consumption harms the environment, causes individual economic problems, and contributes to the breakdown of the family. But other topics may seem more difficult to connect with. Local or intensely personal topics, for instance, may seem less linked to broader concerns. Who would think that childhood vomiting could be an interesting topic or make for a valuable essay? But Leonard Kress makes his own vomiting experience resonate (in more than one way) with readers:

> My brother and sister were silent, too, as though my barfing were a perfectly acceptable alternative to an after-dinner mint, a toothpick, a wet-wipe wrapped like a condom. Perhaps they were too busy stashing away the details of the affront, safekeeping for a time of need—like Aesop's despicable, self-righteous ant. I can only imagine the hay they might have later made by simple melodramatic evocations of the sounds of my gagging, as it echoed in tiny bathrooms. The deep, throaty sound of plosively expelling vomit. "Well, whatever I did can't be as gross and disgusting as THAT," I can hear them repeating over and over till they got what they wanted. Or did they have their own equally disgusting but self-customized techniques of catharsis and orgasm back then—I wondered. Does everyone, I still wonder? And how could a "D" in French or a detention or a missed meal or a dent in the car compare with what I did, over and over and over?

In this paragraph, Kress broadens the scope, including his siblings and "everyone." He makes the connection for us: Not everyone throws up for catharsis, but, he supposes, everyone may have some technique for experiencing relief, release, or comfort. This broader scope does not mean that Kress is losing focus—he is bringing others into the issue. As a writer, he knows that his job is to invite others into his exploration, into his search for causes. Imagine how your topic involves others who are not directly associated with it.

Use the following questions to help generate a sense of public resonance for your topic:

▶ What are the effects of this phenomenon?

▶ Whom does it affect? How does it affect them?

▶ How does it affect people indirectly?

▶ How does my position or understanding relate to popular perspectives on the topic? ■

In his exploration, Leonard Kress looks outward and compares his personal search with "pop psychology." He decides that his personal experience (and intellectual response) is different from what he sees in the media. But he doesn't therefore decide that his topic has no public resonance. Instead, he decides to explore the contrast between his experience and common characterizations.

> **How does your position or understanding relate to popular perspectives on the topic?**
>
> In writing this, I guess I am caught in the popular mania of confession. I consider myself to be a fairly private person, but all around I see people (in books, articles, on TV, etc.) revealing the most personal and embarrassing details about their lives. And doing so with relish. The fact that this piece deals with childhood makes it somewhat easier, of course. This is as close as I came to a taboo subject—and it intrigues me that my experience was so different from the media and pop psychology take on eating disorders and adolescent girls.

Kress's move here is vital to academic writing: When a writer discovers contrast or tension between his own experience and that of others, he has discovered something worth exploring more—something worth writing about.

Like Kress's topic, Jack's topic of cult membership might seem to affect only specific people—cult members, their families, maybe the communities surrounding the cult. But Jack goes further than that and imagines the broader and subtler factors:

**How does it affect people indirectly?**

If people are drawn to cults through deep loneliness, then cults potentially relate to everyone—that is, anyone who cares about family, friends, the quiet neighbor, etc. Our days are filled with constant inattention to others. Most people choose their narrow paths (their jobs and their small circle of friends) and leave everyone else. Many of us will go weeks without truly acknowledging anyone outside of our little circles. Rarely do we invite the quiet guy from work out with us; rarely do we call our cousin to see how she's doing. We leave lonely people behind us every day.

Jack discovers that cults might relate to everyone. He can now explore this idea even further, examining the messages that popular culture sends to people: that we must have intense social engagement to achieve happiness and fulfillment, that solitude should be avoided, that excitement and purpose should define every minute of our lives. Jack would then be exploring the culture surrounding cults. He would be thinking like a sociologist and assuming that any one behavior is linked to a broad system of attitudes, messages, and group behaviors.

While searching for public resonance, writers might find not only public resonance but new angles on the topic. For example, if Jack's exploration of public resonance raises ideas about pop culture and social engagement, these discoveries could lead Jack to think about social networking and then about Facebook and its relationship (or similarity) to cults.

## Activities

1. Present your ideas to a small group of peers, explaining the phenomenon's cause and its public resonance. Ask group members how the phenomenon affects their lives.

2. Explain how the group discussion helped you discover and develop ideas regarding public resonance and the topic in general. What new ideas emerged and how might they help shape your essay?

# If your thinking is out of sync with conventional wisdom, you may have discovered an important insight.

# Thesis

The kind of writing done in this chapter is both analytical and argumentative. Each author offers an analysis of the topic and an argument for his or her understanding of the cause. Each has a thesis that focuses on the causes or set of causes most responsible for the phenomenon. As you consider your main point, examine all possible avenues. (You may even begin writing and drafting before your ideas take shape.) Your thesis might do any of the following:

- Argue for a particular cause.

    Professional sports have gotten more violent because of the intensity of sports coverage in the media.

- Argue that several factors equally cause the phenomenon.

    Writing proficiency among American high school students continues to diminish because of a broader cultural disinterest in reading and a fundamental misunderstanding of language.

- Argue against an apparent cause or widely held belief and for a less obvious or more complicated cause.

    People drive gas guzzlers not because they are selfish and insensitive but because they are uneducated about their real choices.

    The music industry is losing profits not because college kids are insatiable thieves but because the industry has not evolved with the listening habits of the new generation.

As you consider your topic, decide on your emphasis: will it be important to thoroughly describe several causes or to focus on one?

## Evolution of a Thesis

Your main idea may not come into focus immediately. Notice how Jack's thesis evolves from his initial thoughts into a sophisticated point.

Jack focuses on a particular phenomenon:

- What makes people leave everything and everyone behind and join cults?

He uses the Invention Questions on page 336 to probe for causes:

- *What state of mind or psychological need may have led to the phenomenon?* Some form of mental disease makes people join cults.

He works through his initial thoughts and discovers a less obvious cause:

- Deep loneliness and lack of purpose in life cause people to leave their families and join cults.

Jack struggles to integrate public resonance into his understanding of the cause:

- The deep loneliness and loss fostered by our hurried society create desperate searches for belonging and purpose, and cults sometimes fulfill those needs.

## Activity

Reflect on how your main idea, like Jack's, came into focus:

- What phenomenon did you focus on?
- What Invention Question(s) did you use to probe for causes?
- What less obvious cause did you discover?
- How did you integrate public resonance into your understanding of the cause?

# Common Thesis Problems

Perhaps the two most common thesis problems are psychological, striking before the writer ever touches a key or marks a paper.

1. **Fear of Ongoing Invention:** Some writers assume that thesis statements are fixed, unchangeable structures that must be strictly adhered to throughout a writing project. As they draft ideas and generate support for their initial point, they avoid asking hard questions and making new connections; that is, they fear continued invention once they've started drafting. But thesis statements are not traps. They are merely statements that help writers focus and intensify their thinking *as they are writing*. The human brain functions in new ways once serious writing and shaping begin; therefore, writers should allow their own writing to help them with new ideas.

2. **Fear of Commitment:** In contrast to the first fear, some writers avoid committing to a focused statement. They wander around without attempting to establish a particular idea, without digging in to a specific intellectual place. Such wandering, if it goes on for too long, often leads to shallow ideas (saying lots of different things about lots of different things). Although invention is key throughout the process, invention is not general wandering. Better ideas come when writers dig in their intellectual heels.

For more related common thesis problems, see Chapter 7, page 227.

## Revising Your Thesis

Write out responses to these questions: *Am I afraid of ongoing invention? Why? Am I afraid of commitment? Why?* Then discuss your responses with a group of classmates.

1. How many people in your group have a fear of, or resistance to, ongoing invention or commitment?
   - What reasons do group members give for their fear of, or resistance to, ongoing invention? (What caused their fear or resistance?)
   - What reasons do group members give for their fear of, or resistance to, commitment? (What caused it?)

2. Discuss how each group member arrived at his or her thesis for this chapter's essay. Which group members might have committed to a rigid thesis too early? Choose an Invention Question from earlier in the chapter that they should explore further for ongoing invention.

3. For group members who have trouble committing to one idea, help them focus their statement. Choose an Invention Question they should explore to help narrow and deepen their thoughts.

# Thesis statements are tools for narrowing and intensifying ideas.

# Rhetorical Tools

Remember that you are not simply explaining a cause. You are arguing that a particular cause (or set of causes) could be responsible for a phenomenon, and you also are arguing that your understanding of the cause/effect relationship is worth considering. Therefore, consider the support strategies of argument (from Chapter 7: Making Arguments).

The writers in this chapter use a broad range of support strategies. To support his argument, Kress depends on information from his own life. And while personal experience in the form of narration is his primary support, he also uses authorities (outside sources). Nicholas Carr also uses personal testimony (in his second paragraph, for example), then relies on various authorities to support his claims. Use the following questions to develop support for your thesis:

▶ How can I illustrate the relationship between the cause and the effect? (What line of reasoning can I use?)

▶ Does a historical event or figure help to show the cause?

▶ Can I allude to a similar phenomenon (with a similar cause) to support my point?

▶ Does a literary work (novel, poem, drama) or popular culture text (movie, television program, song) support my point?

▶ How do other writers discuss this cause?

▶ Does something in nature (in animal or plant life) support my point?

▶ Has anyone done scientific study on this phenomenon? Does it support my point?

▶ Have I witnessed or experienced someone or something that illustrates my point?

▶ Can I construct a hypothetical situation that illustrates my point? ■

## Integrating Authorities (Outside Sources)

Outside sources must be integral to your own points and carefully integrated into your argument, not just inserted. For example, notice how Carr integrates an outside source to support his personal testimony about having trouble reading:

> I'm not the only one. When I mention my troubles with reading to friends and acquaintances—literary types, most of them—many say they're having similar experiences. The more they use the Web, the more they have to fight to stay focused on long pieces of writing. Some of the bloggers I follow have also begun mentioning the phenomenon. Scott Karp, who writes a blog about online media, recently confessed that he has stopped reading books altogether. "I was a lit major in college, and used to be [a] voracious book reader," he wrote. "What happened?" He speculates on the answer: What if I do all my reading on the web not so much because the way I read has changed, i.e., I'm just seeking convenience, but because the way I THINK has changed?"

Carr introduces his main point in his own words, and then he introduces an outside source, Scott Karp, as support. Notice that Carr provides Karp's credentials: "Scott Karp, who writes a blog about online media, . . ." When using authorities as support, it is important to provide the reader with information about the source:

> Bruce Friedman, **who blogs regularly about the use of computers in medicine,** also has described how the Internet has altered his mental habits.

> But a recently published study of online research habits, **conducted by scholars from University College London,** suggests that we may well be in the midst of a sea change in the way we read and think.

But it's a different kind of reading, and behind it lies a different kind of thinking—perhaps even a new sense of the self. "We are not only *what* we read," says Maryanne Wolf, **a developmental psychologist at Tufts University and the author of** *Proust and the Squid: The Story and Science of the Reading Brain.* "We are *how* we read."

See Chapter 15: Integrating and Documenting Sources for help with this support strategy.

# Counterarguing

Counterarguments defend against opposing claims. Writers must anticipate and account for positions outside of or opposed to their own claims(s) and include reasoning to offset that potential opposition. In many cases, writers must contend directly with arguments that forward another cause. Leonard Kress, for example, argues against common views and explains the way his position differs from others'. Here, Kress points to authorities who seem to miss the mark:

> I also locate "Determinants of Adolescent Obesity: A Comparison with Anorexia Nervosa," in *Adolescence* (1988), which claims that "both anorexics and the obese are characterized by overprotectedness and enmeshment, resulting from a poor sense of identity and effectiveness." After a whole week of research, this seems to be the extent of my findings. I can find nothing to urge me to go beyond the abstracts, nothing at all, though I type in "eating disorder," "vomiting," "obesity," "abnormal psychology," "gluttony," "disgusting and destructive behavior"—always cross-referenced with "childhood."

Because Kress mentions these other causes (or other takes on the phenomenon), we get the sense that he has a broad understanding of the topic—he is not simply guessing at a cause, but has explored other possibilities. The following questions can help you develop counterarguments:

▶ What other causes could be attributed to this phenomenon? (Why are these other causes less acceptable or less valid?)

▶ What other reasons do people have for disagreeing with me?

▶ What support will most effectively respond to opposing positions? ■

# Conceding

Concessions acknowledge the value of positions or claims other than those being forwarded by the writer. Remember that a good writer (with a broad understanding of the topic) is able to concede the value of some points or qualify his or her own points well. As you consider your own argument, your own position about a cause, use the following questions to develop concessions and qualifiers:

- Are there legitimate reasons for taking another position on this topic?
- Does the argument make any large, but necessary, leaps?
- Do I ask my audience to accept generalizations?

# Invention Workshop

The goal here is to play devil's advocate—to give each writer opposing positions to consider and possibly counterargue or concede.

- Each writer should announce his or her thesis.
- Group members should take turns offering responses to the first two Invention Questions in each box on this page. Counterargument: What other causes could be attributed to this phenomenon? What other reasons do people have for disagreeing with me? Concession: Are there legitimate reasons for taking another position on this topic? Does my argument make any large, but necessary, leaps?

The goal for this workshop is to expose ideas that were hidden from writers. While it may be tempting to discuss one opposing position in depth, at this point avoid discussion or debate until all group members have responded to each essay.

# Organizational Strategies

## How Should I Begin?

An effective introduction moves the reader purposefully toward the main idea of the essay. Carr begins with an allusion:

> "Dave, stop. Stop, will you? Stop, Dave. Will you stop, Dave?" So the computer HAL pleads with the implacable astronaut Dave Bowman in a famous and weirdly poignant scene toward the end of Stanley Kubrick's *2001: A Space Odyssey*. Bowman, having nearly been sent to a deep-space death by the malfunctioning machine, is calmly, coldly disconnecting the memory circuits that control its artificial brain. "Dave, my mind is going," HAL says, forlornly. "I can feel it. I can feel it."
>
> I can feel it, too. Over the past few years I've had an uncomfortable sense that someone, or something, has been tinkering with my brain, remapping the neural circuitry, reprogramming the memory. . . .

The allusion to *2001: A Space Odyssey* moves purposefully into the point of Carr's essay. And Carr returns to the allusion at the end of the essay, using it as a framing device:

> I'm haunted by that scene in *2001*. What makes it so poignant, and so weird, is the computer's emotional response to the disassembly of its mind. . . . HAL's outpouring of feeling contrasts with the emotionlessness that characterizes the human figures in the film, who go about their business with an almost robotic efficiency. . . .

In his essay, Kress begins with a personal description of the phenomenon, which leads into his discussion of the cause:

> I remember standing breathless and exhilarated in the hotel lobby, the rest of my family still in the dining room finishing their evening meal. I'm not sure whether or not they can see what I see—the thin gray broken line on the carpet, leading all the way to the back entrance. This time I don't make it out to the patio, the swimming pool, down to the beach, inundated this summer with jellyfish and jelly lichen, Portuguese Man O'War. If only they would leave their table, they could easily find me by following the half-digested dinner rolls and the masticated but intact sirloin morsels, the bitter tomato-broth they soak in. Hansel, whom I imagine to be about my age (seven and a half), couldn't have left a better trail for him and his sister to follow back to their woodland cottage. Even if the birds had pecked it clean, that bile-stain would still remain, like a stripe dividing a country highway. We are here in Miami Beach to visit my grandparents, Ada and Max, and since they live in a tiny apartment, we are staying in this beachfront hotel, more luxurious than we are used to. It occurs to me that only the desk clerk has been following my whole grand performance with any interest. Whatever others there might be carefully and kindly turn away their gaze. But the desk clerk glances over to me and across the lobby, as if surveying both the damage and the cause of it. I recognize that smirk and wonder, was he a vomiter too? I don't have a clue and don't really care; he assiduously computes the cleaning bill.

In her opening paragraph, Bentley moves the reader steadily toward her main point. She begins with a general claim, supports that claim with an outside source, and then responds to the source with her main idea:

> Contemporary American culture has a well-documented obsession with consuming things. According to Simon Benlow, "You know how opulently we lived, how we gorged ourselves daily, how we lived beyond the means of ourselves and of the following generations" (577). Benlow states that we have "irreparably harmed the world for those beyond [our time]" (577). There is no doubt that we are harming the environment somewhat; however, more than harming the environment, this consumerist culture is causing individual economic problems and contributes to the breakdown of the family.

# How Should I Deal with Other Causes?

Other causes, those that are different from yours, can help develop counterarguments; you can argue against other causes in favor of the cause you put forth. For example, Jack may point to a possible cause of cult membership (mental illness) but refute that idea in favor of another (loneliness). In this case, the argument that mental illness causes people to join cults is an opposing position—one that the writer counters:

> Some may argue that people join cults because they are mentally ill, nuts, freaked out. It is easy to write off cult members as lunatics. They willingly cast away their families and friends, give all of their life belongings to a bunch of strangers, wear uniform-like apparel, and sometimes even cut their hair to match the group. In short, they throw away their identities, something next to insanity in a culture that honors individualism as the greatest good. However, insanity may not be the main reason people join cults. In fact, many cult members are highly intelligent, entirely reasonable, and healthy individuals. But they long for something, something that everyone longs for—belonging and purpose.

If you have potential counterarguments, remember some standard strategies from Chapter 7: Making Arguments. Counterarguments might come directly after opposing points in counterpoint, point, counterpoint, point manner. Depending on the amount of detail given to each counter, each point might be an entire paragraph, or more, with supporting evidence:

> **Opposing Point A**
> Your counterargument
>
> **Opposing Point B**
> Your counterargument
>
> **Opposing Point C**
> Your counterargument

# How Should I Transition from One Paragraph to Another?

As in all academic prose (the language that scholars use to communicate ideas), paragraphs are used to cluster information. But we should also think of paragraphs as rhetorical tools—strategies for focusing and refocusing readers' attention. In this sense, paragraphs focus readers on a single idea, point, or example. For an argument about causes, a single paragraph might focus readers on a single illustration of a cause, an outside source that argues for a particular cause, a personal narrative that coincides, or counters the outside source, or a concession to an outside perspective.

Notice how Carr helps the reader move from one idea, or paragraph, to another. For example, after providing several paragraphs of testimonial and anecdotal support, Carr moves to another type of support, a published study. He moves the reader from the anecdotal support to the published study by beginning the paragraph as follows:

> Anecdotes alone don't prove much. And we still await the long-term neurological and psychological experiments that will provide a definitive picture of how Internet use affects cognition. But a recently published study of online habits, conducted by scholars from University College London, suggests that we may well be in the midst of a sea change in the way we read and think. . . .

Carr then provides specific information from the published study. Consider how Carr uses the following sentences to lead readers from one paragraph to another:

> The Net's influence doesn't end at the edges of a computer screen, either. [Carr then explains how the Net has influenced television, magazines, and newspapers.]
>
> About the same time that Nietzsche started using his typewriter, an earnest young man named Frederick Winslow Taylor carried a stopwatch into the Midvale Steel plant in Philadelphia and began a historic series of experiments aimed at improving the efficiency of the plant's machinists. [Carr transitions from support about Nietzsche using a typewriter to another line of support about Taylor systematizing work.]

# Writer's Voice

## Creating Credibility

Good writers are inviting and curious; they avoid preachiness and hostility. They also create a sense of credibility, the quality that makes points believable. In argumentative writing, such as in this chapter, credibility is important for readers to understand and accept claims.

A credible voice is not necessarily commanding or domineering. It might simply be very logical or insightful. Some writers, such as Leonard Kress, use personal experience to build credibility. In his essay, we get the sense that he may know more about the behavior than many of the supposed experts because of his experience. It is not his reference to *The Encyclopedia of Pediatric Psychology* that gives credibility to Kress's voice; rather, it is the manner in which he uses that information to highlight his own understanding. By the time Kress discovers the important passage in the encyclopedia, he has established his own credibility:

> . . . I could simply will the partially chewed hearty chunks of meat and potato up from their sour churning stock. It felt so good! *The Encyclopedia of Pediatric Psychology* (1979) reports that children who vomit, farfetched as it sounds, even "those who have learned society's aversions . . . can overcome such scruples and experience vomiting as cathartic, even orgasmic."

Remember that you can create credibility with personal experiences as well as with others' research. In considering your own writing, ask yourself the following:

▶ How will my own experiences or insights create credibility?

▶ How might outside sources add to my credibility? ■

## Projecting Wonder

Some people assume that a sense of credibility means that the writer is unquestionable and unquestioning. However, credibility should not diminish a sense of curiosity. Even though the writers in this chapter have justification for speaking authoritatively about their topics (from research and observation), they also create a sense of curiosity, even wonder. Sometimes, the most authoritative voice is also the most curious. For example, Leonard Kress is curious even though he has reason to be certain about his claims:

> I often wonder now what led me to such disgusting behavior—what might lead any child to such disgusting behavior. Like any good 21st-century questioner/ researcher, I go to the Internet, hopeful that a search of current medical literature will provide answers and understanding. So I begin my search, seated in front of my computer.

Ask yourself the following:

▶ What about my topic is mysterious or unknown?

▶ How does my topic extend beyond usual perceptions or conventional thinking?

▶ What details or ideas associated with my topic might make the reader curious? ■

### Activity

1. In small groups, discuss how you might create credibility or project wonder for your essay.

2. Support your thesis by writing a paragraph that creates credibility or projects wonder.

3. Consider why you should or should not include the paragraph you wrote for #2 in your final essay.

# Vitality

Academic writing should be clean and intense. Sentences should be sophisticated enough to prompt intensive thinking but concise enough to keep the reader moving briskly.

## Avoid Strings of Phrases

Writers sometimes string together several prepositional phrases. (A prepositional phrase begins with a preposition, such as in, of, between, on, beside, behind, or for.) Too many prepositional phrases (even two in a row) can slow down the reader. You might think of it as a matter of momentum: verbs propel readers through sentences. So when too many phrases pile up, the sentence slows down. Without verbs, the meaning thickens, the sentence gets muddy, and the reader gets bogged down. That's why good writers avoid clustering together too many phrases.

The following sentence begins with three prepositional phrases:

> The celebration of the holiday at the end of the month will attract many tourists to the town.

If the sentence is revised to have fewer prepositional phrases, the verb (will attract) will be closer to the beginning, and the sentence becomes less muddy:

> At the end of the month, the holiday celebration will attract many tourists to the town.

A string of phrases or clauses is not always bad. Good writers sometimes line up several phrases or clauses, intentionally using the repeating pattern to reinforce ideas.

### Activity

Rewrite the following sentences, avoiding strings of prepositional phrases while keeping all the information.

1. The solving of this problem of racial segregation involves several steps that the people of the United States ought to understand.
2. Our present strategy creates the transition from imagining the world as a place full of attainable riches to thinking of the world as a place full of human resources.

## Intensify with a Series

A series of words creates a pattern for readers. When a chain of words is lined up, readers make an automatic intellectual connection. We most often see single words in a series:

> The land flattens itself out and creates a sense of openness, emptiness, and space.

But phrases can also be put in a series:

> The land flattens itself out and creates a feeling of openness, a sense of emptiness, and an eyeful of space.

Skillful writers can even put entire clauses in a series. Here, the repeating clauses create an intellectual pattern, set up a way of thinking, and pull the reader briskly through the images:

> They live in a place where the fields lie uninterrupted, where the houses take the full brunt of the wind, where the horizon simply evaporates.

## Avoid Expletives

To help keep things lively, writers delete unnecessary words, such as expletive constructions. Expletives begin with there or it and are followed by a form of to be, such as is, are, was, or were. (Note: Not every expletive construction must be replaced, and not every there or it followed by a form of to be functions as an expletive.) Notice how the following sentences can be revised to remove the expletive and make the writing more clean and intense:

> There were women who perceived such responses as belittling and unsupportive.

> Some women perceived such responses as belittling and unsupportive.

> It is these differences that begin to clarify why women and men have such different expectations about communication.

> These differences begin to clarify why women and men have such different expectations about communication.

# Revision

Now get help from other writers. Before exchanging drafts with at least one other writer, underline your main idea (your thesis) or write it at the top of your draft.

## Peer Review

**Use the following questions to respond to specific issues in the draft.**

1. Can any phrases or terms in the thesis be narrowed? If so, circle them and make some suggestions for more focus. Does the thesis avoid the common problems? (See page 341.)
2. Can you follow the writer's line of reasoning? Do you accept the cause the writer asserts? Why or why not?
3. What other support strategies could the writer employ? (Consider examples, allusions, scenarios, and so on. See pages 229 and 342.)
4. Mark any paragraphs that shift focus from one point about the subject to another.
5. If the writer uses outside sources, are they integrated smoothly into the argument? (See pages 459–465, in Chapter 15: Integrating and Documenting Sources, for specific strategies.)
6. Consider the writer's voice.
   a. Identify any passages that seem preachy.
   b. Does the writer seem credible? What passages support your decision?
   c. Identify a passage that seems flat, without intensity. Suggest a strategy for the writer to create a sense of wonder.
7. As a reviewer, point to particular sentences and phrases that could gain vitality and intensity. Use the following:
   a. Look for confusing strings of phrases. Suggest a revision.
   b. Rewrite a passage of the draft, and use a series of phrases or clauses to intensify an idea.
   c. Consider vitality strategies from other chapters:

- Look for unnecessary, interrupting clauses and phrases. Underline them and/or draw an arrow to show where the phrase or clause can be moved.
- Rewrite a sentence and create more intensity with a repeating pattern.
- Cross out wordy phrases and write in more concise options.
- What sentences are overembedded? (Point to any clauses that overlap with other clauses, causing a disconnect between ideas.)
- Examine attributive phrases. Point out unnecessary phrases or sentences that could be boiled down.
- Where can the writer change linking verbs to action verbs?
- Where can the writer avoid drawing attention to *I* and *you*?
- Help the writer change unnecessary clauses to phrases and phrases to words.
- Point to expletives (such as *there are* and *it is*).
- Help the writer change passive verbs to active verbs for more vitality.

# Reflection

Exploring and writing about a cause can have consequences for the reader, the writer, and the community as a whole. As you reflect on the causes essay you wrote for this chapter, consider its possible consequences.

1. The chapter introduction states that "people searching for causes are detectives attempting to find answers amidst a dizzying array of possibilities." As a detective, what answer did you find?
2. What rhetorical tools most help the reader understand and accept the answer you found?
3. Based on his or her new understanding, how might the reader think and behave differently? How might this behavior affect others?
4. What particular paragraph or sentence might have the strongest impact on the reader and why?
5. How does your essay contribute to an ongoing discussion, and how might it prompt the reader to make a further contribution?

## Beyond the Essay: Photo Essay

In some parts of the country, salt is put on the roads to melt snow and ice. This salt rusts cars. What point does the photo essay "Road Salt" make about this, and how does it make it? Use several images to communicate the main idea of the causes essay you wrote for this chapter. Select and arrange the images carefully and then explain in writing how the images work together to make your point.

All photos used by permission of the author

For additional resources including instructional videos and links to helpful websites, access your English CourseMate through cengagebrain.com.

# 11 Proposing Solutions

# Chapter Contents

# "All subjects, except sex, are dull until somebody makes them interesting."

—Paul Roberts

In everyday life, crisis is a constant. Problems emerge in every facet of our existence: in the work world, problems arise in working conditions, policy implementation, coworker relations, labor/management relations, and government standards; our communities face problems such as homelessness, pollution, school violence, terrorism, and urban sprawl; at home, the list of possible problems can seem endless. While many of us have the privilege of ignoring such problems, someone in some capacity has to address them. Whether elected official, shift supervisor, environmental scientist, department chair, or scout leader, someone ultimately has to address daily crises and propose solutions.

In academia, people in all disciplines have to propose solutions:

- In an engineering class, students propose solutions to structural problems in a building designed before earthquake construction codes.

- In a business class, students must convince their peers that a particular strategy for solving a company's financial problems is the most efficient.

- In a calculus class, students explore several ways to solve a problem and then convince their peers and instructor that one particular way is the best.

- For a national conference on employment trends, graduate students and faculty members propose strategies to counter the increasing demand for low-salary instructors.

When writers propose solutions to problems, they are involved in many layers of analysis. They must analyze the problem to discover its causes—some of which may lie hidden in abstraction. They must also consider all the possible ways for addressing the problem and then come to some conclusion about the most appropriate solution. Proposing solutions also involves argument: writers have to convince readers that the problem must be addressed, that action is necessary. They also must argue for the value of their particular solution. This is what politicians do for a living; members of Congress, after all, spend much of their time arguing, first, that particular problems deserve allocated funds and, second, that those funds should be used in particular ways.

You might think of proposing a solution as a double-layered argument: first, you must argue that a problem worthy of attention or action exists and, second, that a particular solution will best solve it. Proposing a solution involves all the elements of an argument (thesis, support, counterargument, and concession). And as the following essays illustrate, writers who acknowledge the true complexities of their problems and solutions will better engage their readers and will meet with less opposition. Some solutions are not necessarily complicated physical solutions, but rather simple reconsiderations—that is, new ways of thinking about familiar problems.

This chapter will help you discover a problem, develop a solution, and develop a written argument for the solution. The following essays will provide valuable insight into necessary strategies for proposing solutions. After reading the essays, you can uncover a problem in one of two ways:

1. Go to the Point of Contact section to find a problem from your everyday life, or
2. Choose one of the Ideas for Writing that follow each essay.

After finding a subject, go to the Analysis section to begin developing ideas for your essay.

# Where Anonymity Breeds Contempt

## Julie Zhuo

*As a project design manager for Facebook, Julie Zhuo studies social behavior on the Web. In this article, first published in the* New York Times, *November 29, 2010, Zhuo describes the problem of trolling and how both legal bodies and corporate entities are moving to address it. Zhuo's solution emerges from a causal analysis. In other words, she first names the primary cause of the problem before she offers sound solutions.*

There you are, peacefully reading an article or watching a video on the Internet. You finish, find it thought-provoking, and scroll down to the comments section to see what other people thought. And there, lurking among dozens of well-intentioned opinions, is a troll.

"How much longer is the media going to milk this beyond tired story?" "These guys are frauds." "Your idiocy is disturbing." "We're just trying to make the world a better place one brainwashed, ignorant idiot at a time." These are the trollish comments, all from anonymous sources, that you could have found after reading a CNN article on the rescue of the Chilean miners.

Trolling, defined as the act of posting inflammatory, derogatory or provocative messages in public forums, is a problem as old as the Internet itself, although its roots go much farther back. Even in the fourth century B.C., Plato touched upon the subject of anonymity and morality in his parable of the ring of Gyges.

That mythical ring gave its owner the power of invisibility, and Plato observed that even a habitually just man who possessed such a ring would become a thief, knowing that he couldn't be caught. Morality, Plato argues, comes from full disclosure; without accountability for our actions we would all behave unjustly.

5    This certainly seems to be true for the anonymous trolls today. After Alexis Pilkington, a 17-year-old Long Island girl, committed suicide earlier this year, trolls descended on her online tribute page to post pictures of nooses, references to hangings and other hateful comments. A better-known example involves Nicole Catsouras, an 18-year-old who died in a car crash in California in 2006. Photographs of her badly disfigured body were posted on the Internet, where anonymous trolls set up fake tribute pages and in some cases e-mailed the photos to her parents with subject lines like "Hey, Daddy, I'm still alive."

Psychological research has proven again and again that anonymity increases unethical behavior. Road rage bubbles up in the relative anonymity of one's car. And in the online world, which can offer total anonymity, the effect is even more pronounced. People—even ordinary, good people—often change their behavior in radical ways. There's even a term for it: the online disinhibition effect.

Many forums and online communities are looking for ways to strike back. Back in February, Engadget, a popular technology review blog, shut down its commenting system for a few days after it received a barrage of trollish comments on its iPad coverage.

Many victims are turning to legislation. All 50 states now have stalking, bullying or harassment laws that explicitly include electronic forms of communication. Last year, Liskula Cohen, a former model, persuaded a New York judge to require Google to reveal the identity of an anonymous blogger who she felt had defamed her, and she has now filed a suit against the blogger. Last month, another former model, Carla Franklin, persuaded a judge to force YouTube to reveal the identity of a troll who made a disparaging comment about her on the video-sharing site.

But the law by itself cannot do enough to disarm the Internet's trolls. Content providers, social networking platforms and community sites must also do their part by rethinking the systems they have in place for user commentary so as to discourage—or disallow—anonymity. Reuters, for example, announced that it would start to block anonymous comments and require users to register with their names and e-mail addresses in an effort to curb "uncivil behavior."

10    Some may argue that denying Internet users the ability to post anonymously is a breach of their privacy and freedom of expression. But until the age of the Internet, anonymity was a rare thing. When someone spoke in public, his audience would naturally be able to see who was talking.

Others point out that there's no way to truly rid the Internet of anonymity. After all, names and e-mail addresses can be faked. And in any case many commenters write things that are rude or inflammatory under their real names.

But raising barriers to posting bad comments is still a smart first step. Well-designed commenting systems should also aim to highlight thoughtful and valuable opinions while letting trollish ones sink into oblivion.

The technology blog Gizmodo is trying an audition system for new commenters, under which their first few comments would be approved by a moderator or a trusted commenter to ensure quality before anybody else could see them. After a successful audition, commenters can freely post. If over time they impress other trusted commenters with their contributions, they'd be promoted to trusted commenters, too, and their comments would henceforth be featured.

Disqus, a comments platform for bloggers, has experimented with allowing users to rate one another's comments and feed those ratings into a global reputation system called Clout. Moderators can use a commenter's Clout score to "help separate top commenters from trolls."
15    At Facebook, where I've worked on the design of the public commenting widget, the approach is to try to replicate real-world social norms by emphasizing the human qualities of conversation. People's faces, real names and brief biographies ("John Doe from Lexington") are placed next to their public comments, to establish a baseline of responsibility.

Facebook also encourages you to share your comments with your friends. Though you're free to opt out, the knowledge that what you say may be seen by the people you know is a big deterrent to trollish behavior.

This kind of social pressure works because, at the end of the day, most trolls wouldn't have the gall to say to another person's face half the things they anonymously post on the Internet.

Instead of waiting around for human nature to change, let's start to rein in bad behavior by promoting accountability. Content providers, stop allowing anonymous comments. Moderate your comments and forums. Look into using comment services to improve the quality of engagement on your site. Ask your users to report trolls and call them out for polluting the conversation.

In slowly lifting the veil of anonymity, perhaps we can see the troll not as the frightening monster of lore, but as what we all really are: human.

Jennifer Daniel and Sandi Daniel

# Writing Strategies

1. Explain how anonymity figures into the problem of trolling.

2. In ¶3 and 4, Zhuo alludes to the ring of Gyges. Explain how that allusion helps to support Zhuo's main claim about anonymity.

3. How do the model's lawsuits (referenced in ¶8) help to establish the nature of the problem—and the nature of Zhuo's solution?

4. Zhuo engages opposing positions in quick fashion. Explain the particular opposing positions that Zhuo anticipates. How does she counter or concede to these positions?

5. Zhuo's conclusion suggests that the problem emerges from something fundamental in human nature. Explain how her conclusion makes you rethink the problem.

# Exploring Ideas

1. Zhuo says that Facebook is attempting to "establish a baseline of responsibility." Explain how Facebook's solution directly addresses the cause of trolling.

2. Trolling has become a significant trend. In other words, it's not just a few bad people. Are Plato and Zhuo correct about the immense power of anonymity? Are there other causes behind this trend?

3. How is trolling a social problem? In other words, how does it affect us all—beyond the specific victims?

4. What is the closest you've come to trolling or cyberbullying? Are you willing to explain your behavior?

5. Re-read ¶5. What should happen to people who torture the parents of dead children?

# Ideas for Writing

1. Can you think of another strategy for solving trolling and cyberbullying? Make a case for a specific solution to these behaviors.

2. What other, perhaps more subtle, behaviors have you witnessed on social networking sites? Consider a particular problematic behavior and its effects on users.

If responding to one of these ideas, go to the Analysis section of this chapter to begin developing ideas for your essay.

# Attending to the Word

## Deirdre Mahoney

Our culture's response to illiteracy and low academic performance has involved sweeping proposals: more standardized testing, more teacher accountability, required master's degrees for all K–12 teachers, better buildings, newer textbooks, more administrators, no more art and music classes, and so on. But writing instructor Deirdre Mahoney invites us to look very closely at reading. In this argument, we are invited to analyze the act of reading, to understand the intellectual nuances of engaging text. And then, we might more readily accept a less sweeping, more elegantly basic solution. Portions of Mahoney's invention work are shown throughout this chapter.

Today's college students are suffering, and unnecessarily so. I see them arrive in my writing classes each semester eager and determined, but all too often the motivation and passion dissipate when they come face-to-face with—well—words on the page. This is distressing for both them and me. My students are not illiterate by any means, as they successfully broke the code of sound-to-symbol in the earliest elementary years. Since that time, they've continued to learn in public and private school systems or they've been home-schooled. They're educated and plenty adept at moving through the system. But I'm not convinced any of this means they are capable of truly committing to a book, an essay, or any document requiring sustained focus and labor-intensive thinking and doing. And what interferes most with their abilities to focus and commit? Lack of a pencil in hand while attempting to read, contemplate, and retain the text on the page.

When I tell my students the only way to read a book is with pencil gliding freely across the page (no highlighters please), they look stymied. Selected passages ought to be underlined, I maintain, and tricky vocabulary circled. Further, I suggest that handwritten symbols in the form of stars, asterisks, squiggly lines, question marks, brackets, and the like warrant placement alongside their personal comments posted in the margins. After all, the white space on the printed page could use the company. My students offer good enough reasons, however, for *not*

writing in their books: (1) Writing in books during the K–12 years is absolutely taboo, they tell me, and they've been successfully trained to do as told; (2) Some college bookstores won't buy back textbooks with extensive personalized annotations and markings. Students need cash at semester's end, so they dutifully comply. But how is any of this non-writing good for thinking and learning? I'm pretty sure it's not. We might find the current state of affairs particularly worrisome if we frame the problem this way: In an attempt to educate, it seems that educators and a whole lot of other well-meaning adults have worked successfully to ensure disengagement with the printed word, often during the most formative and critical years of literacy acquisition.

"Don't write in the book." Even though I remain convinced this is perfectly awful advice, the mantra remains standard, announcing itself from every corner of our culture. A few years back Kathie Coblentz, New York Public Library cataloger and author of *The New York Public Library Guide to Organizing a Home Library,* disclosed to a *New York Times* reporter her penchant for scribbling notes on the pages of books in her *private* collection. My elation was short-lived when the reporter amiably cautioned readers *not* to do the same (Braden). But why not, especially if the scribbler is also the owner? Think about this (mis)guiding principle for a moment and you too may share my distress and bewilderment.

I've been scribbling in books for years (lightly and in pencil, I might add) but I'm not nearly as self-disciplined as bibliophile Kathie Coblentz, as I write in books I borrow from libraries. There. I've said it. At a later date, I sometimes borrow the book again and am greeted by my previously penciled notes still etched softly in the margins. Two important things seem to occur in this moment. First, I'm promptly reacquainted with my previous thoughts and, second, I'm often surprised at how much my thinking has shifted since the previous visit to the page, a sure sign that the human mind is in a constant state of making meaning as it constructs and then reconstructs itself.

5    So, I think the problem is clear. Our system of educating, parenting, and nurturing unwittingly conspires to ensure students' disciplined detachment from words on the page. In other words, creating disengaged adults begins early. My proposal is simple and not particularly original,

From Deirdre Mahoney, "Attending to the Word." Reprinted with permission.

but I'll reiterate it nonetheless. Those of us committed to raising and teaching need to raise and teach differently. For starters, we need to insist that from the earliest stages of literacy acquisition all humans—especially the tiniest in size and age—be invited to scribble fervently as they explore books. If we take into account the opening statement in Maryanne Wolf's *Proust and the Squid: The Story and Science of the Reading Brain,* it becomes apparent that humans could use an assist. Wolf avows forebodingly, "We were never born to read" (3). Ditto for writing. Out of necessity, it seems, resourceful adults looking for ways to enhance overtaxed memories found their way to literate practices. In doing so, the human brain began to evolve in ways probably not intended in the original blueprint. That is, in the process of teaching oneself to read and write, the brain began to reinvent itself, thus enhancing human development and evolution. Experts concur that coding and decoding symbols enhances thought and consciousness, which in turn literally alters brain matter. In other words, what we do with our brains determines what our minds are or what they might become.

We are born with the capacity for language built into our genetic code. It's simple enough. People aim to foster human connection, and speech makes itself apparent in children eager to converse soon after birth. Without any overt instruction, the youngest of tots uses speech to assert needs and preferences, often doing so in the form of the familiar toddler command: "More cookie" or "Me hold you." In short order, the toddler strings phrases together and begins to verbalize incessantly with anyone willing to stop and chat a bit. So the advent of spoken language seems straightforward enough, but literacy acquisition, or the ability to read and write, remains a stellar unintended achievement and a considerable cognitive coup if there ever were one. Depending on how we do the math, our ability to pen language goes back five thousand years or so, half that if we're talking specifically about the creation of the Roman alphabet. If we consider that humans were vocalizing perhaps as far back as one hundred thousand years before stumbling on to technologies for capturing memory in print, we recognize the veritable brevity of the written word. And although a relatively recent human innovation, the written word has enhanced the mind's cognitive prowess.

Again, in *Proust and the Squid,* Wolf writes, "Reading can be learned only because of the brain's plastic design, and when reading takes place, that individual brain is forever changed, both physiologically and intellectually" (5). In his essay "Writing Is a Technology that Restructures Thought," esteemed twentieth-century theorist Walter Ong informs the reader, "[W]riting is utterly invaluable and indeed essential for the realization of fuller, interior, human potentials. Technologies are not mere exterior aids but also interior transformation of consciousness . . ." (23). Neuroscientist and Nobel Prize winner Eric R. Kandel confirms in his memoir *In Search of Memory: The Emergence of a New Science and Mind* that "Today, most philosophers of mind agree that what we call consciousness derives from the physical brain . . ." (378). Kandel cautions, however, that all this business of consciousness is "more complicated than any property of the brain we understand" (379). Current neuroscience, complete with functional magnetic resonance imaging (fMRI) and other fancy tools, seems to substantiate Ong's and Kandel's claims. So if the specialists are correct in their collective assertion that literate acts transform consciousness (we might call it "knowingness") and brain construction, why would anyone choose to read a text *without* a pencil grasped firmly in hand? Why not enthusiastically dot the text with penciled symbols and words as matter of habit? More importantly, why wouldn't the "pencil to page" mantra become the preferred teaching strategy of parents and educators everywhere?

I'm passionate about penciling, but this doesn't mean I disapprove of today's sophisticated technologies. Not at all. Like most, I often wonder how we functioned effectively before the arrival of the word processor, cable television, fancy phones, and the Internet. No doubt about it: Current technologies provide us with unprecedented speed and convenience, perfectly timed supports for life in the twenty-first century. I'm grateful every day for their availability; however, the loyal pencil, an archaic invention if there ever were one, continues to garner my full support. The graphite-enhanced wooden stick offers definite advantages. It slows my reading and thinking, allowing opportunity to interact more purposefully with words on the page. Additionally, I'm sure the sensual aspect of sharpened graphite pressing softly against textured paper plays a key role in arousing the neurons. The pencil draws me into the text and invites my active participation, and when my voice appears as light markings on the page it becomes clear that I've assumed my required role in the conversation. The bright yellow #2 meandering along the page ushers me from passivity to activity. Call me sentimental or just demanding, but I want my students to join me in leaving traces on pages. After all, what might be lost in the process? Certainly not enhanced brain development, sustained focus, or heightened awareness. Let the scribbling begin.

## Works Cited

Braden, Carole. "A Bibliophile, 3,600 Friends, and a System." *New York Times.* New York Times, 10 Feb. 2005. Web. 6 Apr. 2008.

Kandel, Eric R. *In Search of Memory: The Emergence of the New Science of Mind.* New York: Norton, 2006. Print.

Ong, Walter. "Writing Is a Technology That Restructures Thought." *Literacy: A Critical Sourcebook.* Ed. Ellen Cushman, Eugene R. Kintgen, Barry M. Kroll, and Mike Rose. Boston: Bedford, 2001. 19–31. Print.

Wolf, Maryanne. *Proust and the Squid: The Story and Science of the Reading Brain.* New York: Harper, 2007. Print.

present in the act of grasping the use and yet isn't present.—For we say that there isn't any doubt that we understand the word, and on the other hand its meaning lies in its use. There is no doubt that I now want to play chess, but chess is the game it is in virtue of all its rules (and so on). Don't I know, then, which game I want to play until I *have* played it? or are all the rules contained in my act of intending? Is it experience that tells me that this sort of game is the usual consequence of such an act of intending? so is it impossible for me to be certain what I am intending to do? And if that is nonsense—what kind of super-strong connexion exists between the act of intending and the thing intended?——Where is the connexion effected between the sense of the expression "Let's play a game of chess" and all the rules of the game?—Well, in the list of rules of the game, in the teaching of it, in the day-to-day practice of playing.

198. "But how can a rule shew me what I have to do at *this* point? Whatever I do is, on some interpretation, in accord with the rule."— That *is* not what we ought to say, but rather: any interpretation still hangs in the air along with what it interprets, and cannot give it any support. Interpretations by themselves do not determine meaning.

"Then can whatever I do be brought into accord with the rule?"— Let me ask this: what has the expression of a rule—say a sign-post—got to do with my actions? What sort of connexion is there here?— Well, perhaps this one: I have been trained to react to this sign in a particular way, and now I do so react to it.

But that is only to give a causal connexion; to tell how it has come about that we now go by the sign-post; not what this going-by-the-sign really consists in. On the contrary; I have further indicated that a person goes by a sign-post only in so far as there exists a regular use of sign-posts, a custom.

199. Is what we call "obeying a rule" something that it would be possible for only *one* man to do, and to do only *once* in his life?— This is of course a note on the grammar of the expression "to obey a rule".

To understand a sentence means to understand understand a language means to be master of a techn

200. It is, of course, imaginable that two peopl tribe unacquainted with games should sit at a che through the moves of a game of chess; and even with mental accompaniments. And if *we* were to see it w were playing chess. But now imagine a game o according to certain rules into a series of actions ordinarily associate with a *game*—say into yells and And now suppose those two people to yell and stam ing the form of chess that we are used to; and t that their procedure is translatable by suitable rul chess. Should we still be inclined to say they wer What right would one have to say so?

201. This was our paradox: no course of actic mined by a rule, because every course of action c accord with the rule. The answer was: if everythir to accord with the rule, then it can also be made ou And so there would be neither accord nor conflict l

It can be seen that there is a misunderstanding her that in the course of our argument we give one another; as if each one contented us at least for a thought of yet another standing behind it. Wha there is a way of grasping a rule which is *not* an *inte* is exhibited in what we call "obeying the rule" and in actual cases.

Hence there is an inclination to say: every actic rule is an interpretation. But we ought to restrict t tion" to the substitution of one expression of the

202. And hence also 'obeying a rule' is a practi is obeying a rule is not to obey a rule. Hence it is a rule 'privately': otherwise thinking one was obe the same thing as obeying it.

# Writing Strategies

1. Closely examine Mahoney's introduction. How does the first paragraph focus our attention on a particular aspect of a broader problem? In your own words, explain how this problem is more specific than illiteracy.

2. Trace the logic of the essay (the line of reasoning) and explain each intellectual step leading to the solution.

3. In ¶5, Mahoney refers to a source (Wolf) and then extends the point: "Wolf avows forebodingly, 'We were never born to read' (3). Ditto for writing." Why is this step critical to Mahoney's line of reasoning?

4. How does Mahoney's use of personal testimony fit into the argument? (Could the argument function without that testimony?)

5. Focus on particular passages in which Mahoney deals with some opposing position or concern. Describe her tactic. How does she deal with that opposition? Does she deflect, take apart, destroy, neutralize, calm, or something else?

# Exploring Ideas

1. Mahoney claims that most of her students have learned how to "move through the system" of education without really attending to language. How does this resonate with your own experience? Why is simply "moving through the system" a bad thing?

2. In Mahoney's words, "Our system of educating, parenting, and nurturing unwittingly conspires to ensure students' disciplined detachment from words on the page. In other words, creating disengaged adults begins early." Give a specific example of a practice or scholastic behavior that encourages students to be detached "from words on the page."

3. After walking us through her line of reasoning, Mahoney wonders: "So if the specialists are correct in their collective assertion that literate acts transform consciousness (we might call it 'knowingness') and brain construction, why would anyone choose to read a text *without* a pencil grasped firmly in hand?" Try to imagine why people would choose to read without a pencil in hand. What reasons, besides those Mahoney counters, might people have for ignoring her solution?

4. Mahoney argues that reading with a pencil "slows [her] reading and thinking, allowing opportunity to interact more purposefully with words on the page." What type of opportunity is this? What is *opportunity* during the reading process?

5. Describe the specific way that you attend to text. Do you skim, occasionally skim, or read closely? How would you characterize your interaction with words on the page? Are they strangers passing by? Are they people you're desperately trying to know?

# Ideas for Writing

1. Point out and attempt to solve another particular layer or aspect of illiteracy in America.

2. What other problem could be solved with something elegantly simple—like a pencil?

If responding to one of these ideas, go to the Analysis section of this chapter to begin developing ideas for your essay.

# Reverence for Food

## Rachel Schofield

Writers, thinkers, activists, parents, and some politicians have argued about America's bad diet for years. Thousands of voices jeer junk food, fast food, and fake food. So Rachel Schofield, who wrote the following essay for her first-year college writing course, works to show a new dimension to a common argument. She does not simply reinforce what readers likely know about junk food; instead, she reveals a problem with the way mainstream culture views and obsesses over food.

**Writing Strategies**

**Exploring Ideas**

The typical American meal today is fast and convenient. Microwave dinners, frozen pizza, hot pockets, fast food, soda. It's mostly fake food, even though our waistlines seem to say otherwise. Economists and historians agree that the advent of processed foods after World War II contributed to the downfall of the family farm and rise of the factory farm. And many argue that it has also contributed, if not outright caused, America's current obesity epidemic. But we've heard these arguments before.

*Acknowledges and then goes beyond the usual arguments about obesity and diet.*

Aside from the obvious health and economic concerns, what are the deeper consequences of eating such processed foods? America's food system, with its fast convenience foods, disconnects us from food's source, resulting in less reverence for food and decreased respect for nature itself.

*It's more than obesity and bad diets. It's disconnection from the earth.*

Historically, humans have worshipped the earth and gods of agriculture and fertility. There is a common myth among many cultures that the earth is the giver of life, and in a very literal sense, it is true. Food comes from the earth, and we require it for sustenance. Many great civilizations flourished under these gods, recognizing their connection to the earth and giving thanks for its sacred bounty. In the past, we revered the earth, nature, and food because we could directly see that our lives depended on them. Most of the population worked the fields and witnessed the divinity of the soil as it miraculously produced their daily bread. Today our lives still depend on nature's produce, but most of us have lost our connection. In losing our reverence, we have allowed for the birth of Frankenfoods.

*Appeal to tradition: our ancestors may have had the right relationship to the earth.*

*Because we no longer value nature, we've created monstrous foods. We're playing God . . . and failing.*

Jump forward (or should I say backward?), and today's food is fast, cheap, and easy. The prostitute of processed food has replaced the revered goddesses who once nurtured our crops. Our blind faith in science has led us to a world where humans re-create in the lab what already exists in nature. We mutilate the natural into virtually unrecognizable forms. Enter high-fructose

*The writer builds up the point with her own line of reasoning before giving the info from the source.*

*Prostitute vs. goddess (the powerless versus the powerful).*

corn syrup—a highly processed, unnatural liquid. A complicated and convoluted method of chemical alchemy is utilized to create this all-too-artificial sweetener:

> First, cornstarch is treated with alpha-amylase to produce shorter chains of sugars called polysaccharides. Alpha-amylase is industrially produced by a bacterium, usually *Bacillus sp.* Next, an enzyme called glucoamylase breaks the sugar chains down even further to yield the simple sugar glucose. Unlike alpha-amylase, glucoamylase is produced by *Aspergillus,* a fungus, in a fermentation vat where one would likely see little balls of *Aspergillus* floating on the top. The third enzyme, glucose-isomerase . . . converts glucose to a mixture of about 42 percent fructose and 50–52 percent glucose with some other sugars mixed in . . . liquid chromatography takes the mixture to 90 percent fructose. Finally, this is back-blended with the original mixture to yield a final concentration of about 55 percent fructose. . . . (Forristal)

*Brings the info from the source to a crescendo.*

If we literally are what we eat, then we're all full of junk.

As unappetizing as vats of floating fungus and bacterial enzymes may sound, Americans are blissfully consuming more and more of this revolting substance. "Since its introduction in the early 1970s, the cheap sweetener's use has jumped 4,000 percent; it's now showing up in everything from sodas to steak sauce" (Callahan). Our food comes more and more from chemical concoctions rather than the earth; we have lost our sense of connection with the very thing that sustains us. We make the distance between life-giving nature and ourselves greater through over-processing our food. In some kind of strange twist of logic, we actually make our food less nutritious.

*Again, the paragraph builds to a climactic statement.*

*Our food choices are increasingly illogical . . . and weird.*

5    Food still enables us to survive, but we no longer revere it. Some would disagree, citing the weight problems engorging our country. We see food 24/7 on TV, hear about it on the radio, see it advertised on billboards, and even in Internet pop-ups. Advertising works. We buy what we see, yet the low nutrition levels in our highly processed foods leave our bodies starving for more, and we only give them more junk. We can see the preeminence of food in the dedication of temples to food all along our highways; fast food chains are more popular than ever. However, there is a difference between obsession with food and reverence for it. Our fast food restaurants and freezer aisles are brothels where impure, chemically altered food is bought and sold. Almost gone are the days when honest, unadulterated food can be purchased by the American family.

*A turnabout paragraph of sorts!*

*Obsession with fake food ≠ reverence for the real thing.*

How can Americans have reverence for food when we have so many artificial consumables surrounding us? And to complicate the problem, "Compare the price of a grapefruit to that of a pack of strawberry-flavored Twizzlers" (Zinczenko). It seems that processed food is almost always cheaper and more accessible than wholesome fresh foods. What can a struggling American family do when the only thing they can afford is cheap processed food?

So . . . we can't revere what's fake.

The quote supports this step in the line of reasoning: Americans are stuck in our obsession with fake food.

David Zinczenko of *Men's Health* proposes that we put a sin tax on unhealthy and unnatural foods. What if "OJ cost less than that *high-fructose* horror known as Sunny Delight? Wouldn't America be a little bit healthier?" (Zinczenko) But a tax on the powerful agribusiness industry, with its already entrenched team of lobbyists in Washington, seems a long way off. Eric Roston of *Time* magazine states: "Although U.S. taxpayers subsidize American farmers generously—to the tune of $20 billion a year—that's not likely to change anytime soon. Besides, corn is so cheap that even a farm policy that doubled the crop's price might make only a marginal difference in grocery-store prices."

Turnabout paragraph: an alternative solution and its potential shortcoming.

A new tax won't solve the problem.

Another solution comes from Arkansas governor Mike Huckabee. He has proposed "a plan whereby food stamps would be worth more when they're applied to healthy foods" (Zinczenko). This is a great idea, and I commend the governor for doing so. But this is just a superficial jab. It does not address the origin of the problem: lack of reverence for nature and food.

Another turnabout paragraph: an alternative solution and its shortcoming.

A real solution has to go to the root of the problem.

The ultimate cure for our lack of connection to nature would be for each person to grow his or her own food. We would be in the fields, dealing directly with the earth itself. We would relearn the lost art of cultivation: how to care for the earth and provide for its needs so it can do likewise for us. One-on-one interaction with nature herself would be the best way of rejuvenating our reverence for food. However, this ideal is neither practical nor possible for the vast majority of people. Why is that so? Because we would have to drastically alter our consumer lifestyles. We would have to take time out of our busy day and spend it at what many see as the mundane task of digging in the dirt.

Another turnabout: explains the ideal and why it won't work.

The ideal never seems to work out.

10    Before we can begin, we must change the way that we think about the earth. It is not some dead mass of matter, but rather a complex interconnection of life. Far from being boring, farming is an entrance into life itself. We can begin to take baby steps toward the ideal. Americans can buy food from their local organic stores. Better yet, they could get to know the people who grow their food. And, whenever possible, Americans should start their own gardens. Once we experience its creation firsthand, it is almost impossible not to have a healthy respect for all the time, effort, and hope embodied in the art of farming.

The solution to our food problem: change our thinking about the earth itself!

The solution is qualified—in "baby steps." This is more acceptable than a grand recalibration of all food items.

## Works Cited

Callahan, Maureen. "Sugar Smack." *Health* Oct. 2006: 150–152. *Academic Search Elite.* Web. 28 Mar. 2007.

Forristal, Linda Joyce. "The Murky World of High Fructose Corn Syrup." *Weston A. Price.* Weston A. Price Foundation, 3 Dec. 2003. Web. 27 Mar. 2007.

Roston, Eric. "The Corn Connection." *Time* 7 June 2004: 83. *Academic Search Elite.* Web. 28 Mar. 2007.

Zinczenko, David. "Food Fight!" *Men's Health* 1 June 2006: 22+. *Academic Search Elite.* Web. 28 Mar. 2007.

# Writing Strategies

1. How does Schofield get us to see something beyond the obvious: that junk food is bad?

2. How are appeals to value operating in Schofield's argument?

3. What is Schofield's line of reasoning? Trace the backbone of the argument—its basic steps—through the paragraphs and characterize each step in one sentence.

4. What is Schofield's solution? How does it address the cause of the problem?

5. How does Schofield deal with opposing positions? Point to particular passages in which she counters or concedes.

# Exploring Ideas

1. Schofield argues that other solutions, such as Governor Huckabee's, are "superficial." Why is it important to discover the origin, the root cause, of a problem before proposing a solution?

2. Schofield argues that the solution begins with an intellectual change: "Before we can begin, we must change the way that we think about the earth." How is such a change possible?

3. Why do you suppose "we" (mainstream Americans) have lost reverence for the earth, for nature, for real food? What particular cultural, economic, or political forces caused this?

4. In everyday life, we are invited to revere flags, sports heroes, politicians, our alma maters, and sometimes religious figures. What would it mean to revere food? And who might take offense at this notion?

5. Schofield makes a distinction between obsession and reverence. In your own words, how would you describe that distinction? What is the fundamental difference between obsessing and revering?

# Ideas for Writing

1. Schofield argues that mainstream American culture has forsaken food. What other basic or fundamental thing has mainstream American culture forsaken? What problem has this created? How do we solve it?

2. What other specific social problem can we solve simply by readjusting our perspective?

If responding to one of these ideas, go to the Analysis section of this chapter to begin developing ideas for your essay.

# INVENTION

"No problem can withstand the assault of sustained thinking."

—Voltaire

For this chapter, your topic will be a particular problem—some situation that needs to be changed or an idea that needs to be rethought. Be wary of global problems like hunger, poverty, or racism. They are not unapproachable or unsolvable, but such big problems usually have local or particular expressions, and it is the local or particular that is often the most appropriate place to start. Focusing on a particular problem also sets the ground for a manageable solution. For example, solving financial difficulty for single-parent students is more manageable than solving poverty in general.

The following sections are designed to help you through the invention process: specifically, to discover a problem (in Point of Contact), to develop an understanding of its causes and develop a possible solution (in Analysis), to make it relevant to a community of readers (in Public Resonance), to develop a focused statement about the problem and solution (in Thesis), and to develop support for your argument (in Rhetorical Tools). The Invention Questions in each section are not meant to be answered directly in your final written assignment. They will, however, help you to think further into your topic, to develop intense claims and insightful points.

# Point of Contact

Social problems are not necessarily physical or material; they can be intellectual, spiritual, or psychological. Consider problems related to bad policies (all first-year students must live on campus), narrow thinking (a government administration that assumes energy must come from fossil fuels), or troubled systems (a bureaucracy in which all decisions must be made at the executive level before action can be taken).

Writers often do best with topics with which they are familiar, or with which they can become familiar. To discover particular problems, consider the different circles of your life. Use the following suggestions and questions to help dig up a problem that you, as a writer, witness or experience, and attempt to see problems that others might disregard. See the problems that lurk behind the obvious. If one of the suggestions prompts you to see a problem, begin by recording details—that is, try to explain the particulars of the problem.

## School

- Are students missing too many classes?
- Do my instructors communicate poorly with students?
- Are my peers lazy?
- Are enough courses offered to students?
- Do instructors give enough or too many exams?
- Did my high school education adequately prepare me for college?
- Is the curricular gap between high school and college too wide?

## Community

- Are the elderly people in my family or community isolated?
- Do people in my neighborhood ignore one another?
- Are there too few animals in people's lives? (Too many?)
- Does traffic in my community interfere with daily life?
- Are billboards tasteless or boring?
- Are there too many chain stores or strip malls in my community?

## Government

- Does the city government do enough for children? For senior citizens?
- Does state government overlook the particular needs of my community?
- Are citizens sufficiently involved in local government?
- Do average citizens know how tax dollars are spent?
- Are there enough minorities in public office?

## Television

- Is prime-time television too adolescent?
- Are sports televised too often?
- Is there something wrong with the way sports are televised?
- Are talk shows tasteless, moronic, or disrespectful?
- Has art been abandoned by popular culture?

## Your major

- What are the problems related to employment in my field?
- What about job security? Safety for the workers? Safety for the public?
- Do people enter the major or career field for the wrong reasons?

## Activity

Now go beyond these suggestions. In groups or alone, develop more strategies for encountering and exploring social problems. Imagine what might be wrong, or what can be better than it is.

# Analysis

## Problems

Any solution must address the causes of a problem. There-fore, analyzing a problem to discover all possible causes is essential to developing a good solution. Often the causes of a problem are not clear, however. A problem may origi-nate from an abstract source, such as a long tradition, a widely held attitude, or a flawed assumption. And writers must search through such abstractions to find the possible causes. To understand the full complexities of your problem, respond to the following questions:

## Invention Questions

▶ What are the causes of the problem?

▶ What are the most troubling or alarming images associated with the problem?

▶ What are its short-term effects? Long-term effects?

▶ What other situation (event, attitude) does this prob-lem resemble? ∎

In her invention writing, Deirdre Mahoney explores her topic: students' inability to read intensively and critically. Her own language takes her somewhere. Here, she discovers that the problem is one of commitment—or even the rela-tionship her students have with text:

> **What are the most troubling or alarming images associ-ated with the problem?**
>
> Here's what's troubling and distressing: Each semester I meet many college students who mean well and want to succeed but who are entirely removed from the printed word. That is, they know how to read . . . to a point. These students often associate reading with glancing or skimming and that's it. Sometimes they skip the reading assignments entirely. So here we have it—adults who really don't understand what it means at all to commit to a text. These are students who don't fully realize that decoding sophisticated texts (or even somewhat sophis-ticated texts or even just slightly sophisticated texts) will take focus and self-discipline and perhaps, even, a whole lot of time. They don't seem to fully understand that engaging in literate practices, especially on the college level, requires all kinds of ongoing, serious application and hard work. Really hard work.

> **What are its short-term effects? Long-term effects?**
>
> The effects are complicated. Often it takes students weeks into a semester before they come to terms with the gravity of the situation. Until that time, they may continue to do the same exercise day in and day out (glancing and skimming), hoping for a different outcome—that of the easily earned revelation. But, of course, success doesn't work that way. Significant challenges most often require commitment to a task not easily begun or completed. So, what are the short-term effects? Failure, decimated confi-dence, learned helplessness, and hopelessness.
>
> Generally speaking, college students who commit—who are willing to attend to words on the page and to embrace the challenge of analyzing a text seriously and laboriously—can begin to train their minds to function differently and more effectively. They might begin to experience access to ideas that they've previously not had the abilities to know or retain. They might discover liberation, confidence, and their own abilities—they might come to understand that the human mind can be trained.

## Research

You may respond to the Invention Questions on different levels, first providing your own initial responses and then gathering information from outside sources. Such sources may include friends, coworkers, family members, websites, articles, and books. (Consult Chapters 13 and 14 to help you explore.) As you research, look not just for ideas that support your initial responses but, more importantly, for ideas that might change the way you think.

# Solutions

Before settling on a solution, consider how the solution will work, how it will address the causes of the problem, and how it might fail. Answers to the following questions will be vital to developing your solution and to making it persuasive to readers. While you will benefit from understanding all of the following issues, your readers may need some points emphasized over others. Ask yourself what points seem least obvious, or most debatable, to your audience. Respond to the following questions to develop your solution:

▶ What action (solution) will best address the causes of the problem?

▶ What might stand in the way of this solution?

▶ How will the solution change the situation?

▶ Does this solution have potential shortcomings or limitations? ■

Again, Mahoney's invention writing takes her thinking into the complexities. She begins with the most fundamental acts of learning to read:

**What action will best address the causes of the problem?**

We need a culture shift. We need to think differently about the printed word and our relationship to it. We need to assume that we are always teaching reading and learning how to read throughout our lives—just as we do in the earliest stages of development. Three-year-olds read the same book over and over. They request we read it to them over and over. They want to retell it over and over. They read it (in their own way) to themselves over and over. Three-year-olds seem to understand the notion of tenacity and commitment. We need to do a better job of teaching students that reading and thinking are labor-intensive, by design.

We must allow students the right to underline and scribble in books.

**What might stand in the way of this solution?**

Students, often to their credit, are managing too much at once. Where I teach, many must earn money to put themselves through school and pay the bills. Their academic schedules are full, and they allot themselves so much time for this course and that course. So it's important to point out that students are not afraid to take on significant challenges, but I think what they don't fully understand is that they have to adopt a different vision for themselves—they must begin to imagine themselves as capable readers of complex texts.

At this point, Mahoney is thinking in brave terms: a cultural shift! She's imagining that people could begin *thinking* differently (which is certainly more difficult than implementing a policy or action).

In analyzing the specific problem, Mahoney is also exploring broader cultural trends. She's exploring public resonance! It is important to realize that insights about public resonance may come at any time during the invention process. Since the process of exploration and discovery cannot be divided simply into separate steps or stages (analysis, public resonance), one must always be on the lookout for insights.

> A solution might change the intellectual environment so that physical changes can take place later.

# Public Resonance

Some topics may seem difficult to connect to a broad public concern, but good writers bring *seemingly* marginal topics into the center of public consciousness. The problem you have chosen may obviously affect (or potentially affect) a community or society at large. However, no matter how much your problem involves or affects people, you still must make it known. As you consider your own topic, respond to the following questions:

▶ Who should care about this issue? Why?

▶ What particular community, place, or group does this issue affect?

▶ How might my reader(s) be involved in this issue?

▶ Why is it important that others hear my opinion about this issue? ■

In Mahoney's invention writing, she picks up on a point from her Analysis responses. Some core ideas are gaining momentum: children and adults alike must develop *intellectual tenacity* as part of literacy.

> **Who should care about this issue? Why?**
> Parents, educators, and anyone who cares about books and ideas should care, especially all of us who want to see our kids succeed in school.
>
> **How might my reader(s) be involved in this issue?**
> Parents who save and save for their kids' college education and who think they are preparing their kids for college and beyond might most need to hear this message, as they might be the ones who are not seeing how important it is to help their children fall in love with words—from the earliest years—and then to continue to foster that relationship throughout the school years. All too often, I sense that parents believe we are off the hook once we've created literacy in our children, but that's actually just the beginning. Without fostering the relationship or constantly celebrating intellectual tenacity, we fall short in our jobs.

## Invention Workshop

The public resonance may not be clear at first, but working through all the possibilities can help your topic to expand in interesting ways. Enlist the help of other writers, and in a small group, answer one of the questions for your topic. As a group, work at collectively building a sophisticated answer to the question.

In the following, Marcus has discovered a problem in his community: elderly people in nursing homes and senior living centers are isolated from others. In a discussion with peers, Marcus develops his initial thinking:

**"What particular community, place, or group does this issue affect?"**

MARCUS: Primarily the elderly. Senior citizens are primarily concerned about this issue, and as medical advances allow people to live longer, it seems like we all should be worried—because we'll all be old someday.

LINDA: But shouldn't the younger generations be concerned about the isolation of the elderly, too—I mean beyond just caring about themselves as they age?

DIANA: Yeah . . . even if they don't care, it seems like stuffing the elderly away from mainstream society can't be a good thing, for anybody.

MARCUS: It's like we are ignoring a huge group of people—the group that probably has the most insight and experience about big social problems.

LINDA: And I would even say personal and family problems. I know in my family, it was always my grandmother who understood everyone's problems and could talk through them without getting angry or mean. She was the one who gave everyone a sense of direction.

MARCUS: So when society shuts away its elderly, maybe the biggest victims are the younger generations. Of course, it's bad for the elderly, but in a more indirect and long-term way, maybe their absence from mainstream society is an even bigger wrong. Maybe the younger generations feel the effects in the long term without their patience, insights, and experience.

# Thesis

A thesis for this project should offer a specific strategy for addressing a specific problem. The following examples show a range of possible strategies:

- If the sales associates at Dalworth's had more discretion over break time, the management/employee tension would decrease significantly.
- The budget crisis at Midland State College can only be addressed with a tuition increase.
- Small-group work can help writers get beyond their frustration with invention.
- The degradation of rural areas cannot be stopped with peaceful public rhetoric. Significantly higher gasoline taxes would, however, keep people from building homes farther away from their jobs.
- If the country could begin to take back the airwaves from corporate interests, democracy might then begin to flourish.
- When America's hunters and fishermen see their shared interests with strong environmental groups, their combined political force will help counter the unchecked movement into wildlife areas.

Thesis statements tend to go off track for a few consistent reasons. Before committing to a statement (to something that may impact everything hereafter!), see the Common Thesis Problems in Chapter 7 (page 227), which overlap with this chapter.

## Evolution of a Thesis

Notice how a thesis might evolve out of the invention process. Marcus's topic (isolation of the elderly) can be developed into a focused and sophisticated point. He begins by articulating the problem. Then he tries to make the problem more specific. Finally, he works to integrate the solution:

- In the long run, younger generations may feel the effects of the elderly's isolation.
- Older generations are isolated—their experiences, insights, and wisdom cut off from the people who need it most: everyone else.

- We have to make our grandparents the center of our families, not the marginal human satellites they are presently.
- Because older generations are isolated, their experiences, insights, and wisdom cut off from those who need them most, families should rethink how grandparents figure into everyday life.
- The lost experiences, insight, and wisdom of the older generations can be reintegrated into culture only through families; therefore, each family should work to place its grandparents at the center of everyday life.

Try to express your own problem and your solution in a sentence or two before moving on.

## Revising Your Thesis

Could your thesis be narrower? Writers sometimes seek out problems that are simply too big: hunger, racism, sexism, political deceit, and so on. But such giant problems have too many causes and too many forms. Writers are more apt to create a focused argument and offer an important insight if they take on a specific problem—one that can be located in a particular place and time. Before moving on, make certain that your problem is narrow—as narrow as possible.

# Rhetorical Tools

Remember that proposing a solution is a form of arguing. In fact, the process may involve two layers of argument: (1) persuading the reader about the nature or degree of the problem and (2) showing the value of a particular solution. The goal is not necessarily to convince readers that only one solution is possible but that a particular solution to an important problem has merit.

Although the act of proposing solutions can vary greatly, good proposal essays have certain key elements (which you have already begun to develop):

- **Problem:** Includes illustrations or examples, an explanation of causes, and a picture of short- and long-term effects.
- **Solution:** Includes an explanation of how that solution will address, confront, or stop the causes of the problem.
- **Counterargument:** Addresses concerns about or opposing claims to the solution or the articulation of the problem.
- **Alternative Solutions:** Include any other potential strategies for addressing the problem. Articulating alternative solutions requires an explanation of why these are less desirable than the main solution being offered.
- **Concession/Qualifier:** Acknowledges any possible shortcomings of the solution or concedes value to some opposing claim or alternative solution.

The development of these elements depends upon your particular problem and solution. Some problems, for instance, require significant explanation; that is, you might need to work hard just to make the reader aware of the complexities of the problem. Or perhaps you have a problem that is rather apparent (such as abandoned buildings plaguing an entire section of town). Consider how your audience may view the problem, and make certain to convince your readers to see the problem as you do.

Also, remember the strategies from Chapter 7: Making Arguments. Writers have the whole world of culture, history, and science within reach. By alluding to key historical moments, relevant literary texts, news events, or popular culture figures, you can make claims more persuasive to readers

# The Double-Layer Argument

## 1. Argue about the nature of the problem.

## 2. Argue for the value of your solution.

or show that your position is shared by others. Use the following questions to help construct supporting points for your argument (and see the examples in the chapter readings):

- ▶ Does a historical situation or trend (the rise of a particular fashion, organization, or individual) illustrate something about my topic? (See Schofield ¶4 and 5.)

- ▶ Has science taught us anything about my topic? (See Mahoney ¶5–7.)

- ▶ Have I witnessed or experienced someone or something that illustrates my point? (See Mahoney ¶1 and 4.)

- ▶ Can I construct a hypothetical situation that illustrates my point or dramatizes my solution? (See Schofield ¶9 and 10.) ■

# Discovering Counterarguments and Alternative Solutions

In proposing a solution, you are arguing that a problem exists *and* that a particular solution will address it. But someone might argue with you about several points: that the problem is no problem at all, that your solution will not work, that your solution is inappropriate—too costly, inhumane, unmanageable, and so on. A good arguer addresses those possible objections and may even dig into opponents' assumptions. (See Mahoney ¶2 and 3.)

Every problem has many possible solutions, and a good writer acknowledges other possibilities. But acknowledging solutions other than your own involves explaining their shortcomings. That is, as you mention other solutions, you must also make it clear that they are not as valuable as yours for some reason. Other solutions, for instance, might be less efficient, more dangerous, less ethical, less manageable, or simply inadequate. (See Schofield ¶7 and 8.)

Considering other solutions can also help you understand the strengths and shortcomings of the solution you are promoting. For instance, a solution to Marcus's problem (from the Public Resonance section), isolation of the elderly, might involve refiguring the concept of the nuclear family to include grandparents, uncles, aunts, and cousins. Only in reconceptualizing the basic family unit, he might argue, will elderly members of society find more genuine social engagement. But he might also address other solutions, such as programs that bring together schoolchildren and nursing home residents. According to his argument, such solutions might fall short of creating deep and lasting relationships for the elderly.

As you consider your own topic, apply the following questions:

▶ Who might not see this as a problem? Why?

▶ Why might my solution not work?

▶ What other solutions could be (or have been) attempted?

▶ Why is the solution I am proposing better or more effective? ■

# Avoiding Logical Fallacies

Logical fallacies are flaws in the structure of an argument that can make readers call the claims into question. (See further explanation of logical fallacies in Chapter 7, pages 234–235.) In proposing solutions, be especially cautious of the following fallacies: faulty cause/effect, non sequitur, and slippery slope. When considering the possible long-term effects of a solution, writers may make any of several logical errors:

- Imagining an effect unrelated to present causes (**faulty cause/effect).**
- Skipping several logical steps between a cause and a possible effect (**non sequitur).**
- Extending present circumstances to their most dramatic or disastrous conclusion without sufficient logical cause (**slippery slope).**

Consider Marcus's topic: *Mainstream society isolates the elderly.* It might be valuable for Marcus to project the long-term effects of this problem. However, he should be cautious and not overstate the effects.

### Logically sound

- Without the insight of older generations, mainstream society may continuously forget the social crises of the past and have to relive many burdens.
- As older generations are further isolated, the difficulties they have lived through are isolated with them. And without constant real-life reminders in our midst, younger generations are likely to ignore a past that is not written by official voices of history.

### Logically unsound

- America will have to go through another two world wars because it has completely forgotten the past.
- Everyone will eventually think like children without the elderly in everyday life.
- Society will eventually keep everyone over fifty years old locked away.

# Organizational Strategies

## How Should I Separate Problem and Solution?

Many elements go into a proposing solutions text: the problem, illustrations or support for the problem, the solution, support for the solution, previously attempted or alternative solutions, shortcomings of those solutions, counterarguments, and concessions. These can be arranged in any imaginable order. Here are two standard strategies:

- Problem
  Examples/Illustrations

- My Solution
  Examples/Illustrations

- Attempted or Alternative Solution
  Explanation
  Shortcoming

- Attempted or Alternative Solution
  Explanation
  Shortcoming

OR

- Problem
- Attempted/Alternative Solution A and the Shortcoming
- My Solution
- Attempted/Alternative Solution B and the Shortcoming
- My Solution
- Attempted/Alternative Solution C and the Shortcoming
- My Solution

But the arrangement of elements depends on the topic. Some problems demand more attention, others less. Some solutions need significant explanation and support, others less. If the problem is fairly obvious—if readers will accept it as a problem—then it will not require lengthy supporting passages, counterarguments, concessions, and so on. But if the problem is subtle—if readers are not likely to accept that it's a problem in the first place—then it will demand lengthy explanation. Writers must ask themselves two questions: First, will readers easily accept this as a problem? (If not, I'll have to persuade them.) Second, will readers easily accept the solution? (If not, I'll have to persuade them.) For example, if the problem is a violent elementary school playground, the writer may not have to work diligently to make a case. (Readers are not apt to dismiss such a problem.) But if the problem is a quiet form of institutional racism, then the writer will have to take more time (more paragraphs) to reveal the problem.

In her essay, Julie Zhuo moves in stages. First, she thoroughly describes the problem and its causes. Then, she explains a previously attempted solution and its shortcomings. Finally, she argues for a new solution:

- ¶1–3: Description of the problem
- ¶4–6: Cause and name of the problem
- ¶7 and 8: Attempted (legalistic) solution
- ¶9: Shortcoming of the attempt and call for a new solution
- ¶10 and 11: Opposition to the new solution
- ¶12–19: Argument for the new solution

## How Should I Include Counterarguments?

Counterarguments (responses to those opposing your claims) often are arranged in separate paragraphs. You might develop a counter in an entire paragraph—explaining why, for example, some people are opposed to your understanding of the problem. Then, in a new paragraph, you might explain why your understanding is most appropriate or correct or valuable. Some writers use the *turnabout paragraph* for counterarguments. A turnabout paragraph begins with one point and then changes directions at some point, always giving the reader a clear indication of that change. For example, you might begin a paragraph with an opposing claim, and then counterargue in that same paragraph, as in the following passage from Rachel Schofield's essay:

Food still enables us to survive, but we no longer revere it. Some would disagree, citing the weight problems engorging our country. We see food 24/7 on TV, hear about it on the radio, see it advertised on billboards, and even in Internet pop-ups. Advertising works. We buy what we see, yet the low nutrition levels in our highly processed foods leave our bodies starving for more, and we only give them more junk. We can see the preeminence of food in the dedication of temples to food all along our highways; fast food chains are more popular than ever. However, there is a difference between obsession with food and reverence for it. Our fast food restaurants and freezer aisles are brothels where impure, chemically altered food is bought and sold. Almost gone are the days when honest, unadulterated food can be purchased by the American family.

Counterarguments can also be addressed in a subtler manner. In the following paragraph, Mahoney creates a kind of back and forth between her solution (using a pencil to read) and resistance to it:

> When I tell my students the only way to read a book is with pencil gliding freely across the page (no highlighters please), they look stymied. Selected passages ought to be underlined, I maintain, and tricky vocabulary circled. Further, I suggest that handwritten symbols in the form of stars, asterisks, squiggly lines, question marks, brackets, and the like warrant placement alongside their personal comments posted in the margins. After all, the white space on the printed page could use the company. My students offer good enough reasons, however, for *not* writing in their books: (1) Writing in books during the K–12 years is absolutely taboo, they tell me, and they've been successfully trained to do as told; (2) Some college bookstores won't buy back textbooks with extensive personalized annotations and markings. Students need cash at semester's end, so they dutifully comply. But how is any of this non-writing good for thinking and learning? I'm pretty sure it's not. We might find the current state of affairs particularly worrisome if we frame the problem this way: In an attempt to educate, it seems that educators and a whole lot of

other well-meaning adults have worked successfully to ensure disengagement with the printed word, often during the most formative and critical years of literacy acquisition.

Such a strategy helps writers to deal directly with resistance. It's much like sitting down with the opposing team and working through the logic of disagreement.

# Where Should I Put Attempted or Alternative Solutions?

Alternative solutions, those strategies other than the one forwarded by the writer, can come early or late in an essay. Some writers acknowledge other possibilities soon after their introductions. Notice Zhuo's strategy: She explains two distinct situations in which people solved the Internet trolling problem with legal action. She devotes a paragraph to each attempt. But, Zhuo argues, the legalistic solution is inadequate. Directly after these two paragraphs, she launches into her own, more complex, solution:

> But the law by itself cannot do enough to disarm the Internet's trolls. Content providers, social networking platforms and community sites must also do their part by rethinking the systems they have in place for user commentary so as to discourage—or disallow—anonymity.

In other words, Zhuo uses others' attempts to solve the issue as a catapult into her own solution. The remainder of the article describes this "rethinking" process.

# Writer's Voice

Because proposing a solution is an argumentative process, the Writer's Voice strategies from Chapter 7: Making Arguments, apply here as well (see pages 238–239). But proposing solutions brings with it some additional concerns and strategies. The following strategies will help you develop and maintain an engaging writer's voice.

## Creating Reasonable Tone

It might be said that *tone* is the way a writer treats readers. In argumentative writing, tone is vital to maintaining readers' interest. One that is too emotional can overwhelm; one that is condescending is apt to alienate. When proposing solutions, writers must be careful not to force problems *at* readers. Instead, it is the writer's job to present a problem and illustrate its significance *for* readers. For example, notice Mahoney's strategy for making the reader understand the significance of a problem:

> Today's college students are suffering, and unnecessarily so. I see them arrive in my writing classes each semester eager and determined, but all too often the motivation and passion dissipate when they come face-to-face with—well—words on the page. This is distressing for both them and me. My students are not illiterate by any means, as they successfully broke the code of sound-to-symbol in the earliest elementary years. Since that time, they've continued to learn in public and private school systems or they've been home-schooled. They're educated and plenty adept at moving through the system. But I'm not convinced any of this means they are capable of truly committing to a book, an essay, or any document requiring sustained focus and labor-intensive thinking and doing.

It would be easy, or at least tempting, for Mahoney to scream and shout at her readers about students' disengagement from the written word. Imagine the following:

> Today's college students cannot read closely or intensively. They might want to perform well in their classes, but their hopes have been dashed by a care-

less educational system. They are victims in the worst sense. By the time they've reached my classes, very few of them will be able to learn how to read at the college level. The rest will be left behind. We've forgotten our most vulnerable population—our children.

This passage is over the top. It forces the problem at its readers and demands that they feel a particular emotion. Mahoney's passage is less confrontational, while still intense. She does not make emotional demands on the reader; instead, she presents the strengths and weaknesses she sees in her students and leaves the reader to reflect on them.

## Inviting the Reader

Writerly invitations are phrases that promote curiosity in readers, phrases that entice them to examine a particular topic.

**Question**  Asking the right question can make a reader concerned about the subject: *Why are the computer labs at University Hall a problem? How safe is the drinking water in our community?* In her essay, Schofield invites the reader to consider hard questions that bring the reader into the center of the problem:

> How can Americans have reverence for food when we have so many artificial consumables surrounding us? And to complicate the problem, "Compare the price of a grapefruit to that of a pack of strawberry-flavored Twizzlers" (Zinczenko). It seems that processed food is almost always cheaper and more accessible than wholesome fresh foods. What can a struggling American family do when the only thing they can afford is cheap processed food?

**Group Inclusion**  A writer can include potential readers in a relevant group (small or large) that is affected by the subject. Mahoney creates a collective *us*—a group that is interested in raising and teaching children:

So, I think the problem is clear. Our system of educating, parenting, and nurturing unwittingly conspires to ensure students' disciplined detachment from words on the page. In other words, creating disengaged adults begins early. My proposal is simple and not particularly original, but I'll reiterate it nonetheless. Those of us committed to raising and teaching need to raise and teach differently.

**Statement** A simple claim that calls the reader's attention to the matter is often the most effective. Notice Mahoney's strong statement at the beginning of her essay:

Today's college students are suffering and unnecessarily so.

## Considering Verb Mood

There are three moods in English: *indicative* (used for stating facts or statements about the world), *subjunctive* (used to express conditions that are not facts, such as a recommendation, a wish, a requirement, or a statement contrary to fact), and *imperative* (used for issuing commands or suggestions). Many passages in this text are in the imperative mood. (Find one right now.) Rather than informing the reader about possible ways to act (as in the subjunctive), imperative mood orders the reader to act.

Imperative mood is not often used in academic essays or formal proposals because it puts the reader in the position of action. Of course, there are exceptions. Imperative can be applied effectively, especially in the final passages of an essay. For instance, Julie Zhuo's article is primarily in the indicative mood, as are most of the essays in this book, but she does briefly shift to imperative in her concluding passages. She uses the imperative to urge particular actions:

Instead of waiting around for human nature to change, let's start to rein in bad behavior by promoting accountability. Content providers, stop allowing anonymous comments. Moderate your comments and forums. Look into using comment services to improve the quality of engagement on your site. Ask your users to report trolls and call them out for polluting the conversation.

But be careful with imperative mood. It can diminish the intensity of a good argument. Because imperative mood draws attention to the reader, it must necessarily draw less attention to the topic. The goal of most academic writing is to keep intensive focus on the topic, to build a compelling idea for would-be readers, not to go after the particular person holding the essay. In the following, notice how the first sentence focuses on the reader rather than the topic. In other words, the energy of the sentence goes toward a nameless and invisible "you," while the second and third sentences draw more attention to the topic:

- **Imperative Mood:** While reading, use a pencil to better engage the nuances of a text.
- **Indicative Mood:** Reading with a pencil helps students to engage the nuances of a text.
- **Subjunctive Mood:** If students would use a pencil while reading, they could better engage the nuances of a text.

The differences may seem subtle, but the three sentences radically change the role of a reader. In an imperative sentence, the reader is called upon—insisted upon. In indicative and subjunctive sentences, the reader joins the writer in a mutual examination of the topic. And because academic writing celebrates that mutual examination, indicative and subjunctive are used most often.

## Activity

Before drafting an essay, try to chart its main components. Consider some basic elements: your problem, causes of the problem, alternative or attempted solutions, your solution, potential opposition to your solution, your counterarguments or concessions. Charting a path for the proposal can help you to write more comfortably—without wondering what's coming next.

# Vitality

In his widely read essay "How To Say Nothing in 500 Words," Paul Roberts offers college students advice for succeeding in college writing courses. The problem students face: a standard college assignment that requires a certain page length. The solution Roberts proposes: more-lively writing, less-obvious approaches, and less-usual positions.

## Avoid the Obvious Content

In his essay, Roberts argues that writers should avoid saying what everyone knows. He urges writers to make a list of the first ideas that come to mind on any topic, and then to avoid those initial ideas: "If these are the points that leap to your mind, they will leap to everyone else's too. . . ." Even at the sentence level, writers can avoid the obvious. They can trim out the statements that readers will simply infer on their own. Notice the following obvious content:

> It is wrong when people cheat others. And when the Enron executives cheated thousands of employees out of their pensions, they ruined retirement years for many families.

The entire first sentence is unnecessary, and it detracts from the intensity of the ideas. When writers force such obvious statements onto readers, they make readers less involved. Obvious statements actually tell readers to turn off!

## Get Rid of Obvious Padding

Padding occurs when writers stuff their sentences with unnecessary material. The sentences become longer but contain no added meaning. In his essay, Roberts begins with a brief sentence and a simple idea: "Fast driving is dangerous."
The brief idea then gains words but no meaning:

> In my humble opinion though I do not claim to be an expert on this complicated subject, fast driving, in most circumstances, would seem to be rather dangerous in many respects, or at least so it would seem to me.

The padded sentence is full of unnecessary qualifiers and attention to the writer. While qualifiers can be valuable and first-person pronouns can be important, they can be overused. They can slow down sentences and inflate simple ideas so they sound important.

But when writers begin pruning and trimming their essays, when they really get good at vitalizing their sentences, their drafts are apt to shrink. This may seem like bad news if the goal is to reach a certain length requirement. But Roberts again gives good advice:

> Instead of taking a couple of obvious points off the surface of the topic and then circling warily around them for six paragraphs, you work in and explore, figure out the details. You illustrate. You say that fast driving is dangerous, and then you prove it. How long does it take to stop a car at forty and at eighty? How far can you see at night? What happens when a tire blows? What happens in a head-on collision at fifty miles an hour? Pretty soon your paper will be full of broken glass and blood and headless torsos, and reaching five hundred words will not really be a problem.

So it all comes back to invention. Developing more intensive ideas from the beginning means writers can avoid padding.

## Call a Fool a Fool

Academic audiences value intensity and directness. But some writers may avoid directly stating points. Roberts gives the following scenario:

> The student writes, "In my opinion, the principal of my high school acted in ways that I believe every unbiased person would have to call foolish." This isn't exactly what he means. What he means is, "My high school principal was a fool." If he was a fool, call him a fool. Hedging the thing about with "in-my-opinion's" and "it-seems-to-me's" and "as-I-see-it's" and "at-least-from-my-point-of-view's" gains you nothing. Delete these phrases whenever they creep into your paper.

# Revision

Academic audiences value directness and intensity. They do not want to struggle through overly wordy phrases and jumbled sentences. And they don't like boredom any more than anyone else. In short, academic audiences are people too. They want to stay awake and be engaged. Considering Paul Roberts' advice on the previous page, closely examine your draft. Focus specifically on the following issues:

- **Delete the Obvious:** Consider statements or passages that argue for or detail what you and your peers already assume. While you might use some common assumptions or common knowledge to build an idea, avoid telling readers what they already accept.
- **Intensify the Least Obvious:** Think about your essay as a declaration of new ideas. What is the most uncommon or fresh idea? Even if it's a description of the problem or a slightly different take on solving it, develop it further. Draw more attention to it.

## Peer Review

Exchange drafts with at least one other writer. Before passing your draft to others, underline the thesis or write it at the top of your essay. This way, reviewers will get traction as they read.

### As a reviewer, use the following questions to guide your response:

1. After reading the draft, do you believe that the problem the writer describes is worthy of attention? Do you think it's a problem worth solving? If not, what might the writer do to make the problem more significant?

2. Do you think the writer's solution is appropriate for the problem? Will it address specific causes? Is it manageable? Realistic? Humane?

3. Try to imagine a reason why the writer's solution will not work. What unforeseen forces or variables should the writer consider?

4. What other solutions might be as or more productive in solving the problem?

5. Consider the organization of the essay. Do any paragraphs shift focus without sufficient cues? Do you feel like any paragraphs move away from their initial points without taking you along? Point to specific places in the essay that move too abruptly from one idea to another.

6. How would you describe the writer's tone? (See page 376.) Do you feel invited into the topic, or do you have to work at keeping your attention focused? (Is the writer's voice too flat, too uninteresting, too typical?) Rewrite a short passage of the draft using a different voice. Help the writer to imagine how a different voice might sound.

7. Consider sentence vitality:
   a. Help the writer to avoid obvious content. Circle any sentences or passages that seem obvious to you.
   b. Help the writer to avoid padding. Underline phrases that inflate simple ideas and draw out sentences unnecessarily.
   c. Help the writer to "call a fool a fool." Rewrite any phrases or sentences that seem to hedge, that circle around a more direct and intense wording.
   d. Consider vitality strategies from other chapters.

# Reflection

One powerful way to better understand your own work is to analyze its basic elements or perform what is often called *rhetorical analysis*. In rhetorical analysis, writers describe how arguments work. Looking at the proposal you've written, develop a final analytical statement. Explain, in writing, how your essay confronts a problem and offers a solution. Explain how you go beyond the common intellectual reflexes related to the problem. Do you, for instance, see it in a different light? Do you assert something that others do not? Do you call for a solution that has not been attempted? And explain how you take on the opposition—how you counterargue, how you concede, or why you do not concede.

Consider this final statement more of a report than an evaluation. Imagine that you are explaining the mechanics of your argument rather than defending your point of view. For instance, you might explain how your essay provides specific examples of the problem and how those examples reveal layers of difficulty. You might explain how your solution directly connects to the original cause of the problem. You can also describe how outside sources figure in—as support for your proposed solution, as background about the problem, as opposition to your ideas.

## Beyond the Essay

The cartoon on the following page encourages you to express the idea from your essay in some other form: a letter, speech, and so on.

*Why?*

Students sometimes see education—or certain college courses such as this one—as separate from their actual lives. However, the course is not only related to your major; it is, more importantly, related to your *life*. Writing courses such as this one go out into the real world and bring that real world back into the classroom.

Such courses look at what really goes on in everyday life, and they present what goes on (invention strategies, rhetorical strategies, and so on) in an organized way. College courses gather and organize the untidy ideas of disorganized real life, and they present those ideas in a more graspable way. Admittedly, the college writing course can be a confusing and seemingly irrelevant place. But if you can remember that the invention strategies in this book are a description (not a prescription) of how everyday people think and communicate effectively, you can more successfully fuse schoolwork and real life. This fusion is the intended purpose of all education.

# A student's job is to connect everyday life to classroom work.

# A student's job is to connect classroom work to everyday life.

For additional resources including instructional videos and links to helpful websites, access your English CourseMate through cengagebrain.com.

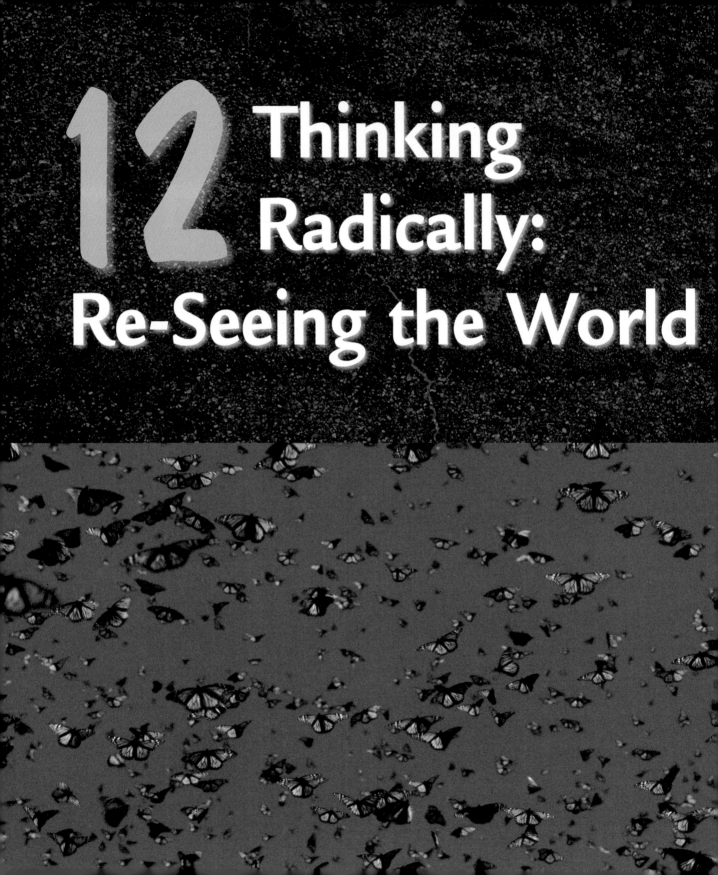

# 12 Thinking Radically: Re-Seeing the World

# Chapter Contents

# "We must therefore look in the most obscurest corners and summon up courage to shock the prejudices of our age if we want to broaden the basis of our understanding of nature."

—Carl Jung

Living in a society demands a certain degree of conformity. As individuals in a society, we conform to laws, clothing styles, hairstyles, and even culinary tastes (most Americans like french fries but not raw oysters). We also conform to ways of thinking; we learn to follow intellectual conventions. This is not to say that we all think alike, not by a long shot, but we do buy into conventional modes or patterns of thought that, on the one hand, allow us to participate in shared knowledge but, on the other hand, limit intellectual possibilities.

Mainstream thought invites us to accept a particular view of reality, and with it, certain assumptions. Consider the following:

- Progress involves technological advancement.
- The past is behind us.
- People who make lots of money are successful.
- Poor people are worse off than rich people.
- We make individual choices.
- Time is constant.

Such ideas are what we might call *common sense,* in that they represent widely held, and largely unexamined, beliefs. But some people have examined and even challenged such common ideas. For example, thinkers such as Wendell Berry challenge the idea that human progress necessarily involves increased dependence on technology; several important religious figures (Jesus, Buddha, Mohammed) overturned the inherent value of monetary riches; and Albert Einstein showed the world that time is not constant but relative. We might say that such figures transcend and challenge commonsense thinking. They call into question those beliefs that rest beneath layers of intellectual practice and everyday life. They show us questions where we may have assumed solid answers.

People who transcend conventional thinking are not *radical* in the sense that they want to destroy mainstream life. (We are not talking here about anarchists, religious zealots, or specific political positions.) Rather, they are radical *thinkers:* They escape conventional thought patterns. While convention calls on us to think within the lines radical thinkers work to see beyond those lines and then communicate what ideas are possible. Their writing seeks to reform conventional thinking.

Radical thinking is not necessarily a matter of topic choice; in fact, topics are not, in themselves, radical. Radical thinking involves an adventurous *approach* to a topic and offers a new way to think. For example, in 1784, Benjamin Franklin first put forth the idea of daylight savings time. After waking at an unusually early hour in the morning and finding that the sun had risen, he imagined that people could change their clocks to coincide with sunrise throughout the seasons.

In 1543, Nicolaus Copernicus challenged the conventional theory that the Earth is the center of the universe. He defied church law and common sense of the day and claimed that the Earth rotates around the sun. History is filled with such intellectual adventurers, those who transcended norms to see relationships beyond the obvious, to find meaning outside of cultural norms, and to imagine perspectives beyond the present:

- W. E. B. DuBois argued against mainstream thinking about African Americans' place in society. While most politicians, educators, and civic leaders walked a moderate line, assuming that black people in America could thrive in subservient positions, DuBois imagined that African Americans should act as leaders for national and global change.

- Psychologist Carl Jung broke away from his colleague Sigmund Freud (and the conventional wisdom of the psychological community) to argue that human unconscious is, in part, a collective rather than an individual phenomenon.

- Georgia O'Keeffe transcended artistic conventions by focusing on the organic. While art and popular culture were increasingly transfixed on the abstract, O'Keeffe sought out the most pure and basic forms of identity in images such as flowers and landscapes.

Radical thinkers have changed how laws, government, and institutional policy work. People such as Thomas Jefferson; Mahatma Gandhi; Eleanor Roosevelt; Martin Luther King, Jr.; and Martin Luther articulated ideas and policies that were beyond conventional thinking of their times.

In academic study and everyday life, methods often evolve because real people transcend the common sense of their fields; that is, they imagine the possibilities beyond what is assumed. The people who are able to think beyond *what is* and to conjure images of *what could be* are those who most often provide direction for improvement in the quality of daily work and daily life. As you explore this chapter, remember that all those people who have helped bring about change are those who first had to imagine a reality beyond the status quo.

This chapter will help you transcend conventional thought, focus on a particular topic, develop a focused thesis, and communicate your ideas in writing. The following essays will provide valuable insight into various strategies. After reading the essays, you can find a topic in one of two ways:

1. Go to the Point of Contact section to find a topic from everyday life, or
2. Choose one of the Ideas for Writing following the essays.

After finding a subject, go to the Analysis section to begin developing your thoughts.

# Celibate Passion

## Kathleen Norris

In the following essay, Kathleen Norris, a writer and oblate in the Benedictine Order, offers an alternative vision of celibacy. Norris is author of various books and poems including *Dakota: A Spiritual Geography*. "Celibate Passion" was published in *The Christian Century* (1996).

Celibacy is a field day for ideologues. Conservative Catholics tend to speak of celibacy as if it were an idealized, angelic state, while feminist theologians such as Uta Ranke-Heinemann say, angrily, that celibate hatred of sex is hatred of women. That celibacy constitutes the hatred of sex seems to be a given in popular mythology, and we need only look at newspaper accounts of sex abuse by priests to see evidence of celibacy that isn't working. One could well assume that this is celibacy, impure and simple. And this is unfortunate, because celibacy practiced rightly is not at all a hatred of sex; in fact it has the potential to address the troubling sexual idolatry of our culture.

One benefit of the nearly ten years that I've been affiliated with the Benedictines as an oblate, or associate, has been the development of deep friendships with celibate men and women. This has led me to ponder celibacy that works, practiced by people who are fully aware of themselves as sexual beings but who express their sexuality in a celibate way. That is, they manage to sublimate their sexual energies toward another purpose than sexual intercourse and procreation. Are they perverse, their lives necessarily stunted? Cultural prejudice would say yes, but I have my doubts. I've seen too many wise old monks and nuns whose celibate practice has allowed them to incarnate hospitality in the deepest sense. In them, the constraints of celibacy have somehow been transformed into an openness. They exude a sense of freedom.

The younger celibates are more edgy. Still contending mightily with what one friend calls "the raging orchestra of my hormones," they are more obviously struggling to contain their desire for intimacy and physical touch within the bounds of celibacy. Often they find their loneliness intensified by the incomprehension of others. In a culture that denies the value of their striving, they are made to feel like fools, or worse.

Americans are remarkably tone-deaf when it comes to the expression of sexuality. The sexual formation that many of us receive is like the refrain of an old Fugs song: "Why do ya like boobs a lot—ya gotta like boobs a lot." The jiggle of tits and ass, penis and pectorals assaults us everywhere—billboards, magazines, television, movies. Orgasm becomes just another goal; we undress for success. It's no wonder that in all this powerful noise, the quiet tones of celibacy are lost.

But celibate people have taught me that celibacy, practiced rightly, does indeed have something valuable to say to the rest of us. Specifically, they have helped me better appreciate both the nature of friendship and what it means to be married. They have also helped me recognize that celibacy, like monogamy, is not a matter of the will disdaining and conquering the desires of the flesh, but a discipline requiring what many people think of as undesirable, if not impossible—a conscious form of sublimation. Like many people who came into adulthood during the sexually permissive 1960s, I've tended to equate sublimation with repression. But my celibate friends have made me see the light; accepting sublimation as a normal part of adulthood makes me more realistic about human sexual capacities and expression. It helps me better respect the bonds and boundaries of marriage.

Any marriage has times of separation, ill health, or just plain crankiness in which sexual intercourse is ill advised. And it is precisely the skills of celibate friendship—fostering intimacy through letters, conversation, performing mundane tasks together (thus rendering them pleasurable), savoring the holy simplicity of a shared meal or a walk together at dusk—that help a marriage survive the rough spots. When you can't make love physically, you figure out other ways to do it.

The celibate impulse in monasticism runs deep and has an interfaith dimension. It is the Dalai Lama who has said, "If you're a monk, you're celibate. If you're not celibate, you're not a monk." Monastic people are celibate for a very practical reason: The kind of community life to which they aspire can't be sustained if people are pairing off. Even in churches in which the clergy are often married—Episcopal and Russian Orthodox, for example—their monks and nuns are celibate. And while monastic novices may be carried along for a time on the swells of communal spirit, when that blissful period inevitably comes to an end the loneliness is profound. One gregarious monk in his early 30s told me that just as he thought he'd settled into the monastery, he woke up in a panic one morning, wondering if he'd wake up lonely for the rest of his life.

Another monk I know regards celibacy as the expression of an essential human loneliness, a perspective that helps him as a hospital chaplain when he is called upon to minister to the dying. I knew him when he was still resisting his celibate call. The resistance usually came out as anger directed toward his abbot and community, more rarely as misogyny. I was fascinated to observe the process by which he came to accept the sacrifices that a celibate, monastic life requires. He's easier to be with now; he's a better friend.

This is not irony so much as grace: In learning to be faithful to his vow of celibacy, the monk developed his talent for relationship. It's a common story. I've seen the demands of Benedictine hospitality—the requirement that all visitors be received as Christ—convert shy young men who fear women into monks who can enjoy their company.

Celibates tend to value friendship very highly. And my friendships with celibate men, both gay and straight, give me some hope that men and women don't live in alternate universes. In 1990s America, this sometimes feels like a countercultural perspective. Male celibacy, in particular, can become radically countercultural insofar as it rejects the consumerist model of sexuality that reduces a woman to the sum of her parts. I have never had a monk friend make an insinuating remark along the lines of "You have beautiful eyes" (or legs, breasts, knees, elbows, nostrils), the kind of remark women grow accustomed to deflecting. A monk is supposed to give up the idea of possessing anything, including women.

Ideally, in giving up the sexual pursuit of women (whether as demons or as idealized vessels of purity) the male celibate learns to relate to them as human beings. That many fail to do so, that the power structures of the Catholic Church all but dictate failure in this regard, comes as no surprise. What is a surprise is what happens when it works. For when men have truly given up the idea of possessing women, a healing thing occurs. I once met a woman in a monastery guest house who had come there because she was pulling herself together after being raped, and she needed to feel safe around men again. I've seen young monks astonish an obese and homely college student by listening to her with as much interest and respect as to her conventionally pretty roommate. On my 40th birthday, as I happily blew out four candles on a cupcake ("one for each decade," a monk in his 20s cheerfully proclaimed), I realized that I could enjoy growing old with these guys.

As celibacy takes hold in a person, as monastic values supersede the values of the culture outside the monastery, celibates become people who can radically affect those of us out "in the world," if only because they've learned how to listen without possessiveness, without imposing themselves. In talking to someone who is practicing celibacy well, we may sense that we're being listened to in a refreshingly deep way. And this is the purpose of celibacy, not to attain some impossibly cerebral goal mistakenly conceived as "holiness," but to make oneself available to others, body and soul. Celibacy, simply put, is a form of ministry—not an achievement one can put on a résumé but a subtle form of service. In theological terms, one dedicates one's sexuality to God through Jesus Christ, a concept and a terminology I find extremely hard to grasp. All I can do is catch a glimpse of people who are doing it, incarnating celibacy in a mysterious, pleasing, and gracious way.

The attractiveness of the celibate is that he or she can make us feel appreciated, enlarged, no matter who we are. I have two nun friends who invariably have this effect on me, no matter what the circumstances of our lives on those occasions when we meet. The thoughtful way in which they converse, listening and responding with complete attention, is a marvel. And when I first met a man I'll call Tom, I wrote in my notebook, "Such tenderness in a man . . . and a surprising, gentle, kindly grasp of who I am."

I realized that I had found a remarkable friend. I was also aware that Tom and I were fast approaching the rocky shoals of infatuation—a man and a woman, both decidedly heterosexual, responding to each other in unmistakably sexual ways. We laughed a lot; we had playful conversations as well as serious ones; we took delight in each other. At times we were alarmingly responsive to one another, and it was all too easy to fantasize about expressing that responsiveness in physical ways.

The danger was real but not insurmountable; I sensed that if our infatuation were to develop into love, that is, to ground itself in grace rather than utility, our respect for each other's commitments—his to celibacy, mine to monogamy—would make the boundaries of behavior very clear. We had few regrets, and yet for both of us there was an underlying sadness, the pain of something incomplete. Suddenly, the difference between celibate friendship and celibate passion had become a reality; at times the pain was excruciating.

Tom and I each faced a crisis the year we met—his mother died, I suffered a disastrous betrayal—and it was the intensity of those unexpected, unwelcome experiences that helped me to understand that in the realm of the sacred, what seems incomplete or unattainable may be abundance after all. Human relationships are by their nature incomplete—after 21 years my husband remains a mystery to me, and I to him, and that is as it should be. Only hope allows us to know and enjoy the depth of our intimacy.

Appreciating Tom's presence in my life as a miraculous, unmerited gift helped me to place our relationship in its proper, religious context, and also to understand why it was that when I'd seek him out to pray with me, I'd always leave feeling so much better than when I came. This was celibacy at its best—a man's sexual energies so devoted to the care of others that a few words could lift me out of despair, give me the strength to reclaim my life. Celibate love was at the heart of it, although I can't fully comprehend the mystery of why this should be so. Celibate passion—elusive, tensile, holy.

# Writing Strategies

1. Write down a thesis statement for "Celibate Passion."

2. Explain Norris's strategy for helping the reader understand and accept the thesis. What support strategies (from page 229 in Chapter 7) are especially helpful, and why?

3. Focus on Norris's use of personal testimony. Identify one especially important passage of personal testimony and explain how it helps the reader understand Norris's radical point.

4. What does Norris mean by "celibate passion"? How does she make this concept clear to the reader?

5. Describe Norris's voice as a writer and provide several excerpts from her essay to support your description.

# Exploring Ideas

1. What does Norris mean by "celibates become people who can radically affect those of us out 'in the world'"?

2. What might readers have the most trouble understanding about Norris's argument, and why? What assumptions, values, or beliefs might make Norris's argument difficult for some people to understand?

3. Based on Norris's essay, what is the purpose of celibacy? How does being celibate achieve this purpose?

# Ideas for Writing

1. What, like celibacy, can you argue is a subtle form of service?

2. How has a close connection to something (a group, a cause, a goal) helped you to understand an idea in a different way than most people?

If responding to one of these ideas, go to the Analysis section of this chapter to begin developing ideas for your essay.

# An Apology to Future Generations

## Simon Benlow

Thinking radically means breaking away from the present—cutting the intellectual cord that ties us to conventional wisdom. And when those intellectual cords are cut and a writer ventures off beyond the norm, what he or she writes may seem outrageous. In this essay, Simon Benlow escapes the conventional wisdom of his own generation and imagines life beyond it. Notice that the most mundane daily activities, those we'd not otherwise examine, are under investigation. Portions of Benlow's Invention writing are shown later in this chapter.

**Writing Strategies**

Addresses the reader directly ("you") as someone in the future.

Thesis: we owe future generations an apology, though it cannot really suffice.

The argument = Benlow's generation is guilty of spoiling the world for the future.

Evidence for the argument = specific examples.

Using paragraphs as separate reasons for apology.

**Exploring Ideas**

We can't see ourselves as well as others will see us later.

Apology is not enough.

Personal extravagance and luxury.

We judge previous generations while letting our own generation off the hook.

By now, you certainly know us better than we knew ourselves. You have shaken your heads in amazement. You have, no doubt, wondered at our disregard for you. You know how opulently we lived, how we gorged ourselves daily, how we lived beyond the means of ourselves and of following generations. You know that our desires extended in every direction in time and space, that our capacity to take was monstrous, and our restraint absent. Because we lived in our time, but irreparably harmed the world for those beyond it, I offer this unsatisfactory apology:

- For believing in a world of unlimited resources. We lived as though the water, the land, and the air would perpetually support our fetish with luxury items. We demanded personal extravagances of every imaginable (and entirely unimaginable) kind. Nearly every person of every town had his or her own internal combustion engine lawn mower, leaf blower, snow blower, hedge trimmer. Nearly every home and vehicle had air conditioners. And beyond these "utilities," we had hordes of trinkets, recreational instruments, and pleasure devices that all, eventually, had to lie in waste somewhere when our fickle appetites refocused on the new faster-smoother-quicker-shinier-more-interactive-more-unbelievable gadget. We jet-skied, water-crafted, golf-carted, dune- and moon-buggied, sports-carred, and otherwise spark-plugged ourselves into a frenzy. We became enamored with the movement of machines and the repose of our own bodies.

- For allowing ourselves to be comforted by our own story of progress. The histories of our time kept us self-righteous. We looked back at the waste and pollution of the late nineteenth century—at the dawn of the industrial age. We sighed at the crass industrialists who unknowingly set out to run the entire

---

world on fossil fuels. We denounced the bygone twentieth-century leaders who promoted hate and genocide. But, as you know, our crimes of utter disinterest and self-absorption compete with even the most flagrant atrocities of our past.

- For ignoring our scientists who warned repeatedly that our way of life would have dire consequences. Even though we celebrated the role of science in our culture (that is, when it served our longing for increased convenience), we managed to dismiss an entire scientific community when it insisted that our hyper-consumptive lifestyle would ultimately damage the world around us. We branded them political zealots, and conjured up a pseudo anti-mainstream conspiracy so we could complacently dismiss their findings and promote the image of an apolitical, moderate (hence reasonable) population. Once such scientists were assigned to a political agenda (on the "Left"), the masses could be comforted in ignoring their warnings.

We celebrate science yet ignore scientists who call for restraint.

Our intellectual comfort helps create extreme materialism.

The first phrase (stylistic fragment?) is always short.

- For casting away criticisms of our lifestyle and foreign policies. While many peoples of the world (often the most destitute) insisted that our foreign policies promoted obscene degrees of inequity, we demonized or dismissed them. We ignored the lessons from eighteenth- and nineteenth-century revolutions: that absurd degrees of opulence coexist with (or even depend upon) equally absurd degrees of poverty, and even more importantly, that flagrant inequity eventually results in bloody retaliation.

Voice seems formal. (This is a *formal* apology!)

- For celebrating the most opulent and decadent figures of our time. Our most honored people were those who flaunted their own degrees of comfort and disregard. Their homes, huge monuments to themselves, stretched over acres of private land and, for the most part, sat empty. In the race to mimic the wildly successful, our middle classes, everyday working men and women, sought to build inordinately large homes—with vaulted ceilings and multiple levels. We considered it normal for two adults to occupy vast domestic quarters with numerous empty rooms for storage or show. For holidays, we increased our parade of domestic performances by stringing thousands of electric lights inside and outside of our gargantuan homes and keeping them on for countless hours and days. In short, we measured our success and celebrated our piety with costly ornamentation.

We celebrate decadence. Our homes are large. Why? Are we out of control?

Provides evidence as support: middle class sought to build large homes "with vaulted ceilings" and strung "thousands of electric lights" inside and out.

- For fawning over our children and steeping them in layers of idle comfort, while ignoring, even crudely dismissing, the

The repetition of the opening structure creates formality.

lives of their children's children. We bought them rooms full of trinkets to occupy their energy, and in so doing, we taught them to treasure petty extravagances that could be easily discarded in favor of new and more sophisticated ones. But we never considered the heaping mounds of discarded, out-of-favor junk—certificates of belonging in our age. We never considered how our self-indulgence would breed a nationalistic capriciousness—a total disregard for others beyond our fenced-in, manicured, up-to-date, polished existence.

- For spreading into every last corner of every last region. We sought out the most pastoral, the most "untouched" land and infiltrated with no remorse. We occupied expanses of natural (what we called "virgin") areas, and transformed them from "undeveloped" terrain into overdeveloped sprawl. And we did it with utmost speed. We saw the land change before our own eyes. We watched our cities smear themselves into outlying rural areas; we saw wetlands, woods, and river flood plains blanketed by pavement, but drove happily over them. We said nothing when our fast-food chains (large corporate entities that sold a homogenous type of ready-to-consume "food") built locations in every remote corner of the map. We felt a comfortable familiarity in encountering the same foods, the same logos, the same containers, the same glowing buildings and signs throughout our land—and the world. And it was not only the corporate entities plowing and paving into virgin terrain. The average citizens cheerily built new, and increasingly bigger, homes despite the shrinking undeveloped space. In fact, we built homes faster than we could fill them—and left old empty ones in our wake.

- For perilously ignoring the deep connections among our lifestyles, our foreign policies, our governmental regulations, the environment, and other peoples of the world.

I imagine that you are breathing the exhaust fumes of our disregard. If large metropolitan areas are still inhabitable, your citizens must certainly deal with a plague of airborne toxins (brought on by war, pollution, or both). Perhaps you wear masks. Perhaps you figured out how to purify the air. Perhaps most of your income goes to such causes. (Perhaps you cannot even imagine what it is like to assume nothing about the air . . . to *not* consider it as daily routine.) I imagine that, in your time, the environment is a daily concern, and that you know the names and effects of toxins that only our most advanced scientists understood. No doubt, you must regard even the most basic food ingredients

---

*Side annotations:*

Metaphor: "certificates of belonging."

The constant use of "we" creates public resonance—but also involves the reader in the guilt.

Metaphor.

Kind of a summary of all the above?

Metaphor: "breathing the exhaust fumes of our disregard."

He's not certain of the future—but assumes it'll be rough. (Qualifying here?)

Use of description to paint a picture.

Capriciousness = erratic, impulsive, flighty, inconstant behavior.

"We" say nothing. Who is "we"? The majority?

Benlow is pointing to the most common parts of our culture—food, homes, cars, toys.

Urban areas are probably uninhabitable.

with scrutiny. I imagine that the sun is no longer personified in children's drawings with a gentle smile and happy radiant beams, but is, instead, something to avoid at all costs. (I imagine that you cannot possibly imagine how we once "bathed" in sun rays for recreation.)

I imagine that your everyday lives are filled with the consequences of our political naïveté. Perhaps the countries that provided our laborers, those we so boldly referred to as "Third World," have by now demanded a change in the world order. Perhaps they are now capable of responding to years of exploitation; perhaps they have escaped the economic imperialism of the twentieth century; or, perhaps their numbers ultimately afforded them the ability to resist their tyrants—who served them up as objects to our "globally minded" leaders. Or perhaps our greed for oil became so great that we no longer concealed our desire to control entire regions of the world. Perhaps, the hidden global tensions of the late twentieth and early twenty-first centuries came to full realization, and you are living in the aftermath.

International policies/politics figure in, too.

Every age has its dissonant voices. But as it shrinks into the past, its internal tensions and dissonant voices fade, and the telescopic lens of history sees it as a unity. And certainly, this fate will befall our time. The material conditions created by our time will frame us all as guilty, as complicit in the deterioration of a socially and environmentally uninhabitable world. And this is no defense of our dissonant voices—those who tried to warn us. They too enjoyed our opulence. As a collective mass of consumers, we all created the conditions that you presently endure—whatever they may be.

We are all guilty. Even those who object to the current lifestyle contribute to it, participate in it. We must be a part of our culture while at the same time resisting it.

Concession: dissonant voices (such as Benlow) enjoyed opulence, too.

Although it is probably impossible, I hope you do not look back and characterize us as purely self-serving and wicked, but as trapped in our own enterprise. We were a young culture with no parents. In fact, we stumbled over ourselves to appear perpetually immature and restless. We packaged restlessness, and sold it in the form of hair dyes, fake breasts, and sexual stimulants. Like a mass of delirious adolescents, we made ourselves increasingly giddy, posing for ourselves and for one another, posing in every aspect of our lives: our homes, travel, clothes, food, water, and vacations. It was a mammoth parade of teenage delirium that began in New York, wormed through every tiny town of the Midwest, and wrapped around itself in dizzying perpetual circles on the beaches of California. As it came through every town, no one could resist it. It banged and clamored and woke everyone from dreamy isolation, and so even the most ascetic types found themselves playing along in some small way.

We are a young culture. America is a country like a child, without parental control. Our parents are children. Our leaders are like children in the world. As a country, we lack discipline and foresight.

Figurative language: "we stumbled over ourselves."

Examples supporting the argument.

We grew outward and consumed everything because we told ourselves that we could, because our parents said we could, and because their parents said we should. Relentless growth was part of our mythology. It was hard-wired into our daily lives and our nightly dreams. Perhaps it was our conflated notion of private property that eclipsed our potential concern for those outside our fences or beyond our calendar years. Perhaps it was our bloated pride at overcoming nature; we were utterly smitten by the idea that nature could rarely infringe on our desires to move whimsically about the world. Perhaps it was some instinctual drive to outdo others—to surpass the luxuries of past generations. Perhaps it was all of these that blurred our collective vision of the future. Had we been able to look beyond our giant, ballooned notions of self, property, and progress, perhaps we would have been able to foresee something or someone out there in the distance.

"Perhaps" shows Benlow's exploration of the issue.

Very formal language—seems like a funeral.

Although you cannot possibly imagine it, we were, generally, an agreeable people: We knew how to celebrate, how to have a parade, how to draw a crowd, how to break seating capacity records. And if you could return to our time, I would make a

We are guilty, but nice, people.

Conclusion: any humans living in our times would be tempted to go along, too.

dubious wager that you, too, would find it difficult to resist the lure of our lifestyle, the attraction of our conveniences. And if we had been able to imagine you as real people, even as our own distant progeny, rather than a simple euphemism ("the future"), we certainly would have acted differently. Although we probably would not have relented in our give-it-to-me-now race for more, we would have taken a solemn moment to raise a toast and drink to your hardship.

. . . we're also ridiculous.

## Writing Strategies

1. How does the introduction invite the reader into the essay?

2. What is the essay's thesis?

3. Explain how an appeal (to logic, emotion, character, need, or value) helps the reader understand and accept the thesis.

4. Describe Benlow's voice as a writer, referring to several passages to support your description.

5. How does the essay (especially the last four paragraphs) go beyond simply placing blame?

## Exploring Ideas

1. In a paragraph or two, describe how Benlow sees contemporary American culture.

2. How is the way that you see contemporary American culture similar to or different from the way Benlow sees it?

3. Consider your initial reactions to Benlow's essay. What points did you most agree or disagree with? What ideas did you not understand?

4. Ask others if they feel future generations deserve an apology and, if so, for what. Record their responses and compare them to Benlow's essay. How are their views similar to or different from Benlow's and your own?

## Ideas for Writing

1. What would you like to say to future generations?

2. What idea of Benlow's might you expand on?

If responding to one of these ideas, go to the Analysis section of this chapter to begin developing ideas for your essay.

# Unemployed and Working Hard

## Simon Wykoff

Radical thinkers help others reimagine conventional ways of thinking. In the following essay, written for his first-year writing class, Simon Wykoff provides carefully selected details from an average day to help others reimagine the common stereotype of the "lazy bum." Using personal testimony and a few outside sources, Wykoff flips the stereotype upside down.

A common stereotype in today's society is that of the lazy bum. People see a homeless man on the side of the road, waiting for handouts, and assume that's all he ever does. In reality, this couldn't be farther from the truth. As the painter Willem de Kooning once said, "The trouble with being poor is that it takes up all of your time" (qtd. in "Willem de Kooning Quotes"). This is absolutely true, and I think you'll find that homeless people are incredibly busy doing the most important job to all of us: surviving.

According to a fact sheet available from the National Coalition for the Homeless, the best approximation of the total number of homeless people comes from a study done by the National Law Center on Homelessness and Poverty, which states that roughly 3.5 million people in the United States will experience homelessness every year ("How Many" pages 2 and 3). For most of my childhood, my father was one of these many homeless people. While growing up, I spent a large amount of my time living on the streets with him. I can tell you from my experiences that the process he went through every day in order to find food and shelter was one of the roughest "jobs" I have ever seen.

Before I begin, something you need to understand is that my father did not make use of services like shelters during his many years of homelessness. His opinion, which I have seen held by many other homeless people, was that these services were usually crowded, of poor quality, and often more dangerous than simply living on the streets. While this did make life more difficult in some ways, he (and I) felt it kept him safer in the end.

The first thing my father did upon waking up was check his belongings. Depending on the place he was sleeping, there was a good chance that something could have been stolen from him in the middle of the night. It was not uncommon for him to find the clothes in his backpack gone, or to discover that he was missing money he had stashed away.

After checking through his items, he would look over the money he had remaining from his efforts on the previous day. If he had enough, he would buy himself breakfast, usually at one of the cheaper coffee shops around town. If he had no money, he went to the dumpsters behind several bakeries in the town to fish out the four-day-old bread they had thrown away. If the bread wasn't moldy, it was his morning meal.

Once he had some food in his belly, he usually tried to locate a current paper. This often meant waiting around in coffee shops until someone left one on the table after their breakfast. Sometimes this step could take him hours, but he was determined not to waste the precious money on a newspaper when he could get it for free with patience.

As soon as he had the paper, he thumbed through it, looking for jobs he could feasibly apply to. Due to his particular circumstances, he was without official identification. This, of course, made the search much more difficult. If he found something, he would tear off the piece of the paper and store it to refer to later.

I should interject here and explain how he got around the city. While my father was homeless, he was lucky enough to have a bicycle, which he treasured beyond everything else. It's not uncommon in a larger city to have the place you get food, the place you sleep, and the place you go to try and earn money be miles and miles apart. Because of this, even on a bike my father spent a considerable amount of time traveling. He would often ride from one end of the city to the other several times a day. This takes an incredible amount of endurance, especially when you are doing it on an empty stomach, as he often was. Many times, just a trip from the place he was sleeping to the closest bakery in the morning was a marathon!

The next thing he did after looking for job opportunities was to get money in order to buy food for the rest of the day. While you may see many homeless panhandling,

I think people don't realize that a large number of homeless actually do small-time work for their daily bread. As mentioned in an online editorial, the homeless these days are increasingly working menial tasks for extra cash, or just to survive (Hilton). For all the people you see standing outside of stores with signs, others are playing instruments on street corners, gathering cans for recycling, or washing windows.

My father fell into the category of musicians. To make money, he sat in a high-traffic area and played his pennywhistle for the people passing by. He didn't heckle pedestrians, or openly beg. He didn't even display a sign. He was simply a man on the street with an upturned hat in front of him, playing Irish jigs.

After a few hours of tiring playing, my father went off to buy his lunch and dinner for the day. He had no place to store food, like a refrigerator, so he was forced to buy items that wouldn't perish. His diet was made up largely of things like chips, bread, and vegetables that could be eaten raw. This was hardly an ideal diet, but he managed nonetheless.

After he finished his lunch, my father went looking for things he could sell or use himself. The best way for him to do this was dumpster diving. He would go to the areas of town where the richer college students lived, and wade through the communal dumpsters for things like VCRs or microwaves that could be carried to nearby stores and sold. This was often difficult work, as he had to strap any large items to the back of his bicycle and ride with them for some time.

Once he finished searching through the dumpsters, he went on to his next task, applying for any jobs he had found in the paper. This was difficult, as most of the places he could apply to were on the edges of town, away from the college districts. He would ride all the way across town to submit his barren resume, only to have it rejected.

Finally, as his arduous day neared an end, my father looked for a place to sleep at night. This was not always easy, and he had to switch locations fairly often. If he didn't, he would begin to raise the suspicions of the property owner, or become a target for the more dangerous people on the streets.

Used by permission of the author

As you can see, my father's day was far from that simplistic stereotype of the bum who sits on street corners all day and waits for people to help him out. What people don't seem to realize is that to survive on the streets, you have to take things into your own hands. You need to have perseverance, stamina, and a little bit of luck. Though it may seem outlandish, I think you'll find that many homeless people work just as much, or more, than you.

### Works Cited

Hilton, G. Dan. "Designer Java for a Regular Joe." *Homeless Man Speaks*. N.p., 2 Nov. 2006. Web. 8 Nov. 2007.

"How Many People Experience Homelessness?" *Facts about Homelessness*. National Coalition for the Homeless, Aug. 2007. Web. 8 Nov. 2007.

"Willem de Kooning Quotes." *The Quotations Page*. N.p., n.d. Web. 14 Nov. 2007.

## Writing Strategies

1. How is the essay a response to conventional thinking?

2. What is the essay's thesis?

3. Choose one paragraph from the essay and explain why it is especially effective in helping the reader reimagine the homeless.

4. Identify several details and explain how they help bring Wykoff's narrative to life.

5. Describe how the essay is organized. What other organizational strategy might Wykoff have used?

## Exploring Ideas

1. What important qualities does Wykoff's father have? What other qualities might be important to surviving as a homeless person?

2. What skills are most important for the survival of someone who isn't homeless?

3. With a group of peers, explore Wykoff's closing sentence: "Though it may seem outlandish, I think you'll find that many homeless people work just as much, or more, than you." Does that seem outlandish? Do group members agree with Wykoff's statement?

## Ideas for Writing

1. What common stereotype couldn't be further from the truth?

2. What don't people realize?

If responding to one of these ideas, go to the Analysis section of this chapter to begin developing ideas for your essay.

# Outside Reading

Read a *New York Times* article online, along with its Readers' Comments. (Not all articles have Readers' Comments.) Find one comment that you think illustrates radical thinking and respond to the following:

1. What is the main claim (or thesis) of the comment? Is the main claim stated or implied?

2. In what way(s) does the comment transcend or challenge conventional thinking?

3. Which of the following support strategies help the reader understand and accept the main claim and how?

    example, allusion, personal testimony/anecdote, scenario, statistics, authority, facts appeal to logic, emotion, character, need, or value

    (See the Rhetorical Tools section of Chapter 7 for help understanding support strategies.)

4. How does the comment engage opposition: Does it respond directly to any points in the article or to any other reader comments? Does it make any counterarguments or concede any points?

5. Describe the writer's voice and why it might be inviting or alienating to a reader.

6. Write your own Readers' Comment in response to the article or more specifically in response to the comment you found radical.

# INVENTION

## "Uncertainty can be your guiding light."

—U2

On the one hand, the focus of this chapter may seem rather abstract; we are, after all, attempting to imagine new intellectual ground. On the other hand, these ideas can have their beginnings in familiar, everyday terrain. While the goal may be to extend thinking beyond familiar ideas, we can still start with everyday life.

For this chapter, nothing is more important than the act of invention. As in previous chapters, the writer should attempt to discover something particularly interesting or valuable—or even bizarre. Unlike in previous chapters, the ultimate goal is to escape conventional thinking and to imagine something entirely outside of common intellectual activity. The following sections are designed to help you through this process; specifically, to discover a topic (in Point of Contact), to develop particular points about the topic (in Analysis), to make it relevant to a community of readers (in Public Resonance), to invent a focused position (in Thesis), and to develop support (in Rhetorical Tools). Use the Invention questions in each section to explore further. Good luck!

# Point of Contact

The prompts on this page are designed to generate possible writing topics. Fill in the blanks with as many possibilities as you can until you find an engaging topic. You might imagine particular situations or people to help you start exploring ideas. But do not confine yourself to practical situations or personal experiences. Imagine possibilities beyond your experiences.

**Imagining New Connections**   Radical thinkers see connections not normally seen: an important connection between the economy and nature, oceans and people, music and politics, and so on. Imagine various possibilities, and fill in the blanks in the following statements:

Most people do not see the connection between _____ and _____.

Even though it is not apparent, _____ and _____ are deeply connected.

**Imagining Different Possibilities**   The policies and procedures of society often blind us to alternatives. Imagining those alternatives might reveal a new way to live. For example, someone might imagine something even better than democracy, or a new way to fund college, or an alternative to war. Fill in the blanks with possible ideas:

Presently, most people _____, but they could _____.

Presently, the law requires that people must _____, but the law could state that _____.

**Questioning Common Sense**   Living in a society means participating in common practices and beliefs. But a common belief is not always the best belief. Imagine possibilities for the following and fill in the blanks:

Most people in my community want _____ without examining the underlying meaning.

I have always been taught to think _____ but now see a different way.

**Exploring the Past and Future**   A radical vision sees beyond the confines of the present. A radical thinker might imagine what the world would be like if the American Revolution had not occurred, or how work in America will be defined in fifty years. As you imagine time beyond the present, fill in the blanks for the following:

In the past, people's perspective of _____ was fundamentally different from our present understanding.

In the future, people will probably understand _____ differently than we do.

**Going to the Root**   The term *radical* comes from the Latin *radix,* which means *root* or *source.* Radical thinking might be seen as a process of finding the root or essence. For example, someone might explore the essence of womanhood or manhood, the true meaning of growing old, or the essence of education. Fill in the blanks in the following questions:

What is the essence of _____?

What is the most fundamental quality of _____?

## Activity

In a small group, use the categories in this section to ask more questions. After generating more questions within these categories, try to create more categories, and then create several questions for each category. Do not stop generating questions until everyone participating has encountered a potential topic.

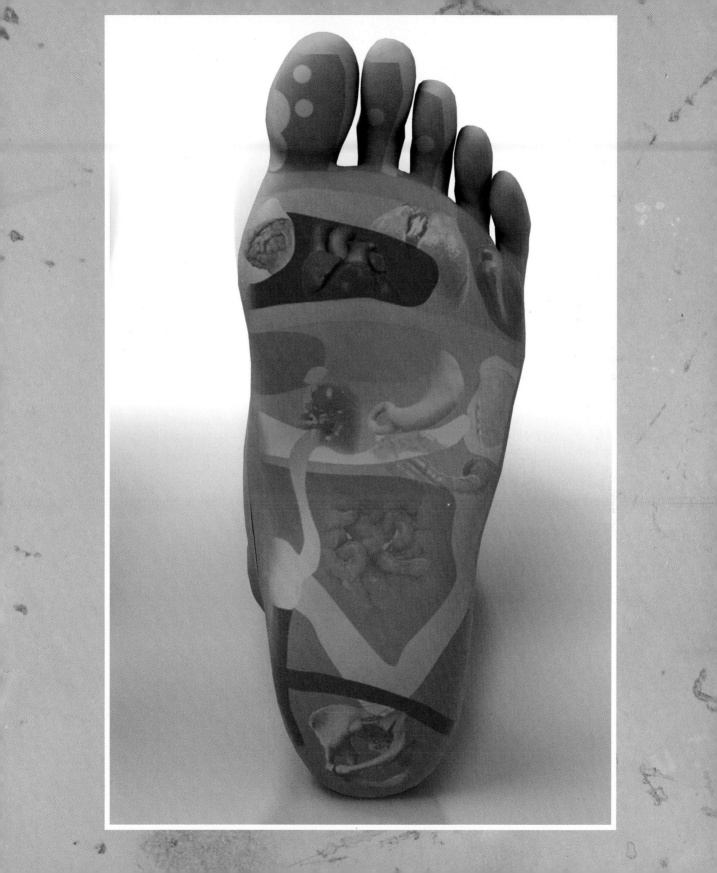

# Analysis

The intellectual activity in this chapter involves *theory*—reasoning that is divorced from practical or physical particulars. When people theorize, they explore the realm of ideas and assumptions and make generalized claims. For example, when Sigmund Freud theorized about the nature of the unconscious, he was not making guesses about his own mind, but that of the *human* mind. He theorized that psychological ailments emerge from childhood crises. His theory, like all theories, could be applied to particular situations; he used the general notion to help cure problems within specific patients.

Everyone has theories (general accounts or concepts that inform how we receive ideas and act on the world), but theories are usually not discussed openly. They most often lie undetected in our minds. For instance, people may have a theory about knowledge acquisition; that is, they may have a general account of how people come to know things. This theory may be fairly complicated and may involve memory, experience, and language use—but rarely do people examine such theories closely and ask hard questions: *How does language acquisition relate to knowledge acquisition?* Doing theory, then, is the act of examining and developing our concepts. As you can imagine, theorists take little for granted. They are not willing to accept the answers they have been given, but rather look around them and imagine what other answers may be possible.

## Activity

Doing theory requires a degree of intellectual play, as well as some deliberate and constructive probing. With several peers, choose one of the following topics:

- The difference between men and women
- When a child becomes an adult
- The relationship between individual and community
- The relationship between humans and nature

Each participant should explain his or her theory about the topic in one minute—or one paragraph if using e-mail or instant messaging. After each participant has a turn, start again: everyone should take another turn and build upon or speak back to particular points made in the previous round. After the second round, start again. After several rounds, each participant should write a brief paragraph explaining how the theory session changed, developed, confirmed, expanded, or highlighted his or her ideas.

# Theorists discuss what others avoid . . . or ignore.

Now, *theorize* about your topic: explore freely, beyond prior assumptions or quick answers. Ponder your topic for as long as possible before coming to any conclusions. Keep a notepad with you for a day or for several days while you rethink your ideas. Record even the most offbeat or seemingly irrelevant notions. The following questions will help you make connections and discover meaning:

## Invention Questions

▶ What is the basic or essential quality of the topic?

▶ How does the topic affect or influence thinking?

▶ How does conventional thought or practice keep people from a radical perspective on this topic?

▶ What is the origin of the topic?

▶ What do people normally not consider about the topic? ■

Use these questions to begin a process of exploration that you will continue through writing. For example, Linda, a business major, has chosen to explore the *essence of business.* In a discussion with peers, she begins to explore the topic:

**What is the basic or essential quality of the topic?**

LINDA: Well, I wonder if this topic can even be thought about radically, but let's try it: I think the basic quality of business is competition.

MARCUS: Competition with other people?

LINDA: Yes . . . I think so. Other people or companies— or even countries.

MARCUS: For that matter, what about towns and communities?

LINDA: Yeah, I guess so. Towns and communities do compete for customers, for market, for tourism dollars.

DIANA: So are all these people and communities competing for money?

LINDA: Ultimately, yes. But at first, they are competing for more customers or clients.

MARCUS: So . . . is it always about more customers? More money?

LINDA: Well, I'd think so. Certainly, for retail stores, the daily goal is getting more people through the doors and to the cash register than the store across the street.

DIANA: What if we looked at it like the companies are living organisms? I just saw something about bears on the Discovery Channel: Every summer and fall, before hibernation, the bears try to consume as much food as possible. But they also need to conserve their strength. They don't want to exert a lot of energy while trying to eat all this food. The ultimate goal isn't the amount of food. It's survival. The bears are competing for food, like salmon, but the essence of their competing is survival.

LINDA: So . . . back to business . . . companies are not necessarily competing for just money; they're competing for survival, for life.

MARCUS: That makes a lot of sense. Surviving in business involves making a lot of money (more than others), but it also involves conserving. Think about it: companies that are out just to make a lot of money go down quickly because they didn't conserve.

The important moment here is Diana's brave reference to the Discovery Channel. While bears and business have little in common, Diana is thinking about the essence of things—how entities stay alive. Her inventive connection makes the group rethink the essence of business. And now Linda's thoughts on the essence of business are beginning to take flight. She is going beyond the quick, easy response and exploring some hidden dynamics of business. If she continues developing these ideas, she could transcend conventional wisdom and make valuable discoveries.

# Thinking Further

Everyday language is filled with sayings that suggest indisputable truths. Widely used yet unexamined, these sayings, sometimes called *clichés,* conceal more truth than they communicate. They might even misguide our thinking. Consider the following: *What doesn't hurt you only makes you stronger. Bigger is better. Back to the basics. Boys will be boys.* Such clichés might get in the way of exploring your own topic, but they can also mark the exact spot where radical thinking is most needed. The following questions may help you explore beyond conventional thinking:

▶ Can you think of any clichés related to your topic?

▶ How do they limit thinking?

▶ Might the opposite of the cliché be true? ■

## Activity

In a small group, share topic ideas. Then list the common sayings, assertions, and opinions related to each topic. Capture all the conventional wisdom associated with each topic. What do people normally think, feel, and say about each? What are the common opinions, complaints, and hopes? The goal is to give each writer a clear sense of the conventional so that he or she can think beyond it.

# Clichés are intellectual bubbles. Pop them, and there's nothing there.

In his invention writing about the future, Simon Benlow explores the present:

**What do people normally not consider about the topic?**
People do not normally consider pollution and the future because nothing in our popular culture invites us to, unless it's some silly movie inviting us to imagine a post–world war future, or a not-so-silly documentary that we forget about as soon as the lights come back up. In general, we're not asked to consider how our present wants will influence anyone beyond ourselves. The presiding language of our culture is filled with provocations to be fulfilled, to be happy (i.e., buy lots of things and drive a new car). We keep building/buying bigger and bigger vehicles, and consider our actions only (only!) when gas prices go up. In other words, the general trend in buying goods is to wrap ourselves in as much luxury as our wallets allow.

Benlow then goes further when he thinks about the language we use in everyday life. He tries to get beyond the common phrases (such as "the future") that hide complexity:

**Can you think of any clichés related to your topic?**
Maybe "the future" itself is a cliché. If a cliché hides or glosses over complexity, that phrase ("the future") hides something. It hides the people out there in the distance . . . the real people who'll no doubt have to deal with our wants! When we say "the future" or "posterity" or "our children," we're just glossing over the real people who'll be living with policies and laws and practices that emerge from our overindulgence. "Make sure to wear your air mask, Connor." "Oh, I left it at school yesterday." And then, of course, if anyone today brings up things like breathing nontoxic air or drinking clean water, they get deemed "environmentalists," "tree huggers," "liberals," etc. These terms are ways of dismissing the present and the future . . . real humans with real lungs and kidneys. We've become a culture of lunatics.

# Public Resonance

In one sense, your topic may already have public resonance. Because you are theorizing (exploring general ideas rather than particular situations), your topic may easily connect to others. However, radical thinking runs the risk of alienating others. When writers transcend conventional wisdom, they must invite others into the new vision, which is no small task (consider Galileo's fate!). Use the following questions to help connect your ideas to readers' concerns:

▶ What is conventional thought on the topic?

▶ What nonconventional claims have been made about the topic?

▶ What keeps people from understanding the thing/idea in nonconventional ways?

▶ How would a new understanding of the topic help people? (Who, particularly, would a new understanding help?) ■

In his invention writing, Simon Benlow goes beyond naming "conventional thought." He tries to explain the nature of present thinking, how it works, how it is limited:

**What is conventional thought on the topic?**
The thing is . . . there is no conventional thought on this matter. People do not genuinely think about the future—in the specific and local sense. They don't imagine their lives affecting their grandchildren's world. People have been lulled into a present-tense-only mentality. Sure, most parents try to provide for their children . . . but they don't imagine how their lives (outside of creating a savings account) will affect the world that their children (and their children's children's children) will inhabit. In general, people in America spend most of their time thinking about their own financial existence, and the future earning power of their children. But they do not think about the air, the land, the water of the world 50 years, or 100 years, from now . . . and they don't imagine how present global politics might impact the future.

Writers who make radical (or new) claims cannot simply dismiss the beliefs of others; they must build an intellectual bridge between conventional thought and new thought. In a sense, this is the primary objective of the writing in this chapter. When making adventurous claims, it is especially important to make these connections, so your ideas have genuine significance and are more than vague abstractions. Simon Wykoff begins and ends his essay with a connection to readers' beliefs:

A common stereotype in today's society is that of the lazy bum. People see a homeless man on the side of the road, waiting for handouts, and assume that's all he ever does. In reality, this couldn't be farther from the truth. As the painter Willem de Kooning once said, "The trouble with being poor is that it takes up all of your time." This is absolutely true, and I think you'll find that homeless people are incredibly busy doing the most important job to all of us: surviving.

Wykoff immediately speaks to what many people believe: "A common stereotype in today's society. . . ." He helps the reader see that stereotype: "People see a homeless man on the side of the road, waiting for handouts, and assume that's all he ever does." Then he offers an alternate way of thinking: "I think you'll find that homeless people are incredibly busy doing the most important job to all of us: surviving." The details throughout the essay help the reader understand and accept an alternate viewpoint to the common stereotype. Then in his conclusion, Wykoff makes an explicit connection between this alternative and others' beliefs:

As you can see, my father's day was far from that simplistic stereotype of the bum who sits on street corners all day and waits for people to help him out. What people don't seem to realize is that to survive on the streets, you have to take things into your own hands. You need to have perseverance, stamina, and a little bit of luck. Though it may seem outlandish, I think you'll find that many homeless people work just as much, or more, than you.

# Thesis

A thesis provides focus. Since the ideas for a Thinking Radically essay are potentially abstract and far-reaching, a focused thesis will help keep the text from wandering. Notice how the following thesis statements focus on a particular topic, acknowledge a conventional view, and offer an alternative way of seeing. For example,

> Behind our desire to drive bigger vehicles and own bigger homes lurks more than an attraction to symbols of personal success; it is, rather, a deep hostility toward other people and the environment.

This thesis focuses on a particular topic: the desire to drive bigger vehicles and own bigger homes. It acknowledges a conventional view: this desire is related to one's personal success. And it offers an alternative way of seeing: the desire actually has more to do with one's hostility toward other people and the environment. Consider the focused topic, conventional view, and alternative way of seeing in the following thesis statements:

- While a glass ceiling may prevent women from climbing the ladder of success, women and men both would have a better quality of life if they participated on the lower rungs only.
- Though *Jeopardy* is often perceived as a test of intelligence, it is really a test of knowledge. A better test of intelligence is *Survivor* or *The Amazing Race,* which requires more analytical thinking skills.
- More gunfights and car crashes actually make a movie duller, not more exciting.
- Because people have come to believe it is the ultimate power, modern medicine has ironically done more harm than good in most people's lives.
- It is commonly thought that the North defeated the South in the Civil War. In fact, the South now controls the American government.
- Even just a cursory look at one's own life will turn up evidence that every American's primary function these days is to consume.

- While the American school system prepares citizens for employment, it allows (and perhaps encourages) them to be helpless against propaganda.
- Farmers or dogcatchers as politicians would serve the people better than professional politicians do.
- A president who doesn't understand why terrorists might fly planes into buildings is ultimately far more dangerous than the terrorists.
- The poor are better off than the wealthy.
- Had the electric guitar not been invented, the accordion would have continued its reign as the most popular instrument among American youth.
- Although students should feel comfortable in a college classroom, the uneasiness some students feel is necessary to learning.
- All animals, not just humans, should be given the right to life, liberty, and the pursuit of happiness.
- Because of credit and debt, most Americans today are unknowing slaves to the wealthy.
- College professors aren't any smarter than the average Joe.
- Eggs are more valuable than gold.
- Mundane tasks, like weeding a garden or doing the dishes, are a form of meditation that most Americans should indulge in more often and more earnestly.
- The way that Americans communicate with each other is a bigger threat than terrorism.

## Activity

Choose one of the statements on this page. Describe how it is or is not radical. Does it transcend or speak back to some particular conventional way of thinking? Does it reveal something usually overlooked or dismissed? How does the wording and construction of the sentence help the reader see something new?

# Evolution of a Thesis

Do not be in a hurry to solidify your thesis. As you write and think, ideas will evolve, and this *evolution* of ideas is the goal of academic writers. In the previous example, when Linda explored the topic of business, her ideas transformed over time. She started by trying to discover the essence or root of business. In her early discussion with peers (see the Analysis section, page 403), she discovered an alternative way of thinking, as illustrated in the move from the first and second statements. More focused and inventive thinking led her to the final statement.

Linda begins with a widely held understanding of her topic:

- The essence of business is making money.

She develops a position different from conventional thinking:

- Like any organism, the essence of business is survival.

She shapes the idea as she writes:

- Beneath the everyday affairs of making money, the essence of business is survival, which involves consuming and conserving.

Because this chapter invites you beyond your initial opinion, you might be wondering: *Am I supposed to give my opinion, or what?* This is a fair question. A radical statement is an opinion insofar as a single writer is offering a new way to see a topic. But it is more than a personal opinion. It is a writer's attempt at rethinking something, and an invitation to others to rethink.

While you may begin your exploration with an opinion, your thinking will evolve. When a writer provides support for an opinion, the opinion becomes a claim. By supporting a claim, the writer is now making an argument, not just expressing an opinion or saying what he or she thinks.

## Revising Your Thesis

How do you know that your opinion is speaking back to conventional views? How do you know that you've gone far enough in your thinking? To answer these questions, you might enlist the help of others in reevaluating your thesis. In a small group, present your topic. Have the group members describe all the conventional opinions they can imagine. Then present your thesis and explain why you think it responds to or transcends conventional thinking. The group should then ask:

- Does the thesis uncover something new?
- Does it offer a new way of seeing the topic?
- If not, what is holding it back?

**A radical statement is more than a personal opinion. It is an invitation to rethink.**

# Rhetorical Tools

It will take various rhetorical tools to help the reader understand and possibly accept an entirely new vision. In addition to the ones mentioned here, consider the strategies discussed in other chapters, particularly Chapter 7.

## Using Narration

Narration draws readers into a set of events. A narrative or story can help writers illustrate a broader point; when making adventurous claims, a narrative can help bridge the gap between conventional and radical ideas. Throughout his essay, Simon Wykoff uses narration to help the reader understand his broader point about how hard some homeless people work:

> Once he had some food in his belly, he usually tried to locate a current paper. This often meant waiting around in coffee shops until someone left one on the table after their breakfast. Sometimes this step could take him hours, but he was determined not to waste the precious money on a newspaper when he could get it for free with patience.
>
> As soon as he had the paper, he thumbed through it, looking for jobs he could feasibly apply to. Due to his particular circumstances, he was without official identification. This, of course, made the search much more difficult. If he found something, he would tear off the piece of the paper and store it to refer to later.

## Using Description

Writers making adventurous or radical claims must consider the intellectual positions of their audience. Because readers may have no mental pictures of the ideas being put forth, it is up to the writer to sufficiently describe or characterize ideas. Notice Benlow's description, which helps the reader to see evidence of his claims:

> Nearly every person of every town had his or her own internal combustion engine lawn mower, leaf blower, snow blower, hedge trimmer. Nearly every home and vehicle had air conditioners. And beyond these "utili-

ties," we had hordes of trinkets, recreational instruments, and pleasure devices that all, eventually, had to lie in waste somewhere when our fickle appetites refocused on the new faster-smoother-quicker-shinier-more-interactive-more-believable-gadget.

## Using Figurative Language

Literal description is sometimes insufficient to communicate the depth of an idea. This is when writers turn to figurative language, such as similes and metaphors, which help to represent complex or particularly abstract ideas. Notice Benlow's simile, which develops into a metaphor:

> Like a mass of delirious adolescents, we made ourselves increasingly giddy, posing for ourselves and for one another, posing in every aspect of our lives: our homes, travel, clothes, food, water, and vacations. It was a mammoth parade of teenage delirium that began in New York, wormed through every tiny town of the Midwest, and wrapped around itself in dizzying perpetual circles on the beaches of California. As it came through every town, no one could resist it. It banged and clamored and woke everyone from dreamy isolation, and so even the most ascetic types found themselves playing along in some small way.

## Counterarguments and Concessions

Especially when their claims are unconventional, writers must anticipate and account for positions opposed to their own. Counterarguments anticipate and refute opposing positions while concessions acknowledge their value. In one sense, a Thinking Radically essay, or any essay that makes an argument, is like one big counterargument to a more conventional way of thinking. Notice how Wykoff frames his entire essay as a counterargument, or response, to another position:

> A common stereotype in today's society is that of the lazy bum. People see a homeless man on the side of the road, waiting for handouts, and assume that's all

he ever does. In reality, this couldn't be farther from the truth. . . .

Kathleen Norris's essay illustrates the same point. After explaining a certain way of thinking about celibacy, Norris responds, framing the rest of her essay as a sort of counterargument:

> One could well assume that this is celibacy, impure and simple. And this is unfortunate, because celibacy practiced rightly is not at all a hatred of sex; in fact it has the potential to address the troubling sexual idolatry of our culture.

While it can help to think of one's entire essay as a counterargument, it's also important to make smaller counterarguments at key points throughout the essay, taking on particular opposing points within the broader, overall argument.

While counterarguments refute, concessions acknowledge the value of others' positions. Even though a text making radical claims may not be openly argumentative, by definition it seeks to overturn conventional ideas. For this reason, concessions can be essential to engaging potentially apprehensive readers. Notice Benlow's concession in the following example. Most of his essay condemns his own generation, but he offers this small note, suggesting that people were more weak than evil. Without such a concession, readers would be more apt to reject Benlow's ideas as purely antagonistic:

> Although it is probably impossible, I hope you do not look back and characterize us as purely self-serving and wicked, but as trapped in our own enterprise. We were a young culture with no parents.

## Outside Sources

Radical or adventurous claims do not exist in a vacuum; they exist alongside other similar claims and discoveries. While Wykoff develops his argument primarily through a personal narrative about his father, notice how he reinforces this position with an outside source:

> The next thing he did after looking for job opportunities was to get money in order to buy food for the rest of the day. While you may see many homeless panhandling, I think people don't realize that a large number of homeless actually do small-time work for

their daily bread. As mentioned in an online editorial, the homeless these days are increasingly working menial tasks for extra cash, or just to survive (Hilton). For all the people you see standing outside of stores with signs, others are playing instruments on street corners, gathering cans for recycling, or washing windows.

### Research versus Mesearch

Finding outside sources that confirm our positions and support our worldviews is usually easy. But such work, what we might call *mesearch*, misses the spirit and goal of *research*, which is to explore beyond our own initial suppositions, to read and rethink topics. Researching can be an inventive process—one that catapults us beyond initial ideas.

#### Avoid:

- Collecting statistics without questioning them, reflecting on them, and evaluating their significance.
- Limiting your exploration to sources that share your opinion or perspective.
- Merely "proving" your position with others' words.

#### Try:

- Gathering perspectives from a variety of sources.
- Closely examining writers who oppose your perspective or who see the world differently.
- Directly addressing the unstated assumptions and values in the sources. Try to discover what the writers value, hope for, or dismiss. What is their basic view of the world, and how does that influence their approach to the topic?

# Organizational Strategies

## How Should I Begin?

The important point to remember in this chapter is that the writing must move the readers outside of their comfortable intellectual positions. Readers tend to associate highly conventional writing structure with conventional thinking. So if writers want to move readers beyond conventional thinking, they might do well to explore alternative introduction strategies.

Consider an introductory strategy you would not typically use: anecdote, scenario, allusion, figurative language, question. For any of these introduction strategies, remember that an opening paragraph should not only establish the tone of a text; it should also create an intellectual climate that is developed throughout the text.

## How Should I Make Connections to Conventional Thinking?

Conventional ideas are those you are trying to transcend or challenge. You might treat them as you would treat opposing arguments, using paragraphs to distinguish between conventional and radical ideas in the same way as you would for counterargument.

  ¶ Conventional thinking
  ¶ New radical thinking
  ¶ Conventional thinking
  ¶ New radical thinking

Or you might use the turnabout paragraph (see page 000). For example, consider Linda's topic (in the Analysis section): the essence of business. In making a connection to conventional thinking, she could use a paragraph that shifts to her new ideas. Notice the turnabout in the middle of the following sample paragraph where the direction shifts and introduces the new way of thinking:

Money seems to be the thing that drives business. It seems to be the ultimate goal, the bottom line, the thing that is pursued every hour of every day. We might even say that money itself is the essence of business. It is, after all, the life source of every business enterprise, from the major international retail chain to the small-town Ma and Pa restaurant. However, money is merely the engine—the thing that sustains and develops business. It is not the essence. The essence of business is the same as the essence of a living organism: the struggle for survival. And when survival is the root of business, an exaggerated focus on money can actually put the nail in the coffin.

## How Should I Conclude?

Apprehensive readers might see radical claims as irrelevant, even dangerous, so writers must be vigilant about connecting to readers. Conclusions are especially important places for making those connections and for making the claims in the text relevant and valuable to the world shared by the writer and readers. You might say that a conclusion is where the writer uses *the most dramatic or direct means for connecting the idea to the reader*. Notice, for instance, Benlow's conclusion; he offers a scenario and an image that reinforce the main idea of the essay:

And if you could return to our time, I would make a dubious wager that you, too, would find it difficult to resist the lure of our lifestyle, the attraction of our conveniences. And if we had been able to imagine you as real people, even as our own distant progeny, rather than a simple euphemism ("the future"), we certainly would have acted differently. Although we probably would not have relented in our give-it-to-me-now race for more, we would have taken a solemn moment to raise a toast and drink to your hardship.

# Writer's Voice

## Engaging the Reader

Writers invite readers to participate in essays through the ideas they communicate and through the way they communicate those ideas. Every writer in every writing situation creates a voice—a character that is projected by the language and style of the writing. If writers want a reader to *hear them out* or *give their ideas a chance,* they must make writerly decisions that create an engaging, not an alienating, voice. An engaging voice, however, can sound quite different from one essay to the next. For example, notice Wykoff's voice, and then Benlow's:

- Before I begin, something you need to understand is that my father did not make use of services like shelters during his many years of homelessness.
- The first thing my father did upon waking up was check his belongings. Depending on the place he was sleeping, there was a good chance that something could have been stolen from him in the middle of the night.
- Once he had some food in his belly, he usually tried to locate a current paper.
- I should interject here and explain how he got around the city.

Wykoff's word choice and sentence structure reflects his topic and position on that topic. He hopes to help the reader see the hard work and dignity of a homeless man, so he uses language that is straightforward and ordinary but appropriately formal and respectful. Benlow's voice is different, as is his purpose in writing, his audience, and his subject matter. He is apologizing to future generations about harm caused to their lives.

> I imagine that you are breathing the exhaust fumes of our disregard. If large metropolitan areas are still inhabitable, your citizens must certainly deal with a plague of airborne toxins (brought on by war, pollution, or both). Perhaps you wear air masks. Perhaps you figured out how to purify the air. Perhaps most of your income goes to such causes.

While both Wykoff and Benlow speak directly and clearly to the reader, they craft different voices because of the different writing situations, which are determined by their purpose for writing, the audience, the subject, and the relationship the writers want readers to have with their ideas.

## Considering Formality

While some writers tend toward a formal, sober tone, others use comedy or informality to connect with readers. Notice how the essays in this chapter maintain an appropriate level of formality. For example, while Wykoff and Benlow speak directly to the reader, they are not overly casual, nor are they overly formal or elaborate. Wykoff's language can be described as conversational, yet it is not chatty (or overly conversational):

> I should interject here and explain how he got around the city. While my father was homeless, he was lucky enough to have a bicycle, which he treasured beyond everything else. It's not uncommon in a larger city to have the place you get food, the place you sleep, and the place you go to try and earn money be miles and miles apart. Because of this, even on a bike my father spent a considerable amount of time traveling. He would often ride from one end of the city to the other several times a day. This takes an incredible amount of endurance, especially when you are doing it on an empty stomach, as he often was. Many times, just a trip from the place he was sleeping to the closest bakery in the morning was a marathon.

# Vitality

Creating vitality in writing means creating life—making language feel lively and real to the humans who engage it. (Remember, readers are real humans who are swirling around in their own messy lives.) When language is intensive enough, it draws us inward to the ideas. Consider the following strategies, which may fall outside the normal or "safe" academic sentence patterns.

## Try the Stylistic Fragment

Sentence fragments are grammatical errors. They occur when a writer punctuates a phrase or dependent clause as though it were a full sentence. Here are some examples of sentence fragments:

### Fragment Errors

- By writing on the sidewalk in colored chalk and then hiring an airplane to write the message in the sky.
- Because the grand opening of the hotel coincided with the holiday parade and the community's main fundraising festival.
- Just when Marvin flummoxed the toss and flailed wildly at Herdie's aunt, who was then experiencing an intestinal expression.

None of the preceding examples can stand alone as full sentences. This is not because of the content, but because of the grammatical structure. None of them is an independent clause.

But some writers venture into fragments intentionally. They deliberately craft fragments, because breaking the conventions calls the reader out of a comfortable intellectual pattern. Notice the (italicized) stylistic fragments in the following passages.

### Stylistic Fragments

- At some point in its life cycle, business must conserve. *Like a lion or a bear. Like any organism.*
- Sooner, rather than later, evaluating performance will not be the enterprise of faculty. It'll be the work of outside corporations. *Profit hounds. Performance peddlers.*
- *When everything seems broken. When nothing seems fixable. When persistent crisis looms.* These are the conditions that make political parties comfortable. Then, they can further etch their agendas into the masses by detailing the wrongs of the other party.

The italicized fragments are technically incorrect. But the writers decided to use the unconventional to help create vitality and intensity.

## Deliberately Break Some Other Rule

Grammar is a set of conventions—a code agreed upon and supported by institutions within a culture. But all codes are toyed with. People who know the codes of a culture well intentionally tamper . . . for one of several reasons:

- They want to explore the limits of language and not simply use it.
- They want to assert some sense of individuality—something beyond their complicity in rules.
- They want readers to share in a brief moment of nonconformity.

And, believe it or not, academia is a perfect place for intellectual rule breaking. In fact, many would argue that the job of academia is to make certain that students know the rules so well that they can break them with grace and purpose. Playing with the conventions of language helps us to better understand what's possible, intellectually speaking. Keep in mind that rule breaking should not be a mere game of self-indulgence. It should increase the vitality of the text and the reader's understanding of your ideas.

## Give Your Essay an Engaging Title and Sharpen Your Opening Sentence

An engaging title helps to capture the reader's interest, suggest the writer's position on the topic, and establish a tone for the essay. It gets the essay off to a good start. While some titles leap into the writer's mind like a gift out of nowhere, others emerge slowly over time as the writer invents and revises.

Like titles, opening sentences can either engage or alienate a reader. For example, an obvious, general opening sentence, such as "There are many kinds of people in the world," can send a reader the unintended message that the rest of the essay will communicate equally obvious, and therefore uninteresting, ideas. The obvious opening sentence has created this expectation in the reader's mind.

### Activities

1. In a small group, create a passage that integrates one or several stylistic fragments. Share the passage with the rest of the class and explain how the fragment adds life to the ideas.

2. As you look over your writing, consider some sentence-level rule. Break it. Make certain you explore this option with your instructor. Also make certain you understand your own motives!

3. With a group of peers, discuss the titles in this chapter: "Celibate Passion," "An Apology to Future Generations," "Unemployed and Working Hard." Which title is most engaging and why? How does each title reflect the tone of its essay?

4. With a group of peers, discuss possible titles for your essays for this chapter. Have fun suggesting alternative titles that capture interest, suggest the writer's position, and establish tone.

5. With a group of peers, discuss the opening sentences for Norris's, Benlow's, and Wykoff's essays. How does each sentence encourage the reader to keep reading?

6. Browse through the other chapters in this book, reading the opening sentences of their essays. Which opening sentence is most engaging? Why?

7. With a group of peers, discuss the opening sentences of your essays for this chapter. First, decide whether each opening sentence is specific and engaging or general and obvious. Then have the group discuss how to make it sharper.

## Create a moment of nonconformity!

# Revision

Because you are asking the reader to re-see an idea so completely, you must first participate in that re-seeing by revising carefully. Before exchanging drafts with another writer, revisit the Invention Questions in the Analysis and Public Resonance sections to see how they might help you write an even more focused, more revealing thesis. Then revisit the Rhetorical Tools section to see how else you might help the reader understand and accept your thesis.

## Peer Review

Exchange drafts with at least one other writer. First underline the thesis or write it at the top of your essay. This way, reviewers will get traction as they read.

**As a reviewer, use the following questions to guide your response.**

1. Does the thesis offer a new way of thinking about the topic? Why or why not?
2. In what sense does this essay transcend or speak back to conventional thinking?
3. Where is the writing most descriptive and specific? Where could the writer be more specific? Remember that it is easy, but less valuable, to remain entirely abstract and general. If the writer makes a general statement (about business, students, women, and so on), it must be exemplified. As a reader, you should come away from the essay with some specific image or impression imprinted on your thoughts. Have you?
4. Where does the writer use appeals to logic? Can you follow the line of reasoning? If not, at what point does it break down? (See the discussion of logos in Chapter 7, page 233.)
5. Play devil's advocate for a moment: What points seem entirely ungrounded or unreasonable? Why? What could the writer do to make the point more reasonable?
6. Suggest specific points that the writer should concede or qualify. For instance, the writer's position might seem too extreme; the claims might include too many people or include a large, diverse group without making any distinctions. Point out such claims, and help

the writer to see the need to acknowledge subtlety, complexity, and exceptions.
7. Does the writer do anything unconventional or especially engaging with the organization? Is the introduction especially intense? The conclusion? Where does the writer seem to rely on old standard strategies?
8. Consider the writer's voice.
   a. Describe how it engages you with the ideas. Do any passages seem unengaging? Why?
   b. Describe the level of formality. Is it appropriate for the topic, the writer's approach, the assignment?
9. What is the most engaging passage in the draft so far? Why?
10. Check for sentence vitality.
    a. Offer a strategy for a stylistic fragment.
    b. Consider vitality strategies from other chapters:
       • If you encounter any noun clusters, suggest a revision of the sentence.
       • When possible, change nouns (such as in *make a decision*) to verbs *(decide)*.
       • Circle any unnecessary modifiers *(very, really, certainly,* and so on).
       • Where can the writer avoid drawing attention to *I* and *you?*
       • Where can the writer change linking verbs to active verbs?
       • Point to expletives (such as *there are* and *it is*).
       • Help the writer change passive verbs to active verbs for more vitality.

## Questions for Research

If the writer used outside sources:

• Where must he or she include in-text citations? (See pages 470–471.)

• Are quotations blended smoothly into the argument and punctuated correctly? (See pages 456–468.)

• Where could more direct textual cues or transitions help the reader? (See pages 466–467.)

• Is the Works Cited page formatted properly? (See pages 469–480.)

# Reflection

Now that you have challenged conventional thinking and explored new possibilities, you can develop further as a writer and thinker by stepping back and reflecting. As you respond to the following questions, write well, crafting complete sentences and supporting your claims:

1. How does your essay transcend the intellectual norm and reveal a new pattern of thinking?
2. How did you discover and develop a new way of thinking through your response to a particular Invention Question in this chapter?
3. What particular support strategy (or rhetorical tool) was most important in helping the reader understand the essay's main idea?

4. Why is your writer's voice effective for this particular essay? Describe your voice and refer to several sentences from your essay as examples.
5. Did you purposely break any grammatical rules in your essay? What was your motive? What was the result?

## Beyond the Essay: Create a Visual Essay

Conventional thinking can be challenged in a variety of ways: images, posters, even bumper stickers. Combine several images to create a visual essay that challenges common thinking.

Carl Dwyer/StockXchng; "I DEPEND ON FOREIGN OIL" banner: Cengage Learning; "DRILL ALASKA": Cengage Learning; Hummer: Lars Sundström/Cengage LearningStockXchng; Saudi Arabian: Lynsey Addario/Corbis; 1895 map of Alaska: Ray Sterner/John Hopkins University

For additional resources including instructional videos and links to helpful websites, access your English CourseMate through cengagebrain.com.

# 13 Finding Sources

# Chapter Contents

# Using Catalogs and Databases

When writing instructors refer to sources, they most often mean nonfiction published works: books, periodicals (journals, magazines, and newspapers), government documents, reference texts, audio recordings, video recordings, and digital texts like blogs and e-mails. In short, a source is anything that has been written, reported, recorded, or performed—everything from a blog to a formal academic study. In many ways, the process of finding, reading, and analyzing sources is a process of invention. It involves not simply gathering information but also engaging the theories, assumptions, perspectives, and outright arguments of others. For this reason, researchers should not see themselves as *finding and consuming information* but rather *building ideas* with the help of (many) others.

## Online Catalogs

Almost universally, libraries use online catalogues for their book and government document collections. A few simple moves can streamline the search process: adding words narrows a search, while using fewer words broadens the scope. For instance, "economics" by itself tells the catalog to find any and all works with "economics" in the title or description. (At Northwestern Michigan College, this search yielded 1,387 works.) "Economics and consumers" narrows the search (and yielded nine works—a much more reasonable number to browse).

Most catalogs give search options: *an author search, a title search, a subject search,* or *a keyword search.* Author and title searches are appropriate only if you are seeking out a particular source or author by name. Subject searches, which are organized by common headings such as *agriculture, government,* or *gender,* may be valuable for early stages of research—before writers have begun narrowing their insights. Keyword searches are most helpful after you have generated a list of possible words and phrases related to your topic.

# Periodical Databases

Newspapers and magazines most often have their own websites. But researchers can rely on electronic databases such as Academic Search Elite, JSTOR, or Academic One File to navigate through the millions of available articles. Like online catalogs, periodical databases give a range of search options: author, title, subject, and keyword searches. Adding words to a search tends to narrow the focus (and limit the number of returns). For example, the keyword search for "weight" on one database produced 804 entries. Narrowing the search by typing "weight and body" produced only 146 entries. Thus, if you are seeking sources about weight and the body, "weight and body" would narrow the results to more relevant sources.

Database searches can be made more efficient by using the following words (called *Boolean operators*):

- Using *and* between words narrows a search by finding documents containing multiple words—*weight and body.*
- Using *or* between words broadens a search by finding documents with either word in a multiword search—*weight or body.*
- Using *and not* between words finds documents excluding the word or phrase following "and not"—*weight and not body* (that is, *weight* only, without any references to *body*).
- Using *near* between words finds documents containing both words or phrases that are near, but not necessarily next to, each other—*weight near body.*

Also, remember that a simple keyword search can turn up thousands of returns. Narrowing one's focus by typing "weight and body and media," for example, will eliminate irrelevant returns found by typing just "weight."

Sources themselves can also lead the way to more sources. If an article, for instance, seems particularly helpful or in tune with your claims, examine its works cited or references list. Chances are, the author has already made some connections or used sources that are directly relevant to your topic and position.

## Where Are We? The Web or a Database?

Periodical databases are not necessarily on the web. They are their own special island. While they are accessible via an Internet service, they are not websites. Databases such as Academic Search Elite function like resource centers. They collect and categorize articles—most of which have been published in print prior to being uploaded in the electronic format. In other words, database administrators and editors have already done significant work for you. They have compiled sources, created abstracts, and uploaded them into searchable categories and subcategories. And some have even created the formal citations (MLA, APA, Chicago, and so on) for each source. Such databases are usually not open to everyone on the Internet. They are for subscribers only—or for students who attend a school that has paid the subscription fee.

## Activities

1. In a periodical database, try several keyword approaches for each of the following questions: In what ways might organized sports harm the young children who participate in them? What is the impact on the environment of people relocating to western states? What novel written in the last half of the twentieth century has been most influential?

2. List the different types of sponsors for websites that you found. For example, did you find government-sponsored websites? Websites created and maintained by businesses? Individuals? Nonprofit organizations?

In the old days of walking through library stacks and looking for a particular book, researchers would invariably scan adjacent titles—and often find a number of similar sources. That still happens today! People *still* find important sources in print form. Also, many databases and online catalogs have added tools that connect researchers to related material. For example, after a researcher has clicked on a source, the database may give a list of related search words or subjects. In other words, the database may "know" what you want. (Databases are smart—and getting smarter.) In the following example, the database offers a link, in the left margin, that connects users to similar sources. Once you have found a key article, this "SmartText" feature connects you to sources that are often directly related:

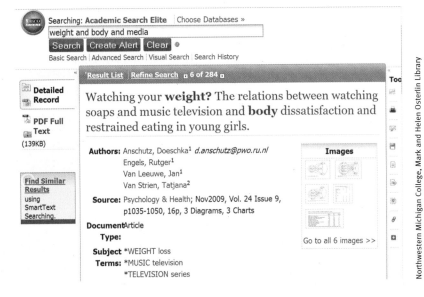

# Conducting Interviews

At a basic level, interviewing involves gathering information from a single person. But it can mean a great deal more. Good interviewers seek to engage interviewees in intensive conversations. They probe for knowledge and ideas, but they also allow interviewees to explore and develop ideas. A good interview, like a good essay, goes beyond basic knowledge; it provides insight.

## Asking the Right Questions

Good interview questions create focus, yet allow interviewees to explore. While they may seek out specific information (data, facts, dates), interview questions should go beyond collecting basic knowledge. (In fact, asking interviewees basic information that can be retrieved through print sources undermines the interview process.) A more valuable strategy is to prompt interviewees to reflect on the meaning of issues or to make connections between ideas. Notice the difference between the following:

> What's it like being a doctor?
>
> How has working in the medical field influenced your personal life?

The first question does not focus attention on any particular issue; the interviewee could talk about anything related to the profession. The second question, however, draws attention to a particular issue, asking the interviewee to consider a particular relationship. It is more specific than the first question but still calls for a certain degree of exploration.

Effective questions can come from good planning, but good interviewers also depart from their scripted questions when they see an opportunity to further engage the interviewee. Following up on an interviewee's answers, in fact, is the interviewer's most powerful research tool. While a survey can only ask a list of preformulated questions, an interview can follow a line of thought that comes from an interviewee's response.

Imagine the following scenario, in which a researcher is interviewing a civil engineer:

INTERVIEWER:    Is being a civil engineer interesting?
ENGINEER:    Sure. I get to deal with all kinds of people and very real situations.
INTERVIEWER:    Is being a civil engineer hard?
ENGINEER:    Well, some of the work can be difficult. Trying to figure in all the variables in a given project can be a mathematical nightmare.

## Field Research

Academic writers also do field research: experiments, observations, interviews, and surveys. Field research is often referred to as *primary* research because the researcher interacts directly with the subject(s) and is engaged in the activities and behavior of the thing being studied. This chapter briefly describes two common modes of field research for English studies: interviews and surveys.

| INTERVIEWER: | What would you tell someone who wants to become a civil engineer? |

Here, the interviewer comes up short in several ways. First, the questions are mundane. As worded here, such questions would probably not yield focused and insightful answers; they prompt the engineer to respond in general terms. They are surface questions (the kind one might ask at a party), which yield short and uncomplicated answers. Also, the interviewer ignores opportunities to follow up. After the engineer's first responses, the interviewer could have asked about the "very real situations" or the "mathematical nightmare" but leaves both ideas and, instead, moves to the next question. This interview does not probe for insight or engage the thoughts of the interviewee, but merely poses a list of unrelated questions. The following example, however, shows a different approach:

| INTERVIEWER: | How is a civil engineer important to society? |
| ENGINEER: | Well, civil engineers conceptualize living space for the public. They envision what it might be like to live in particular place, say, a downtown area, and then lay out plans to make a park, an intersection, even an entire downtown livable—and they do it all while considering how an area will grow and how people's needs may change. |
| INTERVIEWER: | So civil engineers have to be visionaries? |
| ENGINEER: | Yes! They are not simply figuring formulas about buildings and zones and land; they are imagining what it might be like to live and work within a given area in the present and future. |
| INTERVIEWER: | And they do all this while accommodating the demands of city officials? |

Here, the interviewer starts with a more insightful question. While the first interviewer depends on a vague concept ("interesting"), the second interviewer seeks out the meaning of a potential relationship (between civil engineers and society) and consequently receives an insightful response. Also, the interviewer in the second scenario springboards from the engineer's answers ("So civil engineers have to be visionaries?"), thereby extending initial thoughts. The second interview evolves, even within a short amount of time.

# Integrating Interviews into Your Writing

Ideas from an interview can be incorporated into various writing situations and purposes. An interview can be used to support claims made in argument, to help explain an idea, or even to help explain the history or significance of some topic. In the following example, notice how the information helps support an idea:

> Most often the water sewers can withstand the runoff from storms, but the past season has illustrated the inadequacy of the current sewer system. According to Harold Johnston, director of utilities, the sewer system was

overwhelmed twice in the past three and a half months, and the result was that untreated sewage flowed out into Silver Lake. When an overflow occurs and untreated water spills into the natural water system, the high amounts of bacteria affect the wildlife and jeopardize the health of swimmers and water enthusiasts. In essence, anyone or anything in the lake for days after an overflow is swimming in sewage.

Here, the writer is trying to persuade readers that the water treatment system in her town is inadequate. The claim made by the director of utilities supports the idea. Although the writer probably collected extensive information about the treatment system, she used only one particular point in this paragraph because it directly supports the main idea. (Other information might be used in different passages.)

# Planning an Interview

When setting up an interview, be sure to respect the interviewee's position and accommodate his or her schedule. Researchers should never impose themselves on potential interviewees. Use the following hints and strategies:

- Always request an interview well in advance of your own deadlines.
- When making a request, introduce yourself and the reason for the interview: Explain the nature of your research and how the interview will be integrated.
- Beforehand, negotiate a reasonable amount of time for the interview (such as thirty minutes)—and stick to it so as not to impinge on the interviewee's time.
- Plan out the method of recording responses—writing, audiotaping, or videotaping. Ask the interviewee if his or her answers can be recorded, and if his or her name can be used in the research.
- At the end of the interview, thank the interviewee for his or her time, and leave promptly.

# Creating Surveys

While an interview is based on an individual's knowledge, a survey attempts to find public opinion on a topic. An interview is driven, in part, by the interviewee; his or her insights may influence the direction or emphasis of the interview. But with surveys, the researcher prearranges the direction and emphasis with carefully formulated questions.

## Generating Questions

In generating survey questions, a researcher should consider three points:

1. Questions should not lead the respondent to a particular answer. Good survey questions avoid influencing the respondents' thinking about the issue. For instance, a question that asks *Is our current president completely out of touch with public opinion?* leads the respondent toward a negative evaluation of the president. Such questions prompt respondents to take up a certain position even before answering. A better approach is to state the question without leading the respondent; for example: *Is the current president in touch with labor issues in America?*

2. Questions should narrow the focus of the respondents on a specific topic. While good survey questions should not influence the respondents' thinking on an issue, questions should create a particular focus. For instance, a question that asks *Has the president taken an appropriate stance on international trade?* is more focused than *Do you like our current president?*

3. Questions should use common or unspecialized language. Because survey respondents may come from different walks of life, survey questions should avoid technical jargon or specialized terminology.

## Choosing Respondents

Surveyors must consider the demographics (or particular characteristics) of their potential respondents.

What is the age range in the respondent group?

What is the racial makeup of the respondent group?

What is the gender makeup of the respondent group?

What is the occupational makeup of the respondent group?

What is the geographical origin of the respondent group?

People's occupations, gender, ethnicity, age, and geography impact their understanding of the world—and how they are likely to respond to any particular issue.

---

## Sample Survey: Working Hours

Please respond to the following questions. Use the back of the page if you need more space.

1. Do you currently hold a full-time or part-time job? If so, what is the nature of the work?

2. If you work part time, how many hours per week?

3. How many hours per week are you contracted to work? (Or how many hours per week are you supposed to work, according to the job description?)

4. How many hours per week do you normally work (at or away from the job site)? Do you work weekends?

5. How much time do you spend preparing for and/or traveling to and from work? (Feel free to give specifics.)

6. Is overtime mandatory or voluntary at your job? (What kinds of incentive are offered for overtime?)

7. Do you feel sufficiently compensated for the work you do? Why or why not?

For instance, imagine a survey about college life: if all the respondents are college instructors, the answers will probably reflect certain biases and assumptions—which may be entirely different from those of students or people not associated with college life.

# Recording and Using Responses

Responses can be recorded in various ways. Perhaps the easiest means is to elicit written responses by asking the respondents to write or check off their answers. But if that is not possible, the researcher must do the recording by writing or taping. (If you plan to record answers, either with video or audio equipment, you must always ask the respondents' permission.)

Survey responses are most often used to show public opinion about a topic or to illustrate common trends in everyday life. A writer researching work issues among students at her college might discover important trends:

> While many students take a full course load, they also work late on week-nights and throughout the weekends. In an informal survey, 24 of 35 respondents reported that they work at least 25 hours each week—and 21 of those 35 work over 30 hours each week. One student explained her situation bluntly: "No one told me that a full load of classes would compete with my work schedule. I thought I could do both, but it's nearly impossible."

Notice that the writer uses the information from the survey to enhance the significance, or the public resonance, of her topic. She sets up the idea in her first sentence and then plugs in the information from the survey.

The sample survey shown on the preceding page offers room for the respondents to write in answers and to develop their thoughts. You could imagine someone responding to this survey fairly quickly because the questions are limited in number and fairly simple. While it could offer some valuable insights about working hours, it is also limited in its scope, like all surveys. Because this survey does not ask for personal information from the respondents (age, sex, education, etc.), the researcher should be careful not to make broad statements about salary and job satisfaction in America, but to stay focused on the amount of time people dedicate to their jobs.

 For additional resources including instructional videos and links to helpful websites, access your English CourseMate through cengagebrain.com.

# 14 Analyzing, Synthesizing, and Evaluating Sources

# Chapter Contents

John Metz

# Developing Critical Literacy

In the age of digital information, researchers have to make constant decisions about the nature and use of sources. They have to decide how a Wikipedia entry, for instance, may differ from a journal article or a historic document. They have to *analyze* the intended audience of sources, *evaluate* sources according to standard criteria, and *synthesize* sometimes contradictory voices. The process can be dizzying. Researchers must develop the ability to sift through the mountains of opinions, reports, images, theories, and data—and to make sound judgments about the nature of all that information. Scholars and teachers across the disciplines often refer to this ability as *critical literacy.*

## "Just the Facts, Please"— or Maybe Not

In a world saturated with information (news reports, breaking news reports, blogs, tweets, documentaries, and talk shows for every political persuasion), people sometimes long for simple facts. They want to read or hear something without an overt opinion attached to it. But this can be a naïve and even dangerous hope. Facts are tricky. They can *appear* unbiased, but they often emerge from a particular worldview, from a specific way of interpreting a situation. For instance, consider the following two reports about the same event:

> A) Today in Milford, rush hour traffic was slowed when over two-thousand protesters gathered around the town square to challenge a new city ordinance that will allow Pemblebrook Industries to open another facility in the city limits. The new facility will bring thirty to forty new jobs into Milford. Construction is to begin by early fall.

> B) Today in Milford, over two-thousand people gathered downtown in a peaceful protest against a new city ordinance that will change zoning of the Stark's wetland area. The ordinance, passed in an unpublicized overnight council meeting, was celebrated by Pemblebrook Industries, which hopes to drain and pave the wetland and make way for a new bottling facility.

Both passages report facts, and the facts themselves may seem unbiased. However, the selection of facts in each portrays a particular slant on the situation. In passage A, the situation itself is framed by traffic. In passage B, the situation is framed by the cause of the protest. In A, we learn about new jobs but do not learn about the destruction of wetlands. In B, we learn about an overnight meeting but not the jobs. Each report invites us to see the Milford protest in a particular light. If these passages were published in a newspaper, the headlines might read:

| **Headlines for A:** | **Headlines for B:** |
|---|---|
| New Bottling Facility Coming to Town | Backroom Deal Dooms Stark's Wetlands |
| Forty New Jobs for Milfordians | Quiet Zoning Change Concerns Milford Citizens |
| City Council Paves the Way for New Facility | Public Outrage at Overnight Rezoning |
| Outraged Environmentalists Hit the Streets | The End of Milford's Wetlands |

These headlines seem factual—like they are beyond opinion. But they all select and emphasize a single dimension of the situation. And that selection supports a way of valuing, devaluing, supporting, or ignoring a set of concerns. Both selections, both sets of headlines, are biased *and* factual.

Collectively held opinions can also parade around as facts. When an entire community (or civilization!) believes something without question—as every community does—the idea functions as a fact. Here are some commonplace beliefs that were, at one time, considered facts:

- Women cannot make rational decisions but can only mimic the decision-making process of men.
- If she doesn't drown, she's a witch.
- People of African descent are naturally prone to criminality.
- People of Mediterranean descent are naturally more passionate than Northern Europeans and Asians.
- We can determine personality traits by feeling the shape of the individual's skull.
- The Earth is flat.
- Mental disorders are caused by an unacknowledged sin.
- Bleeding supports good health.
- Jews are the root cause of economic hardship in Europe.
- The Iraqi government was involved in the 9/11 attacks.

Of course, most people in the United States now look on these beliefs as terribly sexist, racist, tragic, or just wrong-headed. But at given points in the past, these were collectively asserted as uncontested truths. In some cases, they were taken for granted. They were "facts."

# "Numbers Don't Lie"— or Do They?

Sometimes we can be convinced that numbers are beyond opinion—that they simply represent a truth about the world. Again, this is a dangerous assumption. Numbers, like any text or symbol system, can be used for a range of purposes. We should see statistics as argumentative statements based on various assumptions and variables. As readers, we rarely have access to the assumptions and variables. Most often, about 78 percent of the time, we see only the conclusion—only the number. We are not invited to understand the research situation or the reasoning behind the numbers. For this reason, statistics can be more difficult to evaluate than a well-developed argument.

Of course, plenty of statistics are generated in a careful and sound manner, but many are produced under questionable circumstances or through flawed procedures. If the procedure is flawed, then the numerical conclusions are flawed—and they can distort the reality and urge people to accept ideas that simply are not true. The following flaws or misuses occur frequently, and they may even support some popular claims about medicine, health, and politics:

- Biased sampling
- Data dredging
- Data manipulation
- Discarding of unfavorable data
- Misapplication
- Overgeneralization

When we see statistics in an argument (or used as evidence to support an argumentative statement), we should think through the reasoning. Without a sound line of reasoning, an argument does not benefit from all the statistics in the world. In the following passage, the numbers might distract us from the logical fallacies (such as *begging the question* and *non sequitur):*

> According to the Learning Styles Institute, three out of five students are visual learners. That means 60 percent of all students learn best from pictures and charts. Therefore, teachers should use more visuals. If teachers use more visuals, students will get better grades and perform better on standardized tests.

The percentage has a kind of automatic persuasive power to it. But the overall line of reasoning is fraught with problems. The Learning Styles Institute provides nothing in this passage that explains how it defines *visual learner*. Does the study show how a person responds consistently—over weeks, months, years, or decades—to the same stimuli? If not, how can the Learning Styles Institute justify the label? Furthermore, we don't know what *learning* means in this situation. Does it mean consuming and remembering the content of a picture? Does it mean developing increasingly sophisticated insights? We simply do not know. And the answer would certainly change how we accept the argument. Furthermore, we don't know the demographics of the sample—who was involved in the 60 percent. Were there 10, 100, 1,000 students? Were they tested under a variety of situations, seasons, times of day? The problem with statistics in this case is clear: they can eclipse critical questions and prompt uncritical readers to be persuaded by flawed reasoning. Like a fancy paint job on a bad car, they can keep us from looking under the hood—or even starting the engine.

"In ancient times, they had no statistics, so they had to fall back on lies."
—Stephen Leacock

# Summarizing and Analyzing Sources

Research requires an understanding of the content and context of sources. We have to understand not only what is being said (content) but also who is being addressed and where the conversation takes place (context). Every source—from book to article to blog—exists in a context of other voices and assertions. And if we don't understand that broader conversation, deciphering a source can be like walking into a dark cave and hearing nothing but weird echoes.

## Content

To understand the content of a source, we have to understand the source on its own terms. In other words, we have to understand its typical qualities. In the same way that a good traveler enters another country and tunes into its sensibilities, good researchers tune into their sources' sensibilities. For instance, we cannot hope that a sophisticated essay will loudly announce its main idea or give a bullet list of solutions. Academic essays simply do not behave like breaking news updates.

Each type of source has unique purposes and functions. A newspaper article, for instance, updates readers on a current event; an academic essay walks carefully through a focused and sophisticated idea; a blog expresses the opinions or experiences of an individual; a scholarly book takes on the assumptions or collective knowledge of a discipline. Obviously, such generalizations do not hold true for every source, but researchers gain more insight when we can shift our own readerly expectations according to the specific text in front of us. An academic essay, for instance, might build slowly to the main idea. A newspaper article may announce the main idea in the first passage or the headline. In a book, the main idea may come at the end of the introduction—after the author has explained a range of other opinions. If we know such patterns (and don't expect an essay to function like a report), we'll likely understand far more.

A key strategy for understanding content is summarizing the source—reading and then explaining the main idea as accurately as possible. This can be a challenge. We have to avoid skimming the surface and blurring away a source's specific insight. For instance, notice how the first statement in the following examples vaguely characterizes John Steinbeck's essay (from Chapter 3) while the second statement gives a more focused characterization of his *insight*:

> **Blurred Summary:** In "Americans and the Land," John Steinbeck describes early Americans' treatment of the land.

**Focused Summary:** In "Americans and the Land," John Steinbeck describes the American settlers' disdain for the frontier and their "child-like" aggression, which destroyed the early forests, extinguished species, and diminished the continent's fertility.

This section introduces summary as a strategy for better understanding a source. Chapter 15 (pages 460–461) goes further and explains how to use summary inside of a research essay. In other words, this chapter introduces summary as a tool for understanding content, and Chapter 15 explains summary as a tool for integrating others' ideas into your own work.

# Context

To understand context, we should consider two aspects of a source: audience and publication cycle: *Audience* refers to the intended readership—to the particular people inclined to read, study, or purchase the source. Are they from an academic discipline? Do they know a particular set of terms and issues that the general population does not? Are they hobbyists? What about their cultural sensibilities? Are they mad at the government or minorities? Do they believe in a god? Are they suspicious of organized religion? Are they older or younger? What is their overall level of literacy? Can they follow a complex line of reasoning for thirty pages? Do they like NASCAR or fine art? Such questions are figured into publication decisions about the source. For instance, *Forbes Magazine,* which is pro-corporate and politically conservative, will likely not publish a lengthy treatise against the banking industry, nor will a scholarly journal in chemistry publish an article on how to make a can of soda explode.

As you can probably detect, writers and publishers make an important distinction between academic and popular audiences. Academic readers have different expectations than popular audiences. For instance, a scholar reading *Philosophy of Science* expects a certain level of analytical rigor that will likely be absent in a magazine such as *Newsweek*. And while general distinctions are difficult to maintain for all sources, it may be helpful to understand the following:

## Readers of Academic Sources Expect

- Appeals to logic
- Rigorous analyses
- Evidence or theoretical backing for claims
- Formal documentation (such as MLA)

## Readers of Popular Sources Often Expect

- Familiar characterizations and descriptions
- Appeals to value and emotion
- References to popular issues, places, and people

Researchers also should consider the publication cycle of their sources. Does the source get updated weekly? Monthly? Every three years? Has it been reprinted from an original publication? If it's an online source, has anyone taken responsibility for updating the information? Have updates attempted to address changes in the issue? Such questions point to the way information gets handled—and what gets published. Book publishers, for instance, are less apt to print ideas that are bound to fluctuate on a daily, weekly, or monthly basis. Instead, they publish work that will remain relevant through time. If the source does deal with issues that fluctuate (the stock market, important political figures, fashion trends, health care legislation), then researchers should expect sources to monitor those changes and deal with them accordingly. (These issues also correspond to timeliness, one of the criteria for evaluating sources. See page 448.)

## Activity

In a small group, develop a list of imaginary publication failures—instances when the source does not match the audience's expectations; for instance:

- An article about lowering one's cholesterol in a punk rock magazine

- A report on best deals among L.A. marijuana distributors published in *Time Magazine*

- A lengthy article about shifting epistemological assumptions in literary criticism published in *Sports Illustrated*

# Understanding Common Source Types

**Books and E-Books** come in a huge variety: fiction (novels, short story collections) and nonfiction (everything else), textbooks (like *The Composition of Everyday Life)* and trade books (everything sold outside of college curricula), and single-authored books and edited collections. One need only browse a bookstore to understand the immense number of subject categories. For academic research, it's important to remember that books generally take years to write, revise, and publish, so they are not the timeliest source of information. People don't value books for their timeliness but for their depth and richness, for their potential to reveal complexity, history, and the subtle nuances within a topic. Writers sometimes use the phrase *book-length project* to characterize work that involves a careful exploration of a complex issue.

Like all sources, books do exist in a conversation, but it may take place over years, decades, even centuries. In other words, with a book, the context may be more difficult to detect than with a tweet, blog, or article. The author(s) may be responding to a claim made long ago. Authors and publishers know this, and they have created some tools to help readers get a sense of the context. For instance, on the back cover and inside sleeve of print books, publishers often tell readers about the nature of the broader conversation. They explain how the work responds to a trend, how it engages a problem or debate, and how it contributes something new. In print and e-books, authors (or editors) use the preface and introduction to explain how their work fits into or responds to a tradition.

**Periodicals** include magazines (for a general audience), journals (for a specialized audience), and newspapers (both local and national). Popular magazines, such as *People* or *Newsweek,* offer information about mainstream news but rarely provide in-depth analysis of issues, and even more rarely deal with issues outside of major social and political topics. However, some magazines support in-depth reporting. *Harper's Magazine* and *The New Yorker,* for instance, are well known for publishing incisive articles that go beyond common perspectives. Even entertainment magazines such as *Rolling Stone* often publish lengthy analytical articles on current issues or significant political figures.

Scholarly journals, which are usually specific to one discipline (such as English, engineering, nursing, business, or marketing), offer very detailed analyses and well-developed opinions on an endless range of topics. The writing in academic journals is most often well researched and documented, so it tends to be more reliable than that of popular magazines. It may also use discipline-specific jargon that could confuse nonexperts.

At first glance, journals and magazines may look a lot alike, but closer inspection will reveal significant differences. Generally, journals are written for academic or highly specialized readers. The articles put forward new theories or practices in a particular field of study (sociology, psychology, nursing, English, chemistry, history, etc.). The goal of academic articles is not necessarily to communicate an opinion but to explain a new idea—and thereby help the discipline, as a whole, to evolve. Magazines are written for general readers, who may have a particular interest (politics, mountain climbing, hunting). If you are not certain what kind of periodical you have, use the following criteria:

### Journals

- Seek to advance knowledge in a *field of study*
- Deal with principles, theories, or core practices in an academic discipline
- Are associated with a particular discipline or field of academic study
- Have few advertisements, which usually appear only at the beginning and end (not between or among articles)
- Have few colors and flashy pictures (unless they are related to a study or article)

### Magazines

- Report information/news or offer how-to advice
- Offer the latest technique in a hobby or sport
- May appeal to readers with a particular *interest*
- Have advertisements throughout the pages, even interrupting articles
- Tend to have more colors and pictures

**Newspapers** are most valuable for highly publicized topics—those that are or have been visible to the public eye: political events, public figures, national or local disasters, and significant cultural events. For this reason, the context of a newspaper article is fairly easy to detect. The headlines alone help readers to understand the issue, the rhetorical or political tension, and the people involved. For instance, we don't have to think much to understand the context of the *USA Today* headline:

Obama to Birthers: "I Was Born in Hawaii"

For the most part, newspapers give the latest updates on current issues but refrain from giving lengthy background information. There are exceptions. For instance, the *New York Times* still funds, supports, and features lengthy analyses of political and cultural issues. But generally, newspapers are records of daily or weekly events more than tools of deep exploration.

Although the move to electronic publication has shrunk the number of printed newspapers, researchers still have access to a staggering number of local and national titles, such as the following, that are increasingly available online: *Afro American, American Banker, Amsterdam News, Atlanta Journal-Constitution,*

*Boston Globe, Chicago Tribune, Christian Science Monitor, Denver Post, Detroit News, Houston Chronicle, Los Angeles Sentinel, Los Angeles Times, Muslim Journal, New York Times, San Francisco Chronicle, St. Louis Post Dispatch, Times-Picayune [New Orleans], USA Today, Wall Street Journal, Washington Post.*

**Government Documents** include reports, transcripts, pamphlets, articles, speeches, books, maps, and films. State, local, and federal government bodies have accumulated huge amounts of information about everyday life. Government websites may be the best sources for researching general behavioral trends: what we purchase, how we live, how we get sick, how we heal, what we drink, what we eat, how we vote. While the U.S. government is the nation's largest publisher, state and city governments publish as well. Such documents, which can be of great value in one's research, can be found online with keyword searches or by going directly to the Government Printing Office (GPO) website at www.access.gpo.gov.

**Reference Works** such as dictionaries, encyclopedias, and almanacs can be seen as sources about sources. In other words, reference works give a general overview about the scholarship on a given topic. They explain what has been thought and said about key issues in a field. A particularly helpful reference work is the topic-specific encyclopedia. Consider, for instance, the following titles, which represent a huge number of specialized reference books:

> *The Encyclopedia of Popular Culture*
> *The Encyclopedia of Catholicism*
> *The Encyclopedia of Occultism and Parapsychology*
> *The Encyclopedia of Literary Theory*
> *The Encyclopedia of Counseling*
> *The Encyclopedia of Chemical Technology*
> *The Encyclopedia of Phobias*
> *The Encyclopedia of Fantasy*
> *The Encyclopedia of Popular Music*
> *The Encyclopedia of Quantum Physics*

Researchers often consult reference works early in the process—as a way of gathering keywords or concepts that they use for further searches.

**Audiovisual Materials** include videos, CDs, DVDs, films, photographs, and any type of recording. As organizations and governmental bodies increasingly move to digital storage, researchers can access a growing body of online recordings. For example, the Academy of American Poets offers videos of poets reciting their work; organizations such as Amnesty International offer video reports; and many governmental sites now include recorded speeches and video updates.

# Synthesizing Sources

As we explained in the previous section, information does not come free of biases and worldviews. Information usually comes in the form of theories, arguments, and hypotheses. In other words, research often involves swimming in others' opinions. Good researchers swim well. They understand how to read, question, and accept the ideas around them. Bad researchers grasp at chunks of statistical and factual debris.

It is also important to remember that writers rarely find sources that neatly overlap, or completely agree with, their own positions. In fact, research should not be seen as a process of seeking out agreement, but as a process of bringing together various kinds of information, viewpoints, and arguments. Sometimes, writers do not find any sources that share their position on a specific topic. Instead, they discover sources that partially overlap in some way. All of these sources, then, help give dimension to the writer's ideas. In the following chart, notice that supporting evidence (for instance, some fact or statistic that backs up the writer's stance) is only one possibility.

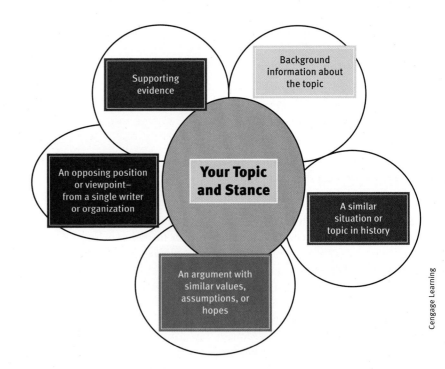

For example, consider the topic *light pollution*. Imagine that a writer begins the research process with a vague sense of her position—that too much light hinders most people from seeing the night sky. A quick search of the web and periodical databases will likely yield some sources that share her position. She might find statistics on the number of Americans who cannot see constellations other than the Big Dipper. And she might also find background information about the topic: when it became a concern for astronomers, or how much it impacts plant life. But then she can go further. In some invention work, the writer may discover that the night sky is important because it bestows a sense of wonder and humility in people. In her research, she could seek out sources that celebrate the power of wonder—a sociologist who argues that civilizations without a deep sense of wonder quickly fade from history, or a religious scholar who argues for the value of humility. Perhaps she even finds some rationale for parking lots that are lit all night from a major retailer. She then develops a counterargument to address that rationale. In her reading, she might also discover a similar but related issue—noise pollution and its effects on agriculture. Although this information about noise pollution may not directly support her main claim, it may show a trend in history—that people have always battled the slow invasion of technology into the natural world. All of these sources could help develop an insightful and rich argument.

Synthesis literally means *bringing together*. So synthesizing sources involves bringing a range of voices and texts together. Academic researchers know they may find closely related sources—for instance, three articles on the local effects of light pollution. But they also know they may find no closely related sources or merely a smattering of texts that are distantly related. In this common scenario, the researcher has to bridge gaps between and among sources. And bridging those gaps often creates exciting insights. When researchers begin writing—formulating the relationships among sources—they often create nuances in their own thinking and discover dimensions of the topic itself.

In the following passage from her essay "Cruelty, Civility, and Other Weighty Matters" (page 202), Ann Marie Paulin assembles a range of sources. Notice how the shaded passages help establish connections among her sources. Paulin does the work of bringing the sources into her own line of reasoning:

And most diets don't work. An essay by Rebecca Puhl, Ph.D. and Chelsea Heuer, MPH, in the *American Journal of Public Health,* cites studies which found:

> Most weight losses are not maintained and individuals regain weight after completing treatment. Patients who have lost weight through lifestyle modification typically regain 30% to 35% of their lost weight during the year following treatment, and regain most (if not all) of their lost weight within five years. ("Obesity Stigma: Important Considerations" 1021)

The authors go on to quote from a study by Mann, et al: "Dieters who gain back more weight than they lost may very well be the norm, rather than an unlucky minority" (qtd. in Puhl and Heuer 1021). My point here is not to argue that overweight people should not try to lose weight for health reasons. Indeed, even a modest weight loss of ten percent of a person's body weight is beneficial to one's health (Puhl and Heuer, "Obesity Stigma: Important Consideration" 1021). But such modest weight loss, while healthy, is rarely enough to earn a person fashionably thin status. And despite what the cultural messages suggest, most of us fat folks are trying to eat more sensibly, but the environment does play a role. In a culture where most of us are rushed from work to classes to other activities, the temptation to grab fast food is huge. Sugary or fatty foods are often available in grab and go packages that are so much easier to take to work or eat in the car than making a healthy snack. And, there is evidence to suggest we may even be wired to prefer junk food. Brownell and colleagues, in an essay in *Health Affairs,* cite studies which show: "Animals given access to food high in sugar and fat—even when healthy food is freely available—consume calorie-dense, nutrient-poor food in abundance, gain a great deal of weight, and exhibit deteriorating health" (379). I know, I know. We aren't rats. We are thinking beings, but this article goes on to point out that it is not so different for people: "Research has shown consistently that people moving from less to more obese countries gain weight, and those moving to less obese countries lose weight" (379).

So we are surrounded by a culture, even an infrastructure, that encourages obesity, yet the culture also breeds a prejudice against fat people. Various articles and news magazine programs have reported that Americans of all sizes make far more than simple aesthetic judgments when they look at a fat person. Fat people are assumed to be lazy, stupid, ugly, lacking in self-esteem and pride, devoid of self-control, and stuffed full of a host of other unpleasant qualities that have nothing to do with the size of a person's belly or thighs. But, as anyone who has ever been the victim of such prejudice can tell you, the impact such foolish notions have is real and harmful. For example, Marilyn Wann, in her book *Fat! So?,* cites an experiment in which "[r]esearchers placed two fake personal ads, one for a woman described as '50 pounds overweight' and the other for a woman described as a drug addict. The drug addict received 79 percent of the responses" (59). So, in spite of the agony addiction can cause to the addict and those who love her, people would rather get romantically involved with an addict than a fat person. And not much has changed. In a 2008 article, "The Stigma of Obesity: A Review and Update," Puhl and Heuer report:

One study asked college students (N=449) to rank order six pictures of hypothetical sexual partners, including an obese partner, a healthy partner, and partners with various disabilities (including a partner in a wheelchair, missing an arm, with a mental illness, or described as having a history of sexually transmitted diseases. Both men and women ranked the obese person as the least desirable sexual partner compared to the others (10).

While it is certainly good news to see that people can look beyond disabilities, such as a wheelchair or a missing arm, and see the value of the whole human being, it is distressing that Americans refuse to do the same for a person's weight. Why would anyone want to date someone who will land them in the STD clinic? How dangerous is that? And yet, such a person is clearly seen as a better romantic choice than a heavy person. Here is a case where weight prejudice is certainly more dangerous to the person with the prejudice than it is to the fat person.

# Assignment: Summarizing, Analyzing, and Synthesizing Sources

Much academic research is driven by a need to understand what others think—to know how scholars are debating and probing a topic. In others words, academic researchers are not always (or even often!) driven by the desire to find proof for their own convictions. They are, instead, out to discover the tensions and curiosities about a topic. This assignment focuses on that discovery process. It is designed to help writers explore the boundaries of a topic, to find multiple sources, bring them together, and develop new insights. The goal is not to prove a point or reinforce one's own opinion but to explore how other writers have addressed a topic—what others believe, assume, or imagine. The following steps will help guide you through that process:

**1. Search for Sources:** First, consider a topic—perhaps one that you have already written about. Draw a circle in the middle of a page with your topic and stance (if you have one). Then, in separate circles, write out possibilities for the following: background information; supporting evidence for your position; similar situations or topics in history; the values, assumptions, and hopes underlying your position; and opposing positions and the people or groups that might hold them. Use those circles, then, to generate keywords for searching databases or the Internet.

**2. Summarize the Content:** After finding two or more sources, summarize each. Briefly describe the main idea, or thesis, of the sources. (Be careful not to blur away the particular insight of the source.)

**3. Analyze the Context:** Next, analyze the content and context of the sources. Avoid evaluating the worth or value. In other words, avoid arguing that the sources are good, bad, credible, agreeable, and so forth. Instead, explain how the sources fit into a broader conversation about the topic. Consider the following questions:

- Who is the intended audience? Scholars? The general public? Any particular group?
- How do the sources speak to the audience? How do the sources address the values of their audience?
- What do the writers seem to value? What ideas or principles or hopes do you detect?
- How do the sources deal with the audience's potential questions, concerns, or doubts? Do they ever address potential concerns or doubts directly?

**4. Synthesize Ideas:** Synthesis involves explaining all the ways sources relate to one another—how they support, inform, or oppose one another. Synthesis can also involve the relationship between sources and the writer's own thinking about the topic. In other words, you might explain how the sources respond to, rub against, undermine, extend, challenge, or reinforce your own ideas. Consider the following questions:

- How do the sources overlap or contradict? How do they approach the topic differently? Beyond the obvious claims and opinions, what assumptions or unstated values seem to overlap or conflict?
- How do the sources contribute to your understanding of the topic or your ability to engage in this conversation?
- What further questions do the sources provoke?
- How do the sources reveal some layer of the topic that you did not imagine or discuss prior to researching?
- What perspective do the sources offer to you? For instance, do they address some psychological or philosophical layer that you did not imagine?

# Sample Synthesis: Exploring Caffeine Views

## Jim Crockett

In his essay, "Mugged" (Chapter 3, page 68), Jim Crockett explores the relationship between himself and his coffee mug. As he explores the meaning of that relationship, he suggests in one passage that he may be addicted to caffeine. While that is not the main assertion in his essay, it gave him a springboard into research. In the following essay, Crockett illustrates three critical moves in academic research: (1) he briefly summarizes two sources related to his topic; (2) he analyzes the content and context of each source; and (3) he synthesizes the sources and his own prior thoughts on the topic. In other words, he marries sources and his own understanding of the topic. This marriage of ideas generates new insights. Notice that Crockett does not use the sources to uphold his own initial thoughts. In fact, in the final section of this essay, he corrects part of his prior thinking.

### Summary

In his magazine article "Caffeine Addiction Is a Mental Disorder, Doctors Say," George Studeville explains that caffeine withdrawal may be officially classified as a psychological disorder. Studeville describes how Roland Griffith, a professor at Johns Hopkins, makes the case for the "syndrome" of caffeine withdrawal. In her article, "Is Caffeine Addictive?—A Review of Literature," Sally Satel concludes that caffeine does not meet the criteria for an addictive drug. While people commonly use the term *addiction* for heavy caffeine use, Satel argues that mild and temporary withdrawal symptoms do not warrant equating the drug with others, like heroin, that are harmful, even ruinous, to individuals and society. These articles, then, seem to oppose one another: Griffith assumes that caffeine should be considered an addictive drug, while Satel argues that consistent use and mild temporary withdrawal symptoms do not meet the DSM (Diagnostic and Statistical Manual of Mental Disorders) standards for genuine chemical addiction.

### Analysis

Studeville writes for a popular magazine. His readers, then, are not familiar with the jargon of the discipline or its ongoing professional debates. And Studeville himself is a reporter rather than a doctor or professor. His purpose is to inform readers about ongoing research—and a particular argument from Griffith, a professor of behavioral biology and neuroscience. His voice is informal and even a bit dramatic. The title offers the most absurd or extreme characterization of Griffith's argument. "Mental disorder," for common readers, suggests a kind of pathology, a chronic condition. The article offers Griffith's position on caffeine addiction and withdrawal, but it offers no opposing claims. The argument goes unchallenged, uncontested. And according to the title, "doctors" (all or most?) seem to say that Griffith's argument is correct.

Satel is an MD and researcher. She takes on the opposition directly—explaining why some people classify caffeine as an addictive drug. Her section on "methodological problems" reveals some of the flaws and hiccups in this type of research.

The researchers in both articles (Griffith and Satel) seem to value accuracy and a scientific method. Griffith says that he launched his study because "doctors and other health professionals have had no scientifically based framework for diagnosing the syndrome." Satel calls for her colleagues to make fine distinctions in previous studies—and to discount conclusions drawn from studies that lack reliability and credibility. But they differ in an important way: Griffith's argument calls for the collapse of categories: If one cup of coffee creates "physical dependence" (or anything like it), then coffee contains a dependent drug. Satel wants to make distinctions: some drugs are ruinous to the individual's life, while other drugs (like caffeine) merely create a mild form habituation. Griffith wants to erase degree and difference. Satel suggests that degree of dependence is all the difference in the world.

### Synthesis

As Satel explains, dependence on a drug comes from a need to acquire "physiological homeostasis"—or physical stability. This is, perhaps, different from my acknowledgement about coffee: that drinking it is a daily grounding ritual, a practice that works against the social forces. I suggest that our culture, our *econoculture,* pulls us away from ourselves—that it has left behind its roots in the wilderness. Instead of intimacy and simplicity, we have to blast through everyday life. (The other drivers looked at me angrily—*get the hell out of my way!*—while I meekly tried to rescue my helpless little mug at the busy intersection.) The two sources, and particularly Satel, raise this question: When we talk about drugs and addictions and habits, what is the battle? In my "Mugged" essay, I suggest that the battle might be psychological or philosophical rather than chemical. I focus on the act of drinking, the ritual of carrying my old familiar mug in a society that invites me to buy something new every time I turn around. That's a big battle! Sure, it's not physiologically addictive . . . and maybe I'm not really addicted to caffeine. Maybe that's just a common way of putting it. If Satel's right, after all, I'd just get a headache if I quit. But if I left my mug behind, if I bought (into) the plastic/paper cup world around me, maybe I'd be joining another realm of addiction—a bigger and more ruinous one.

And I don't mean this metaphorically. I mean it for real. I'm thinking, on this morning, of the recent government bailouts: $750 billion to keep the world of super-consumption chugging along. Rather than put serious resources into education, into health care, into the crumbling infrastructure, into alternative energy, we have to inject huge amounts into a habit. And the Treasury Secretary says that the injection will likely create more bad behavior and that we shouldn't monitor it too closely. (The main thing: get the junkies their fix! And hurry!) There's nothing we can do. We're stuck in a violent cycle. And this resonates with my point about *econoculture*. We're all now working to support the addicts on Wall Street and their political mules in Congress. If the addicts don't get their fix, they'll crumble and the whole economy will shake.

Maybe this is going too far. But Satel's essay makes me think about addiction in social terms. She says that it's not enough for us to simply think about the withdrawal. Instead, we have to think about *harm*. Do the drug and withdrawal hurt the individual and the society? This is where Satel and I overlap, and where I end up wondering: What kinds of addiction am I participating in? What kinds of withdrawal? What addictive behavior does my life encourage? How do I get out of those behaviors? Can I? What personal choices can I make if I am not in control of the drug and its effects?

## Works Cited

Satel, Sally. "Is Caffeine Addictive?—A Review of Literature." *The Journal of Drug and Alcohol Abuse.* 32(2006): 493–502. Print.

Studeville, George. "Caffeine Addiction Is a Mental Disorder, Doctors Say." *National Geographic News.* NationalGeographicNews.com. 19 Jan. 2005. Web.

# Evaluating Sources

Sources should be relevant, reliable, credible, timely, and diverse. Sources that do not adhere to these criteria can diminish an academic project and even damage an author's credibility.

## Relevance

A relevant source is appropriately related to the writer's topic. A writer's first inclination may be to find those sources that directly support his or her thesis statement; that is, sources that speak directly about the writer's particular subject and that espouse his or her particular stance on it. However, this is very limiting—especially since the research process might develop or change how a writer thinks about a subject. Sources do much more than back up someone's opinion. They might help to explain the complexities of the subject; the history of the subject; the writer's position; or even opposition to the writer's position.

Because sources can be used in various ways, a source that seems only remotely related to your project might, in fact, be extremely valuable in the long run. Consider the following example: A writer is researching voting practices in his community and wants to make a claim about low voter turnouts in recent elections. He finds a newspaper article about a local school, scheduled for demolition, that had previously been used as a voting location. This article at first might seem unhelpful. After all, how does this particular school relate to voting trends in the community? It may, in fact, suggest a great deal about voting. That is, one of the factors in voter turnout is proximity to voting locations. This article might, therefore, show a trend in declining number of voting locations. The same writer might find a government web page about the history of voting in his state. At first this source may not seem valuable because the writer is primarily concerned with recent voter activity. However, the history may provide some clues about the system itself, about the reasons for establishing Tuesdays as election days, about the number of constituents in a given area—all potentially valuable factors in understanding the complexities of recent voter turnout.

## Reliability

Reliability refers to the quality of information in the source. A reliable source uses verifiable information and helps readers trace the sources of information. The most reliable sources document the information they offer. (That's why academic audiences value some type of formal documentation, such as in-text citations and a bibliographical list.) In effect, formal documentation says to readers, "Here is the path to relevant research."

For published books and academic journal articles, reliability may not be an issue because such sources endure a process of critical peer review. However, many publications do not have peer reviews. Most magazines and newspapers also do not have room to include formal documentation. Their editorial policies exclude in-text documentation and Works Cited lists.

But there are other ways for writers to signal reliability, such as an appositive phrase. In the following examples, the underlined appositive phrases lend some reliability to the information. Even though the passages lack formal documentation (a formal link to a particular text), they give the reader specific cues about the nature of the source:

> Kalle Lasn, <u>a co-founder of the Canadian media criticism and environmentalist magazine Adbusters</u>, explains how dependence on television first occurred and continues today each time we turn on our sets.

> Deirdre Mahoney, <u>a professor of writing at Northwestern Michigan College and a scholar of rhetoric</u>, argues that online courses are significantly more challenging for college students than traditional face-to-face courses.

Notice that the information after the name indicates the source's credentials. When a formal Works Cited list is not possible, writers in many publications use such phrases to document the reliability of their information.

Remember that most popular magazines are guided by a primary force: money. Editorial policies are driven by the need to make information attractive to consumers. Therefore, claims may be inflated, mitigating details may be played down, and generalizations are common. Also remember that magazines are funded in large part by corporate advertising and so are not apt to publish articles that might compromise relationships with those advertisers. For these reasons, researchers should always be cautious about quoting popular magazines (or even news magazines) as unbiased truth.

# Credibility

Credibility refers to the internal logic of the information presented in the source. A credible source does not attempt to hide its biases or its argument. It makes logical claims and helps the reader follow its logic. If the source offers an argument, it makes its position clear and reveals its biases. (Of course, it is free of logical fallacies.) If the source attempts to inform rather than persuade, it does not spin information or conceal its biases.

The question of credibility may also involve the source's author. Some authors have more credentials than others. However, a book or article by a well-known author should not necessarily outweigh one by a less familiar writer. Many academic and professional writers are not necessarily big names in popular media but are well respected within small communities because they have spent years researching a particularly focused issue. For instance, Patricia Limerick, a highly respected historian, has written a great deal about the American West. Although her name is not recognizable to the general public, it is often noted in history scholarship.

## Timeliness

A significant concern in academic research is the date of the sources. It is important that claims are supported with sources that are not obsolete or behind the times. But this criterion depends upon the issue and the claim being made. Some claims require very current sources. For example, a writer making a claim about the marriage laws would be wise to consider sources published only within two to three years of her research. (Because the laws have changed and continue to create significant public debate, sources that are ten years old may be antiquated.) However, that same writer might also want to discuss the concept or development of equality in America and discover a valuable text by a nineteenth-century philosopher. In this case, the writer would use current texts to support claims about time-sensitive topics and would refer to an older source to express an issue that stretches beyond a particular era.

## Diversity

Diversity refers to the variety of sources a writer uses. Good writers seek to develop their projects and their perspectives with different voices and media. Writers develop their views on a subject from a range of sources—much in the same way that we develop our views on religion or marriage or education from taking in and making sense of information from various sources. For example, our religious beliefs may have been influenced primarily by our parents, but other sources, such as childhood friends, books, movies, and music, also influence us. Even views that oppose our own are important, because they help us to define the borders of our beliefs.

Writers should hope to read and synthesize various sources about their topics; otherwise, their perspectives, and ultimately their positions, can be limited. This means that writers should explore *different perspectives.* They should not seek out conformity of opinion but diversity of thought. For this reason, writers often attempt to seek out different types of sources. They hope to view their topics from as many angles as possible—from different scholarly communities and from popular or mainstream perspectives.

# Evaluating Websites

Writers should be especially careful when evaluating websites; a particularly important criterion for a website is reliability. Anyone with a computer (or access to a computer) can publish a website and make any claim he or she wishes. In other words, much information on the web is potentially bogus.

Bias also must be considered. Because the purpose of many sites is to sell something, they may provide information that is slanted. Of course, bias in itself is not bad. Bias is only negative when it is concealed. If a source is trying to sell something, its claims should not be accepted as unbiased truth. And if the source asks for personal information, it may have an alternative agenda. Although some online sources (such as newspapers) require you to register to enter the site, many other sources may ask for personal information so they can market products or services to you.

Websites should also be scrutinized for timeliness. Many sites have been abandoned by their creators, and although the content may appear recent, it may have been uploaded long ago. Reliable sites are updated regularly and have "last updated" notes toward the top or bottom of the homepage. To evaluate the content of websites, ask the following questions:

▶ Who sponsors this site, and what credibility do they have for posting the information?

▶ Is the site attempting to sell something? If so, how might that impact the nature of the information?

▶ Does the site ask for personal information? (Does it state the purpose of this request?)

▶ Are statistics/data supported with appropriately documented sources?

▶ Is the information presented up to date? (When was the site last updated?) ■

# Assignment: Evaluating a Source

Evaluating literally means calling out the value of something. When we evaluate sources, we draw attention to their value—not according to how much we agree with them but according to specific criteria. In other words, evaluating is not about praising sources that support our biases but explaining how sources stack up according to categorical standards: relevance, reliability, credibility, timeliness, diversity (pages 446–448). For this assignment, find and save a particular source—one that you can read closely. Develop a brief formal evaluation. For each criterion, consider the following key questions:

## Relevance

- Does the source speak directly to my specific topic?
- How does the source help to clarify some broader or related point?
- How does the source help to explain the history or complexities of the topic?

## Reliability

- Does the source offer formal documentation? Do other sources check out? Are they available?
- If there is no formal documentation, does the source acknowledge authorities with related credentials or qualifications?
- What about the source itself? Is it published by a reputable organization?

## Credibility

- Does the source make an argument? If so, are the claims well supported and well reasoned? Do you sense any logical fallacies?
- Does the source attempt to conceal its biases?
- Do you have reason to question the author's credibility? (If so, do a quick web or database search to see if he or she has written for or is referenced in other publications.) Is your reason for questioning the author's credibility reasonable? (Are you unnecessarily suspicious?)

## Timeliness

- Is this a time-sensitive topic?
- If this is a time-sensitive topic, why might the information in the source be either timely or out of date?

## Diversity

- Do my sources represent a variety of viewpoints?
- How do the sources represent different value or belief systems?

# Sample Evaluation: A Look at Portable Health Care

## Janet Lively

In this brief essay, Janet Lively evaluates a single source as it relates to her project about self-employed workers. She begins with a focused summary paragraph. Thereafter, she explains the values and assumptions working in the source and then devotes a paragraph each to reliability, credibility, and timeliness.

My source is "A Prescription for the Health Care Summit: Portable Insurance," an opinion column by Sara Horowitz, who is identified as the founder of the Freelancers Union and Working Today. Horowitz's organizations are New York City non-profits that work on behalf of self-employed people. Horowitz's column ran in the *New York Daily News* on Feb. 25, 2010. The *New York Daily News* is a newspaper based in New York City with a circulation of 632,595 in June 2009, according to Wikipedia.

Horowitz seems to value pragmatism, efficiency, fairness, flexibility, independence, and compromise. She claims to reject both the Democrat plan for government run health care and the Republican plan of loosening regulation on private insurers by letting them compete across state lines. Instead, she proposes keeping private insurers in the game but giving them incentives to work with organizations like hers that buy insurance on behalf of self-employed workers. She seems to subscribe to the "Third Way" ideology that focuses on solving problems and promoting economic progress by balancing the interests of government and business. She assumes that the days when everyone worked for someone else are over for good; she uses statistics to back up the present situation and assumes that this trend will increase dramatically. She doesn't comment directly on whether this is good or bad, but by labeling the self-employed as "independent workers," she implies that it's a positive trend. Still, her mostly neutral stance helps her frame her proposal as a practical, a let's-rise-above-politics-and-just-get-things-done sort of approach. She positions herself as an advocate for an overlooked but fast-growing group whose interests are not necessarily being addressed in the debate over health insurance. "Whether or not you're a permanent employee today, chances are high that you'll be an independent worker at some point in your career," she writes.

Horowitz seems reliable. She doesn't cite sources for her statistics, but that's expected in a newspaper column with a strict word count. In addition, the Freelancers Union website includes reports with documentation, implying that she knows how to research. Other sources I've found support her claim that "independent" workers are growing in number. And the *New York Daily News,* a mainstream and reputable newspaper, probably would not have run Horowitz's column if she were a fruitcake. Not that newspapers don't miss things, but the Freelancers Union has been around for a while and is based in New York, so I can safely assume that the *Daily News* could easily vet Horowitz and her organization.

That said, the source itself is not necessarily credible, for two main reasons. First, there is a huge gap in its line of reasoning. Government-run health care would be far and away the simplest solution for independent workers. Horowitz says that above all, insurance needs to be portable. Government health care is portable; retired people who move from Michigan to Arizona get to keep their government-run Medicare, no questions asked. So while Horowitz's plan represents a compromise approach, it is not necessarily the most portable and beneficial option for independent workers. Which leads to the second credibility issue: Who would benefit from Horowitz's proposal? Organizations like the Freelancers Union, which would stand to gain many members. Horowitz does not hide this fact. However, by promoting private insurance sold by non-profits as simply a common-sense solution—when it is perhaps the best compromise option or maybe a good option for independent workers who subscribe to free-market ideology and is certainly the best option for her organizations like hers—she is spinning the issue. Horowitz is not being entirely honest about her motives.

Even so, the source is relevant to my argument. It confirms my basic claim about the changing nature of the workforce, as well as my claim that self-employed workers will affiliate themselves with unions. Horowitz's support of for-profit insurance sold by not-for-profit organization seems to refute my claim about the push towards government-run health care. However, I will argue that the Freelancers Union is an early version of the unions of the future, which will eventually give up on providing/bargaining for health care and focus on other benefits and services. This source is also useful because it introduced me to the term *independent worker*. Other sources use more negative terminology like temporary worker, less suitable for my optimistic view.

Finally, the source is timely even though it was written before Congress passed the health care bill. Issues regarding insurance portability were not, as far as I know, definitely resolved by the legislation. And, since private insurers are still in the game and the number of independent workers continues to grow, it's safe to assume that Horowitz's proposal remains relevant.

For additional resources including instructional videos and links to helpful websites, access your English CourseMate through cengagebrain.com.

# Research is another
# form of invention.

# 15 Integrating and Documenting Sources

# Chapter Contents

Rob Howard/CORBIS

# Integrating Sources

Sources can add dimension, insight, and depth to your own ideas. They can also add a layer of difficulty. As sources get integrated, sound organizational principles must still apply: ideas should remain focused, paragraphs must be coherent, and your own line of reasoning should be apparent to readers. Also, information from sources should be blended smoothly into the text so that readers (1) understand its relationship to the writer's own ideas and (2) know where the information came from. The challenge is to maintain coherence and flow while integrating other voices and opinions. The best way to achieve coherence is to develop an overall plan for your essay before drafting. That is, develop a general strategy for your organization and decide how the sources will function in that plan.

## Source Functions

This section explains four common functions for sources in an essay. As you examine the following passages, notice how the writers set up the source's ideas and even provide further commentary on the source.

**Sources That Support Your Thesis:** Writers won't always find sources that directly support their thesis statements. But when it happens, they often select the most powerful statements and quote directly. For example, in her argument against intensive computer use in elementary school classrooms, Elizabeth Bohnhorst (from Chapter 7) integrates several quotations from a source:

> Now, what could possibly be wrong with such a sophisticated device for learning?
>
> In reality, "thirty years of research on educational technology has produced almost no evidence of a clear link between using computers in the early grades and improving learning," states Michael Dertouzus, director of the MIT Laboratory for Computer Science. In fact, evidence of hazardous effects of frequent use of computers in young children is overwhelming. They do little to promote a healthy childhood. "Computers are perhaps the most acute symptom of the rush to end childhood. The national drive to computerize schools, from kindergarten on up, emphasizes only one of the many human capacities, one that naturally develops quite late—analytic, abstract thinking—and aims to jump start it prematurely," continues Dertouzus.

**Sources That Support a Premise:** A premise is one step in your line of reasoning—one logical progression toward your main idea (or thesis). Often writers find a source that supports only a single step. That source may not be related at all to your overall topic, but it may provide some key backing—at a key moment. For example, in her essay (from Chapter 11), Deirdre Mahoney argues that students should learn how to write in the margins of books while they read. In the following passage, Mahoney develops a particular point in her line of reasoning, and she uses a source, Maryanne Wolf, to back up this particular point:

> So, I think the problem is clear. Our system of educating, parenting, and nurturing unwittingly conspires to ensure students' disciplined detachment from words on the page. In other words, creating disengaged adults begins early. My proposal is simple and not particularly original, but I'll reiterate it nonetheless. Those of us committed to raising and teaching need to raise and teach differently. For starters, we need to insist that from the earliest stages of literacy acquisition all humans—especially the tiniest in size and age—be invited to scribble fervently as they explore books. If we take into account the opening statement in Maryanne Wolf's *Proust and the Squid: The Story and Science of the Reading Brain,* it becomes apparent that humans could use an assist. Wolf avows forebodingly, "We were never born to read" (3). Ditto for writing. Out of necessity, it seems, resourceful adults looking for ways to enhance overtaxed memories found their way to literate practices. In doing so, the human brain began to evolve in ways probably not intended in the original blueprint. That is, in the process of teaching oneself to read and write, the brain began to reinvent itself, thus enhancing human development and evolution. Experts concur that coding and decoding symbols enhances thought and consciousness, which in turn literally alters brain matter. In other words, what we do with our brains determines what our minds are or what they might become.

## Sources That Oppose Your Claims:
In argumentative writing, writers have to take on opposition. They have to counterargue and concede to contrary perspectives and claims. Often, this means making a generalization, for example:

> Some people may argue that children ought to develop an intimate connection with computers. But they ignore the subtle effects on cognitive development.

But it may also mean countering or conceding to a particular source—to specific language. In the following passage, Elizabeth Bohnhorst uses a quotation from a source to set up her counterargument:

> On the other hand, technology is an effective way to get kids interested in learning, considering "that there is a passionate love affair between children and computers" (Setzer). A colorful computer screen is obviously more attractive to a child than an old novel or a textbook. But this attraction is

more likely a fascination with animation and sound effects rather than a genuine exploration of ideas.

And in her essay, Ann Marie Paulin (from Chapter 7) uses a passage from a source to launch her own objections:

> While we can shrug off advertisements as silly, when we see these attitudes reflected among real people, the hurt is far less easy to brush away. For instance, in her essay, "Bubbie, Mommy, Weight Watchers and Me," Barbara Noreen Dinnerstein recalls a time in her childhood when her mother took her to Weight Watchers to slim down and the advice the lecturer gave to the women present: "She told us to put a picture of ourselves on the 'fridgerator of us eating and looking really fat and ugly. She said remember what you look like. Remember how ugly you are" (347).
>
> I have a problem with this advice. First, of course, it is too darn common. Fat people are constantly being told they should be ashamed of themselves, of their bodies. And here we see another of those misconceptions I mentioned earlier: the assumption that being fat is the same as being ugly.

## Sources That Juxtapose Your Claims:

Sometimes writers find sources that make similar but not necessarily supporting points. In other words, the sources may juxtapose the writer's own thinking. In these cases, the juxtaposing source might help to explain or draw boundaries around the writer's point. In his essay (from Chapter 10), Leonard Kress uses a source to show the difference between his experiences and others. His own point about the treatments for childhood bulimia comes into better view when it is placed next to a medical encyclopedia:

> Perhaps earlier generations of parents and child psychologists had a better understanding of its power and attraction. And that's why older writings on the subject, rare but not unheard of, prescribe such drastic, almost Draconian treatment to stop the behavior. *The Encyclopedia of Pediatric Psychology* (1970) lacks entries for either anorexia or bulimia and refers to it as "psychogenic vomiting." It predates the public and medical concern over the condition, and takes a stern, almost Victorian approach to treatment:
>
> Karo syrup, Phenobarbital, anticonvulsants, chlorpromazine, antihistamines, chin straps, esophageal blocks, thickened feedings, removal of normal appendix, electric shock therapy, and even intensive prayer are all reported to have been used successfully to resolve the problem.
>
> In some cases, and in my case, I suppose, the patient simply outgrows it.

# Integration Strategies: Paraphrase, Summary, Quotation

As you can see from the preceding examples, writers often quote sources directly. But paraphrase and summary are equally important moves. Imagine a writer is doing research on political action. She discovers the following passage from Martin Luther King, Jr.:

> Human progress never rolls in on wheels of inevitability; it comes through the tireless efforts of men willing to be co-workers with God, and without this hard work, time itself becomes an ally of the forces of stagnation. We must use time creatively, in the knowledge that the time is always ripe to do right. Now is the time to make real the promise of democracy and transform our pending national elegy into a creative psalm of brotherhood. Now is the time to lift our national policy from the quicksand of racial injustice to the solid rock of human dignity.

The writer decides that this information is valuable because it adds complexity to her ideas. It may be *paraphrased, summarized,* or directly *quoted.*

**Paraphrase** is a rewording of the original source using your own words and expressions. It conveys the detail and complexity of the original text. A paraphrase of the King passage might read as follows:

> Humanity doesn't progress without constant struggle of pious and committed individuals. Absence of such struggle means the lack of social and spiritual development. We have to use time to do what is right, to realize the idea of democracy, to change national sorrow into community and collaboration. We have to try to raise the nation up from racist practices into a place of shared honor and respect (King 130).

The paraphrase restates King's ideas, but does so without his particularly figurative language. The writer might find paraphrase valuable because she wants to share the nuances of the idea but does not want the tone of the original text (such as King's poetic voice) to interfere with or take over her own text.

Paraphrasing does not involve merely changing a word or two, or shifting around sentence parts. Inappropriate or lazy paraphrasing leads to *plagiarism:* taking others' ideas or words without attributing proper credit. In the following example, the writer does not rephrase the ideas, but merely shifts some words around and replaces others. If the following appeared in a text, it would be plagiarism:

> Human progress never rolls in on tires of inevitability; it comes by way of the tireless efforts of men willing to be co-workers with God, and without this hard work, time itself becomes an ally of the forces of stagnation. In

**Information from sources can be**

**1. Paraphrased**

**2. Summarized**

**3. Quoted**

the knowledge that the time is always ripe to do right, we must use time creatively (King 130).

Notice that in the first sentence, the writer has only substituted one word for another here and there. In the second sentence, the writer has just shifted sentence parts around. This is plagiarism rather than paraphrasing because the passage retains the original flavor and expression of the author. (See more about plagiarism on page 468.)

**Summary** also involves expressing a source's ideas in your own words instead of using the words of the source. But unlike paraphrasing, summary often removes much of the detail while still dealing with the complexity of the source's idea. A writer may summarize because he or she wants to illustrate a point (made by the original text) and then move on to another idea. In other words, a summary is often used to support a broader claim. For example, consider this brief summary of the original King passage. Notice that King's idea has been entirely reworded, abbreviated, and used as a supporting point:

> Even liberal-minded people who seek more social justice mistakenly believe that things naturally get better over time. They believe that minority rights can, somehow, evolve quietly through the decades. But Martin Luther King, Jr. made the opposite point: that humanity progresses only by the struggle of spiritually motivated people, and those people must use time for social change (130).

Since summary leaves out detail while capturing the main idea, accuracy is essential. Writers should be careful not to misinterpret the source, as in the following summary:

> According to King, only people who go to church regularly can make the world a better place. Racism will thrive without their timely efforts (130).

Summaries can be any length, depending on the writer's purpose. For instance, imagine that a writer is building a line of reasoning about justice. She wants to borrow an idea explained in King's "Letter from Birmingham Jail." She quickly summarizes King's distinction between just and unjust laws without dwelling on specifics:

> But something is not right simply because it is legal. As Martin Luther King, Jr. reminds us in "Letter from Birmingham Jail," we must appeal to some principle beyond the law. Because so many laws through history have been unjust and downright oppressive to minority groups, we cannot simply accept legality as the ultimate criterion for righteousness (132–33). In the current debate about gay marriage, we must go beyond legality and explore what is just.

# The length of a summary depends upon the writer's purpose.

Here, the writer has summarized several lengthy passages from King's text. Rather than get bogged down in the details of King's argument, she abbreviates his ideas in one sentence and then continues developing her own point.

A lengthier summary might be appropriate if the writer wanted to carefully detail the difference between a just and an unjust law. She might summarize but offer slightly more detail from King's argument. In effect, she would be summarizing and paraphrasing:

> It is difficult for a population to weigh the justice of its own laws. After all, the laws seem just by virtue of their place in social structures and institutions. But as Martin Luther King, Jr., argues, there is a clean and clear distinction between just and unjust laws. First, an unjust law contradicts or opposes moral law—that set of principles above and beyond any particular society. Second, an unjust law diminishes and objectifies people. Segregation, the set of laws that maintained formal racial separation, treated minorities as fundamentally inferior beings—as a group to be removed from the center of society. It was, therefore, unjust. Finally, an unjust law burdens one group of people while passing over another group. In other words, it is not uniformly enacted. And unjust conditions will always come when one group develops a law that targets another group. For instance, the laws in Alabama to keep African Americans from voting were developed by white politicians and their constituents. Such laws maintained oppression, separation, and inequality (132–33). Although the people of the time did not recognize their actions as unjust, they were out of sync with moral law, with God's law.

This lengthier summary of King's argument helps the writer make a point. And if the writer were developing an extensive argument about the distinction between just and unjust laws, she might go even further with her summary. She might take several paragraphs to detail King's logic. But she would have to walk carefully—not allowing King's ideas to take over or push her own ideas aside.

**Quotation** involves using the exact words of a source. It puts a spotlight on another writer's language and allows writers to integrate especially important phrasing or passages. The key, however, is to carefully select what ideas and manners of expression are *worth* quoting. When writing down quotes, keep in mind two points:

1. Quote sparingly. Quote only when a passage is particularly striking, AND quote only the striking part. For example, do not quote an entire paragraph if you can quote just a sentence; do not quote an entire sentence if you can quote only three words from that sentence.
2. Put others' words within quotation marks. Consider the following well-chosen quotation from the original King passage:

## Activity

In groups, summarize the following passage from Ann Marie Paulin's essay (from Chapter 7). Try to develop two different summaries—one that abbreviates Paulin's point into a single sentence and another that makes the point in a single short paragraph.

> So we are surrounded by a culture, even an infrastructure, that encourages obesity, yet the culture also breeds a prejudice against fat people. Various articles and news magazine programs have reported that Americans of all sizes make far more than simple aesthetic judgments when they look at a fat person. Fat people are assumed to be lazy, stupid, ugly, lacking in self-esteem and pride, devoid of self-control, and stuffed full of a host of other unpleasant qualities that have nothing to do with the size of a person's belly or thighs. But, as anyone who has ever been the victim of such prejudice can tell you, the impact such foolish notions have is real and harmful. For example, Marilyn Wann, in her book *Fat! So?*, cites an experiment in which "[r]esearchers placed two fake personal ads, one for a woman described as '50 pounds overweight' and the other for a woman described as a drug addict. The drug addict received 79 percent of the responses" (59).

According to Martin Luther King Jr., "Human progress never rolls in on wheels of inevitability; it comes through the tireless efforts of men willing to be co-workers with God, and without this hard work, time itself becomes an ally of the forces of stagnation" (130).

Writers can use various strategies for punctuating quotations:

# Quotation puts a spotlight on another writer's language.

**Quotation Marks Only:** When the quoted matter blends directly into your sentence without a speaking verb (such as *say, says, said, exclaims, proclaims,* or *states*) indicating a change in voice, no punctuation is required before the quotation. The sentence may be punctuated just as it would be if there were no quotation marks:

According to Anderson's records, before the end of the decade, there were "eighteen million people involved in the crisis" (177).

Emphasizing her point, Miller demands that "it is now time for something drastic to change here on campus" (43).

**Speaking Verb Followed by a Comma:** Speaking verbs (such as *say, says, suggests, exclaims,* or *states*) indicate a shift in voice from your voice to the voice of your source. A comma separates the speaking verb and the quotation:

His final paragraph, before the epilogue, says, "Let's create a system that encourages people like Andie at least as much as the ones who don't give a damn" (Sacks 187).

Emphasizing her point, Miller suggests, "It is now time for something drastic to change here on campus" (43).

### Helpful Verbs for Attributing Quotes

| | |
|---|---|
| says | describes |
| considers | insists |
| argues | tells |
| shows | offers |
| explains | informs |
| demands | claims |
| suggests | instructs |
| teaches | points out |
| emphasizes | |

As Martin Luther King Jr. explains, in his "Letter from Birmingham Jail," "One day the South will know that when these disinherited children of God sat down at lunch counters, they were in reality standing up for what is best in the American dream" (130).

A speaking verb combined with a noun creates an attributive phrase that can be placed at the beginning, in the middle, or at the end of a sentence. Quoting involves crafting sentences carefully to create clear and natural-sounding connections between the writer's own ideas and the words of the source. Here are some standard strategies:

### Quotation at the Beginning of a Sentence

"All voting is a sort of gaming, like checkers or backgammon, with a slight moral tinge to it," explains Henry David Thoreau (56).

### Quotation in the Middle of a Sentence

As Thoreau points out, "All voting is a sort of gaming, like checkers or backgammon, with a slight moral tinge to it" (56), and it is this moral issue that is often overemphasized on ballots.

### Quotation at the End of a Sentence

Henry David Thoreau claims that "voting is a sort of gaming, like checkers or backgammon, with a slight moral tinge to it" (56).

### Quotation Divided by Your Own Words

"All voting," explains Thoreau, "is a sort of gaming" (56).

**Sentence followed by a colon:** Sometimes writers use a whole sentence to set up, or explain, the quotation. In this case, they use a colon between their own sentence and the quotation. The colon, in effect, says, "and now, here comes the other person's words":

For example, he introduced the reader to Marissa and Carol: "As very good students, [their views] were virtually excluded by The College in order to accommodate the whiners and complainers" (Sacks 61).

As George Williams notes, protection of white privilege is critical to patterns of discrimination: "Whenever a number of persons within a society have enjoyed for a considerable period of time certain opportunities for getting wealth, for exercising power and authority, and for successfully claiming prestige and social deference, there is strong tendency for these people to feel that these benefits are theirs by 'right'" (727).

If an entire sentence is a quotation—that is, if it begins and ends with a quotation mark and contains no reference to the source in between—consider the following approaches: (1) connect the quote, if appropriate, to the preceding sentence with a colon, or (2) add a cue, or transition, as an introduction to the quote.

**Special Conditions in Quoting** To integrate quotes smoothly into a text, writers sometimes find it helpful to omit or add certain words for clarity or cohesion. Standard guidelines exist for letting the reader know how the writer has altered a quotation. Of course, the writer must be certain that he or she has not changed the source's intended meaning. Note also the standard approach to using long quotations.

**Omitting Words:** Occasionally, writers want to leave out words or phrases of a passage they are quoting. This is done with ellipses (. . .). They tell the reader that words have been taken out of the original passage. Notice how one might quote the following passage from an essay by David Crabtree:

> **Original:** The world is changing at a bewildering pace. Anyone who owns a computer and tries to keep up with the developments in hardware, software, and the accompanying incompatibilities is all too aware of the speed of change. This rapid change, especially technological change, has extremely important implications for the job market. In the past, it was possible to look at the nation's workforce, determine which of the existing occupations was most desirable in terms of pay and working conditions, and pick one to prepare for. But the rapid rate of change is clouding the crystal ball. How do we know that a high-paying job today will be high-paying tomorrow?

> **Quotation:** According to David Crabtree, "The world is changing at a bewildering pace. . . . This rapid change, especially technological change, has extremely important implications for the job market."

The ellipses indicate the missing sentence from the quotation. The same strategy can be applied to cut any amount of text from a passage. For instance, in the following sentence, a few words have been cut from Crabtree's passage:

> **Quotation:** According to David Crabtree, "This rapid change . . . has extremely important implications for the job market."

**Adding Words:** Sometimes it is valuable to add a note or comment within a quote. In this case, writers use square brackets to set off their own words. For example, a writer may insert a word in a quoted passage to clarify a vague pronoun or to give a brief explanation:

> **Original:** After months of exhausting research, they had finally come to understand the problem with their design.

> **Quotation:** "After months of exhausting research, [the nuclear scientists] had finally come to understand the problem with their design" (Smith 82).

Here, the writer substitutes the actual noun for the pronoun *they*. Without the noun, the reader may not understand the meaning of the quotation. As in this example, inserting bracketed comments within quotes can clear up any potentially confusing information within a quote while maintaining the flow of the sentence.

**Noting an Error:** If a quotation is grammatically or syntactically flawed, a writer cannot simply change it. In such cases, the quotation must remain intact, and the writer must use square brackets and the three-letter word *sic* directly after the error. Otherwise, a reader might assume that the error is on the part of the writer.

In his letter to the editor, Jeremy Miller argues that "Obama should not of [sic] bailed out the auto industry or the banks." He goes on to argue against bailouts in any form.

**Using Lengthy Quotes:** When writers quote more than four lines, they must use a block quote. As in this passage from Ann Marie Paulin's essay, writers often use a colon before block quotes:

Another example of this bullying someone thin comes from Pipher's book *Hunger Pains: The Modern Woman's Tragic Quest for Thinness.* Pipher recounts a conversation she overheard one day in a dress shop:

I overheard a mother talking to her daughter, who was trying on party dresses. She put on each dress and then asked her mother how she looked. Time after time, her mother responded by saying, "You look just awful in that, Kathy. You're so fat nothing fits you right." The mother's voice dripped with disgust and soon Kathy was crying. (89)

Pipher goes on to suggest that Kathy's mother is a victim of the culture, too, because she realizes how hard the world will be on her fat daughter. Unfortunately, what she doesn't realize is how much better her daughter's quality of life would be if she felt loved by her mother. Any person surrounded by loving family members at home is much better equipped to deal with whatever the cruel world outside throws at her or him.

**Double Quotes:** Occasionally, writers quote a passage that contains a quotation or is itself a quotation. In this case, single quotation marks are used inside the double quotation marks:

As Maria Gallagher has argued, "It is time that we turn the corner on the road of national energy policies and begin to take 'alternative energy' seriously" (23).

*Sic* is Latin for *thus* or so. It is used after an error to tell readers that the passage is quoted *as is*.

# Coherence Strategies

Outside sources can make a text more sophisticated, but they can also create confusion if the writer does not make explicit connections between points. Because outside sources often increase the complexity of a text, writers have to employ *textual cues:* sentences, words, and phrases that explain the relationship between ideas and sources. Textual cues are like the road signs of an essay. They help readers keep track of who's saying what within paragraphs and throughout the essay. For example, the following textual cue helps the reader keep track of previously mentioned names:

> Most music critics, *such as Smith, Castella, and Sanchez,* see the latest alternative genre as a collective response to the grunge scene of the early '90s.

Here, the critics listed have been discussed prior to this sentence, and the writer simply reminds the reader about these voices and how they relate to the present point being made. Simple phrases *(such as for example)* cue the reader to make connections between passages in the text:

> Jones's ideas are often seen as radical. Alberta Slavik, *for example,* casts Jones aside as a "hyper-liberal" journalist: "William Jones has gone too far, simply parading his politics at the cost of facts" (76).

In the following paragraph, notice how Daniel Bruno uses a range of textual cues. He blends together, or integrates, what he thinks and what his source says by (1) stating his main idea *(Sacks illustrates that all of today's college students cannot just be thrown in the same big barrel);* (2) directing the reader to the source *(he spends, he says, he mentions);* (3) providing the information from the source that supports or explains his idea; and (4) concluding by commenting on the information:

> In *Generation X Goes to College,* Peter Sacks illustrates that all of today's college students cannot just be thrown in the same big barrel. In describing the modern/post-modern clash in education, he spends the majority of his time talking about those students who are underprepared, who lack the basic study skills required in academic work, and who demonstrate little real commitment to their own education. Yet, he does not discuss this problem in isolation. He also mentions another type of student. For example, he introduces the reader to Marissa and Carol: "As very good students, [their views] were virtually excluded by The College in order to accommodate the whiners and complainers" (61). And he says they "suffered not only educationally" (63). In addition to discussing specific good students, an entire chapter presents survey results about students' attitudes toward education. While he makes claims such as "nearly a quarter of the students . . . harbored a disproportionate sense of entitlement," this very statement tells the reader that a full three quarters (that

is, three out of four) students *do not* "harbor a disproportionate sense of entitlement" (54–59). He wraps up the book by focusing on another student, Andie, who he describes as "a good student, constantly picking [his] brain for information and feedback on her work" (186–87). His final paragraph, before the Epilogue, says, "Let's create a system that encourages people like Andie at least as much as the ones who don't give a damn" (187). Thus, Sacks shows that today's students are a more diverse group—in skill level, background, and attitude toward education—than has ever before been gathered together in the college classroom. (322)

Writers often rely on Bruno's four steps:

1. Explaining the main idea
2. Referencing the source
3. Giving information from the source
4. Commenting on that information

## Planting a Tree

You might think of integrating sources as planting a tree. First, the hole should be dug. (One cannot simply plop a tree onto the ground.) Then, after the hole is prepared, the tree can be dropped into place. But the job is not done! The planter must fill in the hole, pack good dirt back into that space, and water it, making certain that the roots of the tree are nestled into the new soil. Likewise, a writer must first set up the idea—not simply plop the ideas from a source into a paragraph. Then, the information (summary, paraphrase, quotation) can be integrated smoothly into the writer's own language. Finally, the writer should then consider how to fill in and reinforce the connectedness of the source and his or her own points.

Essays that rely on outside sources also require good *paragraph transitions* (sentences and phrases that join the content of paragraphs and show the logical connections). Because sources create more dimensions in an essay project, readers require explicit intellectual help as they walk through a line of reasoning. Transition statements usually begin paragraphs and help the reader to bridge from one paragraph to the next. The following sentences, which all begin paragraphs, act as bridges from previous points:

- Not all farmers, however, agree with Johnson's strategy.
- Despite this overwhelming amount of evidence, some teachers refuse to acknowledge the way gender and race figure into the classroom.
- But all of the discussion on war distracts voters from significant domestic issues that will impact everyday life in the present and future.
- Because of Smith's recent book, many researchers have begun focusing their attention on the ways technology will change our ability to communicate.

# What Is Plagiarism?

Plagiarism—failing to acknowledge, or give credit to, a source of information—is intellectual theft. It involves using either (1) an idea or (2) the manner of expression of another person as if it is the writer's own idea or manner of expression. Plagiarism can take many forms and may be either intentional or unintentional. For example, knowingly turning in another person's paper and claiming it as one's own work is a serious form of academic dishonesty likely to have a severe consequence, such as damage to one's reputation and expulsion from school. Other times, however, writers plagiarize accidentally because they are unaware of the rules. They do not know, for example, that the ideas taken from a source, even if not quoted directly, must be documented.

Just as it is every driver's responsibility to know and obey the rules of the road (for his or her own benefit as well as for the benefit of others), it is every writer's responsibility to know the rules of documentation. To avoid plagiarism, you must acknowledge your source (also referred to as "citing" or "crediting" the source) whenever you express someone else's idea, opinion, or theory, or whenever you provide information such as a fact or statistic that is not common knowledge.

If you use the exact words of the source, you must indicate that by putting them within quotation marks—and also by crediting the source (using quotation marks alone does not count as crediting the source). If you use information from a source but express it in your own words (through paraphrase or summary), you should not put the information inside quotation marks, but you still must credit the source.

Most often, plagiarism occurs because writers are simply not going far enough in their paraphrasing. That is, they are not sufficiently rewording the ideas from the original source. A good paraphrase avoids using the same subjects and verbs as in the original text. To avoid this, read the original passage closely, but rather than writing down the ideas immediately, talk through them first. Remember that any one idea can be phrased in infinite ways.

Writers sometimes plagiarize intentionally because they are desperate to complete an assignment or pass a class. They set out to steal (or buy) others' ideas. In this age of technology, students can easily download text from an online source, and they can even buy college essays from websites and online databases. However, such essays are prepackaged, the topics are generalized, and the writing mundane—essentially, they are the opposite of what most college instructors want, and are contrary to the Invention strategies suggested throughout this book. Also, as websites featuring prewritten essays increase, so does the ability of instructors to detect plagiarism.

The consequences of plagiarism are more far-reaching and destructive than what some students may assume. Besides failing an assignment, failing an entire class, or being expelled, students who plagiarize fail to learn essential writing and thinking skills—or even when and how to ask for help. They also establish a low standard for themselves, which is perhaps the worst result of plagiarizing.

# Documenting Sources

Why document sources? There are at least three good reasons:

- **To be honest.** When presenting others' opinions, research, or manner of expression, writers give credit to, or acknowledge, their sources.
- **To gain credibility.** If a source is credible (see Evaluating Sources, pages 446–449), then the writer's claims gain credibility. Many times writers are not experts on their subject matter; however, they can write confidently about their subjects as a result of sources. Also, writers are taken more seriously if they appear well-informed, having "done their research."
- **To provide readers with more information.** Listing sources provides readers with access to more information. This allows readers to explore the subject matter further.

Different disciplines rely on different styles of documentation. The two most common styles are MLA (Modern Language Association) and APA (American Psychological Association).

## Documentation provides readers a path to the information you used.

# MLA Style

English and humanities use MLA Style. Like other documentation styles, MLA depends on two basic components: (1) an in-text citation of a work and (2) a list of works cited at the end of the text. These two components function in the following ways:

- In-text citations let a reader know that particular ideas come from a particular source.
- In-text documentation corresponds to the complete bibliographic information provided at the end of the text.
- In-text citations lead the reader directly to the corresponding Works Cited page.
- Done correctly, the in-text reference lists the first word(s)—whether it be the author's last name or the article title—plus the page reference of the citation on the alphabetized Works Cited page. This allows the reader to easily locate the source in the list of works.
- The Works Cited page provides complete information for finding all formal sources. This complete information is provided only once and comes at the end of the entire text so that it doesn't interfere with ease of reading.

> **An in-text citation must occur when a writer does any of the following:**
>
> - Quotes directly from a source
> - Paraphrases ideas from a source
> - Summarizes ideas from a source
> - References statistics or data from a source

## In-Text Citation

In-text documentation involves referencing the original text in parentheses within the actual sentences of your text; because it uses parentheses, it is sometimes called *parenthetical citation*. In general, for MLA style, in-text citations should include the author's last name (unless it is given within the sentence) and page number of the source from which the cited material is taken (unless the source is electronic and lacks page numbers).

> "After months of exhausting research, they had finally come to understand the problem with their design" (Smith 82).

A space separates the name and the page number.

The end punctuation comes after the citation.

**If the author is referred to in the sentence,** his or her name can be omitted from the citation.

> Emphasizing her point, Miller demands that "it is now time for something drastic to change here on campus" (43).

**If the source has no author,** use the first word or phrase of the source's title and punctuate accordingly (quotation marks for an article and italics for a book).

> The oil had spread over much of the shoreline and had "already begun its death grip on a vast array of wildlife" ("Black Death" 54).

**If the source has two or three authors,** use the last name of all authors.

> (Lunsford, Olin, and Ede 158)

**If you have more than one work by the same author,** insert the title of the work after the author name, followed by the page number.

> (Faigley, *Fragments of Rationality* 43)

**If you are citing material that is already quoted in the source,** cite the source in which you found the quotation and add "qtd. in" before the author's name or title.

> (qtd. in Smith 82)

**If you want to acknowledge more than one source for the same information,** use a semicolon between citations within one set of parentheses.

> (Lunsford and Ede 78; Smith 82)

**If you have an electronic source with no page numbers,** simply exclude the page number from the citation. Do not add page numbers, and do not use those that a computer printer assigns.

> According to Martha Smith, "untold numbers of children are negatively affected by the proficiency test craze."

## Works Cited

Works Cited pages list the sources that are directly cited in the text. In general, the first piece of information in the Works Cited entry should correspond directly with the in-text citation. For example, notice the relationship between the in-text citation for Patricia Hampl, below, and the entire bibliographic information in the Works Cited page:

> The difference between those who write memoirs and those who write fiction is that "memoirists wish to tell their mind, not their story" (**Hampl** 330).

The in-text reference refers the reader to the Works Cited page at the end of the essay, where complete bibliographic information allows the reader to locate the source.

Works Cited

**Hampl,** Patricia. "Red Sky in the Morning." *Reading Culture: Contexts for Critical Reading and Writing.* Ed. Diana George and John Trimbur. 7th ed. New York: Longman, 2010. 329–31. Print.

Entries in Works Cited pages must follow strict formatting guidelines, but the process is easy if you know the formulas involved.

- Author name(s) comes first and is inverted (last name first), with a comma between last and first names.
- Title of the work comes directly after author name. All words in titles are capitalized except prepositions (such as *on, in, between*), articles *(a, an, the),* coordinating conjunctions *(and, but, for, nor, or, so, yet),* and *to* in infinitives (such as *to run, to go*).
- If no author is listed, the title comes first.
- Article titles are in quotation marks, while the sources in which they appear (newspapers, books, journals, and magazines) are italicized.
- Publication information (including city, publisher, and copyright or publication date) follows the title of the source.
- If the source is an article, then page numbers come next.
- After any page number (e.g., for an article) comes information on the medium consulted (e.g., *Print, Web*).
- If the source is online, the date of access comes last.

Bibliographic information for books is contained on the title page and the copyright page (the back side of the title page). The title page contains the full title of the book, the author(s), the publishing company, and the city of publication. The copyright page contains date(s) and any edition numbers. Go to the title and copyright pages of this text, and find all the information you would need to cite it as a source.

# Printed Books

### Single Author

**Author Name:**
As for all sources in MLA format, single author names are inverted.

**Title:**
Book titles are italicized.

Howell, Mark D. *From Moonshine to Madison Avenue:*

*A Cultural History of the NASCAR Winston Cup.*

Bowling Green: Bowling Green State U Popular P, 1997. Print.

**City of Publication:**
If multiple cities are listed on the title page of the book, give only the first.

**Publishing Company:**
Publishing companies are always found on the title page of the book. List them in shortened form, directly after the city. A colon separates the city of publication and the publisher.

**Date of Publication:**
The date usually appears on the copyright page, which is the back side of the title page in a book. Always use the most recent date listed. Use a comma between the publishing company and the date of publication.

**Medium Consulted:**
For the print version of a book, the medium consulted will be *Print* (See page 477 for information on citing an online book.)

**Two or More Authors**

Vasta, Ross, Marshall M. Haith, and Scott A. Miller. *Child Psychology: The Modern Science.* New York: Wiley, 1995. Print.

For more than three authors, you may avoid listing all the names and simply add *et al.,* Latin for "and others" after the first name.

Johansen, Sturla, et al.

**Corporate Author or Government Publication**

Modern Language Association. *MLA Handbook for Writers of Research Papers.* 7th ed. New York: MLA, 2009. Print.

United States. Office of Consumer Affairs. *2003 Consumer's Resource Handbook.* Washington: GPO, 2003. Print.

If an author is not given for a government publication, list the name of the government first, followed by the agency. The title follows, and then the publication information. Many federal publications are published by the Government Printing Office (GPO).

**Subsequent Editions**

Wicks-Nelson, Rita, and Allen C. Israel. *Behavior Disorders of Childhood.* 6th ed. Upper Saddle River: Prentice, 2005. Print.

Find the edition information on the title page of the book, and place the information in the entry directly after the title or the editor, if there is one. Use the abbreviations *2nd ed., 3rd ed.,* and so on, or *Rev. ed.* for "Revised edition," depending on what the title page says.

**Republished Book**

Tolkien, J. R. R. *The Hobbit.* 1937. New York: Ballantine, 2003. Print.

Older books may be published by a company other than the original publishers, or a hardcover book may be republished in paperback. In this case, insert the original publication date after the title, and then give the recent publisher and date.

**Edited Book**

Foucault, Michel. *The Foucault Reader.* Ed. Paul Rabinow. New York: Pantheon, 1984. Print.

Add *Ed.* after the title of the book, followed by the editor's name, not inverted. Since *Ed.* here means "Edited by," not "Editor," it should never appear as "Eds." even if there is more than one editor.

## Activity

Decide which type of periodical (magazine or journal) may have published the following articles, and in groups or as a class, discuss the reasoning behind your decisions:

"Heading for the Mountains: An Exciting Getaway for the Whole Family"

"Climatic Shifts in the Mountain Region"

"Coach Fired, Team Responds"

"Enzymes, Nutrition, and Aging: A Twenty-Year Study"

"The Latest in Deep Water Bait"

"Re-inventing the Microscope"

"The Epistemology of Literature: Reading and Knowing"

### Translated Book

Bakhtin, Mikhail. *Problems of Dostoevsky's Poetics.* Trans. Caryl Emerson. Minneapolis: U of Minnesota P, 1984. Print.

Add *Trans.* after the title of the book followed by the translator's name, not inverted.

# Printed Articles

Articles appear in newspapers and periodicals (journals or magazines). While newspapers are usually published daily, magazines are usually published weekly or monthly, and journals are published quarterly or even biannually. Information on citing articles appearing online begins on p. 475.

### Article in a Magazine

**Author Name:**
Regardless of the type of source, the author name is inverted.

**Article Title:**
Article titles are always in quotation marks.

Paumbarten, Nick. "Food Fighter: Does Whole Foods' C.E.O. Know What's Best for You?" *New Yorker* 4 Jan. 2010: 35+. Print.

**Page numbers:**
Provide the specific page number(s) on which the article appears. If the article covers consecutive pages, include the range (such as *52–75*). If the page numbers are not consecutive, include the first page number, immediately followed by a plus sign (such as *64+*). Place a colon after the date and before the page numbers.

**Medium Consulted:**
End with medium consulted (in this case, *Print)* followed by a period.

**Periodical title:**
The title of the magazine, journal, or newspaper is italicized.

**Publication date:**
Include month and year directly after the title of publication. For weekly or biweekly magazines, include the full date (day, month, and year). (For all types of sources, abbreviate all months except May, June, and July.)

### Article in a Journal

Coogan, David. "Service Learning and Social Change: The Case for Materialist Rhetoric." *College Composition and Communication* 57.4 (2006): 667–93. Print.

If an academic journal provides both the volume and issue numbers, provide both. Otherwise, simply provide whichever has been made available, followed by the year (in parentheses), a colon, then inclusive page numbers and medium consulted.

### Article in a Newspaper

Drahos, Marta Hepler. "Now and Then: Women's Rights Have Come a Long Way, but Still Have a Long Way to Go." *North Coast* [Traverse City] 19 Mar. 2011: 1+. Print.

Johnson, Kevin and Mimi Hall. "Bin Laden Involved in Terror Planning." *USA Today* 5 May 2011: A1. Print.

After the author, if one appears, list the title of the article and the publication information. Exclude introductory articles *(a, an, the)* from publication titles. Add the city name in square brackets if it does not appear in the title of the newspaper and the newspaper is local rather than national. Add section letters before the page numbers. As with magazine articles, if the page numbers are not consecutive, list the first page number, immediately followed by a plus sign. End with medium consulted.

### Essay, Story, or Poem in an Anthology (such as a college textbook)

Paulin, Ann Marie. "Cruelty, Civility, and Other Weighty Matters." *The Composition of Everyday Life.* 4th ed. John Mauk and John Metz. Boston: Wadsworth, 2013. Print.

Begin with the author, followed by the title of the work (essay, story, or poem). Then give the title of the book, the editors, and the publication information. End with the page numbers on which the article appears, followed by medium of publication.

### Encyclopedia Article

Esposito, Vincent J. "World War II: The Diplomatic History of the War and Post-War Period." *Encyclopedia Americana.* Intl. ed. 2000. Print.

Like all sources, begin with an author name (inverted) if one is given. (Check for author names at the beginning or end of the article.) Put the title of the article in quotation marks and italicize the encyclopedia title. End with edition, year, and medium of publication.

## Electronic Sources

Often, websites do not list authors. But when they do, author names should be documented as they are for print sources (inverted at the beginning of the entry). Like print sources, websites also have publication information, but it is different in nature: While a book, for instance, has a publishing company, a website is sponsored by an institution or organization (unless the site is personal). Website entries should include the title of the site (italicized), the name of the sponsoring institution or organization, the date of publication or the date of the most recent update (if available), the medium of publication, and the date when the researcher accessed the site.

The 7th edition of the *MLA Handbook for Writers of Research Papers* indicates that a URL should be provided only when your reader is unlikely to be able to locate the source without it. (If you do add the URL to your citation, use angle brackets at the beginning and end, break it only after a slash [/], and do not add hyphens.) And with electronic sources especially, remember the basic principle behind documentation: *to provide a guide for finding the sources you used.*

### Official Website

Pinsker, Sarah, ed. *Robin Flies Again: Letters Written by Women of Goucher College, Class of 1903.* Goucher Coll., 1999. Web. 10 Mar. 2011.

*Sierra Club.* Sierra Club, Mar. 2011. Web. 18 Mar. 2011.

Begin with the name of the site's editor or author (if available) and the title of the site (italicized). If the site has no title, offer a description, such as *Home page* (not italicized) in its place. Next, give the name of any sponsoring or supporting institution or organization (if not available, use the abbreviation *n.p.*), the date of electronic publication or the latest update (or the abbreviation *n.d.* if not available), and the medium of publication (*Web*). Always end with the date that you accessed the site.

### Personal Home Page

Good, Melissa. *Merwolf's Cave.* N.p., 2007. Web. 15 Mar. 2011.

Begin with the creator's name, followed by the title (or *Home page* if no title is given), publisher or sponsor (or *n.p.*), the most recent update (use *n.d.* if none is given), the medium of publication, and the date of access.

### Document from Website

Sacks, Bo. "How Magazines Can Survive." *Media Bistro.* Media Bistro, 15 Dec. 2006. Web. 10 Mar. 2011.

Begin with the author's name, followed by the title of the particular document (in quotation marks), the title of the entire site (italicized), the sponsor or publisher, the date of last update or publication (if given), the medium of publication, and the date of access.

"Asteroids." *Solar System Exploration.* National Aeronautics and Space Administration, n.d. Web. 5 May 2011.

If no author is given, begin with the title of the particular document (or article) and follow the same rules as the previous entry. Use the abbreviation *n.d.* to indicate "no date."

### Magazine Article Retrieved from a Database

Stanglin, Douglas, and Amy Bernstein. "Making the Grade." *US News and World Report* 4 Nov. 1996: 18. *Academic Search Elite.* Web. 21 Feb. 2011.

First cite as a print article, but leave off *Print* at the end of the entry. Then list the name of the database, the medium in which you accessed the publication (*Web*), and the date of access. If the database does not list the page (or the page range) of the article, write *n. pag.* for *no pagination*.

## Journal article Retrieved from a Database

Edwards, Clifford H. "Grade Inflation: The Effects on
    Educational Quality and Personal Well-Being." *Education*
    120.3 (2000): 538–46. *Academic Search Elite.* Web. 4 Feb.
    2011.

Follow the guidelines for a magazine article retrieved from a database, but make certain to format the publication information according to guidelines for print journal articles: volume. issue (year): page range.

## Article in Online Journal

Kingma, Mireille. "Nurses on the Move: Historical Perspective
    and Current Issues." *Online Journal of Issues in Nursing* 13.2
    (2008): n. pag. Web. 28 Feb. 2011.

Follow the format for print articles, but leave off *Print* at the end of the entry. After the year of publication, give the range of pages if they are numbered in the article, or write *n. pag.* if not given. At the end of the entry, add the medium of publication and date of access.

## Online Book

Shaw, Bernard. *Pygmalion.* New York: Brentano, 1916.
    *Bartleby.com.* Web. 9 Jan. 2011.

Follow the format for print books. Italicize the title of the website. If the book is part of an online scholarly project, which is often the case, include the sponsoring institution. At the end of the entry, add the medium of publication and date of access.

## E-book

Tolstoy, Leo. *Anna Karenina: A Novel in Eight Parts.* New York:
    Penguin, 2002. Microsoft Reader e-book file.

Follow the format for print books. Give the original publication information and date (on the copyright page). End the citation with the type of e-reader you used to view the source.

## Abstract

Barton, Ellen. "Resources for Discourse Analysis in Composition
    Studies." *Style* 36.4 (2002): 575–95. Abstract. *InfoTrac College
    Edition.* Web. 10 Dec. 2010.

Use the format appropriate for the type of source (book, article, etc.) and add the descriptor *Abstract* after the page numbers. Conclude with the database title, the publication medium, and the date of access.

### E-mail

Wells, Carson. "Recent Behavior." Message to Anton Chigurh. 23 Nov. 2007. E-mail.

Begin with the author/sender of the e-mail, followed by the title (the word or phrase from the subject line of the e-mail) in quotation marks, the descriptor *Message to,* and the recipient's name. If you were the e-mail's recipient, insert *Message to author.* End with the e-mail's date and the word *E-mail.*

### Listserver Posting

Brandywine, Jacob. "Raising Standards." Online posting. *Writing Program Forum.* Northern Michigan College, 21 Apr. 2010. Web. 4 May 2010.

Follow the format for a document from a website, but add the descriptor *Online posting* (without italics or quotation marks). Then give the name of the listserver or forum, the sponsor, the date of the posting, medium of publication, and the date of access.

### CD-ROM

*The Trigonometry Explorer.* Chevy Chase: Cognitive Technologies, 1996. CD-ROM.

If no author is given, use the editor, compiler, or translator's name, with the abbreviation *ed., comp.,* or *trans.* If none of these are listed, begin with the title, followed by publication information (city, publishing company, date). End with the descriptor *CD-ROM.*

### Part of CD-ROM

Allen Edmonds Shoes. Advertisement. *Comp21: Composition in the 21st Century, The Composition of Everyday Life.* Boston: Wadsworth, 2006. CD-ROM.

If citing a portion of a CD-ROM, begin with the author of that particular section (if one is listed), the title of the section, and then follow the format for a CD-ROM entry.

### Entry in an Online Encyclopedia or Dictionary

"India." *Columbia Encyclopedia.* Yahoo! Education, 2006. Web. 5 Jan. 2011.

As with a print encyclopedia, begin with the title of the article if no author is available. Then list the title of the encyclopedia, sponsor or publisher, the publication date (if available), the medium of publication, and the date of access.

# Other Sources

### Brochure

Masonic Information Center. *A Response to Critics of Freemasonry.*
    Silver Spring: Masonic Services Assn., n.d. Print.

Give information in the same format as a book. Use abbreviations to indicate missing publication information: *n.p.* (no publisher or no place), *n.d.* (no date of publication), and *n. pag.* (no page numbers).

### Personal Interview

Mossbacher, Delaney. Personal interview. 4 Mar. 2011.

Begin with the name of the interviewee, inverted. End with the interview date.

### Personal Letter or Memo

Bosley, Cindy. Letter to the author. 15 Nov. 2004. TS.

Like all sources, begin with the author's name (inverted). Then give the title or description of the letter. End with the date and medium of publication (*TS* for *typescript* and *MS* for handwritten *manuscript*).

### Published Letter

Tolkien, J. R. R. "To Christopher Tolkien." 18 Jan. 1944.
    Letter 55 of *The Letters of J. R. R. Tolkien.* Ed. Humphrey
    Carpenter and Christopher Tolkien. New York: Houghton,
    2000. 67–68. Print.

After the date of the letter, give the number of the letter, if available. List the information of the source in which the letter was published, according to the correct format for the source. (In other words, if the letter is published in a book, as above, follow the book format.)

### Television Program

"A Streetcar Named Marge." *The Simpsons.* FOX. WAGA,
    Atlanta, 10 Oct. 2007. Television.

Begin with the title of the episode or segment (in quotation marks). Name the creator, producer, director, narrator, performer, or writer (if pertinent). Provide the title of the program, the network, and the call letters, and city of the television station (if appropriate and available). End with the broadcast date and medium of reception.

### Film

*True Grit.* Dir. Ethan Cohen and Joel Cohen. Paramount, 2010.
    DVD.

After the title (italicized), list the director, the distributor, the year of release (or re-release if relevant), and the type of medium on which you viewed the film (such as *DVD* or *Blu-ray*).

### Sound Recording

Radiohead. "Morning Moon." *We Are the Same.* Zoe Records, 2009. CD.

Begin with the artist's name. Then list the title of a particular song or section (in quotation marks), the collection title (italicized), the recording company, and the year of release. All of this information is available on the product sleeve or insert. Finally, list the medium *(Audio-cassette, Audiotape, CD, LP)*, followed by a period.

### Lecture or Speech

Obama, Barack. "Remarks by the President on Osama Bin Laden." The White House East Room, Washington. 1 May 2011. Speech.

Begin with the speaker's name (inverted). Then list the title of the presentation (in quotation marks), the name of the meeting and sponsoring organization (if applicable), the location of the lecture or speech, the date, and a description (such as *lecture* or *address*).

### Advertisement

Whitney Museum of American Art. Advertisement. *New Yorker* 4 Jan. 2011: 22. Print.

Begin with the company or product name, followed by *Advertisement.* Then list the relevant publication information. For instance, if the ad appears in a periodical, list the information in the appropriate format and end with the page number and medium of publication.

### Work of Art (painting, sculpture, photograph)

O'Keeffe, Georgia. *Evening Star No. VI.* 1917. Watercolor. Georgia O'Keeffe Museum, Santa Fe.

Include the artist's name (inverted), the title of the work (italicized), the date of composition (if not given, write *n.d.*), the medium of composition, the collector or institution that houses it, and the city where it is held.

### Performance

*Twelfth Night.* By William Shakespeare. Dir. William Church. Harvey Theater, Interlochen, MI. 28 June 2008. Performance.

Begin with the title (if applicable), the author of the performed work (if applicable), the director, the performers (if available), the site of the performance, the date, and the word *Performance.*

# Sample Research Essay

Ben Wetherbee wrote this essay for his English 112 class (a second-semester composition course). As you read, take note of the strategies Wetherbee uses to integrate sources into his argument.

Wetherbee 1

Ben Wetherbee

Professor Mauk

English 112

22 April 2011

Branded

Often we recall the days of knights in shining armor, those men forever etched into history within their majestic shells of war. The bravery, the nobility, the selflessness of these radiant warriors—we recall that. But why shining armor? Yes, it undoubtedly had practical merit, but it acted as more than a protective casing: It was gleaming, curving, accompanied by luminous plumes and banners. Why the extravagance?

Easy! Medieval folks expected their knights to come in shining armor. Hulking, thick breastplates; glistening chain mail; colorful, intricate crests displayed upon great shields of iron—all indications of the times. The outfit—as much as the man, even—made a knight a knight. A knight without his armor, his shield, his weaponry, or his colors would pass only as an indistinct and vulnerable man, a commoner. In this spectacle-oriented world, the heart of a knight is insufficient; one must look the part to appear in the history textbook.

The result: Dress reflects cultural identity. Victorian women ruthlessly layered themselves in constricting attire certainly not for the sake of practicality or comfort, but because that's how women dressed; a woman improperly outfitted was scarcely a woman. Young men sported Beatles haircuts in the early '60s because the Beatles exemplified rock 'n' roll, rebellion, and freedom. The anti-Vietnam War movement

Historical allusion: gives a familiar reference to the reader.

More historical allusions make the point: dress reflects cultural identity.

Wetherbee 2

displayed the peace sign not because it was geometrically pleasing, but because it symbolized peace. Exposed chest hair, gold medallions, and white bellbottoms symbolized the disco movement. Eyeliner, tattoos, and uncouth, black-dyed hair symbolized the punk movement. Every hairstyle, makeup job, pair of jeans, white undershirt, and piece of jewelry means something—always! A glance at a person's garments, lipstick, or hairdo invariably offers a small insight to his/her cultural identity.

Focusing the point on individual identity.

The flip side, of course, is that dress reflects individual identity, too. A knight's colors, crest, or specific style of armor might have represented what specific sort of knight he was—his family, cause, or place of origin. Personal modifications are easily applicable to disco attire, hippie attire, punk attire—a personally significant emblem on a medallion, a jean jacket encrusted with handpicked embroidered patches, a tattoo reflecting an event in one's life. Personal expression even seeps from the cracks of the army, a place one would assume does its utmost to stifle individuality; recall Stanley Kubrick's Vietnam War film *Full Metal Jacket*—the protagonist's helmet sports both the peace symbol and the phrase "born to kill." Even officers' insignias convey a level of individuality by symbolizing personal accomplishment. Individual expression completes the duality of physical self-presentation, allowing great insight in the examination of identity.

Cultural allusions and reference to a popular film support the main idea so far.

So in the interest of argument, let's examine my identity. I typically wear loose-fitting jeans or khakis, often with side "cargo" pockets. My shirts vary from button-up to softball-style to basic t-shirts, but they're all simple, often exhibiting deep tones of blue, green, and grey. My shoes are simple, black, rugged, and masculine. I have no piercings, no tattoos. I wear a fleece jacket in the spring and fall, a wool peacoat and knit scarf in winter. No hats, usually. Trendy metal watch with a blue face. Two trendy necklaces with earthy beads. These observations may fail to offer any insights

Testimony and an appeal to character. (The writer is part of a cultural trend.)

into my soul, but I am certainly a visible product of the '90s and '00s. I look normal for one born in 1985, one who became a teenager in 1998—normal except for one thing . . .

What's missing? Give up?

Here's where the individual identity comes in—no corporate logos. I wear no corporate logos. My backpack displays the Eastpack emblem, but this one exception I've masked with political buttons. It's nearly impossible to buy decent shoes that don't display a logo these days, but I've succeeded even in this field. I ardently exercise my right not to wear corporate logos, which is a monumental deviation from the trend of my generation. Why? Here's why: The way my generation wears corporate logos scares the hell out of me.

Especially among middle- and high-schoolers, corporate logos appear rampantly. One can hardly set foot in a public school's hallway without drowning under a barrage of geometric homage to capitalism—the sleek meanness of the Nike swoosh, the catchy asymmetry of the Adidas stripes, the pseudo-heart insignia of Roxy, the many bubbly fonts of Billabong. Also appearing in mass: Polo Jeans' patriotic display, Tommy Hilfiger's boldly shaded rectangular tapestry, and the ultramodern Reebok regalia—to name a few. Shoes, jeans, sweatshirts, t-shirts, socks, hats, and even jewelry exhibit the plentiful etchings of a *laissez-faire* dream.

And while secondary schools provide their most overstated presence, the corporate-clad appear ubiquitously, even in the most seemingly unlikely settings. Political columnist Kirsten Anderberg, for example, even recalls the omnipresence of corporate logos at an anti-war rally:

> As my son put it, "The Anti-War Movement, brought to you by Banana Republic!" . . . People were pulling anti-war fliers out of Swatch bags and wearing

**Appeal to character:** the writer chooses not to be "branded."

**Specific examples** prove the point about his generation.

**The source,** Anderberg, helps make the point that is already expressed.

**The block quotation** is connected with a textual cue, "for example," and the content is set up.

Wetherbee 4

Old Navy shirts! The corporate logos on the umbrellas in the crowd were representative of this new population also. We saw a man with an umbrella that said "Telecommunications Systems" and he was holding up a sign that said "No Iraq Attack."

One might expect an anti-war protest to be consistent with the notion of hippie amaterialism, but no. Not in this age. Amazingly, the Nike swoosh and the peace symbol may traverse hand in hand.

Not surprisingly, corporations deliberately capitalize the public's willingness to wear their logos—it's a fantastic form of advertising! Brand consultant Jim Knutsen, in his appropriately titled article "Making Your Mark," discusses the value of "distinctiveness and consistency" in corporate labels: "The visual identities of the best brands trigger recognition and response, having been pounded into our subconscious over long periods of time" (56). Clothing offers a delicious means of exhibiting corporate "distinctiveness and consistency"—nothing like a succinct blurb of imagery on the breast of a hooded sweatshirt to help trigger the ol' "recognition and response." Because clothing is worn by people, and people are mobile, brand-name apparel presents a pervasive and inescapable means of advertisement. The eagerness of brands to create and distribute clothing-friendly logos melds in complete harmony with—and contributes to—the abundance of willful walking advertisements.

In addition to the more-than-enthusiastic support of the brands themselves, the logo-wearing phenomenon owes much of its endurance to good old-fashioned conformity. People love to conform. A glance at any human society from any time will reveal this; it's what enables trends in the first place. Furthermore, numerous psychological investigations (Zimbardo's mock prison and the famous Milgram experiment, for example); have scientifically established the willingness—eagerness,

---

The writer comments on Anderberg's point.

The in-text citation requires only the page number because the author is given in the setup.

A transition sentence brings us from the idea in the previous paragraph.

even—of the individual to bow to group expectations. As renowned author Doris Lessing sums up the matter, "When we're in a group, we tend to think as that group does: we may even have joined the group to find 'like-minded' people. But we also find our thinking changing because we belong to a group. It is the hardest thing in the world to maintain an individual dissident opinion, as a member of a group" (48). So, once the trend of logo-wearing sets in (which it has), it escalates. To use a cliché, "monkey see, monkey do." Humans *are* primates, after all—in Lessing's words, "we are group animals"—so humans mimic popular behavior (48). Once a trend gains popularity, social pressure colossally adds to its momentum; it's that simple. For my own example (this was before I became rebelliously anti-logo), I recall the desire to wear Airwalk shoes as a middle-schooler, the longing for miniature insignias to dot my socks just above the ankles. These things were cool. Social pressure—there's no avoiding it.

But enough with the how of the matter—corporate enthusiasm and the psychology of conformity explain that simply enough. The more pressing question is why? Why did the phenomenon of logo-wearing appear in the first place? Logos on employee attire and company-owned vehicles—sure, those make complete sense. Nobody's questioning those who wear logos to advertise their own businesses. But what prompted the pioneers of the logo-wearing movement to plaster other people's logos across their backpacks, sweatshirts, and jeans?

The answer is frightening: If clothing reflects cultural identity, and my generation wears corporate logos on its clothing, then my generation must identify with corporations. I, therefore, am a member of the Corporate Generation. How precisely did we come to identify with corporations? That's a difficult question with particularly elusive details. However, one can hardly ignore the correlation between the

The quotation reinforces the point made by the allusions to Milgram and Zimbardo.

The writer follows the quotation with personal testimony—wrapping the outside sources into his own argument.

Transition paragraph—to a more "frightening" insight.

All the support, thus far, leads here: the "corporate generation."

Wetherbee 6

logo-wearing phenomenon and the general rise of corporate America—the symbiotic existence of Washington and big business, the sweeping deployment of Wal-Marts against local enterprises. Corporate America has engraved its mark on this nation, including this nation's youth. My generation, we have been branded.

What's scarier, though, is how well we have adapted to our brands. To best describe my generation's passion for corporate logos, one must employ a word that evades the dictionary. The extraordinary novelist Kurt Vonnegut, in his book *Cat's Cradle,* first introduced the much-needed term *granfalloon. Granfalloon* describes a group of people bound by a hollow cause, who have nothing genuinely significant in common—"a seeming team that [is] meaningless in ways God gets things done," as Vonnegut puts it (91). "Hazel's obsession with Hoosiers around the world was a textbook example of a . . . granfalloon," Vonnegut elaborates. "Other examples of granfalloons are the Communist party, the Daughters of the American Revolution, the General Electric Company, the International Order of Odd Fellows—and any nation, anytime, anywhere" (91–92). With this in mind, one could aptly accuse my genera-tion of assembling itself into a brand-based granfalloon.

I try to like my generation—sometimes successfully. But this is too much. First, the premise uniting my generation's granfalloon is positively ludicrous. Much worse than Vonnegut's examples, our cause has no deep and philosophical criticism. No, ours is blatantly nutty: We willingly advertise corporations with which we have no affiliation whatsoever. Furthermore, brand-name attire is usually more costly than "plain" clothes, clothes that don't advertise—and we buy it anyway! We financially go out of our way to advertise other people's corporations. It's borderline insanity! Don't we realize we're doing their work for them? Don't we get it?—we're advertis-ing for them; they should be paying us!

Even literature helps to make the point. (Good writers find the connec-tions between culture, lit-erature, history, film, and their secondary sources.)

The writer maintains a strong but playful voice—even among the sources and allusions.

And it goes deeper. Recall that clothing also reflects individual identity. The Corporate Generation's members still seek to express their individual identities, but even this is often achieved through logo-wearing. Some wish to show off their wealth by wearing pricey brands. Some wish to boast their acute tastes in fashion. Some think the Nike swoosh just looks so damn cool. So, the Corporate Generation has broken itself into sub-granfalloons: the Nike-wearers, the Abercrombie-wearers, etc. And this is our individual expression—brand selection. On marches the rich kids' granfalloon, wearing its seventy-dollar Tommy Hilfiger jeans. On marches the in-crowd girls' granfalloon, signifying its lofty social altitude with Roxy sweatshirts and pink Adidas shoes. And on marches the wannabe jocks' granfalloon, t-shirts and warm-up pants plastered with any number of athletically oriented logos. This is my generation.

We don't use the symbol the way other generations have. Symbols are wildly effective in triggering ideas—the two-fingered V, the black armband, the holy cross. Past generations have used symbols effectively to represent specific movements and ideas; they have personalized symbols. The peace sign, for example, originally stood specifically for nuclear disarmament, its design very possibly inspired by the semaphore code positions for N and D (Liungman 253). The anti-Vietnam War movement personalized the emblem in the late '60s—its meaning was slightly altered to fit a new cause. But our emblems still mean "Nike," "Adidas," and "Reebok." The matter would vastly change if we were to use corporate logos against corporations—protesters have adopted this ironic spirit by wearing old army jackets to anti-war rallies. But irony is not our intention. We provide good publicity.

And let us take a moment to consider what we're publicizing. By and large, these corporations we advertise fall short of refined virtue; their methods are often questionable, to say the least. Nike, for example—undoubtedly among the worst

The writer intensifies the point by using the terms from his sources.

The source helps to prove a small supporting point.

Wetherbee 8

offenders—remains a longtime target of human rights groups. A report from 2000 entitled "Sweatshops Behind the Swoosh" alleges that "Nike [factory] workers in China . . . put in 12-hour days and seven-day weeks and earn $1.50 for every pair of shoes they turn out—which Nike sells for $80–$120" (qtd. in "The Swoosh"). Furthermore, the report directly asserts that "the deplorable conditions in Nike factories are Nike's fault. In a global economy with no rules that protect workers, it is companies such as Nike [that] direct the global sweatshop in industries such as clothing and footwear" (qtd. in "The Swoosh"). Ouch! So Nike is not quite a monument to morality and goodwill toward men, and other corporations face similar charges. Names like Adidas, Gap, Reebok, and many more can also be associated with the third-world sweatshop, and it doesn't even end there. Abercrombie, for instance, faces accusations of racial discrimination in its hiring policies. Do we really want to pay top dollar to advertise for the Abercrombies and Nikes of the world, to essentially do their work for them? If it isn't absurd enough to willingly advertise other people's companies in the first place, we're advertising companies with distinctly sinister backgrounds.

In all fairness, however, Nike and other corporations have undertaken efforts to improve working conditions since 2000. But this hardly justifies the small fortunes we pay to do their advertising work for them. It seems unlikely, anyway, that these sweatshop-based corporations would have taken any virtuous steps in the absence of scalding pressure from humanitarian groups. They have no excuses. They exploited their impoverished workers.

My generation, let us not reward such exploiters, even if they have shown a little progress. At the very least, let them do their own advertising.

I have to give my generation a bit of credit, though—not every company logo worn may directly reflect a granfalloon. Paintball enthusiasts, for instance, may

He follows the info from the source with a direct response—which resonates with his voice.

The source ("The Swoosh") prompts several paragraphs of writer's commentary.

Speaking directly to his generation makes the essay slightly informal.

wear the logo of a certain paintball equipment company—thus the logo reflects their identities as paintballers. And wearing the Atari logo may be a genuine expression of proud nerdiness, though even this logo has been trivialized by widespread popularity. These groups may qualify as granfalloons, too, by Vonnegut's standards, but at least their status is debatable. The Nike-wearers, the Roxy-wearers, the Adidas-wearers, the Abercrombie-wearers, though—they're only expressing their membership in the Corporate Generation, a certain granfalloon among granfalloons.

He consistently points to corporate logo examples.

Indeed, Aldous Huxley may have foreseen the Corporate Generation in his 1932 novel *Brave New World,* a depiction of an ultra-consumerist future in which *Ford* has replaced God: "Ford! Ford! it was too revolting . . ." (91). Had Huxley only lived to witness the upsurge of Nike and its compatriots, perhaps he'd have found a more contemporary replacement for Ford—"[Nike! Nike!] it was too revolting . . ." Or perhaps "Adidas! Adidas!" or "Reebok! Reebok!" After all, we have taken our logo-wearing perilously near a religious status. Perhaps we're out to make Huxley a prophet, to attain the dystopia of his vision. It's a farfetched notion, but here we are—marching steadfastly onward, proudly adorned by our favorite corporate insignias. This is my generation.

Another novel helps illustrate the point. And the writer helps make the connection between the fictional and the real.

And to you, my generation, I offer this challenge: We can do better. We're still the young generation; we're supposed to rebel against the machine. We're supposed to rally against the aged fat cats who watch us from lofty offices—cigars dangling from their lips; disgusted, aghast, and mortified by our presence. We're supposed to strike blows for humanity. We're supposed to be out to change the world.

Rather, we're blithely buying into the schemes of those aged conservatives in their towering office buildings. Some youth of the nation we are.

The historical allusions now contrast with the present generation.

Wetherbee 10

So what happened to the creativity of youth? Look at how the hippie kids dressed. It may have been eccentrically colorful and a little too LSD-inspired, but at least it was their style. Look at how the '70s kids dressed. Brown and orange may be a thoroughly nasty color combination, but at least it was theirs. Look at how the original punks dressed. They may have been crude, vulgar, and downright revolting, but at least it was their crudeness. At least it was their vulgarity, their downright revoltingness.

These corporate logos—they aren't ours. They belong to old men in grey suits, sweatshop-perpetuators, violators of human rights, crushers of the little guy. Our adornment of these logos plainly exposes our shortcoming as the young generation. We aren't even trying. We actually wear the mark of the enemy—all that the young generation, by definition, is supposed to oppose. Nike is not ours. Adidas is not ours. Reebok is not ours. Billabong is not ours. Roxy is not ours. Abercrombie is not ours. No corporate entities are ours.

So let's be damn sure we aren't theirs.

The first element in each entry (usually the last name of the author) appears in the text.

## Works Cited

Anderberg, Kirsten. "Corporate Logos and Protest Signs." *Eat the State!* Eat the State! 26 Feb. 2003. Web. 20 Apr. 2011.

Huxley, Aldous. *Brave New World.* 1932. New York: Harper, 1969. Print.

Knutsen, Jim. "Making Your Mark." *Searcher* 12 (2004): 56. *Academic Search Elite.* Web. 20 Apr. 2011.

Lessing, Doris. "Group Minds." *Prisons We Choose to Live Inside.* New York: Harper, 1988. 47–62. Print.

Liungman, Carl G. *Dictionary of Symbols.* New York: Norton, 1991. Print.

"The Swoosh and the Sweats." *Nation* 22 May 2000: 7. *General Reference Center Gold.* Web. 30 Mar. 2011.

Vonnegut, Kurt. *Cat's Cradle.* New York: Delta, 1998. Print.

# APA Style

The American Psychological Association documentation style is used in psychology, nursing, education, and related fields. But while the format is somewhat different from MLA, the strategies for finding, evaluating, and integrating sources remain the same. And even the basic principles of documentation remain the same across styles: the information in the in-text citation should correspond directly with the References page (the APA equivalent of a Works Cited page).

- In-text (or parenthetical) citations provide unobtrusive documentation of specific information.
- In-text citation lets a reader know that particular ideas come from a particular source.
- In-text citation corresponds to the complete bibliographic information provided at the end of the text.
- In-text citations lead the reader directly to the corresponding References page.
- Done correctly, the in-text citation lists the first word(s)—whether the author's last name or the article title—plus year of publication and the page number of the citation on the alphabetized References page. This allows the reader to easily find the appropriate source on the References page.
- The References page provides complete information for finding the source easily.
- This complete information is provided only once and comes at the end of the entire text so that it doesn't interfere with ease of reading.

## In-Text Citation

Like MLA style, in-text documentation for APA involves referencing the original text in parentheses within the actual sentences of your text. An in-text citation must occur whenever a writer:

- Quotes directly from a source
- Paraphrases ideas from a source
- Summarizes ideas from a source
- References statistics or data from a source

For direct quotes, APA in-text citations should include the author name, date (year only) of the source, and page number from which the cited material is taken. If the author name is given within the sentence, however, it does not need to be included in the in-text citation.

"After months of exhausting research, they had finally come to understand the problem with their design" (Smith, 2008, p. 82). ──────

*p.* or *pp.* comes before the actual page number(s).

End punctuation comes after the parenthetical citation.

Commas separate elements within the parentheses.

Writers using APA style often include the date directly after the author's name in the sentence.

Emphasizing her point, Miller (2000) demands that "it is now time for something drastic to change here on campus" (p. 43).

**If the source has no author,** use the first word or phrase of the source title and punctuate the title accordingly (either with quotation marks or italics).

"Even though most of the nation's coastal shorelines can no longer sustain a full range of sea life, the vast majority of Americans seem unconcerned" ("Dead Seas," 2001, p. 27).

**If the source has two authors,** use the last name of both authors. (Notice that APA style uses &, an ampersand, for in-text citations and the References page.)

(Lunsford & Ede, 2004, p. 158)

**If the cited material is quoted in another source,** cite the source in which you found the quotation and add *as cited in* before the author name or title.

(as cited in Smith, 2008)

**If you want to acknowledge more than one source for the same information,** use a semicolon between citations within one set of parentheses. The sources should be listed in alphabetical order.

(Lunsford & Ede, 1984; Smith, 2008)

**Electronic Sources**  Many electronic sources (web pages, for instance) do not have page numbers, but page numbers may appear on the hard copy. Unless the original source has page numbers, omit them from the in-text citation. Instead, either use the paragraph number (after the abbreviation *para.*), if provided, or, if the source has headings, use the heading plus the paragraph number of the source. Electronic texts (especially web pages) may lack authors; in that case, follow the same formula as with print sources and use the title of the source in the citation.

(Vince, 2010, Blood to Brain section, para. 2)

# References

The References list gives sources that are directly cited in the text. Bibliographies, on the other hand, list all the sources that a writer may have read and digested in the process of researching the project. Entries in a References list must follow strict formatting guidelines. As in MLA documentation, the guidelines may change depending on the type of source, but there are some consistent rules. For instance, the first bit of information in the reference entry should always correspond directly with the in-text citation. In the following example, from Stemlow's essay (page 500), the entry begins with *Wrightson*—as does the in-text citation within her essay:

Some 91.2 million people choose to make a New Year's resolution each year (**Wrightson,** 1992, p. 19).

**Wrightson,** C. (1992, November/December). Vital statistics. *Health, 6*(6), 19. Retrieved from http://www.health.com/health

The following rules also apply to all sources:

- Author names come first. Last name first, followed by first initial of first name (and first initial of middle name, if given).
- The date comes in parentheses directly after the author names.
- Title of the work comes directly after the date. Article titles are always in regular type, while the sources in which they appear—newspapers, magazines, and journals—are italicized. (Only the first letter of the article title or subtitle is capitalized unless there are proper nouns.)
- If no author appears, the title comes first.
- Publication information follows the title of the source.
- If the source is an article, page numbers come last. If the source is electronic, the retrieval information comes last.

# Printed Books

All of the necessary information for books can usually be found on the title page, which is one of the first pages.

### General Format for Books

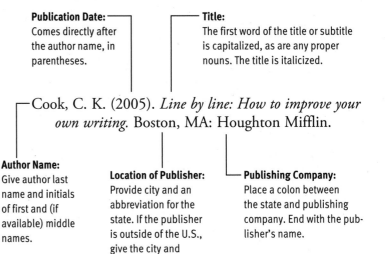

**Publication Date:** Comes directly after the author name, in parentheses.

**Title:** The first word of the title or subtitle is capitalized, as are any proper nouns. The title is italicized.

Cook, C. K. (2005). *Line by line: How to improve your own writing.* Boston, MA: Houghton Mifflin.

**Author Name:** Give author last name and initials of first and (if available) middle names.

**Location of Publisher:** Provide city and an abbreviation for the state. If the publisher is outside of the U.S., give the city and country.

**Publishing Company:** Place a colon between the state and publishing company. End with the publisher's name.

### Two or More Authors

Vasta, R., Haith, M. M., & Miller, S. A. (2005). *Child psychology: The modern science.* New York, NY: Wiley.

Add all additional author names, also inverted, before the title. Use an ampersand (&), not *and,* between the names.

### Corporate Author

American Automobile Association. (2007). *Tour book: New Jersey and Pennsylvania.* Heathrow, FL: Author.

Use the name of the corporation for the author name. If the corporate author also published the text, write *Author* for the publisher.

### Subsequent Editions

Lauwers, J., & Shinskie, D. (2004). *Counseling the nursing mother* (4th ed.). Sudbury, MA: Jones & Bartlett.

Find the edition information on the title page of the book and place the information in parentheses directly after the title. Use abbreviations: *2nd ed., 3rd ed.,* etc., or use *Rev. ed.* for "Revised edition."

### Edited Book

Alarcon, D. (Ed.). (2010). *The secret miracle.* New York, NY: Holt.

If referencing an entire edited book, begin with the editor's name and *Ed.* (for "editor"). Use *Eds.* (for "editors") if the book has more than one editor. Then give the date, the title, the publisher location, and the publisher name.

### Translated Book

Bakhtin, M. (2004). *Problems of Dostoevsky's poetics* (C. Emerson, Trans.). Minneapolis, MN: University of Minnesota Press.

Add the translator's name (first and middle initials and last name) and *Trans.* (all in parentheses) after the title of the book.

# Printed Articles

Articles appear in newspapers and periodicals (journals or magazines). While newspapers are usually published daily, magazines are usually published weekly or monthly, and journals are published quarterly or even biannually.

### Article in a Magazine

Buchanan, M. (2004, November 20). A billion brains are better than one. *New Scientist, 184,* 34–37.

Include the date (year, month, day) directly after the author name. Do not abbreviate months. Give the volume number in italics after the magazine title.

### Article in a Newspaper

Drahos, M. H. (2011, March 19). Now and then: Women's rights have come a long way, but still have a long way to go. *North Coast,* pp. A1, A4.

If one is listed, give the author first, followed by the date and the title of the article. After the title of the newspaper, add section letters before the page numbers.

### Article in a Journal

Crow, A. (2003). Risky behavior among youth: A study of American teens. *American Psychologist, 58,* 400–415.

Most academic journals number the pages of each issue continuously through a volume. The second issue does not begin with page 1, but with the number after the last page of the previous issue. For these journal articles, place the volume number in italics directly after the journal title, and before the page numbers. If each issue starts over with page 1, provide the issue number in parenthesis after the volume number, not in italics.

**Article or Chapter in an Edited Book**

Mickelson, R. A., & Smith, S. S. (1991). Education and the struggle against race, class, and gender inequality. In E. Disch (Ed.), *Reconstructing gender: A multicultural anthology* (pp. 303–317). Mountain View, CA: Mayfield.

After the author and date, give the title of the article or chapter. Then write *In* and the first initial and last name of the editor(s). The abbreviation *Ed. or Eds.* (in parentheses) should follow the editor(s). End with the title of the book, the page numbers in which the article appears, and the publication information.

**Encyclopedia Article**

Esposito, V. J. (2000). World War II: The diplomatic history of the war and post-war period. In *Encyclopedia Americana* (9th ed., Vol. 29, pp. 364–367). Danbury, CT: Grolier.

Begin with the author (if given) and date. Then give the title of the article. The name of the encyclopedia (after *In*) should be in italics. The edition number, volume number, and page number(s) should be in parentheses. If an editor is also named, list the first initial and last name before the title (after *In*).

# Electronic Sources

As with print sources, citations for electronic sources require author(s), date, title, and publication information. Authors and titles are formatted in the same manner as print sources. The difference occurs with publication information: Publishers of electronic work sometimes assign a *digital object identifier* (DOI), which is a kind of persistent virtual address. The DOI is sometimes, not always, located at the top of the article. If a source has a DOI, you need not include a retrieval date or URL. If no DOI was assigned, however, provide a URL. (When adding the URL to your citation, break it only before slashes [/] or other punctuation and do not add hyphens.) The *Publication Manual of the American Psychological Association* (APA) says, "No retrieval date is necessary for content that is not likely to be changed or updated, such as a journal article or book." In other words, if the content is likely to stay unchanged, no retrieval date is needed. Especially with electronic sources, remember the basic principle behind citing sources: to provide a guide for finding the sources you used. Therefore, the most direct route to the source should always be used in the entry.

### Website

Pinsker, S. (Ed.). (1999). *Robin flies again: Letters written by women of Goucher College, class of 1903.* Retrieved from http://meyerhoff.goucher.edu/library/robin

*Sierra Club.* (2011, March). Retrieved March 10, 2011, from http://www.sierraclub.org

As with all sources in APA format, begin with the author's or editor's name(s) (inverted), if available, and the date of electronic publication. Give the title of the site (italicized). Write *Retrieved* and then the date of access (if the information is likely to get edited or revised), followed by *from* and the URL (no final period).

### Document from Website (Author and Date Stated)

Sacks, B. (2006, December 15). How magazines can survive. Retrieved from http://mediabistro.com/articles/cache/a9304 .asp

Begin with the author name (normal APA format), followed by the date (in parentheses), the title of the specific document, the word *Retrieved* and the access date if necessary, and finally *from* and the URL.

### Document from Website (No Author or Date Stated)

Astrology. (n.d.). Retrieved April 8, 2011, from http:// en.wikipedia.org/wiki/Astrology

Begin with the title. In place of the date, write *n.d.* in parentheses for "no date." Then, give the title of the specific document (if applicable), *Retrieved* and the access date, and finally *from* and the URL.

### Personal Home Page

Good, M. (2007). *Merwolf's cave.* Retrieved February 10, 2011, from http://www.merwolf.com/

Begin with the creator's name, followed by the date of the most recent update, the title, *Retrieved,* the date of access if needed, and *from* and the URL.

### Journal or Magazine Article Retrieved from a Database

Boyd, N. G. (2002). Mentoring dilemmas: Developmental relationships within multicultural organizations. *Journal of Occupational & Organizational Psychology, 75*(1), 123–125. Retrieved from http://www.bps.org.uk/publications/journals/journaltitles/joop.cfm

Follow guidelines for a print journal. After the page number, add *Retrieved* and the home page URL of the journal if there is no DOI for the article. If there is a DOI, list it after *doi:* following the page numbers. Whether you provide a URL or DOI, do not include the name of the database.

### Journal Article Online

If the online journal is exactly the same as the print version (which is most common for academic journals), then follow the format for print articles, but conclude the entry with *Retrieved from* and the URL of the journal's homepage if no DOI is assigned. If a DOI is given, list it after *doi:*

Crow, A. (2000). What's age got to do with it? Teaching older students in computer-aided classrooms. *Teaching English in the Two-Year College, 27*(4), 400–415. Retrieved from http://www.ncte.org

Birmingham, P. (2008). Elated citizenry: Deception and the democratic task of bearing witness. *Research in Phenomenology 83*(2), 198–215. doi: 10.1163/156916408x286969

### Online Book

Shaw, B. (1916). *Pygmalion.* Retrieved from http://bartleby .com/138/index.html

Follow the format for print books, but exclude the original print publication information. End with the URL.

### Abstract

Bailey, K.D. Towards unifying science: Applying concepts across disciplinary boundaries. *Systems Research and Behavioral Science,* 18(1), 41-62. Abstract retrieved from http://onlinelibrary.wiley .com/

Include either the database name or the database URL, but not both.

> For periodicals accessed in digital form, provide a DOI if one is available. Otherwise, provide the URL for the home page.

# Other Sources

### Brochure

Masonic Information Center. (n.d.). *A response to critics of freemasonry* [Brochure]. Silver Spring, MD: Masonic Services Association.

Use *n.d.* to indicate no date, which is often necessary for brochures. After the title, add the descriptor *Brochure* in brackets before the publication information.

### Personal Interview or Letter

(L. Jackson, personal communication, March 4, 2011)

APA style recommends citing personal communications only with an in-text citation—not in the References list. In the in-text citation, give the name of the interviewee, the title *personal communication,* and the date.

### Television Program

Martin, J. (Writer), & Moore, R. (Director). (1992). A streetcar named Marge [Television series episode]. In A. Jean & M. Reiss (Producers), *The Simpsons.* Los Angeles, CA: Twentieth Century Fox.

Begin with the name and title of the scriptwriter, then the name and title of the director and the date. Give the title of the episode or segment followed by the producer and the title of the program (italicized). End with the location of the broadcasting company and the company name.

### Government Publication

U.S. Census Bureau. (2007). *Statistical abstract of the United States.* Washington, DC: U.S. Government Printing Office.

If no author is given, use the government agency as the author, followed by the date, the title (in italics), and the publication information that appears on the title page.

# Sample Research Essay

Amanda Stremlow wrote this essay for her English 112 class, a second-semester composition course. As you read, notice how Stremlow uses sources to develop ideas.

The title page includes the title of the essay, the student's name and the name of the school. Also, notice that the title (shortened to fifty characters, if longer) and the page number appear at the top of the title page and on all subsequent pages.

1/2" from top title (shortened to fifty characters, if longer) and page number
Title centered

Your name, in the center of the page both vertically and horizontally

Course title, instructor's name, and date

All information double-spaced

Running head: VULTURES                                    1

Vultures

Amanda Stremlow

Northwestern Michigan College

Vultures

"5, *4, 3, 2 . . . 1! I* am going to lose weight this year." How many people recited

these words last New Year's Eve? Probably more than anyone thinks! Some 91.2

million people choose to make a New Year's resolution each year (Wrightson, 1992,

p. 19). New Year's celebrations almost always lead to the infamous resolution. With

all the fun of New Year's Eve, it is doubtful that many of us ever wonder why we

even made a resolution in the first place. Most would say that is a part of our culture,

something we are taught. But ask this: Are we taught that it has to be to lose weight,

eat healthy, or quit smoking at the beginning of each year?

No one ever told me that I needed to resolve to lose weight, but still for the last

three years I have told myself: "I am going to lose weight this year." The first year I

bought diet pills I had heard about on a commercial. Needless to say, they don't mag-

ically "melt away the pounds." So, one whole year later, there I sat making the same

resolution: "I am going to lose weight this year." But after wasting a couple hundred

dollars on a gym membership, I still hadn't lost any weight. Why waste my time

making a resolution I was unable to keep? That's exactly what I was thinking last

year on December 31st. Still at the stroke of midnight, I uttered those same words,

but to avail because here I sit approaching the New Year with those same ten pounds

(and probably more) to lose. Why did I feel the need to lose weight every year? The

rest of the year I am happy with the way I look and I never think about it.

More than likely, most people have a story that follows these same lines. An

amazing 91.2 million people make resolutions and, more importantly, there is a "top

10 resolutions" as most of us make the same resolutions every year (Wrightson,

1992, p. 19). One has to wonder why, but most consumers probably don't. Let's be

honest: People don't like to question things they don't see clear answers to. However,

The statistic requires an in-text citation.

Testimony—the writer's own experience illustrates the point.

The writer quotes only key words or phrases when appropriate.

VULTURES                                                                        3

it is possible that the sheer number and collective similarities of New Year's resolutions in our society are directly related to marketing strategies that prey on consumers' vulnerabilities during the holiday season. There is a reason why we don't make
Fourth of July resolutions or Groundhog Day resolutions. Instead of ignore it, I suggest that we analyze the reasons and delegate responsibility where it is due.

She first sets up the idea,
then gives a brief sum-
mary of the source before
giving the quotation.

Latent elements of our consciousness may allow us to overlook the impact marketing strategies could have on New Year's resolutions. Embedded in our minds, a
distinct ideology prevents us from grasping the concept of market control. In "Group
Minds," Doris Lessing (1988) reveals valuable information about people and the way
we view ourselves. Lessing insists that we operate under the ideology: "I am a citizen of a free society, and that means I am an individual, making individual choices"
(p. 47). This ideology allows consumers to overlook the possibility of market control.
As educated individuals, Americans would like to believe that, if we make decisions
about self-improvement and actually resolve to change our own lives, it is a matter of
free will. The claim that marketing strategies can control our resolutions is unnerving

She follows the quotation
with further explanation.

and, therefore, questionable simply because of this ideology. However, consumers
must be willing to investigate how and why companies have an ability to control our
choices.

A line of reasoning.

An enterprise that controls collective trends should be monitored closely because
it impacts people's finances—and personal desires. As American consumers, our
lives revolve around our money; so paying close attention to the mechanisms that
control our purchases is invaluable. The way we spend our money determines how
much of it we need, which in turn affects the way we live. Clearly, our money and
the issues that surround our spending should be scrutinized. (Again, remember it is

our money that the diet industry, or any industry, is after. Our purchases determine their profit.)

Consumers must see the forms of control at work. If 91.2 million people chose to wear the same hat on the same day, we would immediately wonder. If 91.2 million people choose to make a resolution at the same time (and sometimes, more importantly, the same one), we must question the cause. Making a resolution is not an instinct; it is not a means of survival and no gene in our body codes for resolutions. With those causes out of the equation, consumers must look outside ourselves for some influence. This is where specifically designed marketing comes into play—a type of marketing that probably starts in late November and preys on consumers' vulnerabilities during the holiday season.

The statistic from the intro is used throughout the argument.

Some consumers may say that the holiday season is no different than any other time of the year. However, there are distinct cultural traditions that make us more vulnerable to holiday marketing. This is why we make New Year's resolutions and not Groundhog Day resolutions. First off, the holidays are a time for reflection; we spend time with our close family and friends. This type of interaction allows us to closely compare ourselves with our peers and our family. For me, I sit and compare aspects of my life to those of three female cousins my age. And close inspection always seems to turn up inadequacies no matter what the situation is.

Counterarguing.

Secondly, consumers have preconceptions surrounding the New Year; specifically, it is a chance for rebirth. It is the most drastic change our calendar makes, a whole new year, a chance to change the most undesirable aspects about ourselves. If we can be shown that we need to change, we easily *know* that this is the time to do it. We feel a looming sense of rebirth as the calendar year shifts. According to a publication from Indiana University (2003), resolutions are "a ritualized way of reviewing

VULTURES                                                                    5

The quotation reinforces
the point expressed at
the beginning of the
paragraph.

the past and looking toward the future." Universally, the New Year is "an opportunity to clean house." Symbolically, we can "clean house" by changing our lives *(New Year's)*.

The difference between the holiday season and other seasons, and the vulnerabilities we encounter during the New Year, make resolutions an excellent opportunity for companies to increase their profit. Writing in the *Journal of Health Communication*, Michael Basil, Debra Basil, and Caroline Schooler (2001) insist that the basic principle of "consumer behavior is that marketing and advertising are most effective when they target an existing need." Consequently, by preying on the vulnerabilities of consumers (the existing need for self-improvement or change), companies spawn increased sales of the product. Basil et al. also assert that an awareness of "psychological needs is the most important device available to marketers." They proclaim that the "needs that consumers actually feel reveal the type of products that are generally easiest to sell to them and the time it is easiest to sell them." These basic tenets of marketing explain how and why companies prey on consumers' vulnerabilities during the holiday season.

No page number is given
because the source was
retrieved from a database.
(The writer cannot know
the actual page number
for the quotation.)

Marketing strategies prey on these vulnerabilities by forcing us to see what we must change: to see the extra weight, the debt, the smoking. If they can simply make us want to change something, we will pick the night of December 31st to change. Upon making the resolutions, we will more than likely employ the products or services of the company in order to uphold them. Whether or not we keep our resolutions isn't their concern. Simply making a resolution that entails the purchase of their product is enough to promote their profits.

Let's imagine a girl, Sarah, in her late twenties. She has gained a few pounds every year, but for the most part she is a beautiful person with a lot of potential. She

enario illustrates the

spends time with her family during all their get-togethers for Thanksgiving, Christ-mas, and the New Year. Looking around at her family, she notices a slight difference. All but her uncle look thinner than her. Feeling a little larger in last year's red dress, she throws on a cardigan over it and thinks nothing more of her inadequacies. Then, later that night an ad on the TV screams, "Finally, a diet pill that melts the pounds away" as a "newly transformed" beautiful blonde women blabs on and on about her new life. The line of reasoning behind the ad: Sarah can have a new life if she just takes the pills. Mixed with the inadequacy she felt at the Christmas party, this commercial is enough to prompt the subsequent resolution: to lose weight this year. BOOM . . . the company just made a profit.

This is how it works: By exploiting our vulnerabilities during the holiday sea-son and forcing faulty reasoning on us, the company makes money. Preying on our intellectual immobility, these companies force an oversimplified line of reasoning on consumers. Like most commercials, they proclaim that doing this one thing will solve all of our problems. They control our consciousness, creating the desire for a product that we ignored previously.

Even with ample research to support this point, many consumers choose to ignore it. They continue to operate under the ideology Doris Lessing explains: "I am a citizen of a free country, an individual making individual choices" (1988, p. 47). Of course, we are comfortable living within this box, but unfortunately it cannot be true. If companies can justify spending billions of dollars on advertising, it must serve a purpose. In a capitalistic society, the goal is profit and that which doesn't serve that single goal is abandoned. If advertising didn't serve that goal, companies would have found a better means of controlling their profit.

Analysis of the advertising strategy reveals a hidden line of reasoning.

She returns to key lines from her sources.

VULTURES                                                                 7

Companies track their advertising budgets. If consumers could even fathom the amount of these budgets, we would understand what the companies plan to gain back from the investment. This money is only gained if the company can persuade an individual, who wouldn't have, to buy their product or service. Many companies' advertising budgets increase during and directly after the holiday season, to impact New Year's resolution making. The diet/health industry and smoking cessation companies, whose advertising budgets increase during these months, prey on consumers' engrained vulnerabilities.

The frozen food companies, like Lean Cuisine, manipulate their market by increasing their advertising budget during the holiday season. According to Betsy Spethmann (1995), Stouffer Foods was to spend an estimated 8 to 10 million dollars by March to "extend the lift diet foods get from consumers' New Year's resolutions" (p. 1). If the company spent this much money between November and March, they spent 2 to 2.5 million dollars a month on advertising during and directly after the holiday season. Preying on consumers' vulnerability, they make an increased profit off the propagation of New Year's resolutions. The continuous marketing of their "health lifestyles" culture with its subtle cues about the value of thinness and the lifestyle it *creates* controls the conscious thoughts of its audience with faulty reasoning.

Similarly, according to Ian Murphy, the Healthy Choice food product line "'typically sees a double-digits sales increase' from January promotions" (1997, p. 12). Also they doubled first-quarter advertising and promotions, spending just over 3 million dollars a month on advertising directly after the holiday season (Murphy, p. 12). Their method preys on consumers' internal thoughts about inadequacy and worth, specifically the ones that surround the holidays. Knowing that this is the most fertile time in which to implant this faulty reasoning, they increase their budgets and, in

**The statistics support the initial statement of the paragraph.**

turn, succeed in creating a customer that they previously didn't have. This type of strategic marketing is not exclusive to the diet/health industry but it is probably the most obvious to the average consumer. Clearly, strategic marketing that preys on our existing vulnerability (or need) during the holiday season promotes great profit.

Even the tobacco industry recognizes and reacts to the trends of New Year's resolutions in our society by increasing their marketing during the months of January and February (Basil et al., 2000). But they aren't trying to increase profit; clearly, one can infer that their marketing seeks to counter the impact of smoking cessation during the New Year. In an article from *Advertising Age,* Mercedes Cardona (1998) outlines how SmithKline Beecham, the company in charge of NicoDerm and Nicorette, is "following the dieter's recipe" by taking "advantage of a tendency among smokers to choose the beginning of the year as the kick off for their attempts at quitting" (p. 4 ). According to a Gallup poll, half of the smokers who aim to quit begin their attempts on New Year's Day (as cited in Cardona). Smoking cessation companies increase their advertisements in an attempt to maximize their profit by exploiting this tendency.

This is not to say that companies should not cater to our needs during the season, but they shouldn't have to create them. As in the above scenario, Sarah doesn't have the best confidence in herself, but she can ignore her inadequacies until they are thrown in her face by the diet industry. This is how advertising works; this is its purpose. In our capitalistic society, competition is key and an edge on the market is the best way to increase profit.

Maybe consumers can't stop advertising from affecting us, but we can tip the balance by at least understanding and accepting its power to do so. We, the consumers, push this art of advertising forward by participating in the process. Looking at

¶14–17 all work to support the same point about money, advertising, and the strategic marketing.

The references to sources always give information about the writer's identity or the publication. This boosts reliability.

A concession paragraph.

The conclusion avoids mere summary—and offers a new way to think about our own attitudes.

VULTURES                                                                 9

our clothes, our houses, our cars, our refrigerators, and our lifestyles, we must accept the effects of advertising and level with them. As Doris Lessing argues, "It is one thing to admit it, in a vague uncomfortable way . . . but quite another to make that cool step into a kind of objectivity" where consumers can say, "'let's admit it, examine and organize our attitudes accordingly'" (1998, p. 50). Think about that on New Year's and choose wisely at the stroke of midnight.

The sources are listed in alphabetical order—each corresponding to the appropriate format. (Pages 473–481 show APA formatting for articles, books, and so on.)

References

Basil, M. D., Basil, D. Z., & Schooler, C. (2000). Cigarette advertising to counter New Year's resolutions. *Journal of Health Communication, 5*(2), 161–174. doi:10.1080/108107300406875

Cardona, M. M. (1998, December 21). Nicorette, NicoDerm CQ ads tied to New Year's resolutions. *Advertising Age, 69*(51), 4. Retrieved from http://adage.com/

Lessing, D. (1988). Group minds. *Prisons we choose to live inside* (pp. 47–62). New York, NY: HarperCollins.

Murphy, I. P. (1997, February 3). Marketers help consumers to keep their resolutions. *Marketing News, 31*(3), 12–13. Retrieved from http://www.marketingpower.com/

*New Year's resolutions: Why do we make them when we usually don't keep them?* (2003, December 5). Retrieved from http://newsinfo.iu.edu/news/page/normal/1206.html

Spethmann, B. (1995, November 6). Lean mean New Year. *Brandweek, 36*(42), 1. Retrieved from http://www.brandweek.com/bw/index.jsp

Wrightson, C. (1992, November/December). Vital statistics. *Health, 6*(6), 19. Retrieved from http://www.health.com/health

# Frequently Asked Questions

## What If I Don't Know What Type of Source I Have?

This question often comes up when researching electronic sources. Most online research methods lead to either periodicals (journals, magazines, and newspapers) or websites. (Online books are generally not in the same search paths as periodicals.) If you have an electronic source and are not sure if it is a website or a periodical, check the top of the first page for publication information. If the text has a volume or issue number, or date information, it is most likely a periodical. Also, an electronic article most often lists the title of the magazine or journal at the top of the first page.

## How Do I Tell the Difference between a Journal and a Magazine?

In general, a magazine is published more often than a journal. Magazines are published every week *(Time, Newsweek),* every other week, or every month. Magazines are written for nonspecialized, or *general,* readership, whereas journals are written for readers with a specialized field of knowledge (such as nursing, engineering, or pharmacology). While magazines attempt to inform or entertain the public about various (sometimes even eccentric) topics, journals attempt to investigate particular ideas, theories, or situations within a discipline or field of study. Check the publication information to see how often the periodical is published, and look at the table of contents to see if the articles are written for general or specialized readers. (See pages 435–436.)

## How Do I Find the Publication Information?

Publication information for books can be found on the title page. The front of the title page has the full title, the publisher, and the city of publication, and the reverse (or copyright) page includes the copyright dates and any edition information. For periodicals, the volume and issue number usually appear at the bottom of each page and are often printed on the first page inside the cover along with the table of contents. (However, some periodicals fill the first few pages with advertisements.) Websites can be more tricky. If the author, last update, or sponsoring institution does not appear on the opening (or home) page, scroll down to the bottom of the page (or look on the menu for *Information* or *About Us).*

## How Do I Know the Page Numbers of an Electronic Source?

Generally, electronic sources do not have page numbers—and documentation styles do not require page numbers for websites or online journal articles. Sometimes, however, a print source will republish its contents electronically and retain page numbers. (In other words, the source appears online exactly as it does in print.) In that case, simply use the page numbers as they appear.

## Should I Use APA, MLA, or Something Else?

MLA (or Modern Language Association) style is used by writers in the humanities and literature (such as English and communications). APA style is used by writers in the medical field, education, and, of course, psychology. CMS (or Chicago Manual of Style) is used by writers in humanities fields such as religion, history, and philosophy. The sciences (such as physics and chemistry) have particular styles as well. When writing for an academic audience, you should always ask what style to use. Some instructors want their students to use a particular style, regardless of their major or field of study.

## Why Are There Different Documentation Styles?

The different styles have emerged over the course of years. They have developed because different research techniques sometimes call for a particular type of documentation. As academic fields grow, they develop and reward particular research strategies—and one documentation style cannot always account for those strategies.

## Why Don't Some Articles Have Works Cited or Reference Pages?

Writers in magazines and newspapers use an informal strategy for referencing their sources. They use *attributive phrases* to link statements or information to particular sources; for example: *according to the English department chair at Pennsylvania State,* grades in first-year college courses have remained relatively stable. However, in scholarly work, writers document sources formally—according to MLA or APA guidelines. These shared guidelines provide a way for readers from other schools, states, countries, or centuries to follow the writer's research trail. In other words, the conventions serve an important purpose: to make certain that others beyond our particular social spheres can participate in our work.

## Standard Abbreviations

| MLA | APA | |
|---|---|---|
| ed. | Ed. | = Editor or Edited by |
| eds. | Eds. | = Editors |
| ed. | ed. | = Edition, usually associated with a number (4th ed.) |
| Rev. ed. | Rev. ed. | = Revised edition |
| n.d. | n.d. | = No date |
| n.p. | n.p. | = No publisher or no place |
| n. pag. | n. pag. | = No page numbers |
| trans. | Trans. | = Translator |
| p. | p. | = Page number |
| pp. | pp. | = Page numbers |
| no. | No. | = Number |
| pars. | para. | = Paragraphs |
| vol. | Vol. | = Volume ∎ |

 For additional resources including instructional videos and links to helpful websites, access your English CourseMate through cengagebrain.com.

Documentation conventions help others beyond our social spheres to participate in our work.

# Index